The Face of
New Testament
Studies

The Face of New Testament Studies

A Survey of Recent Research

Edited by

Scot McKnight

and

Grant R. Osborne

Baker Academic

Grand Rapids, Michigan

APOLLOS

© 2004 by Scot McKnight and Grant R. Osborne

Published by Baker Academic
a division of Baker Publishing Group
P.O. Box 6287, Grand Rapids, MI 49516-6287
www.bakeracademic.com

and

Apollos (an imprint of Inter-Varsity Press)
38 De Montfort Street, Leicester, LE1 7GP, England
email: ivp@uccf.org.uk
website: www.ivpbooks.com

Printed in the United States of America

Library of Congress Cataloging-in-Publication Data
The face of New Testament studies : a survey of recent research / edited by Scot McKnight
    and Grant R. Osborne.
        p.   cm.
    Includes bibliographical references and indexes.
    ISBN 0-8010-2707-1 (pbk.)
    1. Bible. N.T.—Criticism, interpretation, etc. I. McKnight, Scot. II. Osborne,
Grant R.
BS2393.F33 2004
225.6—dc22   2003062949

British Library Cataloguing-in-Publication Data
A catalogue record for this book is available from the British Library.
    ISBN 1-84474-039-0

Contents

Contributors

Craig L. Blomberg (Ph.D., University of Aberdeen) is distinguished professor of New Testament at Denver Seminary, Denver, Colorado.

Darrell L. Bock (Ph.D., University of Aberdeen) is research professor of New Testament studies at Dallas Theological Seminary, Dallas, Texas.

Peter G. Bolt (Ph.D., University of London) is head of New Testament at Moore Theological College, Sydney, Australia.

Bruce Chilton (Ph.D., Cambridge University) is Bernard Iddings Bell Professor of Religion at Bard College, Annandale-on-Hudson, New York.

Gregory A. Clark (Ph.D., Loyola University Chicago) is professor of philosophy at North Park University, Chicago, Illinois.

David A. deSilva (Ph.D., Emory University) is professor of New Testament and Greek at Ashland Theological Seminary, Ashland, Ohio.

James D. G. Dunn (Ph.D., Cambridge University) is Emeritus Lightfoot Professor of Divinity at the University of Durham, England.

Craig A. Evans (Ph.D., Claremont Graduate University) is Payzant Distinguished Professor of New Testament at Acadia Divinity College, Wolfville, Nova Scotia, Canada.

David A. Fiensy (Ph.D., Duke University) is professor of New Testament and Greek at Kentucky Christian College, Grayson, Kentucky.

Bruce N. Fisk (Ph.D., Duke University) is associate professor of New Testament at Westmont College, Santa Barbara, California.

Sean Freyne (S.T.D., Saint Thomas University, Rome) is director of Mediterranean and Near Eastern studies at Trinity College, Dublin, Ireland.

George H. Guthrie (Ph.D., Southwestern Baptist Theological Seminary) is chair and Benjamin W. Perry Professor of Biblical Studies at Union University, Jackson, Tennessee.

Donald A. Hagner (Ph.D., University of Manchester) is George Eldon Ladd Professor of New Testament at Fuller Theological Seminary, Pasadena, California.

Scot McKnight (Ph.D., University of Nottingham) is Karl A. Olsson Professor of Religious Studies at North Park University, Chicago, Illinois.

Grant R. Osborne (Ph.D., University of Aberdeen) is professor of New Testament at Trinity Evangelical Divinity School, Deerfield, Illinois.

Stanley E. Porter (Ph.D., University of Sheffield) is president, dean, and professor of New Testament at McMaster Divinity College, McMaster University, Hamilton, Ontario, Canada.

Eckhard J. Schnabel (Ph.D., University of Aberdeen) is associate professor of New Testament at Trinity Evangelical Divinity School, Deerfield, Illinois.

Klaus Scholtissek (Ph.D., University of Münster) is professor of biblical theology at the University of Cologne, Germany.

Klyne R. Snodgrass (Ph.D., University of St. Andrews) is Paul W. Brandel Professor of Biblical Literature at North Park Theological Seminary, Chicago, Illinois.

Graham H. Twelftree (Ph.D., University of Nottingham) is professor of New Testament at Regent University School of Divinity, Virginia Beach, Virginia.

Steve Walton (Ph.D., University of Sheffield) is senior lecturer in Greek and New Testament Studies at London School of Theology, England.

Robert L. Webb (Ph.D., University of Sheffield) is adjunct professor of New Testament at Tyndale Seminary, Toronto, Ontario, Canada.

Preface

One of the editors of this volume has a friend who is a touring professional golfer, Kermit Zarley. He once asked Kermit a question about putting. What Kermit said was impressive indeed, but the editor had no idea what he meant by his careful description. And it certainly did not help the amateur in his amateurish putting. Many students of the NT are similarly bewildered in reading commentaries, monographs, and journal articles. They ask, "Who is this scholar? What is that movement of scholarship about? Where do I find that source? How can I figure out what is going on?" But it is not just students who are bewildered by the intricacies and delicacies of scholarship. Fellow scholars are often bewildered by their comrades in pens! What the Jesus scholar says can be totally perplexing to the Pauline scholar and to the Johannine scholar and to the Petrine scholar and to the scholar of the Letter to the Hebrews, to name but a few.

The contributors to this volume provide "macroscopic" overviews of the field and give students a handle on the most important voices in the discipline. Our purpose in this companion to *The Face of Old Testament Studies* (ed. David W. Baker and Bill T. Arnold) is to provide students and scholars alike with a handbook of "what is going on" in NT scholarship.

What is going on is mentioned briefly in the first paragraph: NT scholarship is neatly divided into groups of scholars who (to continue with our athletic metaphor) are sitting in their respective and highly respected (!) box seats in the front row of the "game of scholarship." They tend to chat only with those nearby, but they know scholars who are sitting elsewhere. There are special sections for historical Jesus scholars, scholars on individual Gospels (Matthew, Mark, Luke, John), some generalists on the Synoptic Gospels, Pauline scholars, scholars of early Christian history, Petrine scholars (with a very few who focus on Jude or 2 Peter), scholars on the Letter to the Hebrews, Johannine literature scholars, and experts on the Apocalypse (Revelation). Surrounding these boxed sections are other scholars who watch from their own special seats. Some are grammarians of NT Greek, who have mastered the Greek language, or NT textual critics, who study the thousands of ancient manuscript witnesses to the NT text. Others focus on (what used to be called) "backgrounds"—they know the OT (and how it is used in the NT), Jewish sources (OT apocryphal or pseudepigraphical writings, the Dead Sea Scrolls, or the various layers and types of rabbinic literature), archaeological/epigraphical sources, or Greco-Roman sources. Others apply modern theories of knowledge (say, sociology) to ancient texts. And then there are the very few who sit in the upper deck and discuss NT theology and whether one "does NT theology" by synthesizing the various authors or by setting them all out in separate boxes. This, then, is how the seats are organized around the scholarly field of NT studies.

The most intelligent way for students to find out what is going on, at the specific level, is to read *New Testament Abstracts* (to name but one abstracting source) and to read the best studies firsthand. *New Testament Abstracts*, published three times per year, "abstracts" virtually all journal articles and books that appear in a given year. The volumes now average about two hundred pages, and combined they abstract some two thousand articles and around a thousand books per year. Each abstract is a short paragraph. A year with *NTA* does not a scholar make, but it makes a student aware of what scholars are doing. However, it is often wiser for the student to get the bigger picture before plunging into the intricacies of scholarship, and we seek to provide that bigger picture in this volume.

Since scholars are organized by fields, it is the scholars in their boxes that is the organizing principle of this volume. In what follows we have asked well-known scholars to provide for students and scholars alike a summary of what is going on in their respective fields of expertise. We gave each scholar the freedom to pursue the task with some flexibility—some essays focus on scholars in a given field, some on trends, and some on the content. We are confident, however, that the student who uses this volume will be exposed to the finest and latest of what is going on in NT scholarship—not everything, of course, but a sampling of what is going on in each field. This volume also pays occasional attention to the contribution of evangelical scholarship, which, though hardly always at the forefront of NT studies, has blossomed in the last four decades into a flowering plant in the midst of a bouquet of options.

The editors will be more than satisfied if students and their fellow scholars find in these articles a shortened path to the destination of biblical and theological knowledge, without which the church empties its gospel of content and context. We invite students and scholars alike to join us in this ever-blossoming field of NT studies.

Scot McKnight
Grant R. Osborne

Abbreviations

Bibliographic and General

AB   Anchor Bible

ABD   *The Anchor Bible Dictionary,* ed. D. N. Freedman et al., 6 vols. (New York: Doubleday, 1992)

ABG   Arbeiten zur Bibel und ihrer Geschichte

ABRL   Anchor Bible Reference Library

ACCS   Ancient Christian Commentary on Scripture

ACNT   Augsburg Commentaries on the New Testament

AGJU   Arbeiten zur Geschichte des antiken Judentums und des Urchristentums

AJBI   *Annual of the Japanese Biblical Institute*

ALGHJ   Arbeiten zur Literatur und Geschichte des hellenistischen Judentums

AnBib   Analecta biblica

ANRW   *Aufstieg und Niedergang der römischen Welt: Geschichte und Kultur Roms im Spiegel der neueren Forschung,* ed. H. Temporini and W. Haase (Berlin, 1972–)

ANTC   Abingdon New Testament Commentaries

ANTF   Arbeiten zur neutestamentlichen Textforschung

AR   *Archiv für Religionswissenschaft*

ASNU   Acta seminarii neotestamentici upsaliensis

AsTJ   *Asbury Theological Journal*

AUS   American University Studies

AUSS   *Andrews University Seminary Studies*

BA   *Biblical Archaeologist*

BAC   Biblioteca de autores cristianos

BAFCS   The Book of Acts in Its First Century Setting

BAR   *Biblical Archaeology Review*

BASOR   *Bulletin of the American Schools of Oriental Research*
BBB   Bonner biblische Beiträge
BBR   *Bulletin for Biblical Research*
BBRNT   Bibliographies for Biblical Research: New Testament Series
BCH   *Bulletin de correspondance hellénique*
BCILL   Bibliothèque des Cahiers de l'Institut de linguistique de Louvain
BECNT   Baker Exegetical Commentary on the New Testament
BETL   Bibliotheca ephemeridum theologicarum lovaniensium
BGBE   Beiträge zur Geschichte der biblischen Exegese
BHT   Beiträge zur historischen Theologie
Bib   *Biblica*
BIBALDS   BIBAL Dissertation Series
BibOr   Biblica et orientalia
BICS   *Bulletin of the Institute of Classical Studies*
BIS   Biblical Interpretation Series
BJRL   *Bulletin of the John Rylands University Library of Manchester*
BJS   Brown Judaic Studies
BL   *Bibel und Liturgie*
BLG   Biblical Languages, Greek
BLit   *Bibliothèque liturgique*
BNTC   Black's New Testament Commentaries
BR   *Biblical Research*
BRev   *Bible Review*
BSac   *Bibliotheca sacra*
BTB   *Biblical Theology Bulletin*
BTZ   *Berliner theologische Zeitschrift*
BZ   *Biblische Zeitschrift*
BZNW   Beihefte zur Zeitschrift für die neutestamentliche Wissenschaft
CBC   Cambridge Bible Commentary
CBET   Contributions to Biblical Exegesis and Theology
CBQ   *Catholic Biblical Quarterly*
CBQMS   Catholic Biblical Quarterly Monograph Series
CC   Continental Commentaries
ChrCent   *Christian Century*
CIJ   *Corpus inscriptionum judaicarum* (Rome: Pontificio Istituto di Archeologia Cristiana, 1952)
CJA   Christianity and Judaism in Antiquity
CJT   *Canadian Journal of Theology*
CNT   Commentaire du Noveau Testament
ConBNT   Coniectanea neotestamentica
CRBR   *Critical Review of Books in Religion*
CRINT   Compendia rerum iudicarum ad Novum Testamentum

CSHJ Chicago Studies in the History of Judaism
CSL Cambridge Studies in Linguistics
CTL Cambridge Textbooks in Linguistics
CTR *Criswell Theological Review*
CurBS *Currents in Research: Biblical Studies*
CurTM *Currents in Theology and Mission*
DBSup *Dictionnaire de la Bible: Supplément,* ed. L. Pirot and A. Robert (Paris, 1928–)
DNP *Der neue Pauly: Enzyklopädie der Antike,* ed. H. Cancik and H. Schneider (Stuttgart, 1996–)
EdF Erträge der Forschung
EHS Europäische Hochschulschriften
EKKNT Evangelisch-katholischer Kommentar zum Neuen Testament
EncJud *Encyclopaedia Judaica,* 16 vols. (Jerusalem, 1972)
ENF Estudios de filología neotestamentaria
ESI *Excavations and Surveys in Israel*
ETL *Ephemerides theologicae lovanienses*
ETS Erfurter theologische Studien
ETSMS Evangelical Theological Society Manuscript Series
EvQ *Evangelical Quarterly*
ExpTim *Expository Times*
FF Foundations and Facets
FRLANT Forschungen zur Religion und Literatur des Alten und Neuen Testaments
FzB Forschung zur Bibel
GBS Guides to Biblical Scholarship
GNS Good News Studies
GuL *Geist und Leben*
HBS Herders biblische Studien
HBT *Horizons in Biblical Theology*
HDR Harvard Dissertations in Religion
HNT Handbuch zum Neuen Testament
HTKNT Herders theologischer Kommentar zum Neuen Testament
HTR *Harvard Theological Review*
HUT Hermeneutische Untersuchungen zur Theologie
IBS *Irish Biblical Studies*
ICC International Critical Commentary
IEJ *Israel Exploration Journal*
INJ *Israel Numismatic Journal*
Int *Interpretation*
IRT Issues in Religion and Theology
IVPNTC IVP New Testament Commentaries
JAAR *Journal of the American Academy of Religion*
JAC *Jahrbuch für Antike und Christentum*

JBL	*Journal of Biblical Literature*
JBLMS	Journal of Biblical Literature Monograph Series
JBTh	*Jahrbuch für biblische Theologie*
JETS	*Journal of the Evangelical Theological Society*
JFSR	*Journal of Feminist Studies in Religion*
JHC	*Journal of Higher Criticism*
JJS	*Journal of Jewish Studies*
JPT	*Journal of Pentecostal Theology*
JPTSup	Journal of Pentecostal Theology: Supplement Series
JQR	*Jewish Quarterly Review*
JR	*Journal of Religion*
JRA	*Journal of Roman Archaeology*
JRH	*Journal of Religious History*
JSJ	*Journal for the Study of Judaism*
JSJSup	Journal for the Study of Judaism: Supplement Series
JSNT	*Journal for the Study of the New Testament*
JSNTSup	Journal for the Study of the New Testament: Supplement Series
JSOT	*Journal for the Study of the Old Testament*
JSOTSup	Journal for the Study of the Old Testament Supplement Series
JSP	*Journal for the Study of the Pseudepigrapha*
JSPSup	Journal for the Study of the Pseudepigrapha: Supplement Series
JSS	*Journal of Semitic Studies*
JSSR	*Journal for the Scientific Study of Religion*
JTS	*Journal of Theological Studies*
KEK	Kritisch-exegetischer Kommentar über das Neue Testament (Meyer-Kommentar)
LD	Lectio divina
LEC	Library of Early Christianity
LQ	*Lutheran Quarterly*
LXX	Septuagint
LXXA	Septuagint text of Codex Alexandrinus
LXXB	Septuagint text of Codex Vaticanus
MNTC	Moffat New Testament Commentary
MS/MSS	manuscript/manuscripts
MT	Masoretic Text
MTZ	*Münchener theologische Zeitschrift*
NA[26]	*Novum Testamentum Graece,* ed. K. Aland et al., 26th ed. (Stuttgart, 1979)
NA[27]	*Novum Testamentum Graece,* ed. B. Aland et al., 27th ed. (Stuttgart, 1993)
NAC	New American Commentary

NBL	*Neues Bibel-Lexikon*
NCB	New Century Bible
NEAEHL	*The New Encyclopedia of Archaeological Excavations in the Holy Land,* ed. E. Stern, 4 vols. (Jerusalem, 1993)
NEB	New English Bible
NEBNTSup	Die neue Echter-Bibel: Ergänzungsband zum Neuen Testament
NedTT	*Nederlands theologisch tijdschrift*
Neot	*Neotestamentica*
NewDocs	*New Documents Illustrating Early Christianity,* ed. G. H. R. Horsley and S. R. Llewelyn, 9 vols. (North Ryde, N.S.W., 1981–)
NICNT	New International Commentary on the New Testament
NIGTC	New International Greek Testament Commentary
NIV	New International Version
NIVAC	NIV Application Commentary
NovT	*Novum Testamentum*
NovTSup	Novum Testamentum Supplements
NRSV	New Revised Standard Version
NSBT	New Studies in Biblical Theology
NT	New Testament
NTAbh	Neutestamentliche Abhandlungen
NTD	Das Neue Testament Deutsch
NTDH	Neukirchener theologische Dissertationen und Habilitationen
NTG	New Testament Guides
NTOA	Novum Testamentum et Orbis antiquus
NTS	*New Testament Studies*
NTT	New Testament Theology
NTTS	New Testament Tools and Studies
OT	Old Testament
ÖTK	Ökumenischer Taschenbuch-Kommentar
OTM	Oxford Theological Monographs
PNTC	Pelican New Testament Commentaries
QD	Quaestiones disputatae
QR	*Quarterly Review*
RAC	*Reallexikon für Antike und Christentum,* ed. T. Kluser et al. (Stuttgart 1950–)
RB	*Revue biblique*
RBL	*Review of Biblical Literature*
ResQ	*Restoration Quarterly*
RevExp	*Review and Expositor*
RevQ	*Revue de Qumran*

RGG	*Religion in Geschichte und Gegenwart,* ed. K. Galling, 3rd ed., 7 vols. (Tübingen, 1957–65)
RHPR	*Revue d'histoire et de philosophie religieuses*
RNT	Regensburger Neues Testament
RRelRes	*Review of Religious Research*
RSR	*Recherches de science religieuse*
RSV	Revised Standard Version
RThom	*Revue thomiste*
RTR	*Reformed Theological Review*
RVV	Religionsgeschichtliche Versuche und Vorarbeiten
SBAB	Stuttgarter biblische Aufsatzbände
SBB	Stuttgarter biblische Beiträge
SBEC	Studies in Bible and Early Christianity
SBG	Studies in Biblical Greek
SBL	Society of Biblical Literature
SBLDS	Society of Biblical Literature Dissertation Series
SBLMS	Society of Biblical Literature Monograph Series
SBLRBS	Society of Biblical Literature Resources for Biblical Study
SBLSP	*Society of Biblical Literature Seminar Papers*
SBLSymS	Society of Biblical Literature Symposium Series
SBS	Stuttgarter Bibelstudien
SBT	Studies in Biblical Theology
SD	Studies and Documents
SEÅ	*Svensk exegetisk årsbok*
SemeiaSt	Semeia Studies
SFSHJ	South Florida Studies in the History of Judaism
SJLA	Studies in Judaism in Late Antiquity
SJT	*Scottish Journal of Theology*
SNT	Studien zum Neuen Testament
SNTA	Studiorum Novi Testamenti Auxilia
SNTG	Studies in New Testament Greek
SNTSMS	Society for New Testament Studies Monograph Series
SNTSU	Studien zum Neuen Testament und seiner Umwelt
SNTW	Studies of the New Testament and Its World
SP	Sacra Pagina
SPA	Studien der patristischen Arbeitsgemeinschaft
SPB	Studia Post-biblica
SR	*Studies in Religion*
SSEJC	Studies in Early Judaism and Christianity
StTh	Kohlhammer Studienbücher Theologie
SVTQ	*St. Vladimir's Theological Quarterly*
SwJT	*Southwestern Journal of Theology*
SWR	Studies in Women and Religion
TAPA	*Transactions of the American Philological Association*

TBei   *Theologische Beiträge*
TC   *TC: A Journal of Biblical Textual Criticism* (online)
TDNT   *Theological Dictionary of the New Testament,* ed. G. Kittel and
G. Friedrich, trans. G. W. Bromiley, 10 vols. (Grand Rapids:
Eerdmans, 1964–76)
TGl   *Theologie und Glaube*
Them   *Themelios*
THKNT   Theologischer Handkommentar zum Neuen Testament
ThTo   *Theology Today*
TJ   *Trinity Journal*
TNTC   Tyndale New Testament Commentaries
TP   *Theologie und Philosophie*
TPINTC   Trinity Press International New Testament Commentaries
TRev   *Theologische Revue*
TRu   *Theologische Rundschau*
TS   *Theological Studies*
TSAJ   Texte und Studien zum antiken Judentum
TSR   *Trinity Seminary Review*
TTZ   *Trierer theologische Zeitschrift*
TU   Texte und Untersuchungen
TUMSR   Trinity University Monograph Series in Religion
TynBul   *Tyndale Bulletin*
TZ   *Theologische Zeitschrift*
UBS[3]   *The Greek New Testament,* ed. K. Aland at al., 3rd ed. (New
York: United Bible Societies, 1975)
UBS[4]   *The Greek New Testament,* ed. K. Aland at al., 4th ed.
(New York: United Bible Societies; Stuttgart: Deutsche
Bibelgesellschaft, 1993)
UTB   Uni-Taschenbücher
VCSup   Vigiliae Christianae Supplements
VF   *Verkündigung und Forschung*
WBC   Word Biblical Commentary
WTJ   *Westminster Theological Journal*
WUNT   Wissenschaftliche Untersuchungen zum Neuen Testament
ZBKNT   Zürcher Bibelkommentare: Neue Testament
ZDPV   *Zeitschrift des deutschen Palästina-Vereins*
ZNW   *Zeitschrift für die neutestamentliche Wissenschaft und die Kunde
der älteren Kirche*
ZPE   *Zeitschrift für Papyrologie und Epigraphik*
ZRGG   *Zeitschrift für Religions- und Geistesgeschichte*
ZTK   *Zeitschrift für Theologie und Kirche*

Ancient Sources

ʾAbot	tractate *ʾAbot*
ʾAbot R. Nat.	*ʾAbot de Rabbi Nathan*
Ann.	Tacitus, *Annales*
Ant.	Josephus, *Jewish Antiquities*
b.	Babylonian Talmud
Ben.	Seneca, *De beneficiis*
Cels.	Origen, *Contra Celsum*
Dial.	Justin Martyr, *Dialogue with Trypho*
Diatr.	Epictetus, *Diatribai (Dissertationes)*
En.	*Enoch*
Geogr.	Srabo, *Geographica*
Hist.	Tacitus, *Historiae*
Hist. eccl.	Eusebius, *Historia ecclesiastica*
Inst.	Quintillian, *Institutio oratoria*
J.W.	Josephus, *Jewish War*
Legat.	Philo, *Legatio ad Gaium*
Life	Josephus, *The Life*
m.	Mishnah
Meg.	tractate *Megillah*
Meʿil.	tractate *Meʿilah*
Mek.	*Mekilta*
Midr.	*Midrash*
Nat. fac.	Galen, *De naturalibus facultatibus*
Naz.	tractate *Nazir*
Pesaḥ.	tractate *Pesaḥim*
Pesiq. Rab.	*Pesiqta Rabbati*
QE	Philo, *Questions and Answers on Exodus*
Rab.	*Rabbah*
Sanh.	tractate *Sanhedrin*
Sat.	Juvenal, *Satirae*
Sem.	tractate *Semaḥot*
Sukk.	tractate *Sukkah*
t.	Tosefta
Tg. Isa.	*Targum Isaiah*
Tg. Neof.	*Targum Neofiti*
Tg. Ps.-J.	*Targum Pseudo-Jonathan*
Vesp.	Suetonius, *Vespasianus*
y.	Jerusalem Talmud

Part 1

Context of the New Testament

1

Galilee and Judea

The Social World of Jesus

Sean Freyne

The interest in Galilee in NT scholarship today is largely related to the renewal of the quest for the historical Jesus. Galilee was also the home of rabbinic Judaism in the period after the second Jewish revolt (132–35 C.E.), and it was there, in the schools of Sepphoris and Tiberias, that such classic texts of Judaism as the Mishnah and the Palestinian Talmud were produced between the years 200–450 C.E. This essay will concentrate on Galilean life of the first century C.E. Yet, as we will see, the issue of the Jewish character of the region is highly significant for that period also. In order to explore this aspect properly, we must give special attention to the ongoing relationship with Jerusalem.

Modern scholarship has portrayed Jesus in many different roles, everything from Zealot revolutionary to Cynic sage, and each of these accounts presumes a different picture of the Galilean social world that is deemed to have played a decisive role in determining the contours of his ministry. In order to obtain some objectivity, therefore, we must bracket concerns with Jesus in the first instance and attempt a description of the Galilean social world insofar as is feasible from writings other than the Gospels. In addition, a considerable body of archaeological evidence from the region relating to the Hellenistic and Roman periods has emerged over the past twenty-five years. Apart from the Synoptic Gospels, the writings of Josephus are of prime importance, but these are not unproblematic. In particular, his account of the first revolt (the *Jewish War*) and his self-defense against the defamation of one Justus of Tiberias (the *Life*), both dealing with his own period in Galilee as commander on behalf of the Jewish revolutionary council in Jerusalem, are, to say the least, not unbiased accounts. In order to obtain some perspective, therefore, we will need a brief overview of the previous history of Galilee from the eighth century B.C.E.

Galilean History in Outline

The name *Galilee,* meaning "the circle," in all probability is derived from the experience of the early Israelites inhabiting the interior highlands and surrounded by Canaanite city-states. Judea, on the other hand, is a tribal name that came to particular prominence in the monarchic period because David was of Judean origin. The first Galilean tribes were Zebulun, Naphtali, and Asher, with the tribe of Dan migrating north later. The various accounts of the different tribes and their characteristics (Gen. 49; Deut. 33; Judg. 5), though dated to the period of the judges, may well reflect later situations where the issue of ethnic identity came under threat from various sources.[1] Certainly the north bore the brunt of the Assyrian onslaught of the eighth century B.C.E., with Tiglath-pileser III's invasion resulting in the destruction, and possibly the depopulation, of many centers in upper and lower Galilee (2 Kings 15:29; Isa. 9:1). However, unlike the case of Samaria some ten years later (2 Kings 17:24), there is no mention of a foreign, non-Israelite population being introduced to Galilee at that time. A century and a half later, Judah succumbed to the Babylonians, with the destruction of the temple and the deportation of the king and the leading members of the Judean aristocracy to Babylon in 582 B.C.E. Restoration occurred quickly under the Persians, with the edict of Cyrus in 515 B.C.E. allowing the successors of the deportees to return and rebuild the temple and reestablish the Persian province of Yehud (Judea). According to Josephus, it was from that time that the name *Ioudaioi* (Jews) was given to the inhabitants of the temple state (*Ant.* 11.173).

Galilee next appears in the historical record in the mid–second century B.C.E., when an independent Jewish state emerged under the successors of the Maccabees, the Hasmoneans. They initiated campaigns of expansion that eventually led to the establishment of a kingdom that territorially was as extensive as that of David and Solomon in the ninth century. For the first time in almost a millennium, therefore, Galilee and Judea were under the same native rulership, with Jerusalem again the political as well as the religious capital. At the same time, the name *Ioudaios* began to be used not just for the inhabitants of Judea, but for all who embraced the Jewish temple ideology

1. Sean Freyne, *Galilee from Alexander the Great to Hadrian: A Study of Second Temple Judaism* (1980; reprint, Edinburgh: Clark, 2000), 3–21; Rafael Frankel, "Galilee: Prehellenistic," *ABD* 2:879–94.

by worshiping in Jerusalem.[2] By the mid–first century B.C.E., however, Rome was emerging as master of the eastern Mediterranean, and the Hasmoneans had been replaced by the Herodians, an Idumean dynasty entrusted by Rome to maintain its interests in the region as client kings. Galilee, with Sepphoris, close to Nazareth, as the administrative center for the region, was recognized as a Jewish territory, together with Judea proper and Perea beyond the Jordan. They were, however, soon incorporated into the kingdom of Herod the Great and were expected to make their contribution to the honoring of his Roman patron, Augustus.

The long reign of Herod as king of the Jews (40–4 B.C.E.) made a deep impact on every aspect of both Galilean and Judean society. When Herod died, Augustus refused to appoint any of his sons as his successor, assigning instead different regions to each: Galilee and Perea to Antipas; Judea to Archelaus; and to Philip, Batanaea, Trachonitis, and Auranitis in northern Transjordan, territories that Augustus had granted to Herod the Great as a reward for fidelity. Galilee was once again, therefore, administratively separate from Judea, something reflected in Matthew's Gospel in explaining how Jesus, though born in Judea, came to live there: Joseph, "hearing that Archelaus ruled in Judea in the place of Herod, his father," took Jesus and his mother to Galilee, and they came to live at Nazareth (Matt. 2:22–23). Josephus gives a broader background to this information. Archelaus had so outraged his subjects that he was deposed by Rome in 6 C.E., and thereafter Judea was ruled as a procuratorship, or Roman province of second rank, with the governor resident in Caesarea Maritima, and Jerusalem acting as the temple city controlled by the priestly aristocracy.

Antipas aspired to, but was never given, the title of king, but only that of tetrarch. He ruled in Galilee and Perea until 39 C.E., when he too was deposed and his territory was handed over to his nephew Agrippa I. Despite this lesser status, he continued with the style and policy of his father in ensuring that Roman concerns were taken care of in his territories. John the Baptist suffered at his hands, probably not for the reason given in the Gospels (Mark 6:13–29), but for that given by Josephus, namely, that John's popularity and espousal of justice for the poor gave cause for concern that an uprising might occur (*Ant.* 18.116–119). This would have been deemed a serious failure in imperial eyes, since client kings were tolerated only if they could be seen to ensure stability and loyalty to Rome and its values. Apart from the Jerusalem temple, Herod the Great had confined his major building projects to the periphery of the Jewish territories: Samaria was renamed Sebaste (Latin: Augustus), and a temple to Roma and Augustus was built there, as also at Caesarea Maritima on the coast, where a magnificent harbor was developed. In the north a temple to Augustus was built at Paneas, which his son, Philip, later renamed Caesarea (Philippi).

---

2. Sean Freyne, "Behind the Names: Galileans, Samaritans, *Ioudaioi*," in *Galilee through the Centuries: Confluence of Cultures,* ed. Eric M. Meyers (Winona Lake, Ind.: Eisenbrauns, 1999), 39–55.

Antipas also continued this tradition of honoring the Roman overlords through monumental buildings in Galilee. Sepphoris was made "the ornament of all Galilee" and called *autokratoris*, probably alluding to Augustus as sole ruler (*Ant.* 18.27). In 19 C.E. he founded a new city, Tiberias, on the lakefront, honoring Augustus's successor as emperor.

This brief account of Galilean history is crucial for a correct understanding of the social world of Palestine in the first century C.E. Historical factors were largely determinative of shifting population and settlement patterns in the different regions, thereby explaining the religious and cultural loyalties also. Economic conditions were dependent on the political realities of the day, since all ancient economies were to a considerable extent politically controlled. It is to these topics that we now turn, focusing on Galilee and Judea separately, while also highlighting aspects of the relationship between them based on a shared religious tradition.

Who Were the Galileans? Religious and Cultural Affiliations

The inhabitants of Galilee are described in the sources as Galileans. But who were they? What was their provenance, what social and economic strata did they represent, and what were their religious and cultural affiliations? Definitive answers to questions such as these are hard to achieve, but the effort to address them adequately can offer some criteria for evaluating different proposals. Briefly, one can distinguish three broad lines of response in the contemporary discussions to the questions posed, with minor variations to each.

1. One proposal, by the German scholar Albrecht Alt, maintains that the Galileans of the later sources are direct descendants of the old Israelite population, who had remained undisturbed, it is claimed, in the first wave of Assyrian conquest of the north, and who had maintained their essential Yahwistic beliefs over the centuries. The inhabitants of Galilee freely and naturally joined the *ethnos tōn Ioudaiōn* when the opportunity arose after the Hasmonean expansion to the north, bypassing their historical, religious, and cultic center of Samaria within the old northern kingdom.[3] More recently, Richard Horsley also has espoused the notion of the old Israelite population remaining undisturbed in Galilee, but he sees the situation in the Hasmonean times quite differently. Over the centuries the Galileans had developed their own customs and practices that made them quite different from the Judeans, despite their sharing of the same Yahwistic beliefs based on the Pentateuch. Thus, according to Horsley, the Hasmonean expansion represented not a liberation but

3. Albrecht Alt, "Galiläische Probleme 1937–40," in *Kleine Schriften zur Geschichte des Volkes Israels,* 3 vols. (Munich: Beck, 1953–64), 2:363–435.

an imposition on the Galileans of the laws of the Judeans, laws that he regards as restrictive and designed to serve the material needs of the aristocracy of the Judean temple state.[4]

2. The opposite view is held by other scholars who accept the phrase "Galilee of the nations" (Isa. 9:1; 1 Macc. 5:15) as an accurate description of the population of the region and its cultural affiliations, especially from the Hellenistic period onward. This view reached its most extreme expression with the claim by Walter Grundmann in 1941 that Galilee was pagan, and therefore that Jesus in all probability was not a Jew.[5] Not everybody who accepts the notion of pagan influences in Galilee goes quite that far. Instead, Galileans are seen as having been more exposed to Hellenistic culture generally, so that they espoused a more open form of Judaism, influenced as they were, it is claimed, by the ethos of the surrounding cities.[6] Most recently this emphasis on Greco-Roman culture in Galilee has taken the form of the claim of Cynic influences on the population there. This was a countercultural movement within Greco-Roman society, similar, it is claimed, to that of Jesus and his followers.[7] Since the Cynics were an urban phenomenon, proponents of a Cynic presence there speak also of an urbanized Galilee, but with little support for such claims from the available evidence.

3. A third position, the one that in my opinion best corresponds to the archaeological evidence, speaks of the Judaization of Galilee from the south by the Hasmoneans, as they triumphantly marched north and east. Again, however, there are variations to this account. Some scholars have accepted uncritically Josephus's version, according to which the Hasmonean Aristobulus I had, in 104 B.C.E., forcibly circumcised the Itureans, a seminomadic Arab people who had infiltrated into upper Galilee (*Ant.* 13.319).[8] Such a

---

4. Richard Horsley, *Galilee: History, Politics, People* (Valley Forge, Pa.: Trinity, 1995), 34–62.

5. Walter Grundmann, *Jesus der Galiläer und das Judentum* (Leipzig: Wigand, 1941).

6. Walter Bauer, "Jesus der Galiläer," in *Festgabe für Adolf Jülicher* (Tübingen: Mohr, 1927), 16–34; W. Bertram, "Der Hellenismus in der Urheimat des Evangeliums," *AR* 32 (1935): 265–81.

7. Burton L. Mack, *A Myth of Innocence: Mark and Christian Origins* (Philadelphia: Fortress, 1988), 53–97; idem, *The Lost Gospel: The Book of Q* (San Francisco: HarperSanFrancisco, 1993), 51–68; John D. Crossan, *The Historical Jesus: The Life of a Mediterranean Jewish Peasant* (San Francisco: HarperSanFrancisco, 1991); Leif Vaage, *Galilean Upstarts: Jesus' First Followers according to Q* (Valley Forge, Pa.: Trinity, 1994); F. G. Downing, *Cynics and Christian Origins* (Edinburgh: Clark, 1994), 115–68. For a detailed criticism of the hypothesis, see Hans D. Betz, "Jesus and the Cynics: Survey and Analysis of a Hypothesis," *JR* 74 (1994): 453–75.

8. Emil Schürer, *History of the Jewish People in the Age of Jesus Christ*, rev. ed., 3 vols. (Edinburgh: Clark, 1973–87), 2:7–10. Cf. W. Schottroff, "Die Ituräer," *ZDPV* 98 (1982): 125–47; M. Hartel, *Northern Golan Heights: The Archaeological Survey as Source for Local History* (Qatsrin: Israel Department for Antiquities and Museums); Shimon Dar, *Settlements and Cult Sites on Mount Hermon, Israel: Iturean Culture in the Hellenistic and Roman Periods*, BAR International Series 589 (Oxford: Tempus Reparatum, 1993).

background, if correct, would have made the Galilean Jews, as recent converts, suspect in the eyes of their southern coreligionists, thus explaining some later disparaging remarks by the rabbis about the Galilean lack of piety.[9] Other scholars, on the basis of the material culture, believe that Galilee was settled from the south in the wake of the Hasmonean conquests.[10] This would explain their loyalty to Jerusalem and its worship documented in the literary sources, since they would have been of Judean stock originally and were sent to Galilee because of their support for the Hasmoneans.[11] A further variation on the Galilean Jews is the view that suggests a Babylonian influence in view of indications from the later literary sources of contacts between Galilean and Babylonian rabbis.[12]

In principle there is nothing to preclude the Galilean population from including Israelite, Iturean, Judean, and even Babylonian strands in the ethnic mix by the first century C.E., and it would be somewhat unrealistic to exclude such elements entirely. However, certain claims can be ruled out as unlikely or overstated on the basis of our present knowledge of the situation. The case for a pagan Galilee is poorly supported by the literary evidence and receives no support whatsoever from the archaeological explorations. Nor is there any evidence of a lasting Iturean presence in the region, even though they may have infiltrated upper Galilee for a time. There are also several problems with the idea of Galilean Israelites, not least of which is the likelihood of a largely peasant population maintaining a separate Yahwistic identity over the centuries in the absence of a communal cultic center.[13] Thus, the theory of the Judaization of Galilee from the south appears to be the most likely hypothesis in our present state of knowledge. Surveys have shown a marked increase of new foundations from the Hasmonean period onward, and at the same time the destruction of older sites, such as Har Mispe Yamim, which had a pagan cult center.[14] Excavations at sites such as Sepphoris, Jotapata, Gamala, and Meiron, as well as lesser sites, have uncovered artifacts of the distinctive Jewish way of life such as ritual baths, stone jars, and natively produced ceramic household

9. Adolf Büchler, *Der Galiläische 'Am ha-'aretz des Zweiten Jahrhunderts* (1906; reprint, Hildesheim: Olmsz, 1968).

10. Mordechai Aviam, "Galilee: the Hellenistic and Byzantine Period," in *The New Encyclopedia of Archaeological Excavations in the Holy Land*, ed. E. Stern, 4 vols. (Jerusalem: Israel Exploration Society, 1993), 2:455–58; Jonathan L. Reed, *Archaeology and the Galilean Jesus* (Harrisburg, Pa.: Trinity, 2000), 23–61.

11. Freyne, "Behind the Names," 39–56.

12. Etienne Nodet, "Galilee from the Exile to Jesus," in Etienne Nodet and Justin Taylor, *The Origins of Christianity: An Exploration* (Collegeville, Minn.: Liturgical Press, 1997), 127–64.

13. Freyne, "Behind the Names," 41–44; Philippe Bruneau, "Les Israelites de Delos et la Juivre Delienne," *BCH* 106 (1982): 465–504; A. Thomas Kraabel, "New Evidence of the Samaritan Diaspora Has Been Found on Delos," *BA* (1984): 44–46.

14. Rafael Frankel, "Har Mispe Yamim—1988/89," *ESI* 9:100–102; Rafael Frankel and Rafael Ventura, "The Mispe Yamim Bronzes," *BASOR* 311 (1998): 39–55.

wares—all indicators of a concern with ritual purity emanating from Jerusalem and its temple and an avoidance of the cultural ethos of the encircling pagan cities and their lifestyles.[15]

Social Stratification: A Pyramid of Power

Most recent social historians of Roman Palestine adopt Gerhard Lenski's model of agrarian empires as their working hypothesis. This envisages a pyramidal view of society in which most of the power, prestige, and privilege resides at the top among the narrow band of ruling elite and native aristocracy, if and when these are to be distinguished. Beneath these are the retainer classes, which help to maintain the status quo on behalf of the elites, thereby gaining for themselves some measure of relative prestige. On a further rung down the ladder, as the base broadens, are the peasants, the free landowners who are the mainstay of the society but who cannot aspire to a higher place on the social scale. Instead, they are in constant danger of being demoted to the landless poor and destitute due to increased taxation, a bad harvest, or aggrandizement of property by the ruling elites for their own purposes. Such a model certainly fits well in general terms with what we know of Roman Galilee, once certain adjustments are made to this ideal picture to account for local circumstances.

Though Antipas never was given the title of king but simply that of tetrarch, there is no doubt that within Galilee itself he and his court represented the ruling elite. In one sense they could be said to be retainers on behalf of the emperor, but once Antipas was prepared to accept the role that Roman imperial policies in the East had dictated for him, his role was assured.[16] Josephus informs us that he "loved his tranquillity" (*Ant.* 18.245)—a characterization that fits well with the Gospel portraits, despite his attempts to upstage at Rome the governor of Syria on one occasion (*Ant.* 18.101–104). Augustus had decreed that he could have a personal income of two hundred talents from the territories of Galilee and Perea, and presumably he could also introduce special levies for building and other projects, especially when these were intended to honor the imperial household (*Ant.* 17.318). Not merely did Antipas and his

15. Jonathan Reed ("Galileans, 'Israelite Village Communities' and the Sayings Gospel Q," in Meyers, *Galilee through the Centuries,* 87–108), gives the most detailed and up-to-date report of the evidence. Cf. Eric Meyers, James Strange, and Denis Groh, "The Meiron Excavation Project: Archaeological Survey in Galilee and Golan, 1976," *BASOR* 233 (1978): 1–24; Eric Meyers, Ehud Netzer, and Carol Meyers, *Sepphoris* (Winona Lake, Ind.: Eisenbrauns, 1992); David Adan-Bayewitz and Mordechai Aviam, "Iotapata, Josephus and the Siege of 67: Preliminary Report of the 1992–94 Seasons," *JRA* 10 (1997): 131–65; Shmaryahu Gutman, "Gamala," in *NEAEHL* 2:459–63.

16. The most detailed study of Antipas is that of Harold W. Hoehner, *Herod Antipas: A Contemporary of Jesus Christ,* SNTSMS 17 (Cambridge: Cambridge University Press, 1972).

immediate family benefit from these concessions, but also a new class seems to have emerged around him, called in the Gospels the Herodians, presumably as a replacement for the older, native Hasmonean aristocracy, which had disappeared after Herod the Great's takeover.[17]

One passage that opens up an interesting perspective is the account of Herod's birthday where the list of guests is described as "the courtiers, the military officers, and the leading men of Galilee" (Mark 6:21). The *chiliarchoi* clearly are military personnel of some kind, suggesting that the tetrarch had a permanent army, however small, distinct from the militia, which he might call up for a particular engagement (*Ant.* 18.251–252). There is nothing unusual about such a force, nor does it necessarily imply a huge burden on the natives, as would be the case when soldiers were billeted in a region. The *chiliarchoi* attending the king's banquet were in all probability in charge of local policing and border posts and responsible for the personal protection of Antipas himself and his household. They thus belong to the retainer level rather than the aristocratic level on Lenski's model.

The *prōtoi tēs Galilaias* are also known to us from Josephus's writings. Two particular incidents involving their role are significant (*Ant.* 18.122, 261–309). In both incidents, the *prōtoi* clearly are influential Jews concerned about religious values, ostensibly at least, but they were also interested in the maintenance of law and order and the payment of the tribute to Rome. Josephus uses the term seventy-five times in his writings, and in the vast majority of uses it refers to "men who held official positions of authority among the Jews."[18] As such, they are to be distinguished from two other groups mentioned frequently, the *dynatoi* and the *hoi en telei,* the former referring to an aristocracy of power, as distinct from one of birth, and the latter to those holding some official office.

The third group mentioned by Mark are the *megistanes,* meaning "great ones" or "grandees." Thus, one might be tempted to identify them as courtiers as in Dan. 5:23 LXX. Josephus uses the term to refer to noblemen who at the outbreak of the revolt fled from the territory of Agrippa II, bringing their horses, their arms, and their possessions (*Life* 112). This seems to indicate local lords on whom the ruler normally could rely for active support at times of crisis, rather than court officials or administrative officers. It is not certain whether they could be identified with the Herodians who appear elsewhere in the Gospels (Mark 3:6; 12:13). The Latin ending to their name, *-ianoi,* suggests adherents or supporters of a person, and presumably, therefore, includes a wider circle than the immediate household. Indeed, at the time of the first revolt there are two people bearing the name of Herod, numbered among the ruling class of Tiberias, who recommended loyalty to Rome and who owned property across the Jordan. On that understanding, therefore,

---

17. Ibid., 331–43.

18. William Buehler, *The Pre-Herodian Civil War and Social Debate* (Basel: Rheinhardt, 1974), 20–53.

the Herodians in Galilee and elsewhere in the country could be described as wealthy landowners who presumably depended on benefactions from Herod the Great and his sons for their opulence. Inevitably, they would be stoutly loyal to the Herodian house and its policies, and could, arguably, be seen as the new Galilean aristocracy.

I have already suggested that the *chiliarchoi* of Mark's list belonged to the retainer class rather than to the ruling elite. Other functionaries who would fit into this same category also appear in the literature. Mention of the *archeia* in Sepphoris immediately suggests keepers of official records and scribes of various kinds, such as the *kōmogrammateis* "from every village of Galilee" to whom Luke refers (Luke 5:17). Justus of Tiberias, Josephus's rival in Galilee, had a good Greek education and was in the service of Agrippa II, presumably as a high administrative officer within his realm. Likewise, John of Gischala, Josephus's implacable enemy in 66 C.E., seems to have had some official role in the Roman administration of upper Galilee (*Life* 73). We can also assume a whole network of lesser officials within the highly bureaucratic structures that had been put in place from the early Hellenistic period by the Ptolemies, and that simply would have been inherited by successive regimes thereafter.[19] These officials would have included market managers (*agoranomoi*), tax collectors (*telōnai*), estate mangers (*oikonomoi*), judges (*kritai*), prison officers (*hypēretai, praktōres*), all of whom (or their equivalents) are alluded to in the Gospels. The tax collectors appear to be ubiquitous—an indication perhaps of the demands that were being made on people, not just to meet the tribute due to Antipas himself, but also various other levies and tolls that were imposed.[20] The payment at least of the *tributum soli,* or land tax, was in kind, as indicated by the mention of imperial granaries in upper Galilee at the outbreak of the first revolt. Presumably there were others throughout the region also (*Life* 71.119). In addition, there was the *tributum capitis,* or personal tax, which was a regular feature of the Roman tax system, and the collection of this would have imposed another layer of bureaucratic retainers within the Galilean social structure.

Beneath the retainers comes the peasantry, according to Lenski's model. These may include owners of small, family-sized holdings (ten to fifteen hectares), or tenants who engaged in subsistence farming while paying a rent, usually in kind to an absentee landowner. Ideally, all Jews were intended to participate in the use of the land, and the whole structure of tithing and agricultural offerings for the temple was built on that assumption. However, imperial domination had seen the emergence of large estates in Palestine, as elsewhere, and this inevitably put pressure on the traditional landowning system, as can

---

19. George McLean Harper, *Village Administration in the Roman Province of Syria,* Yale Classical Studies 1 (Princeton: n.p., 1928), 107–68; Victor Tcherikover, *Palestine under the Ptolemies: A Contribution to the Study of the Zenon Papyri,* vols. 1–4 of *Mizraim* (New York: Steichert, 1937).

20. Fritz Herrenbrück, *Jesus und die Zöllner,* WUNT 41 (Tübingen: Mohr, 1990).

be seen by the land reform of Nehemiah, already in the Persian period (Neh. 5:1–12). Though the Hasmoneans subscribed to the Israelite ideal of "each man under his own vine" (1 Macc. 14:12), there is plenty of evidence that they too continued the policy of large estates in the conquered territories, as did the Herodians also.[21] This pressure on the system meant that more and more people were driven off the land and reduced to penury.

The results of this sketch, patchy though it is, suggest that there was a mixed pattern of landownership in Galilee in the first century. Undoubtedly, the trend was toward larger estates, and thus a move away from mere subsistence farming of the traditional Jewish peasant class. The foundation of Tiberias is a good example of how pressure could come on small landowners as the ruling aristocracy's needs had to be met. In a preindustrial situation, land was the primary source of wealth, but this was in short supply in a Galilee that was thickly populated by the standards of the time (*J. W.* 3.41–43). Increased taxation to meet the demands of that lifestyle meant that many were reduced to penury, thus reaching the lowest level on Lenski's pyramid, that occupied by the landless poor and the urban destitute classes (*Life* 66–67). The slide from peasant owner to tenant to day laborer was inexorable for many, thus giving rise to social resentment, debt, banditry, and in the case of women, prostitution. All these social types can be documented from the Gospels either as typical characters in the parables of Jesus or as real-life figures for whom his movement offered a radical alternative to the harsh realities of daily life in Herodian Galilee.

Economic Systems

The problem of landownership in Galilee raises immediately the question of the economic situation there, since in preindustrial societies land was the primary resource. Relatively speaking, Galilee was well-endowed with natural resources. The melting winter snows from Hermon and seasonal rains ensured good growth and the production of a variety of crops. Josephus waxes lyrical about the climatic conditions of the plain of Genessar in the region of Capernaum, with its luxuriant range of fruits (*J. W.* 3.506–521). But the valleys of lower Galilee also yielded a variety of grain crops as well as flax, according to both Josephus and the rabbinic sources (*J. W.* 3.42–43).[22] The slopes of upper Galilee were suitable for the cultivation of grapes and olives, supporting the production of wine and oil, so graphically illustrated in the entrepreneurial activity of John of Gischala, as reported by Josephus (*Life* 74–75; *J. W.* 2.259–260).[23] In addition to the agricultural activity, the lake was a natural resource

---

21. See David A. Fiensy, *The Social History of Palestine in the Herodian Period: The Land Is Mine* (Lewiston, N.Y.: Mellen, 1991).

22. See Ze'ev Safrai, *The Economy of Roman Palestine* (London: Routledge, 1994).

23. Rafael Frankel, "Some Oil Presses from Western Galilee," *BASOR* 286 (1992): 39–71.

that supported a robust fishing industry, giving rise to the need for specialized services such as ceramic making for export of liquid products, as well as boat builders and net makers for the fish industry.[24]

The pertinent question that most concerns students of the Galilean economy is the extent to which the benefits of these products accrued to the peasants themselves, or whether they were creamed off by the ruling elite in taxes and other exactions.[25] Was the Galilean economy a politically controlled one to the extent that the peasants were mere serfs? In whose interest were the primary resources utilized? If, as I suggested, the Galilean landownership pattern represented a combination of large estates and family-run holdings, then it seems that some degree of commercial independence should be granted to the Galilean peasants. However, the refurbishment of Sepphoris and the building of Tiberias must have marked a turning point in terms of the Galilean economy. This was a watershed that coincided with Jesus' public ministry and provides the most immediate backdrop to his particular emphasis on the blessedness of the destitute and the call for trust in God's provident care for all.[26] The new Herodian class had to be accommodated with adequate allotments in order to maintain a luxurious lifestyle (cf. Matt. 11:8), and inevitably this meant pressure on the peasants. Debt was followed by appropriation of property, with slavery or brigandage as the only alternative ways of life.[27]

Yet this picture has to be balanced by the evidence from admittedly later sources that shows that a Jewish peasant class did survive the crisis of the two revolts. We find the rabbinic sources replete with references to markets, village traders, and laws to do with buying and selling.[28] This cannot be dismissed as mere idealization of later generations, but is rather a continuation of patterns that we can already discern in first-century sources such as the Gospels and Josephus's writings. However, the dividing line between subsistence and penury was a thin one, as the threatened strike by the Galilean peasants that occurred in the reign of the emperor Gaius Caligula (39 C.E.) demonstrates. In protest at the proposed erection of the emperor's statue in the Jerusalem temple, they decided not to till the land, and significantly, some members of the Herodian family were dismayed, fearing a consequence of insufficient resources to pay the annual tribute, thus leading to social anarchy (*Ant.* 18.273–274). Julius Caesar had recognized the problem for Jewish peasants by his restoration in 47 B.C.E. of their rights to support their temple, and consequently he reduced

24. K. C. Hanson, "The Galilean Fishing Economy and the Jesus Tradition," *BTB* 27 (1997): 99–111.

25. Horsley, *Galilee*, 202–22.

26. Sean Freyne, "The Geography, Politics, and Economics of Galilee and the Quest for the Historical Jesus," in *Studying the Historical Jesus: Evaluation of the Current State of Research*, ed. Bruce Chilton and Craig Evans, NTTS 19 (Leiden: Brill, 1994), 75–124.

27. Richard Horsley and John Hanson, *Bandits, Prophets, Messiahs: Popular Movements in the Time of Jesus* (Minneapolis: Winston, 1985).

28. Safrai, *Economy of Roman Palestine*, 224–72.

the annual tribute due to Rome (*Ant.* 14.190–216). Now, however, Antipas was annually entitled to two hundred talents (the equivalent of six hundred thousand Tyrian silver shekels) from Galilee and Perea as a personal income. This compares favorably with his brother, Philip, in the neighboring territory, who was allowed only one hundred talents. But Archelaus, before his deposition in 6 C.E., had been granted six hundred talents from Judea, Samaria, and Idumea, together with the coastal towns of Strato's Tower (Caesarea Maritima) and Joppa (*Ant.* 17.318–320). Antipas's income was still a considerable demand on the Galilean populace, however, and a direct tribute to Rome was, presumably, still applicable, even though this is not mentioned explicitly.[29]

The use of money is essential for any developing economy, since as stored value it allows for a far wider and more complex network of trading than does the barter of goods, which can occur only at a local level. Josephus does mention that John of Gischala used Tyrian money in his transactions with his fellow Jews from Syria. This piece of information is in line with archaeological evidence from various sites where Tyrian coinage seems to dominate the numismatic finds at locations not just in upper Galilee, such as Meiron, Gischala, and Khirbet Shema, but even at Gamala and Jotapata as well, both of which were lower Galilean strongholds of Jewish nationalism in the first revolt.[30] This suggests trading links with the important Phoenician port, despite the cultural differences between the city and its Jewish hinterland, which often boiled over into open hostility (*J. W.* 4.105). Most surprising is the fact that the Tyrian half-shekel was deemed to be "the coin of the sanctuary," which all male Jews were obliged to pay for the upkeep of the Jerusalem temple. The usual reason given is that the Tyrian money had retained a constant value in terms of its silver content for over a century and a half (126 B.C.E.–56 C.E.), whereas other currencies in the region had been debased. It may also have been due to the fact that Tyrian money was in far greater supply than any other currency, native or foreign. The Tyrian mint was recognized by Rome as the most important one in the region, and the Herodians were not allowed to produce silver coins. Thus, we cannot infer from the quantity of coins alone that Galilean commercial relations were concentrated on that one Phoenician city. In antiquity, coins remained in circulation for a very long time after their date of issue, and they may have served transactions at several different locations along the way, not just at the places of production and final deposition.

The Galilean economy was motivated by values and attitudes that were directly opposed to those of the Jewish religious worldview that both the Galilean peasants and their Jerusalem religious leaders espoused, at least in

29. Hoehner, *Herod Antipas*, 298–301.

30. Richard Hanson, *Tyrian Influence in the Upper Galilee* (Cambridge, Mass.: ASOR, 1980); Joyce Raynor and Yakov Meshorer, *The Coins of Ancient Meiron* (Winona Lake, Ind.: Eisenbrauns, 1985); D. Barag, "Tyrian Coinage in Galilee," *INJ* 6–7 (1982–83): 7–13; D. Syon, "The Coins of Gamala: an Interim Report," *INJ* 12 (1992–93): 34–55.

theory. In order to maintain their elite lifestyle, the Herodians creamed off the wealth of the land for their own benefit without giving anything back in return. The Jewish ideal, on the other hand, espoused an inclusive community in which all shared in the blessings of the land and its fruits. It was during the long reign of Antipas that this conflict became apparent for the Galilean peasants in the changing ethos represented by Sepphoris and Tiberias.[31] These two centers and their upkeep drained the countryside of its resources, natural and human, thereby causing resentment and opposition. This opposition comes into clear light during the first revolt, when both were attacked by Galileans who sought to vent their resentment on the aristocratic inhabitants and their opulent lifestyles (*Life* 66.301, 373–380). However, this feeling of distance, even resentment, can be detected some forty years earlier during the ministry of Jesus to the villages of Galilee. Neither Herodian center is mentioned in the Gospels, and the lifestyle of those dwelling "in the houses of kings" is viewed critically when contrasted with the values that both Jesus himself and his mentor, John the Baptist, espoused (Matt. 11:8).[32]

Galilee and Jerusalem

If the Galilean peasants were opposed to the two Herodian cities and their values, Jerusalem, the holy city, represented in their expectations a very different reality. The temple in Jerusalem may have been a source of awe and wonder for Galilean peasants at first sight (Mark 13:1), but as the symbol of a shared universe that included shared stewardship of the land of Israel, it was meant to provide them with "long-lasting feelings of attachment and motivation" that were to express themselves in pilgrimage and offerings freely given.[33] The problem was that Jerusalem and its native aristocracy had suffered a fatal blow with the advent of Herodian rule. Even though Herod the Great had endowed the city with some magnificent buildings, in particular the greatly extended and refurbished temple complex itself, his espousal of other centers, notably Caesarea Maritima, indicates that there was a separation between the religious and political authority.[34] This considerably circumscribed the sphere of influence of Jerusalem—a situation that was further accentuated after the introduction of direct Roman rule in 6 C.E. with the deposition of Archelaus.

31. Sean Freyne, "Herodian Economics in Galilee: Searching for a Suitable Model," in *Galilee and Gospel: Collected Essays* (Tübingen: Mohr Siebeck, 2000), 86–113.

32. Gerd Theissen, *The Gospels in Context: Social and Political History in the Synoptic Gospels* (Edinburgh: Clark, 1992), 25–42; Sean Freyne, "Jesus and the Urban Culture of Galilee," in *Galilee and Gospel*, 183–207.

33. Sean Freyne, "The Geography of Restoration: Galilee-Jerusalem Relations in Early Jewish and Christian Experience," *NTS* 47 (2001): 289–311.

34. Doron Mendels, *The Rise and Fall of Jewish Nationalism* (New York: Doubleday, 1992), 277–332.

Herod had also sought control of the religious institutions, especially the office of the high priest, by introducing his own appointees from the Diaspora, and thereby eroding the effectiveness of the office for inner-Jewish life. None of the usual status criteria of Greco-Roman society, such as wealth or claims to noble lineage, could indefinitely cloak the historical realities.[35] The life of luxury lived by the Jerusalem aristocracy, as evidenced by the recent excavations of their residences in the Jewish quarter, meant that even violence could be used in order to extract the dues from an increasingly disaffected peasantry (*Ant.* 20.180–181, 206–207).

It is not surprising, therefore, that the first century saw an increase in social turmoil of various kinds in the Judean countryside: banditry, prophetic movements of protest, and various religious ideologies that can be directly related to the prevailing social conditions.[36] Thus, the Essenes' practice of the common life in the Judean desert away from the city, and the Pharisees' espousal of a modest lifestyle (*Ant.* 18.12, 18), represent the classic countercultural response to the prevailing aristocratic ethos by treating poverty as an ideal rather than as shameful. However, as in Galilee, so in Judea, it is with the various revolutionary groups and their strategies, which come into full view at the outbreak of the revolt in 66 C.E., that one can best judge the resentment of the aristocracy and its elitist behavior. The refusal to pay the tribute, the cessation of "the loyal sacrifice" on behalf of Rome, and the burning of the debt records (*J. W.* 2.404, 409, 427) were acts prompted by hatred of the Roman governor, Florus, yet they had a strong social and class component also.[37] Josephus says that the chief priests, by a display of public piety, which was as contrived as it was personally motivated, sought in vain to persuade the people to accept the Roman troops (*J. W.* 2.321–324). The real reasons for their trying to placate Florus were later revealed to Agrippa: "being men of position and owners of property, they were desirous of peace" (*J. W.* 2.338). In fact, a political revolt had become a social revolution in which the chief targets were not the Romans, but the high priests and their immediate followers. Thus, in 67 C.E., as Vespasian advanced on Jerusalem, supported by "brigands" from the countryside, the Zealots occupied the temple and elected by lot a country villager with no legitimate credentials as replacement for the high priest Ananus, whom Josephus describes as "a most wise man, who might possibly have saved the city, had he escaped the conspirators' hand" (*J. W.* 4.151).

Since Judea, like Galilee, was a rapidly changing society in the first century C.E., it seems clear that the systemic causes of the breakdown of Judean society, so graphically illustrated during the revolt, were already operative in the early provincial period. To some extent these were the legacy of Herod the Great's

---

35. Martin Goodman, *The Ruling Class of Judaea: The Origins of the Jewish Revolt against Rome, A.D. 66–70* (Cambridge: Cambridge University Press, 1987), esp. 29–75.

36. Horsley and Hanson, *Bandits, Prophets, Messiahs*.

37. Goodman, *Ruling Class of Judaea*, 152–95.

domination of the religious institutions of Judaism for his own political ends. By his strong-arm tactics he was able to contain any show of dissent, to the point that no protest was possible. The reaction among the Jewish people upon his death, and the failure of Archelaus to maintain order, are clear indications that Judean society was already in turmoil in a way that Galilee was not. This was the world in which Jesus grew up and that shaped his distinctive understanding of Israel's destiny and his own role in it. In Galilee he sought to address the social needs of the village culture, whose lifestyle and values were being eroded by the new level of Herodian influence there as a result of Antipas's presence. However, as a *Jewish* prophet, he also had to address the center of his own religious tradition in Jerusalem. Like other country prophets before and after him, he had the unenviable task of having to declare judgment on the temple and the city that he loved (Luke 13:34–35).[38]

38. Gerd Theissen, "Die Tempelweissagung Jesu: Prophetie im Spannungsfeld zwischen Tempel und Land," *TZ* 32 (1976): 144–58; Sean Freyne, *Galilee, Jesus and the Gospels: Literary Approaches and Historical Investigations* (Minneapolis: Fortress, 1988), 224–39.

2

The Roman Empire and Asia Minor

David A. Fiensy

The people of Asia Minor witnessed some of the more important events in the development of early Christianity. Many of the NT books were addressed to persons, cities, or provinces of this region: Philemon, 1–2 Timothy, Ephesians, Colossians, Revelation, Galatians, and 1 Peter; and Paul was at Ephesus when he wrote 1 Corinthians (1 Cor. 15:32; 16:8). Further, the Book of Acts narrates Paul's missionary travels through Galatia and Asia, two provinces in Asia Minor. Christian tradition locates the Johannine community, which produced the Fourth Gospel and the three Johannine Epistles, in Ephesus. Finally, one of the greatest leaders of the early Christian movement, Paul the apostle, and other Christian workers of less importance (Timothy [Acts 16:1]; Epaphras [Col. 4:12]) came from Asia Minor. And this list does not even touch upon the numerous second-century Christian leaders (both "orthodox" and heretical) who were born there.[1]

It is appropriate, then, to survey the work done in investigating Asia Minor because of this region's importance in early Christian history. The wealth of

---

1. Papias, Polycarp, Melito, Polycrates, Montanus, Irenaeus, Cerinthus, Quadratus, and Marcion were born in Asia Minor. Aquila, an important translator of the Hebrew Bible, came from Pontus in Asia Minor. Further, three notable Greek philosophers originated from Asia Minor: Epictetus, Diogenes of Sinope, and Peregrinus.

newly published inscriptions and other archaeological finds in recent decades also makes such a survey particularly desirable at this time. Ongoing excavations in several parts of Asia Minor have brought to light numerous texts and other material remains that are yielding important results for NT study.[2]

Added to the new materials is the new trend in NT studies to consider these materials alongside the texts. When a noted NT scholar turns to editing collections on the epigraphy and archaeology of Ephesus and Pergamum, one senses a shift in the discipline.[3]

We will consider relevant works from roughly the last three decades that have appealed to the new evidence to interpret the NT. Generally, we will not consider commentaries and works of introduction (about authorship, etc.) except when they speak to our theme of using archaeology, epigraphy, and numismatics to illumine the NT texts.

The Scholarly Legacy

Although we want to consider the work done in the last three decades or so, we cannot ignore the major resources before that. Those working in the sources today cite some authors repeatedly. First of all is W. M. Ramsay, the patriarch of Asia Minor studies. Often, scholars today are only acting on leads that he provided in his numerous publications both on ancient history and NT. A classicist who traveled extensively in Turkey in the late nineteenth century, Ramsay wrote *The Historical Geography of Asia Minor* in 1890.[4] Two other authors of notable standard works are T. R. S. Broughton[5] and D. Magie.[6] The former traces the economic development of the region, while the latter provides an exhaustive history from the death of Attalus (133 B.C.E.) to 285 C.E.

2. G. H. R. Horsley ("The Inscriptions of Ephesos and the New Testament," *NovT* 2 [1992]: 121) reports that there were, at the time the article was written, around 3,750 inscriptions from Ephesus alone.

3. See H. Koester, ed., *Ephesos, Metropolis of Asia: An Interdisciplinary Approach to Its Archaeology, Religion, and Culture* (Valley Forge, Pa.: Trinity, 1995); idem, *Pergamon, Citadel of the Gods: Archaeological Record, Literary Description, and Religious Development* (Harrisburg, Pa.: Trinity, 1998).

4. W. M. Ramsay, *The Historical Geography of Asia Minor* (London: John Murray, 1890). See also Ramsay, *The Letters to the Seven Churches of Asia and Their Place in the Plan of the Apocalypse* (London: Hodder & Stoughton, 1904); idem, *The Cities of St. Paul: Their Influence on His Life and Thought* (London: Hodder & Stoughton, 1907). On Ramsay's contribution to NT study in general, see W. W. Gasque, *Sir William Ramsay: Archaeologist and New Testament Scholar* (Grand Rapids: Baker, 1966).

5. T. R. S. Broughton, "Roman Asia Minor," in *Economic Survey of Ancient Rome*, ed. T. Frank (Baltimore: Johns Hopkins University Press, 1938).

6. D. Magie, *Roman Rule in Asia Minor*, 2 vols. (Princeton, N.J.: Princeton University Press, 1950).

Notable Resources

S. E. Johnson attempted to present all the relevant publications on the study of Asia Minor in three essays, the last of which was in 1975. Johnson reported on archaeological excavations as well as works specifically on NT and Christianity in Asia Minor.[7] *Aufstieg und Niedergang der römischen Welt,* a series devoted to ancient Roman history, has in addition produced several essays on Asia Minor. In 1980 two appeared, one on Galatia and one on the cities of Asia Minor,[8] and in 1990 R. Oster's essay on Ephesus as a religious center was published.[9] The *American Journal of Archaeology* has published reports of archaeological work in Asia Minor/Turkey almost yearly from 1956 to 1997.[10] Finally, the ongoing publication of inscriptions under the title *Inschriften griechischer Städte aus Kleinasien* seeks to collect the new materials pertaining to Asia Minor.

The Acts of the Apostles

The God-Fearers/Worshipers

In the Book of Acts, whenever Paul entered a new town in Asia Minor, he almost always found a significant population of Jews. He went into the synagogues (13:14; 14:1; 18:19; 19:8), and he also interacted with Jews in various other ways (16:1; 19:13). The epigraphic sources confirm that a large number of Jews lived in Asia Minor during the events narrated in Acts.[11] Although the new evidence may call for rethinking our views about the nature of the Jewish

---

7. S. E. Johnson "Asia Minor and Early Christianity" in *Christianity, Judaism, and Other Greco-Roman Cults,* ed. J. Neusner, 4 vols., SJLA 12 (Leiden: Brill, 1975), 2:77–145. See also Johnson, "Laodicea and Its Neighbors" *BA* 13 (1950): 1–18; "Early Christianity in Asia Minor," *JBL* 77 (1958): 1–17; "Unsolved Questions about Early Christianity in Anatolia," in *Studies in New Testament and Early Christian Literature,* ed. D. E. Aune, NovTSup 33 (Leiden: Brill, 1972), 181–93; "The Apostle Paul and the Riot in Ephesus," *Lexington Theological Quarterly* 14 (1979): 79–88.

8. S. Mitchell, "Population and the Land in Roman Galatia," in *ANRW* 2.7.2:1053–81; A. D. Macro, "The Cities of Asia Minor under the Roman Imperium," in *ANRW* 2.7.2:658–97.

9. R. Oster, "Ephesus as a Religious Center under the Principate, Paganism before Constantine," in *ANRW* 2.18.3:1661–728. See also Oster, *A Bibliography of Ancient Ephesus* (Metuchen, N.J.: Scarecrow, 1987).

10. The reports until 1993 were done by M. J. Mellink. From 1994 to 1997 they were written by Marie-Henriette Gates.

11. See M. Stern, "The Jewish Diaspora," in *The Jewish People in the First Century,* ed. S. Safrai and M. Stern, 2 vols., CRINT 1.1–2 (Philadelphia: Fortress, 1974), 1:143–55; E. Schürer, *The History of the Jewish People in the Age of Jesus Christ (175 B.C.–A.D. 135),* ed. G. Vermès et al., 3 vols. in 4 (Edinburgh: Clark, 1973–87), 3.1:17–36; A. T. Kraabel, "Judaism in Western Asia Minor under the Roman Empire" (Ph.D. diss., Harvard University, 1968); P. R. Trebilco, *The Jewish Communities in Asia Minor* (Cambridge: Cambridge University Press, 1991); P. W. van der Horst, "Jews and Christians in Aphrodisias in the Light of Their Relations in Other Cities

Diaspora,[12] it certainly does in general support the information in Acts and Josephus about Jews in this region.

But another group of persons seemed less confirmed by the evidence until an inscription was found in Aphrodiasias. This group is referred to in Acts in several verses. These persons are called "those fearing God" (οἱ φοβούμενοι τὸν θεόν, *hoi phoboumenoi ton theon*) or "one fearing God" in some passages (10:2, 22, 35; 13:16, 26), and "those worshiping (God)" in others (οἱ σεβόμενοι [τὸν θεόν], *hoi sebomenoi [ton theon]* [13:43, 50; 16:14; 17:4, 17; 18:7]). After narrating the conversion of the first God-fearer, Cornelius of Caesarea (chs. 10–11), Luke tells the story of Paul and Barnabas in Antioch of Pisidia in Asia Minor (ch. 13). There, Paul preached in the synagogue to both Israelites and those fearing God (13:16, 26), and when the Israelites did not believe, Paul and Barnabas turned to the Gentiles (evidently the God-fearers) to minister (13:46–48). Thus, the full Israelites did not accept Paul's message, but the God-fearers did. Based on these references and a few texts outside the NT (mainly Josephus, Philo, Juvenal, Epictetus, and the Talmud[13]), the scholarly consensus said that attached loosely to the synagogues in the Diaspora was a group of Gentiles who studied the Torah and lived a life ethically acceptable to Jews but did not accept circumcision. These, so the consensus maintained, were half-Jews who would have been more open to Paul's preaching than the Jews.

But some challenges have been made against the consensus. First, M. Wilcox doubted that Acts was describing a group such as the consensus had imagined. Only Acts 16:14 and 17:4 perhaps refer to such a group, but even here the texts are unclear. The references seem to Wilcox to speak only about a person's piety and not about membership in "a fringe group of Gentile synagogue adherents." Wilcox concludes that without further external evidence, one should not interpret these texts as referring to a class of Gentiles who regularly worship at the synagogue.[14]

---

in Asia Minor," *NedTT* 43 (1989): 106–21; F. F. Bruce, "Jews and Christians in the Lycus Valley," *BSac* 141 (1984): 3–15.

12. See A. T. Kraabel, "The Roman Diaspora: Six Questionable Assumptions," in *Diaspora Jews and Judaism,* ed. J. A. Overman and R. S. MacLennan, SFSHJ 41 (Atlanta: Scholars Press, 1992).

13. See the impressive evidence collected by F. Siegert, "Gottesfürchtige und Sympathisanten," *JSJ* 4 (1973): 109–64. Also see B. Lifshitz, "De nouveau sur les 'Synmpathisants,'" *JSJ* 1 (1970): 77–84; L. H. Feldman, "The Omnipresence of the God-Fearers," *BAR* 12, no. 5 (1986): 58–69; J. G. Gager, "Jews, Gentiles, and Synagogues in the Book of Acts," in *Christians among Jews and Gentiles,* ed. G. W. E. Nickelsburg and G. W. MacRae (Philadelphia: Fortress, 1986), 91–99. The texts usually cited (see the above works for others) are Josephus, *Ant.* 14.110; 20.34–38, 195; Philo, *QE* 2.2.; Juvenal, *Sat.* 14.96–106; Epictetus, *Diatr.* 2.9.19–21; *Deut. Rab.* 2.24; *b. Sanh.* 70b; *Mek.* on Exod. 22:20; *y. Meg.* 1.11.

14. M. Wilcox, "The 'God-Fearers' in Acts—A Reconsideration," *JSNT* 13 (1981): 102–22. This same observation had been made similarly by L. H. Feldman, "Jewish 'Sympathizers' in Classical Literature and Inscriptions," *TAPA* 81 (1950): 200–208; and by K. Lake, "Proselytes and God-Fearers," in *The Beginnings of Christianity,* ed. F. J. Foakes-Jackson and K. Lake, 5 vols. (Grand Rapids: Baker, 1979), 5:74–96.

A more serious challenge to the thesis has come from A. T. Kraabel. For a number of years, Kraabel worked on the excavations at Sardis and found no clear references or evidence for such a group of Gentiles connected to the worship of the synagogue. In examining over one hundred synagogue inscriptions both from Sardis and elsewhere, one can find no expressions such as those in Acts, although one does find a somewhat similar expression, θεοσεβής (*theosebēs*). Kraabel began to question the consensus and decided that although Luke does seem to be describing a group of Gentile synagogue adherents, Luke was not writing history at this point. Rather, the God-fearers were an effective theological construction for Luke to use in explaining how the gospel was rejected by the Jews and accepted by the Gentiles. Thus, the God-fearers were not an actual historical group, but Luke's literary invention.[15] Further, the sources outside the NT that supposedly refer to God-fearers are always interpreted from the perspective of Acts. If one reads them without the influence of Acts, they do not clearly refer to such a group. Kraabel concludes that the God-fearers, "if they existed at all . . . were isolated and did not have the effect that many suppose. In a sense they were a figment of the scholarly imagination."[16] These articles were written before the publication of the Aphrodisias inscription, but by 1992 Kraabel was still hesitant to accept the received view on the God-fearers. In an article published that year, he granted that there is a kernel of truth behind the God-fearers pictured in Acts, but he maintained that Luke took over that kernel and exaggerated it. Kraabel has seemed to see something anti-Jewish in the thesis. What Luke wanted, Kraabel maintained, was to show how Judaism was superseded. Yet he admitted, "There surely were some Gentiles interested in their Jewish neighbors and their piety."[17]

Since the publication of the synagogue inscription from Aphrodisias, a city in western Asia Minor, the question of the existence of a group of God-fearers attached to the synagogue has been settled for most scholars. A stone pillar inscribed on two sides lists the donors to the local Jewish soup kitchen, according to J. Reynolds and R. Tannenbaum, who give the inscription with commentary.[18] On one side of the pillar are listed members of the δεκανία (*dekania*), or special company or class of those pursuing study of Torah and

---

15. See A. T. Kraabel, "The Disappearance of the 'God-Fearers,'" *Numen* 28, no. 2 (1981): 113–26; idem, "Greeks, Jews, and Lutherans in the Middle Half of Acts," in *Christians among Jews and Gentiles,* ed. G. W. E. Nickelsburg and G. W. MacRae (Philadelphia: Fortress, 1986), 147–57; and Kraabel with R. S. MacLennan, "The God-Fearers—A Literary and Theological Invention," *BAR* 12, no. 5 (1986): 46–53, 64.

16. Kraabel and MacLennan, "God-Fearers," 48.

17. Kraabel, "The God-fearers Meet the Beloved Disciple," in Overman and MacLennan, *Diaspora Jews and Judaism,* esp. 282. Kraabel also refers to an offensive statement written by M. Hengel to the effect that the God-fearers show how Judaism in the Diaspora had to make "constant and ultimately untenable compromises" to survive. See Kraabel, "Disappearance of the 'God-fearers,'" 129.

18. J. Reynolds and R. Tannenbaum, *Jews and God-Fearers at Aphrodisias: Greek Inscriptions with Commentary* (Cambridge: Cambridge University Press, 1987). See also R. Tannenbaum,

prayer. Listed among the mostly Jewish names are three persons called proselytes (προσήλυτος, *prosēlytos*) and two (named Emmonius and Antoninus) called God-worshipers (θεοσεβής, *theosebēs*). Obviously, the two God-worshipers have attracted much attention. They are singled out from the others by this title, and yet they have joined the others in study and worship. These certainly sound like the God-fearers of Acts. On the other side of the pillar are two longer lists of names separated by an empty space in the inscription. The upper list contains mostly Jewish names, and the lower list is introduced by the words "and as many as are God-worshipers." Again, these persons, since they are separated from the other names and introduced by the title "God-worshipers," seem to have been like the God-fearers in Acts. The support for these conclusions has been strong, and one can safely say that the consensus about the God-fearers—perhaps with some modifications[19]—has been confirmed by the Aphrodisias inscription.[20] C. K. Barrett's cautious conclusions about this matter seem appropriate: (1) some Gentiles were attracted to Jewish ethics,

---

"Jews and God-Fearers in the Holy City of Aphrodite," *BAR* 12, no. 5 (1986): 54–57. Other inscriptions containing the term *theosebēs* have been found, but it is debatable whether these refer to God-fearers in the sense of that expression in Acts. For a survey of these inscriptions, see P. Trebilco, *Jewish Communities in Asia Minor*, SNTSMS 69 (Cambridge: Cambridge University Press, 1991), 155–65; Irina Levinskaya, *The Book of Acts in Its Diaspora Setting*, BAFCS 5 (Grand Rapids: Eerdmans, 1996), 59–70.

19. Siegert ("Gottesfürchtige und Sympathisanten," 147–49, 163) wants to differentiate between God-fearers and sympathizers of the synagogue. The former were adherents of Judaism but not full Jews. The latter did not necessarily honor the God of the Jews but may have either adopted certain Jewish customs such as Sabbath observance or had a politically friendly attitude toward Jews. Such a division is, in effect, advised by J. Murphy-O'Connor ("Lots of God-Fearers? *Theosebeis* in the Aphrodisias Inscription" *RB* 2 [1992]: 418–24), who surmises that the two God-worshipers, Eummonius and Antoninus, who were studying Torah were actual God-fearers, but those listed on the other side of the pillar were mere contributors to the soup kitchen. Perhaps an excellent example of a sympathizer is Julia Severa, who in Acmonia during the reign of Nero was both a priestess of the emperor cult and the patroness of the Jewish synagogue. See Kraabel, "Judaism in Western Asia Minor," 46, 78; Trebilco, *Jewish Communities in Asia Minor*, 59.

20. Those who support the existence of God-fearers as a group of synagogue adherents include Levinskaya, *The Book of Acts*, 80; Trebilco, *Jewish Communities in Asia Minor*, 164; Gager, "Jews, Gentiles, and Synagogues"; Feldman, "Omnipresence of the God-Fearers"; Lifshitz, "De nouveau sur les 'Sympathisants'"; Siegert, "Gottesfürchtige und Sympathisanten"; Schürer, *History of the Jewish People*, 3.1:165–72; J. A. Overman, "The God-Fearers: Some Neglected Features," *JSNT* 32 (1988): 17–26; B. Witherington III, *The Acts of the Apostles: A Socio-rhetorical Commentary* (Grand Rapids: Eerdmans, 1998), 343; P. W. van der Horst, "Juden und Christen in Aphrodisias im Licht ihrer Beziehungen in anderen Städten Kleinasiens," in *Juden und Christen in der Antike*, ed. J. van Amersfoort and J. van Oort, SPA 1 (Kampen: Kok, 1990), 130; and S. McKnight, *A Light among the Gentiles: Jewish Missionary Activity in the Second Temple Period* (Philadelphia: Fortress, 1991), 110–14. Those who reject the thesis—in addition to Kraabel—include M. Goodman (*Mission and Conversion: Proselytizing in the Religious History of the Roman Empire* [Oxford: Clarendon, 1994], 47), who posits that such groups did not appear until the second century, and Murphy-O'Connor ("Lots of God-Fearers?"), who accepts only a highly modified version of the God-fearer construct.

theology, and worship but did not become proselytes; (2) in one place at least
(Aphrodisias), they formed a recognized element in the synagogue; (3) such
Gentiles presented a great opportunity to Christian evangelists; (4) Luke was
aware of this.[21]

Paul in Ephesus

As part of his third missionary tour, Paul spent an extended amount of
time in the city of Ephesus (Acts 19:10; 20:31). There, he taught in the Jewish synagogue for a while, encountered some Jewish exorcists, and witnessed
an anti-Christian riot. The material remains confirm that Jews had a presence
in Ephesus but do not provide many details. To date, only three inscriptions
referring to Jews and some objects with Jewish symbols have been found. The
synagogue so far has eluded discovery.[22] Luke then says that Paul removed
himself from the synagogue to teach in the lecture hall of Tyrannus (19:9). A
person named Tyrannus has been attested in an inscription, but we cannot be
certain that this is the same one as in Acts. Additionally, an inscription referring
to an αὐδειτώριον (audeitōrion, from the Latin auditorium) has been found.
This was a lecture hall adjacent to the library.[23]

The riot (19:23–40) has attracted attention due to the numerous epigraphical and classical parallels to the text of Acts. The details of this section
lead to the conclusion that the author at least knew the culture of Ephesus
and may have been present at the riot.[24] The reference to Ephesus as a νε-
ωκόρος (neōkoros), or "temple warden," city (19:35); the mention of the
clerk or scribe of the people (γραμματεύς, grammateus [19:35]); the several
reminders that Artemis was acclaimed as "great" by the Ephesians (19:27,
28, 34, 35); the statement that Artemis was honored in many other places
(19:27); the reference to silversmiths (ἀργυροκόπος, argyrokopos [19:24]);
and calling the regular assembly of Ephesus the ἔννομος ἐκκλησία (ennomos

---

21. C. K. Barrett, *A Critical and Exegetical Commentary on the Acts of the Apostles*, 2 vols.,
ICC (Edinburgh: Clark, 1994), 1:501. See also the conclusions of T. M. Finn ("The God-fearers
Reconsidered," *CBQ* 47 [1985]: 75–84): (1) the term "God-fearers" was not a technical term at
the time of Acts; (2) Luke does overly simplify the process of the evangelization of the Gentiles in
Acts; (3) the literary evidence corroborates Acts regarding the God-fearers; and the conclusions of
McKnight (*Light among the Gentiles*, 110): (1) there was a group of Gentiles attached to Judaism
that may be called sympathizers; (2) the term "God-fearer" was not a technical one.

22. Horsley, "Inscriptions of Ephesos," 122–25. The objects are four oil lamps with menorahs;
a piece of glass with a menorah; an ethrog, a lulab, and a shofar painted on it; a menorah carved
on a step in front of the library; and a gem with a scriptural reference. See also E. M. Yamauchi,
New Testament Cities in Western Asia Minor (Grand Rapids: Baker, 1980), 110.

23. C. J. Hemer, *The Book of Acts in the Setting of Hellenistic History,* WUNT 49 (Tübingen:
Mohr, 1989), 120–21; Yamauchi, *New Testament Cities*, 100.

24. H. Koester, "Ephesos in Early Christian Literature," in Koester, *Ephesos, Metropolis of
Asia,* 119–40. Koester notes that the details demonstrate Luke's knowledge of Ephesian religious
and political life but affirms that these details do not prove that the story is historical.

ekklēsia [19:39])—these are all attested word for word in the inscriptions from Ephesus.[25]

Although no silver shrines have yet been found like those named in Acts 19:24, the oft-cited Salutaris inscription from Ephesus describes a golden statuette of Artemis. In addition, terra-cotta figurines of Artemis standing in a niche have been found that roughly correspond to that indicated in Acts.[26] Further, the zeal with which the Ephesians defended the cult of Artemis in the riot described in Acts 19 is well known from an inscription. According to this text, they sentenced forty-five persons to death for mistreating sacred items from Artemis.[27]

More generally, historians have noted the frequent attestation of labor guilds, such as the silversmiths' guild to which Demetrius belonged (19:24–27). The inscriptions from Asia refer to guilds of all kinds, including silversmiths. Further, other incidents of rioting at the instigation of these labor unions are indicated in the inscriptions.[28] The gathering of labor unions, it seems, often could result in outbreaks of unrest in the cities of Asia Minor. Thus, the story of the riot in Ephesus narrated in Acts 19 seems plausible.

The intent of those scholars investigating the details of Acts 19:23–40, then, has been to demonstrate that they are paralleled in the material remains from the region and thus fit easily into the history and culture of Ephesus.

The Asiarchs

One of the passing remarks in the riot narrative has sparked controversy. In Acts 19:31 Luke writes, "Certain also of the Asiarchs, since they were friends

25. Koester, "Ephesos," 130; Hemer, *The Book of Acts,* 121–23; R. Oster, "A Historical Commentary on the Missionary Success Stories in Acts 19:11–40" (Ph.D. diss., Princeton University, 1974), 112–15; P. Trebilco, "Asia," in *The Book of Acts in Its Graeco-Roman Setting,* ed. D. W. J. Gill and C. Gempf, BAFCS 2 (Grand Rapids: Eerdmans, 1994), 291–362, esp. 318–56; W. W. Gasque, "The Historical Value of the Book of Acts," *TZ* 28 (1972): 186.

26. Oster, "Historical Commentary," 71–73; Hemer, *The Book of Acts,* 121; Trebilco, "Asia," 336, 356; G. Mussies, "Pagans, Jews, and Christians at Ephesus," in *Studies on the Hellenistic Background of the New Testament,* ed. G. Mussies and P. W. van der Horst, Utrechtse theologische reeks 10 (Utrecht: Faculteit der Godgeleerheid van de Rijksuniversiteit, 1990), 189. The Salutaris inscription was published with translation by J. H. Oliver, *The Sacred Gerusia* (Baltimore: American School of Classical Studies, 1941). An excerpt from this inscription is given in *NewDocs* 4:46–47.

27. Oster, "Historical Commentary," 97–98; Trebilco, "Asia," 331. Could their zeal for Artemis have been fueled also by identification of the goddess with Agrippina, the wife of Claudius, as indicated on Ephesian coins? See L. J. Kreitzer, "A Numismatic Clue to Acts 19:23–41: The Ephesian Cistophori of Claudius and Agrippina," *JSNT* 30 (1987): 59–70.

28. Trebilco, "Asia," 336, 338; Oster, "Historical Commentary," 75–77. Horsley ("Inscriptions of Ephesos," 127–33) draws important conclusions of a different nature from an inscription about a fishermen's guild. The guild had members from slaves to the well-to-do and a surprising number of Roman citizens. Was the same pattern true for early Christianity? Also see Horsley's "A Hellenistic Cult Group and the New Testament Churches," *JAC* 24 (1981): 7–41, in which he examines an inscription about a pagan cult with features remarkably similar to early Christianity.

of [Paul], sent word to him and urged him not to go into the theater." Historians have some questions about this statement: (1) Who were the Asiarchs? Specifically, were they the high priests of the imperial cult in Asia? (2) Is this reference anachronistic? In other words, can we find attestation of Asiarchs present during the time when Paul was in Ephesus (mid-fifties C.E.)? Since the literary references to Asiarchs are few (Acts 19:31; Strabo, *Geogr.* 14.1.42 [referring to the time of Pompey—i.e., the late republic]; *Digest* [quoting Modestinus] 27.1.6.14), we must rely heavily on the material remains to answer these questions.

The older view is that the Asiarchs were also the high priests of Asia.[29] In 1974 M. Rossner gave seven arguments for this identification based on her examination of the inscriptions and coins available at that time.[30] But since then several more inscriptions have expanded the list of known Asiarchs to over two hundred; of these, 106 were from Ephesus. Only seventy-four of those from Ephesus were known to Rossner.[31] From the new evidence, both R. A. Kearsley and S. J. Friesen have argued that the two offices were not the same.[32]

The question of whether or not the reference is anachronistic is unsettled. The coins and inscriptions begin to refer to Asiarchs in the late first century, after the time when Paul was in Ephesus. Kearsley has attempted to calculate backward from an inscription that she dates to 114 C.E. This inscription and others related to it trace a family's history, showing that the family produced several Asiarchs down through the years and would have had one at the time of Paul. Kearsley's case, however, depends on the correct dating of the inscription to 114 C.E.[33] Friesen disputes the dating (he dates it to 170 C.E.), locating the first Asiarch in the family no sooner than the 80s, after Paul was in Ephesus. He believes that the office of Asiarch, which was an archaic office found in Asia

---

29. See Lily R. Taylor, "The Asiarchs," in Foakes-Jackson and Lake, *The Beginnings of Christianity,* 5:256–61; Oster, "Historical Commentary," 104–5; S. R. F. Price, *Rituals and Power: The Roman Imperial Cult in Asia Minor* (Cambridge: Cambridge University Press, 1984), 60. Magie (*Roman Rule,* 2:1298–301) surveys various views.

30. M. Rossner, "Asiarchen und Archiereis Asias," *Studii Clasice* 16 (1974): 101–43. Her arguments are the following: (1) Modestinus seems to have identified them; (2) a high priestess of Asia can be the spouse of both the high priest and the Asiarch; (3) additions on titles listed in temples appear by both officials; (4) titles such as Asiarch of Asia may correspond to titles of high priest of Asia; (5) both sponsored gladiatorial contests; (6) there are no lists of official offices in which high priests and Asiarchs are listed separately; (7) the same persons often are called by both titles either at different times or contemporaneously. Rossner's extensive list of attested Asiarchs (112–41) has been substantially expanded by S. J. Friesen, *Twice Neokoros: Ephesus, Asia, and the Cult of the Flavian Imperial Family,* Religions in the Graeco-Roman World 116 (Leiden: Brill, 1993), 189–208.

31. See Horsley, "Inscriptions of Ephesos," 137.

32. See R. A. Kearsley, "The Asiarchs," in Gill and Gempf, *The Book of Acts,* 363–76; idem, "Some Asiarchs of Ephesus," in *NewDocs* 4:46–55. For Friesen, see *Twice Neokoros,* 92.

33. R. A. Kearsley, "A Leading Family of Cibyra and Some Asiarchs of the First Century," *Anatolian Studies* 38 (1988): 43–51. Horsley ("Inscriptions of Ephesos," 138) seems to support Kearsley.

in the days of the old Roman republic (the Strabo reference), was revived in the age of the Flavian emperors.[34] There is, therefore, no scholarly consensus on this issue. I would observe, however, that a revival in the importance of this office does not mean that it had ceased to exist between the time of Pompey (mid–first century B.C.E.) and the time of Domitian (late first century C.E.).

Roman Roads

One reads that Paul passed through Pisidia, Cilicia, Phrygia, Galatia, and Asia (Acts 13:4; 15:41; 16:6; 19:1) without knowing how he traveled. Did he climb mountains? Did he follow goat paths? Did he use well-paved roads?

The discovery and publication of Roman milestones in Asia Minor make it possible to trace the probable route of some of the roads in use when Paul was traveling through the region. D. French has published the inscriptions and the corresponding maps. He distinguishes among paved roads, unpaved but constructed roads, and mere tracks and paths.[35] The highways (the paved, broad roads) available to Paul in Asia Minor were few. There was a road from the republican period (the inscriptions date 129–126 B.C.E.) in western Asia Minor leading from Dorylaeum and Apamea to Ephesus and on north to Pergamum. In the Augustan period (the inscriptions date 6 B.C.E.) the Via Sebaste, or Augustan road, was built, which connected Cremna, Comama, Parlais, Antioch, Iconium, and Lystra (Roman colonies).

One can then both answer some questions and raise others. Since the Via Sebaste seems to have joined Roman colonies, we can understand why Paul followed it to Antioch, Iconium, and Lystra. But why, then, did he go on to Derbe, which was off the road?[36]

In heading west on the second journey, Paul would have found it much easier to transfer from the Via Sebaste to the old republican road and then on

34. Friesen, *Twice Neokoros,* 215. See his list of attested Asiarchs, which begins 80–90 C.E. See also P. Herz ("Asiarchen und Archiereai: Zum Provinzialkult der Provinz Asia," *Tyche* 7 [1992]: 93–115, esp. 97), who agrees generally with Friesen. He dates the family eighty years later than does Kearsley.

35. D. French, "The Roman Road System of Asia Minor," in *ANRW* 2.7.2:698–729; idem, "Acts and the Roman Roads of Asia Minor" in Gill and Gempf, *The Book of Acts,* 49–59. French actually lists six categories of roads. See also his publication of milestones in *Roman Roads and Milestones of Asia Minor,* 2 parts, BAR International Series 105, 392 (Oxford: BAR, 1988). Ramsay (*Historical Geography,* 22) also has a map of ancient roads, which he divides into three chronological categories: pre-Greek, Roman, and Byzantine-Turkish.

36. The location of Derbe is debated. See B. van Elderen, "Some Archaeological Observations on Paul's First Missionary Journey," in *Apostolic History and the Gospel,* ed. W. W. Gasque and R. P. Martin (Exeter: Paternoster, 1970), 151–61. S. Mitchell (*Anatolia: Land, Men, and Gods in Asia Minor,* vol. 2, *The Rise of the Church* [Oxford: Clarendon, 1993], 6–7), working from a number of inscriptions, concludes that the family of Sergius Paulus (Acts 13:7, 12), though ultimately of Italian origin, was native to Pisidian Antioch and thus invited Paul to proceed to his homeland.

to Ephesus. Why, then, did Paul think that the Spirit was forbidding him to travel through Asia (Acts 16:6)? What sort of unpaved path or track must he have used to head toward Troas?[37] As French observes, one cannot conclude that Paul traveled only the Roman roads.[38]

Pauline Epistles

Women Leaders

At least two NT epistles associated with Asia Minor reveal important attitudes about women's roles in the early church. Paul wrote in 1 Cor. 14:34–35 (written at Ephesus) that women should be silent in the assembly. The Pauline or deutero-Pauline letter sent to Timothy in Ephesus (1 Tim. 1:3) requires women to receive instruction quietly and forbids women to teach men (1 Tim. 2:11–12). One could conclude from these texts that women in Asia Minor generally were denied leadership roles and that Judaism maintained this practice in the synagogue—a practice that Christianity imitated.

But work based on the inscriptions in the last thirty years leads to other conclusions. The Book of Acts and the Gospels refer to men who were called "leaders of the synagogue" (ἀρχισυνάγωγος, *archisynagōgos*).[39] Inscriptions from the Greco-Roman world also refer to the *archisynagōgos*. These men had responsibilities, evidently, for managing the synagogue worship, education, and finances.

The surprise is that two inscriptions from Asia Minor and one from Crete name women as *archisynagōgoi*.[40] Rufina of Smyrna, who is called both a Jewess and an *archisynagōgos,* is named in an inscription from the second century C.E., and Theopempte of Myndos of Caria is also so named in an inscription from the fourth or fifth century.[41] These two inscriptions are interesting for two reasons: (1) there are seven references to *archisynagōgoi* from Asia Minor,

37. See W. P. Bowers, "Paul's Route through Mysia: A Note on Acts XVI.8," *JTS* 30 (1979): 507–11; French, "Acts and the Roman Roads," 57. Bowers maintains that Paul intended all along to go to Macedonia by ship and thus avoided the republican road as too far out of the way. French maintains that Paul avoided the road because of trouble in Antioch.

38. French, "Acts and the Roman Roads," 56.

39. Mark 5:22, 35, 36, 38; Luke 8:49; 13:14; Acts 13:15; 18:8, 17. On this synagogue official in rabbinic literature, see *m. Yoma* 7.1; *m. Soṭah* 7.7, 8; *b. Pesaḥ.* 49b.

40. See Kraabel, "Judaism in Western Asia Minor," 43–48; Bernadette J. Brooten, "Inscriptional Evidence for Women as Leaders in the Ancient Synagogue," *SBLSP* 20 (1981): 1–17; idem, *Women Leaders in the Ancient Synagogue,* BJS 36 (Chico, Calif.: Scholars, 1982); Trebilco, *Jewish Communities in Asia Minor,* 104–26; W. Horbury, "Women in the Synagogue," in *The Cambridge History of Judaism,* ed. W. D. Davies et al., 3 vols. (Cambridge: Cambridge University Press, 1999), 3:358–401.

41. See, for Rufina, J. B. Frey, *CIJ* 741. Trebilco (*Jewish Communities in Asia Minor,* 104) also gives the Greek text. For Theopempte, see *CIJ* 756, and Trebilco, *Jewish Communities in*

five to men and two to women; (2) the only other place where a woman was called an *archisynagōgos* was Crete. Thus, as Trebilco and Kraabel suggested, it seems plausible that women were allowed a greater role in some synagogues in Asia Minor.[42]

Added to the above inscriptions are three others that interest us. From Phocaea comes mention of one Tation, who was given the chief seat in the synagogue because of a donation she made. Julia Severa, a Gentile sympathizer to Judaism (or a God-fearer), built the synagogue at Acmonia and was given honors. Finally, the Aphrodias inscription described above mentions someone named Jael as the "president" or "patron" (προστάτις, *prostatis*) of the synagogue.[43] Was Jael a woman, named after the famous person of Judg. 4:17–22, or a man? Opinions vary,[44] but if this person was a woman, she functioned as an important synagogue leader.

The main debate is whether these titles and others[45] were given to women because (1) their husbands or sons held the office, or (2) they were simply honorific, given because of a donation but not carrying an actual leadership function. B. Brooten has argued that the inscriptions do not usually mention a husband or son, and thus we cannot be sure that the women were married at the time. Second, even if the title was in some sense honorific, that does not exclude a leadership role of some kind.[46] Brooten appears to have convinced most scholars writing on the subject.[47] The only factor to give the NT student

---

Asia Minor, 107. For the inscription from Crete, see Brooten, "Inscriptional Evidence," 2. In the last inscription a woman is called both elder and *archisynagōgos*.

42. Kraabel, "Judaism in Western Asia Minor," 46; Trebilco, *Jewish Communities in Asia Minor,* 112.

43. Tation (third century): *CIJ* 738; Julia Severa (first century): *CIJ* 766; Jael (third century): Reynolds and Tannenbaum, *Jews and God-Fearers.*

44. Trebilco (*Jewish Communities in Asia Minor,* 107–9) and Schürer (*History of the Jewish People,* 3.1:25) think that the name is feminine. Reynolds and Tannenbaum (*Jews and God-Fearers,* 101) and Horbury ("Women in the Synagogue," 395) think that it is masculine because all the other names in the list are masculine. For an important woman as *prostatis* in the NT, see Rom. 16:2.

45. Of the other titles discussed by Brooten, the most important one for NT students is "elder." See Brooten, "Inscriptional Evidence," 4; *Women Leaders,* 41–55. R. Kraemer found an additional inscription referring to women elders (Brooten had cited seven). See Kraemer, "A New Inscription from Malta and the Question of Women Elders in the Diaspora Jewish Community," *HTR* 78 (1985): 431–38. Since none of these inscriptions is from Asia Minor, I do not discuss them here.

46. Brooten, *Women Leaders,* 6–7. The same sort of questions are asked about the titles of pagan women in Asia. See Herz, "Asiarchen und Archiereiai," 100.

47. See Kraemer, "New Inscription from Malta," 431–38; Horbury, "Women in the Synagogue," 358–401 (but with some modifications); Trebilco, *Jewish Communities in Asia Minor,* 104–26. But M. Williams ("The Contribution of Jewish Inscriptions to the Study of Judaism," in Davies et al., *Cambridge History of Judaism,* 3:80), on the other hand, writes of the title *archisynagōgos* applied to women, "That their titles . . . were anything other than honorific has yet to be proved."

pause is the dates of these inscriptions (most of them from the second to the fourth centuries). Still, anyone who would discard or otherwise interpret this evidence certainly must accept the burden of proof.

Thus, if Jewish women in Asia Minor were being granted greater authority than generally allowed them elsewhere, what do we make of the text from 1 Corinthians, and especially that from 1 Timothy, which was directed to churches in Ephesus? Did the author(s) intentionally oppose a trend in the synagogues in Asia Minor? Or do we perhaps need to reflect anew on what the texts were saying? At any rate, the inscriptions should serve as the background out of which we understand early Christian teaching on the role of women in the church.

The Galatian Letter

In recent years most of the attention has been given to western Asia Minor due to the excavations in that region. Therefore, the interpretation of NT documents that relate to that region has been most affected by the new materials. Yet, one issue that relates to central Anatolia has again been examined on the basis of inscriptions and classical sources.

In 279 B.C.E. a large body of migrating Celts (or Galatians) left the Danube valley and crossed into Asia Minor. They finally settled in the north-central part of Asia Minor, primarily in and around the three cities of Pessinus, Ankyra, and Tavium. In 25 B.C.E. the Celtic settlement, along with parts of Phrygia, Pisidia, Lycaonia, and Isauria, were made into one Roman province called Galatia. The question concerning the Epistle to the Galatians is whether Paul sent his letter to the ethnic Galatians (Celts), and thus to the northern part of the new province, or to the Roman province of Galatia, including the southern part of the province, where the cities of Antioch, Iconium, and Lystra were located—cities we read about in Acts (13:14–14:24; cf. 2 Tim. 3:11).

The ancient interpreters believed that the letter had been sent to northern Galatia. W. M. Ramsay, however, although not the first to argue for a southern destination, probably first gave the hypothesis its best statement. J. Moffatt vigorously opposed Ramsay's conclusions.[48] There is still no consensus on this issue.[49]

---

48. See W. M. Ramsay, *A Historical Commentary on St. Paul's Epistle to the Galatians* (London: Hodder & Stoughton, 1899), and J. Moffatt, *An Introduction to the Literature of the New Testament* (Edinburgh: Clark, 1918).

49. Among those recently advocating the northern Galatia view are H. D. Betz, *Galatians,* Hermeneia (Philadelphia: Fortress, 1979), 4–5; J. L. Martyn, *Galatians,* AB 33A (New York: Doubleday, 1997), 15–17; J. Murphy-O'Connor, *Paul: A Critical Life* (Oxford: Oxford University Press, 1997), 161–62; J. B. Polhill, "Galatia Revisited: The Life-Setting of the Epistle," *RevExp* 69 (1972): 437–48. Among those holding to the southern Galatia view are F. F. Bruce, *The Epistle to the Galatians,* NIGTC (Grand Rapids: Eerdmans, 1982), 3–18; G. W. Hansen, "Galatia," in Gill and Gempf, *The Book of Acts,* 378–79; S. Mitchell, *Anatolia,* 2:3; Hemer, *The Book of Acts,* 278; B. Witherington III, *Grace in Galatia* (Grand Rapids: Eerdmans, 1998), 2–8.

Two of the more important questions in the determination of the destination of the epistle have received some epigraphical light. First, can the word Φρυγία (*Phrygia*) in Acts 16:6 (cf. 18:23) be an adjective ("Phrygian" country), or must it be a noun? Proponents of the South Galatian theory point out that Acts never records Paul's traveling to northern Galatia (an argument from silence). Advocates of the North Galatian theory respond that the two verses from Acts indicate that Paul traveled through "Phrygia [an old territory west of Galatia] and the Galatian country [a territory in the north]." The South Galatian theorists maintain that the verses should be understood as stating that Paul traveled through "the Phrygian-Galatian country," or the part of the province of Galatia that used to be the old territory of Phrygia (Phrygia Galatica; thus, in the south).

The common belief held by the North Galatian proponents has been that the word "Phrygia" could only be a noun, because in the first century the word used only two terminations and not three. But C. J. Hemer has found examples of the term used as an adjective with three terminations in several classical sources and in inscriptions from Athens, Delphi, Ephesus, Erythrae, Rhodes, Lindos, and Camirus, and from Panticapaeum.[50] Thus, we should conclude that the word may well have been used by Luke as an adjective (but, of course, was not necessarily used adjectivally).

The second question is Would someone call the residents from the southern part of the Roman province of Galatia "Galatians" (= Celts)? Paul called his readers "foolish Galatians" in Gal. 3:1. Since he called his readers Galatians, must they have been ethnic Galatians? Again, the proponents of the northern Galatia view have maintained that "Galatians" must refer to ethnic Celts, and thus the letter must be addressed to people living in northern Galatia.[51]

But S. Mitchell, G. W. Hansen, and especially C. J. Hemer have cited inscriptions that clearly indicate that non-Celts from the Roman province often were called Galatians. It was common to refer to all of the Roman province as Galatia, notes Mitchell.[52] Further, in two inscriptions persons from southern Galatia call themselves Galatians even though their names were Greek and not Celtic.[53] An inscription on the southern edge of Pisidia designated the city

---

50. Hemer, The *Book of Acts,* 283; idem, "The Adjective 'Phrygia,'" *JTS* 27 (1976): 122–26; "Phrygia: A Further Note," *JTS* 28 (1977): 99–101. The classical authors whom Hemer cites are Pseudo-Aristotle, Apollodorus, Strabo, Dio Chrysostom, Pollux, Alciphron, Arrian, Aelian, Athenaeus, Diogenes Laertius, Pseudo-Lucian, and also the *Sibylline Oracles.* In all, Hemer cites thirty-one examples of Φρυγία as a feminine of a three-termination adjective from the fourth century B.C.E. to the fourth century C.E.

51. Martyn (*Galatians,* 16) contends, "It is a very unlikely way of speaking to persons living in the southern part of the Roman province, where there were few if any Celts." Cf. the view of R. E. Brown (*Introduction to the New Testament* [New York: Doubleday, 1997], 476): "[The term Galatians] is more appropriate for people who were ethnically of that descent than for the hellenized city populace to the south." Murphy-O'Connor (*Paul,* 161) understands this argument to be invalid.

52. Mitchell, *Anatolia,* 2:3. Mitchell cites two inscriptions.

53. Hansen, "Galatia," 389.

of Pednelissus as Galatian. Ten slaves receiving sacral manumission at Delphi were called Galatians in inscriptions even though eight of them had Greek names and two had Phrygian names. Resident aliens in both Athens and on the island of Rhodes called themselves Galatians in inscriptions even though their names were Greek and not Celtic.[54] Thus, it appears that this argument against the southern Galatia theory has been effectively refuted.

Although one cannot conclude that Hemer, Hansen, and Mitchell have proved once and for all the southern Galatia theory, they have removed from the discussion two of the most common arguments used against it. Of course, just because "Phrygia" could be an adjective does not mean that Luke so used it in Acts 16:6. Nor does the possibility that "Galatians" could refer to residents of southern Galatia mean that it did in Gal. 3:1. But a certain weight of inevitability seems to have shifted toward the southern Galatia view. One is left wondering: If no good arguments are left to oppose southern Galatia as the destination of the Galatian epistle,[55] why would one want to consider northern Galatia, since we have no clear indication anywhere that Paul was ever there?

The Book of Revelation

The Character of Emperor Domitian

The consensus at the time of this writing seems to be that the Book of Revelation was composed during the reign of Domitian.[56] The questions that remain about Domitian are (1) Did he demand that people acclaim him lord and god? In other words, was he a megalomaniac who destroyed anyone not according him divine honors? and (2) Did he initiate an official persecution of Christians?[57]

Although there is no unanimity on these issues, the discussion now centers on the views of L. L. Thompson. Thompson's line of argument is as follows: First, the ancient authors (Pliny the Younger, Suetonius, Tacitus, Dio Cassius) who describe Domitian as morally profligate and as a megalomaniac, demanding to be addressed as *dominus et deus* ("lord and god"), were writing with a strong bias. They cannot be trusted to give us the facts during the reign of

---

54. Hemer, *The Book of Acts,* 301–3.

55. Both Murphy-O'Connor and Hansen attempt to argue from geography. Would Paul have gone out of his way to travel through northern Galatia (Hansen, "Galatia," 378–79)? Perhaps Paul's illness (Gal. 4:13) caused him to divert his natural route (Murphy-O'Connor, *Paul,* 162).

56. D. E. Aune (*Revelation,* 2 vols., WBC 52A–B [Dallas: Word, 1997], 1:lvii) observes that most interpreters today hold to a Domitianic date, but a minority accept a Neronian period. Aune seeks to combine the views.

57. These are the questions asked by D. A. deSilva, "The 'Image of the Beast' and the Christians in Asia Minor: Escalation of Sectarian Tension in Revelation 13," *TJ,* n.s., 12 (1991): 198.

Domitian, because they seek revenge for their friends and associates harmed under his reign. Second, when one reads authors who wrote during Domitian's reign (Statius and Quintilian), and when one examines the coins, inscriptions, and medallions from Domitian's reign, an entirely different picture emerges. These sources do not present Domitian as demanding to be addressed as "lord and god"; they show him to have been concerned for the weak and poor in the provinces, and they indicate that his reign was economically and militarily a success. For Thompson, Domitian was not a monster but a fairly good emperor. He cannot, then, have been the foil in the Book of Revelation. We should look to the local pagan religions as background to Revelation and less to the emperor cult.[58]

Thompson is not alone in drawing these conclusions, many of which have been maintained by classicists for years,[59] but not everyone has interpreted the data the same way. D. L. Jones, writing in 1980, before Thompson's works were published, accepts the traditional view of Domitian. He has no difficulty with the classical authors' bias (e.g., Suetonius, who claimed that Domitian demanded to be addressed as lord and god) and notes that coins struck by the emperor picture him as father of the gods. Jones accepts that Domitian persecuted the church and affirms that he wanted "to crush Christianity."[60]

Others have sought to accept Thompson's views but with modification. Both T. B. Slater and D. A. deSilva hesitate to diminish the role of the emperor cult in the background of Revelation. The description of Domitian that we get from authors of his own time is not that positive after all. Martial's poetry does refer to Domitian often as lord and god, and even Quintilian believed that the emperor was worthy of divine honor. Further, even if the emperor did not officially persecute Christians in the empire, the devotees of his cult in Ephesus may have done so.[61]

Thompson's work has furnished important correctives (Domitian was probably no more zealous to be worshiped than were other emperors), but the diminished stress on the threat of the emperor cult as the driving force

58. See L. L. Thompson, "A Sociological Analysis of Tribulation in the Apocalypse of John," *Semeia* 36 (1986): 147–74; idem, *The Book of Revelation: Apocalypse and Empire* (New York: Oxford University Press, 1990), 96–106.

59. See the important article by P. Prigent, "Au temps de l'Apocalypse, I: Domitien," *RHPR* 54 (1974): 455–83. Prigent makes many of the same points as Thompson. See also T. B. Slater, "On the Social Setting of the Revelation to John," *NTS* 44 (1998): 232–56. Slater notes that classicists had long questioned the idea that Domitian persecuted Christians, and that many of the members in the SBL seminar devoted to the Book of Revelation agree with Thompson's conclusions both on Domitian's character and on his alleged persecution of the church. Among these are Adela Yarbro Collins, *Crisis and Catharsis: The Power of the Apocalypse* (Philadelphia: Westminster, 1984), 69, 72; Aune, *Revelation,* 1:lxvii–lxix.

60. D. L. Jones, "Christianity and the Roman Imperial Cult," in *ANRW* 2.23.2:1023–54, esp. 1033. P. W. Barnett ("Revelation in Its Roman Setting," *RTR* 50 [1991]: 59–68), although writing after Thompson's publications, also accepts the traditional view of Domitian.

61. Slater, "Social Setting," 236–38; deSilva, "Image of the Beast," 199.

behind the Book of Revelation is forced. S. J. Friesen, based on his study of the cult of the Sebastoi at Ephesus, formed three conclusions that offer a more balanced understanding of the situation: (1) worship of the emperor in Asia played an increasingly important role in society at many levels; (2) worship of the emperor had wide support; (3) the cult was most popular not in Rome but in the provinces.[62] Thus, the establishment of a new cult in Ephesus would have been a significant event in that city's (and province's) life. The pressure on Christians living in that region must have been great. It is to this theme that we now turn.

The Emperor Cult in Ephesus

The study of the imperial cult as background to the Book of Revelation[63] has received important encouragement through an essay by P. Prigent, the publications of S. J. Friesen, and especially through a monograph by S. R. F. Price.[64] Price's research, which is synchronic but has much to say about the time of Revelation, has advanced the study in many ways. He has used cultural anthropology in the examination of ritual; he has dispelled several conceptual errors about the cult (that the adherents did not really believe it or "feel" religious emotion; that this phenomenon was merely politics disguised as religion; that the imperial priests used trickery to do signs and wonders); and he has provided useful maps of Asia Minor indicating locations of imperial cults. As Price observes, the imperial cult seems to have been most popular in Asia Minor.[65] Both Price and Prigent describe the ritual of the imperial cult, which included processions, sacrifices, choral singing, and carrying images of

---

62. S. J. Friesen, "The Cult of the Roman Emperors in Ephesus" in Koester, *Ephesos, Metropolis of Asia,* 249–50. See also Friesen, "Ephesus: Key to a Vision in Revelation," *BAR* 19, no. 3 (1993): 34. There Friesen maintains (I think correctly) that John was not condemning one particular emperor but was condemning the entire imperial cult system.

63. The study of the imperial cult informs our interpretation not only of Revelation, but of other NT texts as well. S. Mitchell notes that Paul would have seen the temple of Augustus at Antioch of Pisidia on his first journey, and also there, on his second journey, the copy of the *res gestae Augusti* (an inscription detailing Augustus's deeds as savior of the world). "One cannot avoid the impression that the obstacle which stood in the way of the progress of Christianity . . . was the public worship of the emperors" (*Anatolia,* 2:10). Also, B. Allen ("Luke-Acts and the Imperial Cult in Asia Minor," *JTS* 48 [1997]: 411–38), suggests, "The immediate historical and social context in which Theophilus and his circle found themselves was one in which the values of Imperial Order were reflected in the developing Imperial Cult in Asia Minor" (412).

64. P. Prigent, "Au temps de l'Apocalypse, II: Le culte impérial au 1er siècle en Asie Mineure" *RHPR* 55, no. 2 (1975): 215–35; Friesen, *Twice Neokoros;* "Roman Emperors in Ephesus"; "Ephesus: Key to a Vision," 24–37; S. R. F. Price, *Rituals and Power: The Roman Imperial Cult in Asia Minor* (Cambridge: Cambridge University Press, 1984); idem, "Rituals and Power," in *Paul and Empire: Religion and Power in Roman Imperial Society,* ed. R. A. Horsley (Harrisburg, Pa.: Trinity, 1997), 47–71.

65. Price, *Rituals and Power,* 7, 10, 15, 198. See also Prigent, "Le culte impérial," 233, for a good discussion concerning what the ancients believed about the cult and the signs and won-

the emperor and his family. Ritual would have been the most dangerous part of the cult for Christians because they could not participate and could not tolerate images of the emperor in their houses. As the processions passed their houses, they were supposed to offer a sacrifice to the emperor. Failure to participate in these activities would have been obvious to the community.[66]

Friesen has focused on the establishment of the cult of the Sebastoi (Augusti) at Ephesus in 89–90 C.E. (according to his dating). In particular he has analyzed the thirteen dedicatory inscriptions (set up by various cities in the province of Asia), the temple of the Sebastoi (and its colossal statues), and the bath-gymnasium complex built about the same time to honor Domitian as Zeus-Olympios. According to Friesen, the cult was established to honor all the Flavian emperors (i.e., Vespasian, Titus, Domitian) and perhaps even Domitian's wife, Domitia, but would have focused mainly on the living emperor, Domitian. The thirteen inscriptions indicate that the establishment of this cult was very important not only for Ephesus but also for the entire province of Asia. As Friesen notes, no other province had two emperor cults at this time. With the establishment of the cult of the Sebastoi at Ephesus, Asia now had three.[67] Thus the civic pride in Ephesus with the new cult and the title of imperial neokorate (temple warden of the imperial temple) would have made the residents even more intolerant of those not wishing to participate in the cult. It was the local persecution that the Christian felt, not the official Roman persecution.[68]

It is hard to deny—and Price and Friesen do not—that the establishment of the new emperor cult in Ephesus in 89–90 C.E. lay behind the Book of Revelation. Thus, they give a rather similar interpretation of Rev. 13 and the beasts from the sea and land. The beast from the sea is the power of Rome. The beast from the land is the local aristocracy—among whom is the imperial high priest—which seeks to advance the worship of the emperor.[69] The seer, John, has witnessed the festivals, the games associated with the emperor cult, the processions, sacrifices, the colossal images[70] of the imperial family,

---

ders that accompanied it. Price and Prigent would disagree with Elisabeth Schüssler Fiorenza (*Revelation: Vision of a Just World* [Minneapolis: Fortress, 1991], 85), S. J. Scherrer ("Signs and Wonders in the Imperial Cult: A New Look at a Roman Religious Institution in the Light of Rev 13:13–15," *JBL* 103 [1984]: 599–610), and G. R. Beasley-Murray (*The Book of Revelation* [Greenwood, S.C.: Attic, 1974], 217), all of whom suggest that trickery was involved.

66. Prigent, "Le culte imperial," 221, 223; Price, *Rituals and Power,* 104–12.

67. Friesen, *Twice Neokoros,* 155; "Ephesus: Key to a Vision," 34. The other two imperial cults in Asia were at Pergamum (cult of Roma and Augustus, established in 29 B.C.E.) and at Smyrna (cult of Tiberius, established in 26 C.E.). See also Prigent ("Le culte imperial," 216–17), who gives a different date for the Tiberius cult.

68. See Friesen, *Twice Neokoros,* 36–38, 48, 140, 155.

69. Price, *Rituals and Power,* 197; Friesen, "Ephesus: Key to a Vision," 37. Compare also Jones ("Christianity," 1035), who gives a similar interpretation.

70. A head and part of one arm of a statue have been found and are displayed in the Ephesus museum at Selcuk, Turkey. The museum and other sources identify these pieces as part of the

and even worse, the local aristocrats competing for the honor of being named high priest of the cult and then prosecuting the cult with enthusiasm—and he is appalled.[71] For him, there must be no compromise within the Christian community; Christians do not offer sacrifices to the emperor.

The works of these three scholars, which establish that the belief in the emperor cult in Asia in the first century was pervasive, have provided interpreters new insights into the socioreligious world of John the seer. Further, they give us a specific event that might have elicited John's condemnation: the establishment of the new cult in 89–90 C.E. One surely can find solutions to many of the puzzling conundrums in Revelation by a more careful scrutiny of these publications.

Local References in the Letters to the Seven Churches

At least since the time of Ramsay a school of thought has existed that believes that John wrote his letters to the seven churches in Rev. 2–3 with subtle references to local events and culture. Ramsay wrote, "It may be said that the author of the Seven Letters . . . imparts to them many touches, specially suitable to the individual churches, and showing his intimate knowledge of them all." He maintained that the letters had been written by someone who was familiar with the "situation, character, the past history, the possibilities of future development, of those Seven Cities."[72] Ramsay's own publication in 1904 sought to point out these references by culling the inscriptions and observing the topography.

Since that time some have attempted to continue Ramsay's work, while others have insisted that the local references were more imagined than real.[73] In recent years the debate has been revived by the publication of C. J. Hemer's monograph on the same topic.[74] Some scholars remain doubtful of Hemer's

---

colossal statue of Domitian, but Friesen maintains that they are from a statue of Titus and there would have been similar colossal statues for Vespasian and Domitian. See Friesen, *Twice Neokoros,* 60–62; "Ephesus: Key to a Vision," 32. Cf. S. Erdemgil et al. (*Ephesus* [Istanbul: Do-Gu Yayinlari, 2000], 87), who identify the remains as being from a statue of Domitian.

71. P. W. Barnett ("Revelation in Its Roman Setting," 61) speculates that John began to voice objections to the emperor cult in the streets of Ephesus and had been exiled to Patmos to get him out of the way. R. Oster ("Numismatic Windows into the Social World of Early Christianity: A Methodological Inquiry," *JBL* 101 [1982]: 195–223, esp. 219) notes that the "iconographic technique" of Revelation (referring to beasts, censers, altars, crowns, thrones, lightning) is also found on the coins of Ephesus. We can suggest that these symbols, many of which related to the emperor cult, must have been quite offensive to a person such as John.

72. William Ramsay, *The Letters to the Seven Churches of Asia* (New York: Hodder & Stoughton, 1904), 39–40.

73. C. H. H. Scobie ("Local References in the Letters to the Seven Churches," *NTS* 39 [1993]: 614) cites J. Moffatt ("The Revelation of St. John the Divine," in *The Expositor's Greek Testament,* ed. W. R. Nicoll, 5 vols. [London: Hodder & Stoughton, 1920], 5:285) as one who rejected Ramsay's conclusions.

74. C. J. Hemer, *The Letters to the Seven Churches of Asia in Their Local Setting,* JSNTSup 11 (Sheffield: JSOT Press, 1986).

collection of alleged references, and others deny that there are any such references at all.[75]

C. H. H. Scobie has collected a "checklist" of at least fifty alleged local references in the letters to the seven churches. He has sought to take the middle ground between Hemer, whom he characterizes as a maximalist on this issue, and Prigent, who denies the existence of any local references in the letters. Scobie has categorized the alleged references into three groups: (1) references to local events, (2) references to topographical features, (3) references to contemporary life.[76]

I present here a small sampling of the suggested local references. John writes in Rev. 2:13 to the church of Pergamum, "I know where you dwell, where the throne of Satan is." Is this a reference to some topographical site in Pergamum? Suggestions include the altar of Zeus on the acropolis, the acropolis itself, the theater on the acropolis (from a distance, it looks like a large chair), and the emperor cult.[77]

The seer writes in 3:16 to the church at Laodicea, "Because you are lukewarm and neither hot nor cold, I will spit you out of my mouth." A popular suggestion now is that the author was contrasting the tepid waters of Laodicea with the hot springs of Hierapolis and the cold springs of Colossae. Thus, the water at Laodicea was rather ineffective (not good for medicinal purposes or for drinking).[78]

In 2:7 the author writes to the church at Ephesus, "To the victor I will grant to eat from the tree of life in the paradise of God." Although the reference seems obviously from Gen. 2, Hemer maintains that there was also a local implication in the words. He connects the description of eating from a tree in paradise to a tree shrine of Artemis and the sacred precincts that surrounded it as pictured in coins.[79]

How should one evaluate the alleged subtle references? A complete rejection of them is extreme. Yet one can see how these suggestions can become far-fetched. Scobie's conclusions are appropriate: (1) some of the suggestions regarding local references are not convincing; (2) but there is "at least a core of local references in the letters"; (3) although identifying local references usually does not affect the interpretation of the text, sometimes it does (e.g.,

---

75. Thompson (*Book of Revelation*, 202–4) evaluates Hemer's work, deciding that "the connections often remain very tenuous." P. Prigent (*L'Apocalypse de Saint Jean* [Lausanne: Delachaux and Niestlé, 1981]) "strongly denies the existence of any local references," according to Scobie, "Local References," 606.

76. Scobie ("Local References," 606–24) notes that Hemer had collected between thirty and thirty-five such references.

77. See Scobie, "Local References," 610; Hemer, *Letters to the Seven Churches*, 87; Adela Yarbro Collins, "Pergamum in Early Christian Literature," in *Pergamon, Citadel of the Gods*, ed. Koester, 176–84; Jones, "Christianity and the Roman Imperial Cult," 1034.

78. Yamauchi, *New Testament Cities*, 141; Scobie, "Local References," 623.

79. Hemer, *Letters to the Seven Churches*, 44–45.

"lukewarm" refers to the Laodicean church's ineffectiveness, not to its lack of zeal).[80]

Conclusions

The use of inscriptions and other material remains (even topography) has made a contribution toward our understanding of early Christianity in Asia Minor as this movement has been reflected in the NT texts. Here, I list three categories of results:

Issues That the Material Remains Have Settled

1. There were at least a few God-fearing Gentiles attached to the synagogues.
2. Details of Paul's Ephesian ministry (Acts 19) are culturally plausible.
3. The Asiarchs were not the same as the imperial cult high priests.
4. We should modify our view of the emperor Domitian. He probably was not a mad persecutor of Christians.
5. But we must also stress the appeal of the emperor cult in Asia Minor as background to Revelation.

Issues for Which the Material Remains Have Offered Progress

1. At least two of the standard objections to the southern Galatia view for the destination of Galatians have been removed.
2. Some of the alleged local references in Revelation may be valid, but many (perhaps most) are not.

Issues for Which the Material Remains Have Only Raised More Questions

1. The Roman roads do not tell us which way Paul traveled on the second and third journeys.
2. The greater authority allowed to Jewish women in Asia Minor (at least from the second century on) contrasts with 1 Corinthians and 1 Timothy.

---

80. Scobie, "Local References," 624. Scobie decides on probable or possible for six references, and he adds two "test cases" to these and finally yet another example (thus equaling nine in all?) (see 618–20, 623). Not all of the alleged local references are found in the letters to the seven churches. R. Bauckham ("Eschatological Earthquake in the Apocalypse of John," *NovT* 19 [1977]: 224–33) suggests that Rev. 8:5; 11:19; 16:18–21 have in mind the earthquakes in Sardis (17 C.E.) and Laodicea (60 C.E.).

Part 2

New Testament Hermeneutics

3

Textual Criticism

Recent Developments

Eckhard J. Schnabel

Textual criticism of the NT is the endeavor to ascertain from the divergent copies—5,500 Greek MSS and perhaps nine thousand versional MSS, displaying roughly three hundred thousand variant readings—"which form of the text should be regarded as most nearly conforming to the original."[1] In the past twenty-five years, since the publication of the twenty-sixth edition of the *Novum Testamentum Graece* (the "Nestle-Aland," NA[26]) in 1979 and the third edition of the *Greek New Testament* (UBS[3]) in 1975,[2] numerous advances have taken place in the study of the manuscript tradition of the NT. New MSS were discovered, revised editions were published, new theories of the history of the manuscript tradition were suggested, the methodology of textual criticism continues to be discussed, and theological issues raised by text-critical issues are being explored. In what follows, I attempt to present the major significant developments and contributions.[3]

1. Bruce M. Metzger, *The Text of the New Testament: Its Transmission, Corruption, and Restoration*, 3rd ed. (New York and Oxford: Oxford University Press, 1992), v.
2. Kurt Aland et al., eds., *Novum Testamentum Graece*, 26th ed. (Stuttgart: Deutsche Bibelgesellschaft, 1979); idem, *The Greek New Testament*, 3rd ed. (New York: United Bible Societies, 1975).
3. For an excellent survey, see the essays in Bart D. Ehrman and Michael W. Holmes, eds., *The Text of the New Testament in Contemporary Research: Essays on the Status Quaestionis*, SD 46 (Grand Rapids: Eerdmans, 1995); see also Metzger, "Advances in Textual Criticism of the New Testament, 1964–1990," in *Text of the New Testament*, 260–97.

New Manuscripts

Before the labors of Count Constantin von Tischendorf (1815–74), the number of known Greek MSS of the NT was a mere one thousand. Caspar Gregory's prolegomena to Tischendorf's eighth edition of 1869–94[4] lists a total of 3,060 MSS. Through the efforts of Kurt Aland, about one thousand new MSS were discovered (first reporting in 1953). During the last twenty-five years there have been no discoveries as dramatic as Tischendorf's discovery of Codex Sinaiticus in the monastery of St. Catherine on Mt. Sinai in 1844/1859; the papyrus discoveries of B. P. Grenfell, A. S. Hunt, and others at Oxyrhynchus since 1897; the discovery of the Chester Beatty papyri in the 1930s; or the publication of the Bodmer papyri between 1956 and 1961. Still, several new MSS have been identified since 1970.

The twenty-sixth edition of the *Novum Testamentum Graece* (1979) listed eighty-eight papyri; the twenty-seventh edition (1993, NA[27]) took the list up to ninety-eight MSS.[5] As a result of seventeen fragments published in volumes 64–66 of *The Oxyrhynchus Papyri* (1997–99),[6] the official list of papyri stands now at 115 MSS. Since 1979, the register of majuscule (uncial) MSS has grown from 274 to 306.[7] The register of minuscules lists 2,812 MSS. The register of Greek lectionaries, which have not been presented systematically in any edition of the Greek text of the NT (NA[27] lists only nine Greek lectionaries) stands at approximately 2,281 MSS. The "official" registry of the Institute for New Testament Textual Research at Münster listed 5,664 MSS in 1994.[8] J. K. Elliott produced a helpful survey of MSS used in editions of the Greek NT.[9]

Electronic study of the manuscript tradition of the NT is, unfortunately, not yet possible. High resolution images of the newly published $\mathfrak{P}^{99}$–$\mathfrak{P}^{115}$ can be found on the Oxyrhynchus website.[10] If basic textual research of Greek NT MSS is to find broader appeal, it seems necessary to have all papyri, majuscules, and a representative selection of minuscules available on a searchable CD-ROM.

4. Constantin von Tischendorf, *Novum Testamentum Graece, I–II: Editio octava critica maior, Prolegomena scripsit C. R. Gregory* (Leipzig: Giesecke & Devrient, 1869–94); see also C. R. Gregory, *Die griechischen Handschriften des Neuen Testaments* (Leipzig: Hinrichs, 1908).

5. Kurt Aland, *Kurzgefaßte Liste der griechischen Handschriften des Neuen Testaments,* ANTF 1 (Berlin: de Gruyter, 1994), 3–16, lists ninety-nine papyri, adding P. Chester Beatty 1499, fol. 11–14.

6. For details on P.Oxy 4401–6, 4445–9, 4494–5, and 4497–9, and for bibliographical information, see Peter M. Head, "Some Recently Published NT Papyri from Oxyrhynchus: An Overview and Preliminary Assessment," *TynBul* 51 (2000): 1–16; also J. K. Elliott, "Seven Recently Published New Testament Fragments from Oxyrhynchus," *NovT* 42 (2000): 209–13.

7. Aland, *Kurzgefaßte Liste,* 44; NA[27], 689–703, lists 301 majuscules.

8. Aland, *Kurzgefaßte Liste.*

9. J. K. Elliott, *A Survey of Manuscripts Used in Editions of the Greek New Testament,* NovTSup 57 (Leiden: Brill, 1987).

10. Online: www.csad.ox.ac.uk/POxy.

New Editions of the Greek New Testament

The most widely used edition of the Greek NT was the *Novum Testamentum Graece,* a pocket edition originally prepared in 1898 by Eberhard Nestle, who produced his text by comparing the texts of Tischendorf and of Westcott/Hort; when these two texts differed, he consulted a third edition (first, Richard Francis Weymouth's second edition of 1892; after 1901, Bernhard Weiss's 1894–1900 edition, which relied heavily on Codex B). Thus, the Nestle text reflected the consensus of nineteenth-century scholarship. Since the thirteenth edition of "the Nestle," prepared by Erwin Nestle in 1927, a separate critical apparatus allows users to evaluate textual decisions independently. Beginning with the twenty-first edition (1952), Kurt Aland became copublisher; starting with this edition, the information of the critical apparatus was checked using the originals, and the readings of the papyri were added. When he published the twenty-fifth edition (1963), he presented a revised critical apparatus, collated against original sources, with an expanded number of witnesses (particularly the newly published Bodmer papyri). The twenty-sixth edition (1979)[11] presented a new text, constructed without reference to earlier editions (whose readings were listed in an appendix: "Editionum differentiae"). The typesetting was improved, and the newly prepared critical apparatus presented an impressive amount of information. The twenty-seventh edition (1993) reproduces the text of the twenty-sixth edition unchanged, while the critical apparatus was revised with the goal of making it more reliable and more convenient to use.

The committee that Eugene Nida assembled in 1955 to produce a Greek NT that would be of use to Bible translators consisted of Matthew Black (St. Andrews), Bruce M. Metzger (Princeton), Allen Wikgren (Chicago), and Kurt Aland (Münster). The first edition of *The Greek New Testament* was published by the United Bible Societies in 1966, the first critical edition of the Greek NT to list all known papyri. The Greek text was newly reconstructed, using basically the criteria of Westcott/Hort, although their concept of a "neutral text" was abandoned. Decisions on textual variants were made by majority vote. The critical apparatus listed only such variants that were directly relevant for the work of translators—that is, variants that would lead to divergent meanings. The total number of textual variants that the UBS text listed was fewer than fifteen hundred (the Nestle-Aland text listed several thousand). The variants were linked with a "grade" (A, B, C, or D) indicating the degree of certainty that the committee members attached to each variant, reviving in a modified form the practice of J. A. Bengel. Due mostly to the superior Greek types that the UBS text used, this edition quickly became the most popular edition among theological students, and not a few professors, in the English-speaking world. The second edition, with Carlo M. Martini added to the committee, appeared in 1968. The text of the third edition (1975, corrected 1983), which embodied

---

11. Beginning with this edition, Barbara Aland was coeditor with Kurt Aland.

the work of the Institute for New Testament Textual Research at Münster, saw over five hundred changes made and is identical with NA[26]. The fourth edition (1993) removed 273 sets of variants and added 284 new sets of variants; the text itself remained unchanged. The degree of certainty for most passages has been raised (many C evaluations were raised to the level of B), and D ratings have virtually disappeared.[12] Moisés Silva, in a recent survey of modern critical editions, joins "the chorus of complaints regarding the popularity of the UBS editions among NT scholars. While it is true that most of the variants listed in NA[26] have little claim to originality—and thus appear to be somewhat irrelevant for NT exegesis—students make a grave mistake if they fail to become familiar with the realities of textual history broadly considered."[13]

One of the most significant publications of the twenty-first century will be the *Editio Critica Maior* by the Institute for New Testament Textual Research at Münster, the long-awaited "new Tischendorf" that was announced by Kurt Aland in 1969,[14] with the first installment, containing the Epistle of James, published in 1997.[15] The *Editio Critica Maior* seeks to provide "the full range of resources necessary for scholarly research in establishing the text and reconstructing the history of the New Testament text during its first thousand years."[16] This edition provides a new text established on the basis of all the evidence presented in the critical apparatus. For the textual witnesses cited in the apparatus, the Münster Institute collated all 522 available text MSS of the Catholic Epistles in ninety-eight test passages and found that 372 MSS attest the Majority text in at least 90 percent of the test passages.[17] All the remaining MSS—that is, those that differ from the Majority text in more than 10 percent of the text passages—are included in the edition of James. Of the 182 MSS included in the edition of James—about eight times as many as cited consistently in NA[27]—ninety-seven MSS represent the Byzantine tradition; in addition, twenty lectionaries were consulted. The edition includes all Greek patristic quotations to the time of John of Damascus (7/8th cent.)—over one hundred church fathers. The Latin, Coptic, and Syriac versions are fully cited as witnesses to the Greek text, the Greek base of each version having been reconstructed. In James 2:1–11, the *Editio Critica Maior* presents sixty-nine

12. See the critique by Kent D. Clarke, *Textual Optimism: A Critique of the United Bible Societies' Greek New Testament,* JSNTSup 138 (Sheffield: Sheffield Academic Press, 1997).

13. M. Silva, "Modern Critical Editions and Apparatuses of the Greek New Testament," in Ehrman and Holmes, *Text of the New Testament,* 290–91.

14. K. Aland, "Novi Testamenti Graeci Editio Maior Critica: Der gegenwärtige Stand der Arbeit an eine neuen großen kritischen Ausgabe des Neuen Testaments," *NTS* 16 (1969): 163–77.

15. *Novum Testamentum Graecum Editio Critica Maior,* vol. 4.1, *Die Katholischen Briefe,* ed. B. Aland et al. (Stuttgart: Deutsche Bibelgesellschaft, 1997). See the description by B. Aland in *TC* 3 (1998), and the contributions by P. H. Davids, B. D. Ehrman, D. C. Parker, W. L. Petersen, and K. Wachtel in *TC* 3.

16. *Novum Testamentum Graecum Editio Critica Maior,* 4.1, 11.

17. K. Aland, *Text und Textwert der griechischen Handschriften des Neuen Testaments,* vol. 1, *Die Katholischen Briefe,* ANTF 9–12 (Berlin: de Gruyter, 1987).

units of variation, NA[27] only twenty-two (and UBS[4] only one).[18] The newly established text differs from NA[27] (UBS[4]) in only two instances, which is criticized by J. K. Elliott,[19] but defended by Barbara Aland as not being due to "any unwillingness on the part of the editors to make changes but rather to the relative integrity of the tradition and also to the quality of scholarship in the Nestle-Aland and UBS editions."[20] Further installments of the *Editio Critica Maior* will include the Epistles of Peter, of John, and of Jude; then the text of the Acts of the Apostles will be published. Supplemental volumes provide fuller information on the apparatus as well as lists of abbreviations used and of the MSS represented in the edition.

The Greek text with critical apparatus of José Maria Bover, first published in a bilingual edition in 1943, has seen a fifth edition in the trilingual NT (Greek, Latin, and Spanish) edited by José O'Callaghan in 1977.[21] The text of Augustin Merk, first published through the Pontifical Biblical Institute in Rome in 1933, recently has appeared in a bilingual edition with the New Vulgate text and the Clementine Vulgate text,[22] in 1990 with an Italian translation.[23] The attempt to rehabilitate the Textus Receptus[24] has produced two editions. The edition of Z. C. Hodges and A. L. Farstad seeks to reconstruct the "majority text"—that is, the prevailing form of the Greek text in church history—on the basis of a reconstruction of manuscript stemmata, while M. A. Robinson and W. G. Pierpont follow the majority of MSS virtually at all costs.[25]

The International Greek New Testament Project, directed by American and British committees of scholars since 1948, originally under the leadership of Ernest Colwell, endeavors to produce a full critical apparatus of the Greek NT. Editors involved in this project were J. N. Birdsall, J. K. Elliott, E. J. Epp, G. D. Fee, B. M. Metzger, and G. Willis. The aim is to provide

18. B. D. Ehrman, *TC* 3 (1998).

19. J. K. Elliott, *TC* 3 (1998).

20. B. Aland, *TC* 3 (1998): par. 9.

21. José M. Bover and José O'Callaghan, eds., *Nuevo Testamento trilingüe*, 2nd ed., BAC 400 (Madrid: Biblioteca de Autores Cristianos, 1988).

22. Gianfranco Nolli, *Novum Testamentum Graece et Latine: Textus Graecus, cum apparatu critico-exegetico, Vulgata Clementina et Neovulgata* (Vatican City: Libreria editrice vaticana, 1981).

23. A. Merk and Giuseppe Barbaglio, eds., *Nuovo testamento greco e italiano*, 3rd ed. (Bologna: Edizioni Dehoniane, 1993).

24. For a critical discussion, see D. B. Wallace, "The Majority Text Theory: History, Methods, and Critique," in Ehrman and Holmes, *Text of the New Testament,* 297–320; D. A. Carson, *The King James Version Debate: A Plea for Realism* (Grand Rapids: Baker, 1979).

25. Zane C. Hodges and Arthur L. Farstad, eds., *The Greek New Testament according to the Majority Text* (Nashville: Nelson, 1982; 2nd ed., 1985); Maurice A. Robinson and William G. Pierpont, eds., *The New Testament in the Original Greek according to the Byzantine/Majority Textform* (Atlanta: Original Word, 1991). The Hodges/Farstad text differs from the Textus Receptus in 1,838 places, and from the UBS text in 6,577 places; see D. B. Wallace, "Some Second Thoughts on the *Majority Text*," *BSac* 146 (1989): 271–90.

an objective presentation of the textual evidence, and not to construct a
new text. Thus, the collating base text is not a critically reconstructed text,
but the Textus Receptus (of the edition published by Clarendon Press, Oxford, in 1873, a reprint of an edition published in 1828 that ultimately is
based on the third edition of Stephanus published in 1550). The apparatus
incorporates evidence from all Greek papyri and all majuscule MSS, from
128 minuscule MSS selected by means of the Claremont Profile Method
(see below), and from about forty lectionaries from early versions in ten languages and the patristic evidence. The first two volumes were published in
1984 and 1987, presenting the textual evidence for the Gospel of Luke.[26] In
1995, W. J. Elliott and D. C. Parker published a first volume on the Gospel
of John.[27] The International Greek New Testament Project edition presents
many more variant readings than NA[27]; for example, for Luke 2:1–14, the
edition needs nine large pages, listing close to two hundred variant readings, whereas NA[27] has twenty variants. The volumes of this edition are of
inestimable value to the textual critic, and one hopes that future volumes
are produced more quickly.

French scholars Marie-Émile Boismard and Arnaud Lamouille published
in 1984 a critical text of the Acts of the Apostles,[28] displaying the Alexandrian
and the Western (D) text in parallel columns, with an extensive apparatus with
annotations in the second volume. Even though their "working hypothesis"
that both text forms go back to Luke himself (a view championed by F. Blass
in 1895 and supported by Th. Zahn in 1916) will not convince many scholars, their inventory of witnesses to the text of Acts, particularly early and later
versions, as well as their extensive list of stylistic characteristics of Luke, are of
lasting significance.[29] The International Project on the Text of Acts, directed by
C. Osburn and Th. Geer, also seeks to produce an exhaustive edition of the text
of Acts.[30] Reuben Swanson has published the manuscript evidence for the Greek
text of the Gospels and the Acts of the Apostles in a novel format: the text of
Vaticanus is printed in full as the lead line for each grouping of parallel lines

26. *The New Testament in Greek III: The Gospel according to St. Luke,* ed. American and British
Committees of the International Greek New Testament Project, 2 vols. (Oxford: Clarendon,
1984–87).

27. *The New Testament in Greek IV: The Gospel according to John,* vol. 1, *The Papyri,* ed. W. J.
Elliott and D. C. Parker, NTTS 20 (Leiden: Brill, 1995).

28. M.-É. Boismard and A. Lamouille, *Le Texte occidental des Actes des Apôtres: Reconstitution
et réhabilitation,* vol. 1, *Introduction et textes;* vol. 2, *Apparat critique, Index des caractéristiques sty-
listiques, Index des citations patristiques* (Paris: Éditions Recherche sur les Civilisations, 1984).

29. Metzger, *Text of the New Testament,* 294–95; cf. C. K. Barrett, *The Acts of the Apostles,*
2 vols., ICC (Edinburgh: Clark, 1994–98), 1:24–25. The recent discussion on Codex Bezae
is summarized in D. C. Parker and C.-B. Amphoux, eds., *Codex Bezae: Studies from the Lunel
Colloquium, June 1994,* NTTS 22 (Leiden: Brill, 1996).

30. See Carroll D. Osburn, "The Search for the Original Text of Acts—The International
Project on the Text of Acts [1991]," in *New Testament Text and Language: A Sheffield Reader,* ed.
S. E. Porter and C. A. Evans (Sheffield: Sheffield Academic Press, 1996), 17–33.

that report "all variants of every kind from each source."[31] In the Acts volume, he uses (and prints in parallel lines) ten papyri, fifteen majuscules, thirty-five minuscules, and the quotations of Clement of Alexandria. This format allows the user to take note of variants such as orthographical errors, differences in spelling, and so on that are omitted from the traditional critical apparatus. Swanson seems to believe that his volumes are an improvement on the work of Westcott/Hort, Nestle/Aland, and the UBS committee, whose editions "all have originated from the Textus Receptus of 1633."[32] He claims that his work is more accurate than the apparatus of Nestle-Aland, but, curiously, cautions the user "to check the data by personally consulting the manuscript(s) whenever the information is to be used authoritatively."[33] Because Swanson worked from microfilmed copies of the MSS, one can hardly be confident that his edition is more accurate than the work of scholars who in many cases work directly with the original MSS. The electronic lists of errata[34] register too many errors for these volumes to be of any practical help. P. W. Comfort and D. P. Barrett published transcriptions of the fifty-five Greek MSS—fifty papyri and the majuscules 0162, 0171, 0189, 0220, 0232—that were produced before 300 C.E., seeking to provide "the complete text of the earliest New Testament manuscripts."[35] The selection of MSS is somewhat arbitrary—for example, $\mathfrak{P}^7$, dated to the third/fourth century in the Münster *Liste*, is excluded, whereas six papyri with the same dating are included, as have been four papyri that the *Liste* dates to the fourth century. D. C. Parker discovered ten errors in fifteen pages of the text of the Gospel of John, and also notes that the original MSS have not consistently been used.

Theories of the History of New Testament Manuscripts

The study of the papyri MSS of the NT has resulted in the rejection of previously held views, at least in one important respect. One of the "assured results" of textual criticism was, for a long time, the conviction that Hort's "Neutral" (Egyptian) text type was a scholarly recension created in Alexandria in the late

31. R. J. Swanson, ed., *New Testament Greek Manuscripts: Variant Readings Arranged in Horizontal Lines against Codex Vaticanus: The Acts of the Apostles* (Sheffield: Sheffield Academic Press; Pasadena: William Carey International University, 1998), xix. The volumes on the Gospels were published in 1995. Bruce M. Metzger has provided a foreword for each volume.

32. Ibid., xiv.

33. Ibid., xvi.

34. Online: www1.uni-bremen.de/~wie/texte/Swanson-errata.html (accessed August 2001).

35. Philip W. Comfort and David P. Barrett, eds., *The Complete Text of the Earliest New Testament Manuscripts* (Grand Rapids: Baker, 1999). For the following comments, see the review by D. C. Parker in *TC* 4 (1999). Comfort and Barrett's book was later published as *The Text of the Earliest New Testament Greek Manuscripts* (Wheaton: Tyndale, 2001). Page references in the present chapter are to the Baker edition.

third or early fourth century. This view gained acceptance after W. Bousset used
the evidence of early papyri finds to show that these early texts evidenced a much
more fluid and "mixed" state of textual transmission than Hort had proposed.[36]
The recensional activity of Christian scribes in Alexandria produced the text
of Codex B and also of Codex A.[37] Such a recension often was associated with
the name of Hesychius, who died as a martyr in the persecution of Diocle-
tian. As scholars came to see that none of the fourth-century text types was
found in the early papyri in a "pure" state, they spoke of "pre-recensional" or
"proto-Alexandrian" texts.[38] Since our critical texts—Westcott/Hort, Nestle/
Aland, UBS—resemble Codex B, this would mean that we rely on a text that
is generally acknowledged to be edited. The dilemma then seems to be that
we seem merely to be "pursuing the retreating mirage of the 'original text.'"[39]
When, in 1961, $\mathfrak{P}^{75}$ was published, a late second- or early third-century MS
containing substantial portions of the Gospels of Luke and John, the question
of the text of the second/third century was put into a new perspective.[40] The
study of C. M. Martini on this papyrus's text of Luke demonstrated that the
close relationship between this papyrus and Codex B rules out the assumption
that Codex B reflects a late third- or early fourth-century recension.[41] Studies
on the text of John demonstrated the same.[42] The discovery of $\mathfrak{P}^{75}$ showed that
the text of Codex B existed already in the second century. This fact raises the
question whether the text of $\mathfrak{P}^{75}$ itself is recensional. "If so, there are only two
alternatives. Either it was a recension created in the second century (= a revised
text), or else it was the culmination of a process (= G. Zuntz's "Euthalian"
edition), but a process which had very little time to develop."[43] Gordon D.
Fee shows that a study of the Greek text of Origen, who is thought to be the
mind behind the production of the Alexandrian recension, and of $\mathfrak{P}^{66}$ shows
that historical probability favors neither of these two alternatives (both $\mathfrak{P}^{75}$
and $\mathfrak{P}^{66}$ date before Origen). Further, $\mathfrak{P}^{75}$ is not itself a recension. This is dem-

36. Wilhelm Bousset, *Textkritische Studien zum Neuen Testament: Die Recension des Hesychius*,
TU 11.4 (Leipzig: Hinrichs, 1894).
37. Kurt Aland and Barbara Aland, *The Text of the New Testament: An Introduction to the
Critical Editions and to the Theory and Practice of Modern Textual Criticism* (Grand Rapids:
Eerdmans, 1987), 50–51.
38. Metzger, *Text of the New Testament*, 215–16.
39. Kenneth W. Clark, "The Theological Relevance of Textual Variation in Current Criticism
of the Greek New Testament," *JBL* 85 (1966): 15.
40. For the following, see Eldon J. Epp and Gordon D. Fee, *Studies in the Theory and Method
of New Testament Textual Criticism*, SD 45 (Grand Rapids: Eerdmans, 1993), 251–56.
41. Carlo M. Martini, *Il problema della recensionalità del codice B alla luca del papiro Bodmer
XIV*, AnBib 26 (Rome: Biblical Institute Press, 1966).
42. Calvin L. Porter, "A Textual Analysis of the Earliest Manuscripts of the Gospel of John"
(Ph.D. diss., Duke University, 1961); idem, "Papyrus Bodmer XV (P75) and the Text of Codex
Vaticanus," *JBL* 81 (1962): 363–76.
43. Gordon D. Fee, "The Myth of Early Textual Recension in Alexandria [1974]," in Epp
and Fee, *Theory and Method*, 256. The following remarks rely on this study.

onstrated by two factors. First, the presence of at least seventy-six uncorrected nonsense readings in the MS indicates that the scribe produced not a serious revision. Second, both the close relationship of the papyrus with Codex B and the nature of the existing disagreements suggest a common ancestor. If the text of $\mathfrak{P}^{75}$ is neither a recension (a revised text) created in the second century nor the culmination of a process of revision, then we must conclude that a third option is more likely: Hort was basically correct when he surmised that the Egyptian text type is a carefully preserved tradition and not a recension at all. "These MSS seem to represent a 'relatively pure' form of preservation of a 'relatively pure' line of descent from the original text."[44]

Despite the fact that detailed studies of individual MSS of the Greek NT text have been undertaken, there is no consensus at present concerning a coherent view of the transmission of the text.[45] Clearly, text critics today no longer operate with the Westcott/Hort view[46] of the history of the text. The papyri MSS have, for example, demonstrated the antiquity of some Byzantine readings. The Alands offered a comprehensive description,[47] "notable for its confidence in the witness of the Egyptian papyri, its distinctive view of the so-called Western textual tradition, and its attempt to describe the surviving MSS from the earliest centuries in terms of scribal characteristics rather than text-types or textual traditions."[48] Eldon J. Epp suggests a "dynamic view of textual transmission."[49] He speaks of three groups of early texts: (1) A "B" text group. This is the clearest cluster of early MSS, which can be identified in the $\mathfrak{P}^{75}$—B line (along with $\mathfrak{P}^{66}$, $\aleph$ [except in John], L, 33, $\mathfrak{P}^{46}$, and 1739 for Paul). This group is traditionally known as Egyptian, Alexandrian, or Neutral. (2) A "D" text group, formed by three or four papyri and one majuscule prior to the fourth century containing portions of Luke-Acts ($\mathfrak{P}^{48}$, $\mathfrak{P}^{38}$, $\mathfrak{P}^{69}$, 0171). This group has traditionally been called Western. (3) A "C" text group, which stands midway between the B text and the D text, extant in a cluster (for the Gospels) in $\mathfrak{P}^{45}$ and W (with, e.g., f^{13}). It should be no longer called Caesarean text. In addition, Epp speaks of a fourth group, an "A" text group, called thus in recognition of Codex Alexandrinus; it is not among the early clusters, and therefore it has no early papyrus representatives. It has supporting witnesses among the papyri from the sixth century onward: $\mathfrak{P}^{84}$,

---

44. Ibid., 272.

45. See Michael W. Holmes, "Reasoned Eclecticism in New Testament Textual Criticism," in Ehrman and Holmes, *Text of the New Testament*, 336–60.

46. See Metzger, *Text of the New Testament*, 131–34.

47. Aland and Aland, *Text of the New Testament* (the German original was published in 1981).

48. Holmes, "Reasoned Eclecticism," 351.

49. Eldon J. Epp, "The Significance of the Papyri for Determining the Nature of the New Testament Text in the Second Century: A Dynamic View of Textual Transmission," in Epp and Fee, *Theory and Method*, 274–97; idem, "The Papyrus Manuscripts of the New Testament," in Ehrman and Holmes, *Text of the New Testament*, 3–21.

$\mathfrak{P}^{68}$, $\mathfrak{P}^{42}$. This is the only text type that the Alands recognize before the fourth century. Epp argues that these groups represent three identifiable text types that existed around 200 C.E. "Several hints, found in the NT (and in other Christian) papyri themselves, suggest that standardization procedures were in existence already in the late first or early second century for the transmission of Christian texts, such as the codex form, the *nomina sacra* techniques, and the possible presence of scriptoria. These standardization procedures permit us to claim that our very earliest NT papyri had antecedents or ancestors as much as a century earlier than their own time."[50] Since we find among the earliest MSS of the NT textual tradition clear concentrations of MSS with similar characteristics, since the early papyri can be linked with major MSS of the third and fourth century that have recognizable textual complexions, and since those "lines of trajectory identify clusters that in turn differentiate themselves sufficiently from other clusters, the claim that at least three 'text-types' existed in the dynamic Christianity of the second century may be made with considerable confidence."[51]

Michael Holmes commented recently on the situation:

> In these circumstances, only a few hardy souls have attempted more than a simple sketch of the history of the text. . . . One has reason, however, to think that change is afoot. A growing number of scholars have made probes into the history of the text that illuminate specific areas or problems and that contribute important data that will eventually enable the larger picture of the whole to be sketched. This number includes Epp, Parker, B. Aland, K. Aland, and Fee; and, in a series of patristic analyses . . . Ehrman, Fee, and Holmes. At the present moment, studies such as these hold the most promise of enabling us to break out of our current straits and eventually to write a history of the text.[52]

Attempts to redate $\mathfrak{P}^4$, $\mathfrak{P}^{64}$, and $\mathfrak{P}^{67}$—C. P. Thiede suggested a date in the first century, eventually dating $\mathfrak{P}^{64}$ before 50 C.E.[53]—have met with general resistance, as the script of the papyrus is closer to later parallels dated around 200 C.E. than to first-century MSS, some of which Thiede overlooked.[54] The efforts of J. O'Callaghan and C. P. Thiede to identify 7Q5 as a NT papyrus

---

50. Epp, "Significance of the Papyri," 295–96.

51. Ibid., 297.

52. Holmes, "Reasoned Eclecticism," 351–52.

53. Carsten P. Thiede, "Papyrus Magdalen Greek 17 (Gregory-Aland P64): A Reappraisal," *ZPE* 105 (1995): 13–20; idem, "Papyrus Magdalen Greek 17 (Gregory-Aland P64): A Reappraisal," *TynBul* 46 (1995): 29–42; Thiede with M. D'Ancona, *Eyewitness to Jesus: Amazing New Manuscript Evidence about the Origin of the Gospels* (New York: Doubleday, 1996).

54. See Peter M. Head, "The Date of the Magdalen Papyrus of Matthew (*P. Magd.* G.R. 17 = P64): A Response to C. P. Thiede," *TynBul* 46 (1995): 251–85; D. C. Parker, "Was Matthew Written before 50 C.E.? The Magdalen Papyrus of Matthew," *ExpTim* 107 (1996): 40–43; G. Stanton, "A Gospel among the Scrolls?" *BRev* 11 (1995): 36–42; Comfort and Barrett, *Earliest New Testament Manuscripts*, 18, 40–43; D. C. Parker, *TC* 4 (1999): par. 7.

(containing Mark 6:52–53)[55] has been rejected on paleographical grounds by most scholars.[56] The proposal of Y. K. Kim, who wants to date $\mathfrak{P}^{46}$ to the "later first century," also has not found general approval.[57]

Approaches to the Praxis of New Testament Textual Criticism

Textual criticism is "the science that compares all known manuscripts of a given work in an effort to trace the history of variations within the text so as to discover its original form."[58] One way of approaching this task is the attempt to reconstruct the history of the NT by tracing the lines of transmission from our extant MSS back to the earliest stages, and then choose the reading that represents the earliest attainable level of the textual tradition. This approach requires the scholar to organize all extant MSS into groups or clusters, each of which has a very similar type of text. Then one could identify some clusters of MSS that represent the earliest known group. This method may be called "external textual criticism," as it relies heavily on external evidence. Or it may be called the "historical-documentary method," because this is the "traditional" method of textual criticism, emphasizing the age and provenance of a MS and the general quality of its scribe and text. Or it may be called the "historical-genealogical method," as it attempts to trace the chronological succession of text types and readings. This approach was followed by Kenneth Clark and Ernest Colwell. "In an ideal text-critical world, this method would be largely adequate by itself."[59] A strict genealogical method has not been feasible in NT textual criticism because there is too much textual mixture in the complex array of NT MSS, too many gaps in the transmission of NT MSS, and often little information on the provenance of the early MSS.[60]

55. C. P. Thiede, "7Q—Eine Rückkehr zu den neutestamentlichen Papyrusfragmenten in der siebten Höhle von Qumran," *Bib* 65 (1984): 538–59; idem, *Die älteste Evangelien-Handschrift? Das Markus-Fragment von Qumran und die Anfänge der schriftlichen Überlieferung des Neuen Testaments* (Wuppertal: Brockhaus, 1986–94); in English, *The Earliest Gospel Manuscript? The Qumran Papyrus 7Q5 and Its Significance for New Testament Studies* (Exeter: Paternoster, 1992).

56. See Metzger, *Text of the New Testament*, 264 n. 5, for the older literature; see also H.-U. Rosenbaum, "Cave 7Q5! Gegen die erneute Inanspruchnahme des Qumran-Fragments 7Q5 als Bruchstück der ältesten Evangelien-Handschrift," *BZ* 31 (1987): 189–205; D. B. Wallace, "7Q5: The Earliest NT Papyrus?" *WTJ* 56 (1994): 173–80; W. R. Telford, "Mark, Gospel of," in *Encyclopedia of the Dead Sea Scrolls*, ed. L. H. Schiffman and J. C. VanderKam, 2 vols. (Oxford: Oxford University Press, 2000), 1:510–11.

57. Young Kyu Kim, "Palaeographical Dating of P[46] to the Later First Century," *Bib* 69 (1988): 248–57; see Metzger, *Text of the New Testament*, 265–66; Comfort and Barrett, *Earliest New Testament Manuscripts*, 18, 194–97.

58. G. D. Fee, "Textual Criticism of the New Testament," in Epp and Fee, *Theory and Method*, 3.

59. E. J. Epp, "Textual Criticism. New Testament," *ABD* 6:431.

60. E. J. Epp, "Decision Points in Past, Present, and Future New Testament Textual Criticism," in Epp and Fee, *Theory and Method*, 17–44, esp. 31–36.

Quantitative methods such as the Claremont Profile Method (CPM) are used to measure manuscript relationships, particularly relationships among the hundreds of Byzantine MSS, and to determine textual affinities of patristic writers and versions. The goal of the CPM is "to find groups of MSS that are close enough in text so that an entire group can be represented by a few of its members in an *apparatus criticus*," and thus "to organize the mass of witnesses to a text into a manageable whole."[61] F. Wisse demonstrated the usefulness of the CPM in his study of 1,385 MSS of Luke. Together with Paul McReynolds, he fully collated five hundred MSS in three chapters of the Gospel of Luke (Luke 1; 10; 20) and devised a system of test passages made up of all the genealogically significant units of variation. After the test readings were selected, the available MSS were profiled—that is, their agreement with the chosen variants against the Textus Receptus were listed in terms of the numbers assigned to the test readings. Thus, the test passages served as "a grid or screen on which the profiles of the individual MSS are projected," meaning that they were used to establish manuscript groups. The secondary group readings serve to spot subgroups and to study the relationships between groups. Groups often share some group readings, but "each bona fide group displays a distinctive pattern of agreement with and variation from the TR that distinguishes it from other groups." "A group profile requires a large degree of internal agreement among its members," and "a group profile must differ significantly from the profiles of other groups."[62] The application of the CPM to 1,385 MSS of the Gospel of Luke identified fourteen groups.

Most scholars work with what is called the "eclectic" method. "Essentially, this means that the 'original' of the NT is to be chosen variant by variant, using all the principles of critical judgment without regarding one MS or text-type as necessarily preserving that 'original.'"[63] The differences that remain result from the degree of weight given to the external evidence. Scholars who adopt the readings of the Egyptian witnesses when all other criteria are equal (thus following Hort) practice what has been called the "eclectic Egyptian method." This may be observed to a greater degree in the UBS first edition, and to a lesser degree in the Greek texts behind RSV and NEB, which give a little more consideration to early Western witnesses. Scholars such as M.-É. Boismard used an "eclectic Western method," advocating a greater emphasis on preference for the shorter readings as they are found in various Western witnesses, especially early versions and citations from certain church fathers. G. D. Kilpatrick and his student J. K. Elliott are committed to a "rigorous eclectic method": they give no weight to the MSS at all, but make text-critical choices solely on the basis of internal principles. "The cult of the best manuscripts gives way to the

61. Frederik Wisse, *The Profile Method for the Classification and Evaluation of Manuscript Evidence*, SD 44 (Grand Rapids: Eerdmans, 1982), 41.

62. Ibid., 37, 40–41.

63. Fee, "Textual Criticism," 15; q.v. for the following remarks.

cult of the best reading."[64] They search the papyri or uncials as well as the late Byzantine MSS for readings that might be original.[65] The main difficulty with this approach is that the results depend on the scholar's preference of internal criteria, which in the case of Kilpatrick and Elliott "seems to be for variants in an author's style as over against the questions of transcriptional probability."[66] Most scholars follow a "reasoned eclectic method," an approach that seeks to combine the documentary method and the eclectic method, taking into account both the manuscript tradition as well as all relevant internal criteria.

> When faced with any variation-unit, we would choose the variant reading that appears to be in the earliest chronological group *and* that also makes the best sense when the internal criteria are applied. Moreover, if no one cluster or type of text can be identified unambiguously as the earliest, then we would choose the variant reading in any given case that is in *one* of the earliest clusters *and* that best fits the relevant internal considerations. . . . In this method it is recognized that no single criterion or invariable combination of criteria will resolve all cases of textual variation, and it attempts, therefore, to apply evenly and without prejudice any and all criteria—external and internal—appropriate to a given case, arriving at an answer based on the relative probabilities among those applicable criteria.[67]

This approach was followed by the editors of NA[27] and UBS[4] and is advocated by scholars such as E. J. Epp and G. D. Fee.[68] The external and the internal criteria used for determining the reading that is most likely original do not need to be repeated here, as they have essentially remained the same.[69]

The fresh examination of the NT manuscript tradition by the editorial committee of the *Editio Critica Maior* made virtually no impact on the reconstructed text itself, as has been noted above. B. D. Ehrman observes that even though some scholars may deplore this, we are "not going to get much closer to the original text than we already are. Barring some fantastic manuscript discovery (like the autographs) or some earth-shattering alterations in text-critical method, the basic physiognomy of our texts is never going to change. . . . At this stage, our work on the *original* amounts to little more than

---

64. J. K. Elliott, "Rational Criticism and the Text of the New Testament," *Theology* 77 (1972): 340.

65. See J. K. Elliott, "Thoroughgoing Eclecticism in New Testament Textual Criticism," in Ehrman and Holmes, *Text of the New Testament,* 321–35.

66. Fee, "Textual Criticism," 15.

67. Epp, "Decision Points," 35.

68. See Eldon J. Epp, "Textual Criticism in the Exegesis of the New Testament, with an Excursus on Canon," in *A Handbook to the Exegesis of the New Testament,* ed. S. E. Porter, NTTS 25 (Leiden: Brill, 1997), 45–97.

69. See Bruce M. Metzger, *A Textual Commentary on the Greek New Testament,* 2nd ed. (Stuttgart: Deutsche Bibelgesellschaft; United Bible Societies, 1994), 10–14; Epp, "Textual Criticism," 61–73.

tinkering."[70] Instead of fretting about this state of affairs, text critics should study the manuscript tradition with the goal of establishing the transmission of the text over the centuries—that is, the new task is the study of the scribal alterations of the text "to see how the text was re-read and re-created once it left the hand of its 'original' author, to see what kinds of social, historical, and theological influences affected its transcribers."

With regard to standard introductions to NT textual criticism, the following deserve mention. In North America, the standard text still is Bruce Metzger's *Text of the New Testament,* published in a third, enlarged edition in 1992, with an appendix discussing "advances in textual criticism of the New Testament, 1964–1990."[71] In England, the standard introduction now is the volume presented by Keith Elliott and Ian Moir.[72] In Germany, Kurt and Barbara Aland's *Der Text des Neuen Testaments* continues to be the traditional handbook for students and exegetes alike and exerts a much wider influence in the world through its English translation.[73] Christian-Bernard Amphoux has revised and updated Leon Vaganay's introduction to NT textual criticism and thus presents the latest teaching in France about the subject.[74]

Centers of Research

In the years around the time of World War II, the "Chicago School" of NT textual criticism was linked with scholars such as D. W. Riddle, E. C. Colwell, and M. Parvis. Major North American textual critics today are B. D. Ehrman (Chapel Hill, North Carolina), E. J. Epp (Cleveland, Ohio), G. D. Fee (Vancouver, British Columbia), M. W. Holmes (St. Paul, Minnesota), F. Wisse (Montreal, Quebec), and, of course, Bruce M. Metzger (Princeton, New Jersey). The Ancient Biblical Manuscript Center at the Claremont School of Theology (Claremont, California), directed by M. B. Phelps, is the official repository of the microfilm collection of the International Greek New Testament Project, circulating films from its collection of MSS to the project collators, and providing access to photographic and digital images of MSS from

70. B. D. Ehrman, *TC* 3 (1998): par. 22.

71. Metzger, *Text of the New Testament,* appendix, 260–97.

72. J. Keith Elliott and Ian A. Moir, *Manuscripts and the Text of the New Testament: An Introduction for English Readers* (Edinburgh: Clark, 1995).

73. Kurt Aland and Barbara Aland, *Der Text des Neuen Testaments: Einführung in die wissenschaftlichen Ausgaben sowie in Theorie und Praxis der modernen Textkritik* (Stuttgart: Deutsche Bibelgesellschaft, 1982); in English, *The Text of the New Testament: An Introduction to the Critical Editions and to the Theory and Practice of Modern Textual Criticism,* trans. E. F. Rhodes, 2nd ed. (Leiden: Brill; Grand Rapids: Eerdmans, 1989).

74. L. Vaganay, *Initiaton à la critique textuelle du Nouveau Testament,* 2nd rev. ed. (Paris: Cerf, 1986); in English, Léon Vaganay and Christian-Bernard Amphoux, *An Introduction to New Testament Textual Criticism,* trans. J. Heimerdinger, 2nd ed. (Cambridge: Cambridge University Press, 1991).

Jewish and Christian antiquity.[75] B. Warren coordinates the Center for New Testament Textual Studies for the New Orleans Baptist Theological Seminary. At Andrews University (Berrien Springs, Michigan), W. L. Richards directs the Greek Manuscript Research Center.

The most productive research center for NT textual research has been the Institut für neutestamentliche Textforschung (Institute for New Testament Textual Research) in Münster, Westphalia, founded in 1959 and directed for many years by the late Kurt Aland, now under the supervision of Barbara Aland. The scholars working at the Münster Institute edited and continue to improve the *Novum Testamentum Graece,* on whose Greek text most translations and revisions of older translations of the NT are based, and they edit the *Editio Critica Maior,* a project that has initiated the publication of many specialized studies of the scholars associated with the Institute, including studies on the early versions and the NT text(s) used by the church fathers. The Institute houses a microfilm collection of 90 percent of the over five thousand NT MSS and maintains the international registry of the Greek MSS of the NT. Regular reports provide information about the work of the Institute.[76] The Institute is linked with a "Bibelmuseum" that seeks to make the work of the Institute accessible for the larger public and presents the history of the Bible through displays of original MSS and early publications.

Other centers of text-critical research exist in the Netherlands (Utrecht, T. Baarda), Belgium (Leuven, J. Delobel and F. Neirynck), England (Leeds, J. K. Elliott), and France (Centre Jean Duplacy pour l'étude des manuscrits de la Bible, established in 1984 by Christian Amphoux). Articles relevant for research into the textual tradition of the NT appear in all learned journals, particularly journals devoted to biblical studies in general and to the NT specifically. Since 1996, the journal *TC: A Journal of Biblical Textual Criticism* is published electronically.[77]

Historical and Theological Issues

The task of textual criticism defined as "discovering the original form of the text" is significant for at least three reasons:[78] (1) Textual criticism seeks to determine the authentic words of the original author. Before one can ask the question "What does the text mean?" one needs to ask, "What does the text say?" And this question implies the basic question "What is the text?" (2) Textual criticism provides a firm foundation for Bible translation. Since the majority

75. Online: www.abmc.org.
76. For example, *Bericht der Hermann Kunst-Stiftung zur Förderung der neutestamentlichen Textforschung für die Jahre 1995 bis 1998* (Münster, 1998).
77. Online: http://rosetta.reltech.org/TC/TC.html.
78. See Fee, "Textual Criticism," 3–16.

of Christians have access to the NT only via translation, the results of textual criticism are of fundamental importance, as Bible translations seek to represent as accurately as possible the original text of the author. (3) Textual criticism allows the interpreter to see how the early church interpreted the text. This is the case in those places where scribes intentionally changed the wording of the text. Thus, textual criticism can put the interpreter in touch with an early phase of historical exegesis (or *Wirkungsgeschichte*).

In recent years, some textual critics have been reexamining the assumptions that underlie the concept of "original text." H. Koester suggests that textual critics of the NT writings were naive in not recognizing that the first century of the transmission of classical texts is the period in which the most serious corruptions occur. Thus, the "text of the Synoptic Gospels was very unstable during the first and second centuries. With respect to Mark, one can be fairly certain that only its revised text has achieved canonical status, while the original text (attested only by Matthew and Luke) has not survived."[79] B. D. Ehrman argues that the scribes of the second and third centuries altered the texts they copied in order to make them more orthodox or less susceptible to heretics.

> The history of exegesis is the history of readers interpreting different forms of the text, since throughout this history, virtually no one read the NT in its original form. . . . It is important for social historians and historians of doctrine to identify the social and theological movements that affected the texts, through the scribes who modified them. Given these historical concerns, there may indeed be scant reason to privilege the "original" text over forms of the text that developed subsequently.[80]

D. C. Parker suggests two reasons why the task of textual criticism does not have to be the recovery of the original text: (1) the diversity of variant readings in the Gospel texts reveals a text that grew freely as "sayings and stories continued to be developed by copyists and readers," and (2) there are important texts such as the Lord's Prayer in which the multiplicity of variant readings demonstrates the extent of substantial variation even in "popular" texts. Parker concludes that "there is no authoritative text beyond the manuscripts which we may follow without further thought. . . . The concept of a *canon* that is fixed in shape, authoritative, and final as a piece of literature has to be abandoned."[81] Recently, E. J. Epp argued similarly that textual critics should not and cannot

---

79. Helmut Koester, "The Text of the Synoptic Gospels in the Second Century," in *Gospel Traditions in the Second Century: Origins, Recensions, Text, and Transmission,* ed. W. L. Petersen, CJA 3 (Notre Dame, Ind.: University of Notre Dame Press, 1989), 37.

80. B. D. Ehrman, "The Text as Window: New Testament Manuscripts and the Social History of Early Christianity," in Ehrman and Holmes, *Text of the New Testament,* 361 n. 1.

81. David C. Parker, *The Living Text of the Gospels* (Cambridge: Cambridge University Press, 1997), 45f., 93; cf. Eldon J. Epp, "The Multivalence of the Term 'Original Text' in New Testament Textual Criticism," *HTR* 92 (1999): 264–65.

ignore the compositional levels of the NT books. "Any search for textual *pre*formulations or *re*formulations of a literary nature, such as *prior* compositional levels, versions, or formulations, or *later* textual alteration, revision, division, combination, rearrangement, interpolation, or forming a collection of writings, legitimately falls within the sphere of text-critical activity *if such an exploration is initiated on the basis of some appropriate textual variation or other manuscript evidence.*"[82] Thus, for example, hypotheses concerning the early sayings traditions, or about the sources of the Gospels, suggest that an "original" had earlier "originals," as textual variants attest to "predecessor literary activity." Further, early Christians "would have treated as 'canon' whatever text-form of a gospel or letter had reached them in the transmission process."[83] Since each of the some 5,300 Greek NT MSS is an "original," each was considered "canonical," as all were used in the worship of a church. This means that since the concept of "original" is multivalent, the concept of "canon" cannot escape multivalence either. "Our multiplicities of texts may all have been canonical (that is, authoritative) at some time and place. . . . The text-critical discipline per se carries with it no normative implications and imposes no theological overlay onto such a text or variant."[84] Epp "allows" textual critics the "full freedom to perform his or her text-critical work within any chosen theological framework, but that choice constitutes a fully separate, voluntary, additional step and one not intrinsic to or demanded by the discipline."[85] Although this last assertion certainly is correct, Epp's understanding of the concept of "original text" in NT textual criticism, advocating the abandonment of the concept of an authoritative canon, is not an "additional" step but a presupposition that has already led G. E. Lessing to question the validity of the NT canon. For those who do not work within a theological framework, the multiplicity of textual variants renders the notion of an authoritative canon spurious. Scholars who study the NT as a historical and literary corpus of texts but also study as Christians who believe that God has spoken and continues to speak in and through the books of the NT recognize the multiplicity of variant readings in the manuscript tradition as another illustration of the human face of God's revelation. At the same time, they acknowledge the advances in the study of the NT text over the last two hundred years that have brought us as close to the original text (i.e., the autographs) as we probably will ever get, and many of them probably would assert that the thousands of variant readings neither "explode" the concept of an original text "into a complex and highly unmanageable multivalent entity"[86] nor challenge the theological convictions of those who hear in and through the NT books the *viva vox evangelii.*

82. Epp, "Multivalence," 268.
83. Ibid., 274.
84. Ibid., 278–79.
85. Ibid., 279.
86. Ibid., 280.

4

Greek Grammar and Syntax

Stanley E. Porter

One of the most important and yet often neglected areas of NT study today is Greek grammar and syntax. The NT was written in Greek, and it demands to be studied in Greek to appreciate fully what it offers the exegete. Exegesis involves much more than thorough knowledge of the Greek NT, but it demands nothing less. However, many exegetes never get beyond a fairly rudimentary, textbook knowledge of the Greek language (even if they can translate it at sight, so that it sounds like the RSV), and fewer still are aware of the tremendous advances that have been made—including a number of significant proposals by evangelical scholars—in the last thirty years. In fact, in the last thirty years, some of the most significant innovations in the study of Greek language and linguistics, as well as in the realm of NT study as a whole, have occurred in the area of NT Greek.

In this essay, I wish, first, to describe and assess some of the basic tools available for the study of Greek,[1] and, second, to introduce a number of recent

---

1. A major, complex topic that will not be discussed in this essay, due to limitations of space, is the controversy regarding the nature of the Greek of the NT (including possible Semitic influence) and how this relates to the overall development of the Greek language. Those interested can pursue such issues in S. E. Porter, ed., *The Language of the New Testament: Classic Essays,* JSNTSup 60 (Sheffield: JSOT, 1991), with a selection of representative essays by scholars such as G. A. Deissmann, J. H. Moulton, C. C. Torrey, M. Black, J. A. Fitzmyer, H. S. Gehman, N. Turner, L. Rydbeck, and M. Silva, and an introduction by the editor; G. Horrocks, *Greek: A History of the Language and Its Speakers* (London: Longman, 1997); S. E. Porter, *The Criteria for Authenticity in Historical-Jesus Research: Previous Discussion and New Proposals,* JSNTSup 191 (Sheffield: Sheffield Academic Press, 2000), esp. 126–80. Two recent studies that attempt to

linguistically based innovations that represent significant advances in Greek study.

Traditional Tools for Study of the Grammar and Syntax of the Greek New Testament

The traditional tools for study of the grammar and syntax of the Greek NT consist of a number of reference grammars, supplemented by a limited number of monographs on specialized topics.[2] Both of these types of resources will be described and assessed, since they are the major means by which most students of the NT gain access to discussion of the Greek language. However, as this survey will show, the nature and limitations of these tools have also led to a lethargy in which it is sometimes thought that there are no advances to be made in Greek grammatical study. I am often amazed to find in a large number of exegetically based works, including not only commentaries but also other works, even those by authors regarded as major scholars, that unfounded or poorly supported linguistic judgments about the Greek language are made, in most instances without reference even to the standard grammatical tools surveyed here (or with the occasional reference to Blass's grammar—see below). One of the most obvious features that emerges from a study of the history of Greek grammatical discussion is that grammatical studies have a close relationship to the theoretical linguistic orientation of their times. In other words, there is no such thing as Greek grammar in and of itself or in the abstract, as if it is a

---

integrate historical discussion with grammatical issues are S. E. Porter, "The Greek Language of the New Testament," in *Handbook to Exegesis of the New Testament,* ed. S. E. Porter, NTTS 25 (Leiden: Brill, 1997), 99–130; idem, "Greek of the New Testament," in *Dictionary of New Testament Background,* ed. C. A. Evans and S. E. Porter (Downers Grove, Ill.: InterVarsity, 2000), 426–35.

2. A second important topic not discussed here due to space limitations is lexicography. A history of traditional NT Greek lexicography is found in F. W. Danker, *Lexical Evolution and Linguistic Hazard* (Chicago: University of Chicago Press, 1999), and represented in W. Bauer, *A Greek-English Lexicon of the New Testament and Other Early Christian Literature,* 3rd ed., rev. and ed. F. W. Danker (Chicago: University of Chicago Press, 2000). New developments are represented by the underrated but invaluable and innovative work by J. P. Louw and E. A. Nida, *Greek-English Lexicon of the New Testament Based on Semantic Domains,* 2 vols. (New York: United Bible Societies, 1988); cf. E. A. Nida and J. P. Louw, *Lexical Semantics of the Greek New Testament,* SBLRBS 25 (Atlanta: Scholars Press, 1992). This work in many ways renders traditional lexicography redundant. See also the semantically well-grounded and innovative volume by J. Mateos and J. Peláez, eds., *Diccionario Griego-Español del Nuevo Testamento: Análisis semántico de los vocablos, Fascículo 1: Ἀαρών-αἱματεκχυσία* (Cordova: Ediciones El Almendro-Fundación Épsilon, 2000), with supporting monographs by each of the editors (in Spanish). Developments in lexicography are discussed in S. E. Porter, *Studies in the Greek New Testament: Theory and Practice,* SBG 6 (New York: Lang, 1996), 49–74. An attempt to integrate lexicon and grammar is found in S. E. Porter, "Aspect and Lexicography," in Frederick Danker's Festschrift (forthcoming).

self-evident thing that requires no interpretation. Greek grammar is as theory-based as any intellectual discipline, and knowledge of the development of this discipline is necessary to understand its major contributors. Therefore, it is entirely right that discussion of Greek grammar and syntax be thought of as a hermeneutical enterprise.[3]

New Testament Greek Reference Grammars

The earliest Greek grammarians were the Greeks themselves. The first Greek grammar was written by Dionysius Thrax (second century B.C.E.), who laid out a very basic manual of the various formal elements of the language. Apollonius Dyscolus (second century C.E.) is attributed with writing the first syntax of Greek. These grammatical works, and others besides, are invaluable for a serious student of Greek, and one thing that they demonstrate is how much has been learned about Greek since that time.[4] With the rise in importance of Latin as the language of the church and scholarship, work on Greek faded in significance until the Renaissance, when Greek began to be studied in a more intense way. In terms of grammars of the Greek NT, there have been a number written in the last several centuries. Virtually all of them have much valuable information in them and reward study, not least as representatives of the grammatical perspective and concerns of their age.

In the eighteenth and nineteenth centuries, a relatively large number of NT Greek grammars were written. Some of the most well known are those by Georg Winer, Moses Stuart, and Alexander Buttmann.[5] To varying degrees, they represent the linguistic approaches to ancient Greek of these two centuries, including belief in rationalistic patterns of language usage and change, attention to classical philology, and, in the later nineteenth century especially, comparative philology.[6] Winer's grammar is probably

---

3. Such recognition is seen in the title of a recent book, E. J. Bakker, ed., *Grammar as Interpretation: Greek Literature in Its Linguistic Contexts* (Leiden: Brill, 1997).

4. For a recent study, see S. E. Porter, "Grammarians, Hellenistic Greek," in Evans and Porter, *Dictionary of New Testament Background,* 418–21.

5. G. B. Winer, *Grammatik des neutestamentlichen Sprachidioms als sichere Grundlage der neutestamentlichen Exegese* (Leipzig: Vogel, 1822), which went through eight German editions, the seventh being issued by G. Lünemann in 1866, and the eighth being revised (but not completed) by P. W. Schmiedel in 1894–98, and, among others, three related English translations by E. Masson (Edinburgh: Clark, 1865); J. H. Thayer (Andover: Draper, 1870); and W. F. Moulton (*A Treatise on the Grammar of New Testament Greek* [Edinburgh: Clark, 1870; 3rd ed., 1882]), who offers a survey of previous grammars (1–11); M. Stuart, *A Treatise on the Syntax of the New Testament Dialect, with an Appendix, Containing a Dissertation on the Greek Article* (Edinburgh: Clark, 1835); A. Buttmann, *Grammatik des neutestamentlichen Sprachgebrauchs* (Berlin: Weidmann, 1859); in English, *A Grammar of the New Testament Greek,* trans. J. H. Thayer (Andover: Draper, 1895).

6. For a brief and useful discussion of the history of this period in linguistics, see R. H. Robins, *A Short History of Linguistics,* 2nd ed. (London: Longman, 1979), chs. 1–2.

the best known of the above and the only one still cited with any regularity. Winer's grammar reflects the rationalistic framework of the nineteenth century, with its formulation of ineluctable rules regarding language. Thus, for example, the present tense-form "expresses present time in all its relations," and "strictly and properly speaking, no one of these tenses can ever stand for another," so that the present tense is "used for the future in appearance only."[7] His rationalist framework will not allow a tense-form labeled "present" to be anything other than present-referring. Most of the grammars of this time period, including Winer's, viewed the Greek of the NT in direct relation to classical Greek. Thus, Buttmann's grammar was an adaptation of his father's classical Greek grammar to the Greek of the NT. This framework had both positive and negative effects. The advantage was the amassing of interesting and potentially useful linguistic parallels to inform study of NT Greek, while the disadvantage was that the classical categories frequently were determinatively used to assess NT usage, often to its detriment, with the Greek seen to be inferior to the great works of literature created in fifth-century Athens.[8]

In 1896, the first edition of what has become the standard NT Greek reference grammar was published by Friedrich Blass.[9] Blass was a well-known classical Greek scholar who is still recognized for his work on Greek style, textual criticism of classical texts, and even some Gospel criticism.[10] It is surprising that his grammar has become the standard reference tool for NT studies, however, since it provides merely a brief and succinct (and far from complete) analysis of the Greek of the NT based upon direct comparison with classical Greek and in terms of the long-enshrined categories of classical Greek philological study. This grammar has gone through a number of editions, with the comparative philologist Albert Debrunner taking over editorial responsibilities with the

7. Winer and Moulton, *Treatise*, 331.

8. One of the pitfalls of comparing classical Greek texts with the Greek of the Hellenistic period, including that of the NT, is that one is comparing unlike things. Classical Greek is represented virtually exclusively by literary texts written in a dialect not used by the majority of people of a single relatively small but significant city. These texts were written around half a millennium earlier than the mix of literary, nonliterary, and even vulgar Greek texts written in the lingua franca of a variety of peoples extended around the Mediterranean in Greco-Roman times. On some of the issues involved in assessing literary Attic, see K. J. Dover, "The Colloquial Stratum in Classical Attic Prose," in *Classical Contributions: Studies in Honour of M. F. McGregor*, ed. G. S. Shrimpton and D. J. McCargar (Locust Valley, N.Y.: Augustin, 1981), 15–25; S. J. Teodorsson, "Phonological Variation in Classical Attic and the Development of Koine," *Glotta* 57 (1979): 61–75.

9. F. Blass, *Grammatik des neutestamentlichen Griechisch* (Göttingen: Vandenhoeck & Ruprecht, 1896).

10. For example, F. Blass, *Die Rhythmen der asianischen und römischen Kunstprosa* (Leipzig: Deichert, 1905); idem, ed., *Demosthenis Orationes*, rev. Wilhelm Dindorf, 4th ed., 3 vols. (Leipzig: Teubner, 1885–89); idem, *Philology of the Gospels* (London: Macmillan, 1898). He is also noted in early volumes of the published Oxyrhynchus papyri as having provided helpful emendations and suggestions on the decipherment of a number of literary manuscripts.

fourth edition (1913),[11] the LXX scholar David Tabachovitz providing an appendix to the twelfth edition (1965), and the NT scholar Friedrich Rehkopf becoming the editor with the fourteenth edition (1976). Despite these editorial changes (many of the editions are simply reprints with slight changes), and despite some changes in formatting, this grammar remains in most essential characteristics the same one that it was in 1896. These features include an emphasis upon comparison with the standards of classical Greek, a lack of a systematic approach to language structure (seen especially in dealing with tense, case, and voice, etc.), a lack of rigorous and explicit semantic terminology, and a tendency to understand Greek by means of German or English (depending upon the version).[12] The first English translation was made of the first and second German editions, and the well-known and widely used English translation by Funk, which has become the standard for English exegesis, was made of the tenth edition with Debrunner's notes for the eleventh, and published in 1961.[13] Despite its concision and reference to some papyri and early Christian writers, this grammar is predicated upon knowledge of classical Greek, and it maintains the kind of grammatical categories inherited from language study in the nineteenth century. This grammar is over a century old in orientation, even though later versions make it appear to be more up-to-date.

In 1906, under the influence of two major factors—(1) recent developments in continental comparative linguistics, especially by the so-called "New Gram-

11. Debrunner was one of the most important influences upon Greek grammar in the twentieth century, but he worked with the nineteenth-century model of comparative philology. According to Robert Funk, his major changes to Blass's grammar were in terms of phonology, accidence, and word formation (F. Blass and A. Debrunner, *A Greek Grammar of the New Testament and Other Early Christian Literature,* trans. and ed. Robert W. Funk [Chicago: University of Chicago Press, 1961], xi). Debrunner's influence can be seen in the fact that he not only edited Blass's NT Greek grammar, but also edited the second volume, *Syntax und syntaktischer Stilistik* (1950), of E. Schwyzer's *Griechische Grammatik auf der Grundlage von Karl Brugmanns Griechische Grammatik,* 4 vols. (Munich: Beck, 1939–71; vols. 3 and 4 are indexes added later). As the title implies, this work is a revision of Karl Brugmann's *Griechische Grammatik* (Munich: Beck, 1885; 4th ed., rev. A. Thumb, 1913). These remain important grammars of classical Greek, along with those of R. Kühner (*Ausführliche Grammatik der griechischen Sprache,* I. *Elementar- und Formenlehre,* 2 vols. [Hannover: Hahnsche, 1834; rev. F. Blass, 1890–92]; II. *Satzlehre,* 2 vols. [Hannover: Hahnsche, 1834; rev. B. Gerth, 1898–1904]) and J. M. Stahl (*Kritisch-historische Syntax des griechischen Verbums der klassischen Zeit* [Heidelberg: Winter, 1907]). English-language classical scholarship has never been as productive of full-scale reference grammars. The standard works are W. W. Goodwin, *A Greek Grammar* (London: Macmillan, 1870; rev. C. B. Gulick [Boston: Ginn, 1930]), and H. W. Smyth, *Greek Grammar* (Cambridge: Harvard University Press, 1920; rev. G. M. Messing, 1956), along with B. L. Gildersleeve and C. W. E. Miller, *Syntax of Classical Greek from Homer to Demosthenes,* 2 vols. (New York: American Book Company, 1900–1911). French scholarship has been limited, but the works astute. See, for example, J. Humbert, *Syntaxe Grecque,* Tradition de l'Humanisme 8 (Paris: Klincksieck, 1945; 3rd ed., 1960).

12. For a fuller study, see S. E. Porter and J. T. Reed, "Greek Grammar since BDF: A Retrospective and Prospective Analysis," *Filología Neotestamentaria* 4 (1991): 143–64, esp. 143–56.

13. F. Blass and A. Debrunner, *A Grammar of New Testament Greek,* trans. and rev. R. W. Funk (Chicago: University of Chicago Press, 1961).

marians" such as Karl Brugmann,[14] and (2) the discovery and publication of the Greek documentary papyri[15]—James Hope Moulton published his *Prolegomena to A Grammar of New Testament Greek.*[16] Moulton envisioned a multivolume work that encompassed the best of recent study in the Greek of the NT. His *Prolegomena* is in many ways a model grammar, since it introduced to the English-speaking world important developments on the continent, such as the concept of *Aktionsart* (originally formulated by Brugmann in his grammar—see below on verbal aspect), and shifted the point of comparison for the Greek of the NT from classical Greek to the contemporary documentary papyri. Moulton did not hesitate to introduce the latest in linguistic thought to the English-speaking world (although much of this work has been surpassed by now), and he used as his major point of comparison the evidence of contemporary Greek usage in the documentary papyri of Egypt. As a result, the Greek of the NT was being studied in terms of other documents of roughly the same period, and many syntactical and grammatical phenomena previously thought to be Semitically motivated were seen to be acceptable usage in other Hellenistic Greek of the time.[17] This was an important advance whose implications have not been fully realized in NT study, where the tendency still is to look to a Semitic substratum to explain Greek grammatical phenomena.

Moulton's *Prolegomena* gives a useful taste of the kind of creative and innovative work that could have continued in subsequent volumes of his grammar. Moulton wrote several sections of a second volume, on accidence and word formation,

14. Brugmann was a part of the diachronically based and rule-governed nineteenth-century New Grammarians. See K. R. Jankowsky, *The Neogrammarians: A Re-evaluation of Their Place in the Development of Linguistic Science* (The Hague: Mouton, 1972).

15. The discovery of the papyri and their importance for NT Greek study are conveniently told in E. G. Turner, *Greek Papyri: An Introduction* (Oxford: Clarendon, 1968), 17–41; W. F. Howard, *The Romance of New Testament Scholarship* (London: Epworth, 1949), 111–37. The two standard grammars of the Greek papyri are E. Mayser, *Grammatik der griechischen Papyri aus der Ptolemäerzeit,* 2 vols. (vol. 1.1, rev. H. Schmoll; Berlin: de Gruyter, 1906–34, 1970); F. T. Gignac, *A Grammar of the Greek Papyri of the Roman and Byzantine Periods,* 2 vols. (Milan: Istituto Editoriale Cisalpino, 1976–81); and the study of the verb by B. G. Mandilaras, *The Verb in the Greek Non-literary Papyri* (Athens: Hellenic Ministry of Culture and Sciences, 1973).

16. J. H. Moulton, *Prolegomena,* vol. 1 of *A Grammar of New Testament Greek* (Edinburgh: Clark, 1906; 3rd ed., 1908). This grammar was originally meant to be a revision of Winer's grammar, translated by Moulton's father. One can see that developments in linguistic perspective, and the shift from classical to contemporary documents, would have made such revision difficult. A German grammar that tries something similar is L. Radermacher, *Neutestamentliche Grammatik,* HNT 1 (Tübingen: Mohr [Siebeck], 1911; 2nd ed., 1925).

17. In lexicography, a similar accomplishment was made by G. A. Deissmann, in his *Bibelstudien* (Marburg: Elwert, 1895) and *Neue Bibelstudien* (Marburg: Elwert, 1897); in English, *Bible Studies,* trans. A. Grieve (Edinburgh: Clark, 1901); and his *Licht vom Osten* (Tübingen: Mohr [Siebeck], 1908; 4th ed., 1923); in English, *Light from the Ancient East,* trans. L. R. M. Strachan (London: Hodder & Stoughton, 1910; 4th ed., 1927); as well as by Moulton in J. H. Moulton and G. Milligan, *The Vocabulary of the Greek Testament Illustrated from the Papyri and Other Non-Literary Sources,* 8 vols. (London: Hodder & Stoughton, 1914–29).

before he was killed in 1917 crossing the Mediterranean, returning from a trip to India.[18] This volume was continued by Moulton's student W. F. Howard, who was more of a biblical scholar than a language specialist like Moulton, and finally published in 1929.[19] The subsequent volumes of the series remained uncompleted until Nigel Turner undertook to publish *Syntax* in 1963 and *Style* in 1976.[20] Although the series finally stands complete, it must be noted that Turner's orientation is to attribute to the Greek of the NT a unique status as a special dialect of Semitically influenced Greek.[21] This reflects a very different orientation from that of Moulton, so much so that it must be asked whether the third and fourth volumes belong in the same series with the first two. Students of the Greek NT need to be aware of these differences, and they should not use the volumes together as if they are a common voice on issues of NT Greek. There have been a number of other criticisms of some of the particular features of Turner's work,[22] but two loom largest. The first is that Turner's *Syntax* volume does not push forward methodological discussion, but relies upon an almost haphazard classification of examples, often invoked in defense of his hypothesis regarding the unique nature of the Greek of the NT. The second criticism is that his *Style* volume is not a study of the concept of style per se, but more a reclassification of the data from his *Syntax* volume according to the usage of the individual writers of the NT. In some ways, the discussion in these two volumes seems older and more dated than that found in Moulton's *Prolegomena*. It certainly reflects an older orientation to language than does Moulton's work.

At about the same time as Moulton was working on his *Prolegomena*, and after also abandoning an attempt to revise Winer's grammar, A. T. Robertson undertook to produce a grammar of the Greek NT along historical and comparative lines.[23] In other words, he attempted to do for NT Greek what had been done in nineteenth-century comparative philology for other languages. The result is a monument to human industry of over twelve hundred pages, not counting additional notes and indexes. In many ways, Robertson's gram-

---

18. Moulton was an active Christian who had been doing work under the auspices of the YMCA in India. He was also the recipient of a D.Theol. degree from Berlin University. It is tragic that he was killed at the height of his powers, and by a German submarine.

19. J. H. Moulton and W. F. Howard, *Accidence and Word-Formation*, vol. 2 of *A Grammar of New Testament Greek* (Edinburgh: Clark, 1929). This was originally published in three separate fascicles, in 1919, 1920, and 1929.

20. N. Turner, *Syntax*, vol. 3 of *A Grammar of New Testament Greek* (Edinburgh: Clark, 1963); idem, *Style*, vol. 4 of *A Grammar of New Testament Greek* (Edinburgh: Clark, 1976). See also his *Grammatical Insights into the New Testament* (Edinburgh: Clark, 1965), esp. 174–88.

21. There have been a number of versions of this theory, which essentially argues that the Greek of the NT is a special form of Semitically influenced Greek, perhaps even a Holy Spirit–inspired form of Greek. This view apparently harks back to the nineteenth century. For discussion, see the introduction in Porter, *Language of the New Testament*, 27–31.

22. See *NewDocs* 5:49–65.

23. A. T. Robertson, *A Grammar of the Greek New Testament in the Light of Historical Research* (New York: Hodder & Stoughton, 1914; 4th ed., Nashville: Broadman, 1934).

mar is still the most useful of all of the reference grammars, since he has some kind of comment on what seems to be virtually every verse in the NT. He also has extensive reference to continental linguistic scholarship of the nineteenth and early twentieth centuries. However, this exhaustive work comes at a price. Robertson often is unfocused in his discussion, occasionally treating the same passage in different ways in different parts of the book, and often giving the impression that he has dealt more with the secondary scholarship than he has with extrabiblical primary sources. And despite all of this, his perspective is bounded by nineteenth-century language study.

These grammars constitute the major reference grammars commonly avail-able to the student of the Greek NT. Thus, the situation is that the major reference grammars of the Greek NT are roughly one hundred years old and reflect scholarship of the nineteenth century. The only exceptions are Turner's volumes, but these hark back to the earlier method and in many ways are not as advanced as Moulton's volume, which instigated the series. In some respects, this is not that much different from English-language classical scholarship, which also is limited in many of its tools. German scholarship is only moderately better off. However, the situations being similar does not excuse the fact that most NT Greek reference grammars have entirely missed out on the advent and development of modern linguistic study (see below). More than that, the basic premises and orientations of the grammars often are out of character with current NT scholarship. The contrast is even more striking when one considers that in many other areas NT scholarship has attempted to utilize the best in methodological developments—redaction criticism, social-scien-tific criticism, literary criticism, and ideological criticism[24]—while allowing its linguistic tools to languish behind.[25] This does not mean that these reference

---

24. For representative essays in these and other areas, see Porter, *Handbook to Exegesis,* esp. part 1, on method.

25. It is therefore not surprising that for the most part beginning or elementary grammars of NT Greek do not represent significant advances either. For discussion, see Porter, *Studies in the Greek New Testament,* 39–48. Many intermediate-level grammars offer little better, utilizing traditional categories often gleaned from the reference grammars, and some even resisting the insights of recent linguistic thought. These include H. E. Dana and J. R. Mantey, *A Manual Grammar of the Greek New Testament* (New York: Macmillan, 1927 [with many reprintings]); W. D. Chamberlain, *An Exegetical Grammar of the Greek New Testament* (New York: Macmillan, 1941; reprint, Grand Rapids: Baker, 1979); C. F. D. Moule, *An Idiom Book of New Testament Greek* (Cambridge: Cambridge University Press, 1953; 2nd ed., 1959); M. Zerwick, *Biblical Greek,* trans. J. Smith (Rome: Pontifical Bible Institute, 1963), although this grammar has an uncommonly large number of insights; J. A. Brooks and C. L. Winbery, *Syntax of New Testament Greek* (Washington, D.C.: University Press of America, 1979); W. J. Perschbacher, *New Testament Greek Syntax* (Chicago: Moody, 1995); D. B. Wallace, *Greek Grammar beyond the Basics* (Grand Rapids: Zondervan, 1996). There are a few useful exceptions, however. S. E. Porter, *Idioms of the Greek New Testament,* BLG 2 (Sheffield: JSOT Press, 1992; 2nd ed., 1994), introduces re-cent developments in linguistic thought, including discourse analysis (see below); R. A. Young, *Intermediate New Testament Greek: A Linguistic and Exegetical Approach* (Nashville: Broadman & Holman, 1994), does similarly, often exploring exegetical insights of the analysis.

grammars are not full of useful information, including citation of useful parallels of syntactical phenomena. However, their explanations often are couched in outmoded terms, without clearly indicating the linguistic significance of the element being discussed. Those using these tools must be aware of their methodological approaches and the limitations of such approaches. Further, one must realize that any significant conceptual developments since these works were written are, of course, not incorporated and utilized. As I discuss below, there have been a number of significant developments in recent study of the Greek NT that demand inclusion in future analysis of the Greek of the NT, and ultimately inclusion in major reference tools available to those other than specialists.

Other Grammatical and Syntactical Studies

In the course of studying the Greek of the NT, there are other studies that one is bound to come across, often in journals, and occasionally in monographs devoted to particular grammatical issues. Unfortunately, when compared with the studies generated in other areas of Greek scholarship, the number of devoted treatments of the Greek of the NT is relatively small. Nevertheless, several of these studies merit attention here. This is not a comprehensive list (and it ignores journal literature almost entirely), and other studies could have been mentioned as well, such as the major sections on Greek usage in some commentaries. Commentaries written in the early part of the twentieth century tended to have more comprehensive discussions of Greek usage, while later commentaries tend to focus on nonlinguistic issues, thus shifting the terms of discussion away from treatment of the language itself to an often contextually isolated discussion of a single grammatical feature.

The earliest study to mention here is that by Ernest De Witt Burton on the moods and tenses of NT Greek.[26] Paralleling the work of Goodwin on the same topic for classical Greek,[27] Burton incorporates recent developments of the late nineteenth century regarding kind of action into his taxonomy of the Greek tense-forms according to tense and mood. The application of these categories is systematic and often insightful, rewarding study for the exegete, but what is missing is an explicit theory of action with regard to the tense-forms, and modality with regard to the moods. As a result, one cannot determine whether his description of what is being conveyed by a given verb is based upon morphology (i.e., the tense-form) or lexis (i.e., the action that the verb describes).

26. E. D. W. Burton, *Syntax of the Moods and Tenses in New Testament Greek* (Edinburgh: Clark, 1888; 3rd ed., 1898).

27. W. W. Goodwin, *Syntax of the Moods and Tenses of the Greek Verb* (London: Macmillan, 1860; rev. ed., 1875).

The next important study is that of Margaret Thrall on NT Greek particles.[28] Again in some ways patterned after work in classical studies,[29] Thrall's work has many virtues, not least of which is that it is one of the few studies dedicated to the use of the particles in Hellenistic Greek.[30] As a result, much can be gained from her treatment. However, in the light of recent developments in Greek linguistics, there are also some limitations to her approach. Thrall approaches the particles in the NT in relation to earlier classical usage; that is, she takes a classical comparative philological approach to the Greek of the NT. This, of course, is to be expected for a study written in that era, using an approach to the study of the NT described above. Nevertheless, this is a distinct limitation, since it indicts the Greek of the NT as in some ways limited in its numbers and types of particles and hence expressively inferior to earlier, classical Greek, rather than evaluating the language on its own merits, attempting to describe its system of usage of particles. Furthermore, Thrall's treatment is not comprehensive, being limited to a small number of particles that have exegetical significance (e.g., γάρ and δέ). Thus, theology and exegesis take precedence over linguistics.

A third study to note is John Doudna's on the language of Mark.[31] Working within the classically based philological tradition, Doudna examines a range of grammatical and syntactical phenomena in Markan usage and the papyri, stating and then exemplifying these various elements of usage in terms of conformity and departure from Attic norms. The comparative approach means that he does little to explore the classificatory principles or means by which these categories are determined or defined. However, a major strength of Doudna's treatment is his incorporation of instances of these phenomena from the papyri. One senses that much of the discussion is motivated by the larger issue of adjudicating the dispute over how much Semitic influence there is in the Greek of the NT, in particular Mark's Gospel, with parallels from the papyri used to counter and temper such a notion.[32]

A fourth study is Murray Harris's treatment of the prepositions of the Greek NT.[33] This study has rightly been used by numerous scholars in their treatment

28. M. E. Thrall, *Greek Particles in the New Testament,* NTTS 3 (Leiden: Brill, 1962).

29. See J. D. Denniston, *The Greek Particles* (Oxford: Clarendon, 1934; rev. K. J. Dover, 1954).

30. The most important is J. Blomqvist, *Greek Particles in Hellenistic Prose* (Lund: Gleerup, 1969); see also idem, *Das sogenannte Kai Adversativum: Zur Semantik einer griechischen Partikel,* Acta Universitatis Upsaliensis: Studia Graeca Upsaliensia 13 (Stockholm: Almqvist & Wiksell, 1979).

31. J. Doudna, *The Greek of the Gospel of Mark,* JBLMS 12 (Philadelphia: SBL, 1961).

32. Cf. E. C. Maloney, *Semitic Interference in Marcan Syntax,* SBLDS 51 (Chico, Calif.: Scholars, 1981). Maloney reflects an apparent change of approach in twenty years by beginning with alleged Semitisms.

33. M. J. Harris, "Appendix: Prepositions and Theology in the Greek New Testament," in *New International Dictionary of New Testament Theology,* ed. C. Brown, 3 vols. (Grand Rapids: Zondervan, 1978), 3:1171–215. Cf. M. J. Harris, *Jesus as God: The New Testament Use of Theos in Reference to God* (Grand Rapids: Baker, 1992), 301–13, which has an appendix on the Greek article that reflects classical philology. The classic work on the article in the Greek of the NT is

of prepositions in the Greek NT because Harris often goes into detailed treatment of the usage of a given preposition, especially in terms of its theological significance. This, however, points out the limitations of such a study. One is that theology seems to be the driving force in much of the discussion. There is not a comprehensive study of the prepositions in their own right as a system of function words in the language, as one might expect from a linguistic perspective. This may well be because Harris does not view the language of the NT in these modern linguistic terms. However, it seems to me that this is the only way that one can at least begin to approach the subject, by first seeing how the prepositions divide up the sphere of connecting word functions.[34] A second limitation—and one that emerges clearly in examining a number of the examples that Harris discusses—is that the theological issues raised take one far beyond simply the use of the prepositions into other grammatical issues, text-critical problems, and a range of theological topics (e.g., treatment of 2 Cor. 5:18–21).[35] In some instances, it might even be the case that theology dictates grammar.

The fifth and final treatment I wish to include here is the analysis of Pauline style by Aída Besançon Spencer.[36] Spencer's treatment of Pauline style might well have been better placed in the next section, since it attempts an innovative approach to the notion of style and its application to three short passages of approximately five hundred words each in the Pauline letters (2 Cor. 11:16–12:13; Rom. 8:9–39; Phil. 3:2–4:13). Spencer adopts a set of ten procedural steps for assessing the style of a passage,[37] with her criteria coming mostly from recent work in English stylistics. She then applies these categories to the Pauline passages. Spencer well illustrates the importance of utilizing research from other disciplines as a means of advancing NT research, yet she also shows that any attempt to come fully to terms with such a discipline requires a thorough immersion in that discipline—an effort that many scholars who have mastered one discipline probably are not willing to make. Despite her innovations, the notion of style that she uses is one that

T. F. Middleton, *The Doctrine of the Greek Article*, rev. H. J. Rose (Cambridge: Deighton; London: Rivington, 1833). The complexities of the Greek article have never been fully resolved.

34. See Porter, *Idioms*, 142–79; influenced by J. P. Louw, "Linguistic Theory and the Greek Case System," *Acta classica* 9 (1966): 73–88.

35. Harris, "Prepositions and Theology," 1192–93; cf. S. E. Porter, Καταλλάσσω *in Ancient Greek Literature, with Reference to the Pauline Writings,* ENF 5 (Cordova: Ediciones el Almendro, 1994), 127–43.

36. A. B. Spencer, *Paul's Literary Style: A Stylistic and Historical Comparison of II Corinthians 11:16–12:13, Romans 8:9–39, and Philippians 3:2–4:13,* ETSMS (Jackson, Miss.: Evangelical Theological Society, 1984). Cf. M. Reiser, *Syntax und Stil des Markusevangeliums im Licht der hellenistischen Volksliteratur,* WUNT 2.11 (Tübingen: Mohr, 1984); K. J. Dover, *The Evolution of Greek Prose Style* (Oxford: Clarendon, 1997).

37. The fact that Spencer uses clear criteria for defining style is an advance over many previous stylistic studies of ancient Greek. See, e.g., Turner, *Style,* and J. D. Denniston, *Greek Prose Style* (Oxford: Clarendon, 1952).

comes from English literary studies, and it is not clear that all of the criteria are applicable. For example, she posits that normal English and Greek word order are similar.[38] One might also question whether the three sections that she studies are large enough to draw significant findings from them, when many stylistic studies claim that much larger samples are needed to arrive at significant results.[39]

In many disciplines the specialist studies are on the cutting edge of what is being done in that area of research. In some ways that is the case with the studies noted above, in that they have pushed beyond what is found in the standard reference grammars in analysis of particular phenomena, such as the use of certain particles and prepositions, or the marshaling of further papyrological evidence. However, most studies that I have encountered in NT Greek research are methodologically bound to their predecessors, such that it provides a hindrance to conceptual innovation. Some may resist such innovation, firmly entrenched in the belief that nineteenth-century-based philological study is the most theory-neutral approach to the language. However, in the light of what has been said above, it is hard to accept such an assumption. Studies such as Spencer's, as well as the clear limitations of some other studies cited, point to the need for a thorough rethinking of Greek linguistic study.

Linguistically Based Innovations in the Study of the Greek of the New Testament

One of the most significant developments in the study of the Greek of the NT over the last thirty years is the application of recent work in linguistic theory to the study of the Greek NT. As we saw in the preceding section, most of the standard tools used in study of the Greek NT, current and timely though they once may have been, were written within an earlier conceptual framework of classical philology or nineteenth-century rationalist and/or comparative linguistics. However, with the advent of modern linguistic theory in the early years of the twentieth century, a fundamental shift occurred in how language was viewed. The paradigm for linguistic investigation of the nineteenth century had been comparative and historical. That meant that many studies were concerned to see how similar phenomena in a variety of

38. For a study of Greek word order, see S. E. Porter, "Word Order and Clause Structure in New Testament Greek: An Unexplored Area of Greek Linguistics Using Philippians as a Test Case," *Filología Neotestamentaria* 6 (1993): 177–206; cf. K. J. Dover, *Greek Word Order* (Cambridge: Cambridge University Press, 1960).

39. See M. B. O'Donnell, "Linguistic Fingerprints or Style by Numbers? The Use of Statistics in the Discussion of Authorship of New Testament Documents," in *Linguistics and the New Testament: Critical Junctures,* ed. S. E. Porter and D. A. Carson, JSNTSup 168, SNTG 5 (Sheffield: Sheffield Academic Press, 1999), 206–62, esp. 245–51.

languages were related to each other, often in terms of function, but also in terms of historical development. Often, philological interests accompanied this study, concentrating on making value judgments in terms of what were deemed the best examples of use of these languages. Modern linguistics has been marked by a very different set of criteria. Even though significant variation exists among various schools of linguistic thought, several common features emerge. These include an empirical and explicit approach to the data, a systematic approach to language and a concern for structure in language, an emphasis upon synchronic over diachronic analysis, and descriptive over prescriptive interests.[40] As a result, no particular set of texts is privileged (in fact, modern linguistics has concentrated on speech rather than on written usage), but the range of usage is explored, for the NT in terms of Hellenistic Greek usage.[41] These several common features represent a radical departure from previous study and point out some potential major shifts in study of the Greek of the NT.

As we noted above, there has been a revival of interest in Greek linguistic study in the last thirty years or so. Four areas can be noted where serious innovations have occurred. Not all of them can be classified as grammar or syntax in the way that the terms traditionally have been used, but this shift illustrates the new perspective on Greek grammar that is emerging in some circles. These areas have been developed to varying degrees, with some of the work advanced enough that it can be and should be incorporated into mainstream exegesis. Some of the work is still in its developmental stages and provides a challenge for future research and implementation. One of the challenges of future work in the Greek of the NT is for exegetes not only to be aware of recent innovations in linguistic research, but also to apply such research in their own exegesis. This means more than simply checking the indexes of these works to see if reference is made to a particular verse being examined. It means trying to come to terms with the methodological framework, scrutinizing the text in terms of this framework, and being open to new insights as a result. There is, of course, a risk in such exegesis, since it might result in conclusions that do not answer the standard or usual questions of traditional exegesis, or might even come up with new and challenging perspectives and conclusions. The possibility of new insights into the text is too inviting an opportunity to pass over by simply settling for restatement of tried-and-true conclusions. The fact that evangelical scholars have been at the forefront of much of this recent research adds to the challenge to test the findings of their work.

40. See S. E. Porter, "Studying Ancient Languages from a Modern Linguistic Perspective," *Filología Neotestamentaria* 2 (1989): 147–72, esp. 151–54.
41. Significant studies that have attempted this kind of program include C. Brixhe, ed., *La Koiné grecque antique*, 3 vols. (Nancy: Presses Universitaires de Nancy, 1993–98).

Verbal Aspect Theory

Development of verbal aspect theory in English scholarship in the 1980s was a natural development from previous research into verbal semantics. In the nineteenth century, Greek verbal structure was seen to be time-based, but in the late nineteenth and early twentieth centuries, due in large part to the work of Brugmann and Moulton, came the recognition that verbs were used in relation to how actions occurred, not strictly when. This came to be known as *Aktionsart* theory. *Aktionsart* theory was restricted by the fact that it attempted to characterize actions as they objectively took place (e.g., instantaneously, incrementally, etc.), but there simply were not enough verb forms in any language, including Greek, to describe the multifarious ways in which action occurs. Therefore, it was a natural step to develop aspect theory, which states that verbal tense-forms are selected by language users not on the basis of the action in itself but on the basis of how they wish to conceive of and conceptualize an action.[42]

In the 1970s, the first important English-language work on verbal aspect was written. This included both a monograph devoted to the topic by the linguist Bernard Comrie (who also a short time later wrote a monograph on tense),[43] and work by a number of Greek scholars. K. L. McKay was the leader in this area, through a number of important journal articles and a classical Greek grammar that described how interpretation was affected by choice of aspect.[44] The first major monograph in English on NT Greek verbal aspect theory was my monograph,[45] and this soon was followed by a major monograph by Buist Fanning.[46] Since that time, McKay has published a syntax of the verb in NT Greek that focuses on aspect theory, Mari Olsen has published a work on the semantics and pragmatics of the Greek verb, and Rodney Decker has published a detailed study of deixis that examines the

42. Some of the history of this discussion is found in Porter, *Studies in the Greek New Testament,* 14–17.

43. B. Comrie, *Aspect: An Introduction to the Study of Verbal Aspect and Related Problems,* CTL (Cambridge: Cambridge University Press, 1976); idem, *Tense,* CTL (Cambridge: Cambridge University Press, 1985). See also J. Holt, *Études d'aspect,* Acta Jutlandica Aarskrift, Aarhus Universitet 15.2 (Aarhus: Universitetsforlaget, 1943).

44. From among his numerous publications, note K. L. McKay, "Syntax in Exegesis," *TynBul* 23 (1972): 39–57; *Greek Grammar for Students: A Concise Grammar of Classical Attic with Special Reference to Aspect in the Verb* (Canberra: Australian National University, 1974), 136–48, 214–24; "Aspect in Imperatival Constructions in New Testament Greek," *NovT* 27 (1985): 201–26; "Aspectual Usage in Timeless Contexts in Ancient Greek," in *In the Footsteps of Raphael Kühner,* ed. A. Rijksbaron et al. (Amsterdam: Gieben, 1988), 193–208; "Time and Aspect in New Testament Greek," *NovT* 34 (1992): 209–28.

45. S. E. Porter, *Verbal Aspect in the Greek of the New Testament, with Reference to Tense and Mood,* SBG 1 (New York: Lang, 1989; 2nd ed., 1993).

46. B. M. Fanning, *Verbal Aspect in New Testament Greek,* OTM (Oxford: Clarendon, 1990).

basis of my theory as it applies to the exegesis of Mark.[47] Other supporting studies have appeared as well, too numerous to mention here.

There are a number of points of agreement among these works and a number of points of dispute.[48] Rather than treat each study independently, I will summarize these issues and then offer a description of the potential use of aspect theory in exegesis. The major points of agreement among these scholars is that aspect theory is important—indeed, vital—for understanding Greek verb usage. Although the verb forms are called "tenses," this has perhaps unduly influenced interpreters (such as Winer, but many since) into thinking that time is the most important, if not the only, semantic category associated with the use of these forms. Advocates of aspect theory (in fact, aspect theory is where the vast majority of work in Greek verbal study has occurred, in both NT and other Greek research)[49] are agreed that the perspectival view of tense-form usage is at the heart of how verbs were used by ancient Greeks. A further point of agreement is that context is important for understanding what the semantic contribution of the use of a given verb form is. The context helps to establish the parameters of the contribution of the verb form in terms of the time of the action and how it is seen in relation to other actions depicted. These two concepts have still to be fully integrated into NT exegesis.[50]

The points of disagreement among these works should be noted as well. Whereas advocates of aspect theory are agreed that aspect is the major semantic category for Greek verb usage, they are divided on whether the tense-forms

47. K. L. McKay, *A New Syntax of the Verb in New Testament Greek: An Aspectual Approach*, SBG 5 (New York: Lang, 1994); M. J. B. Olsen, *A Semantic and Pragmatic Model of Lexical and Grammatical Aspect*, Outstanding Dissertations in Linguistics (New York: Garland, 1997); R. J. Decker, *Temporal Deixis of the Greek Verb in the Gospel of Mark with Reference to Verbal Aspect*, SBG 10 (New York: Lang, 2001). An application to the Greek of the LXX has been made by T. V. Evans, *Verbal Syntax in the Greek Pentateuch: Natural Greek Usage and Hebrew Interference* (Oxford: Oxford University Press, 2001).

48. A summary of some of the points of agreement and disagreement is found in S. E. Porter and D. A. Carson, eds., *Biblical Greek Language and Linguistics: Open Questions in Current Research*, JSNTSup 80, SNTG 1 (Sheffield: JSOT Press, 1993), 18–82, in a section on verbal aspect where Porter and Fanning discuss their perspectives, which are evaluated by Daryl Schmidt and Moisés Silva.

49. See M. S. Ruipérez, *Estructura del Sistema de Aspectos y Tiempos del Verbo Griego Antiguo: Análysis Funcional Sincrónico*, Theses et Studia Philologica Salmanticensia 7 (Salamanca: Colegio Trilingue de la Universidad, 1954); P. Friedrich, "On Aspect Theory and Homeric Aspect," *International Journal of American Linguistics*, Memoir 28, 40 (1974): S1–S44; J. Mateos, *El Aspecto Verbal en el Nuevo Testamento*, Estudios de Nuevo Testamento 1 (Madrid: Ediciones Cristiandad, 1977); H. Hettrich, *Kontext und Aspekt in der altgriechischen Prosa Herodots* (Göttingen: Vandenhoeck & Ruprecht, 1976); M. Delaunois, *Essai de syntaxe grecque classique: Réflexions et recherches* (Brussels: Facultés universitaires Saint-Louis; Leuven: Peeters, 1988); C. M. J. Sicking and P. Stork, *Two Studies in the Semantics of the Verb in Classical Greek* (Leiden: Brill, 1996), esp. 1–118.

50. A number of commentaries make reference to some of the works cited, but few have fully integrated the framework endorsed.

retain any sense of temporal reference. Since at least the time of Moulton, there has been fairly consistent agreement among grammarians (though not necessarily all exegetes realize this) that the tense-forms in Greek in the nonindicative moods (including the participle and infinitive) make no assertion about reality and hence are not time-bound,[51] but there is dispute among aspect scholars on whether verbs are time-based in the indicative mood. My systemic-linguistic perspective has emphasized the semantic structure of Greek verbal usage, and I have suggested that work in corpus linguistics and discourse analysis would provide the larger context for seeing how Greek tense-forms are used. I argue that context determines the temporal values of a discourse, not the use of the individual tense-forms. My work recently has been expanded and supported by Decker's analysis of temporal deixis, in which he notes the various types of indicators that determine temporal values for a given stretch of language. McKay seems to be in sympathy with such a perspective, but without wishing to abandon completely the deeply enshrined temporal perspective, while Fanning clearly wishes to maintain the temporal framework in the indicative. A second point of dispute is the meaning of the various aspects. To some extent this is merely a problem of formulation in the metalanguage (the language used to describe the meanings of the tense-forms) of what all of the scholars believe to be the case. However, at a couple of points major differences appear. One is in the estimation of the perfect tense-form. Following McKay,[52] I wish to see this as a distinct verbal aspect grammaticalizing stative aspect—that is, the state of the action depicted. Fanning rejects this estimation and wishes to argue for two aspects in Greek—represented by the aorist and present stems—with the perfect tense-form being a merging of the meaning of the two, resulting in the traditional estimation of the perfect as indicating abiding results of an action. Aspect scholars also disagree over definition of the meaning of the aorist and present tense-forms, as well as the troublesome future form—whether it is more of a tense-form or a mood-form. All of these issues are still under debate in some circles.

It would be easy for an exegete to back away from incorporating the insights from recent developments in aspectual theory because there is still disagreement among scholars on specific definitions of important concepts. However, such a response would mean that one would be unlikely ever to benefit from aspect theory, since with any theory disagreements are bound to occur. To begin to appreciate the significance of aspect theory requires the exegete to take a fundamentally different approach to the structure of the Greek verb system.

51. Among NT grammarians, see Moulton, *Prolegomena,* 164; Robertson, *Grammar,* passim.

52. See K. L. McKay, "The Use of the Ancient Greek Perfect Down to the End of the Second Century A.D.," *BICS* 12 (1965): 1–21; "On the Perfect and Other Aspects in the Greek Non-Literary Papyri," *BICS* 27 (1980): 23–49; "On the Perfect and Other Aspects in New Testament Greek," *NovT* 2 (1981): 289–329.

Rather than begin with questions of time (when did this action occur, and can the tense-forms show this?), or even theological questions (does the use of this tense-form equate with a particular interpretation of a passage?), the exegete must begin by appreciating the perspectival nature of Greek usage. An author who uses an aorist tense-form is choosing to depict the action in a particular way. Although scholars differ somewhat in how they describe this, the aorist generally is said to describe an action as complete or whole, viewing it in its integrity and from the outside. Many describe this as perfective aspect, and note that this kind of depiction often is found in narrative literary types, or where a relatively undifferentiated background to events or descriptions is being created. The present tense-form is used to describe an action as in progress, evolving, or developing, viewing the action from its internal constituency. Many describe this as imperfective aspect and note that this kind of depiction often is used to highlight an action within a narrative or to describe or exposit a set of actions or events. The interplay of these two major tense-forms is what is used to shape and structure a discourse (see below on discourse analysis). Temporal issues, such as when such actions occurred, are determined by other factors, such as the discourse itself, or other indicators that place the events in relation to each other and external reality (called deictic indicators). Exegetes need to be sensitive to these uses of the tense-forms, and especially the larger patterns of usage within a given discourse, rather than utilizing the tense-forms simply as ciphers for temporal values. This much is agreed on by virtually all scholars doing recent research into the Greek verbal system.

Register Studies

The traditional approach to language variation has been in terms of dialects, or permanent kinds of varieties on the basis of features such as geography, time, and social factors. The classical Greek period is often called the dialect period because it was dominated by various regional dialects, with the Attic/Ionic being the most important due to a variety of large-scale geographical and social patterns. The Greek of the Hellenistic period does not have the same kinds of dialect differences as the earlier period did. For the most part, the Greek of the Hellenistic period represents a single dialect form, although admittedly there are some regional peculiarities in some instances.[53] However, there are still a number of transient differences in the type of language used by various speakers and writers of Hellenistic Greek. These differences reflect changes according to a variety of factors, including personal choices, literary type, subject matter, and the like. These differing levels of usage are referred to as register.[54]

53. See L. R. Palmer, *The Greek Language* (London: Duckworth, 1980), 176.
54. See S. E. Porter, "Dialect and Register in the Greek of the New Testament: Theory," in *Rethinking Contexts, Rereading Texts: Contributions from the Social Sciences to Biblical Interpreta-*

The linguist Michael Halliday has been instrumental in defining register studies.[55] He argues that a given context of situation ("context of situation" is a technical term for the immediate environment in which a given discourse occurs, to be distinguished from "co-text," or the immediately surrounding words, and the larger and pervasive context of culture) sets the parameters for the kind of language that one will use. In other words, register helps to define the factors in the situation that evoke the linguistic expression. The context of situation consists of three major conceptual categories: field, tenor, and mode. The field of the discourse is realized by the ideational semantic component. The ideational component is concerned with the subject matter and how this subject matter is expressed in concrete grammatical constructions. In other words, the field of discourse is concerned with many of the major areas of traditional grammatical study, such as lexis and syntax. The notion of field is more complex than simply lexis and syntax as usually understood, however, since it relies upon notions such as semantic domain theory of lexis[56] and the transitivity network. Transitivity is how the various syntactical constructions convey who is doing what to whom and in what way, and it takes into account concepts such as aspect, voice, agency, and the like. All of these are integrated into a complex expression of how the various participants and actions are related grammatically. The tenor of the discourse is realized by the interpersonal semantic component. The interpersonal component is concerned with the participant structure of the discourse. Here the various participants (both extra- and intralinguistic), how they are related (by status, role, and permanence), and how they are invoked (full reference, reduced reference in terms of a pronoun or the like, and implied reference through a verb form) are analyzed. Mode of discourse is realized by the textual semantic component. The textual component is concerned with the physical expression of the discourse. This includes factors such as the literary type, its permanence (whether an ephemeral letter or a treatise meant for posterity), and even the medium of conveyance. It also includes

---

tion, ed. M. D. Carroll R., JSOTSup 299 (Sheffield: Sheffield Academic Press, 2000), 190–208. Register is related to the issue of diglossia, or varieties of the same language. See the classic essay by C. A. Ferguson, "Diglossia," *Word* 15 (1959): 325–40; and several more recent studies: J. Niehoff-Panagiotidis, *Koine und Diglossie,* Mediterranean Language and Culture Monograph 10 (Wiesbaden: Harrassowitz, 1994); J. W. Watt, *Code-Switching in Luke and Acts,* Berkeley Insights in Linguistics and Semiotics 31 (New York: Lang, 1997); and S. E. Porter, ed., *Diglossia and Other Topics in New Testament Linguistics,* JSNTSup 193, SNTG 6 (Sheffield: Sheffield Academic Press, 2000), 17–89.

55. There is no systematic or comprehensive discussion of register in Halliday, but perhaps the best is M. A. K. Halliday and R. Hasan, *Language, Context, and Text: Aspects of Language in a Social-Semiotic Perspective* (Geelong, Victoria: Deakin University Press, 1985). See also M. Gregory and S. Carroll, *Language and Situation: Language Varieties and Their Social Contexts* (London: Routledge & Kegan Paul, 1978), esp. ch. 6.

56. Cf. the lexicon of Louw and Nida, *Greek-English Lexicon of the New Testament Based on Semantic Domains.*

the linguistic means by which the discourse is held together, or is made to cohere. Cohesion is a crucial concept in what it means for a discourse to be a discourse, and various linguistic means are used to create cohesion. These include noun referents both external and internal to the discourse, their pronouns, and various patterns of connection between them (e.g., ellipsis, when direct reference is excluded).

A number of important register studies have attempted to incorporate this perspective into NT research.[57] Early on, I suggested the importance of register for the study of verbal aspect,[58] and then, after explicating the concept for NT Greek study (see above), I applied the notion in three studies. The first two were concerned with the Gospel of Mark. In the first,[59] after surveying recent work on Mark's Gospel, I offer an overview of that Gospel in terms of register analysis. I describe the mode of discourse in terms of its being a written text meant to be read, in the form of a narrative, with connective descriptive subunits involving both actions and dialogue, following an apparently roughly chronological order. A number of repeated features are used to cohere the discourse, such as the use of the connective "then," the nonperiodic syntax, and the third-person verb. The tenor of discourse revolves around a predominant use of the third person except for Jesus, who uses first, second, and third person. The role relationships are complex, with groupings revolving around Jesus and his associates, and Jesus and his adversaries. The field of discourse is established at the outset as "the gospel of Jesus Christ [Son of God]" (Mark 1:1), an idea that is developed at two key points in the discourse (1:15; 15:39). The transitivity network shows how the tense-forms are used to convey the narrative, using an interplay of the perfective (aorist) and imperfective (present and imperfect) aspects. The broad results of this study encouraged me to develop in a subsequent work a new criterion for historical-Jesus research based upon register analysis.[60] I briefly explored this in an analysis of Mark 13 in which I show that register analysis has potential for establishing evidence by which one can differentiate between different discourse types even within a single book. The result is that I argue that Mark 13 is an integral discourse that is to be distinguished from the discourse type of the surrounding narrative, and hence possibly material attributable to the historical Jesus. In the third study, I invoke register analysis to analyze differences in some of Paul's let-

---

57. Besides those listed below, see J. T. Reed, *A Discourse Analysis of Philippians: Method and Rhetoric in the Debate over Literary Integrity*, JSNTSup 136 (Sheffield: Sheffield Academic Press, 1997), esp. 53–57; idem, "Language of Change and the Changing of Language: A Sociolinguistic Approach to Pauline Discourse," in Porter, *Diglossia*, 121–53; and S. E. Porter and M. B. O'Donnell, "Semantics and Patterns of Argumentation in the Book of Romans: Definitions, Proposals, Data and Experiments," in Porter, *Diglossia*, 176–89, esp. 176–89.

58. Porter, *Verbal Aspect*, 151–54.

59. S. E. Porter, "Register in the Greek of the New Testament: Application with Reference to Mark's Gospel," in Carroll R., *Rethinking Contexts*, 209–29.

60. Porter, *Criteria for Authenticity*, 210–37.

ters.[61] Utilizing register criteria for differentiating between spoken and written language first developed by the linguist Douglas Biber,[62] I have adapted these criteria to the context of ancient Greek usage and created a set of standards by which the different registers of the Pauline Epistles can be analyzed. Placed within the context of discussion of diglossia, I differentiate linguistic elements in terms of six dimensions of register analysis: (1) personal interaction versus informational production, (2) narrative or nonnarrative, (3) explicit versus nonexplicit reference, (4) overt expressions of persuasion, (5) abstract versus nonabstract information, and (6) elaboration. The complex calculus developed allows for nuanced differentiation of features among a number of the Pauline Epistles and helps the interpreter to move beyond generalizations to be able to substantiate perceived differences in the Pauline Epistles.

The most important single study of register in NT studies to date is probably that by Gustavo Martín-Asensio on the Book of Acts.[63] Martín-Asensio utilizes a Hallidayan model of transitivity to explore patterns of action in a number of major episodes in the Book of Acts: Acts 27 and Paul's shipwreck, Acts 6–7 and the Stephen episode, Acts 13:16b–25 and Luke's survey of Israel's history, Acts 21–22 and Paul's arrest and defense, and Acts 2 and the Pentecost episode. Martín-Asensio draws heavily also on the work of Hopper and Thompson,[64] who in their detailed exposition of transitivity help to define criteria for establishing foregrounding of elements in a discourse. Martín-Asensio's thesis is that the Lukan perspective can most fully be appreciated when one sees how in Luke's choice of particular linguistic structures he capacitates or incapacitates, foregrounds or backgrounds, various actions or comments by the participants. For example, in the shipwreck episode in Acts 27, Martín-Asensio shows that Paul is not a motivator of action but an interpreter of the divine perspective for others. Martín-Asensio does this by showing how various linguistic features are motivated in the discourse.

Martín-Asensio's study is a model for the integration of well-grounded linguistics and exegesis. He does not hesitate to approach well-studied passages and to conclude where he thinks that the evidence leads. His approach also serves as a model for others who wish to present well-established and well-grounded arguments for their exegetical conclusions. His model begins by having a clear linguistic theory in mind. In a very real sense, the study of transitivity is part

61. S. E. Porter, "The Functional Distribution of Koine Greek in First-Century Palestine," in Porter, *Diglossia,* 53–79.

62. D. Biber, *Variation across Speech and Writing* (Cambridge: Cambridge University Press, 1988); cf. idem, *Dimensions of Register Variation: A Cross-Linguistic Comparison* (Cambridge: Cambridge University Press, 1995).

63. G. Martín-Asensio, *Transitivity-Based Foregrounding in the Acts of the Apostles: A Functional-Grammatical Approach to the Lukan Perspective,* JSNTSup 202, SNTG 8 (Sheffield: Sheffield Academic Press, 2000).

64. P. J. Hopper and S. A. Thompson, "Transitivity in Grammar and Discourse," *Language* 56 (1980): 251–99.

of a revised and expanded, and linguistically informed, notion of syntax. As Martín-Asensio points out at a number of places in his study, many commentators, including those who have written most recently, rely heavily upon the standard traditional grammars (discussed above), which severely limits the nature and depth of their grammatical insights. Martín-Asensio not only develops a model that pushes forward recent linguistic thought in new ways for studying the Greek of the NT, but also exegetes these passages in the light of this model. His close attention to the detail of the text, including the very wording used to convey the concepts (e.g., choice of aspect, voice, person, etc.), cannot be ignored. He arrives at plausible and defensible theological conclusions, but only after he has engaged in detailed linguistic analysis that places individual linguistic constructions in their proper semantic framework.

Discourse Analysis

Discourse analysis, or text-linguistics, is perhaps one of the few modern linguistic methods that a number of NT exegetes are familiar with. This is probably because various text-linguistically based methods have been utilized in a number of circles for some time. In one sense, discourse analysis is too large a concept to include in a discussion of grammar and syntax, since by definition it includes all that constitutes analysis of discourse. In another sense, it is entirely appropriate to discuss here because it includes within a more appropriate linguistic context—that of the discourse—assessment of grammar and syntax. The major tenet of discourse analysis is that whether one studies discourse from the top down or the bottom up, the discourse, rather than smaller units such as the sentence or the word (the traditional domains of language study), provides the appropriate context for investigation. In the larger field of linguistics there are a number of approaches to discourse analysis, many of them based upon conversational analysis.[65] In NT studies, at least four major schools of discourse analysis are currently being employed. Summarizing work that I have done previously,[66] I will present each one briefly and then refer to some of the most important recent studies in NT research.

The four schools of thought in NT studies are, first, the North American model used by the Summer Institute of Linguistics. Influenced by a number of important North American linguists, and more recently incorporating catego-

---

65. See D. Schiffrin, *Approaches to Discourse* (Oxford: Blackwell, 1994). Of the several introductions to discourse analysis, one of the best is G. Brown and G. Yule, *Discourse Analysis*, CTL (Cambridge: Cambridge University Press, 1983). An excellent recent work is M. Hoey, *Textual Interaction: An Introduction to Written Discourse Analysis* (London: Routledge, 2001).

66. S. E. Porter, "Discourse Analysis and New Testament Studies: An Introductory Survey," in *Discourse Analysis and Other Topics in Biblical Greek*, ed. S. E. Porter and D. A. Carson, JSNTSup 113, SNTG 2 (Sheffield: Sheffield Academic Press, 1995), 14–35. I will note below only a few key and recent studies by members of these four schools of thought.

ries from psycholinguistics,[67] this model has often had questions of translation in mind. However, the work has been wide-ranging in scope.[68] The second is that of the English and Australian model that utilizes the work of Halliday (see above) and his followers in the systemic-functional school of linguistic thought. This discourse model has taken a number of different forms but has especially emphasized the social semiotic function of language.[69] The third model is that of continental European discourse analysis, with its two major and related branches being the Scandinavian school and the German school. The emphasis here has been upon integrating communications theory, semantics and pragmatics, and rhetorical study into a single discourse model.[70] The fourth and final method is that of the South African school. The earliest of the four models, and pioneered by Johannes Louw, this approach is based upon what is called the colon, or a unit that is formed around a nominative and predicate structure, and the meaningful relations that exist between them.[71]

One of the most important recent studies in this area is the treatment of the question of the literary integrity of Philippians by Jeffrey Reed.[72] Reed's volume is essentially divided into two parts. The first is a thorough exposition of a Halliday-inspired form of discourse analysis, drawing heavily upon his

67. For example, relevance theory. See D. Sperber and D. Wilson, *Relevance Theory: Communication and Cognition,* 2nd ed. (Oxford: Blackwell, 1995).

68. See the following essays in S. E. Porter and J. T. Reed, eds., *Discourse Analysis and the New Testament: Approaches and Results,* JSNTSup 170, SNTG 4 (Sheffield: Sheffield Academic Press, 1999): R. E. Longacre, "A Top-Down, Template-Driven Narrative Analysis, Illustrated by Application to Mark's Gospel," 140–68; idem, "Mark 5:1–43: Generating the Complexity of a Narrative from Its Most Basic Elements," 169–96; R. J. Erickson, "The Damned and the Justified in Romans 5:12–21: An Analysis of Semantic Structure," 282–307; S. H. Levinsohn, "Some Constraints on Discourse Development in the Pastoral Epistles," 316–33; J. Callow, "Where Does 1 John 1 End?" 392–406.

69. See the work of Reed below; see also S. E. Porter, "Is Critical Discourse Analysis Critical? An Evaluation Using Philemon as a Test Case," in Porter and Reed, *Discourse Analysis,* 47–70; T. Klutz, "Naked and Wounded: Foregrounding, Relevance and Situation in Acts 19:13–20," in Porter and Reed, *Discourse Analysis,* 258–79; E. Adams, "Ideology and Point of View in Galatians 1–2: A Critical Linguistic Analysis," in Porter, *Diglossia,* 205–54.

70. See, for example, J. G. Cook, *The Structure and Persuasive Power of Mark: A Linguistic Approach,* SemeiaSt (Atlanta: Scholars Press, 1995); W. Schenk, "The Testamental Disciple-Instruction of the Markan Jesus (Mark 13): Its Levels of Communication and Its Rhetorical Structures," in Porter and Reed, *Discourse Analysis,* 197–222; B. Olsson, "First John: Discourse Analyses and Interpretations," in Porter and Reed, *Discourse Analysis,* 369–91.

71. See, for example, in Porter and Reed, *Discourse Analysis:* J. P. Louw, "A Discourse Reading of Ephesians 1:3–14," 308–15; E. R. Wendland, "'Let No One Disregard You!' (Titus 2.15): Church Discipline and the Construction of Discourse in a Personal, 'Pastoral' Epistle," 334–51; A. H. Snyman, "Hebrews 6:4–6: From a Semiotic Discourse Perspective," 354–68.

72. Reed, *Discourse Analysis of Philippians.* Other recent works by Reed worth noting include "Discourse Analysis," in Porter, *Handbook to Exegesis,* 189–217; "The Cohesiveness of Discourse: Towards a Model of Linguistic Criteria for Analyzing New Testament Discourse," in Porter and Reed, *Discourse Analysis,* 47–70; Reed with R. A. Reese, "Verbal Aspect, Discourse Prominence, and the Letter of Jude," *Filología Neotestamentaria* 9 (1996): 181–99.

categories of register, but with further use of work on cohesion by Halliday and Hasan.[73] Then, in the second part of the book, Reed applies his discourse model to the vexing issue of literary integrity. Essentially, Reed subjects the various arguments regarding literary integrity or fragmentation to scrutiny on the basis of his discourse model, and then he performs his own thorough analysis of the Book of Philippians itself. The result is that he shows that many of the arguments often used in such studies are not well conceived linguistically (they tend to be posited in isolation, without regard for the larger context or extrabiblical usage), and could benefit from reformulation in terms of explicit linguistic models. Although Reed's study cannot prove the integrity of Philippians, his method seems to show that those arguing for integrity have the better arguments on their side.

Other recent studies using various discourse analytic or text-linguistic approaches include two collections of essays. The first is a collection of papers by Lars Hartman gathering a number of previously published and some unpublished papers that focus on text-centered questions.[74] The essays are not theoretically oriented so much as examples of how putting text-centered questions to the fore influences exegesis, and they contain important studies of both narrative texts and argumentative texts. Hartman reflects the continental European tradition and usefully draws into discussion material that might otherwise be inaccessible to some English-speaking scholars. The result is some often detailed studies of a number of passages throughout the NT. A second collection represents a mix of approaches (including at least one by each of the four schools of thought described above), arranged by topic and books of the NT.[75] This collection is meant to give some indication of the kinds and range of studies that can be included within a volume on discourse analysis. As a result, there are studies of methodological issues such as cohesiveness and context, as well as several that address topics related to the traditional domain of grammar and syntax, such as the historic present in Matthew, the semantic structure of Rom. 5:12–21, a reading of Eph. 1:3–14, and the question of where 1 John 1 ends. What distinguishes the essays throughout is their "exegetical payoff"—that is, the application of theory to specific texts and their interpretation.

Discourse analysis has been used in NT studies for a number of years, although it has not become fully integrated into the mainstream. There are several reasons for this. Some scholars probably are wary of the diversity of

73. M. A. K. Halliday and R. Hasan, *Cohesion in English* (London: Longman, 1976).

74. L. Hartman, *Text-Centered New Testament Studies: Text-theoretical Essays on Early Jewish and Early Christian Literature,* ed. D. Hellholm, WUNT 102 (Tübingen: Mohr Siebeck, 1997). There are also several text-linguistic studies in the Festschrift to Hartman: T. Fornberg and D. Hellholm, eds., *Texts and Contexts: Biblical Texts in Their Textual and Situational Contexts* (Oslo: Scandinavian University Press, 1995), esp. the essays by Hellholm, F. Siegert, and to some extent H. Boers and B. Johanson.

75. Porter and Reed, *Discourse Analysis.*

methods available, and without expert knowledge are hesitant to commit themselves to a model that might not have currency tomorrow. There is also the problem of technical vocabulary. Many schools of discourse analysis rely upon technical language for their concepts (such as register, co-text, cohesion, etc.). This, of course, is to be expected with any technical discipline, but it can be discouraging for those who think that they will need to learn an entire new discipline. However, the benefits of discourse analysis make it an attractive interpretative model in NT studies. An important shibboleth in NT studies is that it is essential to interpret in context. Discourse analysis begins from the assumption that communication occurs in discourses, not in isolated or random sentences. This common starting point means that in some ways NT scholars who have been concerned for informed contextual interpretation have already been practicing a form of discourse analysis even if not fully cognizant of larger discourse questions. Discourse analysis itself now has the potential to provide the necessary tools and vocabulary to make more informed treatment of discourse possible. A possible shortcoming of discourse analysis is that it generates too much data and that the amounts of data can be overwhelming and intimidating. To be sure, the amount of data will always exceed what can be treated in a single analysis. However, the kinds of principled and structured analyses suggested above provide a means of differentiating useful from extraneous data, as well as how the useful data can count for evidence. A discourse analyst may wish to plot patterns of connection in a discourse, and so will be concerned with obvious features such as conjunctions, but may also wish to analyze participant structure, the use of full and reduced forms, and so on. On the basis of such findings, an exegete may be able to establish how various ideas are introduced and integrated into a given discourse. In some linguistic circles it has been suggested that in the future linguistics will consist of morphology (i.e., the forms of the language) and discourse. In other words, all interpretation of categories beyond simple formal structures will be done in terms of discourse considerations. This framework has highly suggestive possibilities for NT exegesis, which attempts to be fully integrative in its approach.

Other Studies

Before concluding, I wish to mention several other studies of Greek that have appeared within the last thirty or so years. Though they perhaps have not generated their own critical linguistic legacy (yet), they are of interest and have potential for future work.

No linguist has had a greater impact in recent times than Noam Chomsky.[76] His theories have had pervasive influence especially in psycholinguistic

---

76. This began with his *Syntactic Structures* (The Hague: Mouton, 1957) and was continued with *Aspects of the Theory of Syntax* (Cambridge, Mass.: MIT Press, 1965) and *Topics in the*

circles. The effects of his work in NT studies were seen early on but have not had the kind of abiding significance that they have had in other areas of linguistic endeavor. One of the first works that utilized—or rather, invoked—a Chomskyan framework was a monograph by Johannes Louw, originally written in Afrikaans in 1973, but rewritten in English and published in 1982.[77] In this book he presented Chomskyan tree-diagrams to explain Greek syntax as part of his explanation of the semantics of Greek.[78] A more rigorous use of Chomsky has been made by Daryl Schmidt and, later, by Micheal Palmer.[79] Schmidt's treatment of embedded nominal structures was directly dependent upon the early stages of Chomsky's work, especially his extended standard theory. Here he attempts to account for the phrase structures and transformations that embed clauses in nominal constructions, such as when the Greek complementizer *hoti* is or is not used. Palmer not only utilizes the Chomskyan framework for analyzing constituent structures, especially noun phrases in the Lukan material, and introduces some important recent innovations in terms of X-bar theory,[80] but also shows an important concern for proper procedure in linguistic study.[81]

A full-scale critique of Chomskyan linguistics is impossible here. Suffice it to say that I find the theoretical program problematic, especially in terms of dealing with an ancient language. My orientation is less psycholinguistic than it is functional, concerned with how language is actually used for communicative purposes, rather than dealing with a speculative competence. Nevertheless, Palmer's discussion of procedure reflects important concerns that all exegetes could benefit from. It is not enough simply to think or say that one is going to "use linguistics" in NT exegesis unless one is willing to devote serious attention to developing and understanding a linguistic methodology. This requires learning the categories and language of the discipline and implementing the

---

Theory of Generative Grammar (The Hague: Mouton, 1966). Since then, he has continued in his own work, as well as creating a veritable explosion in linguistic publishing. For an overview of developments in North American linguistics, with Chomsky in view, see P. H. Matthews, *Grammatical Theory in the United States from Blooomfield to Chomsky,* CSL 67 (Cambridge: Cambridge University Press, 1993). See also H. Boers, *The Justification of the Gentiles: Paul's Letters to the Galatians and Romans* (Peabody, Mass.: Hendrickson, 1994). Boers attempts to develop a discourse model, but one based upon Chomskyan notions.

77. J. P. Louw, *Semantics of New Testament Greek* (Philadelphia: Fortress; Chico, Calif.: Scholars Press, 1982).

78. The relation of the semantic component to the syntax has been a highly contentious issue in Chomskyan linguistics, and is beyond the scope for discussion here.

79. D. D. Schmidt, *Hellenistic Greek Grammar and Noam Chomsky,* SBLDS 62 (Chico, Calif.: Scholars Press, 1981); M. W. Palmer, *Levels of Constituent Structure in New Testament Greek,* SBG 4 (New York: Lang, 1995).

80. See R. Jackendoff, *X̄ Syntax: A Study of Phrase Structure* (Cambridge, Mass.: MIT Press, 1977).

81. These questions were first raised in M. W. Palmer, "How Do We Know a Phrase Is a Phrase? A Plea for Procedural Clarity in the Application of Linguistics to Biblical Greek," in Porter and Carson, *Biblical Greek Language and Linguistics,* 152–86.

proper procedures of analysis. Too many studies already are in print in which an exegete simply invokes a recent linguistic study when convenient (e.g., on Greek verbal structure) without asking the larger question of what the implications are of verbal aspectual theory for an entire program of interpretation.

In some ways related to the Chomskyan linguistic framework is case theory. Simon Wong has championed a fairly traditional yet elaborate form of this theory,[82] developed in particular by the linguists Charles Fillmore, Wallace Chafe, and Robert Longacre.[83] Rather than examining morphologically based case forms (the traditional domain of Greek language study), he posits fourteen semantic cases—that is, universal semantic roles or relations that exist in the deep structure. He goes on to combine these semantic cases into what he calls twenty-three verbal frames to account for all of the relations of agents to their actions. Thus, there are agents who do things, patients who receive things, sensers who feel things, and the like. Wong has applied this case analysis to the Pauline corpus. Paul Danove recently has introduced to NT studies a form of case theory called construction grammar.[84] This linguistic model, directly dependent upon the later work of Charles Fillmore, is a descriptive but nontransformational grammar that depends upon the concept of semantic frames and valency—that is, the number and type of complements that each predicator (usually a verb) takes. Danove has diligently analyzed a number of lexical items, especially verbs of experience, in terms of their valency structure. There is much to be commended in case theory, since it explores the notion of causality apart from a rigid dependence upon traditional syntax. However, many interpreters have found the notion of semantic cases too abstract, especially for analysis of an ancient language. Both Wong and Danove seem to have a number of assumptions about how one is able to determine the semantics of case on the basis of various contextual features that are not, in fact, part of the explicit theory. Case theory seems to work best, especially for an epigraphic language, when one begins with grammaticalized case structure and a more rigorous notion of voice before moving to semantic cases.[85]

82. S. Wong, "What Case Is This Case? An Application of Semantic Case in Biblical Exegesis," *Jian Dao* 1 (1994): 49–73; *A Classification of Semantic Case-Relations in the Pauline Epistles*, SBG 9 (New York: Lang, 1997).

83. C. J. Fillmore, "The Case for Case," in *Universals in Linguistic Theory*, ed. E. Bach and R. T. Harms (London: Holt, Rinehart & Winston, 1968), 1–88; W. Chafe, *Meaning and the Structure of Language* (Chicago: University of Chicago Press, 1970); R. E. Longacre, *The Grammar of Discourse* (New York: Plenum, 1983).

84. P. Danove, *The End of Mark's Story: A Methodological Study*, BIS 3 (Leiden: Brill, 1993), esp. 30–48; "The Theory of Construction Grammar and Its Application to New Testament Greek," in Porter and Carson, *Biblical Greek Language and Linguistics*, 119–51; "Verbs of Experience: Toward a Lexicon Detailing the Argument Structures Assigned by Verbs," in Porter and Carson, *Linguistics and the New Testament*, 144–205.

85. For one response, see S. E. Porter, "The Case for Case Revisited," *Jian Dao* 6 (1996): 13–28.

As linguistics continues to develop, other approaches certainly will rightly be brought to bear on NT Greek study.[86]

Conclusion

This essay has sought to chronicle some of the major developments in Greek grammatical study over especially the last thirty years, but also in terms of the last two centuries of investigation. In order to do so, it has been necessary to expand the definition of syntax and grammar to encompass the scope of many of the recent developments. When such a study is under-taken, it becomes clear that Greek grammatical study is not a theory-neutral discipline, but one that has been developing over the course of time and is reflective of the linguistic framework in which the work is undertaken. One of the purposes of this essay will have been realized if exegetes come to recognize that the tools that they use come out of particular frameworks and enshrine elements of that framework in their approach. Many of the standard tools used in the study of the Greek of the NT are heavily depen-dent upon a conceptual framework that was developed in the nineteenth century and that is heavily dependent upon historical and comparative investigation. Despite other recent methodological developments in NT study, it is surprising to see that what can only be described as dated (if not archaic) tools are still invoked as if they have status reflective of the current state of discussion. Exegetes who use these tools must be aware that they are referring to work that is not current and therefore cannot necessarily be relied upon for the purposes for which they are intending it. The last thirty years have seen a number of innovations in Greek grammar and linguis-

---

86. One of the approaches not noted above is that of corpus linguistics. Corpus linguistics is less a linguistic method than an orientation that advocates study of linguistic phenomena over the span of an entire corpus. This raises issues for the study of an ancient language, where the corpus is limited by a variety of historical factors. On corpus linguistics, see D. Biber, S. Conrad, and R. Reppen, *Corpus Linguistics: Investigating Language Structure and Use* (Cambridge: Cambridge University Press, 1998). Computer-aided research is related to corpus linguistics. The NT is arguably a structured corpus (and retrievable through a number of search programs), while the Thesaurus Linguae Graecae corpus is not a structured corpus but an archive. See M. B. O'Donnell, "The Use of Annotated Corpora for New Testament Discourse Analysis: A Survey of Current Practice and Future Prospects," in Porter and Reed, *Discourse Analysis*, 71–117; "Designing and Compiling a Register-Balanced Corpus of Hellenistic Greek for the Purpose of Linguistic Description and Investigation," in Porter, *Diglossia*, 255–97. For work in classical studies, see Y. Duhoux, *Le verbe grec ancien: Éléments de morphologie et de syntaxe historiques*, BCILL 61 (Louvain-La-Neuve: Peeters, 1992), and some of his supporting studies. OpenText.org is a web-based initiative that is attempting to make electronic resources available for NT studies. See M. B. O'Donnell, S. E. Porter, and J. T. Reed, "OpenText.org: The Problems and Prospects of Working with Ancient Discourse," in *Proceedings of the Corpus Linguistics 2001 Conference*, ed. P. Rayson et al., University Centre for Computer Corpus on Language Technical Papers 13 (Lancaster: UCREL, 2001), 413–22.

tics.[87] Much of this material provides a challenge to the exegete at least to recognize the limitations of many of the older tools, even if he or she is not willing to become aware of these newer developments. For those who are willing to learn more about these recent developments, the challenges are formidable. Nevertheless, the potential rewards are great. New grammatical methods and frameworks are not developed simply for their own sake, but because scholars believe that they are gaining insights into the Greek language. These insights must be incorporated into future exegesis in order to appreciate fully the meaning of the Greek text of the NT.

87. Two series are being published that encourage work in NT Greek grammar and linguistics. The first is Studies in Biblical Greek, edited by D. A. Carson and published by Peter Lang, and the second is Studies in New Testament Greek, a subseries of the JSNT Supplement Series, edited by S. E. Porter and published by Sheffield Academic Press.

5

General Hermeneutics

Greg Clark

From its beginnings as a discipline, hermeneutics has reflected on theories of interpretation. Since to interpret is to bring out meaning or to make understandable, hermeneutics has expanded into a general account of the act of understanding and the object of understanding, meaning. What, then, does "to understand" mean? What are the necessary conditions for something to be meaningful? A formal account of the act of understanding says that to understand is to see the relation between a whole and its parts and between a part and its whole. For instance, a good definition places the species (the part) in relation to the genus (the whole) while at the same time distinguishing it from other species.

Opinions differ on what metaphysical status to grant the objects, the wholes and parts, of our understanding. Plato bequeathed to us a tradition in which every word has a clear definition, and the definition in turn points us to an eternal, unchanging idea (or whole). Further, he granted a primacy to the whole as more real and more intelligible (though harder to know) than the part. A philosopher in the Platonic tradition, then, approaches the meaning of a word, including a word such as "hermeneutics," through its definition. This approach, however, is less than successful in making intelligible tokens or historically constituted particulars; it works best with mathematical theorems and with types. Platonism will lead us to think of hermeneutics as the contemplative insight into an eternal and unchanging structure, understanding-meaning.

Hermeneutics grows out of a tradition of nominalism;[1] it deals with ideas and relations between ideas in which the parts and the wholes are historically and socially constructed. Hermeneutists typically begin by tracing the

---

1. Nominalism, sometimes also called terminism, claims that only individual things exist, and all our ideas are of particular things. General terms, then, are *only names or terms* that do not refer to general substances or even general ideas. This position opposes Platonic realism, for which ideas exist independently of individual things; Aristotelian moderate realism, for which universals, such as

etymology of the word they seek to understand, placing it in its linguistic and historical context. The meaning of a word can then be built up by shuttling between the whole(s) and the part, each informing the other, in a process that has become known as "the hermeneutical circle." The word "hermeneutics" comes from the Greek verb *hermeneuein,* which could be translated into English as "to express, to explain, to interpret," or "to translate." In this instance, however, the linguistic context does not tell the historical tale, as it was and is common practice to create modern words out of Greek roots. The Lutheran theologian Johann Dannhauer coined the Latin term *hermeneutica* only in the mid–seventeenth century. Consequently, the history of "hermeneutics" begins rather late in the history of interpretation. Since the late nineteenth century it has become common to locate the beginnings of modern hermeneutics in the Protestant Reformation. To understand the meaning of "hermeneutics," then, we must build it up by layers, relating it to the contexts of which it is a part.

Accordingly, this essay will develop the meaning of hermeneutics by placing it in four different historical contexts: (1) the Protestant Reformation, (2) the Enlightenment, (3) Romanticism, and (4) late Modernism. As we will see, these periods correspond to three different hermeneutical paradigms, each of which remains a live option today: biblical hermeneutics (period 1), hermeneutics as epistemology (periods 2 and 3), and hermeneutics as ontology (period 4).

The Protestant Reformation and Biblical Hermeneutics

Martin Luther (1483–1546) interpreted Scripture, but he did not develop a theory of his practice. Still, the circumstances in which he worked raised complex and difficult issues of historical importance, and so attract later theorists. Both Luther and Rome agreed that reading Scripture in an inappropriate context obscures its meaning, but they disagreed on what constituted Scripture's own proper context. Followers of Rome appealed to Scripture *and* to tradition—to popes and councils—to support their position. Scripture and tradition depend on one another; the tradition of the church recognized Scripture as Scripture, and the church has grown out of its continuous reading of Scripture so that each is intelligible only in light of the other. Both have their source in the Holy Spirit. Luther appealed *only* to Scripture as the unique channel of the word of God. According to Luther, Scripture and tradition are two different principles. This is the meaning of the Lutheran phrases *sola scriptura* and *scriptura scripturae interpres* ("Scripture interprets Scripture").

---

genera and species, really do exist in individual things but as separable for the mind; and conceptualism, for which universals exist only in the mind as abstract ideas. These metaphysical positions have direct implications for how language is meaningful. Platonic realism gives the simplest account of language and knowledge but requires a top-heavy metaphysic. The other accounts pare down the metaphysics but require a more sophisticated account of language and knowledge.

Luther, then, faced the task of "freeing" Scripture from tradition.[2] To liberate the gospel from the Latin Vulgate, Luther translated the Bible into German. Since the Vulgate covered over the original Greek and Hebrew texts, Luther needed his knowledge of the ancient languages to perform this task. Since the Vulgate also hid Scripture from the average German Christian who did not know Latin, Luther needed his considerable gifts with his native tongue as well. Luther's translation illustrates the challenges facing any hermeneutic. The translator does not leave the text in the original language with the impossible request that every reader become a historical and cultural contemporary of the text. Rather, to mediate successfully between the original text and the reader, the translator requires, as Luther says, "great skill, hard work, understanding, and intelligence." However, even a good translation can cover over the text that it was meant to reveal, as did Jerome's (347–420 C.E.) Vulgate by the time of Luther. No translation opens a transparent window onto the meanings of the original text. Translation must also be guided by the characteristics of the intended audience of the translation (e.g., Luther's contemporary Germans). This led Luther to paraphrase large sections of his translation. In "An Open Letter on Translating" (8 September 1530), he says, "The literal Latin is a great barrier to speaking proper German. . . . So I have to let the literal words go and try to discover how the German says what the Hebrew . . . expresses." On the other hand, when some crucial doctrine was at stake, he did not insist on the integrity of the German language. For the sake of clarity in doctrine he would remain very literal, or he would even embellish. Indeed, even Luther's motive to translate the Bible was guided by doctrines such as the priesthood of all believers and the sufficiency and clarity of Scripture.

Hermeneutics as Epistemology

Reason and Biblical Criticism

The Protestants did not break with Rome as totally as the polemics on both sides would lead one to believe.[3] After Luther, Protestant scholasticism

2. For the standard work on Luther's hermeneutics, see Gerhard Ebeling, *Luther: An Introduction to His Thought*, trans. R. A. Wilson (Philadelphia: Fortress, 1970). See also G. S. Robbert, *Luther as Interpreter of Scripture* (St. Louis: Concordia, 1982). For a more general account of the context of Luther's thought, see Heiko Oberman, *The Harvest of Medieval Theology: Gabriel Biel and Late Medieval Nominalism* (Grand Rapids: Baker, 2000). For a fascinating discussion of hermeneutical issues in translation theory with special reference to Luther's Bible, see Martin Buber and Franz Rosenzweig, *Scripture and Translation*, trans. Lawrence Rosenwald with Everett Fox (Bloomington and Indianapolis: Indiana University Press, 1994). For Calvin's hermeneutics, see Thomas F. Torrance, *The Hermeneutics of John Calvin* (Edinburgh: Scottish Academic Press, 1988).

3. For an introductory but excellent treatment of biblical criticism in its political context, see Roy A. Harrisville and Walter Sundberg, *The Bible in Modern Culture: Theology and Historical-Critical Method from Spinoza to Käsemann* (Grand Rapids: Eerdmans, 1995).

developed traditions and doctrines that lay just as heavily on Scripture as did anything in Catholicism. Protestants, it turns out, were opposed to some Roman Catholic traditions and doctrines, and not to tradition and doctrine per se. Also, a functional church authority, and not Scripture alone, supported these Protestant traditions and doctrines, which in turn propped up the authority of the Protestant churches.

From the perspective of the Enlightenment, "Protestant Reformation" names an incomplete project. When we place the Protestant Reformation in the political context of the times, we see that its true meaning and the significance of its hermeneutic was not reforming the church in light of the gospel, but rather establishing liberal democracy. That is, on this interpretation, the Reformation broke the political dominance of the Roman church, established religion as a private arena of conscience separate from politics, lifted up the value of the individual, established the principle of freedom of association, and so on. The Reformers, however, fell short of their true goal. They used the state institutions to achieve a margin of freedom from Rome's power, but they did not establish political freedom for all.

The Protestant biblical hermeneutic was at fault. Under Protestantism, rulers continued to use the Bible to justify social and economic inequities, domestic domination, and interstate warfare. Priests persisted in parading their own opinions as God's commands. As Spinoza complained in his *Tractatus,* "Such persons never display less scruple or more zeal than when they are interpreting Scripture" (I.7.1). In both cases they played on the people's hopes and fears and channeled them into the prejudices and superstitions that provided the mechanism for political domination.

In order to complete the Reformation, Enlightenment thinkers set out to develop a rational reading of the Bible, a hermeneutic free of all dogma. They proposed to overcome the passions with knowledge, to provide a critique of the Bible that would establish its meaning based on knowledge rather than on fear of or hope in the supernatural. The Enlightenment project aimed to found Judeo-Christian morality and polity on reason and not on special revelation. Such a hermeneutic would separate rational politics from sectarian religion and so make appeal to the Bible politically irrelevant. This was the explicit goal of Hobbes's *Leviathan* (1651) and Spinoza's *Tractatus Theologico-politicus* (1670), but also of Locke's less-read *First Treatise on Government* (1690).

How, then, does one read the Bible rationally? All people, regardless of the time or place in which they were born or the language they speak, share reason in common. When the Bible teaches truths known through reason, everyone can, in principle, recognize these truths through the use of their own faculties—though in practice, only those trained in and guided by reason overcome their passions to make such recognition effective. The morality of the NT, which teaches love, joy, peace, patience, kindness, and the like, exemplifies these truths known through reason. Since we can immediately recognize the truth of this morality, we need no special hermeneutic to understand it.

But the seventeenth- and eighteenth-century philosophers never imagined that the Bible was a deposit of pure cosmopolitan rationality. Some of its values, such as the privilege accorded to the particular history of Israel, offended the sensibilities of those in London and Paris, Amsterdam and Berlin. And the miracle stories, though stated as fact, were just plain puzzling. Such features of Scripture did not conform to the standard of universal reason. As such, they were not "true" and did not apply to societies that had natural science. Still, the passages had a meaning for the cultures that produced them, and this meaning could be recovered through a hermeneutic that placed the text in its proper (i.e., its historical and cultural) context.

This new understanding of the proper context of Scripture led the philosophers and Bible scholars to set aside concerns that had been central to Christianity. For instance, they rejected the doctrine, shared by both Catholics and Protestants, that the entire canon constitutes a whole in terms of which one ought to read particular passages. Instead, they treated the Bible as a collection of sixty-six (or more) books by different authors to different audiences. They developed techniques to determine the original form of each book, its sources, and the interests of the editor who cobbled it together. Showing how the message of and about Jesus in the NT fulfilled the expectations of the OT did not figure as an interesting or possible project.

Scientific methods provided biblical scholars with independent access to the historical facts and also to what the authors and original readers of the biblical books would have known. By learning the habits of mind of the people, they could distinguish the facts from the culturally determined and limited interpretation given to the facts by the authors. An example from Spinoza illustrates the point. When a biblical author wrote "God says," he was not reporting a fact that, if we had been there, we could have heard or seen. Rather, this is just the way that people spoke in that culture. "The Jews never make mention of intermediate or particular causes nor pay any heed to them, but to serve religion and piety . . . they refer everything to God. For example, if they make money by some transaction, they say it has come to them from God; if it happens that they desire something, they say that God has so disposed their hearts; and if some thought enters their heads, they say that God has told them this" (*Tractatus,* I.1.15).

The specialized training required to read the Bible took it out of the hands of the laity, and its methods were used to free European politics from interminable religious disagreements—all in the name of completing the Protestant Reformation.

History and Romanticism

Romanticism knew that unaided reason could not unite readers and authors across the chasm of time and language as the Enlightenment asked it to do.[4] F. D. E. Schleiermacher[5] (1768–1834) thought, however, that a universal hermeneutic, which included the historical methods of the Enlightenment, could perform this task. Against the optimism of Enlightenment thinkers, Schleiermacher insisted that in human affairs, misunderstanding is the default setting, but, if something is grammatically original or psychologically unique enough to interest us, we can deepen our understanding of it through special effort. To understand another person, we always require hermeneutics, for the fundamental challenge to understanding another is the difference between any two subjectivities and not just linguistic, cultural, or historical differences. Schleiermacher, then, in the early nineteenth century, was the first to develop a general hermeneutic that applied to all written and spoken communication, not just to Scripture, legal documents, or texts from prior times and other cultures.

For Schleiermacher, to understand is to experience; to understand others is to reexperience or share their experiences. Accordingly, Romantic hermeneutics sets out to reexperience the thoughts of an author and so, as Schleiermacher says, "to understand the text at first as well as and then even better than its author."[6] Put differently, understanding reverses the process of composition in order to re-create the genius's creative act.

Schleiermacher's understanding of understanding establishes the goal of his hermeneutic. It also implies the obstacles that it must overcome, for, while our common human nature should make understanding possible, no one has direct knowledge of another's mind. To understand another, then, we must follow an indirect route. Romantic hermeneutics spells out the epistemology that enables the reader to actually know an individual author's intention. First, the reader needs to use objective, grammatical methods to acquire an exhaustive knowledge of the original languages and the historical and literary contexts of a text. The reader must learn everything the author would have known and "many things of which he himself may have been unconscious."[7] Schleiermacher,

---

4. Standard histories of philosophical hermeneutics make their proper beginning with Schleiermacher and move through Dilthey and Heidegger to Gadamer. For a more complete description of this history, see Paul Ricoeur, "The Task of Hermeneutics," in *From Text to Action: Essays in Hermeneutics II,* trans. Kathleen Blamey and John B. Thompson (Evanston, Ill.: Northwestern University Press, 1991), 53–74; part 2 of Hans-Georg Gadamer, *Truth and Method,* trans. J. Weinsheimer and D. G. Marshall, 2nd rev. ed. (New York: Crossroad, 1989); Richard E. Palmer, *Hermeneutics: Interpretation Theory in Schleiermacher, Dilthey, Heidegger, and Gadamer* (Evanston, Ill.: Northwestern University Press, 1969). Closely parallel is Hans-Georg Gadamer, "On the Problem of Self-Understanding," in *Philosophical Hermeneutics,* trans. David E. Linge (Berkeley: University of California Press, 1976), 44–58. For an alternative to this now canonical history, see Jean Grodin, *Introduction to Philosophical Hermeneutics,* trans. J. Weinsheimer (New Haven: Yale University Press, 1994).

5. The standard English edition of Schleiermacher's work is *Hermeneutics and Criticism,* ed. Andrew Bowie (Cambridge: Cambridge University Press, 1998).

6. Schleiermacher is repeating Kant (*Critique of Pure Reason,* B370), but giving the statement a very different meaning from Kant's.

7. Schleiermacher, *Hermeneutics and Criticism,* 9.18.3.

thus, appropriates the scientific methods that philologists and earlier biblical critics had put to quite different purposes. Historical interpretation in those like Spinoza "is wrong," he says, when used to reduce Christianity to already-present conditions and when used to lock Christianity in those conditions. But this is not the only use of historical interpretation, for the NT is indeed rooted in a time and a place, and knowledge of that time and place can also open up our understanding of those texts.[8] The grammatical method then studies words, the objective expression of thought. Besides the grammatical method, the reader needs a complete knowledge of the author's life and works. This knowledge, combined with imagination and empathy, enables the reader to reexperience the author's intention. Romantic hermeneutics, then, names an infinite task that no reader will ever complete. Still, our knowledge of the texts, their contexts, and their relation to one another can continually improve and bring us ever closer to the mind of the author. And we may even be able to point out where the author's words did not express the intention well—thus understanding the author better than he understands himself.

For Wilhelm Dilthey (1833–1911), Schleiermacher's thought suggested solutions to problems posed by Kant's philosophy. Kant had provided an epistemology for the natural sciences, taking mathematics and physics as his examples, and positivists had insisted that the natural sciences also provided the model for the human sciences. But Dilthey saw that the objectivity of the human sciences differed from that of the natural sciences, and that we needed an epistemology appropriate to the subject matter of the human sciences. For Dilthey, the natural sciences try to explain physical phenomena, while the human sciences try to understand mental phenomena. Schleiermacher's hermeneutics pointed the way to establish the epistemological foundations for the social sciences and the humanities. This required that Dilthey generalize the notion of a text beyond the written and spoken word to include any human "life-expression," including artifacts and actions. But though he reworked and developed hermeneutics beyond Schleiermacher, Dilthey remained committed to the claim that understanding is reexperiencing the intention of another, to methodology as the guarantee of objectivity, and to hermeneutics as liberating interpretation from dogma.

Hermeneutics as Ontology

The purported objectivity of hermeneutical epistemology remained elusive.[9] Illustrations from biblical scholarship are not scarce, but one witness will have

---

8. Ibid., 4.13.1.

9. The word *ontology*, from the Greek *on* and meaning the "science of being," was created about the same time and in the same way as the word "hermeneutics." See Jean-Luc Marion, "Is the Ontological Argument Ontological? The Argument according to Anselm and Its Metaphysi-

to suffice. Albert Schweitzer (1875–1965) famously summed up the research into the life of Jesus at the end of the nineteenth century as follows: "Thus each successive epoch of theology found its own thoughts in Jesus. . . . Each individual created Jesus in accordance with his own character. There is no historical task which so reveals a man's true self as the writing of a Life of Jesus."[10] The appeal to history did not prevent scholars from imposing on the text a foreign context—themselves. Put in a more positive form, the reader of the text played an essential, even dominant, role in determining the text's meaning.

Schweitzer's comments point out the dilemma of hermeneutical epistemologists. They began with the claim that a text's proper context is its historical context. But if the reader of the text belongs to a different historical context, this implies that the text's meaning would be inaccessible, for two separate contexts circumscribe the text's meaning and what is meaningful to the reader. Historicism would lead to historical skepticism. The Enlightenment claimed that superstition, prejudice, and passion hid the true meaning of Scripture, and, to overcome these obstacles, it turned to methods of historical science. The more fundamental dilemma for historical understanding, however, concerns not the difference between reason and superstition, but the difference between historical epochs.

This dilemma repeats, at the level of historical knowledge, the problems built into the ontological tradition that guided the epistemologists' research. According to that ontology, there are two basic kinds of substances: mental subjects and physical objects. While objects causally affect subjects, subjects form representations of objects. Representations, however, are distorted by passions, false beliefs or prejudices, and even the bodily senses of the subject. This Cartesian ontology, then, gives birth to an epistemology charged with developing methods that guarantee objective knowledge by purifying it of subjective elements. But, as with historicism, the threat of incoherence always plagued this ontology.[11] Its real problem was not the subjective distortions of the object, but the fundamental dualism of the subject and the object. How can two things defined as independent of, indeed in opposition to, one another ever come together to account for knowledge? Dualism leads to skepticism.

In practice, philosophers, historians, and biblical scholars cheated. They needed contexts capable of bridging historical differences. Such contexts are, by definition, not fully articulated in the text. The "proper" context for a text is not determined by how one parses a Greek sentence. But neither does

---

cal Interpretation according to Kant," *Journal of the History of Philosophy* 30, no. 2 (April 1992): 201–18.

10. Albert Schweitzer, *The Quest of the Historical Jesus,* trans. J. Bowden (1906; reprint, Minneapolis: Fortress, 2001), 6.

11. For a clear account of the layout of this ontology/epistemology and its ultimate incoherence, see Richard A. Watson, *The Breakdown of Cartesian Metaphysics* (Indianapolis: Hackett, 1987). See also Richard Rorty, *Philosophy and the Mirror of Nature* (Princeton: Princeton University Press, 1979).

hermeneutics offer guidance on how to determine a text's "proper" context. Hermeneutics cannot settle disagreements between Catholic, Lutheran, deist, and historicist readings of Scripture by declaring one of their contexts the proper one. The contexts that scholars developed appealed to the text for justification, but they also bore the imprint of the scholar or scholarly community that produced them. And because they needed to bridge some historical differences, they sometimes claimed to transcend all historical differences. That is, in order to have knowledge, some things must remain the same; we know what happened in the past only if we can assume that, in ways x, y, and z, the past was essentially like the present.[12] Reason, human nature, laws of history, Absolute Spirit, universal life, universal history, and so on—all claim to transcend historical differences in this way. This situation was unacceptable for the historicist. It made exceptions to the historicists' central claim that all meaning is rooted in history, and they had no objective way to determine the proper historical context of any text or event. As a result, their conclusions looked subjective, their proofs circular.

Martin Heidegger (1889–1976) saw that the root of the problem was ontological, not epistemological; the act of understanding is not a psychological act but an ontological act. In *Being and Time*[13] (1927) he developed a hermeneutical ontology in which the act of existence is not substance but the act of understanding. That is, for Heidegger, the hermeneutical circle is not a method to produce objectivity in the human sciences; it describes the structure of human existence (*Dasein*). *Dasein* is neither an object that remains what it is in an ever-recurring present nor a mental subject that must fight to find logical bridges to an outside world. *Dasein* exists as a "thrown project." As "thrown," *Dasein* is finite. It has always already inherited a world that comes laden with a history, structures, and orientations that *Dasein* did not create. This traditioned world in which *Dasein* finds itself also provides the possibilities for its future. *Dasein* "ex-ists" by standing out from its present and projecting itself into its future. As being-in-the-world, *Dasein* is always already dealing with tools, which have their own horizons and so can be used more or less well. Tools become objects when they break, for instance, and we strip them of their functional context. But this does not mean that they are not properly tools or that they are really objects. On the contrary, meaning is the product of *Dasein* and its possibilities, on the one hand, and the object and its horizons, on the other hand. To find the meaning of that which confronts us, we do not need to jump outside of all contexts to an absolute or to reduce the tool

12. As David Hume (1711–76) stated in 1748, without need for any argument, never in any age or any country has a person been observed to rise from the dead (David Hume, *An Enquiry concerning Human Understanding* [Oxford: Oxford University Press, 1999], section 10, part 1).

13. Martin Heidegger, *Being and Time,* trans. J. Macquarrie and J. M. Robinson (New York: Harper & Row, 1962).

to a quantitative description. Rather, the true meaning is accessible only to historically situated, future-oriented *Dasein*. "What is decisive," Heidegger says, "is not to get out of the circle, but to come into it in the right way."[14]

Heidegger never completed the larger projected work of which *Being and Time* was to be only a part, and so he never connects his insights back to the philosophical tradition as fully as one might wish. Thankfully, Hans-Georg Gadamer (1900–2002), in *Truth and Method*[15] (1960), has done some of this work for us. Gadamer points out that the Enlightenment's criticism of nonscientific modes of thought was a "prejudice against prejudice itself, which denies tradition its power."[16] Against the Enlightenment, we have access to things in our world only through prejudgments. On the other hand, hermeneutical ontology insists that while our prejudgments give us initial access to the subject matter, they are not the final standard. Rather, as one would expect in a hermeneutical structure, we must modify them in light of the subject matter. So, then, against the Romantic tradition, the aim of understanding is not the individual author's intent or reliving the experience of the author. Rather, the goal and standard of understanding is the subject matter itself; to understand an author is to come to agreement about the subject matter. However, we do not understand the subject matter by an "objective" representation of it in our minds. We understand when we can find our way around the subject matter, and for this we must relate it to the possibilities of our world. Retrieving an insight of Luther's, Gadamer insists that "application" of a text to the contemporary situation belongs to the essence of understanding and is not a mere addendum. Hermeneutical ontology claims that the differences between the author and the reader produce rather than obstruct meaning, so that understanding is productive and not merely reproductive. The task of hermeneutical ontology is to overcome the epistemologists' psychologism and objectivism, not productive differences.

Albert Schweitzer noted that each epoch and each individual Bible scholar found in Jesus a mirror; "that was, indeed, the only way in which [they] could make him live."[17] All agree that Schweitzer was right, but hermeneutical ontology and hermeneutical epistemology separate over their understanding of his comment. For the epistemologists, Schweitzer indicts biblical scholars for failing to be objective; for the ontologists, Schweitzer merely states the requirements for understanding. That the epistemologists take Schweitzer's comment as a criticism is a symptom of their real failures: they misunderstood the nature of understanding and so held themselves to false and unattainable standards, and they did not allow the text to question their own prejudices as fully as they ought.

---

14. Ibid., H153.
15. Hans-Georg Gadamer, *Truth and Method,* trans. J. Weinsheimer and D. G. Marshall, 2nd rev. ed. (New York: Crossroad, 1989).
16. Ibid., 270.
17. Schweitzer, *Quest of the Historical Jesus,* 6.

Contemporary Hermeneutics

In an overview of the contemporary scene, two movements that trace their roots into hermeneutical ontology deserve special mention. *Reader-response criticism,* as a phenomenology of reading, describes what happens when readers (expected and unexpected) read texts. More boldly, it identifies the meaning of a text with what happens in the reading. More boldly still, some critics claim that the text offers no constraints, that interpretation is an imposition on the text, not a cooperation with it. If the interpretive community imposes a meaning on a text, "success is inevitable."[18] Here a few comments are in order. If the only two operative categories in our ontologies and epistemologies are "subject" and "object," reader-response criticism will look viciously subjective. Within a hermeneutical ontology, only the boldest claims of reader-response criticism are false, because they have forgotten the finitude of the human condition, the complexity of tradition, and the subject matter as the goal of understanding. The boldest forms of reader-response criticism, then, find their philosophical expression not in Heidegger and Gadamer but in popular forms of pragmatism and casual readings of Nietzsche.

Heidegger's hermeneutical phenomenology is also an ancestor of *deconstruction.* While Jacques Derrida[19] (1930–) gave deconstruction its initial formulations, the images of it now circulating in academic journalism often have only a tangential relation to his work. Since there is no danger of clearing up the confusions in a short essay, I will limit my comments to a genealogy of the word "deconstruction." Derrida picks up the word from Heidegger, who uses it to explain his project of reinterpreting or "destroying" the history of ontology.[20] Heidegger, in turn, took it from Luther's translation of 1 Cor. 1:19: "I will destroy the wisdom of the wise; the intelligence of the intelligent I will frustrate." For Luther, and then for theologians such as Adolf von Harnack, this named the project of thinking against Scholastic or Hellenistic philosophy, which had covered over the vital insights of primitive Christianity. Heidegger made this project his own before he decided that the pre-Socratics held more promise than Paul.[21] Deconstruction reinterprets by setting one aspect of the

---

18. Stanley Fish, *Is There a Text in This Class? The Authority of Interpretive Communities* (Cambridge: Harvard University Press, 1980), 105.

19. One should come to Derrida through his earliest work, *Edmund Husserl's Origin of Geometry: An Introduction,* trans. John Leavey (Lincoln: University of Nebraska Press, 1989); idem, *Speech and Phenomena: And Other Essays on Husserl's Theory of Signs,* trans. David B. Allison (Evanston, Ill.: Northwestern University Press, 1973); idem, *Of Grammatology,* trans. Gayatri Chakravorty Spivak (Baltimore: Johns Hopkins University Press, 1998).

20. Martin Heidegger, *The Basic Problems of Phenomenology,* trans. Albert Hofstadter, rev. ed. (Bloomington and Indianapolis: Indiana University Press, 1988), 23. See also idem, *Being and Time,* §6.

21. See Theodore Kisiel, *The Genesis of Heidegger's "Being and Time"* (Berkeley: University of California Press, 1993); "Heidegger (1920–1) on Becoming a Christian: A Conceptual Picture

tradition (e.g., Christianity) against another aspect (e.g., philosophy) in order to free up or to retrieve what the tradition both preserved and covered over. Derrida limits the meaning of deconstruction to its first moment of showing how a tradition or a text, as a structural necessity, includes conflicting elements. The second moment of retrieval never gets underway because notions such as "retrieval," "memory," and even "meaning" themselves belong to conflicted, and so deconstructable, traditions. Derrida's work, then, can be read as a critical rejection of hermeneutics and/or as a radicalization of certain tendencies within hermeneutics.[22]

Secondary sources regularly describe the variety of hermeneutical approaches practiced today as "dizzying." For simplicity, some classify the options according to where they locate meaning: in the author, in the text, or in the reader. Such a classification system assumes that location is both a legitimate and the most illuminating feature of meaning. But this assumption holds only in a metaphysic of substances, where the questions are "Is meaning in the subject or the object?" and "If the subject, which one, the author or the reader?" Even if we insist that the "location" of meaning is meant metaphorically, it covers over rather than illumines the subject matter, for location tends to be exclusive—one cannot be in two places at the same time. If this classification system asked how meaning *depends* on the author, the text, and the reader, many of its critical battles would appear less grave.

I have been concerned to approach hermeneutics historically, and my guiding questions have been "What obstructs meaning?" and "What uncovers meaning?" This approach leads to the three models of hermeneutics sketched above—biblical, epistemological, and ontological. Though the second and third models developed as an interpretation and criticism of the first model, we can see that the three models do not necessarily exclude one another. In practice, the different models often borrow from one another. But theory, too, has not remained ghettoized. Rudolf Bultmann's great, though dated, achievement was to bring all three models together into a seamless whole.[23] By retrieving, with Heidegger and Gadamer, Aristotle's notion of practical reason, Alasdair MacIntyre[24] has shown that Scripture, tradition, and reason are not antithetical terms. Paul

---

Show," in *Reading Heidegger from the Start: Essays in His Earliest Thought,* ed. Theodore Kisiel and John van Buren (Albany: SUNY Press, 1994).

22. See John D. Caputo, *Radical Hermeneutics: Repetition, Deconstruction, and the Hermeneutic Project* (Bloomington and Indianapolis: Indiana University Press, 1987); *Dialogue and Deconstruction: The Gadamer-Derrida Encounter,* ed. D. Michelfelder and R. Palmer (Albany: SUNY Press, 1989).

23. For uncritically using Heidegger's ontology, Bultmann rightly sustained heavy criticism from the other models, but his critics rarely reflected on their own ontological presuppositions or, apart from Barth, offered reasons why they need not do so.

24. Alasdair C. MacIntyre, *After Virtue: A Study in Moral Theory,* 2nd ed. (Notre Dame, Ind.: University of Notre Dame Press, 1984); *Whose Justice? Which Rationality?* (Notre Dame, Ind.: University of Notre Dame Press, 1988); *Three Rival Versions of Moral Enquiry: Encyclopedia,*

Ricoeur (1913–) also has bridged the gap between biblical, epistemological, and ontological hermeneutics. Whereas Heidegger and Gadamer focused on the implications of human finitude, Ricoeur produced a phenomenology of guilt. This led him to explore ways that hiding things from ourselves can systematically distort our views and our traditions. He saw that an ontology of understanding built on human finitude alone will fail to expose this systematic distortion. Along with hermeneutical ontology, then, we need the help of writers such as Marx, Nietzsche, and especially Freud. Rejecting the reductive tendencies of these critics while appropriating their suspicions, Ricoeur gained the ability to expose idolatry in order to think legitimately in the wake of our symbols.

Still, the traditional divisions between hermeneutical models remain powerful, often for good reasons. Hermeneutical ontology receives heavy criticism from the epistemologists. Neo-Marxists, feminists, Afrocentrists, and so forth, all of whom approach the text through ideology critique, disapprove of the ontologists for abandoning any external standard capable of criticizing the tradition,[25] for failing to develop the methodological implications of their position,[26] and for reducing truth to "just another interpretation."[27] Their concerns keep Heidegger's Nazism on the front page and constrain would-be defenders of Heidegger to insist that post-Heideggerian hermeneutics is committed to liberal democracy because it has no substantive commitments other than "dialogue."

Biblical hermeneutics also remains robust. Evangelicals have been divided in their assessment of the more recent developments. Many of the older generation who have fought hard for intellectual respectability see the threat of subjectivism and relativism; some of the younger generation (sometimes called "neo-evangelicals"), who can take for granted what their elders had to earn, spy an opportunity to reclaim precritical readings dismissed by Enlightenment standards of intellectual respectability.[28] Three contemporary authors help to cut through the divisions. Anthony Thiselton,[29] who has presented the disci-

---

Genealogy, and Tradition (Notre Dame, Ind.: University of Notre Dame Press, 1990); *Dependent Rational Animals: Why Human Beings Need the Virtues* (La Salle, Ill.: Open Court, 1999).

25. This is Jürgen Habermas's criticism of Gadamer. See Jürgen Habermas, "A Review of Gadamer's *Truth and Method*," trans. F. Dallmayr and T. McCarthy, in *Hermeneutics and Modern Philosophy*, ed. Brice R. Wachterhauser (Albany: SUNY Press, 1986), 243–76; "On Hermeneutic's Claim to Universality," in *The Hermeneutics Reader,* ed. Kurt Mueller-Vollmer (New York: Continuum, 1997).

26. Gadamer's *Truth and Method,* commentators often say, should have been entitled *Truth OR Method.* Gadamer simply points out, "My real concern was and is philosophic: not what we do or what we ought to do [in terms of method], but what happens to us over and above our wanting and doing" (*Truth and Method,* xvi).

27. Gianni Vattimo, *Beyond Interpretation: The Meaning of Hermeneutics for Philosophy,* trans. David Webb (Stanford, Calif.: Stanford University Press, 1997).

28. See Stephen E. Fowl, ed., *The Theological Interpretation of Scripture: Classic and Contemporary Readings,* Blackwell Readings in Modern Theology (Oxford: Blackwell, 1997).

29. Anthony Thiselton, *The Two Horizons: New Testament Hermeneutics and Philosophical Description with Special Reference to Heidegger, Bultmann, Gadamer, and Wittgenstein* (Grand Rapids:

pline of hermeneutics to a wide readership for over twenty years, deserves high praise for his erudite and balanced accounts. Kevin Vanhoozer[30] follows up on some of Thiselton's suggestions, using speech-act theory and the work of E. D. Hirsch to try to stave off what he sees as the excesses of deconstruction, pragmatism, and reader-response criticism. His ambitious work aims to distinguish "meaning" from "significance," understanding from interpretation—roughly the difference between what a text meant from what that text might mean today. The most significant contribution to the field of hermeneutics comes from Nicholas Wolterstorff's *Divine Discourse*.[31] It brings into focus a question central to the concerns of evangelicals ("How can we say that God speaks?"); presents the work of Jacques Derrida, Paul Ricoeur, and Hans Frei fairly; and offers insightful criticisms that advance the discussion.

In the broader theological arena, Martin Kähler, Karl Barth, Hans Frei, John Howard Yoder, Paul Holmer, George Lindbeck, Luke Timothy Johnson, Stanley Hauerwas, John Milbank, and even René Girard have, in different ways, presented Scripture as the normative context that judges epistemology and ontology. Enlightenment hermeneutics, on some of their tellings, was not the liberation that it claims to be, but rather the means by which the nation-state gained hegemony over the church.[32] Hermeneutical ontology, some would argue, reinforces rather than challenges modernity's attempt to absolutize autonomy, and so be done with that which calls us to responsibility.[33] A general account of "meaning," like our concepts of "religion" and the "nation-state," is a creation of the nineteenth century, and something we had best get over.[34]

Hermeneutics as a discipline is as wild and woolly as it has ever been, and its future shape and even its existence are impossible to predict. But just as biblical scholars created the field, perhaps from them will emerge another Luther who can redeem it.

Eerdmans, 1980); idem, *New Horizons in Hermeneutics: The Theory and Practice of Transforming Biblical Reading* (Grand Rapids: Zondervan, 1992).

30. Kevin Vanhoozer, *Is There a Meaning in This Text? The Bible, The Reader, and the Morality of Literary Knowledge* (Grand Rapids: Zondervan, 1998).

31. Nicholas Wolterstorff, *Divine Discourse: Philosophical Reflections on the Claim That God Speaks* (Cambridge: Cambridge University Press, 1995).

32. John Milbank, *Theology and Social Theory: Beyond Secular Reason* (Oxford: Blackwell, 1990); William Cavanaugh, "'A Fire Strong Enough to Consume the House': The Wars of Religion and the Rise of the State," *Modern Theology* 11, no. 4 (October 1995): 397–420.

33. Emmanuel Lévinas, "Hermeneutics and the Beyond," in *Entre Nous: On Thinking-of-the-Other*, trans. Michael B. Smith and Barbara Harshav (New York: Columbia University Press, 1998); idem, *Totality and Infinity: An Essay on Exteriority*, trans. Alphonso Lingis (Pittsburgh: Duquesne University Press, 1969); Jean-Luc Marion, "'Christian Philosophy': Hermeneutic or Heuristic?" in *The Question of Christian Philosophy Today*, ed. Francis J. Ambrosio (New York: Fordham University Press, 1999), 247–64; idem, *God without Being: Hors-Texte*, trans. Thomas A. Carlson (Chicago: University of Chicago Press, 1991).

34. Gerhard Sauter, *The Question of Meaning: A Theological and Philosophical Orientation*, trans. Geoffrey W. Bromiley (Grand Rapids: Eerdmans, 1995).

6

Embodying the Word

Social-Scientific Interpretation of the New Testament

David A. deSilva

Jesus was a real, live human being who worked miracles, taught, and gathered a community of real people as disciples in the midst of the social, political, economic, and cultural realities that made up first-century Judean and Galilean life. Similarly, the apostles took the message about this Jesus into real cities throughout the Roman Empire, and they planted congregations of people drawn from the spectrum of social and economic levels, each with their social and cultural expectations, and called them to interact with one another and the outside world in specific ways. The NT is not just about the "Word of God" in the sense of divine principles and ideas. It is also about the "Word" of God "made flesh" as Christian leaders used words, symbols, and rituals—each having meaning only because it resonated with the social and cultural contexts of their authors and hearers—to create and give shape to the distinctive social group that we now call the church. It is, moreover, about responding to and living out that "Word" in the midst of real, everyday social interactions, and in the face of real, everyday challenges conditioned by social and cultural factors.

Social-scientific interpretation of the NT provides an array of resources by which professional scholars and other students of the NT can take more seriously and uncover more fully its "real life" dimensions. In the words of Robin Scroggs, "Interest in the sociology of early Christianity . . . should be seen as an effort to guard against . . . a limitation of the reality of Christianity to an inner-spiritual, or objective-cognitive system. In short, sociology of early Christianity wants to put body and soul together again."[1]

Social-scientific criticism is part of the larger enterprise of exegesis, bringing the perspectives, models, questions, and tools of sociological research to bear on the NT texts and the real world of the Christians who composed and read them. "It studies (1) not only the social aspects of the form and content of texts but also the conditioning factors and intended consequences of the communication process [thus becomes a natural ally of rhetorical criticism]; (2) the correlation of the text's linguistic, literary, theological (ideological), and social dimensions; and (3) the manner in which this textual communication was both a reflection of and a response to a specific social and cultural context."[2]

This discipline is itself embedded in historical criticism—a connection made explicit by several of its leading practitioners.[3] It represents an attempt to gain a richer and fuller understanding of the historical context of NT texts, informed by the awareness that ideas, decisions, commitments, rituals, and group affiliations all take place within, and derive their meaning from, a complex web of cultural information and social interaction. Two basic directions are taken in social-scientific study. The first involves the investigation of the social world in which the early church took shape and upon which it, in turn, sought to act. This involves the study of sociological data provided by the NT, the fuller investigation of social *realia* described therein (e.g., the socioeconomic conditions of leather-workers and purple-sellers; the etiquette of a meal in a host's house; the system of almsgiving as a welfare system), the integration of such information into a social history of pertinent regions of the Roman Empire in the first century, the study of "the social organization of early Christianity"—both in terms of what social forces brought the early Christian groups together, and in terms of the way the groups were organized and institutionalized[4]—and the discovery of "the social and cultural scripts influencing and constraining social interaction."[5]

The second focuses on the exegesis of the texts themselves and the ways in which "the research, theory, and models of the social sciences" can assist "in the analysis of biblical texts."[6] Sociology provides NT interpreters with questions to ask of a text, questions that open up the real and dynamic world behind

---

1. Robin Scroggs, "The Sociological Interpretation of the New Testament," *NTS* 26 (1980): 164–79, 165–66.

2. J. H. Elliott, *What Is Social-Scientific Criticism?* (Minneapolis: Fortress, 1993), 7.

3. See ibid. These two disciplines are brought together in Stephen C. Barton, "Historical Criticism and Social-Scientific Perspectives in New Testament Study," in *Hearing the New Testament: Strategies for Interpretation,* ed. J. B. Green (Grand Rapids: Eerdmans, 1995), 61–89.

4. These facets were presented in a programmatic essay by Jonathan Z. Smith, "The Social Description of Early Christianity," *RSR* 1 (1975): 19–25.

5. Elliott (*What Is Social-Scientific Criticism?* 19) makes this helpful addition to Smith's typology.

6. Ibid., 19.

the text that has contributed to the shaping of the text. This in turn provides a context for the early readers to understand the text. Sociology also provides resources for inquiring into how the text seeks to impact social interactions, distribution of goods, and other aspects of that real and dynamic world.

What follows here represents but a sampling of the major approaches and landmark works that have advanced the discussion in this area of biblical scholarship.[7]

Sociology and New Testament Interpretation

The use of sociology as a tool for biblical interpretation has its roots in the second half of the nineteenth century, particularly as it manifested itself in the interest of form critics in the "setting in life" of particular forms of biblical literature and in the ideologically driven work of Friedrich Engels and Bruno Bauer on early Christianity as a movement of the proletariat protesting an ancient bourgeoisie.[8] The growth of this discipline was derailed on the European continent, at least, during the fascination with dialectical theology and existential interpretation, while in America, the "Chicago School," notably in the persons of Shirley Jackson Case and Shailer Mathews, kept sociological investigation of early Christianity alive.[9] Interest in sociological exegesis was reawakened in Europe in the early 1970s by Gerd Theissen; in America, the recent revival of interest in the social context of early Christianity tends to be dated to the work of E. A Judge.[10]

Already in these early works one can discern the two major modes in which social-scientific interpretation has proceeded. Judge worked in the mode of social description, in which the interpreter locates himself or herself primarily in a historical mode of investigation, describing social and cultural *realia* in the course of historical-critical investigation. This mode is followed very success-

7. The reader is referred to the following resources for extensive bibliography and bibliographical guides to the sociological investigation of the NT and its environment: D. J. Harrington, "Second Testament Exegesis and the Social Sciences: A Bibliography," *BTB* 18 (1988): 77–85; Bengt Holmberg, *Sociology and the New Testament: An Appraisal* (Minneapolis: Fortress, 1990); Elliott, *What Is Social-Scientific Criticism?* 138–74; Barton, "Historical Criticism," 84–89; idem, "Social-Scientific Criticism," in *Handbook to Exegesis of the New Testament*, ed. S. E. Porter, NTTS 25 (Leiden: Brill, 1997), 278–89; D. G. Horrell, *Social-Scientific Approaches to New Testament Interpretation* (Edinburgh: Clark, 1999), 361–402.

8. See, for example, F. Engels, "On the History of Early Christianity" (1894), in K. Marx and F. Engels, *On Religion* (Atlanta: Scholars Press, 1964), 316–47.

9. See, for example, Shirley Jackson Case, *The Evolution of Early Christianity* (Chicago: University of Chicago Press, 1914); idem, *The Social Origins of Christianity* (Chicago: University of Chicago Press, 1923); Shailer Mathews, *The Social Teaching of Jesus: An Essay in Christian Sociology* (New York: MacMillan, 1897).

10. E. A. Judge, *The Social Patterns of the Christian Groups in the First Century* (London: Tyndale, 1960).

fully by Martin Hengel, whose work on the cultural as well as the political and linguistic penetration of Hellenism into Palestine remains a landmark to this day, having redrawn the cultural maps of Palestine,[11] and by scholars such as Abraham J. Malherbe, John E. Stambaugh, and David L. Balch. Such scholars often aim at achieving a "thick description"[12] of the period, issue, or social fact that they investigate, so as to make an insider's view or understanding of the phenomenon accessible to outsiders.

The second mode, which is incipient in Theissen's earlier works and becomes much more prominent in his later works, involves the use of social-scientific models to explain behaviors reflected in (or prescribed by) the texts, organizational structures, the legitimation of authority, the cultural patterns that provide the context for meaning, and the like. In this mode, the interpreter locates himself or herself primarily in a sociological, analytical mode of investigation. This mode is prominent in, for example, the work of John Gager, who uses models of authority derived from Max Weber, millenarian sect theories, and cognitive dissonance theory not only to analyze but also to explain phenomena in the early church.[13] The two modes are, of course, complementary and are probably best executed when used in conjunction with one another (as is often the case in the work of Gerd Theissen, John Barclay, and Wayne Meeks, among others).

Gerd Theissen stands near the forefront of the current revival of sociological investigation of the NT. He posited a correlation between the teachings preserved during the phase of oral tradition of the Jesus materials and the lifestyle of the preachers who proclaimed Jesus. Jesus' instructions about poverty, homelessness, and wandering were no longer to be viewed as an "impossible ethic," but as a reflection of the real-life circumstances of those who preached the gospel.[14] It brought them into the orbit of the Cynic philosophers and other itinerants dependent on alms or hospitality, into whose mold they fit, but also from

11. Martin Hengel, *Judaism and Hellenism,* 2 vols. (Philadelphia: Fortress, 1974); *Jews, Greeks, and Barbarians* (Philadelphia: Fortress, 1980).

12. A term used by C. J. Geertz (*The Interpretation of Cultures* [New York: Basic Books, 1973], 3–30) to describe the ethnographer's work.

13. J. G. Gager, *Kingdom and Community: The Social World of Early Christianity* (Englewood Cliffs, N.J.: Prentice-Hall, 1975). Gager used observations about Melanesian cargo cults, for example, to shed new light on the social situation of early Christians. His execution of his working presupposition—namely, that similar religious expressions are likely to stem from similar social situations and stimuli, and therefore can be used to reconstruct those situations—has been subjected to rigorous critique.

14. Most fully developed in G. Theissen, *The Social Setting of Early Palestinian Christianity* (Philadelphia: Fortress, 1978). A similar study of the possible correlation between articulated ideology and social location was undertaken by W. A. Meeks ("The Man from Heaven in Johannine Sectarianism," *JBL* 91 [1972]: 44–72), who argues that the peculiar Christology of John, who describes a messiah who is completely not at home in, and indeed experiences the hostility of, this world, reflects the social identity of the sectarians among whom these christological traditions were at home.

whom they needed to differentiate themselves carefully. Theissen proceeded, then, to analyze the social roles necessary to sustain such an itinerant circle; the socioeconomic, socioecological, sociopolitical, and sociocultural factors that contributed to its formation; and the functional effects upon society of the Palestinian Jesus movement. Theissen's *Social Setting of Early Palestinian Christianity* signaled in many ways the birth of social-scientific analysis of the NT.

A similar study was being simultaneously developed by Howard Clark Kee, focusing on the Gospel of Mark.[15] Kee addressed the form-critical question of the *Sitz im Leben* of Mark by positing a relationship between the kinds of traditions preserved in the Gospel and the life setting of the group that preserved those traditions. He also discovered a community of itinerant teachers at the center of this group and offered an interpretation of Mark's message as it would have applied to them and to the community formed around them.

After his groundbreaking work on the Synoptic Gospels, Theissen followed up with a series of studies on the Christian movement in Corinth.[16] He began with a thick description of the congregation at Corinth, a model of meticulous prosopography that challenged the notion that the early church was drawn mainly from the lowest strata of society. He further analyzed the problems addressed by Paul in Corinth (factions, involvement in eating foods sacrificed to idols, and the inappropriate celebration of the Lord's Supper) as a reflection of the varying practices and expectations of different status groups (mostly caused by the practices and expectations of the rich patrons of the community), and examined the issues of legitimation of authority at work in the conflict between Paul and rival itinerant missionaries.

Social-scientific investigation of Paul and his churches was also considerably advanced first by Bengt Holmberg, who used a Weberian typology of legitimate authority to analyze how Paul and other Christian leaders sought to establish power over particular congregations.[17] Even broader was the contribution by Wayne A. Meeks, who provided a thick description of the urban environment of Pauline Christianity (what was it like to live in a Greek or Roman city, and what would that social and cultural environment contribute to Paul the writer and to the life of the Christian churches who read him?), offered further analysis of the social level of the early Christians—adding the dimension of status inconsistency to the discussion of the strata from which early Christianity drew its constituency—and addressed several other pertinent questions: the group formation, social ethos, and governance of the church; the meaning, effect,

15. H. C. Kee, *Community of the New Age: Studies in Mark's Gospel* (Philadelphia: Westminster, 1977).

16. G. Theissen, *The Social Setting of Pauline Christianity: Essays on Corinth* (Philadelphia: Fortress, 1982).

17. B. Holmberg, *Paul and Power: The Structure of Authority in the Primitive Church as Reflected in the Pauline Epistles* (Philadelphia: Fortress, 1980).

and group-forming power of the rites of baptism and the Lord's Supper; and correlations between beliefs and social realities in the church.

John H. Elliott's work on 1 Peter brought social-scientific interpretation to a new level of methodological clarity. Also most welcome was his text-centered focus—the social sciences were being used here less to get at phenomena extrinsic to the text than to enable a deeper understanding of the strategy within the text and the social-formative power of its language and symbols.[18] Elliott displays a judicious use of appropriate models, seen, for example, in the choice of the model of sectarian tension developed by Rodney Stark and William Bainbridge and refined by Bryan Wilson, which analyzes the relationship of a sect to the host society, over the older model developed by Troeltsch of sect versus church, which would be anachronistic and inappropriate.[19]

Elliott's thick description of the status and situation of the addressees, close analysis of the particular social tensions reflected in 1 Peter, and examination of key terms used by the author to label or give identity to the addressees enable him to describe more fully than any predecessor the way 1 Peter is strategically crafted to help sustain the Christian communities in the face of those challenges. He also introduces rather prominently the "ideological" dimension of the text—the way in which the author or authors have advanced their own interests by means of this communication. Elliott's reflection on his own methodology allowed him to distill into a clear procedure the kinds of questions he has been enabled to ask by sociological exegesis,[20] the examination of which displays most clearly the benefits of this mode of interpretation: we ask questions of the text from angles previously unexplored, and, at least in Elliott's case, produce compelling results that will enrich future readings of the text for quite some time to come.

Perhaps the greatest achievement of social-scientific criticism is the new energy it has brought to biblical studies by means of opening up these new avenues of exploration. Such a pursuit has proved helpful for enriching our understanding of the pastoral and historical settings of churches for which we have no sure geographical location, such as my profile of the congregation(s) addressed by the Epistle to the Hebrews.[21] It continues to draw out from the texts

18. J. H. Elliott, *A Home for the Homeless: A Sociological Exegesis of 1 Peter, Its Situation and Strategy* (Philadelphia: Fortress, 1981; 2nd ed., 1990).

19. E. Troeltsch, *The Social Teaching of the Christian Churches* (London: Allen, 1931); Bryan R. Wilson, "An Analysis of Sect Development," in *Patterns of Sectarianism,* ed. B. Wilson (London: Heinemann, 1967), 22–45; R. Stark and W. S. Bainbridge, "Of Churches, Sects, and Cults: Preliminary Concepts for a Theory of Religious Movements," *JSSR* 18 (1979): 117–33; W. S. Bainbridge and R. Stark, "Sectarian Tension," *RRelRes* 22 (1980): 105–24.

20. See especially Elliott, *What Is Social-Scientific Criticism?* 72–74. Another very helpful resource in this regard is H. C. Kee's methodological introduction to this discipline, *Knowing the Truth: A Sociological Approach to New Testament Interpretation* (Minneapolis: Fortress, 1989), esp. 65–69.

21. D. A. deSilva, "The Epistle to the Hebrews in Social-Scientific Perspective," *ResQ* 36 (1994): 1–21.

new reflections of the situation and important aspects of the pastoral response previously given inadequate attention by a more idea-oriented or theologically focused exegesis. These advances can be seen in the work of J. Andrew Overman on the processes of legitimation and institutionalization at work in the Gospel of Matthew,[22] of Todd D. Still on conflict between the voluntary association called Christianity and the larger society in Thessalonica,[23] and in my articles on the struggle between John and other prophets over authority and the right to determine whether the churches in Asia Minor should move in a denominationalizing direction or remain in a position of sectarian tension toward the host society.[24] The creative use of the social sciences in NT interpretation has spurred on a new generation of students to ask these new questions from the vantage point of the shoulders of the giants of traditional scholarship.

Cultural Anthropology and New Testament Interpretation

In addition to sociological investigation of the NT, cultural-anthropological interpretation of the NT has blossomed in the last two decades. The goals and methods of this subdiscipline are geared toward discovering and explicating the typical roles, values, and cultural matrices of meaning that formed the cultural context of authors and audiences in a given locale in a given period. This enterprise is vital because communication, whether written or oral, leaves out more information than it makes explicit—information that an author or speaker assumes a hearer will be able to understand and supply from their shared cultural matrix. If a modern reader from within his or her cultural matrix fails to "make the leap" to the cultural matrix of those ancient communicators, he or she will supply the wrong information or apply the wrong scenarios to the scenes or exchanges being studied.

Although important precedents exist for using cross-cultural analysis to advance NT interpretation,[25] Bruce J. Malina holds pride of place as the pioneer of this line of investigation. Taking the work of cultural anthropologists such as Mary Douglas, Julian Pitt-Rivers, and J. G. Peristiany, who made substantial contributions to the study of honor, shame, purity, and pollution in Mediterranean and tribal cultures, Malina constructed a series of models of first-cen-

22. J. A. Overman, *Matthew's Gospel and Formative Judaism: The Social World of the Matthean Community* (Minneapolis: Fortress, 1990).

23. T. D. Still, *Conflict at Thessalonica: A Pauline Church and Its Neighbours*, JSNTSup 183 (Sheffield: Sheffield Academic Press, 1999).

24. D. A. deSilva, "The Social Setting of the Apocalypse of John: Conflicts Within, Fears Without," *WTJ* 54 (1992): 273–302; "The Revelation to John: A Case Study in Apocalyptic Propaganda and the Maintenance of Sectarian Identity," *Sociological Analysis* 53 (1992): 375–95; "The Image of the Beast and the Christians in Asia Minor," *TJ* 12, n.s. (1991): 185–206.

25. Notably, K. E. Bailey, *Poet and Peasant* (Grand Rapids: Eerdmans, 1976); *Through Peasant Eyes* (Grand Rapids: Eerdmans, 1980).

tury Mediterranean culture, drawing attention to the vast difference between assumptions and "given" ways of doing things in modern American culture and the ancient world.[26] He invited people to test these models for their ability to help modern readers enter the ancient Mediterranean NT texts more as native listeners, and many scholars responded to the invitation. A spate of articles and books followed, trying out and refining the new set of tools, perhaps the most valuable of which is Jerome H. Neyrey's edited collection of essays by members of the "Context Group."[27] This groundbreaking volume expanded the repertoire of cultural topics presented in Malina's *New Testament World* to include discussions of honor and shame, deviancy and labeling theory, preindustrial urban social relations, the relationship of countryside to city, disease and healing, organization of the temple and the household, patronage, purity codes, and rituals of status transformation, and it explored how each model shed new light on the interpretation of Luke-Acts.

The early work of Malina attracted criticism from both sociologists and other NT interpreters. For example, there was the models' lack of rootedness in ancient sources and texts: they did not derive from a "thick description" of the first century, but ultimately from the "thick description" of modern village life in various communities around the Mediterranean,[28] with the assumption that nothing had really changed much in two thousand years.[29]

Such critique generally has met with social-scientific investigators giving increased attention to grounding their models and analyses in ancient sources (or informants). The work of Carolyn Osiek and David Balch on the household as the matrix of early Christianity, for example, is rich in discussion of, and illustration by, archaeological and literary evidence from the Jewish and Greco-Roman environments,[30] as are several of the essays in Halvor Moxnes's volume on the family in the early church.[31] In my work, I have also sought to anchor the scholarly discussion of honor, patronage, kinship, and purity

26. See, most notably, B. J. Malina, *The New Testament World: Insights from Cultural Anthropology* (Louisville: Westminster John Knox, 1981; 2nd ed., 1993; 3rd ed., 2001). This program is carried forward in B. J. Malina and Richard Rohrbaugh, *Social-Science Commentary on the Synoptic Gospels* (Minneapolis: Fortress, 1992); J. J. Pilch and B. J. Malina, *Biblical Social Values and Their Meaning: A Handbook* (Peabody, Mass.: Hendrickson, 1993).

27. J. H. Neyrey, ed., *The Social World of Luke-Acts: Models for Interpretation* (Peabody, Mass.: Hendrickson, 1991).

28. J. G. Gager, "Culture as the Context for Meaning," review of *The New Testament World: Insights from Cultural Anthropology,* by B. J. Malina, *Int* 37 (1983): 194–97, esp. 196; noted also by Horrell, *Social-Scientific Approaches,* 14.

29. J. J. Meggitt, review of *The Social World of Jesus and the Gospels,* by Bruce J. Malina, *JTS* 49 (1998): 215–19.

30. C. Osiek and D. L. Balch, *Families in the New Testament World: Households and House Churches* (Louisville: Westminster John Knox, 1997).

31. Halvor Moxnes, ed., *Constructing Early Christian Families: Family as Social Reality and Metaphor* (London: Routledge, 1997); see especially the essays by J. M. G. Barclay, S. C. Barton, P. F. Esler, and R. Aasgaard.

in data from a broad spectrum of Jewish, Greek, and Roman literature and to refine the models proposed by Malina in light of this information. I hope in this way to close the gap between cultural-anthropological investigators and scholars who locate themselves in a more traditional paradigm (such as historical criticism).[32] My studies also seek to advance the discussion in the direction about which Stephen Barton raised some concern: "It remains to be seen, perhaps, whether social-scientific criticism will help revitalize New Testament theology and ethics as well."[33] Careful investigation of the cultural and social values of the NT world are shown to "provide models and motivation for believers today in their engagement in, and perhaps also confrontation of, the structures of . . . modern social life."[34]

Assessment

The agenda of sociologists and cultural anthropologists, together with the models derived from their work, have allowed interpreters to investigate the environment of the early church, the life and challenges of the early church, and the NT texts themselves from a variety of enriching angles that never would have occurred to biblical scholars without the interdisciplinary conversation that has emerged. The bibliographies cited earlier attest amply to the fruitfulness of this avenue of research and to the extent to which it has enriched our understanding of how the Word was made flesh in the lives of members of the early Christian communities. Insofar as social-scientific interpretation has opened up new, multidimensional strategies for understanding the NT texts as messages that have grown out of real-life situations and concerns and seek to have an impact on real-life behavior, it has equipped interpreters to become more sensitive hearers of the texts and less likely to impose anachronistic or ethnocentric readings upon the texts. It enables modern readers located in their own particular social and cultural contexts to make the jump more completely and accurately to hearing the NT texts within the framework of their social and cultural contexts, supplying more accurately the missing information shared and assumed by author and audience.

Nevertheless, like all venues of interpretation, this one is not without potential pitfalls. First, critics have questioned whether the nature and quantity of the available data are sufficient for true sociological investigation.[35] Can one do sociology without the possibility of live observation or of testing one's findings

32. D. A. deSilva, *Despising Shame: Honor Discourse and Community Maintenance in the Epistle to the Hebrews*, SBLDS 152 (Atlanta: Scholars Press, 1995); *Honor, Patronage, Kinship, and Purity: Unlocking New Testament Culture* (Downers Grove, Ill.: InterVarsity, 2000).

33. S. C. Barton, "Social-Scientific Criticism," 286.

34. Elliott, *What Is Social-Scientific Criticism?* 13.

35. See, for example, Cyril S. Rodd, "On Applying a Sociological Theory to Biblical Studies," *JSOT* 19 (1981): 95–106.

against living samples? Can one elicit reliable sociological data from texts that do not seek to answer questions posed from our social-scientific agenda (but rather seek to execute their own social and ideological agenda upon their audiences)? The limitations of the data do need to be acknowledged and evaluated carefully,[36] but it is no longer questionable that significant data exist.

Second, there is always the danger that any insufficiency of the data could lead to excessive dependence on models drawn from observation of modern groups to fill in the missing information. Moreover, since social-scientific interpreters generally apply models derived from the observation of modern religious and cultural phenomena to ancient civilizations and groups, the dangers of anachronism must be carefully assessed and guarded against. Gerd Theissen is right to point out, however, that those who use these models tend not to proceed without methodological caution.[37]

Third, several scholars caution against the deterministic use of models, on account of which several studies can be justifiably criticized. The models cease to be heuristic tools and become Procrustean beds upon which the texts are made to lie and to which they are made to conform. Of course, it is not only social-scientific criticism that runs into this danger, and even those who avoid the explicit use of any models still work with ideological or methodological presuppositions that are equally effective devices for making the texts fit their mental beds. Nevertheless, this caution is a welcome reminder of the need to continue to employ the models simply as tools by which to examine and sift the evidence in the texts and as resources by which to bring questions to the texts that we would not otherwise think to ask, as well as tools to discover the peculiarities of each specific situation, place, and culture rather than to make some ancient text a cipher for the model we bring to it (as when texts are used only to prove the validity of the model, rather than models being used to discover more about the text). John Barclay's study of the Mediterranean Diaspora is especially noteworthy as an example of the judicious use of models as heuristic devices to elicit and analyze texts without imposing extraneous meanings or forcing data.[38]

Fourth, there is the common charge of reductionism—making a religious phenomenon nothing more than a social phenomenon or regarding social causes and formative factors as the sum total of the causes and formative factors at work in the production of a text or the actions taken by a group or its members. Depending on one's ideological location, this could be a real danger. Those who deny any validity to the reality and purposes of the divine, or even fail to honor the potential innovations, vision, and achievements of a few creative individuals, could fall into this trap. Elliott rightly

---

36. See the judicious comments in Elliott, *What Is Social-Scientific Criticism?* 92–93.

37. G. Theissen, *Social Reality and the Early Christians* (Minneapolis: Fortress, 1992), 21.

38. J. M. G. Barclay, *Jews in the Mediterranean Diaspora from Alexander to Trajan* (Edinburgh: Clark, 1996).

counters, however, that the proper use of social-scientific interpretation as part of a larger program of exegesis is necessary to guard against another kind of reductionism, namely, seeing the text merely as a depository of timeless, revealed theological ideas and ethical instructions[39]—a reductionism to which evangelicals are particularly prone and against which we must guard as true witnesses to the incarnation.

Fifth, and perhaps the greatest concern about the method, is the ideological roots of sociology in "post-Enlightenment atheistic positivism."[40] It is a truism that sociologists of religion must "bracket out" the divine from consideration as an actor and agent in the phenomena they observe,[41] although this fact is but a methodological institutionalization of a post-Enlightenment worldview. Awareness of this bias, however, can free us from perpetuating it as we still engage social-scientific interpretation, which can be used as a tool for understanding faith rather than deconstructing it, and in fact can be harnessed as a means of discovering the resources used by the early church to nurture faith and develop strong communities of disciples—resources that would be useful for the same ends in new settings.[42]

For many, social-scientific interpretation will provide an avenue for investigating the NT apart from the environment of theology and Christian commitment. For many others, however, it will continue to bring the fruits of sociology and cultural anthropology into the detailed interpretation of the texts themselves, which probably is the central focus at least of evangelical scholarship.[43] As Elliott, one of the discipline's most visible proponents, emphasizes, it is but one phase of the exegetical process.[44] On the one hand, biblical interpreters are gaining greater facility in the field of sociology as the discipline as a whole is maturing, with the result that increasingly nuanced conclusions about the social and cultural contexts of early Christianity will emerge in the decades ahead. On the other hand, the interest in using social-scientific insights specifically to interpret the meaning and effects of the

39. Elliott, *What Is Social-Scientific Criticism?* 90.

40. Barton, "Social-Scientific Criticism," 280.

41. See the discussion of this topic in P. L. Berger, *The Sacred Canopy* (New York: Doubleday, 1967), 179–85.

42. Such a goal underlies the use of social and cultural topics as the context for hearing the NT in deSilva, *Honor, Patronage, Kinship, and Purity;* and idem, *New Testament Themes* (St. Louis: Chalice, 2001), although critical assessment of the achievement of these volumes is not yet available.

43. Perhaps the first full-fledged attempt to analyze the social environment of the early church from an evangelical perspective is Derek Tidball, *The Social Context of the New Testament: A Sociological Analysis* (Grand Rapids, Zondervan, 1984). Also noteworthy is Scot McKnight's contribution to the NIV Application Commentary, *1 Peter* (Grand Rapids: Zondervan, 1996), which fruitfully utilizes the work not only of J. H. Elliott but also of many other social-scientific theorists as he brings the situation and strategy behind 1 Peter to life. These works provide sure evidence that faith commitments and sociological analysis of the NT are not incompatible.

44. Elliott, *What Is Social-Scientific Criticism?* 7.

NT texts will continue to be facilitated through interdisciplinary exegetical paradigms, such as are brought together in the various forms of sociorhetorical interpretation.[45] As evangelicals involve themselves more robustly in this enterprise, moreover, we will be in less danger of recovering the "body" of the early church at the expense of the "soul."

45. This interdisciplinary program of interpretation is laid out in Vernon Robbins, *Exploring the Texture of Texts* (Valley Forge, Pa.: Trinity, 1996); its relationship to the recent and ongoing work of the whole spectrum of biblical scholarship is described extensively in idem, *The Tapestry of Early Christian Discourse* (London: Routledge, 1996); its potential for the interpretation of an entire biblical text is tested in D. A. deSilva, *Perseverance in Gratitude: A Socio-Rhetorical Commentary on the Epistle "to the Hebrews"* (Grand Rapids: Eerdmans, 2000). Ben Witherington III has also woven together social-scientific, rhetorical, and historical criticisms in his masterful exposition of 1 and 2 Corinthians, *Conflict and Community in Corinth* (Grand Rapids: Eerdmans, 1995), and of Galatians, *Grace in Galatia: A Socio-Rhetorical Commentary* (Grand Rapids: Eerdmans, 1999).

7

The Old Testament
in the New

Craig A. Evans

The OT is quoted or alluded to in every NT writing except Philemon and
2 and 3 John.[1] It appears in the NT in every conceivable manner. It is quoted
with introductory formulas ("it is written") and without. It is paraphrased
and alluded to. Sometimes the allusions comprise no more than a word or
two. Other times the NT reflects OT themes, structures, and theology. The
NT writers appeal to the OT for apologetic, moral, doctrinal, pedagogical,
and liturgical reasons. Only the gospel itself makes a greater contribution to
NT thought.

1. For principal bibliography, see C. H. Dodd, *According to the Scriptures* (New York: Scribner,
1952); B. Lindars, *New Testament Apologetic* (Philadelphia: Westminster, 1961); C. K. Barrett,
"The Interpretation of the Old Testament in the New," in *The Cambridge History of the Bible*,
ed. P. R. Ackroyd et al., 3 vols. (Cambridge: Cambridge University Press, 1963–70), 1:377–411;
D. M. Smith, "The Use of the Old Testament in the New," in *The Use of the Old Testament in the
New and Other Essays*, ed. J. Efird (Durham: Duke University Press, 1972), 3–65; H. M. Shires,
Finding the Old Testament in the New (Philadelphia: Westminster, 1974); R. N. Longenecker,
Biblical Exegesis in the Apostolic Period (Grand Rapids: Eerdmans, 1975); A. T. Hanson, *The
New Testament Interpretation of Scripture* (London: SPCK, 1980); D. A. Carson and H. G. M.
Williamson, eds., *It Is Written: Scripture Citing Scripture: Essays in Honour of Barnabas Lindars*
(Cambridge: Cambridge University Press, 1988); D. H. Juel, *Messianic Exegesis: Christological
Interpretation of the Old Testament in Early Christianity* (Philadelphia: Fortress, 1988); E. E. Ellis,
The Old Testament in Early Christianity, WUNT 54 (Tübingen: Mohr Siebeck, 1991; reprint,
Grand Rapids: Baker, 1992); R. Liebers, *"Wie geschrieben steht": Studien zu einer besonderen Art
frühchristlichen Schriftbezuges* (Berlin and New York: de Gruyter, 1993).

Jewish Exegesis in Late Antiquity

In late antiquity, Jewish exegesis took many forms.[2] It was pursued consciously and methodically, sometimes manifesting itself in informal, almost unconscious ways. There was no purely Jewish exegesis; rather, Jewish exegetes adopted and adapted forms and styles of interpretation of sacred literature practiced throughout the eastern Mediterranean world.[3] Nevertheless, a distinctive body of materials did emerge in Jewish circles, exemplifying interpretive approaches also found in the writings of the NT.

1. *Targum*.[4] When the canon of Scripture was viewed as more or less closed, the focus became increasingly textual. One way of interpreting the meaning of the text was to paraphrase it. This form of exegesis appears as *targum*, the Aramaic paraphrase of Scripture. Through paraphrase, text and interpretation are combined. (Even the LXX is a paraphrase, and so, in a sense, is a Targum.) Many of the paraphrasing NT quotations of the OT exemplify this form of Jewish exegesis and at many points reflect specific targumic traditions (compare Mark 4:12 with *Tg. Isa.* 6:10; Luke 6:36 with *Tg. Ps.-J.* Lev. 22:28; or Rom. 10:6–8 with *Tg. Neof.* Deut. 30:11–14).[5]

2. *Midrash*.[6] Midrash ("interpretation"; from *darash*, "to search" [see John 5:39]) entails searching the text for clarification beyond the

2. See G. Vermès, "Bible and Midrash: Early Old Testament Exegesis," in Ackroyd et al., *Cambridge History of the Bible*, 1:199–231; idem, *Scripture and Tradition in Judaism*, SPB 4 (Leiden: Brill, 1973); D. Patte, *Early Jewish Hermeneutic in Palestine*, SBLDS 22 (Missoula, Mont.: Scholars Press, 1975); M. Fishbane, *Biblical Interpretation in Ancient Israel* (Oxford: Oxford University Press, 1985); M. J. Mulder, ed., *Mikra: Text, Translation, Reading and Interpretation of the Hebrew Bible in Ancient Judaism and Early Christianity*, CRINT 2.1 (Assen: Van Gorcum; Philadelphia: Fortress, 1988); D. Boyarin, *Intertextuality and the Reading of Midrash* (Bloomington and Indianapolis: Indiana University Press, 1990); D. Instone Brewer, *Techniques and Assumptions in Jewish Exegesis before 70 C.E.*, TSAJ 30 (Tübingen: Mohr Siebeck, 1992); D. Marguerate and A. Curtis, eds., *Intertextualités: La Bible en échos*, Le Monde de la Bible 40 (Paris: Labor et Fides, 2000).

3. See S. Lieberman, *Hellenism in Jewish Palestine* (New York: Jewish Theological Seminary of America, 1962).

4. See J. Bowker, *The Targums and Rabbinic Literature* (Cambridge: Cambridge University Press, 1969). See now *The Aramaic Bible*, a multivolume set edited by M. McNamara.

5. See M. McNamara, *The New Testament and the Palestinian Targum to the Pentateuch*, AnBib 27 (Rome: Pontifical Biblical Institute, 1966); *Targum and Testament* (Grand Rapids: Eerdmans, 1972).

6. See S. Zeitlin, "Midrash: A Historical Study," *JQR* 44 (1953): 21–36; A. G. Wright, *The Literary Genre Midrash* (Staten Island: Alba, 1967); R. Le Déaut, "Apropos a Definition of Midrash," *Int* 25 (1971): 262–82; R. Bloch, "Midrash," in *Approaches to Ancient Judaism*, ed. W. S. Green, BJS 1 (Missoula, Mont.: Scholars Press, 1978), 29–50; G. G. Porton, "Defining Midrash," in *Study of Ancient Judaism*, ed. J. Neusner (New York: Ktav, 1981), 55–94; R. T. France and D. Wenham, eds., *Studies in Midrash and Historiography*, Gospel Perspectives 3 (Sheffield: JSOT Press, 1983); J. Neusner, *What Is Midrash?* (Philadelphia: Fortress, 1987).

obvious. In reference to the study of Scripture, a student of Hillel once said, "Turn it and turn it again, for everything is in it; and contemplate it and grow gray and old over it and do not stir from it, for you cannot have a better guide than it" (*m. ʾAbot* 5:22). The key statement here is "for everything is in it." This reflects the conviction of the midrashist. Scripture is to be searched and contemplated until the answer is found. Hillel followed seven rules (or *middoth*) for studying Scripture (*ʾAbot R. Nat.* 37; *t. Sanh.* 7.11). The most significant for NT study include *qal wahomer* ("light and heavy"), where what is true in a less important case certainly will be true in a more important case (see Matt. 7:11; Rom. 5:10); *gezera shawah* ("rule of equivalence"), where passages clarify one another if they share common vocabulary (see Rom. 4:7–8; 11:7–10); *kelal upherat* ("general and specific"), where a general rule may be deduced from a specific passage, and vice versa (see Rom. 13:8–10; Gal. 5:14). Jewish exegesis is halakic (i.e., concerned with legal matters, from *halak,* "[how to] walk") and haggadic (i.e., homiletical, from *haggadah,* "explanation," from the verb *nagad,* "to explain"). The former was chiefly the product of the academies, while the latter was chiefly the product of the synagogue, though there was much overlap. Midrash sometimes takes the form of a running commentary. One of the best examples in the NT is seen in John 6:25–59 (commenting on Exod. 16:4; Ps. 78:24; cf. John 6:31).[7]

3. *Pesher.*[8] At Qumran, Scripture was viewed as containing mysteries in need of explanation. The "pesher" was the explanation of the mystery: "the pesher of this [scripture] concerns the Teacher of Righteousness to whom God made known all the mysteries of the words of His servants the prophets" (1QpHab 7:4–5). It was assumed that the text spoke of and to the Qumran community, and that it spoke of eschatological events about to unfold. As in NT exegesis (see Mark 12:10–11 [citing Ps. 118:22–23]; 14:27 [citing Zech. 13:7]; Acts 2:17–21 [citing Joel 2:28–32]), pesher exegesis understands specific biblical passages as fulfilled in specific historical events and experiences.[9]

7. P. Borgen, *Bread from Heaven: An Exegetical Study of the Concept of Manna in the Gospel of John and the Writings of Philo,* NovTSup 10 (Leiden: Brill, 1965). For a survey of examples, see M. Gertner, "Midrashim in the New Testament," *JSS* 7 (1962): 267–92.

8. See J. A. Fitzmyer, "The Use of Explicit Old Testament Quotations in Qumran Literature and in the New Testament," *NTS* 7 (1961): 297–333; M. P. Horgan, *Pesharim: Qumran Interpretations of Biblical Books,* CBQMS 8 (Washington: Catholic Biblical Association, 1979); G. J. Brooke, *Exegesis at Qumran: 4QFlorilegium in Its Jewish Context,* JSOTSup 29 (Sheffield: JSOT Press, 1985); D. Dimant, "Pesharim, Qumran," *ABD* 5:244–51.

9. For a major comparison of pesher with NT exegesis, see K. Stendahl, *The School of St. Matthew and Its Use of the Old Testament,* ASNU 20 (Lund: Gleerup; Copenhagen: Munksgaard; rev. ed., Philadelphia: Fortress, 1968).

4. *Allegory.*[10] Allegorical interpretation involves extracting a symbolic meaning from the text. It assumes that a deeper, more sophisticated interpretation is to be found beneath the obvious letter of the passage. The allegorist does not, however, necessarily assume that the text is unhistorical or without a literal meaning. The exegesis is simply not concerned with this aspect of the biblical text. The best-known first-century allegorist was Philo of Alexandria, whose many books afford a wealth of examples of the allegorical interpretation of Scripture, primarily of the Pentateuch.[11] Allegorical interpretation is found in Qumran and in the rabbis. There is even some allegory in the NT. The most conspicuous example is Gal. 4:24–31, where Sarah and Hagar symbolize two covenants. Another example is found in 1 Cor. 10:1–4, where the crossing of the Red Sea symbolizes Christian baptism (though this aspect may be typological as well), and the rock symbolizes Christ.

5. *Typology.*[12] Typology is not so much a method of exegesis as it is a presupposition underlying the Jewish and Christian understandings of Scripture, particularly its historical portions. Typology is based on the belief that the biblical story (of the past) has some bearing on the present, or, to turn it around, that the present is foreshadowed in the biblical story. Unlike allegory, typology is closely tied to history. Even midrashic exegesis reflects this kind of understanding of Scripture. J. L. Kugel has described midrash as reflecting an "obsession with past events and the necessity of having them bear on the present."[13] He later says that Jewish exegesis wished to make the present "partake of (indeed, be continuous with) that comforting world of biblical history in which events made sense."[14] This is typological thinking, and to a certain extent it underlies pesher and allegorical exegesis as well. Popular Jewish eschatological expectation presupposed a typological understanding of Scripture. For example, in the messianic age, it was believed, the great wonders of the past would be reenacted. But typology is not without biblical precedent;

---

10. See J. Z. Lauterbach, "The Ancient Jewish Allegorists," *JQR* 1 (1911): 291–333; G. L. Bruns, "Midrash and Allegory: The Beginnings of Scriptural Interpretation," in *The Literary Guide to the Bible,* ed. R. Alter and F. Kermode (Cambridge: Harvard University Press, 1994), 625–46; D. M. Hay, "Defining Allegory in Philo's Exegetical World," *SBLSP* 33 (1994): 55–68.

11. See S. G. Sowers, *The Hermeneutics of Philo and Hebrews* (Richmond: John Knox, 1965); J. Morris, "Philo the Jewish Philosopher," in E. Schürer, *The History of the Jewish People in the Age of Jesus Christ (175 B.C.–A.D. 135),* ed. G. Vermès et al., 3 vols. in 4 (Edinburgh: Clark, 1973–87), 3.2:809–89, esp. 871–88.

12. G. von Rad, "Typological Interpretation of the Old Testament," in *Essays on Old Testament Hermeneutics,* ed. C. Westermann (Richmond: John Knox, 1963), 17–39; L. Goppelt, *Typos: The Typological Interpretation of the Old Testament in the New* (Grand Rapids: Eerdmans, 1982); Patte, *Early Jewish Hermeneutic,* 159–67.

13. J. L. Kugel, with R. A. Greer, *Early Biblical Interpretation,* LEC 3 (Philadelphia: Westminster, 1986), 38.

14. Ibid., 46.

it is rooted in the OT itself. The great event of the exodus serves as a type
for the postexilic return to the land of Israel (Isa. 43:16–17). David is a
type of the righteous king who would some day rule over restored Israel
(Isa. 11:1–3, 10; Jer. 23:5–6; Zech. 3:8). Jesus compares the judgment
that fell on Sodom with the coming eschatological judgment (Luke
17:28–30), the experience of Lot's wife with those who lose their life
(Luke 17:32–33), and Elijah with John the Baptist (Mark 9:13). Best
known is the comparison of Jonah's experience with that of Christ's burial
and resurrection (Matt. 12:40; Luke 11:30). Of all the writings in the
NT, Hebrews makes the most extensive use of typology.

Method

To determine how a NT writer has understood the OT passage being quoted
or alluded to, it is necessary to reconstruct as closely as possible the first-century
exegetical-theological discussion surrounding the OT passage in question. How
was the OT passage understood by early Christians and Jews? To answer this
question, every occurrence of the passage should be examined. This involves
study of the ancient versions themselves (MT, LXX, Targum) and citations of
the passage elsewhere in the NT, OT, apocrypha, pseudepigrapha, Qumran,
Josephus, Philo, and early rabbinic sources.[15] Some of these sources will prove to
be utterly irrelevant; others may significantly clarify the NT writer's exegesis. For
example, the citation and interpretation of Ps. 82:6–7 in John 10:34–36 cannot
be adequately explained by an appeal to the OT context alone. But when rabbinic
interpretation of this psalm is considered (*Sipre Deut.* §320 [on 32:20]; *Num.
Rab.* 16.24 [on 14:11]), its relevance to the Johannine context becomes clear.

Examples

We may consider a few examples from Jesus, the evangelists, Paul, and the
author of Hebrews. We will find the methods reviewed above at work in these
authors and writings.

1. *Jesus.*[16] With the resurgence of interest in the historical Jesus has come
a renewal of interest in Jesus' understanding and usage of the OT. Although

15. These respective bodies of literature are summarized and introduced in C. A. Evans,
Noncanonical Writings and New Testament Interpretation (Peabody, Mass.: Hendrickson, 1992).
For further discussion of method, see 1–8.

16. For general studies, see R. T. France, *Jesus and the Old Testament* (London: Tyndale,
1971); J. W. Wenham, *Christ and the Bible* (London: Tyndale, 1972); B. D. Chilton, *A Galilean
Rabbi and His Bible*, GNS 8 (Wilmington, Del.: Glazier, 1984); J. W. Wenham and C. A. Evans,
"Jesus and Israel's Scriptures," in *Studying the Historical Jesus: Evaluations of the State of Current
Research,* ed. Evans and Chilton, NTTS 19 (Leiden: Brill, 1994), 281–335.

not all agree, many have rightly recognized that the Jewish Scriptures lie at the heart of Jesus' message and self-understanding.

In a tantalizing exchange with John, the imprisoned baptizer asks Jesus, through messengers, "Are you the coming one, or shall we look for another?" (Matt. 11:3). Jesus replies with allusions to various passages from Isaiah: "Go and report to John what you hear and see: the blind receive sight and the lame walk, the lepers are cleansed and the deaf hear, and the dead are raised up, and the poor have the gospel preached to them" (Matt. 11:4b–5; cf. Luke 7:22). Jesus has alluded to Isa. 26:19; 35:5–6; 61:1. Jesus clearly means to reply to John's question in the affirmative, but was his reply messianic? Evidently it was, for we find the same passages clustered in a text from Qumran, in which similar activities are understood to take place when God's messiah comes, whom "heaven and earth will obey" (cf. 4Q521 frag. 2 ii 1–12). This scroll, which dates to the middle of the first century B.C.E., provides important documentation of messianic belief held among Jews living in Israel a generation or two before the time of Jesus' ministry. Simply by alluding to the same Isaianic passages, Jesus invoked eschatology and messianism in the minds of his hearers.

In his parable of the wicked vineyard tenants (Mark 12:1–9), the contents and context of which reflect bitter animosity between Jesus and the religious authorities of his day, Jesus alludes to Isaiah's Song of the Vineyard (Isa. 5:1–7), reflecting an understanding that cannot wholly derive from either the LXX or the Hebrew. Why should Jesus' opponents have understood his parable as directed against them (Mark 12:12), when Isa. 5:1–7 is directed against all of Judah? The Targum provides the missing link. According to its paraphrase, God built an "altar" and a "sanctuary" (instead of a "watchtower" and "wine vat") for his people.[17] But because of his people's sin, God will destroy their "sanctuaries." This threat of the destruction of the temple and altar makes the Isaianic passage particularly relevant for the temple authorities of Jesus' day. In view of the Targum's interpretation, therefore, Jesus' use of Isa. 5 in his parable is particularly appropriate, and the hostile reaction of his religious opponents is perfectly understandable.[18] The appearance of a similar understanding of Isa. 5 in 4Q500, which dates to the first century B.C.E., confirms the antiquity of this interpretive tradition.

2. *Matthew.*[19] Matthew's citations of the OT, customarily introduced with a fulfillment formula (Matt. 1:22; 2:15, 17, 23; 4:14; 8:17; 12:17; 13:14, 35;

---

17. The same exegesis appears in *t. Meʿil.* 1.16 and *t. Sukk.* 3.15, where the tower and wine vat are explicitly identified as "temple" and "altar," respectively. In *1 En.* 89.56–73, which probably predates the ministry of Jesus, the first and second temples are also referred to as towers.

18. For further discussion, see C. A. Evans, "On the Vineyard Parables of Isaiah 5 and Mark 12," *BZ* 28 (1984): 82–86; Chilton, *Galilean Rabbi,* 111–16.

19. For general studies, see N. Hillyer, "Matthew's Use of the Old Testament," *EvQ* 36 (1964): 12–26; R. H. Gundry, *The Use of the Old Testament in St. Matthew's Gospel,* NovTSup 18 (Leiden: Brill, 1967); Stendahl, *School of Matthew;* R. S. McConnell, *Law and Prophecy in Matthew's Gospel: The Authority and Use of the Old Testament in the Gospel of St. Matthew,* Theologische Dissertationen 2 (Basel: Reinhardt, 1969).

21:4; 27:9), are among the most controversial in the NT. The two that will be considered here offer an assortment of difficulties and thus, for the purpose of this essay, make excellent test cases.

In Matt. 2:13–15 the evangelist tells the story of Jesus' family's flight to Egypt, the place where they were to remain "until the death of Herod" (v. 15a). Jesus' departure from Egypt, Matthew tells us, fulfills a prophecy: "Out of Egypt I have called my son" (v. 15b). The quotation comes from Hos. 11:1b, but from the Hebrew, not the LXX (". . . I called his children"). Matthew's Greek translation is quite literal, but his application is problematic. Hosea, as the context makes quite clear, is looking back to the exodus, not to a future deliverance. Indeed, the Hosean context is judgmental, not salvific. Moreover, God's "son" is Israel (see Hos. 11:1a), not Israel's messiah. If Hos. 11:1 is not messianic, why has the evangelist applied the passage to Jesus?[20] The reference in Hos. 11:1a to Israel as a "child" (MT: *na'ar*) or "infant" (LXX: *nēpios*) may explain in part why the evangelist perceived the relevance of this passage for the infancy narrative. But by itself the text is neither messianic nor predictive. However, when read in light of the similar passage from LXX Num. 24:7–8a ("There shall come a man out of his seed, and he shall rule over many nations. . . . God led him out of Egypt"), its messianic and predictive potential becomes clear. Matthew is not appealing to Hos. 11:1b only, but to LXX Num. 24:8a as well.[21] Appealing to one text interpreted in the light of another is a form of exegesis that is not foreign to Jewish exegetical practices of the time. A messianic application of the text is also facilitated by the assumption that references to David may sometimes be taken as references to all of Israel. This is seen clearly in *Midr. Ps.* 24.3 (on Ps. 24:1): "Our Masters taught: In the Book of Psalms, all the Psalms which David composed apply either to himself or to all of Israel." The midrash goes on to say that in some instances the Davidic psalm may have application for the "Age to Come" (the messianic age).[22] If David and Israel were thus identified, and if David was also understood as a type for the messiah (see Matt. 1:1, 17), it is not hard to see how Matthew saw messianic potential in Hos. 11:1. The saying of Rabbi Yoḥanan, though uttered in the post-NT era, probably reflects what was assumed by many in the first century: "Every prophet prophesied only for the days of the Messiah" (*b. Ber.* 34b).

---

20. The claim of S. V. McCasland ("Matthew Twists the Scriptures," *JBL* 80 [1961]: 143–48, esp. 144, 145) that the evangelist "misunderstood" the passage is not helpful, for no explanation is offered. We should assume that Matthew followed the exegetical conventions of his day, and therefore Matthean exegesis should be assessed accordingly. McCasland's essay throughout betrays a limited understanding of first-century exegesis and application of Scripture, as well as ignorance of the pluralism of the text of Scripture in pre-70 Israel.

21. So B. Lindars, *New Testament Apologetic* (Philadelphia: Westminster, 1961), 216–17.

22. Quotation is from W. G. Braude, *The Midrash on Psalms*, 2 vols., Yale Judaica 13 (New Haven: Yale University, 1959), 1:338; see also *Midr. Ps.* 4.1 (on 4:1–2); 18.1 (on 18:1); *b. Pesaḥ.* 117a. These texts postdate the NT by several generations but probably preserve some interpretive assumptions that reach back to the first century, if not earlier.

Moreover, rabbinic exegesis of Hos. 11:1 itself may shed further light on why Matthew would apply this OT passage to the infant Jesus. In several passages (*Sipre Deut.* §305 [on 31:7]; *Exod. Rab.* 43.9 [on 32:7]; *Num. Rab.* 12.4 [on 7:1]; *Deut. Rab.* 5.7 [on 16:18]; *Pesiq. Rab.* 26.1–2) the rabbis understand Hosea's reference to "son" as a reference to Israel's innocence and youth, even infancy. Matthew has not exegeted Hos. 11:1 in a strict linguistic, contextual, and historical sense. His is an exegesis of typology and "resignification"—that is, finding a new element or dimension in the older tradition. This aspect of his exegesis conforms completely with what is observed in the Jewish exegesis of his day. Matthew has (re)interpreted Scripture in light of what God has accomplished (or "fulfilled") in his Messiah.[23]

In Matt. 27:3–10 the evangelist tells us that the purchase of the potter's field with the betrayer's thirty pieces of silver fulfilled something spoken by "Jeremiah" (vv. 9–10). The citation, however, is based loosely on Zech. 11:12–13, although it does parallel Jeremiah in places (18:1–3; 19:11; 32:6–15),[24] and possibly borrows from LXX Exod. 9:12 ("as the Lord directed") as well. We face here the same problem as in the preceding example. The passages in Zechariah and Jeremiah are not predictions of the purchase of a potter's field with blood money, whether we take the parts of the quotation separately or in combination. Zechariah describes the prophet's actions of casting thirty pieces of silver into the temple treasury (or to the potter—the MT is uncertain), while Jeremiah makes mention of the potter, a place of burial, and the subsequent purchase of the potter's field. As in the preceding example, Matthew has made use of two or more Scriptures and in doing so has resignified them. Apparently, he has understood the actions of the prophets Zechariah and Jeremiah in a typological or pesher sense. That is, by casting thirty pieces of silver into the temple treasury, and by purchasing the potter's field, Judas and the temple priests have reenacted the scriptural story.[25] It is in this sense that prophecy has been fulfilled.

3. *Mark.*[26] Unlike Matthew and John, Mark rarely quotes the OT outside of what is likely the tradition that he received. Other than the conflated quotation

---

23. For further discussion, see G. M. Soarés Prabhu, *The Formula Quotations in the Infancy Narrative of Matthew*, AnBib 63 (Rome: Biblical Institute Press, 1976), 216–28; R. H. Gundry, *Matthew: A Commentary on His Literary and Theological Art* (Grand Rapids: Eerdmans, 1982), 33–34.

24. Gundry (*Matthew*, 558; *Use of the Old Testament*, 122–27) thinks that the evangelist is dependent on Jer. 19 rather than on Jer. 18:1–3; 32:6–15.

25. One thing seems clear here. The Gospel tradition cannot be based on an inference from OT materials, as McCasland ("Matthew Twists the Scriptures," 145) thinks. The awkward appeal to Zechariah and Jeremiah suggests just the opposite: the evangelist works from Gospel tradition to the OT.

26. For general studies, see H. Anderson, "The Old Testament in Mark's Gospel," in Efird, *Use of the Old Testament*, 280–309; W. S. Vorster, "The Function and Use of the Old Testament in Mark," *Neot* 14 (1981): 62–72; M. D. Hooker, "Mark," in Carson and Williamson, *It Is Written*, 220–30.

of LXX Exod. 23:20//Mal. 3:1//LXX Isa. 40:3 at the opening of Mark (1:2–3), and a few allusions in the passion (15:24, 29, 36), OT quotations are limited to statements of Jesus (e.g., 4:12; 7:6–7, 10; 8:18; 11:17). Even in the case of the citation in 1:2–3 and the allusions in the passion, it is likely that these are traditional elements also. But this is not to say that the OT is unimportant to the evangelist. In many places OT passages and themes underlie the Markan narrative.[27]

A specific example of the allusive presence of the OT is found in the transfiguration story (Mark 9:2–8), which at several points parallels Sinai tradition: (1) The phrase "after six days" (v. 2) alludes to Exod. 24:16, where after six days God speaks. (2) Just as Moses is accompanied by three companions (Exod. 24:9), so Jesus is accompanied by Peter, James, and John (v. 2). (3) In both accounts, an epiphany takes place on a mountain (v. 2; Exod. 24:12) (4) Moses figures in both accounts (v. 4; Exod. 24:1–18). It is interesting to note that on one occasion Joshua (LXX: "Jesus") accompanied Moses on the mountain (Exod. 24:13). (5) Jesus' personal transfiguration (v. 3) probably parallels the transfiguration of Moses' face (Exod. 34:29–30). Matthew and Luke apparently have seen this parallel, for they draw a closer correspondence by noting the alteration of Jesus' "face" (Matt. 17:2; Luke 9:29). (6) In both accounts the divine presence is attended by a cloud (v. 7; Exod. 24:15–16). Some believed that the cloud that had appeared to Moses would reappear in the last days (see 2 Macc. 2:8). (7) In both accounts the heavenly voice speaks (v. 7; Exod. 24:16). (8) Fear is common to both stories (v. 6; Exod. 34:30; cf. *Tg. Ps.-J.* Exod. 24:17). (9) Mark's "Hear him" (v. 7), unparalleled in Exod. 24, probably echoes Deut. 18:15. Again it is likely that Luke has noticed the parallel, for he makes the word order correspond to that of the LXX (Luke 9:35). These parallels, especially that of the injunction to hear, may suggest that the voice that spoke with authority from Sinai now speaks through Jesus the Son.[28]

4. *Luke-Acts.*[29] The OT functions in the writings of the Lukan evangelist in ways that are clearly distinct from the other three Gospels. He does not

27. For studies that claim to have found extensive OT typology underlying Mark, see A. Farrer, *A Study in St. Mark* (New York: Oxford University, 1952); U. Mauser, *Christ in the Wilderness: The Wilderness Theme in the Second Gospel and Its Basis in the Biblical Tradition,* SBT 39 (London: SCM, 1963). These studies, however, have not won general acceptance. However the purpose of the Markan evangelist's usage of the OT is to be understood, certainly numerous allusions to OT passages and themes are present; see H. C. Kee, *Community of the New Age: Studies in Mark's Gospel* (Philadelphia: Westminster, 1977), 45–49.

28. For further discussion, see W. L. Liefeld, "Theological Motifs in the Transfiguration Narrative," in *New Dimensions in New Testament Study,* ed. R. N. Longenecker and M. C. Tenney (Grand Rapids: Zondervan, 1974), 162–79.

29. For general studies, see T. Holtz, *Untersuchungen über die alttestamentlichen Zitate bei Lukas,* TU 104 (Berlin: Akademie, 1968); G. D. Kilpatrick, "Some Quotations in Acts," in *Les Actes des Apôtres: Traditions, rédaction, théologie,* ed. J. Kremer, BETL 48 (Gembloux: Duculot, 1979), 81–87; E. Richard, "The Old Testament in Acts," *CBQ* 42 (1980): 330–41; J. Jervell, "The Center of Scripture in Luke," in *The Unknown Paul* (Minneapolis: Augsburg, 1984),

punctuate the tradition with proof texts as do Matthew and John; rather, he punctuates his narrative with speeches that are often made up almost entirely of OT words and phrases (especially the speeches and canticles in the birth narrative). Another distinctive feature is Luke's dependence upon the LXX. Indeed, the evangelist deliberately imitates the style of the Greek OT.[30] But this imitation does not simply involve style; it also involves substance. One of the clearest examples of this imitation in Luke is seen in Jesus' birth narrative: (1) The angelic announcement of 1:32–33 alludes to the Davidic covenant (2 Sam. 7:9–16) and finds a remarkable parallel in an Aramaic text from Qumran (i.e., 4Q246).[31] (2) The progress reports on Jesus in 2:40 and 2:52 echo the similar reports on the young Samuel (1 Sam. 2:26; 3:19; and on John in Luke 1:80). Indeed, at other points in the narrative, there are echoes of the Samuel story (cf. 1 Sam. 1:22 with Luke 2:22; 1 Sam. 2:20 with Luke 2:34). (3) The Magnificat itself, 1:46–55 (cf. Anna's song in 2:36–38), is modeled to a certain extent after Hannah's song of thanksgiving (1 Sam. 2:1–10), which in the Targum is eschatologized.[32]

Two chapters of birth narratives notwithstanding, Luke views the ministry of John as the beginning of the Gospel story (see Acts 10:37: "beginning from Galilee after the baptism that John preached"; cf. 1:22), so it is likely that redactional activity at this point carries with it implications for his Gospel as a whole. Lukan redaction of Mark's opening citation (Mark 1:2–3; Luke 3:4–6) justifies this claim. Luke omits the Mal. 3:1//Exod. 23:20 preface (which appears later in 7:27), but extends Isa. 40:3 to vv. 4–5, so as to conclude, "and all flesh will see the salvation of God." This part of the quotation, found only in the LXX, obviously contributes to Luke's emphasis on the Gentile mission and the universal proclamation of the gospel (see also Acts 13:23–26; 28:28). Moreover, as is clear from usage at Qumran and elsewhere (1QS 8:12–14; 9:19–20; Bar. 5:7; As. Mos. 10:1–5), Isa. 40:3–5 is understood eschatologically (an understanding clearly presupposed by the NT), and not as a reference to Israel's postexilic restoration (the original import of Second Isaiah). It is ap-

---

122–37; H. Ringgren, "Luke's Use of the Old Testament," *HTR* 79 (1986): 227–35; D. L. Bock, *Proclamation from Prophecy and Pattern: Lucan Old Testament Christology,* JSNTSup 12 (Sheffield: Sheffield Academic Press, 1987); C. A. Kimball, *Jesus' Exposition of the Old Testament in Luke's Gospel,* JSNTSup 94 (Sheffield: Sheffield Academic Press, 1994).

30. This has been commonly observed; see W. G. Kümmel, *Introduction to the New Testament,* trans. A. J. Mattill, 14th rev. ed. (Nashville: Abingdon, 1966), 95, 98; J. A. Fitzmyer, *The Gospel according to Luke I–IX,* AB 28 (Garden City: Doubleday, 1981), 114–16; T. L. Brodie, "Greco-Roman Imitation of Texts as a Partial Guide to Luke's Use of Sources," in *Luke-Acts: New Perspectives from the Society of Biblical Literature Seminar,* ed. C. H. Talbert (New York: Crossroad, 1984), 17–46.

31. See Fitzmyer, *Luke I–IX,* 338; idem, "4Q246: The 'Son of God' Document from Qumran," *Bib* 74 (1993): 153–74.

32. See D. J. Harrington, "The Apocalypse of Hannah: Targum Jonathan of 1 Samuel 2:1–10," in *"Working with No Data": Semitic and Egyptian Studies Presented to Thomas O. Lambdin,* ed. D. M. Golomb (Winona Lake, Ind.: Eisenbrauns, 1987), 147–52.

parent also that Luke weaves key words and phrases from this citation (and Mal. 3:1) into the fabric of other parts of his Gospel.[33] Not only do some of these allusions apply to the Baptist, as one would expect (see 1:17, 76–79), but some of them apply to Jesus as well. This is seen in 2:30–31 ("my eyes have seen your salvation which you have prepared in the presence of [lit., 'in the face of'] all peoples") and in 9:52 ("he sent messengers ahead of him [lit., 'before his face']"). The important point is that Luke has applied this Isaianic text to Jesus, and not only to John (as in the other Gospels). The allusion in the Nunc Dimittis suggests that the theme of Isa. 40 applies to the whole of Jesus' anticipated ministry as much as it does to John's, while the allusion in 9:52 provides a specific example of this theme being actualized. Jesus is now on his way to Jerusalem, and he has sent messengers on ahead to prepare his way. What is important here is to realize that the evangelist Luke has applied the promise of Isa. 40:3–5 to Jesus as well as to John. It is for this reason, as well as for his universal concerns, that he extends the citation to verse 5. Whereas the preparation of the way is John's task, the "salvation of all flesh" is accomplished only in Jesus, John's successor.

5. *John.*[34] At first glance, John's use of the OT appears to be about the same as Matthew's. Like Matthew, John formally quotes the OT several times, many times in "fulfillment" of something. But in other important ways the OT functions in John quite differently. Even in the case of the quotation formulas, John's purpose runs along very different lines. Unlike Matthew, John's formulas appear to make up a pattern, one that accentuates the theological development of the Gospel narrative. In the first half of his Gospel, the evangelist introduces Scripture in a variety of ways, though usually using the word "written" (1:23; 2:17; 6:31, 45; 7:38, 42; 8:17; 10:34; 12:14). In the second half he invariably introduces Scripture "in order that it be fulfilled" (12:38, 39–40; 13:18; 15:25; 19:24, 28, 36, 37).[35] What is the meaning of this pattern? The answer may be deduced from the summary in 12:37 and the citation that follows in verse 38: "Though he had done so many signs before them, yet they did not believe in him, in order that the word of Isaiah . . . be fulfilled. . . ." The "signs" to which reference is made are those of the first half of the Gospel.

33. For a fuller discussion, see K. R. Snodgrass, "Streams of Tradition Emerging from Isaiah 40:1–5 and Their Adaptation in the New Testament," *JSNT* 8 (1980): 24–45, esp. 36–40.

34. For general studies, see C. K. Barrett, "The Old Testament in the Fourth Gospel," *JTS* 48 (1947): 155–69; C. Goodwin, "How Did John Treat His Sources?" *JBL* 73 (1954): 61–75; R. Morgan, "Fulfillment in the Fourth Gospel," *Int* 11 (1957): 155–65; E. D. Freed, *Old Testament Quotations in the Gospel of John,* NovTSup 11 (Leiden: Brill, 1965); G. Reim, *Studien zum alttestamentlichen Hintergrund des Johannesevangelium,* SNTSMS 22 (Cambridge: Cambridge University Press, 1974); C. A. Evans, *Word and Glory: On the Exegetical and Theological Background of John's Prologue,* JSNTSup 89 (Sheffield: JSOT Press, 1993).

35. The verb that is used is πληροῦν, except in 19:28, where the synonym τελειοῦν is used (possibly to complement τετέλεσται ["it is finished"] in vv. 28 and 30). The citations in 12:39 and 19:37 are not exceptions, for they are connected to the citations that precede them (as πάλιν ["again"] makes clear).

The scriptural citations in the first half of the Gospel demonstrate that Jesus conducted his ministry in keeping with scriptural expectation ("as it is written"). For example, Jesus' zeal for the temple is related to Ps. 69:9, the feeding of the five thousand is related to Ps. 78:24, his appeal to the testimony of two witnesses is related to Deut. 17:6 (or 19:15), his claim to be God's Son is related to Ps. 82:6, and his riding the donkey is related to Zech. 9:9. In some of these instances the evangelist could have introduced the OT citation as a fulfillment (cf. the citation of Zech. 9:9 in Matt. 21:4–5), but he did not. It is not until Jesus is rejected, despite his signs, that the Scriptures are said to be "fulfilled." It is in Jesus' rejection and crucifixion that the Scriptures find their ultimate fulfillment. Far from proving that Jesus did not fulfill the Scriptures, and so could not be Israel's messiah, Jewish unbelief and obduracy specifically fulfilled Isa. 53:1 ("Lord, who believed . . . ?") and Isa. 6:10 ("He blinded their eyes . . ."). With each action taken against Jesus, including the treachery of Judas, Scripture is fulfilled. It is apparent that John wishes to show that it is in his passion, Jesus' "hour of glorification" (John 17:1), that the Scriptures are truly fulfilled.[36]

Allusions to the OT also have an important function in John's Gospel. The opening words, "in the beginning," are meant to echo those of Gen. 1:1. According to John 1:1–2, the world is created through an intermediary, the Word (*ho logos*). This concept probably reflects Jewish exegesis of Genesis as seen in *Tg. Neof.* Gen. 1:1: "From the beginning with wisdom the Word [*memra*] of the Lord perfected the heavens and the earth"[37] (see also Prov. 8:22–31; Wisd. 8:3–4). Throughout the creation account it is the "Word of the Lord" that acts.[38] Not only did the Word of the Lord create the light (Gen. 1:3), but also, according to *Targum Neofiti's* expanded paraphrase of Exod. 12:24, "the Word of the Lord was the light and it shone" (see also the *Fragmentary Targum*). Just as God sent light into the world at the time of creation, so at the time of redemption he sent his Son, the light of the world (John 8:12; 9:5),

36. For further details of this exegesis, see C. A. Evans, "On the Quotation Formulas of the Fourth Gospel," *BZ* 26 (1982): 79–83.

37. There is some textual uncertainty here. The opening verse may actually read: "From the beginning with wisdom the Son of the Lord perfected. . . ."

38. In the past it frequently has been claimed that the targumic *memra* has nothing to do with John's prologue, since it is a circumlocution for the divine name and not a reference to an intermediary being. Recent studies, however, have offered compelling evidence and reasons for reassessing this claim; see Le Déaut, "Targumic Literature and New Testament Interpretation," *BTB* 4 (1974): 266–69; McNamara, *Targum and Testament,* 101–6. In my judgment, the Johannine evangelist has taken over the *memra* concept in conjunction with ideas of the personification of God's wisdom (note that the targum says, "In the beginning with wisdom the Word. . . ."). See especially Sir. 24, where Wisdom says that she has come "forth from the mouth of the Most High" (v. 3), has existed from "the beginning" (v. 9), and has pitched her "tent" in Israel (v. 8) and rested in Jerusalem (v. 11). These wisdom parallels certainly form part of the background to the Johannine prologue. But the evangelist has chosen the masculine targumic appellation "Word," rather than the feminine "Wisdom."

to enlighten humankind (John 1:4–5, 9).[39] Significant allusions are found elsewhere in John's prologue. In 1:14–18 the Sinai story is contrasted with Jesus. Whereas the law was given through Moses, grace and truth were made available through Jesus the Messiah (1:17). The words of verse 17, "grace and truth," are first mentioned in verse 14: "And the Word became flesh and dwelt among us, full of grace and truth." The phrase "full of grace and truth" probably is an allusion to the words of Exod. 34:6 (*rab-ḥesed weˀĕmet*), uttered when God passed before Moses. Moses, however, was permitted no more than a fleeting glimpse of God's passing back (Exod. 33:20–23), for no one can see God and live (33:20; cf. also John 12:41 with *Tg. Isa.* 6:1). The only Son, by contrast, not only has seen God (so it is implied), but also eternally resides in the bosom (i.e., the "front side") of the Father (John 1:18; cf. Sir. 43:31).[40] Hence, Jesus is in a position to disclose God's will in a way that not even the great Lawgiver himself can equal.[41]

6. *Paul.*[42] Paul quotes the Scriptures some one hundred times and alludes to them many more times. Both the Dead Sea Scrolls and the Targumim have recently aided our understanding of Paul's use of the OT.

One of the most debated issues in Pauline theology has to do with the background of Paul's criticism of those who advocate "works of law" (*erga nomou*). Is Paul criticizing an actual position held by some of his Jewish contemporaries, or has he created a straw man in his polemic in Gal. 2–3 and Rom. 4? The recent publication of 4QMMT ("some of the works of the law") has offered dramatic proof that the position that Paul attacked was indeed held in his time. According to 4QMMT, if the faithful observe the law properly, especially with respect to the "works of the law," about which the author(s) of

39. For more details of this exegesis, see M. McNamara, "*Logos* of the Fourth Gospel and *Memra* of the Palestinian Targum (Ex 12:42)," *ExpTim* 79 (1968): 115–17; idem, *Targum and Testament,* 101–4.

40. This then explains why the preposition *pros* (instead of *syn,* the usual preposition that means "with") is used in the opening verse of the prologue: "In the beginning was the Word, and the Word was *pros* God"—that is, the Word was *facing* God.

41. For more on this exegesis, see Hanson, *New Testament Interpretation of Scripture,* 97–109. For more on Moses in John, see R. H. Smith, "Exodus Typology in the Fourth Gospel," *JBL* 81 (1962): 329–42; T. F. Glasson, *Moses in the Fourth Gospel,* SBT 40 (London: SCM, 1963); W. A. Meeks, *The Prophet-King: Moses Traditions and the Johannine Christology,* NovTSup 14 (Leiden: Brill, 1967). On John's allusive use of Isaiah, see F. W. Young, "A Study of the Relation of Isaiah to the Fourth Gospel," *ZNW* 46 (1955): 215–33; C. A. Evans, "Obduracy and the Lord's Servant: Some Observations on the Use of the Old Testament in the Fourth Gospel," in *Early Jewish and Christian Exegesis,* ed. C. A. Evans and W. F. Stinespring, Homage 10 (Atlanta: Scholars Press, 1987), 221–36, esp. 226–36.

42. For general studies, see E. E. Ellis, *Paul's Use of the Old Testament* (Grand Rapids: Eerdmans, 1957; reprint, Grand Rapids: Baker, 1981); N. Flanagan, "Messianic Fulfillment in St. Paul," *CBQ* 19 (1957): 474–84; A. T. Hanson, *Studies in Paul's Technique and Theology* (London: SPCK, 1974), 136–278; R. B. Hays, *Echoes of Scripture in the Letters of Paul* (New Haven and London: Yale University Press, 1989); C. A. Evans and J. A. Sanders, *Paul and the Scriptures of Israel,* JSNTSup 83, SSEJC 1 (Sheffield: JSOT Press, 1993).

this letter wrote, they "will rejoice in the end time," when they discover that their obedience "will be reckoned to (them) as righteousness" (4Q398 frags. 14–17 ii 7 = 4Q399 frag. 1 ii 4). Paul, of course, argues in precisely the opposite direction, contending that it is faith, not works of law, that will result in being reckoned righteous. There are only two passages in the Hebrew Bible where we find "reckoned" and "righteousness": Ps. 106:30–31 and Gen. 15:6. In the first passage, Phinehas the priest is reckoned righteous because of his zeal (i.e., his lawful work), while in the second passage, Abraham is reckoned righteous because of his faith in God. Paul appeals to Abraham, while the priestly author of 4QMMT appeals to the example of Phinehas![43]

A second example involves the allusion to Deut. 30:12–14 in Rom. 10:6–8. Paul's exegesis strikes some interpreters as odd. Whereas Moses spoke of God's "commandment" not being too far off (either up in heaven or beyond the sea), so that failure to obey it cannot be excused, Paul speaks of Christ. As unusual as Paul's exegesis appears, it is not entirely novel. The author of Baruch has alluded to this passage from Deuteronomy, and has applied it to Wisdom: "Who has gone up into heaven, and taken her, and brought her down from the clouds? Who has gone over the sea, and found her?" (Bar. 3:29–30). However, Baruch's usage leaves some components of Paul's exegesis unclear.

M. McNamara rightly calls attention to the paraphrase of Deut. 30:12–13 in the *Fragmentary Targum*. He translates (with italics showing departures from the Hebrew): "The Law is not in heaven that one may say: '*Would that we had one like the prophet Moses who would ascend to heaven and fetch it for us* and make us hear the commandments that we might do them.' Neither is the Law beyond the Great Sea that one may say: '*Would that we had one like the prophet Jonah who would descend into the depths of the Great Sea and bring it up for us* and make us hear the commandments that we might do them.'"[44] The point of the Hebrew is that the law has been given once and for all; there is no need for a prophet to ascend to heaven or to traverse the sea to obtain it. The Aramaic paraphrase illustrates this point with two biblical characters whose experiences roughly match the language of the passage. Moses, it was believed, had ascended to heaven when he received the law from God. For example, in *Tg. Ps.-J.* Deut. 34:5 we are told that Moses "brought it [the law] from heaven"; and in *Pesiq. Rab.* 4:2, "Moses went up to heaven" (see also *Bib. Ant.* 15:6; 2 Esdr. 3:17–18). These traditions are based on Exod. 19:3, 20, where God summons Moses to meet him on the mountain. The reference to the sea, of course, provides the link to Jonah. In fact, the Targum's "descend into the depths" draws the OT passage into closer alignment with Jonah's experience, for the prophet did not go across the sea, he went down into it (see the reference to "abyss" in Jon. 2:3; cf. v. 6). In the NT, of course, both Moses and Jonah are compared to Christ, specifically at points that are relevant to

43. See M. G. Abegg, "'Works of the Law' and MMT," *BAR* 20, no. 6 (1994): 52.
44. McNamara, *Palestinian Targum to the Pentateuch*, 74–75.

the traditions just reviewed. Like Moses, Jesus brings a new law from heaven (Mark 9:2–8; John 3:13–14; 1:17); like Jonah, Jesus descends into the abyss (Matt. 12:39–40; 16:4; Luke 11:29–30). Paul presupposes these Jewish and Christian traditions (cf. Eph. 4:8–10) and has combined them in his own way. His point in Rom. 10:4–13 is that Christ has accomplished salvation. All that is now required is faith. No one needs to ascend to heaven to bring Christ down, for he has already descended. No one needs to descend into the abyss to raise him up, for he has already been resurrected. Redemption has been accomplished. All that remains is the confession of faith (Rom. 10:8–10, citing and interpreting Deut. 30:14). By faith in what God has accomplished through Christ, God's righteousness may be obtained.[45]

7. *Hebrews.*[46] Although several studies have looked to Philo[47] or Qumran[48] as the background against which Hebrews might be understood, the exegesis of its author is neither allegory nor pesher. Its author has developed his own style of typological exegesis in which he compares Christ and the church against OT figures and institutions. Unlike midrash, pesher, or even allegory, typology is primarily interested in biblical events, not the biblical text. He cites or alludes to the OT approximately sixty times, usually following the LXX, and often citing the Psalter.[49] His most important typological comparisons include Moses/Christ (3:2–6), Melchizedek/Christ (7:1–28), and old covenant/new covenant (8:1–9:28). The discovery of *Melchizedek* (11QMelch), which anticipates the arrival of an eschatological Melchizedek who in some sense is divine clarifies why the author of Hebrews found it useful to appeal to this OT worthy to develop the theme of Jesus' superior priesthood.

Hebrews' quotation formulas vary considerably. Scripture is the utterance of the Holy Spirit (3:7), or of Moses (12:21). Usually, Scripture is introduced as "he says" or "he said" (1:5, 6, 7, 13; 2:12; 3:15; 4:3, 4, 7; 5:5; 6:14; 7:21; 8:5, 8; 9:20; 10:5, 8, 15, 30; 11:18; 13:5), as though it were spoken by God himself. From this we may infer that the author of Hebrews believed Scrip-

---

45. For more details of this exegesis, see ibid., 70–78.

46. For general studies, see R. Rendall, "The Method of the Writer to the Hebrews in Using OT Quotations," *EvQ* 27 (1955): 214–20; G. B. Caird, "The Exegetical Method of the Epistle to the Hebrews," *CJT* 5 (1959): 44–51; F. C. Synge, *Hebrews and the Scriptures* (London: SPCK, 1959); M. Barth, "The Old Testament in Hebrews," in *Current Issues in New Testament Interpretation,* ed. W. Klassen and G. F. Snyder (New York: Harper & Row, 1962), 65–78; K. J. Thomas, "The Old Testament Citations in Hebrews," *NTS* 11 (1965): 303–25; F. Schröger, *Der Verfasser des Hebräerbriefes als Schriftausleger,* Biblische Untersuchungen 4 (Regensburg: Pustet, 1968); A. T. Hanson, "Hebrews," in Carson and Williamson, *It Is Written,* 292–302.

47. Sowers, *Hermeneutics of Philo and Hebrews;* R. Williamson, *Philo and the Epistle to the Hebrews,* ALGHJ 4 (Leiden: Brill, 1970).

48. Y. Yadin, "The Dead Sea Scrolls and the Epistle to the Hebrews," in *Aspects of the Dead Sea Scrolls,* ed. C. Rabin and Y. Yadin (Jerusalem: Hebrew University, 1958), 36–55; G. Howard, "Hebrews and the Old Testament Quotations," *NovT* 10 (1968): 208–16.

49. See S. Kistemaker, *The Psalm Citations in the Epistle to the Hebrews* (Amsterdam: van Soest, 1961).

ture to be the Word of God. The familiar formulas, "as it is written," "as the scripture says," or "in order that it be fulfilled," do not appear. Many times the citation is woven into the text without an introduction.

Conclusion

As the foregoing examples make evident, NT writers frequently find new meanings in OT passages. This happens not because of careless exegesis or ignorance, but because of the conviction that Scripture speaks to every significant situation. This is especially so if the situation is believed to have eschatological significance. The Scriptures are accordingly searched for clarification. New Testament exegesis is not often concerned with the question of what happened or what the text originally meant. The NT writers, as also their contemporary Jewish exegetes, were chiefly interested in what the Scriptures mean and how they apply. The life, death, and resurrection of Jesus became for early Christians the hermeneutical key for their interpretation and application of the Jewish Scriptures. Since the Scriptures could be relied on for clarification of eschatological events, and since Jesus was the eschatological agent, there could be no doubt that the Scriptures were fulfilled in him.

Part 3

Jesus

8

Jesus of Nazareth

Scot McKnight

And those who believe that in the life and teaching of Jesus God has given a unique revelation of His character and purpose are committed by this belief, whether they like it or not, whether they admit it or not, to that quest. Without the Jesus of history the Christ of faith becomes a Docetic figure, a figment of pious imagination, who, like Alice's Cheshire cat, ultimately disappears from view.[1]

There is much at stake in the study of Jesus,[2] in the attempt to put his mission and message into compelling shape, for in such a synthesis it is impossible for the scholar to avoid enmeshment. Everyone wants Jesus on his or her side—traditionalists and revisionists, fundamentalists and liberals, feminists and chauvinists, mystics and empiricists, cinematographers and novelists, Chris-

---

1. G. B. Caird, *New Testament Theology,* completed and edited by L. D. Hurst (Oxford: Clarendon, 1994), 347.

2. For a general survey of the history of the study, see C. Brown, *Jesus in European Protestant Thought, 1778–1860* (Grand Rapids: Baker, 1988); D. L. Pals, *The Victorian "Lives" of Jesus,* TUMSR 7 (San Antonio, Tex.: Trinity University Press, 1982); W. P. Weaver, *The Historical Jesus in the Twentieth Century, 1900–1950* (Harrisburg, Pa.: Trinity, 1999); W. G. Kümmel, *Dreißig Jahre Jesusforschung (1950–1980),* ed. H. Merklein, BBB 60 (Königstein: Peter Hanstein, 1985); idem, "Jesusforschung seit 1981," *TRu* 53 (1988): 229–49; B. Witherington III, *The Jesus Quest: The Third Search for the Jew of Nazareth* (Downers Grove, Ill.: InterVarsity, 1995); M. A. Powell, *Jesus as a Figure in History: How Modern Historians View the Man from Galilee* (Louisville: Westminster John Knox, 1998); for a handy bibliographic guide, see C. A. Evans, *Jesus,* IBR Bibliographies 5 (Grand Rapids: Baker, 1992). This chapter's bibliography has been ruthlessly selective, and only a small sampling of Jesus studies is presented here.

tians, Jews, Muslims, and New Age proponents. In addition, ideological causes gain in appealing to Jesus: democracy, federalism, republicanism, communism, socialism, Marxism, and capitalism. Psychological theories appeal to Jesus; sociological models justify points in evidence about Jesus; economic decisions find an anchor in the Gospel traditions. Political speeches are punctuated, at least in the United States, by the language, forms, and ideas of Jesus. Jesus is alive and well.

Tout au contraire: the Jesus who is alive among such advocates is so dissimilar to the Jesus who lived in Galilee[3] that he who is considered well is often a weak exploitation. All sectors in the history of the church have exploited Jesus—liberals and evangelicals, critics and conservatives, political movements and clerical movements, women's studies and diversity movements. Scholarship on Jesus can be seen through its tendencies, and in what follows four such tendencies will be canvassed.

Tendency to Modernize

The exploitation of Jesus received an alarm in 1937 from H. J. Cadbury in one of the most important books about Jesus of the twentieth century, *The Peril of Modernizing Jesus.*[4] What Cadbury called "modernization" (making Jesus like us) and "anachronization" (retrojecting our world onto Jesus) might also be called "enmeshment," and his warning to scholars set the tone for the rest of the twentieth century. Prophetically, he wrote a commentary on the trends in the second half of the twentieth century in his book from the first half of that century! Cadbury called for an attempt to bracket off one's presuppositions to the degree that is possible (and he was not naive here),[5] and to go through the painstaking task of historical understanding. In fact, the problem of modernization is no small matter, for it began with the earliest Christians and can be seen in the (redactional) editing of the evangelists. But as "the gospels illustrate the process of modernization at work in the earliest stages, so also they supply the best materials for correcting their more recent successors."[6]

It is not possible here to point to the manifold ways in which Jesus has been captured by moderns for their own agendas. Scholars are not always easy

---

3. Scholars distinguish at times between the "real Jesus" and the "historical Jesus," with the latter referring more modestly to the reconstruction of the real Jesus by historians, hence the "historians' Jesus." In this essay I will use "historical Jesus" for the real figure, recognizing the nuance that every statement about the historical Jesus is a reconstruction by historians. An early clarification can be seen in L. E. Keck, *A Future for the Historical Jesus: The Place of Jesus in Preaching and Theology* (Philadelphia: Fortress, 1980); see also his recent study *Who Is Jesus? History in Perfect Tense* (Columbia: University of South Carolina Press, 2000).

4. H. J. Cadbury, *The Peril of Modernizing Jesus* (New York: Macmillan, 1937).

5. Ibid., 15.

6. Ibid., 26.

on one another, and they have pointed to modernizing features in Günther Bornkamm,[7] Joachim Jeremias,[8] R. A. Horsley,[9] J. D. Crossan,[10] and Marcus Borg.[11] Some might say that the modernizing influence is present in all Jesus scholarship. One area that is particularly illustrative of the force of modernization is the present feminist study of Jesus.

An important, groundbreaking study of Jesus and women was offered by Ben Witherington III in the publication of his Durham dissertation, *Women in the Ministry of Jesus*.[12] Operating with a maximal view of authenticity as well as a rather generous use of Jewish source materials, the author concluded that "in many, though not all, regards, Jesus differed from His Jewish contemporaries."[13] But this bipolar grasp of the issues—Jewish patriarchalism and Jesus' loving relationships with all—partly distorts what can be and ought to be said about Jesus and women.[14] This is not to say that Witherington's study is flawed, but

---

7. Günther Bornkamm, *Jesus of Nazareth*, trans. I. and F. McLuskey, with J. M. Robinson (New York: Harper & Row, 1960). The original German edition appeared in 1956, and, to date, there is a twelfth edition (1980).

8. Jeremias's studies are too numerous to list here. His magnum opus is the first volume of a NT theology (the second volume was never completed), *New Testament Theology: The Proclamation of Jesus*, trans. J. Bowden (New York: Scribner, 1971). Three other studies include his *The Prayers of Jesus*, trans. J. Bowden (London: SCM, 1967); *The Parables of Jesus*, trans. S. H. Hooke, 2nd ed. (New York: Scribner, 1972); *Jerusalem in the Time of Jesus: An Investigation into Economic and Social Conditions during the New Testament Period*, trans. F. H. and C. H. Cave, with M. E. Dahl (London: SCM, 1969).

9. R. A. Horsley, *Jesus and the Spiral of Violence: Popular Jewish Resistance in Roman Palestine* (San Francisco: Harper & Row, 1987).

10. See especially Crossan's *The Historical Jesus: The Life of a Mediterranean Jewish Peasant* (San Francisco: HarperSanFrancisco, 1991). Crossan has published other studies on Jesus of a more popular nature that need not be listed here, though one should be mentioned: *Jesus: A Revolutionary Biography* (San Francisco: HarperSanFrancisco, 1994). For Crossan's use of Cynics, see the trenchant evaluation by David Aune, "Jesus and Cynics in First-Century Palestine: Some Critical Considerations," in *Hillel and Jesus: Comparative Studies of Two Major Religious Leaders*, ed. J. H. Charlesworth and L. L. Johns (Minneapolis: Fortress, 1997), 176–92; on Crossan's method, see the heavy criticisms of D. C. Allison, *Jesus of Nazareth: Millenarian Prophet* (Minneapolis: Fortress, 1998), 10–33; for further critiques of Crossan, see N. T. Wright, *Jesus and the Victory of God*, Christian Origins and the Question of God 2 (Minneapolis: Fortress, 1996), 44–74; Witherington, *The Jesus Quest*, 58–92.

11. Marcus Borg, *Jesus, a New Vision: Spirit, Culture, and the Life of Discipleship* (San Francisco: Harper & Row, 1987); see his earlier *Conflict, Holiness, and Politics in the Teachings of Jesus* (Harrisburg, Pa.: Trinity, 1998; reprint of the 1984 edition with a new introduction); Borg's other small book on Jesus, *Meeting Jesus Again for the First Time* (San Francisco: HarperSanFrancisco, 1994), is more autobiographical and sets the above comments in context.

12. B. Witherington III, *Women in the Ministry of Jesus: A Study of Jesus' Attitudes to Women and Their Roles as Reflected in His Earthly Life*, SNTSMS 51 (Cambridge: Cambridge University Press, 1984). Witherington followed this study up with *Women in the Earliest Churches*, SNTSMS 58 (Cambridge: Cambridge University Press, 1988).

13. Ibid., 125.

14. See my *New Vision for Israel: The Teachings of Jesus in National Context* (Grand Rapids: Eerdmans, 1999), 221–22.

his particular study points to the implications of all study about women and Jesus. What is almost never mentioned in studies of Jesus and women is that Jesus was not known for anything particularly offensive in his attitudes toward, or practices with, women, and negative evaluations of Jesus are not uncommon with respect to his other practices and attitudes (cf. Matt. 11:16–19).

A "hermeneutic of suspicion," as well as explicit social motive, inform the feminist study of Jesus and women. As an example, we note the study of Elisabeth Schüssler Fiorenza, *Jesus: Miriam's Child, Sophia's Prophet,* which overtly seeks to make use of the Jesus traditions while also criticizing those Gospels as sometimes oppressive.[15] This book is less concerned with the historical Jesus and more with how the texts have oppressed women. Also, her concern is how those traditions might still be used, if interpreted historically and shorn of their hierarchical themes, pragmatically for the liberation of women and society.[16] Schüssler Fiorenza contends that the "reconstruction of the Jesus movement as an emancipatory *basileia* movement . . . provides such a different historical frame of reference."[17]

It should be observed here that no feminist scholar, as far as I know, has undertaken a full-scale book on the historical Jesus.[18] The reason for such a lack is due in part to an earlier work of Schüssler Fiorenza, *In Memory of Her,*[19] in which she sketches a proposal that what is most important is not a study of the historical Jesus but the emancipatory movement that crystallized its hopes in and around Jesus. The same motif dominates her newer book *Jesus and the Politics of Interpretation.*[20] This study excoriates recent "Historical-Jesus" research as a discourse and rhetoric of oppression itself: as a discipline, such research sets up categories and pursues questions emerging from what she calls a "kyriarchal" model—a model of knowledge rooted in hierarchy and domination patterns, especially male domination ("kyriarchy" evokes the idea of an order based on lordship). If her own clear motivation is to use Jesus and historical-Jesus research to promote egalitarianism and radical democracy, at least her cards are faceup on the table.

Besides the rather common criticism made of Schüssler Fiorenza's work for a lack of serious historical reconstruction, her work deserves two further criticisms: (1) In her appeal for the importance of Jesus scholars being public

15. Elisabeth Schüssler Fiorenza, *Jesus: Miriam's Child, Sophia's Prophet: Critical Issues in Feminist Christology* (New York: Continuum, 1995).

16. For an excellent typology of feminist hermeneutics, see A. C. Thiselton, *New Horizons in Hermeneutics* (Grand Rapids: Zondervan, 1992), 411–70.

17. Schüssler Fiorenza, *Jesus: Miriam's Child, Sophia's Prophet,* 96.

18. The closest to such a study is D. Sölle and L. Schottroff, *Jesus of Nazareth,* trans. J. Bowden (Louisville: Westminster John Knox, 2002).

19. Elisabeth Schüssler Fiorenza, *In Memory of Her: A Feminist Theological Reconstruction of Christian Origins* (New York: Crossroad, 1983).

20. Elisabeth Schüssler Fiorenza, *Jesus and the Politics of Interpretation* (New York: Continuum, 2001).

intellectuals,[21] her own rhetoric and style remains stubbornly within the style of American upper-class, abstract-concept-loving elites. If *Jesus and the Politics of Interpretation* is a public intellectual book, I know few who could read it without first reading a series of preliminary studies in the abstract rhetoric of hermeneutics, political theory, and historical-Jesus studies. (2) Her kyriarchal paradigm for reading the Gospels and earliest Christianity remains an example of anti-Judaism and anti-Semitism. If the language is one of emancipation versus kyriarchy, then that from which the emancipation is breaking free is kyriarchal, and that from which her so-called emancipation movement around Jesus is breaking free is Judaism. Even if it is *as* a Judaism that the Jesus movement breaks free, it remains a smirch against Judaism to be seen as kyriarchal.

Recently, Ingrid Rosa Kitzberger collected a series of essays that sought to examine once again Jesus and women; the study deserves thorough discussion, but I limit my comments here to one essay.[22] The most important essay in the book is by Amy-Jill Levine, assessing Christian scholarship, feminist and otherwise. The following statement is thunderous: "The suggestion that Jesus was the only Jewish man to treat women with compassion is at best ahistorical-apologetic; the connection between 'friend of women' and 'friend of sinners' is at best overdrawn. The implication that the Jewish system tortured women is slanderous."[23] In short, Levine reminds us, this time in the approach to the question about Jesus and women, we do not need to lionize Jesus by demon-izing Judaism. Levine has in her grasp the eagle's nest, and she reveals that modernizing has infiltrated the feminist agenda.

If the foregoing examples illustrate how some are plugging their ears to what H. J. Cadbury warned scholarship about at the beginning of the century, each of the books also demonstrates a life of research.[24] Lurking behind each of these books are prior conclusions about which sayings and events in the Jesus traditions are authentic and which are secondary to the historical Jesus. The impulse to examine the traditions critically reveals another strand of Jesus scholarship of the last century, and to this theme we now turn.

A Tendency toward Skepticism in Methodology

If Cadbury's 1937 book sounded the alarm about the tendency to modernize Jesus, it was Rudolf Bultmann's *History of the Synoptic Tradition* that sounded out the rally cry to question both the historicity of the Gospels and the legiti-

---

21. Ibid., 74–75.

22. Ingrid Rosa Kitzberger, ed., *Transformative Encounters: Jesus and Women Re-viewed*, BIS 43 (Leiden: Brill, 2000).

23. "Lilies of the Field and Wandering Jews: Biblical Scholarship, Women's Roles, and Social Location," in Kitzberger, *Transformative Encounters*, 334–35.

24. A fine study by a systematic theologian is J. Moltmann, *The Way of Jesus Christ: Christology in Messianic Dimensions*, trans. M. Kohl (Minneapolis: Fortress, 1993).

macy for the historians to shape the foundations for theology and the gospel. But Bultmann was building on the work of others, notably Martin Kähler and Ernst Troeltsch,[25] and they deserve to be reseated at the table of this discussion, mostly because the unexamined presupposition of much modern skeptical study of the Jesus traditions owes its origin to these two scholars.

Troeltsch argued vociferously and effectively (at least in Germany) for a noticeable difference between the "dogmatic" and the "historical" method. Famously, Troeltsch developed and articulated his three items of historical judgment:

> *The principle of criticism*—all historical judgments are more or less probabilistic and not certain, necessitating the subjection of religious texts to judgment.
>
> *The principle of analogy*—all knowledge is rooted in the analogy of all normal events as we have experienced them, implying the similarity of all historical events.
>
> *The principle of correlation*—all events in life are interrelated into a permanent relationship, requiring that a comprehensive wholeness is the only approach to understanding history.

As he says it, "Give the historical method an inch and it will take a mile. From a strictly orthodox standpoint, therefore, it seems to bear a certain similarity to the devil."[26] The implications of Troeltsch's proposal are enormous, beginning with the relativization of everything sacred as well as the debunking of privileged historical judgments in favor of theological belief. On the other hand, the dogmatic method possesses an authority and a certainty that transcends historical judgment through faith. History thus reflects the duality of God: as God transcends, so the dogmatic method transcends the historical method; as God is immanent, so the historical method is subject to these three principles. Troeltsch, committed as he was to the historical method, believed that out of the chaos of history emerges "an orderly sequence in which the essential truth and profundity of the human spirit rise from its transcendent ground."[27]

If Troeltsch frames the picture of what can be known through the historical method, Martin Kähler sets inside this frame a picture of theology that has shaped the understanding of how the historical Jesus might be useful for theology. Kähler's judgment was a disaster. He pretended that dogmatic and historical knowledge are of two such different orders that the former is all that is needed for faith while the latter pales into insignificance for Christian

---

25. See E. Troeltsch, "Historical and Dogmatic Method in Theology," in *Religion in History*, trans. J. L. Adams and W. F. Bense, Fortress Texts in Modern Theology (1898; reprint, Minneapolis: Fortress, 1991), 11–32.

26. Ibid., 16.

27. Ibid., 27.

faith.[28] Besides this epistemological judgment in which "kinds of knowledge" are given absolute separation (can anyone think that theological judgment is without historical judgment, or that historical knowledge does not involve theological judgment?), Kähler argued his case on the basis of theological presupposition (Lutheranism; Kähler was himself a systematic theologian) and in the context of ecclesiastical apologetics (his famous book was addressed to pastors to console them).[29]

Although the epistemological shift that takes place when a person has "faith" may transcend historical knowledge, that shift does not eliminate historical judgment as a foundational feature of that faith. Furthermore, what Kähler and the followers of this rigid demarcation of knowledge avoid is serious interaction with those who do think that historical judgment is part of—conducive for, destructive of—faith. While Kähler was speaking and Bultmann explicating,[30] British scholars were propounding a completely sane alternative to this German "split of the mind"—one thinks here of the majestic scholarship of J. B. Lightfoot, B. F. Westcott, and F. J. A. Hort,[31] not to mention the articulate judgments that were to follow in scholarship such as that of E. Hoskyns and N. Davey,[32] C. H. Dodd,[33] and C. F. D. Moule.[34]

Scholars may debate particulars, but there has been a long and consistent defense (beginning with the apostle Paul in 1 Cor. 7:10, 12 and 15:12–14!) of the groundedness of Christian faith in historical events, the overturning of which would destroy credibility in that faith. Historical judgment may not be identical with faith, but the former plays a role in the latter, and the two need one another. This has been made clear in a recent study by Paul Minear.[35] And there have been many who have argued not only for the importance of history,

28. Martin Kähler, *The So-Called Historical Jesus and the Historic, Biblical Christ*, trans. C. E. Braaten (German, 1896; English, Philadelphia: Fortress, 1964).

29. The tone of the volume is set in the introductory remarks on pp. 42–45; the theological orientation of Kähler, who was hardly a friend to connecting Jesus to Judaism, can be seen in the second essay in this volume, "Do Christians Value the Bible Because It Contains Historical Documents?" which is an orthodox Lutheran discussion of the doctrine of revelation and biblical authority.

30. Cf., for example, the more conservative orientation in M. Dibelius, *Jesus*, trans. C. B. Hedrick and F. C. Grant (Philadelphia: Westminster, 1949).

31. For a readable survey of this Cambridge triumvirate, see S. Neill and N. T. Wright, *The Interpretation of the New Testament 1861–1986*, 2nd ed. (New York: Oxford University Press, 1988), 35–64; see also 252–312, 360–449, where N. T. Wright's contribution is most notable.

32. E. Hoskyns and N. Davey, *The Riddle of the New Testament* (London: Faber & Faber, 1931).

33. C. H. Dodd, *The Founder of Christianity* (London: Collins, 1970); idem, *History and the Gospel* (London: Hodder & Stoughton, 1964).

34. See especially C. F. D. Moule, *The Phenomenon of the New Testament* (London: SCM, 1967); "Jesus in New Testament Kerygma," in *Essays in New Testament Interpretation* (Cambridge: Cambridge University Press, 1982), 37–49.

35. Paul Minear, *The Bible and the Historian: Breaking the Silence about God in Biblical Studies* (Nashville: Abingdon, 2002).

but also for the essential integrity of the Jesus traditions as recorded in the Gospels.[36] To the degree that faith is related to knowledge, and knowledge at times to historical judgment, to that same degree faith is related to historical judgment.

And this last point is what motivated the historical work of Rudolf Bultmann. Bultmann—the story is well known—operated on several fronts. Methodologically and historiographically, Bultmann thought that the Gospel records about Jesus were an expression of faith and not history (again, note the absolute bifurcation), and, as his famous *History of the Synoptic Tradition* shows, careful examination of those records reveals that we can gain but a mere glimpse of the historical Jesus. Bultmann's famous statement about how little we can know about Jesus[37] was directed more at two kinds of scholarship: traditional belief in the records as pure history as well as, and perhaps even more, psychological investigation into the development of Jesus' atittudes and psyche so that a modern biography could be written. For Bultmann, because he was coasting in the streams charted by Troeltsch and Kähler, historical judgment had nothing to do with faith, for the latter was an existentialist commitment rooted in decision and not in history.[38]

Eventually, even Bultmann's students became convinced that the historical Jesus could be known, and that the figure and message of the historical Jesus mattered for Christian faith. The famous lecture of Ernst Käsemann and an early book of Günther Bornkamm[39] set the tone for the next generation of post-Bultmannian scholarship. If it was a chastened form of judgment guiding these scholars who now took up the challenge of seeing what could be known about the historical Jesus because it mattered, it was still a bedrock conviction that what could be known would be foundational for shaping what Christians should believe, even if what is known is the existential encounter with *Geschichte*.[40]

Besides the post-Bultmannian response led by Käsemann and Bornkamm, another line of thinking developed out of the Troeltsch-Kähler-Bultmann

36. Besides the scholars named immediately above, I mention the Tyndale Project, a council of scholars who discussed critical issues touching on the issues of faith and history and who did so in reasonable and evidentiary manner. See the six-volume Gospel Perspectives series edited by R. T. France, D. Wenham, and C. L. Blomberg (Sheffield: JSOT Press, 1980–86); popularized and summarized ably in C. L. Blomberg, *The Historical Reliability of the Gospels* (Downers Grove, Ill.: InterVarsity, 1987).

37. *Jesus and the Word*, trans. L. P. Smith and E. H. Lantero (New York: Scribner, 1934; reprint, 1958), 8.

38. See R. Bultmann et al., *Kerygma and Myth: A Theological Debate*, ed. H. W. Bartsch (New York: Harper & Row, 1961); R. Bultmann, *History and Eschatology: The Presence of Eternity* (New York: Harper, 1957); idem, *Jesus Christ and Mythology* (New York: Scribner, 1958).

39. E. Käsemann, "The Problem of the Historical Jesus," in his *Essays on New Testament Themes*, trans. W. J. Montague, SBT 41 (London: SCM, 1964), 15–47; Bornkamm, *Jesus of Nazareth*.

40. See J. M. Robinson, *A New Quest of the Historical Jesus*, SBT 18 (London: SCM, 1959).

bifurcation of knowledge with an utter commitment to (what is in effect) the dogmatic method against the historical method: narrative criticism. In the 1980s scholarship of all sorts[41] shifted to an interest in the narrative art of the Gospel texts, and within that shift there emerged a tacit and sometimes explicit commitment to the narrative shape as the canonical and confessional shape of the Christian message vis-à-vis the historical method.[42] Few have made a connection between this methodological shift and the Troeltsch-Kähler-Bultmann approach, but the narrative approach could never have risen to the heights it reached without that earlier articulation as an encouragement and legitimation.

Other post-Bultmannians, however, have developed the skeptical orientation of Bultmann's methodology to an extreme. One thinks here, of course, of the Jesus Seminar, as articulated especially by one of Bultmann's students, Robert W. Funk. In essence, the insight of Bultmann that the Gospel records are an expression of faith and not history leads to the conclusion that those same records contain almost no history because they are expressions of faith. The earliest proponent of a radical skeptical approach at the methodological level was Norman Perrin, whose criteria have been swatted back and forth and refined into a fairly acceptable set of criteria used by a wide variety of scholars, including B. F. Meyer, E. P. Sanders, and N. T. Wright, but most completely used recently in the massive undertaking of John P. Meier. We can wind our way through this discussion by beginning with Perrin.[43]

Perrin proposed three basic criteria to which all evidence must submit and which, when passed, are said to indicate what is "authentic." First, *dissimilarity:* evidence is authentic if it is "dissimilar to characteristic emphases both of ancient Judaism and of the early Church."[44] Second, *coherence:* evidence is authentic "if it can be shown to cohere with material established as authentic

41. Some of the most significant early studies may be listed here: D. Rhoads, D. Michie, and J. Dewey, *Mark as Story: An Introduction to the Narrative of a Gospel,* 2nd ed. (Minneapolis: Fortress, 1999); J. D. Kingsbury, *Matthew as Story,* 2nd ed. (Philadelphia: Fortress, 1988); R. C. Tannehill, *The Narrative Unity of Luke-Acts: A Literary Interpretation,* 2 vols. (Philadelphia: Fortress, 1986). For my early assessment of this trend in scholarship, see Scot McKnight, *Interpreting the Synoptic Gospels* (Grand Rapids: Baker, 1988), 121–37.

42. The point is a general criticism of the method itself. A good example of this kind of orientation is J. D. Kingsbury, "The Significance of the Earthly Jesus in the Gospel of Matthew," *Ex Auditu* 14 (1998): 59–65, and the telling response of J. A. Kelhoffer, "Response to Jack Dean Kingsbury's 'The Significance of the Earthly Jesus in the Gospel of Matthew,'" *Ex Auditu* 14 (1998): 66–69.

43. A thorough survey of the historical development of the criteria can be found in S. E. Porter, *The Criteria for Authenticity in Historical-Jesus Research: Previous Discussion and New Proposals,* JSNTSup 191 (Sheffield: Sheffield Academic Press, 2000), 28–123.

44. Norman Perrin, *Rediscovering the Teaching of Jesus* (London: SCM, 1967), 39. This criterion, of course, was fundamentally shaped by R. Bultmann, *History of the Synoptic Tradition,* trans. John Marsh, rev. ed. (Peabody, Mass.: Hendrickson, 1994), 205, and then more radically defined by Käsemann, "Problem of the Historical Jesus," 36–37. It was most widely known in its Perrin form, however.

by means of the criterion of dissimilarity."[45] Third, *multiple attestation:* evidence is authentic if it "is attested in all, or most, of the sources which can be discerned behind the synoptic gospels."[46] Scholarship was aroused by this form of historical judgment for a variety of reasons, including the issue of the burden of proof;[47] historical work requires more "art" and less "science";[48] the criteria run into logical roadblocks themselves;[49] the value of the analogy to textual criticism;[50] the importance of Semitic language reflection in the sayings attributed to Jesus;[51] the criterion of historical plausibility;[52] and the value of recent understandings of Jesus and the Greek language.[53] For instance, what Perrin was able to distill from the Gospel records was a "distinctive" Jesus and not a "characteristic" Jesus, a Jesus who was unlike both Judaism and earliest Christianity but not necessarily the well-rounded picture of a Jesus who was in some senses distinct but in others quite common. Raymond E. Brown called this sort of methodological distillation of Jesus a "monstrosity."[54] Thus, to begin with the dissimilar is to prejudge what will be discovered, and it will find a residue of Jesus that finds no relation to Judaism or to the early church.

A special contribution to the philosophical issues involved in criteria for distinguishing the authentic from the inauthentic in the Jesus traditions came from Canada when Ben F. Meyer published *The Aims of Jesus.* Adapting the dense philosophical studies of Bernard Lonergan, Meyer argued that "critical realism" is the most balanced approach to studying the historical Jesus.[55] He operates with a chastened set of criteria: discontinuity (vis-à-vis the early church and not Judaism), originality (items in the tradition distinctive to Jesus), per-

45. Perrin, *Rediscovering the Teaching of Jesus,* 43.

46. Ibid., 45.

47. H. K. McArthur, "The Burden of Proof in Historical Jesus Research," *ExpTim* (1970–71): 116–19; S. C. Goetz and C. L. Blomberg, "The Burden of Proof," *JSNT* 11 (1981): 39–63.

48. R. S. Barbour, *Traditio-Historical Criticism of the Gospels* (London: SPCK, 1972).

49. M. D. Hooker, "Christology and Methodology," *NTS* 17 (1970–71): 480–87; "On Using the Wrong Tool," *Theology* 75 (1972): 570–81.

50. J. D. Crossan, "Divine Immediacy and Human Immediacy: Towards a New First Principle in Historical Jesus Research," *Semeia* 44 (1988): 121–40.

51. J. Jeremias, *New Testament Theology,* vol. 1, *The Proclamation of Jesus* (London: SCM, 1971), 14–45. B. D. Chilton, ever since publication of his dissertation, is known for the specification of this criterion in the direction of targumic parallels; see his *God in Strength: Jesus' Announcement of the Kingdom,* SNTSU B/1 (Freistadt: Plöchl, 1979); idem, *A Galilean Rabbi and His Bible: Jesus' Use of the Interpreted Scripture of His Time,* GNS 8 (Wilmington, Del.: Glazier, 1984).

52. G. Theissen and D. Winter, *Die Kriterienfrage in der Jesusforschung: Vom Differenzkriterium zum Plausibilitätskriterium,* NTOA 34 (Göttingen: Vandenhoeck & Ruprecht, 1997).

53. S. E. Porter, *The Criteria for Authenticity in Historical-Jesus Research: Previous Discussion and New Proposals,* JSNTSup 191 (Sheffield: Sheffield Academic Press, 2000).

54. R. E. Brown, *An Introduction to the New Testament,* ABRL (New York: Doubleday, 1997), 827.

55. The fundamental discussion can be seen in B. F. Meyer, *The Aims of Jesus* (London: SCM, 1979), 23–110.

sonal idiom (forms in which Jesus spoke), resistive form (forms distinctive of Jesus—e.g., parables), multiple attestation (understood as material found in more than one Gospel source), multiform attestation (material in more than one form), and Aramaic substratum (sayings of an Aramaic nature). For Meyer, history is inferential knowledge gained by hypothesis and verification but not totally opposed to faith (unlike Kähler).

J. P. Meier, in a multivolume work on the historical Jesus,[56] operates as extensively on the basis of the criteria of authenticity as did Perrin, but he does so in light of the intervening discussion and refinement of the tools at hand, with the result that his criteriological approach will lead to a deeper and longer-lasting consensus. If his book lacks imaginative synthesis and ground-breaking paths, it makes gains in the arena of methodological candor and thoroughness. Meier operates with five criteria:[57] (1) embarrassment—those actions and sayings that would have caused embarrassment for the early church; (2) discontinuity—those actions and sayings that cannot be derived from either Judaism at the time of Jesus or from the early church after him; (3) multiple attestation—those actions and sayings of Jesus that are attested in more than one independent literary source of the evangelists; (4) coherence—those actions and sayings that fit well into the already-established data bank; (5) rejection and execution—which historical words and deeds can best explain the trial and execution of Jesus? Meier is looking for actions and sayings that alienate Jesus substantially from the powers of his day. Meier's study uses the criteria in balance with sound exegetical and historical logic, and it sees historiography to be as much an art as it is a science, but that historical judgment is no less certain than other parts of our lives.[58]

If Meier reflects the balanced judgment of a historian, the work of R. W. Funk reflects the skepticism of the post-Bultmannian new quest—with several spices added, including a hostility toward orthodox Christian faith as well as an ability to promote his projects at an international and sensational level.[59] If Funk shows anything, it is that scholarship does not really "make progress" or reach a "consensus." Funk completely rejects the affirmations of the Jesus traditions in the scholarship that followed Bultmann and Käsemann—includ-

56. J. P. Meier, *A Marginal Jew: Rethinking the Historical Jesus*, 3 vols., ABRL (New York: Doubleday, 1991–2001).

57. Ibid., 1:167–95.

58. For another balanced study of the criteria, see C. A. Evans, "Recent Developments in Jesus Research: Presuppositions, Criteria, and Sources," in *Jesus and His Contemporaries: Comparative Studies*, AGJU 25 (Leiden: Brill, 1995), 1–49; an older but still useful survey is C. L. Blomberg, *The Historical Reliability of the Gospels* (Downers Grove, Ill.: InterVarsity, 1987).

59. Three books are worthy of note here: R. W. Funk, *Honest to Jesus: Jesus for a New Millennium* (San Francisco: HarperSanFrancisco, 1996); Funk with R. Hoover et al., *The Five Gospels: The Search for the Authentic Words of Jesus* (New York: Macmillan [Polebridge], 1993); Funk and the Jesus Seminar, *The Acts of Jesus: The Search for the Authentic Deeds of Jesus* (San Francisco: HarperSanFrancisco [Polebridge], 1998).

ing R. Schnackenburg, J. Jeremias, C. H. Dodd, B. F. Meyer, E. P. Sanders, J. P. Meier, and G. Vermès,[60] to name but a few. And what he affirms is an American, postmodern, antiauthoritarian, cynical, comic savant-like Jesus who would cast aspersions on all Christian creedal affirmations.

Funk led the Jesus Seminar to a procedure of voting on the sayings and deeds of Jesus in four categories: authentic, probably authentic, probably inauthentic, and definitely inauthentic—and the vast majority of the Gospel materials fit into the last two categories. However, many of the claims are open to serious debate,[61] and the work has been criticized as knowing in advance the portrait of Jesus it wanted to disseminate.[62] In complete contradiction to E. P. Sanders's approach of beginning with actions, R. W. Funk (and the Jesus Seminar) began with the parables, and then moved to coherence with the authentic parables, and only after this to actions that cohere with the previously established data bank. Furthermore, he proposes the criterion of embarrassment (echoing J. P. Meier), the exclusion of sayings that belong to the fabric of a story—for example, "Get up here in front of everybody" (from Mark 3:3)—as well as those that claim that no auditors were present. Funk wants to "give skepticism rein."[63] In general, Funk's method is little different from any other kind of methodological procedure used in Jesus scholarship. The fundamental problem is his starting place (his presuppositions) and the apparent goal he had in mind before he began—to debunk Christian orthodoxy, which becomes altogether clear at the conclusion of *Honest to Jesus*.[64] It can be said, fairly I think, that Funk transcended his presuppositions less than do most Jesus scholars.

N. T. Wright used several criteria, including an important revision of the criterion of coherence as well as the criterion of dissimilarity, in a breathtaking study of Jesus that has sparked major scholarly discussions.[65] Wright's impressive study operates, like a skilled military plan, on several fronts at once: the history of the discussion since Albert Schweitzer; historiography; the philosophy of

60. I list a single work for each: R. Schnackenburg, *God's Rule and Kingdom*, trans. J. Murray (New York: Herder & Herder, 1963); Jeremias, *The Proclamation of Jesus*; Dodd, *The Founder of Christianity* (Philadelphia: Fortress, 1985); Meyer, *The Aims of Jesus*; E. P. Sanders, *Jesus and Judaism*; Meier, *A Marginal Jew*; and G. Vermès, *The Religion of Jesus the Jew* (Minneapolis: Fortress, 1993).

61. An emotive but trenchant critique of the Jesus Seminar and R. W. Funk is that of Luke T. Johnson, *The Real Jesus: The Misguided Quest for the Historical Jesus and the Truth of the Traditional Gospels* (San Francisco: HarperSanFrancisco, 1996), though Johnson's conclusions are clearly of a Kähler-Bultmann orientation. An early evangelical assessment is the volume edited by M. J. Wilkins and J. P. Moreland, *Jesus under Fire! Crucial Questions about Jesus* (Grand Rapids: Zondervan, 1995).

62. Wright, *Jesus and the Victory of God*, 33.

63. Funk, *Honest to Jesus*, 139 (see 136–39 for discussion of his method).

64. Ibid., 297–314.

65. See especially Wright, *Jesus and the Victory of God*; see also Wright's *The New Testament and the People of God*, Christian Origins and the Question of God 1 (Minneapolis: Fortress, 1992).

how meaning is composed through "story"; Judaism; the historical Jesus; how Jesus' message and mission fit into both OT as well as Jewish traditions; and the development of the Jesus tradition in a Pauline theological direction. This is not to mention the elegant and charming style in which Wright argues his case. Wright's method is a combination of criteria and historical logic, with the latter operating frequently as a massive use of the criterion of coherency. Thus, Wright's case is built by way of "explanation" of a given historical datum (a saying, an action) within the "story" (Judaism's, Jesus') previously established. And, as has been argued throughout the history of historiography, a coherent thesis is superior to an incoherent one. It should be noted that Wright's "story of Jesus" fundamentally builds upon and reworks the scintillating study of C. H. Dodd on Jesus' use of the OT.[66]

In addition to this adaptation of coherency, Wright finds a criterion of double similarity and dissimilarity! That is, "when something can be seen to be credible (though perhaps deeply subversive) within first-century Judaism, *and* credible as the implied starting-point (though not the exact replica) of something in later Christianity, there is a strong possibility of our being in touch with the genuine history of Jesus."[67] This amounts to a subversion of one criterion (dissimilarity) through the use of another (Meier's criterion of rejection and execution) in establishing the former (dissimilarity within similarity through subversion of Judaism). Thus, in Wright's case, the "kingdom of God" is authentic both because it is similar to "Israel's story" and because it is similar to the "early Christian story" while also subverting the former and not quite being the same as the latter! Again, this combines several criteria; we have dissimilarity, embarrassment, and discontinuity operating on the table of sheer historical common sense: Jesus is likely to have shared many common features of Judaism and earliest Christian thinking. In my assessment, this revision of the criterion of dissimilarity is more clever than it is innovative. Wright has reworked the criteria of dissimilarity and coherence into the insights of discontinuities between Jesus and the early church to form one criterion. Historical judgment is an art, not a set of criteria, and what works in one case will not work as well for another. In addition, historical judgment exercises itself with a framework of faith and presupposition, and those a prioris have a significant impact on what counts as knowledge.[68]

Criteriology will not get the final word in the debate. The criteria are a part of historical judgment that is far more complex than the criteria will permit.

---

66. C. H. Dodd, *According to the Scriptures: The Sub-structure of New Testament Theology* (London: Collins, 1952).

67. Wright, *Jesus and the Victory of God,* 132.

68. On this, see C. S. Evans, *The Historical Christ and the Jesus of Faith: The Incarnational Narrative as History* (New York: Oxford, 1996). Evans argues, among many other things, that the "facts" of the story about Jesus are vital to faith and knowable. See also R. G. Gruenler, *New Approaches to Jesus and the Gospels: A Phenomenological and Exegetical Study of Synoptic Christology* (Grand Rapids: Baker, 1982).

For this reason, the scholarship of E. P. Sanders, G. Vermès, G. B. Caird, B. D. Chilton, N. T. Wright, and D. C. Allison is far more methodologically satisfying than that of those preoccupied with establishing what is authentic on the basis of supposedly neutral criteria. And one of the features of the mission and message of Jesus that is durable beyond time is his eschatological vision, to which we now turn.

A Tendency to Begin with Eschatological Imminency

Literal

Students and scholars begin this discussion with Albert Schweitzer, but this mistakes the communicator for the innovator. What Schweitzer made so public, so bold, and so provocative was fashioned earlier at the hands of the more humble, more conservative, and less inflammatory Johannes Weiss.[69] Weiss, son of the conservative German NT scholar Bernhard Weiss,[70] and son-in-law of Albrecht Ritschl, the major exponent of German Lutheran liberalism, steered a difficult course between German liberal theology and straightforward historical exegesis. He pushed the envelope to see an eschatology of Jesus that was much less culturally relevant, morally social, and politically protective and more historically conditioned by Jewish apocalyp-

69. Johannes Weiss published two editions of his famous book on Jesus, *Die Predigt Jesu vom Reiche Gottes,* ed. F. Hahn, 3rd ed. (Göttingen: Vandenhoeck & Ruprecht, 1964). The first edition was published in 1892 and is the only edition translated into English: *Jesus' Proclamation of the Kingdom of God,* trans. and ed. R. H. Hiers and D. L. Holland, Scholars Press Reprints and Translations Series (Philadelphia: Fortress, 1971). The second edition retreated somewhat from the earlier edition.

Albert Schweitzer, whose views were based on the first edition of Weiss's book, published several books on Jesus early in his career: *Das Messianitäts- und Leidensgeheimnis: Ein Skizze des Lebens Jesu* (Tübingen: Mohr, 1901; in English, *The Mystery of the Kingdom of God: The Secret of Jesus' Messiahship and Passion,* trans. W. Lowrie [New York: Dodd, Mead, 1914]); *Die psychiatrische Beurteilung Jesu* (Tübingen: Mohr, 1913; in English, *The Psychiatric Study of Jesus,* trans. C. R. Joy [Boston: Beacon, 1948], the dissertation for his degree in medicine); and the most influential book ever written in historical-Jesus studies, *Geschichte der Leben-Jesu-Forschung,* 9th ed., UTB 1302 (Tübingen: Mohr Siebeck, 1984). The first title of this last book, published in 1906, was *Von Reimarus zu Wrede;* a second edition, with the present title, was published in 1913; in 1966 J. M. Robinson wrote an informative preface to a new edition. There are now two English editions: *The Quest of the Historical Jesus: A Critical Study of Its Progress from Reimarus to Wrede,* trans. W. Montgomery (not mentioned on title page) (Baltimore: Johns Hopkins University Press, 1998); *The Quest of the Historical Jesus,* ed. J. Bowden, trans. W. Montgomery, J. R. Coates, S. Cupitt, and J. Bowden (Minneapolis: Fortress, 2001). This latter new "translation" corrects W. Montgomery's occasional effusions of style and adds the translation of the fuller German second edition.

70. His influential (liberal) "life of Jesus" was a standard read: *Das Leben Jesu,* 2 vols., 4th ed. (Stuttgart: I. G. Cotta, 1902; in English, *The Life of Christ,* trans. J. W. and M. G. Hope, 3 vols., Clark's Foreign Theological Library 14, 16, 17 [Edinburgh: Clark, 1909]).

tic.[71] That Weiss's proposals were historically oriented, theologically explosive, and familially divisive gave the book the impact it had, but it was Schweitzer who so popularized the view of Weiss that the view became connected to the latter's name.[72] In fact, Rudolf Bultmann says that Schweitzer "carried the theory of Weiss to extremes."[73]

It can be said that the eschatological perception of Jesus' message ended Protestant German liberalism, for it forced the meaning of "kingdom of God" out of a cultural grasp into an eschatological, historical, and Jewish grasp that was, in its deepest sense, countercultural. It was Albert Schweitzer who expounded this viewpoint for all to see in such provocative and powerful categories that German theology would never be the same.[74] Schweitzer's views, which had been percolating for some time,[75] moved along the lines of Weiss but with greater force: under his heavy hand, Jesus became a misguided apocalyptic fanatic who had the courage to challenge the nation and God in a last-ditch effort to make God act to usher in the kingdom. Schweitzer's pet verse was Matt. 10:23, which he believed was literal in import and set in Matthew in its original, historical context:[76] "You will not finish going through the cities of Israel before the Son of Man comes." When the disciples returned, sporting some good stories of impact, Jesus realized that the mission was not enough; he would have to give himself in death as an atonement for the kingdom to be realized—hence, the fatal trip to Jerusalem as an enactment of the woes of the tribulation.[77] He died a failure, but nonetheless as a testimony of what the will can achieve.[78]

71. The anti-Semitism of Ritschl, however, influenced this discussion in manifold ways; on this, see S. Heschel, *Abraham Geiger and the Jewish Jesus*, CSHJ (Chicago: University of Chicago Press, 1998), 106–26. And, one is entitled to ask, was the historical Jesus debate as set up by Martin Kähler not also influenced by the same ideological strains? The answer is yes. See Kähler, *The So-Called Historical Jesus*, 47, 54, 64. Heschel explores this matter pointedly in the chapter "The Protestant Flight from the Historical Jesus" (127–61), concluding that the flight was motivated to avoid the realities of a critical approach, including the discovery that Jesus was a Jew.

72. Oddly enough, Weiss's own theology gave shape to a pragmatics: he contended that in spite of Ritschl's unhistorical understanding of Jesus' message of the kingdom, that view of Ritschl remains useful because Jesus' message needs to be constantly readjusted and reinterpreted. This begins to be seen in the second edition of Weiss, *Die Predigt Jesu vom Reiche Gottes*.

73. Rudolf Bultmann, *Jesus Christ and Mythology* (New York: Scribner, 1958), 13.

74. British and American scholarship largely continued on as it had been, though eventually the influence of the eschatological school was felt. For England, one should note the mediator of Schweitzer: W. Sanday, *The Life of Christ in Recent Research* (New York: Oxford, 1907), 37–89. See also the more moderate line taken by E. von Dobschütz, *The Eschatology of the Gospels* (London: Hodder & Stoughton, 1910).

75. See, for example, A. Schweitzer, *Out of My Life and Thought: An Autobiography*, trans. A. B. Lemke (Baltimore: Johns Hopkins University Press, 1998), 5–9, 13–14.

76. Schweitzer is notorious for arguing for the historical veracity of the Markan and Matthean Gospels; see Schweitzer, *Quest for the Historical Jesus*, xxv (noted correctly by Nineham).

77. Schweitzer, *Quest of the Historical Jesus*, ed. Bowden, 347.

78. The second edition omits the famous lines of the first edition about the "wheel of the world" crushing Jesus (Schweitzer, *Quest of the Historical Jesus*, 2nd ed., 370–71; *Quest of the*

What Schweitzer and Weiss achieved was an interpretation of Jesus based on a literal reading of his eschatological sayings, especially those expressing an imminent eschatology (Mark 9:1; 13:30; Matt. 10:23).[79] It can be argued that his literal view of the eschatology of Jesus dominated critical scholarship of the twentieth century with only a few discordant voices being heard. Because this essay is not concerned with every voice heard, I will mention only a few. B. F. Meyer grappled with the nature of prophetic language, found an important insight in the ambiguity of all prophetic expectation, and came to the conclusion that Jesus did not have "determinate" knowledge of what God intended in history.[80] Thus, all prophetic knowledge is "limited knowledge," and imminence ought to be seen for what is, not for what the skeptical critics have claimed that it is.[81]

E. P. Sanders so reinvigorated the literal interpretation of the eschatological imminency of Jesus that he had to spell out his differences with Albert Schweitzer.[82] Sanders disputes the key pillars of Schweitzer's proposals, the events in Jesus' life (such as the mission charge and return, the confession at Caesarea Philippi, etc.) seen as crucial for Schweitzer, and argues for a "restoration eschatology" on other bases; but he still has a Jesus who has an eschatology not unlike that of Schweitzer—literal and imminent and mistaken. Thus, "Jesus looked for the imminent direct intervention of God in history, the elimination of evil and evildoers, the building of a new and glorious temple, and the reassembly of Israel with himself and his disciples as leading figures in it."[83] Along the same lines, but with a profoundly sophisticated interaction of the sociology of millenarian movements with ancient Jewish apocalyptic literature as setting the stage for Jesus' own eschatology, Dale C. Allison has proposed that Jesus had a literal and imminent eschatology, and that eschatology revolved around the judgment, the resurrection, and the restoration of Israel.[84] This language about the future, Allison contends, is not mundane but supernatural.[85] Finally, in

---

Historical Jesus, ed. Bowden, 333; *Geschichte der Lebe-Jesu-Forschung,* 423). On the will, see his conclusion: *Quest of the Historical Jesus,* ed. Bowden, 478–87.

79. For the most important survey of the history of interpretation of these three verses, see M. Künzi, *Das Naherwartungslogion Matthäus 10,23: Geschichte seiner Auslegung,* BGBE 9 (Tübingen: Mohr Siebeck, 1970); *Das Naherwartungslogion Markus 9,1 par: Geschichte seiner Auslegung: mit einem Nachwort zur Auslegungsgeschichte von Markus 13,30 par,* BGBE 21 (Tübingen: Mohr Siebeck, 1977).

80. Meyer, *The Aims of Jesus,* 242–49.

81. Ibid., 246. "If God speaks in prophecy, he speaks in the history that follows on prophecy, and it is history, history grasped within the perspective of faith, that does what the prophet cannot do—namely, decipher prophetic symbol, translating image into event, schematic sequence into actual sequence, and symbolic time into real time" (247).

82. Sanders, *Jesus and Judaism,* 327–30.

83. Ibid., 153. See also the fuller exposition around the category of kingdom in 222–41.

84. Dale C. Allison, *Jesus of Nazareth: Millenarian Prophet* (Minneapolis: Fortress, 1998); see also his earlier book *The End of the Ages Has Come: An Early Interpretation of the Passion and Resurrection of Jesus* (Philadelphia: Fortress, 1985).

85. Allison, *Jesus of Nazareth,* 152–69.

my own study of the eschatology of Jesus, I have tried to steer a path between the radical imminence of Schweitzer and the overly zealous reinterpretation of that language by G. B. Caird and N. T. Wright (see the next section). I argue, with B. F. Meyer and somewhat with D. C. Allison (though his book was unavailable to me when I wrote), that Jesus' language about the future is imminent, but it is so because prophetic language is inherently ambiguous and limited. Jesus' knowledge, like that of those who were prophets before him (in this topic Jesus shows little transcendence of prophetic knowledge), was limited. His language is neither mistaken nor accommodating; it is prophetic language that construes the "next event" on God's big calendar as the "final event" of history—a theory of prophetic knowledge well known to those who are aware of the studies of prophetic language.[86]

Myth and Metaphor

This line of thinking of Jesus' eschatological images as literal has occasionally been bucked the entire century: one thinks here of Rudolf Bultmann's demythologizing program, C. H. Dodd's attempts to use Platonic imagery for Jesus' expectations of the future, and G. B. Caird's and N. T. Wright's appeal to apocalyptic language as metaphor. Fundamentally, each of these scholars thinks that the imminent eschatology was either metaphorical or to be appropriated at a nonliteral level. To be fair, Dodd, Caird, and Wright would not appreciate finding themselves enlisted with Bultmann, but the "use" of Jesus' language remains the same, even though they come to that conclusion from a significantly different direction. Bultmann thought that Jesus' language of imminence was literally intended but an "illusion"[87] because the "course of history has refuted [this] mythology."[88] Hence, demythologizing, we find: God in heaven means the transcendence of God, hell means the transcendence of evil, Satan and demons mean that our actions are puzzling and overwhelming, and the eschatology of Jesus means "to be open to God's future which is really imminent for every one of us; to be prepared for this future which can come as a thief in the night when we do not expect it; to be prepared, because this future will be a judgment on all men who have bound themselves to this world and are not free, not open to God's future."[89]

Dodd himself was not open to Bultmann's future, because he thought that the eschatology of Jesus was less futuristic and more realized.[90] More importantly,

86. McKnight, *A New Vision for Israel: The Teachings of Jesus in National Context* (Grand Rapids: Eerdmans, 1999), 120–39.

87. Rudolf Bultmann, *Theology of the New Testament*, trans. Kendrick Grobel, 2 vols. (New York: Scribner, 1951–55), 1:22.

88. Bultmann, *Jesus Christ and Mythology*, 14.

89. Ibid., 31–32.

90. C. H. Dodd, *The Parables of the Kingdom*, 3rd ed. (London: Religious Book Club, 1942).

Dodd thought that Jesus did envision an imminent wrapping up of God's redemptive plan that was expressed in apocalyptic language and concerned the imminent events connected to Jerusalem's destruction (though Dodd was less confident that Mark 13 reflects the mind of Jesus). These predictions of Jesus "resemble the forecasts of the apocalypses, referring to events of a wholly supernatural order,"[91] and "Jesus pronounced the doom of the temple as an impending event in history."[92] For Dodd, Jesus foresaw an imminent confluence of various features: his own death, the persecution of his disciples, and an upheaval in which Rome would destroy the "Jewish nation, its city and temple."[93] But these are symptomatic of a spiritual judgment, and "foresight is primarily insight" and predictions are "primarily a dramatization of spiritual judgments"[94] as well as a shortening of historical perspective. That occurs when "the profound realities underlying a situation are depicted in the dramatic form of historical prediction, the certainty and inevitability of the spiritual processes involved are expressed in terms of the immediate imminence of the event."[95] Here are Dodd's concluding words, words that show (in my judgment) that Bultmann and Dodd were not as far apart as might at first appear:

> Thus the course of events which outwardly is a series of disasters holds within it a revelation of the glory of God, for those who have insight. This is the "mystery of the Kingdom of God"; not only that the *eschaton, that which belongs properly to the realm of the "wholly other," is now matter of actual experience,* but that it is experienced in the paradoxical form of the suffering and death of God's representative. *Behind or within the paradoxical turn of events lies that timeless reality which is the kingdom, the power and the glory of the blessed God.*[96]

Dodd is even clearer when he comes to his discussion of the Son of Man: "But Jesus declares that this ultimate, the Kingdom of God, has come into history, and He takes upon Himself the 'eschatological' role of 'Son of Man.' *The absolute, the 'wholly other,' has entered into time and space.*"[97] These "supra-sensible, supra-historical realities" have a "corresponding actuality within history."[98] "The historical order however cannot contain the whole meaning of the absolute."[99] These are "eternal realities," and that means that the "Kingdom of God in its full reality is not something which will happen after other things have happened. It is that to which men awake when this order of time and space no longer limits their vision, when they 'sit at meat in the Kingdom

91. Ibid., 52.
92. Ibid., 63.
93. Ibid., 70.
94. Ibid., 70–71.
95. Ibid., 71.
96. Ibid., 79–80 (italics added, except for *eschaton*).
97. Ibid., 107.
98. Ibid.
99. Ibid., 107–8.

of God' with all the blessed dead, and drink with Christ the 'new wine' of eternal felicity. 'The Day of the Son of Man' stands for the timeless fact."[100] This language corresponds to "the spirit of man," which, "though dwelling in history, belongs to the eternal order."[101] I have given this much attention to Dodd's own words because Dodd's theory influenced G. B. Caird, and Caird's understanding of Jesus' imminent language begot the important and widely influential book of N. T. Wright.

Consequently, what Bultmann saw as below, Dodd sees as "behind or within," and what they both do is reinterpret the imminent language of Jesus in a theologically suitable form: for Bultmann, authentic existence is found in the decision for God; for Dodd, ultimate realities about God's ways with humans are found in the language through insight. For Dodd, the ultimate shows itself, for a moment, in time—a Platonic conception if ever there was one; for Bultmann, humans encounter God through this language. For Caird and for Wright, however, this approach needs modification: this language is more historical even if metaphorical. The imminent eschatological language of Jesus refers to the historical plane, not to the existential or eternal order, but it is a specific Jewish idiom for national disaster.

We cannot give much attention to Caird's study, since its brevity permitted only a sketch of what was to become a full picture under the art of N. T. Wright.[102] Caird's chapter on eschatology distinguishes several definitions of that concept: individual (death, judgment, heaven, hell) and historical (goal of history; he develops several strands of thinking within this rubric). For example, the term "resurrection," in Jewish usage, "denoted a single event at the end of the present age or, more commonly, at the end of the world," and therefore (as can be seen in its use for Easter Day), "there is a prima facie case for saying that this is metaphor, the use of end-of-the-world language to refer to that which is not literally the end of the world."[103] Thus, when Jesus refers to the "Son of Man," he is referring to a corporate figure (not just himself, but his followers included) who "would then be the new Israel, which, rejected by the contemporary Jewish generation, was shortly to be vindicated."[104]

It is this transfer of referent that makes Caird's study of eschatology so useful; it maintains a firm anchor in historical realities (resurrection as exegeted by historians) as well as linguistics (resurrection as metaphor). As Caird observes,

100. Ibid., 108.
101. Ibid.
102. See G. B. Caird, *The Language and Imagery of the Bible* (Philadelphia: Westminster, 1980); see also idem, *New Testament Theology*. The world of scholarship owes a debt to L. D. Hurst for devoting so much of his own time to the completion of Caird's important volume on NT Theology. Hurst had to "think Caird" to construct the volume with such expertise. The story is told that a well-known British retired professor commented that a certain sentence in the book was vintage Caird, only to learn that the sentence was spun by Hurst out of Cairdian threads.
103. Caird, *Language and Imagery*, 249.
104. Caird, *New Testament Theology*, 380.

few noted that Dodd was saying that eschatological language was metaphorical.[105] The effect of Caird's view was that writers (read: the historical Jesus) of the first-century Jewish world could use end-of-the-world language metaphorically to refer to significant events in history. This is what Jesus did, argues N. T. Wright, when he spoke the words now found in Mark 13:24–27: these are-end-of-the-world words used metaphorically for political disaster for the Jewish nation. The best parallel to this is the application of Joel 2:28–32 to the Pentecost experience as recorded in Acts 2. Here we have end-of-the-world imagery applied to historical experience; the writer does not think that this is the end of the world, nor does he think that the speaker is wrong because the end of the world did not come, nor does he think that some of this prophecy is still hanging in the air awaiting future fulfillment. He sees Pentecost as an event of divine significance. What he has is "insight" into the significance of a historical event. Caird offers this parting shot: "It appears, then, that Weiss and Schweitzer were right in thinking that eschatology was central to the understanding of biblical thought, but wrong in assuming that the biblical writers had minds as pedestrian as their own."[106]

N. T. Wright, whom Caird would not see as pedestrian, develops the insights of both Dodd and Caird while allowing his lens also to be fully focused on the significance of the destruction of Jerusalem as central to Jesus' eschatology.[107] These two foci of Wright permit some confusion over whether he subscribes to Dodd's realized eschatology or to the consistent eschatology of Weiss and Schweitzer. His focus on 70 C.E. permits the latter, while his focus on metaphorical language sets him in the Dodd camp. Because he refuses to proceed to the conclusion that Jesus was mistaken, Wright seems to fit into the school of realized eschatology (what Wright thinks of Jesus' future eschatology is unclear but will become clearer as he continues to write on these themes).[108] For Dodd, Caird, and Wright, the imminent eschatological language of Jesus, while referring to historical events, is fundamentally imagery and metaphor; for Weiss and Schweitzer, it was historical prediction pure and simple—and mistaken. What Wright (and Caird and Dodd) fail to examine is the historical implication of using end-of-the-world language for 70 C.E.—what's next? and further, when? For Wright, the destruction of Jerusalem is seen as God's vindication of Jesus and his followers—the Son of Man—and this event is of

---

105. He records his debt to Dodd; see Caird, *Language and Imagery,* 253.

106. Ibid., 271.

107. Wright, *Jesus and the Victory of God,* 320–68.

108. In my *New Vision for Israel,* 73, I put Wright, because of his emphasis on the destruction of Jerusalem, into the Weiss-Schweitzer camp. I would do the same for Caird's emphasis on the significance of 70 C.E., but neither of them moves into the consistent eschatology school of thought. Dodd permitted a future dimension to Jesus' view of the kingdom; it is this future dimension that is fully explored in a linguistic format by both Caird and Wright, but within the Dodd rubrics. Dodd, however, gave little attention to that future dimension, and he spent his energy expounding the realized nature of the kingdom.

momentous historical significance.[109] It is God's act on the historical plane. But is the entire future program of Jesus' language a study in a multiple set of unhistorical metaphorical images? Are parousia, resurrection, judgment, and final banquet each simply a metaphor for that vindication? Or, do those images move to a different time frame? The end? In spite of my reservations about the incompleteness of Wright's studies in the eschatology of Jesus, it is to the credit of Dodd and especially Caird and Wright that focus is given to the significance of the national mission of Jesus and the place that 70 C.E. occupies in Jesus' vision for the future (and therefore implications for his present). The language about imminent eschatology is not flat and literal (as it is with Weiss and Bultmann), and neither is it understood without historical sensitivity (Wright anchors the language in Israel's prophetic language). It is referential (it refers to the destruction of Jerusalem) even if it is also metaphorical—this in contrast to Bultmann, who slipped the referential grip of the language.

Inauthentic

Some think that the line taken by Bultmann, on the one hand, and Dodd, Caird, and Wright, on the other hand, is driven by theological needs. In particular, Dodd, Caird, and Wright are accused of saving Jesus at the expense of historical interpretation by appealing to metaphor. If Bultmann recognized the imminent language as an "illusion" on the part of Jesus (but found an underlying hermeneutical core), these other three reinterpret that language sufficiently enough to drive from the desk the notion of illusion. However, another line of thinking, reacting ultimately to Weiss and Schweitzer, is present today among those who think that the imminent language of Jesus is simply inauthentic. It derives from later Jewish Christians who mixed Jesus into a surviving Jewish apocalypse, or from other Christians with an apocalyptic bent. A notable example of this today is Marcus Borg, who thinks that the apocalyptic Jesus needs to be driven from the scene as a historical improbability.[110] Borg's missive to his fellow scholars contends that the "eschatological Jesus" is based on the authenticity of the coming Son of Man passages, the importation of imminency into the kingdom of God texts, and the assumed temporal framework used to understand what Jesus meant by "kingdom." Borg contests each of these conclusions and assumptions. This is an illustration, to be sure, that what counts as authentic determines the depiction of Jesus. Borg, in a second essay on the topic, contends that this view of his is becoming more typical of Jesus scholarship.[111] He is, in fact, correct in assessing one of the trends of

109. See especially Wright, *Jesus and the Victory of God*, 339–43, 360–65.

110. The most convenient study is Borg, "A Temperate Case for a Non-Eschatological Jesus," in *Jesus in Contemporary Scholarship* (Valley Forge, Pa.: Trinity, 1994), 47–68.

111. See Borg, "Jesus and Eschatology: Current Reflections," in *Jesus in Contemporary Scholarship*, 69–96.

contemporary historical Jesus studies, but scholarship can rarely appeal to a consensus for anything other than moral support.

This section can conclude with an examination of the nature of eschatological language.[112] A dominant thread of the Jesus traditions is his expectation of an imminent end: the language itself—whether or not it is pronounced illusory and then demythologized, or reinterpreted in an existentialist, Platonic, or metaphorical direction, and whether or not it is authentic—betrays an expectation of an imminent consummation of God's plans. Dale Allison examines the reinterpretation of the language of Jesus by C. H. Dodd, T. F. Glasson (who is otherwise not discussed here), G. B. Caird, and N. T. Wright. Essentially, these authors believe that first-century Jews would have known a good metaphor when they heard one. Allison responds with four claims, and he supports each one with incontrovertible evidence and logic: (1) many ancient and modern worldviews assert a blissful age to come, a golden age, and for many that age was/is imminent; (2) modern readers and ancient readers sometimes misunderstood metaphors and sometimes altered the meanings of metaphors, but there is a steady stream of evidence that prophetic and apocalyptic texts were understood literally—people "who take their eschatology straight";[113] (3) the struggle with unfulfilled prophecy demonstrates that ancients understood prophetic predictions literally; (4) cognitive dissonance—the condition of living with disappointed expectations—leads frequently to reinterpretation, and Allison thinks that these four scholars exhibit this tendency of religious movements.[114]

A Tendency to Anchor Jesus in Judaism

Because modern scholarship is in a contest to see who can find the most Jewish Jesus (to echo the tiring words of J. D. Crossan in public settings), it may surprise the reader to know that from the time of Bultmann's *Jesus and the Word* (1934) until Géza Vermès's *Jesus the Jew* (1973), nearly four decades of scholarship, Jesus was more or less seen as un-Jewish and was depicted either apart from his Jewish background or over against that background. There were reasons for this, all of them inexcusable.

Without doing any kind of survey of that sort of scholarship, we should note that this period of history also exhibited the modern, heinous tragedy of anti-Semitism in the Holocaust, and the Jesus books of that era, particularly

112. See especially Allison, *Jesus of Nazareth*, 152–69.
113. Ibid., 159.
114. Space prohibits further discussion, but see also J. Becker, *Jesus of Nazareth*, trans. J. E. Crouch (New York: de Gruyter, 1998), 85–224; G. E. Ladd, *The Presence of the Future: The Eschatology of Biblical Realism* (Grand Rapids: Eerdmans, 1974); and especially the insightful Ben Witherington III, *Jesus, Paul, and the End of the World* (Downers Grove, Ill.: InterVarsity, 1992); idem, *Jesus the Seer: The Progress of Prophecy* (Peabody, Mass.: Hendrickson, 1999), 246–92.

but not only German works, often reflected the times and provoked those times to further despicable ideas and acts.[115] Much has been written on this topic, with especially insightful cautions raised about the use of Gerhard Kittel's *Theological Dictionary of the New Testament,*[116] and it does little if any good here to list those German scholars of Jesus who participated in the Third Reich.[117] Books and scholars such as these are guilty not only for the specific claims they make, which can readily be put down, but also for setting up categories that then infiltrate generations of students, pastors, and laypeople and lead them to think that the way to understand something about Jesus is by setting him over against Judaism.[118] The categories remain with us to this day; we are not yet set free from this history of interpreting Jesus. The long story cannot be told in the short space here.

For Christians, the most widely read sources were two: for English readers, Alfred Edersheim's *The Life and Times of Jesus the Messiah,* and for German readers, H. Strack and P. Billerbeck's *Kommentar zum Neuen Testament aus Talmud und Midrasch.*[119] Neither of the studies should be (though both still are!) trusted in the realm of history, since both use Jewish sources indiscriminately and are driven by categories and bipolar oppositions that destroy a genuinely historical picture of Jesus. In contrast to many scholars, however, I am grateful for these works (and others of their ilk could be mentioned) because they put on the table some valuable information that could be used to understand Jesus historically, and because they attempted to raise the issue of the Jewishness of Jesus. Most Christians using these sources came away from them recognizing at least that Jesus was plenty Jewish.

One can say that modern study of Jesus, after Abraham Geiger, starts with Joseph Klausner's appreciative and critical study of Jesus, *Jesus of Nazareth: His Life, Times, and Teaching.*[120] A Lithuanian Jew who moved to Jerusalem in 1920

115. See especially Heschel, *Abraham Geiger and the Jewish Jesus.* See also R. P. Ericksen, *Theologians under Hitler: Gerhard Kittel, Paul Althaus, and Emanuel Hirsch* (New Haven: Yale University Press, 1985).

116. Some years ago I traded to a friend my English edition of Kittel for his German edition. Volume 4, published in 1942, has a list of those who had contributed to previous volumes but who had died in World War II (A. Stumpff, W. Gutbrod, H. Fritsch, and H. Hanse). Kittel, the editor of this (his last) volume of the series (on whom, see Ericksen, *Theologians under Hitler*), speaks of the "witness of the blood-offering" of these soldiers.

117. For names and ideas, see Heschel, *Abraham Geiger and the Jewish Jesus,* esp. 186–228, where the influential works of H. J. Holtzmann, J. Wellhausen, and E. Schürer are detailed.

118. For example, see W. Bousset, *Jesus,* trans. J. P. Trevelyan, ed. W. D. Morrison (London: Williams & Norgate, 1906). Bousset must have thought that the piety of the psalms was atypical of the faith in the "Old Testament" and for those who read it.

119. Edersheim's book was first published in 1883, was updated in 1886, and has undergone numerous reprintings, most recently by Eerdmans (Grand Rapids, 1971). Strack and Billerbeck's *Kommentar,* 6 vols. in 7 (Munich: Beck, 1922–61).

120. Joseph Klausner, *Jesus of Nazareth: His Life, Times, and Teaching,* trans. H. Danby (New York: Macmillan, 1926).

under the vision of Zionism, Klausner penned a book on Jesus that steered a path between polemical options and set out options that have been followed and filled in since his time. Though some fifteen years earlier than Klausner and under a deeper liberal impulse, C. G. Montefiore summarized his commentary work on the Synoptic Gospels with a careful, judicious, and appreciative study of the teachings of Jesus.[121] This line of thinking moves through scholars such as Israel Abrahams, Samuel Sandmel, Schalom Ben-Chorin,[122] and Pinchas Lapide,[123] but the two most important scholars are Géza Vermès and David Flusser.

In 1973 Géza Vermès, who had, advantageously, converted from Judaism to Roman Catholicism and then moved on to a priesthood and then back to Judaism, convinced Jesus scholars, in his nicely written *Jesus the Jew*, that Jesus was thoroughly Jewish.[124] Vermès sought to present Jesus in the context of Jewish charismatic *hasidim*, like Honi the Circle Drawer and Hanina ben Dosa, and did so, to some extent, convincingly. Using an eclectic method not trapped by the criteria of authenticity, Vermès is known for setting Jesus into his Galilean context, for his careful study of "Lord," and for his careful attention to the vernacular nuance of "son of man." Twenty years later, Vermès published a study on the teachings of Jesus, *The Religion of Jesus the Jew*, but his creative impulse had died out, and the book remains little more than an uneventful trip through known territory.[125] Regardless, the world of Jesus scholarship will remain indebted to Géza Vermès's *Jesus the Jew*.[126]

David Flusser, formerly professor of comparative religion at Hebrew University in Jerusalem, published two books on Jesus, with the later book being

121. C. G. Montefiore, *Some Elements of the Religious Teaching of Jesus according to the Synoptic Gospels* (London: Macmillan, 1910).

122. Ben-Chorin's Jesus book recently has been translated into English: *Brother Jesus: The Nazarene through Jewish Eyes*, trans. J. S. Klein and M. Reinhart (Athens: University of Georgia Press, 2001).

123. For a summary of the writings of these four scholars, see D. A. Hagner, *The Jewish Reclamation of Jesus: An Analysis and Critique of the Modern Jewish Study of Jesus* (Grand Rapids: Zondervan, 1984). Hagner summarizes fairly and judiciously the history of the modern discussion while also asserting that the reclamation of Jesus by Jewish scholars is often done at the expense of Jesus' personal claims.

124. Géza Vermès, *Jesus the Jew: A Historian's Reading of the Gospels* (London: Collins, 1973). His desire to sit down "with a mind empty of prejudice" (19) is a noble, if never completely attainable, goal. His autobiography, which indulges in too much self-defense, is *Providential Accidents: An Autobiography* (Lanham, Md.: Rowman & Littlefield, 1998).

125. Géza Vermès, *The Religion of Jesus the Jew* (London: SCM, 1993). In addition, see Vermès, *The Gospel of Jesus the Jew*, Riddell Memorial Lectures 48 (Newcastle upon Tyne: University of Newcastle upon Tyne, 1981); *Jesus and the World of Judaism* (Philadelphia: Fortress, 1983); and *The Changing Faces of Jesus* (London: Penguin, 2000), containing a religious address to Jews, Christians, and those who have lost their faith (269–70).

126. We should note here that the willingness of scholarship to move to Jesus' Jewishness was prepared for by W. D. Davies, *Paul and Rabbinic Judaism: Some Rabbinic Elements in Pauline Theology*, 4th ed. (Philadelphia: Fortress, 1980), who single-handedly dismantled the Bultmannian line on Paul's relationship to the Greco-Roman world of thought.

a culmination of his many studies on Jesus and earliest Christianity.[127] If that book lacks a cohesive presentation of Jesus, it, along with that of Ben-Chorin, makes up for it in independent judgment—especially when it comes to judgments of historicity,[128] clever insights, and lucid comments on the various events and teachings of Jesus. His knowledge of Jewish sources, including a strong command of the Dead Sea Scrolls, and ancient historical sources from the classical world, as well as his appreciation for the Mennonite approach to Christian faith, lead him to present a Jesus who is quite comfortable with both Jews and Christians, ancient and modern, while totally comfortable with neither. A significant feature of Flusser's book is his willingness to let Jesus be Jesus, and that means to let him make his astounding self-claims. For example, Flusser thinks that Jesus may have thought of himself as the Servant of the Lord from his baptism onward.[129] Correctly, I believe, Flusser thinks that the creative moments for Jesus were in his understanding of love, the call for a new morality, and his notion of the kingdom of heaven, and Flusser affirms the view of Abraham Geiger that Jesus was closest to the Pharisees.[130] This movement of Jesus establishing the kingdom led ultimately to the church,[131] even if that church took his message and mission and transformed it—and Flusser particularly takes issue with Jesus thinking of himself as dying for the sins of others.[132] As is the case with most Jewish studies of Jesus, Flusser's devalued the place of Jesus in his own message.[133]

Let me add a third scholar, Paula Fredriksen, a convert from Roman Catholicism to Judaism, who as such neatly bridges the gap.[134] The book has an overly ambitious title, and the focus of the book's question, on why Jesus died and not his followers, permits her to explore many fields not obviously part of the material necessary to answer her question. But what she does explore is nicely written and conversant with a significant strand of Jesus scholarship

127. David Flusser, with R. Steven Notley, *Jesus*, 2nd ed. (Jerusalem: Magnes, 1998). Notley writes an encomium on Flusser in the new edition. In addition, see D. Flusser's collection of essays, *Judaism and the Origins of Christianity* (Jerusalem: Magnes, 1988).

128. For example, that "the Synoptic Gospels are based upon one or more non-extant early documents composed by Jesus' disciples and the early church in Jerusalem" (Flusser, *Jesus*, 21). It is a trait of some of Jewish scholarship, especially with some older scholars who may have lived most of their lives in Israel, that it approaches the Gospels with less skepticism and seeks to explain many of the traditions in light of (sometimes much) later rabbinic sources. I think here of D. Flusser and S. Ben-Chorin, as well as D. Daube, *The New Testament and Rabbinic Judaism*, Jordan Lectures in Comparative Religion 2 (London: University of London, Athlone, 1956; reprint, New York: Arno, 1973; Peabody, Mass.: Hendrickson, n.d.).

129. Flusser, *Jesus*, 42.

130. Ibid., 81–112.

131. Ibid., 111.

132. Ibid., 123.

133. Ibid., 176–77.

134. Paula Fredriksen, *Jesus of Nazareth, King of the Jews: A Jewish Life and the Emergence of Christianity* (New York: Knopf, 1999).

(especially that of E. P. Sanders), and on the whole she tackles what I think to be a fundamental issue: the death of Jesus. Her book does not reveal a specially Jewish Jesus, though in passing she dismisses and destroys many shibboleths of modern Christian scholarship on Jesus—she is especially keen to destroy the notion that Jesus had much to do with Rome and that Jews were especially caught up in xenophobia with respect to Rome. The strength of the book is its weakness: she penetratingly focuses on Jesus through the lens of why he, but not his followers, died; that is its strength, and it confirms J. P. Meier's criterion of rejection/execution. Its weakness is her solution: Jesus died because the (newly acquired) enthusiastic crowds in Jerusalem hailed him as messiah.[135] Death was not part of his mission—at all. "Jesus, the focus of this popular conviction, had in essence lost control of his audience."[136] I doubt this. Jesus was too swift upstairs to give his life accidentally, and he had plenty of opportunity to run had he wanted to. The universal testimony of the Jesus traditions is that Jesus knew that he was to die and stuck his head into the lion's mouth anyway. The concern with Jesus' Judaism continues.

Following Jeremias, and in direct polemic with him, E. P. Sanders essayed a more believable portrait of Jesus by setting him into a more accurate historical construct (restoration eschatology) through examining his actions that can be more or less established with historical probability.[137] Sanders earlier demonstrated, to the satisfaction of a wide variety of scholars, that Christians had misunderstood Judaism for centuries because it had forced Judaism into Martin Luther's polemics with Roman Catholicism.[138] Assuming his earlier study, Sanders then builds a case for Jesus fitting into the same general pattern. If Sanders's method is at times overly skeptical, it cannot be said that he has failed to set Jesus into a credible first-century Jewish context. In particular, Sanders thinks that we have to begin with the observation that Jesus was crucified, and where there is smoke there is fire. His portrait of Jesus is his attempt to figure out what kind of Jesus got himself crucified at the hands of the authorities.

From the most recent decade, I mention the informed study of Michael O. Wise on "Judah Messiah," the founder of the Qumran community,[139] as well as my own book *A New Vision for Israel,* which attempts to explain the teachings of Jesus consistently from the angle of Jesus' mission to Israel in the context of an urgent, prophetic call to repent if Israel wishes to escape the disaster of destruction that he sees on the horizon. And one thinks here of the larger, more comprehensive work of N. T. Wright, whose study of Jesus sets him into a credible, theologically oriented context of addressing the nation and calling it

---

135. The critical chapter, which is the climax of the entire book, is on pp. 235–59.

136. Fredriksen, *Jesus of Nazareth,* 247.

137. Sanders, *Jesus and Judaism.*

138. See E. P. Sanders, *Paul and Palestinian Judaism: A Comparison of Patterns of Religion* (Philadelphia: Fortress, 1977).

139. M. O. Wise, *The First Messiah: Investigating the Savior before Jesus* (San Francisco: HarperSanFrancisco, 1999).

to, among other things, avoid the rush to violence if it wishes to maintain its faithful heritage.[140] D. C. Allison sets Jesus' eschatology into a Jewish context with a further defining apparatus drawn from the world of the sociology of millenarian movements.[141] Finally, a creative attempt for dialogue between Jewish and Christian scholars, done by comparing and contrasting Hillel and Jesus, was attempted in Jerusalem in 1992 and was published in 1997 under the title *Hillel and Jesus*.[142] Among the various topics are the Pharisees, factionalism, the Cynics, Jesus' socioeconomic background, the sayings traditions of Jesus and Hillel, the Golden Rule, and prayer.

The most recent book that sets Jesus into his Jewish context is the sometimes baffling, but always interesting, study of Bruce Chilton, *Rabbi Jesus*.[143] Chilton himself is hard to pin down (if one likes to do such things), for in former works he set out some lines that were not followed here,[144] but some of his earlier adumbrations are now being made clearer. For instance, Jesus is herein stripped of nearly every shade of Christian theological orthodoxy (in the creedal sense)—no virginal conception (he was a *mamzer*, or child of suspect parentage, i.e., a bastard child), no dying for the sins of others, no resurrection—and was instead a Galilean rabbinic mystic[145] who attempted to occupy the temple in order to effect the Zecharian vision of purity. Chilton's method is not the reified criteria approach, but is what he has described as a "generative exegesis" that sets Jesus into a believable Jewish world. Chilton's forte is his command of Jewish Targumim, especially *Targum Isaiah*, and his growing awareness (in close consultation with Jacob Neusner—references omitted!) of the rabbinic corpus. There is much to commend Chilton's portrait of Jesus (style, Jewishness, creativity, etc.), but the independence of lines of thought, not to say eccentricities at times, will lead to further discussion, refinement, and adjustment before Chilton's Jesus will be seen as a major alternative in the scholarly market.

Conclusion

Indeed, there is much at stake in the study of Jesus, but that should not and will not keep us from trying to piece together the puzzles. And the early

---

140. Wright, *Jesus and the Victory of God*.

141. Allison, *Jesus of Nazareth*.

142. J. H. Charlesworth and L. L. Johns, eds., *Hillel and Jesus: Comparative Studies of Two Major Religious Leaders* (Minneapolis: Fortress, 1997).

143. Bruce Chilton, *Rabbi Jesus: An Intimate Biography* (New York: Doubleday, 2000).

144. Chilton has written numerous works on Jesus, and it would be unfair to him not to mention three: *God in Strength: Jesus' Announcement of the Kingdom*, SNTSU 1 (Freistadt: Plöchl, 1979); his published dissertation, *Pure Kingdom: Jesus' Vision of God* (Grand Rapids: Eerdmans, 1996); and the more technical *The Temple of Jesus: His Sacrificial Program within a Cultural History of Sacrifice* (University Park, Pa.: Pennsylvania State University Press, 1992).

145. The informative study here is Chilton, *Rabbi Jesus*, 174–96.

Christian witness to Jesus ought not be stripped bare in the search to come to terms with him. Where have we come? In my judgment, though it has taken nearly a century of badgering and bullying, Christian scholarship has gradually accepted the challenge of Henry J. Cadbury to avoid modernizing Jesus, and has, in a gradual but progressive way, finally offered to the reading public, in as many forms as one might wish, a Jewish Jesus who is credible within first-century Judaism, who gave rise to the basic contours of the early Christian movement, and who can truly be Lord to the church and human enough to be brother to the church as well as all other humans on the face of the earth. If critics and conservatives alike can listen to the discordant voices of this scholarship long enough to hear what is being said, and if theologians and historians can work themselves into a comfortable peace agreement, and if eschatologians can hear what the linguists are saying about prophetic language, then there will be sufficient ground for scholarship to proceed together for a century of multidisciplinary and collaborative efforts.

9

Modern Approaches
to the Parables

Klyne Snodgrass

Throughout much of the church's history the parables of Jesus have been mistreated, rearranged, abused, and butchered. Often they still are today. They are *used* more than they are heard and understood. That there is a long history and tradition of abuse does not make it valid.[1]

The modern period of technical parable research begins with the fierce protest of Adolf Jülicher against the abusive allegorizing of the church.[2] One cannot understand modern research on the parables apart from knowing about the church's allegorizing and Jülicher's protest. Despite objections from luminaries such as John Chrysostom and John Calvin,[3] until the nineteenth century most parable interpretation was mired in theological allegorizing.[4]

1. For longer treatments of the history of parables research, see Norman Perrin, *Jesus and the Language of the Kingdom* (Philadelphia: Fortress, 1976), 89–193; Warren S. Kissinger, *The Parables of Jesus* (Metuchen, N.J.: Scarecrow, 1979), 1–230; Craig L. Blomberg, *Interpreting the Parables* (Downers Grove, Ill.: InterVarsity, 1990), 13–167; and Klyne Snodgrass, "From Allegorizing to Allegorizing: A History of the Interpretation of the Parables of Jesus," in *The Challenge of Jesus' Parables*, ed. Richard N. Longenecker (Grand Rapids: Eerdmans, 2000), 3–29.

2. Adolf Jülicher, *Die Gleichnisreden Jesu*, 2 vols. (Freiburg: Mohr, 1888–89).

3. John Chrysostom, *The Gospel of Matthew*, Homily 64.3; John Calvin, *Calvin's Commentaries*, ed. David W. Torrance and Thomas F. Torrance, vol. 3, *A Harmony of the Gospels: Matthew, Mark and Luke* (Edinburgh: Saint Andrew, 1972), 37–39, on the parable of the good Samaritan.

4. A glance at Stephen L. Wailes's *Medieval Allegories of Jesus' Parables* (Berkeley: University of California Press, 1987) illustrates the problem.

The theology, practice, and issues of the church were read back into Jesus'
parables. Augustine's interpretation of the parable of the good Samaritan is
classic, with virtually every feature in the story standing for some aspect of the
Christian story of salvation. The victim is Adam, and Christ is the Samaritan.
Even the donkey and the innkeeper are given significance, the former standing for the incarnation, and the latter for the apostle Paul. Such allegorizing
was the assumed method of parable preaching from Irenaeus to the end of
the nineteenth century. Connections were drawn that seem strange to us. The
sores on Lazarus in the parable of Lazarus and the rich man (Luke 16:19–31)
could be understood as confession of sins, and the five yoke of oxen in Luke's
parable of the banquet (Luke 14:15–24) as the five senses.[5] The five times
that the owner hires workers in the parable of the workers (Matt. 20:1–16)
can stand for the divisions of world history (from Adam to Noah, etc.) or the
history of individuals.[6] Competing allegories of the same text could coexist
without difficulty.

The church was not alone in allegorizing. This method of interpretation
was well established in Judaism, especially with Philo, but also in Qumran (see
1QpHab XII.2–10), and also practiced by Hellenistic interpreters of Homer
and Plato. It still occurs in modern preaching, but neither ancient precedent
nor modern adaptation gives it legitimacy.

Further, the allegorizers in the church were not ignorant people. They knew,
at least on some level, that they were not merely interpreting the text, for they
did not allow doctrine to be based on allegorizing, and they set limits on who
could allegorize and within what boundaries.[7] They were meditating on the
text, seeing mirrored in the text truth they already knew by other avenues, but
they were not hearing the parables as Jesus or the evangelists intended them.

Adolf Jülicher rejected all allegorizing as distortion, and in the process he
rejected that Jesus told allegories at all. He thought that Jesus' parables were
expanded similes, literal speech, merely simple comparisons with only one
point of correspondence (one *tertium comparationis*) between image (*Bild*)
and reality (*Sache*). They were self-evident and did not need interpretation.
For Jülicher, the one point that the parables make is nearly always a simple,
pious maxim. Allegory, however, is expanded metaphor, indirect speech that
says one thing and means another. Metaphor and allegory hide and need to be
decoded. The evangelists thought that parables were such enigmatic, mysterious speech that needed explanations. Anywhere that allegory is found in the
Gospels, such as with the parable of the sower, where the sowings on various

---

5. Augustine, *Questions on the Gospels*, 2.38, and *Sermon 62* (*A Select Library of the Nicene and
Post-Nicene Fathers of the Christian Church*, first series, ed. P. Schaff [Grand Rapids: Eerdmans,
n.d.], 6:447), respectively. Allegorizing was a result of the belief that the Scriptures had four
levels of meaning (literal, theological, moral, and about heaven), but doctrine could be derived
only from the first.

6. See Wailes, *Medieval Allegories of Jesus' Parables*, 137–44.

7. See David Steinmetz, "Calvin and the Irrepressible Spirit," *Ex Auditu* 12 (1996): 94–107.

soils represent various responses to Jesus' preaching, Jülicher thought that the evangelists are to blame.

Jülicher also established four categories for analysis of parables that are still used: similitudes (such as the leaven), parables, example stories,[8] and allegories—although debate continues whether allegory and example story are legitimate categories. Jülicher also argued that the evangelists altered Jesus' parables, which encouraged attempts to reconstruct the original versions.

Reaction against Jülicher was almost immediate and has continued to the present,[9] but despite the cogency of the arguments against Jülicher, his assumptions still influence much work on parables. Even when people have never heard Jülicher's name, they frequently have repeated the assertion that parables have only one point of comparison. The desire not to allegorize parables as the church had done has caused people to retreat to Jülicher's arms without realizing how inadequate his theory is. Only in the last few decades have the criticisms become so forceful that people now can admit that Jülicher's position cannot be maintained.[10] The rejection of allegorizing—the process of seeing correspondences where they were not intended—has nothing to do with correspondences inherent *in* the stories and in their function as analogies. Gallons of ink have been spilled trying to distinguish parable from allegory, which is impossible, particularly when it is questionable whether allegory is a separate genre at all and not merely a way of thinking.[11] All parables are allegorical to some degree. Parables certainly may have more than one point of correspondence, but interpretation is not about finding points of correspondence so much as determining how the analogy works in each case. In fact, correspondences may be part of the way parables deceive the hearer into the truth.[12] Also obvious with any careful reflection is that parables do not all function the same way. Each must be heard and treated individually.

---

8. These are stories where the figures are positive or negative examples for human conduct. Usually, only four are identified, all in Luke: the good Samaritan, the rich fool, the rich man and Lazarus, and the Pharisee and the toll collector.

9. Among the early dissenters was Paul Fiebig. See his *Altjüdische Gleichnisse und die Gleichnisse Jesu* (Tübingen: Mohr [Siebeck], 1904); *Die Gleichnisreden Jesus im Lichte der rabbinischen Gleichnisse des neutestamentlichen Zeitalters* (Tübingen: Mohr [Siebeck], 1912).

10. See especially Madeleine Boucher, *The Mysterious Parable* (Washington, D.C.: Catholic Biblical Association of America, 1977); Blomberg, *Interpreting the Parables;* David Flusser, *Die rabbinischen Gleichnisse und der Gleichniserzähler Jesus,* part 1, *Das Wesen der Gleichnisse,* Judaica et Christiana 4 (Bern: Lang, 1981); David Stern, *Parables in Midrash* (Cambridge: Harvard University Press, 1991).

11. See Boucher, *The Mysterious Parable,* 17–25; John W. Sider, *Interpreting the Parables* (Grand Rapids: Zondervan, 1995), 18–23.

12. Søren Kierkegaard's language (see Thomas C. Oden, ed., *Parables of Kierkegaard* [Princeton, N.J.: Princeton University Press, 1978], xiii). Note Nathan's parable to David (2 Sam. 12:1–14). There are correspondences between the rich man and David, the poor man and Uriah, and the ewe and Bathsheba. But it is not the ewe that dies in reality; it is the poor man, Uriah.

After Jülicher, the names of C. H. Dodd and especially Joachim Jeremias dominated the parables scene from 1935 to about 1970. Both stood in the Jülicher tradition, both stressed the historical and cultural background of the parables, and both attempted to reconstruct the parables by removing interpretations and allegorical features supposedly added by the church. Both also emphasized the importance of eschatology for understanding Jesus' parables.

Dodd's significance is somewhat surprising in that only a little over half of his small book *The Parables of the Kingdom*[13] actually discusses the parables. No doubt, the impact of this book is partly due to his extreme emphasis on realized eschatology. He argued that with Jesus, the kingdom had come; the harvest began in Jesus' day, not at some future parousia. He argued that the early church altered Jesus' realized eschatology to emphasize present morality and future eschatology. For example, for Dodd, the parable of the talents was originally about the conduct of Pharisees but was changed by the church to address moral responsibility, the problem of the delay of the parousia, and the end judgment at Christ's return.[14]

Jeremias built on Dodd's work and provided a much more substantive treatment of the parables and their background.[15] Jeremias's contribution can be summarized in three main areas: (1) focus on Palestinian culture and background; (2) delineation of ten ways the church altered the parables, which provided a blueprint for reconstructing the original parables and their meanings; and (3) an understanding of the parables as teaching a present kingdom offered to the poor, an offer that was at the same time both grace and crisis. His understanding of eschatology was more nuanced than Dodd's in that he argued that the kingdom was in the *process* of realization in the ministry of Jesus. Jeremias's reconstructions of the parables typically ignored the context in which the parables were placed by the evangelists and removed introductory and concluding material and anything suspected of being a result of the church's theological allegorizing. This practice of reducing parables to a briefer, authentic core continues to the present in many critical studies. The *Gospel of Thomas*, which came to light after the early editions of Jeremias's work, contained just such shortened versions of some parables and seemed for certain scholars to confirm Jeremias's deallegorized reconstructions.

The influence of Jeremias's work has been so strong that Norman Perrin could say, rather foolishly, that future interpretation of the parables should be interpretation of the parables as Jeremias has analyzed them![16] No one would say this today. Jeremias's work is valuable and must be consulted, but it must also be verified and critiqued. His discussion of the ways the church altered

13. C. H. Dodd, *The Parables of the Kingdom* (London: Nisbet, 1935).
14. Ibid., 146–53.
15. Joachim Jeremias, *The Parables of Jesus* (New York: Scribner, 1963).
16. Perrin, *Language of the Kingdom*, 101.

the parables often proceeds on faulty assumptions.[17] Sometimes his facts are not correct, and he—like Dodd before him—often removes allegorizing in analyzing a parable only to restore it when explaining the parable.[18]

Existentialist, Artistic, and Early Literary Approaches

Frustration with current practice leads to new efforts, and that is precisely what happened as Jeremias's influence began to wane. From about 1970 on, no leading figure dominates the scene as Jülicher, Dodd, and Jeremias had done. Several movements or emphases take the stage for a brief period, only to yield to newer emphases. Sometimes the same individuals are involved at several stages of the discussion. Already from the 1960s, dissatisfaction was being voiced for several reasons. The historical-critical method so prized by Dodd and Jeremias did not do enough. The power of the language and the force and beauty of the parables were lost. The historical reconstruction of the parables had left them limp and lifeless. The new approaches, however, still operated under the shadow of Jülicher and with much of the heritage of Dodd and Jeremias.

Most important of the new approaches was the work of Ernst Fuchs and his students Eta Linnemann and Eberhard Jüngel. Their work was still strongly historical in that they were heavily involved in the "new quest" for the historical Jesus, but they were equally involved in the "new hermeneutic." Fuchs brought the concerns of existentialism and the insights of philosophical discussions of language to bear on the interpretation of the parables.[19] Fuchs's thought is complex, but he argued rightly that existence is essentially linguistic. He spoke of the language-character of existence and of the power that language has to create reality. The parables are "language events" (*Sprachereignisse*); their telling brings to expression the reality to which they point. This concept is similar to the idea of "performative utterances," which emphasizes the power of language to accomplish and enact. The parables are a summons to the existence that Jesus embodies and describes.

Eta Linnemann's book on the parables[20] is an attempt at a systematic explanation of the parables following Fuchs's insights, and the concern for language

17. For example, that the shorter version is necessarily the original; that the *Gospel of Thomas* often is earlier; that virtually none of the parables was directed originally to the disciples; that similar parables are necessarily parallels, one or both of which has been altered.

18. See, for example, Jeremias's treatments of the parables of the banquet (Jesus could not have uttered this parable as an allegory of the feast of the time of salvation, but he may well have had it in mind!) and of the wicked tenants (Jeremias, *The Parables of Jesus,* 69, 72).

19. For English translations of some of his most important essays, see Ernst Fuchs, *Studies of the Historical Jesus*, trans. A. Scobie (Naperville, Ill.: Allenson, 1964). See also Jack Dean Kingsbury, "Ernst Fuchs' Existentialist Interpretation of the Parables," *LQ* 2 (1970): 380–95; A. C. Thiselton, "The Parables as Language-Event," *SJT* 23 (1970): 437–68.

20. Eta Linnemann, *Parables of Jesus* (London: SPCK, 1966).

results in the effort to enable people to hear the parables as Jesus' original audience would have heard them. In the end, however, Linnemann was influenced as much by Jeremias as by Fuchs, and despite the focus on language, the power of the parables is not communicated any better than before.

Those emphasizing the artistic quality of the parables were still very much concerned with the existential dimension of the parables (the way they mirror human existence), but the earlier concerns for the historical Jesus were largely abandoned. G. V. Jones sought a wider relevance for the parables because of their artistic, literary, and existential character, but found that relatively few of them (eight of the fifty he considered) were susceptible to wider interpretation. Many were strictly limited by their historical reference.[21] For Dan Via, the parables are autonomous, aesthetic works not bound by the author's intention or by Jesus' original situation.[22] The parables address us because they offer an understanding of existence that calls for decision. Via emphasized that parables cannot be completely translated into another form—a point often repeated—and he distinguished between tragic and comic parables (comic in the sense of a positive movement). His analysis of individual parables has three sections: historico-literary criticism, literary existential analysis (usually the longest section), and existential-theological interpretation. His explanations often are like Jülicher's pious maxims with an existential twist. For example, he suggests that the parable of the wicked tenants is merely a parable about unbelief, and it teaches that sin is a person's self-centered effort to reject any and all limitations that God imposes.[23] Surely, the parable does more than that.

Robert Funk was influential in conveying the impact of Fuchs and his students to the English-speaking world. Like them, he brought existentialist concerns to parables research and emphasized that the parables were language events, but he added a concern for literary analysis that had been neglected.[24] He adapted Dodd's definition of a parable, emphasizing especially that parables are metaphors that arrest by their vividness and that the application of parables is left imprecise to tease hearers into making their own applications. In opposition to Jülicher, Funk, like nearly everyone now, saw parable as an extension of metaphor, not simile. Further, simile was not viewed as superior to metaphor in communicating, for simile merely illustrates, whereas metaphor can create meaning. The hearer's engagement with metaphor as a participant in creating meaning shows that parables cannot be reduced to a single moral point (as Jülicher argued) or to a single eschatological point (as Dodd and Jeremias said). Metaphors are *bearers* of the reality to which they refer, and since parables are extended metaphors, they are not reducible to ideas and are not expendable

---

21. G. V. Jones, *The Art and Truth of the Parables* (London: SPCK, 1964), esp. 141–43.

22. Dan Otto Via, *The Parables* (Philadelphia: Fortress, 1967).

23. Ibid., 137.

24. Robert W. Funk, *Language, Hermeneutic, and Word of God* (New York: Harper & Row, 1966); only pp. 124–222 deal directly with parables.

once meaning has been derived. Both metaphors and parables remain open-ended, with potential for new meaning. Funk was not arguing for uncontrolled creation of meaning, as Jesus' original telling of the parable had an intent that serves as a control over reinterpretation. Like Jeremias, Funk also at times favored the versions of the parables in the *Gospel of Thomas*.

Closely allied with Funk, and also bringing literary concerns to the analysis of parables, is the work of John Dominic Crossan.[25] Convinced, however, that the early church had significantly changed the parables, Crossan also intensified the Jeremias tradition of reconstructing the parables. His formula is common with others as well. Parables are removed from their contexts and shorn of introductions, interpretive conclusions, and any elements suspected of theological allegory. If the *Gospel of Thomas* has the parable, that version is preferred. Crossan viewed the parables as inviting and requiring participation. They convey the reality of the kingdom, not just information about the kingdom. The kingdom is not about time, however, but about an act of God. Crossan argued for a permanent eschatology, one emphasizing "the permanent presence of God as the one who challenges the world and shatters its complacency repeatedly."[26] Crossan divided parables into three categories corresponding to "three modes of the Kingdom's temporality": parables of advent, of reversal, and of action. The parables of reversal were changed by the church into example stories. Crossan is always interesting, and no doubt God's kingdom always shatters our world, but one often feels that the parables have been forced into a mold, and not only have they been shorn of their introductions and conclusions but also deprived of their meanings.[27]

Possibly the biggest detour in parables interpretation came in the forays into "structuralist" approaches (roughly from 1970 to 1980), especially in the SBL Parables Seminar and the early issues of the journal *Semeia*. Via, Funk, and Crossan were participants in these attempts. Structuralists did not seek the historical meaning of Jesus or of the evangelists. Instead, they compared both surface and deep structures of various texts (even from different chronological periods) to chart the movements, motives, functions, oppositions, and resolutions within texts. Rarely did these studies contribute much to understanding; most were burdened with technical jargon. As quickly as structuralist approaches became the trend, they faded from the scene. Perrin's negative assessment is justified: "The contribution this [the literary-structuralist approach] may make to the understanding and interpretation of this or any parable is by no means either obvious or immediate."[28]

---

25. John Dominic Crossan, *In Parables: The Challenge of the Historical Jesus* (New York: Harper & Row, 1973).

26. Ibid., 26.

27. Is the parable of the good Samaritan only a metaphor of the reversal the kingdom brings? Is the parable of the wicked tenants really a story about a successful murder to give an example of people who saw their opportunity and acted upon it? See Crossan, *In Parables*, 66–67, 96.

28. Perrin, *Language of the Kingdom*, 180; see also 181.

By far the most important literary approach to the parables, even though it has not received the attention it deserves, is Madeleine Boucher's *The Mysterious Parable*,[29] a brief book on parable theory and the purpose of parables in Mark 4. With literary sophistication she provides a devastating critique of Jülicher and gives sane discussions of parable and allegory. She, like other literary specialists, argues that allegory is not a literary genre at all, but a way of thinking. With this insight, all the discussions attempting to distinguish parable and allegory are set aside. She knows that parables can be obvious or mysterious and sees nothing inherently objectionable about the presence of interpretations with the Synoptic parables. Her explanation of Mark's redactional shaping of his parable discussion (ch. 4) and its theology of hardness of heart is superb.

Other literary approaches increasingly questioned the legitimacy of Jülicher's distinction between image (*Bild*) and object (*Sache*) in parables and of the search for a *tertium comparationis*.[30] This conclusion is virtually necessitated when one says that metaphor and parable cannot be translated into literal speech. If metaphor must be participated in and cannot be reduced, one cannot leave the image to find an object.

Studies Emphasizing Palestinian Culture and Jewish Parables

Paul Fiebig's early protest against Jülicher argued against the latter's dependence on Greek categories and his failure to consider rabbinic parables. Fiebig was not given sufficient respect, and his studies still merit attention. Since the 1960s, parallel and almost unrelated to other approaches discussed so far, a number of people have argued that the best help for understanding Jesus' parables is the Semitic world. Two scholars emphasized Jewish and Palestinian culture. J. Duncan M. Derrett brought information from ancient (especially rabbinic) law to show attitudes and assumptions about contracts, social relations, and other everyday phenomena that Jesus used in his parables.[31] Kenneth Bailey's works also emphasize Palestinian culture and ancient Jewish sources, but much of his understanding of the Palestinian mind-set is based on his experience with Bedouins as a missionary in Lebanon.[32] Bailey also is adept at

29. Washington, D.C.: Catholic Biblical Association of America, 1977.

30. See Hans Weder, *Die Gleichnisse Jesu als Metaphern* (Göttingen: Vandenhoeck & Ruprecht, 1978), 97.

31. See J. Duncan M. Derrett, *Law in the New Testament* (London: Darton, Longman & Todd, 1970); *Studies in the New Testament*, 2 vols. (Leiden: Brill, 1977–78). Derrett's information is helpful, but his interpretive suggestions stretch credulity.

32. See Kenneth Bailey, *Poet and Peasant: A Literary Cultural Approach to the Parables in Luke* (Grand Rapids: Eerdmans, 1976); *Through Peasant Eyes: More Lucan Parables, Their Culture and Style* (Grand Rapids: Eerdmans, 1980); *Finding the Lost: Cultural Keys to Luke 15* (St. Louis: Concordia, 1992). An earlier effort to interpret the parables from their Jewish backgrounds is W. Oesterley, *The Gospel Parables in the Light of Their Jewish Background* (New York: Macmillan, 1936).

analyzing the structure of the parables. His work is valuable but must be used cautiously, for one cannot assume that modern Bedouin practice is the same as ancient Jewish practice.

Several other studies contribute significantly by analyzing and comparing rabbinic parables with those of Jesus, the most important of which is the work of David Flusser.[33] The rabbinic parables are quite similar to Jesus' parables in form and subject matter. The biggest difference is that rabbinic parables usually serve to explain biblical texts, whereas Jesus' parables rarely do. All of these studies reject the legitimacy of Jülicher's approach, and the more that scholars pay attention to rabbinic parables, the less likely they are to be impressed with arguments to excise the introductions and conclusions of the parables or with the relevance of the *Gospel of Thomas*. Flusser is confident about the reliability of the Gospel tradition, including the contexts of the parables. He also correctly points out that Jesus' parables are more pseudorealistic than realistic. They use everyday materials, but they do not usually narrate everyday events.

Still, rabbinic parallels must be used with caution, for all of them are later than the NT. Other than the parables in the OT,[34] very few Jewish parables can be shown to be earlier than those of Jesus.[35]

From the demise of structural approaches to the present, no dominant trend has taken the stage. Some studies focus on polyvalence and an intentional return to allegorizing, and some on sociocultural reconstruction. Others render the parables toothless, even banal in their intent. With many of these studies, the chance of hearing the voice of Jesus gets lost in the chorus of interpretations.

Polyvalence and Allegorizing

Partly because of modern literary criticism and reader-response approaches to literature, we have come full circle. Some scholars and their followers now allegorize in ways not unlike Augustine's. Seeds planted by Funk and Via have gone to weed. John Dominic Crossan, who had rejected allegory earlier, radically altered his views and argued for a much more positive view of allegory. While not so concerned with finding exact correspondences between image and reality, Crossan argued that a text's meaning is determined by the interac-

33. Flusser, *Die rabbinischen Gleichnisse und der Gleichniserzähler Jesus.* See also the works of Flusser's student Brad Young, *Jesus and His Jewish Parables* (New York: Paulist, 1989); idem, *The Parables: Jewish Tradition and Christian Interpretation* (Peabody, Mass.: Hendrickson, 1998); Stern, *Parables in Midrash;* the collections of parables by Asher Feldman, *The Parables and Similes of the Rabbis* (Cambridge: Cambridge University Press, 1924); Harvey K. McArthur and Robert M. Johnston, *They Also Taught in Parables* (Grand Rapids: Zondervan, 1990).

34. See Klyne Snodgrass, "Parables and the Hebrew Scriptures," in *To Hear and Obey: Essays in Honor of Fredrick Carlson Holmgren,* ed. Bradley J. Bergfalk and Paul E. Koptak (Chicago: Covenant, 1997), 164–77.

35. See 4Q302 and the parable-like sayings of *1 Enoch* and John the Baptist.

tion of the reader with the text. He emphasized that parables are paradoxical and polyvalent, capable of multiple meanings, because they can be read in multiple contexts. Polyvalent narration reveals the play of plot across many levels of reality.[36] An interpreter of parables is a trained player who plays with the narrative in various contexts, and the possibilities are without limit.

Mary Ann Tolbert provides a more substantial defense of polyvalent interpretation. Such an approach is valid for her because equally competent scholars reach different conclusions about meaning anyway. She knows that the more specific the context in which a parable is placed, the more definite is its meaning, but she devalues the Gospels' contexts because the evangelists have placed some of the same parables in different contexts. She is concerned about the integrity of the parables but also argues that the interpreter may choose the context in which they are to be read in order to "exploit" their polyvalency. For example, she interpreted the parable of the prodigal son in terms of Freudian psychology as speaking to the wish of every individual for harmony and unity within. The younger son corresponds to Freud's id, the elder brother to the superego, and the father to the ego. Or, for a different but equally valid Freudian reading, the parable speaks about the painful nature of emotional ambivalence. The excessive love of the father betrays hostility toward the prodigal, and the anger of the elder brother is displaced onto the father.[37] Jülicher has virtually been forgotten, and Augustine, while he may not have understood the Freudian conclusions, would have enjoyed the process!

We may grant that the parables are not merely simple stories and that they contain resonances and nuances not yet grasped, but this kind of polyvalent approach is way out of bounds. With such procedures the interpreter is no longer a hearer of the parables but instead has become a teller of parables. The parables of Jesus have been plagiarized and retold in new contexts. Susan Wittig's defense of polyvalent readings is revealing. She argued that what was signified by the parable becomes a second-order signifier. She granted that the original teller had a meaning system in mind and that from the teller's perspective multiple signifieds are wrong. But "from another, more objective point of view [!], what is demonstrated here is the ability to semantically alter a parabolic sign by embedding it within another belief-system and validating the new significance by reference to those beliefs."[38] Embedding parables in another belief system was exactly what Augustine was doing. Reflecting on

36. John Dominic Crossan, *Cliffs of Fall: Paradox and Polyvalence in the Parables of Jesus* (New York: Seabury, 1980), esp. 96–97; "Parable, Allegory, and Paradox," in *Semiology and the Parables,* ed. Daniel Patte (Pittsburgh: Pickwick, 1976), 247–81, esp. 271–78.

37. Mary Ann Tolbert, *Perspectives on the Parables: An Approach to Multiple Interpretations* (Philadelphia: Fortress, 1979), 30, 52–55, 63–71, 93, 102–7. For another example, see Daniel Patte, who gives three competing but equally valid interpretations of the parable of the unforgiving servant ("Bringing Out of the Gospel-Treasure What Is New and What Is Old: Two Parables in Matthew 18–23," *QR* 10 (1990): 79–108.

38. Susan Wittig, "A Theory of Polyvalent Reading," *SBLSP* 14 (1975): 177.

the significance of a parable in another system is not illegitimate, but it is not interpreting the message of Jesus or discerning the function of a parable.

Even so reputable a scholar as Ulrich Luz has tried to justify allegorizing—both the allegorizing of the ancient church and present-day allegorizing. He is driven in this direction because of his lack of confidence that we can discern the original meaning of the parables and his desire to let the risen Lord create new meaning from the text for new situations. The standard of any new meaning for Luz is the exalted Christ, who is the same as the earthly Jesus.[39] But how he arrives at his understanding of the earthly Jesus is none too clear, especially given his doubts about discerning the original meanings of Jesus. This is no legitimate hermeneutic at work.

Allegory has also been given new respect from an entirely different and much more reasonable direction. Craig Blomberg argues that Jesus' parables *are* allegories and may have more than one correspondence between the image and the reality. A parable has as many correspondences and lessons as it has main characters. Accordingly, he classifies parables according to their complexity into those that have one, two, or three main points.[40] His argument is legitimate if one accepts that allegory is a literary genre, but it seems preferable to view allegory as a literary mode, not a genre, and to see the parables as proportional analogies.[41] That parables may be allegorical and have more than one point, though, should be beyond question. From any perspective, we are far from Jülicher.

Reduction to Banality

Three studies, quite different in their approaches, must be mentioned, but the result of all three is that the parables of Jesus are deprived of any real force and intent. Bernard Scott's work is the most helpful of the three because it is one of the more complete studies of the parables in recent years and the first

39. See the treatment of the parable of the wheat and the weeds in Ulrich Luz, *Matthew: A Commentary,* vol. 2, *Matthew 8–20,* trans. James E. Crouch, ed. Helmut Koester, Hermeneia (Minneapolis: Fortress, 2001), 269–71, esp. n. 36. From different perspectives but still allegorizing—this time psychological allegorizing—are the works of Robert Winterhalter with George W. Fisk, *Jesus' Parables: Finding Our God Within* (New York: Paulist Press, 1993), and Richard Q. Ford, *The Parables of Jesus: Recovering the Art of Listening* (Minneapolis: Fortress, 1997). Ford rejects that the parables offer any conclusive answers and reconstructs them along sociohistorical lines (see below).

40. Blomberg, *Interpreting the Parables.*

41. See Mary Ford, "Towards the Restoration of Allegory: Christology, Epistemology, and Narrative Structure," *SVTQ* 34 (1992): 161–95, esp. 171; Sider, *Interpreting the Parables,* 29–89. Blomberg uses the word "polyvalent" differently than others do. With him, it refers to the multiple perspectives within the story, not to finding new meanings by putting the parables in new contexts. See Blomberg, "Poetic Fiction, Subversive Speech, and Proportional Analogy in the Parables," *HBT* 18 (1996): 123.

part of the book has good information. First, like Jeremias, he reduces parables to an earlier form, attempting to find not the *ipsissima verba* of Jesus but the *ipsissima structura,* the very structure of the parables. The result is not much different. He views the *Gospel of Thomas* as early and, often, a superior source for Jesus' teaching. He accepts that the parables are allegorical and open to polyvalence. His procedure is to analyze the "performance" of a parable by each evangelist as he works back to the simplest form. Second, he analyzes how the originating structure effects meaning. Third, he analyzes the parable's juxtaposition to the kingdom to discover how the parable challenges conventional wisdom. His interpretations regularly reduce the parables to simplistic statements, quite reminiscent of Jülicher's reducing the parables to pious moralisms. If his interpretations are correct, one wonders why the stories were ever told or remembered. For example, the parable of the Pharisee and the toll collector is not an example story and has no lesson. Rather, it subverts the system that sees the kingdom as temple. In the parable, the holy is outside the kingdom, and the unholy is inside the kingdom. The parable of the wicked tenants is understood to question whether the kingdom will go to the promised heirs. *"In the plot the kingdom fails and the inheritance is in doubt."*[42]

Charles Hedrick's work goes against the grain of most parable research—and common sense. He argues that Jesus' parables were indeed banal, originally were not metaphors, and did not reference the kingdom. The evangelists inserted theological and kingdom significance to make the parables relevant. The parables were poetic fictions to stimulate thought and are open to a range of possible meanings. He believes that the contexts of the parables in the life of Jesus are irretrievably lost. The parables are "potentially radical poetic fictions that competed with Judaism's paradigmatic narrative rigidity." With these assumptions, the parable of the good Samaritan is understood to offer two responses to the injured man: callous indifference or outlandish benevolence. The first is wrong, and the second is an impossible ideal. The parable is a parody of the ideal of the righteous person in late Judaism. The parable of the rich fool is about the laughingly inappropriate action of the rich man tearing down barns when he should be harvesting. The parable is ultimately nihilistic and offers no hope, meaning, or theology.[43]

William Herzog assumes that the parables are not theological, moral stories, but political and economic ones. They show how exploitation worked in the ancient world. Herzog uses the work of Paulo Freire, the twentieth-century Bra-

42. Bernard Scott, *Hear Then the Parable* (Minneapolis: Fortress, 1989); for the examples, see 97, 253.

43. Charles Hedrick, *Parables as Poetic Fictions* (Peabody, Mass.: Hendrickson, 1994), 87, 113–16, 158–61. On banality, note Jülicher's claim that Jesus' parables originally were about "trifling matters" and have been given more theological meanings by the evangelists ("Parables," in *Encyclopaedia Biblica,* ed. T. K. Cheyne and J. Sutherland, 4 vols. [New York: Macmillan, 1899–1903], 3:3566). Note that Perrin (*Language of the Kingdom,* 154) wrote of the surprising banality of Via's conclusions.

zilian pedagogue of the oppressed, as a lens to read the parables. He claims that Jesus' parables present situations familiar to the rural poor and encode systems of oppression that controlled peasants and held them in bondage. The parables were to stimulate social analysis, not to teach about theology and ethics. They were discussion starters, and this is why the "conclusions" are often unsatisfying. The Gospel contexts are not viewed as trustworthy, so a new context is provided, that of exploitation. Herzog's sociological reconstruction leads to the assertion that authority figures in the parables (such as owners and fathers) do not refer to God but to oppressors. For example, in the parable of the vineyard workers, the vineyard owner is not God, but is a member of an oppressive elite class. In the parable of the wicked tenants, the tenants are not wicked; they are the original landowners whose land had been usurped, and their violent acts reasserted their honorable status as heirs. In the end, this parable codifies the futility of violence.[44] The parables of Jesus are indeed at times subversive, but with Herzog, they have been subverted. Little of Jesus' intent remains.

Hope for the Future

Arland Hultgren's recent work on the parables[45] is much more sane than the efforts just discussed. Hultgren rejects Jülicher's narrow views and acknowledges the presence of allegorical elements. He also rejects sweeping generalizations such as Jeremias's view that all the parables are Jesus' defense against his critics. Hultgren does not attempt much reconstruction of the parables and deals with most of the issues as he seeks to interpret the parables within their canonical contexts. Though some of his conclusions may be questioned, his discussions are helpful. Also useful and balanced is the work of Peter Rhea Jones.[46] He provides insightful commentary on select parables and demonstrates for pastors and students how the parables function within the message of Jesus.

Reflections

A major issue in parable interpretation is the value of the contexts of the parables in the Gospels.

What is obvious in the works surveyed is that the more one cuts the parables from their contexts in the Gospels, the life of Jesus, and the theology of Israel,

44. William Herzog, *Parables as Subversive Speech* (Louisville: Westminster John Knox, 1994), esp. 27–28, 96, 112–13, 259–61.

45. Arland Hultgren, *The Parables of Jesus: A Commentary* (Grand Rapids: Eerdmans, 2000).

46. Peter Rhea Jones, *Studying the Parables of Jesus* (Macon, Ga.: Smyth & Helwys, 1999), a revision of his earlier *The Teaching of the Parables* (Nashville: Broadman, 1982).

the more one promotes subjectivity and lack of control in interpretation. The theology of the evangelists has been removed, but the ideology or the sociology of the interpreter has been introduced. Scholars have read their own agenda into the parables as frequently as did the patristic church. Neither approach will help us hear the voice of Jesus.

This is not to suggest that we have the *ipsissima verba* of Jesus or every historical context in which parables were told. Many parables have been preserved without specific context, and many would have been told several times, which excludes the possibility of reconstructing a single, original form. But the parables were stories with an intent in the context of Jesus' ministry, and it is the voice and intent of Jesus that we seek to hear.

Parables are not reducible to abstract explanations, but they do point beyond themselves to other realities and can be explained in nonfigurative speech. We must insure that we retain the "language event" character of the parables and understand their theology without reducing them to pious moralisms.

There is no way to justify the allegorizing efforts of the church or the modern focus on polyvalence, renewed allegorizing, or sociohistorical reconstruction. What has become obvious over the past century is that each aberration, each extreme, and each fad—although ignoring the protests raised at its emergence—soon is seen for what it is. Lessons may be learned and insight gained, but with increasing speed what was thought to be the last and final word in parable research is shown to be one-sided, misguided, or simply wrong. The names of Augustine and Gregory, and then of Jülicher, Dodd, and Jeremias, long dominated the scene, but despite the value of their contributions, they cannot be followed. The replacement efforts of Crossan, Via, Scott, Hedrick, and Herzog have far less to offer and more quickly mislead. It is time to give the parables themselves the respect and attention they deserve. They do not need to be treated as mirrors of Christian theology or human psychology, nor do they need to be rewritten, curtailed, and controlled. They need to be heard, heard in the context of Jesus as framed by the evangelists. Granted that respect, once again they will confront and inform as no other genre can, and will reveal that their author deserves not only to be heard, but also followed.

10

The History of Miracles in the History of Jesus

Graham H. Twelftree

In the nineteenth century, the cold winds of English Deism, as well as empiricism and rationalism, blew across the intellectual landscape. This brought the issue of miracle to the center of the study of the historical Jesus.[1] Early in the period, the prevailing view was that the miracles were to be understood rationally.[2] But some suggested that the miracles were invented[3] or had been

1. For histories of the study of the miracles of Jesus, see, for example, E. Keller and M.-L. Keller, *Miracles in Dispute* (London: SCM, 1969); B. Schilling, "Die Frage nach der Entstehung der synoptischen Wundergeschichten in der deutschen neutestamentlichen Forschung," *SEÅ* 35 (1970): 61–78; C. Brown, *Miracles and the Critical Mind* (Grand Rapids: Eerdmans; Exeter: Paternoster, 1984); H. Weder, "Wunder Jesu und Wundergeschichten," *VF* 29 (1984): 25–49; G. Maier, "Zur neutestamentlichen Wunderexegese im 19. und 20. Jahrhundert," in *The Miracles of Jesus,* ed. D. Wenham and C. Blomberg, Gospel Perspectives 6 (Sheffield: JSOT Press, 1986), 49–87; J. Engelbrecht, "Trends in Miracle Research," *Neot* 22 (1988): 139–61; G. Theissen and A. Merz, *The Historical Jesus* (London: SCM, 1998), 285–91.

2. For example, K. F. Bahrdt, *Briefe über die Bibel im Volkston* (Halle: 1702). For other scholarly treatments of a rationalist approach to the miracles, see A. Schweitzer, *The Quest of the Historical Jesus,* trans. W. Montgomery et al., ed. J. Bowden (1913; reprint, London: SCM, 2000), 37–64, discussing K. F. Bahrdt, H. E. G. Paulus, K. A. Hase, and F. D. E. Schleiermacher.

3. For example, H. S. Reimarus, *Fragments,* trans. R. S. Fraser, ed. C. H. Talbert (Philadelphia: Fortress, 1970; London: SCM, 1971), 126–29, 232–33.

imported into the Gospel traditions.[4] Others interpreted the miracles as myths of one kind or another.[5] By early in the twentieth century, a long-held view became established: the kerygma, not the miracles, was to be seen as the essence of the gospel.[6]

By the middle of the twentieth century, the problem of miracle was considered either solved or unimportant and hardly featured in the reconstructed lives of Jesus.[7] Not surprisingly, there had been dissenters who maintained that a miracle-free Jesus tradition never existed[8] and even that the miracles, not the teaching, were what captivated Jesus' audiences.[9]

Particularly with few scholars still following the form critics in believing that the early church provided the matrix for the creation of certain types

4. A view generally associated with the *Religionsgeschichtliche Schule*. In relation to this school and the miracles of Jesus, see W. Kahl, *New Testament Miracle Stories in Their Religious-Historical Setting*, FRLANT 163 (Göttingen: Vandenhoeck & Ruprecht, 1994). Not least because of their links with the *Schule*, the form critics also averred the view. See, for example, R. Bultmann, *History of the Synoptic Tradition*, trans. John Marsh, rev. ed. (New York: Harper & Row, 1976), esp. 231; M. Dibelius, *Jesus*, trans. C. Hedrick and F. Grant (London: SCM, 1963), ch. 6.

5. Especially D. F. Strauss, *Das Leben Jesu*, 4th ed., 2 vols. (Tübingen: Osiander, 1840; in English, *The Life of Jesus, Critically Examined*, trans. George Eliot, ed. Peter C. Hodgson [Philadelphia: Fortress, 1972; London: SCM, 1973]). Although previously, J. G. Herder (1744–1803) had argued that the miracles were to be understood symbolically rather than literally. Cf. Schweitzer, *Quest of the Historical Jesus*, 74; H. Harris, *David Friedrich Strauss and His Theology* (Cambridge: Cambridge University Press, 1973), ch. 23. For others who grappled with the problem of myth in the Gospels, see those cited in C. A. Evans, "Life-of-Jesus Research and the Eclipse of Mythology," *TS* 54 (1993): 5–6 n. 11.

6. For example, Bahrdt, *Briefe*, third letter, cited in Keller and Keller, *Miracles in Dispute*, 67–68; A. von Harnack, *What Is Christianity?* (London: Williams & Norgate: New York: Putnam, 1900); R. Bultmann, *Jesus and the Word* (London: Collins; Glasgow: Fontana, 1958), 124; C. Brown, *Jesus in European Protestant Thought, 1778–1860* (Grand Rapids: Baker, 1988), xxii. J. M. Robinson (*A New Quest of the Historical Jesus* [London: SCM, 1959], 59) gives C. H. Dodd the credit for this centrality of the kerygma in the English-speaking world. But even before Dodd, a number of studies of the historical Jesus subordinated the miracles to the teaching of Jesus—for example, A. C. Headlam, *The Life and Teaching of Jesus the Christ* (London: Murray, 1923; 2nd ed., 1927).

7. For example, G. Bornkamm, *Jesus of Nazareth* (London: SCM, 1960), taken to be the first "life" of Jesus of the "new quest," has only a token mention of Jesus' activities in ch. 8. Cf. Brown, *Jesus in European Protestant Thought*, xxii; G. H. Twelftree, *Jesus the Miracle Worker* (Downers Grove, Ill.: InterVarsity, 1999), 353.

8. For example, A. von Schlatter, *The History of the Christ*, trans. A. Köstenberger (Grand Rapids: Baker, 1997), 191. Cf. B. Weiss, *The Life of Christ*, 3 vols. (Edinburgh: Clark, 1883), 1:151–58; W. Sanday, "Jesus Christ," in *A Dictionary of the Bible*, ed. J. Hastings, 4 vols. (Edinburgh: Clark, 1898), 2:624–28; J. H. Bernard, "Miracle," in Hastings, *A Dictionary of the Bible,* 3:389–90; Headlam, *Life and Teaching of Jesus*, 1–44, 186–92; W. Manson, *Jesus the Messiah* (London: Hodder & Stoughton, 1943), 33, 45–46.

9. See, for example, A. C. Headlam, *The Miracles of the New Testament* (London: Murray, 1914), 242; H. J. Cadbury, *The Peril of Modernizing Jesus* (New York: MacMillan, 1937; reprint, London: SPCK, 1962), 79–80. More recently, see especially Morton Smith, *Jesus the Magician* (London: Gollancz, 1978), 10, 14, 16; and E. P. Sanders, *Jesus and Judaism* (London: SCM, 1985), 164, who also cites M. Hengel, *The Charismatic Leader and His Followers* (Edinburgh: Clark, 1981), 66.

of traditions,[10] and with a renewed interest in the milieu of Jesus' ministry, the problem of miracles has returned to become one of the dividing lines and unsolved issues in present-day Jesus research.[11] On the one hand, J. P. Meier, in the second volume of his three-volume study of Jesus, allocates about one-half of the eleven hundred pages to a discussion of the miracles of Jesus.[12] On the other hand, in Sanders's *Jesus and Judaism,* miracles are handled in one small chapter.[13] Further, for some, it is not even agreed that miracles are an issue.[14] Also, as we will see, there is no agreement on the meaning of the miracles. There is also the question of how Jesus as a miracle worker would have been assessed by his contemporaries. Over all of this is cast the distinct shadow of rationalism or naturalism, making it unclear whether or not what can be recovered of Jesus' "mighty works" were miracles or, as we supposedly can now more clearly see, events that are to be explained otherwise.[15]

In this chapter we will note some of the recent major contributors to the search for Jesus, most of whom have written replete lives of the historical Jesus: Géza Vermès, Morton Smith, Anthony E. Harvey, John P. Meier, E. P. Sanders, N. T. Wright, Marcus J. Borg, John D. Crossan, Markus Bockmuehl, and the Jesus Seminar.[16] These representatives will demonstrate the fluctuating fortunes of ways that the miracles of Jesus have been understood

10. See B. Witherington III, *The Jesus Quest,* 2nd ed. (Downers Grove, Ill.: InterVarsity, 1997), 147 n. 23; M. D. Hooker, "On Using the Wrong Tool," *Theology* 75 (1972): 570–78; G. N. Stanton, "Form Criticism Revisited," in *What about the New Testament?* ed. M. D. Hooker and C. J. Hickling (London: SCM, 1975), 13–27.

11. See J. P. Meier, "Dividing Lines in Jesus Research Today: Through Dialectical Negation to a Positive Sketch," *Int* 50 (1996): 355–72; M. A. Powell, *Jesus as a Figure in History: How Modern Historians View the Man from Galilee* (Louisville: Westminster John Knox, 1998), 176–81.

12. J. P. Meier, *A Marginal Jew: Rethinking the Historical Jesus,* 3 vols., ABRL (New York: Doubleday, 1991–2001), 2:507–1038.

13. Sanders, *Jesus and Judaism,* ch. 5. In *The Historical Figure of Jesus* (London: Penguin, 1993), 132–68, Sanders devotes a chapter to miracles. But this is an uncertain chapter, mixing a treatment of how the NT writers viewed the miracles with those that may originate in Jesus, contributing little to our understanding of the miracles of the historical Jesus. Likewise, in B. F. Meyer, *The Aims of Jesus* (London: SCM, 1979), 154–58, and in L. Houlden, *Jesus: A Question of Identity* (London: SPCK, 1992), little space is given to the discussion of the miracles of Jesus. D. Guthrie did not discuss the miracles in his one-thousand-page *New Testament Theology* (Downers Grove, Ill.: InterVarsity, 1981).

14. Citing H. Braun, *Jesus of Nazareth* (Philadelphia: Fortress, 1979), and R. Bultmann, *Jesus and the Word* (New York: Scribner, 1958), J. Gnilka (*Jesus of Nazareth* [Peabody, Mass.: Hendrickson, 1997], 112 n. 66) notes that in numerous books on Jesus, healing and miracles are omitted; Gnilka himself gives only 22 of 346 pages to the discussion of the miracles of Jesus (112–34).

15. On the definition and possibility of "miracle," see Twelftree, *Jesus the Miracle Worker,* part 1.

16. See Powell (*Jesus as a Figure in History*), who, in addition to covering the Jesus Seminar, discusses J. D. Crossan, M. J. Borg, E. P. Sanders, J. P. Meier, and N. T. Wright as the key modern historians of Jesus.

and treated in the scientific study of the historical Jesus over about the last thirty years.[17]

Jesus as Jewish Holy Man

In *Jesus the Jew* (1973), Géza Vermès asserts that Jesus is to be seen as the paramount example of the early *hasidim,* who made their strongest impact through their miracles.[18] In turn, the key feature of Vermès's portrait of Jesus is that he gives preeminence to the comparison with Jewish miracle workers.[19] Two such important figures were Honi the Circle Drawer, who lived just before Jesus, and Hanina ben Dosa, who was active just after Jesus.

However, the most basic criticism brought to bear on Vermès's work is that his "acritical use of sources undermines his whole argument."[20] That is, Vermès relies uncritically on material, as in the case of the *Pirqe Rabbi Eliezer,* which probably originated in the eighth or ninth century C.E.[21] Further, many of the

17. See B. L. Blackburn, "The Miracles of Jesus," in *Studying the Historical Jesus: Evaluations of the State of Current Research,* ed. B. Chilton and C. A. Evans, NTTS 19 (Leiden: Brill, 1994), 353–94. There has always been a great stream of publications exhibiting a keen interest in the miracles of Jesus, most of which we can omit here. Some have been dedicated to the study of miracles—for example, H. Hendrickx, *The Miracle Stories of the Synoptic Gospels* (London: Chapman; San Francisco: Harper & Row, 1987); R. Latourelle, *The Miracles of Jesus and the Theology of the Miracles* (New York: Paulist Press, 1988); G. Theissen, *Miracle Stories of the Early Christian Tradition* (Edinburgh: Clark, 1983). Some other studies left out of consideration here are from a christotheological perspective rather than from the guild of NT students, as is the case of, for example, W. Kasper, *Jesus the Christ* (London: Burns & Oats, 1976); G. O'Collins, *Interpreting Jesus* (London: Chapman; Ramsey, N.J.: Paulist Press, 1983).

18. Vermès is not the first to compare Jesus with his contemporaries. E. Renan (*The Life of Jesus,* trans. C. E. Wilbour [London: Dent, 1863; reprint, New York: Dutton, 1927], 49) had said, "By his poverty, so meekly endured, by the sweetness of his character, by his opposition to priests and hypocrites, Hillel was the true master of Jesus." See also Schlatter, *The History of Christ,* 176. W. Horbury ("Jesus the Jew," *Theology* 77 [1974]: 227–32) cites Arthur Marmonstein as having compared Jesus with the miracle-working rabbis (229); similarly, L. E. Keck's review of Vermès (*JBL* 95 [1976]: 508) draws attention to R. Otto, *The Kingdom of God and the Son of Man* (London: Lutterworth, 1938). More recently, see also D. Flusser, with R. Steven Notley, *Jesus,* 2nd ed. (Jerusalem: Magnes, 1998); cf. C. A. Evans, *Jesus and His Contemporaries* (Leiden: Brill, 1995), ch. 5.

19. G. Vermès, *Jesus the Jew: A Historian's Reading of the Gospels* (London: Collins/Fontana, 1973; reprint, London: SCM, 1983), 79, 223–24. See also idem, "Hanina ben Dosa: A Controversial Galilean Saint from the First Century of the Christian Era," *JJS* 23 (1972): 28–50; 24 (1973): 51–64.

20. Meier, *A Marginal Jew,* 2:587. For an important critique of Vermès, see S. Freyne, "The Charismatic," in *Ideal Figures in Ancient Judaism,* ed. J. J. Collins and G. W. E. Nicklesburg (Chico, Calif.: Scholars Press, 1980), 223–58.

21. See M. D. Herr, "Pirkei de-Rabbi Eliezer," *EncJud* 13:558–60; H. L. Strack and G. Stemberger, *Introduction to the Talmud and Midrash,* trans. M. Bockmuehl (Minneapolis: Fortress, 1992), 356–58.

stories about Honi and Hanina are no earlier than the Talmuds, and neither of these *hasidim* is characterized as Galilean in the earliest traditions.[22]

These points aside, Vermès must also face the criticism of failing to acknowledge that there were other miracle workers in Palestine in Jesus' time,[23] which means that it is not possible to conclude that the miracles of Jesus simply number him as one of the rabbis. Also, even granting that first-century rabbis conducted miracles, as miracle workers, some important differences existed between Jesus and the rabbis. Even on Vermès's own admission, compared to his portrait of the rabbis, Jesus' healing technique is simplicity itself. Further, the association of miracle and prophecy is not peculiar to the Jewish holy men, for the expectation of prophetic miracles is rooted in the biblical heritage of Jewry as a whole.[24] Also, so far as I know, none of the Jewish holy men made any connection between their miracles and a message. In the end, we can only conclude that the style of the charismatic rabbi is not one that Jesus chose.[25]

Methodological issues notwithstanding, although the nearest parallel to Jesus and his disciples may be the rabbis and their pupils, it is the very miracles on which Vermès relies, as well as the significance that Jesus gave to his miracles, that set Jesus over against other contemporary Jewish holy men.[26]

Jesus as Magician

Although Morton Smith's *Jesus the Magician* (1978) does not propose to give a rounded picture of Jesus, it is an important book, for it marks the transition from focusing on the teaching of Jesus to looking at the activities of Jesus, and at the miracles in particular. Smith viewed Jesus as attracting attention primarily as a miracle worker,[27] and he attempted to show not only that Jesus was portrayed as a magician[28] but also that he was a magician.[29]

---

22. See the discussion by Meier, *A Marginal Jew*, 2:581–88. Cf. Schlatter, *The History of Christ*, 176: "Of the celebrated teachers of Jerusalem and Javne—Hillel, Gamaliel, Yohanan ben Zakkai, or Akiba—there are no miracle stories."

23. See, for example, G. H. Twelftree, *Jesus the Exorcist*, WUNT 2.54 (Tübingen: Mohr, 1993), 22–47.

24. See the review of Vermès, *Jesus the Jew*, in Horbury, "Jesus the Jew," 230.

25. See A. E. Harvey, *Jesus and the Constraints of History* (London: Duckworth, 1982), 107; Witherington, *The Jesus Quest*, 112.

26. See W. S. Green, "Palestinian Holy Men: Charismatic Leadership and Rabbinic Tradition," in *ANRW*, 2.19.2:646–47; Twelftree, *Jesus the Exorcist*, 211.

27. Smith, *Jesus the Magician*, 10—a point picked up by Sanders, *Jesus and Judaism*, 164; Meier, *A Marginal Jew*, 2:3–4; M. J. Borg, *Jesus, a New Vision: Spirit, Culture, and the Life of Discipleship* (San Francisco: Harper & Row, 1987), 60; idem, "The Historian, the Christian, and Jesus," *ThTo* 52 (1995–96): 8–10.

28. So, for example, J. M. Hull, *Hellenistic Magic and the Synoptic Tradition* (London: SCM, 1974).

29. A strong current of scholarship trying to distance Jesus from anything associated with magical techniques flows in the opposite direction. See, for example, E. Fascher, *Die formgeschicht-*

Aside from the devastating critique by Jacob Neusner, Smith's particular program is easily shown to have failed.[30] First, he has not been able to show that Tacitus, Pliny, or Suetonius thought that Jesus was a magician.[31] Second, where the charge of magic is made clear (in Justin Martyr, Quadratus, and Celsus),[32] Smith has not taken into account that these opinions are not from contemporaries of Jesus. Third, Smith has misunderstood that a person generally was judged to be a magician not by technique, but primarily in light of the individual's lifestyle as well as the authenticity and longevity of the results of the person's work.[33]

On a fourth, and important, point there is less agreement among scholars. Smith argues that the Gospels contain charges that Jesus was a magician. Smith contends that the accusation that Jesus was a Samaritan and had a demon (John 8:48) is a charge of being a magician. He draws the same conclusion from the charge that Jesus is said to "have Beelzebul" (Mark 3:22//Matt. 12:24//Luke 11:15). However, a historically informed reading of the texts shows that to have a demon was to be considered possessed, not that one was using or manipulating a demon to perform miracles; and the charge of being a Samaritan was a charge of having an unbelievable message.[34] Also, the charge of being mad (*mainetai* [John 10:20]) is to be seen as a charge that Jesus had an unbelievable message rather than of him being a magician (see Acts 12:15; 26:24–25). Nor can Smith use the Pharisees' charge that Jesus was an impostor (*planos* [Matt. 27:63]) or someone who led people astray to mean that he was a magician.[35] In pre-NT times, the word impostor (*planos*) was used

---

liche Methode: Eine Darstellung und Kritik, zugleich ein Beitrag zur Geschichte des synoptischen Problems (Giessen: Töpelmann, 1924), 127–28; W. Grundmann, "δύναμαι/δύναμις," *TDNT* 2:302; E. Stauffer, "ἰάομαι," *TDNT,* 3:210; S. V. McCasland, *By the Finger of God* (New York: Macmillan, 1951), 110–15; V. Taylor, *The Gospel according to St. Mark* (London: Macmillan, 1952), 176; S. E. Johnson, *The Gospel according to St. Mark* (London: Black, 1960), 48; Latourelle, *The Miracles of Jesus,* 167.

30. J. Neusner, foreword to *Memory and Manuscript,* by B. Gerhardsson (Grand Rapids: Eerdmans, 1998), xxv–xxxii. For what follows, as well as a more detailed critique of Smith, see Twelftree, *Jesus the Exorcist,* 190–207. On the now-famous debate between Smith and Howard Kee at a meeting of the Society of Biblical Literature in New York in 1970, see B. L. Mack, *Myth of Innocence* (Philadelphia: Fortress, 1988), 210.

31. Tacitus, *Ann.* 15.44.3–8; Pliny, *Letters* 10.96; Suetonius, *Nero* 16.2.

32. Justin, *Dial.* 69; Quadratus, cited by Eusebius, *Hist. eccl.* 4.3.2; Celsus, cited by Origen, *Cels.* 1.6, 28 (cf. 38), 68.

33. Twelftree, *Jesus the Exorcist,* 204–6, citing Quadratus (Eusebius, *Hist. eccl.* 4.3.2); Justin, *Dial.* 69; Celsus, cited in Origen, *Cels.* 1.68; cf. D. Aune, "Magic in Early Christianity," in *ANRW* 2.23.2:1538; E. Yamauchi, "Magic or Miracle? Disease, Demons, and Exorcisms," in Wenham and Blomberg, *The Miracles of Jesus,* 142.

34. See J. Bowman, "Samaritan Studies I," *BJRL* 40 (1957–58): 306–8.

35. See P. Samain ("L'accusation de magie contre le Christ dans les Évangile," *ETL* 15 [1938]: 449–90), who argues that although Jesus was never directly charged with being a magician, the charge of impostor (e.g., Matt. 27:63) was an accusation that Jesus performed miracles by magical technique.

primarily in relation to erring from right teaching and never, on its own, to describe the work of a magician until later debates about Jesus.[36] Similarly, Smith cannot use the charge that Jesus was an evildoer (*kakon poiōn* [John 18:30]) as an equivalent for being a magician, as there is no evidence for the use of this in Greek legal terminology.[37] Over and above these considerations we must note that although the NT writers were familiar with the vocabulary of "magician," they never used it either of Jesus[38] or, indeed, in seeking to save him from such an epithet.

A number of other scholars have concluded that Jesus was charged with being a magician.[39] Yet, besides the need to settle whether or not and in what way it is possible to use the debates of the second century to determine the nature of the debates about Jesus among his contemporaries,[40] there also must be more discussion and agreement on the exact nature of magic as it was understood in first-century Palestine.[41] Notwithstanding, because of the unresolved methodological issues and a lack of agreement on definitions, all we can say is that the jury is still out, deciding whether or not Jesus was considered a magician by those who witnessed his miracles. Nevertheless, Smith is to be applauded for helping to bring the activities of Jesus—notably, the miracles—back nearer to the center stage of studies of the historical Jesus.

Miracles Regained

A. E. Harvey's *Jesus and the Constraints of History* (1982) represents a balanced and brilliant product of mainline British NT scholarship at its best. However, he has been criticized from the other side of the Atlantic for not being explicit about the way he brings together historical research and the commitment of faith, as well as because his treatment has been deemed "unduly burdened by his historical either/or apologetic."[42]

36. See the primary evidence in H. Braun, "πλανάω," *TDNT* 6:228–53.

37. Cf. 1 Pet. 2:12, 14, on which, see F. W. Beare, *The First Epistle of Peter*, 2nd ed. (Oxford: Blackwell, 1961), 137–38; J. R. Michaels, *1 Peter*, WBC 49 (Waco: Word, 1988), 266–67.

38. See Meier, *A Marginal Jew*, 2:537–52, esp. 551.

39. For example, Sanders, *Jesus and Judaism*, 169; J. D. Crossan, *The Historical Jesus* (San Francisco: HarperCollins, 1991), 311; G. N. Stanton, "Jesus of Nazareth: A Magician and a False Prophet Who Deceived God's People?" in *Jesus of Nazareth*, ed. J. B. Green and M. Turner (Grand Rapids: Eerdmans; Carlisle: Paternoster, 1994), 178.

40. H. C. Kee, *Miracle in the Early Christian World* (New Haven: Yale University Press, 1983), 211–12 n. 69.

41. For example, D. Aune, "Magic in Early Christianity," in *ANRW* 2.23.2:1507–57; Twelftree, *Jesus the Exorcist*, 190–91; and those cited.

42. See M. E. Boring's review of Harvey in *CBQ* 45 (1983): 690, and D. C. Duling's review of Harvey, "In Quest of the Historical Jesus," *Int* 38 (1984): 72. Cf. the review by B. F. Meyer in *JBL* 103 (1984): 654.

Harvey argues that even though it is possible to take the view that the apparently supernatural events could not have happened and can be left out of account by the historian, there are good reasons why this cannot be the case. Thus, Harvey takes us beyond the constraints of the history-of-religions school and the form critics and their insistence on the accretions of miracles to the core of the Jesus tradition.

Harvey then explores the options open to Jesus as a miracle worker. He demonstrates that Jesus did not take up the option of using his powers to foretell the future and thus be credited as an exceptionally wise and divinely gifted man in line with Hellenistic traditions. Also, "The style of the 'Charismatic' is not the one chosen by Jesus." Nor did Jesus heal by normal medical means, as reported of the emperor Vespasian.[43] Instead, in conducting exorcisms in a world of magicians and sorcerers, Jesus chose a more dangerous and ambiguous form of healing, raising questions about the weapons of the exorcist.

In that, with the exception of John, none of the Gospel writers succeeds in presenting a uniform and consistent account of Jesus' motivation for performing miracles,[44] and that Jesus chose cures such as healing the deaf, mute, blind, and lame, which was without precedent in his culture, he was both breaking new ground and making it difficult for observers to understand his motives. According to Harvey, not only do the miracles that Jesus chose to perform not "run in the channels of known techniques by which his contemporaries believed they could occasionally reverse the impact of the normal course of events," but also they do not seem to have been performed in a spirit of competition with other charismatic figures. Nor do the miracles seem to be a means of drawing attention to the power of the thaumaturge and investing him with unanswerable authority. "Instead, we find an impressive number of them took the form of an attack on the limitations of the human condition which seemed most intractable, most inexplicable, and most stubbornly to prevent mankind from moving into that better world which is surely intended for us in the future purposed of God."[45]

Nevertheless, Harvey does not think that the reports of miraculous activity can provide us with anything of value for determining Jesus' religious significance, for "messiahs must be capable of wonder-working, even if this is not what is primarily stressed in their mission."[46]

43. Harvey, *Jesus and the Constraints of History,* 107–8, citing Solon fragment 13.61–62 (*Iambi et elegi Graeci ante Alexandrum Cantati,* ed. M. L. West, 2nd ed. [Oxford: Oxford University Press, 1989–92], vol. 2); Seneca, *Ben.* 6.16.2; Galen, *Nat. fac.* 3.7; Tacitus, *Hist.* 4.81; Suetonius, *Vesp.* 7.

44. Citing D.-A. Koch, *Die Bedeutung der Wundererzählungen für die Christologie des Markusevangeliums* (Berlin: de Gruyter, 1975), Harvey notes that it is possible to suggest a number of different motives that Mark allows us to infer from the various miracle stories; and citing B. Gerhardsson, *The Mighty Acts of Jesus according to Matthew* (Lund: Gleerup, 1979), he notes that in Matthew the motives are different again. See Twelftree, *Jesus the Miracle Worker,* part 2.

45. Harvey, *Jesus and the Constraints of History,* 118.

46. Ibid., 101, citing B. R. Wilson, *Magic and the Millennium* (London: Heinemann, 1973), 134.

The high-water mark in the present quest for the historical Jesus has come in John P. Meier's *A Marginal Jew: Rethinking the Historical Jesus* (1991–2001), which, in the context of a study of the historical Jesus, contains the most thorough treatment of miracles in recent times. Acknowledging the influence of Smith (though not his equation of miracle and magic), Meier claims that it is the explosive convergence and mutual reinforcement of the usually distinct activities of prophet, gatherer of Israel, and teacher, as well as healer, exorcist, and raiser of the dead, that makes Jesus stand out. Further, like Smith, Meier thinks that miracle-working probably contributed the most to Jesus' popularity as well as the enmity that he stirred up.[47] For this reason, and because in practically all layers of the Gospel tradition there is broad attestation of Jesus' miracle-working activity, he does not want to ignore the miracle stories or give them the polite nod of a mere single chapter.

Though he is keen to "reject an a priori affirmation that miracles do not or cannot happen," Meier argues that the acceptance or rejection of the miracles of Jesus is beyond the ability of historians, it being the province of philosophers and theologians. Thus, Meier makes the crucial observation that although scholars would not deny that Jesus was known as a miracle worker, they object to being able to evaluate individual stories because the material is too meager or dubious for any serious judgment of historicity to be made. While sympathetic to this view, he asserts that his inventory has the positive result of showing that (1) some stories, such as the cursing of the fig tree, appear to have been created by the early church;[48] (2) some stories, such as the healing of Bartimaeus, have a historical foundation in an event in which witnesses believed that Jesus restored sight to a blind person;[49] (3) some stories, such as the feeding of the multitude, may have a symbolic base, in this case a meal that Jesus shared with a large crowd, a meal perhaps only later taken to be miraculous.[50] Meier goes on to conclude that with the exception of the feeding of the multitude, all the so-called nature miracles appear to be the creation of the early church.[51]

Nevertheless, overall Meier concludes, "Any historian who seems to portray the historical Jesus without giving due weight to his fame as a miracle-worker is not delineating this strange and complex Jew, but rather domesticating Jesus." On the significance of Jesus' miracles, he says, "His miracle-working activity not

47. Meier, *A Marginal Jew,* 2:3–4 nn. 4, 14.

48. A view shared by many students of the Gospels; see, for example, R. W. Funk and the Jesus Seminar, *The Acts of Jesus* (New York: HarperSanFrancisco, 1998), 122–23. Further see Twelftree, *Jesus the Miracle Worker,* 323–24.

49. On the possible historicity of Jesus healing the blind, see Twelftree, *Jesus the Miracle Worker,* ch. 13.

50. A rational interpretation long held. See, for example, K. F. Bahrdt's views cited by Schweitzer, *Quest of the Historical Jesus,* 40. See also the discussion of H. E. G. Paulus, *Das Leben Jesu als Grundlage einer reinen Geschichte des Frühchristentums* (1828) in Schweitzer, *Quest of the Historical Jesus,* ch. 5, and a more recent advocacy of rational interpretations of miracles in H. Braun, *Jesus of Nazareth,* and Gnilka, *Jesus of Nazareth,* 133–34.

51. See also below on Crossan. Note that Meier (*A Marginal Jew,* 2:967) says that "the common category called 'nature miracles' is seen to be an illusion." See the discussion in Twelftree, *Jesus the Miracle Worker,* 350–52.

only supported but also dramatized and actuated his eschatological message, and it may have contributed to some degree to the alarm felt by the authorities who finally brought about his death."[52] Generally, Meier's work has been well received. However, according to the current intellectual fashions, Meier's first volume has been criticized for being insufficiently skeptical or objective.[53]

Miracles Marginalized

In *Jesus and Judaism* (1985), E. P. Sanders, like Smith, turns from the teaching to the activities of Jesus for more secure and agreed evidence on which to proceed.[54] Although Jesus cannot be considered simply a teacher, Sanders does not want to build on the miracles, because the principal context of Jesus' work was Jewish eschatology, and there are other facts that fit Jesus better and unmistakably into a context other than that of magic. The key fact for Sanders is the cleansing of the temple, which, he suggests, was an act symbolizing its destruction and was carried out against the background of Jesus' eschatological expectation.[55] This is of a piece with his conclusion that Jesus was a prophet of national restoration. Thus, we have a Jesus bearing a striking resemblance to Albert Schweitzer's eschatological prophet or seer.[56]

Sanders notes that Jesus did not want to rest his case on his miracles but probably saw his miracles indicating that the new age was at hand and that he fulfilled the hopes of the prophets. Those who were close enough to Jesus to be able to put his miracles into the context of his teaching were able to share his perspective, even though they remained uncertain.

In that, for Sanders, miracles do not provide a definition of who Jesus was, or at least of what sort of figure he was, we have one of the reasons why miracles end up not being very important in his discussion. Since miracles meant different things to different people, Sanders rejects Harvey's interpretation that miracles are eschatological. Sanders also rejects Smith's proposal that Jesus was a magician, not because he was not called a magician, but because it leaves out of account the persuasive evidence that makes us look to Jewish eschatol-

52. Meier, *A Marginal Jew,* 2:970.

53. See the reviews of vol. 1 of Meier, *A Marginal Jew,* by B. Capper, *Theology* 95 (1992): 384, and D. Rhoads, *CurTM* 21 (1994): 56–57.

54. In this, Sanders acknowledges his debt to Smith and Harvey, as well as to E. Fuchs, "The Quest of the Historical Jesus" (1956), in *Studies of the Historical Jesus* (London: SCM, 1964), 21. Also on Sanders and the miracles, see Witherington, *The Jesus Quest,* 123–25.

55. Cf. the critique by C. A. Evans, "Jesus' Action in the Temple: Cleansing or Portent of Destruction?" *CBQ* 51 (1989): 237–70; R. J. Miller, "Historical Method and the Deeds of Jesus: The Test Case of the Temple Demonstration," *Forum* 8 (1992): 5–30, esp. 6–14.

56. A. Schweitzer, *The Mystery of the Kingdom of God,* trans. W. Lowrie (London: Black, 1925). Cf. A. J. Hultgren, "Jesus of Nazareth: Prophet, Visionary, Sage, or What?" *Dialog* 33 (1994): 263–73, esp. 267 n. 43, and those cited. On the differences between Sanders's and Schweitzer's Jesus, see Sanders, *Jesus and Judaism,* 327–29.

ogy as defining the general contours of Jesus' career. The view that Jesus was a type of Galilean holy man is also set aside: "I am inclined to put him closer to Theudas than to Honi or to the magicians of the *PGM*."[57]

While Harvey says that Jesus "opted" to perform primarily those miracles that, to his contemporaries, would hold the promise of a new age, Sanders says that it is more likely that Jesus performed the miracles that came to hand, and that nothing can be concluded about Jesus' motives from these diseases that respond to faith-healing and are prominent in pagan sources.

Sanders thinks that the tendency to explain miracles rationally is successful in the case of exorcisms and healings, for they can be explained as having a hysterical or psychosomatic base.[58] Other miracles, such as the stilling of the storm, may have been coincidences. Others only appeared to be miraculous, as in the case of Jesus seen to be walking on water, when he actually was on land.[59] Group psychology may explain the feeding of the multitudes, while Peter's walking on the water may be a pictorial representation of character failing. However, he concludes, some of the miracle stories cannot be explained rationally.

In that the nature miracles lacked impact on the crowd as well as the disciples, and that not many believed in Jesus, Sanders concludes that the Christian tradition later augmented and enhanced the miracle stories to make them more striking, and that "it could be reasoned that historically there was little response because there were few major miracles."[60]

With Sanders's contribution has come the first full-scale, well-rounded technical study of the historical Jesus in the previous two or more decades. Yet, in contrast to the authors of other studies we have sampled, Sanders has marginalized the miracles of Jesus, even though he took the activities of Jesus as his starting point.

In *Jesus and the Victory of God* (1996), N. T. Wright agrees that there has been "a quiet revolution in relation to the 'mighty works' or 'works of power' that Jesus is said to have performed."[61] Sanders said, "There is nothing about miracles which would trigger, in the first-century Jewish world, the expectation that the end was at hand."[62] Over against this, Wright says that the mighty

---

57. Sanders, *Jesus and Judaism*, 172.

58. So also A. Richardson, *The Miracle Stories of the Gospels* (London: SCM, 1941), 126. Cf. McCasland, *By the Finger of God;* T. A. Burkill, "The Notion of Miracle with Special Reference to St. Mark's Gospel," *ZNW* 50 (1959): 33–73. At a more popular, perhaps amateurish, level, see A. N. Wilson, *Jesus: A Life* (New York: Norton, 1992), and the devastating critique it received from L. T. Johnson, "Reshuffling the Gospels: Jesus according to Spong and Wilson," *ChrCent* 110 (1993): 457–58.

59. Here Sanders stands in the long tradition of rationalist interpretations. See, for example, Schweitzer, *Quest of the Historical Jesus*, 40.

60. Sanders, *Jesus and Judaism*, 157. Cf. below on Crossan.

61. N. T. Wright, *Jesus and the Victory of God* (Philadelphia: Fortress, 1996), 186.

62. Sanders, *Jesus and Judaism*, 170.

works "were signs which were intended as, and would have been perceived as, the physical inauguration of the kingdom of Israel's god, the putting into action of the welcome and the warning which were the central message of the kingdom and its redefinition."[63] But Wright gives only a slight discussion to the miracles (eleven of the 662 pages).[64] Along with not integrating the miracles into his picture of the historical Jesus, Wright in this brief treatment allows the miracles to be overshadowed by his attention to the other aspects of Jesus' life. Thus, Wright is another scholar who marginalizes the miracles.

Wright is well aware of this being one of the largest lacunae in his *Jesus and the Victory of God*. However, in response to this criticism he has said that a more substantial discussion was not possible within the already bulky pages of his book. In any case, miracles do not seem to be important to Wright's understanding of the historical Jesus; he says that even if we suppose that Jesus did exactly what the Gospels say he did, little would be proved, because others—magicians as well as prophets—conducted miracles, and "the meaning of Jesus' 'mighty works' must remain . . . a function of the interpretation we give or indeed of the interpretation Jesus himself gave to his life as a whole."[65] But this is to take the unargued position that there was little or no difference between the miracles of Jesus and those of his contemporaries, and that Jesus saw his miracles as secondary and derivative rather than primary and programmatic.[66] Notwithstanding, Wright's slight treatment of miracles may simply be that in distancing himself from supernaturalism, he adopts a form of methodological naturalism.[67]

The Culturally Acceptable Jesus

In *Jesus, a New Vision* (1987), Marcus J. Borg agrees that Jesus was a man of deeds like Hanina ben Dosa and Honi and—over against most of his colleagues in the Jesus Seminar—sees it as virtually indisputable that Jesus was (and was known as) a healer and an exorcist.[68] However, when it comes to what he calls "spectacular" deeds, such as resuscitation of apparently dead people,

63. Wright, *Jesus and the Victory of God*, 196.
64. Already noted by C. S. Evans, "Methodological Naturalism in Historical Biblical Scholarship," in *Jesus and the Restoration of Israel*, ed. C. C. Newman (Downers Grove, Ill.: InterVarsity; Carlisle: Paternoster, 1999), 188–93.
65. N. T. Wright, "In Grateful Dialogue: A Response," in Newman, *Jesus and the Restoration of Israel*, 274.
66. See above on Smith. Cf. Twelftree, *Jesus the Miracle Worker*, 356–68.
67. See Evans, "Methodological Naturalism," 190. Cf. Wright, *Jesus and the Victory of God*, 187.
68. Borg, *Jesus, a New Vision*, 60; see also idem, "The Historian, the Christian, and Jesus," 8–10. Cf. Powell, *Jesus as a Figure in History*, 105.

for example, Borg finds it very difficult to accept them. These stories must remain in a "historical suspense account."[69]

In the end, the miracles of Jesus hardly feature in Borg's image of the historical Jesus. Jesus was a Spirit-filled figure in the charismatic stream of Judaism, a teacher of wisdom, a social prophet, a model for human life, a disclosure of God as compassionate in his healing, and critical of culture in his movement away from securities.[70] In fact, "Borg's Jesus is a 'counterculture Jesus' of the kind that we might have met on the streets of San Francisco in the sixties and can still find in pockets of reaction in the Santa Cruz mountains."[71] The question arises of why we should accept Borg's worldview that shamanistic healings and exorcisms are possible, but not the nature miracles precluded by a rationalist's worldview.[72]

While J. D. Crossan's *The Historical Jesus: The Life of a Mediterranean Jewish Peasant* (1991) has been immensely popular, it has also been widely criticized.[73] Crossan's proposal is that Jesus was a Mediterranean Jewish Cynic peasant whose aims are seen not simply in his teaching, but in his offering of free miracles and in his eating freely with anyone. Crossan says, "Miracle and parable, healing and eating were calculated to force individuals into unmediated physical and spiritual contact with God and unmediated physical and spiritual contact with one another."[74] So, while his treatment of the miracles uses only one of the fifteen chapters of his book, Crossan regards the healings and exorcisms as standing at the heart of Jesus' work and message about the kingdom.[75]

The point of interest for us is Crossan's observation that Jesus spoke of the kingdom as a power that could be felt in the exorcisms and healing and in the radically egalitarian ethos of the movement. Thus, Jesus' understanding of the kingdom of God is not to be interpreted against the background of an apocalyptic longing for a future new kingdom, but against the wisdom tradition's recognition of a present

---

69. Borg, *Jesus, a New Vision*, 67, 70. See further, Twelftree, *Jesus the Miracle Worker*, 354–55.

70. Borg, "The Historian, the Christian, and Jesus," 8–10; cf. M. J. Borg, ed., *Jesus at 2000* (Boulder, Colo.: Westview, 1997), 11.

71. R. G. Hammerton-Kelly, review of *Jesus, a New Vision*, by Marcus J. Borg, *CRBR* 2 (1989): 182–83.

72. See ibid., 183. Also on Borg, see Witherington, *The Jesus Quest*, 93–108; Powell, *Jesus as a Figure in History*, ch. 6.

73. J. D. Crossan, *The Historical Jesus: The Life of a Mediterranean Jewish Peasant* (San Francisco: HarperSanFrancisco, 1991). On what follows, see also Twelftree, *Jesus the Miracle Worker*, 255–56. Cf. H. C. Kee, "A Century of Quests for the Culturally Compatible Jesus," *ThTo* 52 (1995): 17, cited by W. L. Craig, *Will the Real Jesus Please Stand Up? A Debate between William Lane Craig and John Dominic Crossan*, ed. P. Copan (Grand Rapids: Baker, 1998), 31, where severe criticisms of Crossan are cited. See also Blackburn, "The Miracles of Jesus," 391–92; Witherington, *The Jesus Quest*, ch. 3.

74. Crossan, *The Historical Jesus*, 422.

75. See also J. D. Crossan, "The Presence of God's Love in the Power of Jesus' Works," *Concilium* 10, no. 5 (1969): 34–40.

kingdom in which the wise, good, and virtuous share. In turn, this has significant implications for Crossan's view of the miracles of Jesus. Instead of being in some way related to the interruption by God's reign into contemporary life, they are Jesus' response to a colonial people under political and religious pressure.

However, the impression we gain from Crossan's *Historical Jesus* is radically altered when we take into account his eccentric understanding of miracle.[76] In *Jesus: A Revolutionary Biography* (1994), he says with regard to Jesus healing a leper, "I presume that Jesus, who did not and could not cure that disease or any other one, healed the poor man's illness by refusing to accept the disease's ritual uncleanness and social ostracization."[77] Crossan also asserts that the so-called nature miracles should be grouped together with Jesus' postresurrection apparitions.[78] In this way the nature miracles are dispensed with, for they are not concerned with control over nature before Jesus' death but are apparitions with dramatic and symbolic stories about power and authority in the earliest Christian communities.[79] In any case, the nature miracles also are dispensed with: "I do not think that anyone, anywhere, at any time brings dead people back to life."[80] In this way the miracles of Jesus turn out not to be miracles at all, at least not in the generally understood meaning of miracle.

The culturally comfortable Jesus produced by Borg and Crossan is of a piece with the Jesus Seminar, to which both belong. The Jesus Seminar has been heavily criticized not only for its methods but also for its results.[81] Reflecting the opinion of not a few scholars, Jacob Neusner has gone so far as to say that the Jesus Seminar is "either the greatest scholarly hoax since the Piltdown Man or the utter bankruptcy of New Testament studies."[82]

On the historicity of the miracles of Jesus, the fellows of the Jesus Seminar are, on the whole, more positive than they are about the sayings of Jesus. They believe that Jesus practiced exorcism and that during his lifetime Jesus was considered a healer; though from today's perspective, they say, the cures are

76. Among the various definitions for miracles (see Twelftree, *Jesus the Miracle Worker,* 24–27, esp. 24), a generally accepted definition would be something like that offered by Richard Swinburne (*The Concept of Miracle* [London: Macmillan, 1970], 1): "An event of an extraordinary kind, brought about by a god, and of religious significance."

77. J. D. Crossan, *Jesus: A Revolutionary Biography* (San Francisco: HarperSanFrancisco, 1994), 82.

78. Crossan, *Jesus,* 181; cf. Gnilka, *Jesus of Nazareth,* 133.

79. Crossan, *The Historical Jesus,* 186. Cf. Gnilka (*Jesus of Nazareth,* 132), who attempts to sidestep the issue of historicity: "The question to be asked is not what he [Jesus] formerly did and was but rather what he continues to do and be for us."

80. Crossan, *Jesus,* 95. See Crossan's views on miracles collected by Craig, *Will the Real Jesus Please Stand Up?* 30–31.

81. For example, C. Grant, "The Greying of Jesus," *ExpTim* 110 (1999): 246–48; see also L. T. Johnson, *The Real Jesus* (San Francisco: HarperCollins, 1997), and the reply by R. J. Miller, "History Is Not Optional," *BTB* 28 (1998): 27–34; cf. Witherington, *The Jesus Quest,* ch. 2.

82. Quoted in R. N. Ostling, "Jesus Christ, Plain and Simple," *Time* (January 10, 1994): 38.

related to psychosomatic maladies. However, the fellows are unable to endorse any of the nature wonders as historical events, concluding that they are all fictions suggested by extra-Gospel models.[83]

Miracles Partially Recognized

In *This Jesus: Martyr, Lord, Messiah* (1994), Markus Bockmuehl comments, "Scholars are increasingly coming to recognize the historical setting and importance of miracle stories in the ministry of Jesus."[84] In contrast to Sanders, for example, he suggests that the significance of the miracles can be seen in that while "other contemporaries, like Honi and Hanina ben Dosa, had also performed miraculous actions," Jesus, unlike them, "explicitly understood his healings and exorcisms as inaugurating the Kingdom of God and spelling the defeat of the reign of Satan."[85] As profound as were the significance of the miracles, Jesus demonstrated God's kingdom power to drive out evil spirits by appearing to employ magical practices of exorcism, which the theologians regarded as suspect. However, Bockmuehl, having established the importance of miracles in Jesus' work, gives the miracles and miracle traditions almost no part to play in his biography and in the significance of Jesus. In fact, the miracles are not mentioned in his summary of "this Jesus."[86]

Assessment

Debates that raged earlier in the twentieth century have run their course. No longer is the category of myth much discussed as important in understanding the miracles.[87] Similarly, though form criticism was once at the heart of studies of Jesus, some time ago it was said, "Form criticism of the gospels is a stagnant discipline."[88] Though the concept of a "divine man" and its usefulness in accounting for the early Christian miracle traditions still have faithful adherents, the idea is being laid to rest.[89] For there was a diversity among miracle workers

83. Funk and the Jesus Seminar, *The Acts of Jesus*, 530–31.

84. M. Bockmuehl, *This Jesus: Martyr, Lord, Messiah* (Edinburgh: Clark, 1994), 56, noting Evans, "Life-of-Jesus Research."

85. Bockmuehl, *This Jesus*, 56.

86. The same can be said of L. Morris, *Jesus* (Sydney: Acorn, 1994), and of J. D. G. Dunn, "Jesus for Today," *ThTo* 52 (1995–96): 66–74.

87. On the collapse of the mythological debate, see Evans, "Life-of-Jesus Research," 3–36; *Jesus and His Contemporaries*, 2, and those cited.

88. Stanton, "Form Criticism Revisited," 13. Cf. W. R. Telford, "Major Trends and Interpretive Issues in the Study of Jesus," in Chilton and Evans, *Studying the Historical Jesus*, 58.

89. See D. L. Tiede, *The Charismatic Figure as Miracle Worker* (Missoula, Mont.: Scholars Press, 1972); M. Hengel, *The Son of God* (London: SCM, 1976), 31–32; J. D. Kingsbury, "The

performing a diverse range of miracles in an era when divinity was judged and expressed with a range of criteria and terms equally diverse—though rarely using the term *theios anēr*.[90]

Notably, by the end of the twentieth century, the view most clearly expressed by Schlatter had won the day: "The attempt to find a miracle-free Gospel as the first form of Christian tradition to which only later miracle accounts were attached has no chance of success."[91] It is not that the accent of research has now fallen on the miracle traditions.[92] Rather, there is a shift from focusing on the teaching to giving attention to the activities of Jesus—including the miracles—in the hope of finding more solid ground for reconstructions of his life.

There is now almost unanimous agreement among Jesus questers that the historical Jesus performed mighty works.[93] (As Meier noted, however, there is the paradox that while some scholars affirm that Jesus was a miracle worker, when it comes to the evaluation of individual miracle stories, they feel that the material is too meager or dubious for any serious judgment of historicity to be made.[94]) Over and above this, an increasing number of scholars affirm that the miracles in the Gospel traditions are important in understanding and reconstructing the historical Jesus. Yet the so-called nature miracles remain an insurmountable problem;[95] rarely is Jesus clearly credited with being able to, for example, raise the dead or walk on water.

Nevertheless, even with the wealth of data to show that Jesus was being portrayed in the Gospels in a way consistent with other charismatics or holy men of the period, there remain those who not only marginalize Jesus' miracles, but even purge their Jesus of miracles. Thus, I remain convinced that those who recently have produced lives of the historical Jesus are still looking down the well of history and can see only a reflection of themselves, their values, and the religious heroes of our own times.[96]

'Divine Man' as the Key to Mark's Christology—The End of an Era?" *Int* 35 (1981), 243–57; Kee, *Miracle in the Early Christian World*, 297–99; J. D. Kingsbury, *The Christology of Mark's Gospel* (Philadelphia: Fortress, 1983), 33–37, and those he cites (34 n. 42).

90. B. L. Blackburn, "'Miracle Working ΘΕΙΟΙ ΑΝΔΡΕΣ' in Hellenism (and Hellenistic Judaism)," in Wenham and Blomberg, *The Miracles of Jesus*, 185–218; idem, *Theios Anēr and the Markan Miracle Traditions*, WUNT 2.40 (Tübingen: Mohr, 1991).

91. Schlatter, *The History of the Christ*, 174.

92. Contra B. B. Scott, "From Reimarus to Crossan: Stages in a Quest," *CurBS* 2 (1994): 272; Wright, *Jesus and the Victory of God*, 186.

93. Blackburn, "The Miracles of Jesus," 392. Cf. Maier, "Zur neutestamentlichen Wunderexegese."

94. Meier, *A Marginal Jew*, 2:967.

95. See Maier, "Zur neutestamentlichen Wunderexegese," 79. See the attempted solutions by C. L. Blomberg, "New Testament Miracles and Higher Criticism: Climbing Up the Slippery Slope," *JETS* 27 (1984): 425–38; idem, "The Miracles as Parables," in Wenham and Blomberg, *The Miracles of Jesus*, 327–59; Meier, *A Marginal Jew*, vol. 2, ch. 23.

96. See Twelftree, *Jesus the Miracle Worker*, 356, echoing George Tyrrell, *Christianity at the Cross-Roads* (London: Longman, Green, 1910), 44, in his comment on Adolf von Harnack.

The new Jesus who has emerged in recent decades is no longer the super-natural wand-waver of precritical days. Instead, he turns out to be a model of modern spirituality: a man of the Spirit in constant communion with his God, and whose miracles of compassion—so far as they may be important—maintain his popularity on the periphery of society with the other eccentric Cynic-like Jewish holy men. The miracles, for which there are ready rational explanations—they are accomplished by heightened human endeavor—reveal Jesus to be a magician, or at least someone using magic, even if that is not seen as the best overall title for him.

How, then, can we account for the sanctioning of this renewed interest in the miracles associated with the historical Jesus? The preeminent cause is probably the weight of research bringing about the demise of the view kept alive primarily by the *Religionsgeschichtliche Schule* and their heirs, the form critics, that miracles, perhaps in the form of myths, were imported into the miracle-free Jesus tradition or that the traditions have been (re)written in light of contemporary miracle workers.

Also, no longer is the search for the historical Jesus dominated by liberal Protestants;[97] confidence in the historical skepticism of the liberals has faltered, even among those who do not focus on the miracles of Jesus.[98] Concomitantly, in this postmodern era, when a plurality of possible truths can be held,[99] it is now seen as methodologically prudent to hold back from too hasty a judgment on what is and what is not possible in this space-time universe.[100] This caution is warranted in light of at least two factors. One is the long and ongoing defense of the historicity of the miracles of Jesus by scholars using increasingly sophisticated tools for historical study, which is difficult to ignore.[101] The other factor warranting caution in dispensing with the miraculous is the ongoing vigorous philosophical and theological defense of the possibility of miracles.[102] Further, Roman Catholic and Jewish scholars, along with evangelicals and those of no particular religious affiliation, have entered the arena and made significant contributions to the field; yet, we await an evangelical scholar to

97. On which, see A. E. McGrath, *Christian Theology* (Oxford: Blackwell, 1997), 101–4.

98. See Harvey, *Jesus and the Constraints of History*, 2–5; Evans, *Jesus and His Contemporaries*, 8–11, and those cited; Theissen and Merz, *The Historical Jesus*, ch. 4. See also R. Hannaford, "The Legacy of Liberal Anglican Theology," *Theology* 103 (2000): 89–96.

99. See, D. Tracy, *Blessed Rage for Order: The New Pluralism in Theology* (New York: Seabury, 1975; reprint, Chicago: University of Chicago Press, 1996), 3–21.

100. Wright, *Jesus and the Victory of God*, 189; cf. Meyer, *The Aims of Jesus*, 99–104.

101. See, for example, Meier, *A Marginal Jew*, 2:507–1038; Twelftree, *Jesus the Miracle Worker*; Blomberg, "New Testament Miracles," 427; Wright, *Jesus and the Victory of God*, 186.

102. See, for example, R. F. Holland, "The Miraculous," *American Philosophical Quarterly* 2 (1965): 43–51; Swinburne, *The Concept of Miracle*; R. C. Wallace, "Hume, Flew and the Miraculous," *Philosophical Quarterly* 20 (1970): 230–43; R. D. Geivett and G. R. Habermas, eds., *In Defense of Miracles* (Downers Grove, Ill.: InterVarsity, 1997); Twelftree, *Jesus the Miracle Worker*, ch. 2.

contribute a credible life of the historical Jesus that takes seriously into account the miracle traditions.

At the beginning of the twenty-first century there is still much work to be done on the miracles of the historical Jesus. Still to be decided is the fundamental question of the place of miracles in a reconstructed life of Jesus: do they have a place, and if so, are they of central or of peripheral significance? And what, if anything, do the miracles mean? Are they, as Crossan says, to be seen as Jesus' response to a colonial people under pressure? At one level, with Smith, do they mean that Jesus was a magician? At another level, with Harvey, do they mean that Jesus was a (or the) messiah? Or, as Sanders argues, are we unable to learn anything definite from the miracles? Or are the miracles the physical inauguration of the kingdom of Israel's God, as Wright supposes? Further, was Jesus only a healer and exorcist, as most scholars would allow; or was he also able to perform feats unattainable even by heightened human accomplishment, as few if any Jesus questers so far are able to say with confidence?[103]

Of all the aspects of the study of the historical Jesus, that of miracles most sharply reflects philosophical and theological fashions, as well as personal presuppositions. Jesus remains offensive, if not for Schweitzer's reason, then because he was reported to be a miracle worker of extraordinary power and success. No less than in the nineteenth century, the fluctuating fortunes of the way the miracles of Jesus are treated has remained theologically driven[104] and often philosophically shackled by rationalism or naturalism. It cannot be otherwise until historiographers are able to challenge successfully this ascendant paradigm of reality presupposed by most Jesus questers.

103. See Blackburn, "The Miracles of Jesus," 368–72.

104. Clearly illustrated by, for example, Latourelle, *The Miracles of Jesus;* and by Gnilka, *Jesus of Nazareth,* 134, in dealing with the stories of Jesus raising the dead: "Only from the perspective of Easter can the question of death and life be posed radically." Contra Evans, "Life-of-Jesus Research," 34–35; *Jesus and His Contemporaries,* 10–13.

11

John and Jesus

Craig L. Blomberg

The differences between John's Gospel and the Synoptics have been the object of intense fascination throughout church history. John contains no full-fledged parables or exorcisms. He omits Jesus' baptism, his calling of the twelve apostles, the transfiguration, Gethsemane, and the institution of the Lord's Supper. Conversely, he alone includes Jesus' miracle of turning water into wine, the resurrection of Lazarus, Jesus' early ministry in Judea and Samaria, his frequent trips to Jerusalem, and his numerous extended discourses. Only John has Jesus making explicit claims that affirm his divinity. Instead of the gradual self-disclosure of the Synoptics, John's Jesus receives messianic acclaim from the very outset of his public ministry. The central message of the Synoptic Jesus involves the kingdom of God; in John, Jesus talks far more about eternal life. It is only from John that we learn of a roughly three-year ministry. Certain events seem to appear at different times than in the Synoptics—most notably, the temple cleansing, Mary's anointing, and the crucifixion. A policy of excommunicating Jews who confess Christ is described, which seems to correspond better to events at the end of the first century rather than a *Sitz im Leben Jesu*. Finally, John's writing style merges with that of Jesus; the key vocabulary and concepts of the two seem indistinguishable. Given that the Synoptic Gospels have provided most of the foundation for reconstructing the historical Jesus, it is little wonder that the role of the Fourth Gospel has been greatly minimized in that arena of scholarship.[1]

---

1. This brief essay cannot address all of these differences. For additional detail, see Craig L. Blomberg, *The Historical Reliability of John's Gospel: Issues and Commentary* (Downers Grove, Ill.: InterVarsity, 2001).

Background to Recent Scholarship

A century ago, it was widely believed that John was literarily dependent on the Synoptics, so that when he went his own way, he was consciously rejecting or at least supplementing the information found in the first three Gospels. For some, this conviction bolstered confidence in John's historicity: there were so many legitimate angles from which to view Jesus that John had simply picked a different one and did not want to repeat most of what the Synoptics already treated well.[2] For most scholars, however, John's differences reflected less historically accurate information, so that the Fourth Gospel was not a primary source for Jesus research.[3] Percival Gardner-Smith inaugurated a new era in 1938 by convincing many that John was literarily independent of the Synoptics.[4] Gardner-Smith himself believed that this observation opened the door to considering this Gospel to have great historical value, but other scholars were slow to follow him on this point. The next three decades would generate the two massive German commentaries on John by Rudolf Bultmann and Ernst Haenchen, both of which alleged that the historicity of uniquely Johannine material was almost nil.[5] Less heralded works in both the English- and German-speaking worlds, however, would begin to argue for a substantial measure of historicity in John.[6] One of these, by Ethelbert Stauffer, actually took the bold step of incorporating considerable portions of John's unique material, including the high Christology of the "I am" statements, into his overall reconstruction of "Jesus and his story."[7] Nevertheless, as late as 1965, Franz Mussner could write an entire book on *The Historical Jesus in the Gospel of St. John* and conclude that, differing substantially from the Synoptics, in John "the words of the earthly Jesus and of the exalted Christ can no longer be distinguished at all."[8] Indeed,

---

2. See especially William Sanday, *The Criticism of the Fourth Gospel* (Oxford: Clarendon, 1905).

3. See especially Benjamin W. Bacon, *The Fourth Gospel in Research and Debate* (New York: Moffat, Yard, 1910).

4. Percival Gardner-Smith, *Saint John and the Synoptic Gospels* (Cambridge: Cambridge University Press, 1938).

5. Rudolf Bultmann, *Das Evangelium des Johannes* (Göttingen: Vandenhoeck & Ruprecht, 1964; in English, *The Gospel of John* [Oxford: Blackwell; Philadelphia: Westminster, 1971]); Ernst Haenchen, *Das Johannesevangelium* (Tübingen: Mohr, 1980; in English, *John*, 2 vols. [Philadelphia: Fortress, 1984]). Despite the late publication dates, even of the German editions, both works reflected several prior decades of research and publishing. Haenchen's volume was in fact edited posthumously by Ulrich Busse, based on various drafts in various stages, a few unrevised since the 1940s.

6. Especially A. C. Headlam, *The Fourth Gospel as History* (Oxford: Blackwell, 1948); A. J. B. Higgins, *The Historicity of the Fourth Gospel* (London: Lutterworth, 1960).

7. Ethelbert Stauffer, *Jesus: Gestalt und Geschichte* (Bern: Francke, 1957; in English, *Jesus and His Story* [London: SCM; New York: Knopf, 1960]).

8. Franz Mussner, *Johanneische Sehweise und die Frage nach dem historischen Jesus* (Freiburg: Herder, 1965; in English, *The Historical Jesus in the Gosepl of St. John*, trans. W. O'Hara [New York: Herder & Herder, 1967]).

the majority of Mussner's volume is not about the historical Jesus, but about John's understanding of history and inspiration that allowed him to merge these two perspectives.

Meanwhile, winds were changing. As early as 1957, John A. T. Robinson delivered a short but influential paper entitled "The New Look on the Fourth Gospel."[9] In it, he itemized five presuppositions in Johannine research that he sensed were being increasingly questioned: (1) John's dependence on the Synoptics; (2) dramatic redactional differences from his source; (3) his witness to the Christ of faith rather than the Jesus of history; (4) his late position in the evolution of NT theology; and (5) scholarly rejection of apostolic, eyewitness authorship. In 1963, C. H. Dodd proved Robinson's work to be prophetic in several respects. In a major work entitled *Historical Tradition in the Fourth Gospel,* Dodd analyzed in detail John's Passion Narrative, key features of his presentation of Jesus' ministry, his treatment of John the Baptist and the first disciples, and a large cluster of isolated sayings and parable-like accounts. Dodd concluded that there was excellent evidence at each point for John's reliance on early traditions, many of which stood a good chance of being historically accurate.[10] Dodd still found considerable theological overlay throughout the Fourth Gospel, but his relatively conservative conclusions would influence and be echoed in Raymond Brown's major two-volume commentary on the Gospel of John, published in 1966 and 1970.[11]

From a quite different perspective, in 1968, came J. Louis Martyn's *History and Theology in the Fourth Gospel.*[12] Despite its promising title, most of the book was not about the historical Jesus at all, but about how one should

9. At the Oxford Conference on "The Four Gospels in 1957"; subsequently published in *Studia Evangelica,* vol. 1, *Papers Presented to the International Congress on "The Four Gospels in 1957" Held at Christ Church, Oxford,* ed. K. Aland et al., TU 73 (Berlin: Akademie-Verlag, 1959), 338–50.

10. C. H. Dodd, *Historical Tradition in the Fourth Gospel* (Cambridge: Cambridge University Press, 1963). On Dodd's contribution and subsequent influence, see D. A. Carson, "Historical Tradition in the Fourth Gospel: After Dodd, What?" in *Studies of History and Tradition in the Four Gospels,* ed. R. T. France and David Wenham, Gospel Perspectives 2 (Sheffield: JSOT Press, 1981), 83–145. This study in turn led to the exchange reflected in J. S. King, "Has D. A. Carson Been Fair to C. H. Dodd?" *JSNT* 17 (1983): 97–102; and D. A. Carson, "Historical Tradition in the Fourth Gospel: A Response to J. S. King," *JSNT* 23 (1985): 73–81.

11. Raymond E. Brown, *The Gospel according to John,* 2 vols., AB 29–29A (Garden City, N.Y.: Doubleday, 1966–70). See also Brown's earlier essays, "Incidents That Are Units in the Synoptic Gospels but Dispersed in St. John," *CBQ* 23 (1961): 143–60; "The Problem of Historicity in John," *CBQ* 24 (1962): 1–14. Brown's views of the authorship of the Fourth Gospel would later change from belief in, to rejection of, John the apostle as author. But even late in his life, he would synthesize his convictions in his massive *Death of the Messiah* (2 vols. [New York and London: Doubleday, 1994]), with regular sections discussing historicity that remained roughly as confident as his earlier commentary in finding historical cores in most passages.

12. J. Louis Martyn, *History and Theology in the Fourth Gospel* (New York: Harper & Row, 1968). Martyn considerably expanded his work in a second edition (Nashville: Abingdon, 1979).

read most of John's Gospel as a mirror of events affecting a Hellenistic-Jewish audience at the end of the first century. Most influential were Martyn's claims that the hostility between Jesus and the Jewish leaders did not primarily reflect historical controversies in Jerusalem in the late 20s or early 30s, but rather the antagonism between Christianity and Judaism at the end of the first century after the establishment of the *birkat ha-minim* (the "blessing"—as a euphemism for cursing—of the heretics) in the eighteen benedictions of the synagogue liturgy and the practice of excommunicating Christian Jews from synagogues altogether (cf. esp. John 9:22; 12:42; 16:2). Thus, while Martyn spoke of reading John at two levels—that of the historical Jesus and that of the circumstances of the Johannine community two generations later—his attention focused primarily on the latter.[13] From an evangelical perspective, Leon Morris's *Studies in the Fourth Gospel* became the most important book of this era on our topic. The most relevant section for historical-Jesus research was his lengthy analysis of the phenomenon he labeled "interlocking"—passages in John that explained otherwise puzzling features of the Synoptics and vice versa.[14]

1970–85

The 1970s did not produce any major works on the historical Jesus in John, but the "new look" increasingly took on the appearance of a consensus. Ernst Bammel wrote an important article on Jesus' trial narrative in John, vindicating its historical accuracy at crucial junctures.[15] The initial findings of Dead Sea Scrolls research were increasingly synthesized, and James Charlesworth and a team of collaborators could highlight how they reinforced the Jewish nature of John at numerous points where earlier researchers had thought that

13. Not surprisingly, in the same year as Martyn's second edition, Raymond E. Brown would use similar "mirror-reading" to produce an important work (*The Community of the Beloved Disciple* [New York: Paulist Press, 1979]) entirely devoted to discerning the makeup of the Johannine community.

14. Leon Morris, *Studies in the Fourth Gospel* (Exeter: Paternoster; Grand Rapids: Eerdmans, 1969), esp. 40–63. For example, John 3:24 refers to a time before John the Baptist was imprisoned, yet the Fourth Gospel nowhere narrates that imprisonment as the Synoptics do (Mark 6:14–29 pars.). John 11:2 distinguishes Mary of Bethany from other Marys by referring to her role in anointing Jesus as if it were already well known (cf. esp. Mark 14:9). In the other direction, Mark 14:49—on Jesus frequently teaching in the temple—makes better sense if Jesus had made numerous trips to Jerusalem, as in John. Jesus' cryptic saying in John 2:19 about destroying "this temple" accounts for the garbled testimony against him in his Synoptic trial (Mark 14:58–59 par.). Morris supplied numerous additional examples with varying degrees of persuasiveness.

15. Ernst Bammel, "'Ex illa itaque die consilium fecerunt . . . ,'" in *The Trial of Jesus*, ed. E. Bammel (London: SCM; Naperville, Ill.: Allenson, 1970), 11–40. Cf. his later essay "The Trial before Pilate," in *Jesus and the Politics of His Day*, ed. Ernst Bammel and C. F. D. Moule (Cambridge: University Press, 1984), 353–64.

Hellenistic parallels proved closest.[16] Most famous was Qumran's frequent use of the expression "sons of light" and "sons of darkness" and other forms of dualism, predestination, pneumatology, and messianic hope. C. K. Barrett's important commentary charted a judicious middle ground between widespread skepticism and full-fledged historicity, concluding:

> It is evident that it was not John's intention to write a work of scientific history. . . . John's interests were theological rather than chronological. . . . He did not hesitate to repress, revise, rewrite, or rearrange. On the other hand there is no sufficient evidence for the view that John freely created narrative material for allegorical purposes. . . . This means that the chronicler can sometimes (though less frequently than is often thought) pick out from John simple and sound historical material.[17]

In fact, when one works through his commentary passage by passage, one discovers a kernel in a significant majority of John's pericopae that Barrett deems historical. Barnabas Lindars's commentary, reflecting research that ultimately would span four decades, takes much the same tack, with the added feature that he sees Jesus' lengthy discourses as the product of shorter authentic sayings mingled with subsequent Johannine homiletical elaboration.[18] The "double amen" sayings that proliferate throughout the words of Jesus in John he finds particularly promising as the historical kernels of these various "sermons."[19] In Germany, the prodigious three-volume commentary on John by Rudolf Schnackenburg took a similar middle-of-the-road position,[20] while Leon Morris produced a detailed, conservative commentary with comments about the probability of more widespread historicity embedded in his passage-by-passage exegesis.[21]

By the end of the 1970s, then, Stephen Smalley could write a very helpful textbook on the state of Johannine research and defend a moderately evangelical position with considerable credibility.[22] Ongoing research into ancient Judaism

16. James H. Charlesworth, ed., *John and Qumran* (London: Chapman, 1972).

17. C. K. Barrett, *The Gospel according to St. John* (London: SCM; Philadelphia: Westminster, 1978), 141–42.

18. Barnabas Lindars, *The Gospel of John* (London: Marshall, Morgan & Scott, 1972; Grand Rapids: Eerdmans, 1981). Lindars's published works on John spanned the 1960s to the 1990s. Particularly relevant for our topic are *Behind the Fourth Gospel* (London: SPCK, 1971); "Traditions behind the Fourth Gospel," in *L'Évangile de Jean: Sources, rédaction, théologie,* ed. M. de Jonge et al., BETL 44 (Gembloux: Duculot, 1977), 107–24; "John and the Synoptic Gospels: A Test Case," *NTS* 27 (1981): 287–94.

19. See Lindars, "Discourse and Tradition: The Use of the Sayings of Jesus in the Discourses of the Fourth Gospel," *JSNT* 13 (1981): 83–101.

20. Rudolf Schnackenburg, *Das Johannesevangelium,* 3 vols., HTKNT 4 (Freiburg: Herder, 1965–75); in English as *The Gospel according to St. John,* 3 vols. (London: Burns & Oates; New York: Herder & Herder, 1968–82).

21. Leon Morris, *The Gospel according to John* (Grand Rapids: Eerdmans, 1971; London: Marshall, Morgan & Scott, 1972).

22. Stephen S. Smalley, *John: Evangelist and Interpreter* (Exeter: Paternoster, 1978).

discovered parallels to almost every pericope in John, so that Greco-Roman parallels seemed less and less relevant. Confirmation of previously suspect details in the Fourth Gospel continued to emerge, and discussions of criteria of authenticity or historicity became increasingly sophisticated. While by no means universally agreed on, the following elements of John's story of Jesus were widely held to be at least as likely to be historical as the core of authentic Synoptic Gospel data: Jesus and his first disciples emerging out of the circle of followers of John the Baptist; Jesus' early ministry of baptizing; a ministry in Judea and Samaria prior to the Synoptics' "great Galilean ministry"; the overall sequence of events in John 6 (found more spread out in the Synoptics), including the crowd's aborted attempt to make Jesus king; John's chronology, including Jesus' multiyear ministry and multiple trips to Jerusalem in conjunction with the major Jewish festivals; an earlier decision on the part of the Sanhedrin to put Jesus to death at the opportune time as in John 11; and distinctive features of Jesus' Jewish and Roman trials, including the hearing before Annas, the reason for the Jewish leaders sending Jesus to Pilate (they could not instigate the capital punishment they believed he deserved), and Pilate's fear at being called no friend of Caesar as the catalyst for convincing him to crucify someone he believed to be innocent. Smalley's largest personal contribution to this discussion was to argue against those who wanted to dismiss the miracles in John as unhistorical and in favor of a process of composition that saw original, genuinely supernatural events, elaborated over time and couched in Johannine language and conceptual symbolism that made them function somewhat akin to the Synoptic parables.[23]

In a posthumously edited volume, J. A. T. Robinson authored the next "blockbuster" work on the historical Jesus in John. This liberal English bishop had already stunned the scholarly world with his 1976 work *Redating the New Testament,* in which he argued that *every* book in the NT was written before 70 C.E.[24] Now, nearly a decade later, he was arguing for the "priority of John."[25] Not only should John be dated to the 60s, but his independent perspective on Jesus at numerous points proved superior to, and more historical than, the Synoptics' approach. In addition to supporting all the points noted above as part of the "end of the 1970s" trends, Robinson argued that John was right and the Synoptics wrong in the placement of the clearing of the temple and the anointing at Bethany, that the cluster of messianic titles ascribed to Jesus in John 1 reflected conventional nationalistic hopes and could be accepted as authentic in its context, that the distinctive focus on Jesus as "king" in the events from "Palm Sunday" through to Jesus' crucifixion best reflected the historical realities

---

23. Ibid., 169–84. Cf. his parallel treatment of "history behind the discourses" (184–90).

24. J. A. T. Robinson, *Redating the New Testament* (London: SCM; Philadelphia: Westminster, 1976).

25. J. A. T. Robinson, *The Priority of John,* ed. J. F. Coakley (London: SCM, 1985; Oak Park, Ill.: Meyer-Stone, 1987).

of Jesus' downfall,[26] and that the references to the Beloved Disciple throughout the last chapters of John (and to an anonymous disciple elsewhere) reflected eyewitness testimony. Even more controversially, Robinson played down any ontological significance for John of all Jesus' seemingly high christological claims and found them no more lofty or incredible than the regular Synoptic emphasis on Jesus as one sent by his Father as his "agent." Apart from evangelicals, few scholars were willing to accept a majority of Robinson's claims, particularly criticizing him for relying on and trying to rehabilitate numerous older English-language works and not interacting sufficiently with the more liberal *status quaestionis.*[27]

From 1986 to the Present

Perhaps in part due to Robinson's numerous extremely conservative claims, the most recent period of Johannine research has seen a pendulum swing back to highly skeptical positions on several fronts. It also has seen a proliferation of conservative scholarship, along with some studies that cling to an increasingly tenuous middle ground. Without the benefit of knowing the future to determine which perspectives will endure and prove most influential, this recent phase of Johannine scholarship is hardest to characterize. Like NT studies more generally, it seems quite fragmented and even polarized.

Representing the more liberal end of the spectrum, A. T. Hanson published an important work in the early 1990s on the numerous ways the Gospel of John quotes, alludes to, and builds on the OT and subsequent Jewish exegetical traditions so as to set it apart from the Synoptics.[28] Hanson recognizes that John employs traditional material, some of it actually historical, though in general he finds the Fourth Gospel significantly inferior to the Synoptics in this respect. In fact, the anonymous fourth evangelist

> allows himself a very wide license indeed in altering, enriching, transposing and adding to his own tradition from his own resources, which were largely drawn from scripture as he understood it. He has therefore not provided us with a reliable historical account of Jesus. Could he have understood what we mean by "a reliable historical account," he would probably repudiate [*sic*] the suggestion that this is what he was giving us in his Gospel.[29]

---

26. This point was ably developed by Robinson's editor, J. F. Coakley, in a pair of articles on John 12: "The Anointing at Bethany and the Priority of John," *JBL* 107 (1988): 241–56; "Jesus' Messianic Entry into Jerusalem (John 12:12–19 par.)," *JTS* 46 (1995): 61–82.

27. For an important article-length review, see Pierre Grelot, "Problemes critiques du IVe Evangile," *RB* 94 (1987): 519–73. Important authors of a previous era on which Robinson relied heavily included B. F. Westcott, J. B. Lightfoot, and H. Scott Holland.

28. A. T. Hanson, *The Prophetic Gospel: A Study of John and the Old Testament* (Edinburgh: Clark, 1991).

29. Ibid., 318.

Hanson's logic, however, proves to be far from clear. To the extent that John's Jesus consistently shows a mastery of OT and Jewish exegetical traditions, one would have supposed that the case for authenticity/historicity would have been enhanced.

The most highly publicized development of the 1990s, of course, was the publication of the twin volumes by the Jesus Seminar, color-coding first all of the sayings attributed to Jesus and then all of the narrative material in each of the five Gospels, including the *Gospel of Thomas*.[30] In the first volume, the Seminar determined that all but three of the sayings of Jesus in John's Gospel bore no resemblance to his authentic teaching, and thus they were colored black (definitely inauthentic).[31] In the second volume, the Seminar colored sixteen short excerpts—from one line to a few verses in length—of the evangelist's narrative something other than black.[32] With rare exceptions, the appended commentary simply presupposed that when John noticeably differed from the Synoptics, his work was to be considered wholly unhistorical. Only rarely is any additional rationale given for coloring something black; even less common is interaction with any strand of scholarship that disagrees.

Undoubtedly, the fiercest attack on the historicity of John in quite some time appeared in 1996 with Maurice Casey's *Is John's Gospel True?*[33] Casey begins by arguing that John has misplaced Jesus' temple cleansing and altered the date of the Last Supper. These observations alone "show that a conservative evangelical view of scripture is verifiably false."[34] Casey proceeds to present additional ways in which John's Gospel cannot be harmonized with the Synoptics, discussing its Christology, portrait of John the Baptist, style and content of Jesus' teaching, and Passion Narrative. Instead, this Gospel has fabricated its distinctive content in light of the polemics between Christians and Jews at the end of the first century and in keeping with the pseudepigraphical tradition of much of Hebrew Scripture. Casey concludes that John's Gospel "is profoundly untrue. It consists to a large extent of inaccurate stories and words wrongly attributed to people. It is anti-Jewish, and as holy scripture has been used to legitimate outbreaks of Christian anti-Semitism." It is thus unworthy, in Casey's opinion, of inclusion in the Bible![35] While neither Casey nor the Jesus Seminar reflects mainstream Johannine scholarship,[36] both do reflect a clear trend in one im-

---

30. Robert Funk, Roy W. Hoover, and the Jesus Seminar, *The Five Gospels: The Search for the Authentic Words of Jesus* (New York: Macmillan, 1993); Robert Funk and the Jesus Seminar, *The Acts of Jesus: The Search for the Authentic Deeds of Jesus* (San Francisco: HarperSanFrancisco, 1998).

31. Funk, Hoover, and the Jesus Seminar, *The Five Gospels*, 40–170.

32. Funk and the Jesus Seminar, *The Acts of Jesus*, 365–440.

33. Maurice Casey, *Is John's Gospel True?* (London and New York: Routledge, 1996).

34. Ibid., 29.

35. Ibid., 229.

36. For a brief but important critique of Casey, see Ruth Edwards and Eric Franklin, "Two Contrasting Approaches to John's Gospel," *ExpTim* 109 (1998): 242–44.

portant wing of biblical studies internationally: the embracing of increasingly anti-Christian perspectives.

The "middle of the road" perspective is still ably articulated by leading Johannine specialists such as D. Moody Smith and R. Alan Culpepper. Both of these scholars have written prolifically on John throughout distinguished careers. With respect to the historical Jesus, Smith suggests that John's distinctive chronology, geography, portrait of John the Baptist, vignettes about women, and elements of the passion and resurrection accounts all may contain historical material.[37] Culpepper has focused primarily on the Johannine community and literary criticism, but in one short study continues in the tradition of Lindars in seeing historical cores, often related to the "double amen" sayings, in the larger, otherwise more redactional discourses of John.[38] Yet another leading Johannine scholar who identifies a core, underlying historical tradition, while focusing primarily on what he believes are numerous subsequent stages of redactional overlay, is John Ashton.[39] The influential shadow of Martyn's mir-ror-reading continues to loom large and receive further nuancing within this branch of scholarship.

Other substantial numbers of Johannine studies of recent vintage have eschewed historical questions altogether, preferring exclusively redactional/ theological, literary, and/or sociological approaches.[40] In many instances, the assumption, explicit or implicit, is that John's Gospel is for the most part not historical, and therefore other approaches are required. But Derek Tovey has broken fresh ground with a study that seeks to bridge the divide between literary and historical criticisms.[41] Focusing on the close connection between the Fourth Gospel's implied author and its story world, Tovey highlights the distinctions within John between the time of Jesus and the time of the Gospel's composition, and the combination of history and theology that interact with each other throughout. Overall, for Tovey, the literary form of John's narrative falls about one-quarter of the way across a spectrum from pure history, as "an accurate record of the memory of what happened," to pure myth, as "narrative which is neither true nor does it approximate to actual events." It is slightly freer in style than the Synoptics, which resemble "memoirs" or "personal

---

37. D. Moody Smith, "Historical Issues and the Problem of John and the Synoptics," in *From Jesus to John,* ed. Martinus C. de Boer, JSNTSup 84 (Sheffield: JSOT Press, 1993), 252–67.

38. Though not as consistently as Lindars did. See R. Alan Culpepper, "The AMHN, AMHN Sayings in the Gospel of John," in *Perspectives on John: Methods and Interpretation in the Fourth Gospel,* ed. Robert B. Sloan and Mikeal C. Parsons (Lewiston and Lampeter: Mellen, 1993), 57–101.

39. See Ashton, *Understanding the Fourth Gospel* (Oxford: Clarendon, 1991); idem, *Studying John: Approaches to the Fourth Gospel* (Oxford: Clarendon, 1994).

40. The most recent detailed bibliography of Johannine scholarship, providing ample documentation, is Watson E. Mills, *The Gospel of John* (Lewiston and Lampeter: Mellen, 1995).

41. Derek Tovey, *Narrative Art and Act in the Fourth Gospel,* JSNTSup 151 (Sheffield: Sheffield Academic Press, 1997).

reminiscences," but not as disinterested in factual reporting as aretalogy or a historical novel.[42] And in a wide-ranging monograph on ancient Mediterranean historiography, biography, and oral history- or story-telling, Samuel Byrskog observes a balance between a genuine concern for eyewitness information that can be corroborated and interpretive perspectives necessarily imposed on the traditions.[43] Byrskog identifies the Fourth Gospel as an example of "history as authorial legitimation" and finds at the very least a substantial core of credible history.[44] Andrew T. Lincoln's recent *Truth on Trial* agrees that John's theological emphases require at least the basic contours of Jesus' life, especially in the Passion Narrative, to be historically accurate. But he interacts primarily with a different kind of literary critic than Tovey or Byrskog and thus allows for substantially more "fiction" to be interwoven into the Fourth Gospel.[45]

Perhaps the most significant development in Johannine scholarship since the death of Bishop Robinson, however, has been the extraordinary proliferation of evangelical studies. Unfortunately, as in NT scholarship more generally, with important exceptions, these works simply have not received the attention they deserve. A spate of evangelical commentaries has appeared since 1986, including volumes by Beasley-Murray, Carson, Pryor, Witherington, Borchert, Ridderbos, Whitacre, Köstenberger, and Keener.[46] Each of these, to differing extents, includes regular comments about the probable historicity of various

42. Ibid., 273. Mark W. G. Stibbe, in his several works on John, likewise has sought to combine historical and literary concerns, with substantial gains for John's historicity. See especially his *John as Storyteller: Narrative Criticism and the Fourth Gospel* (Cambridge: University Press, 1992). In complementary studies of the Gospel genre, Richard A. Burridge (*What Are the Gospels? A Comparison with Graeco-Roman Biography* [Cambridge: Cambridge University Press, 1992], esp. 220–39) and James D. G. Dunn ("Let John Be John—A Gospel for Its Time," in *Das Evangelium und die Evangelien*, ed. Peter Stuhlmacher [Tübingen: Mohr, 1983], esp. 338–39) have stressed how John remains closer in form to the Synoptics than to any other known work of literature from antiquity.

43. Samuel Byrskog, *Story as History—History as Story: The Gospel Tradition in the Context of Ancient Oral History*, WUNT 123 (Tübingen: Mohr, 2000).

44. Ibid., 235–38.

45. Andrew T. Lincoln, *Truth on Trial: The Lawsuit Motif in the Fourth Gospel* (Peabody, Mass.: Hendrickson, 2000), esp. 369–97. Lincoln recognizes a historical core in John's Gospel but believes that the author was much freer with history, the lawsuit motif notwithstanding, than do many others who have studied the concept of truth and witness in John.

46. George R. Beasley-Murray, *John*, WBC 36 (Waco, Tex.: Word, 1987); D. A. Carson, *The Gospel according to John* (Leicester: Inter-Varsity; Grand Rapids: Eerdmans, 1991); John W. Pryor, *John: Evangelist of the Covenant People* (London: Darton, Longman & Todd; Downers Grove, Ill.: InterVarsity, 1992); Ben Witherington III, *John's Wisdom: A Commentary on the Fourth Gospel* (Louisville: Westminster John Knox, 1995); Gerald L. Borchert, *John*, 2 vols., NAC 25A–B (Nashville: Broadman & Holman, 1996–); Herman N. Ridderbos, *The Gospel according to John: A Theological Commentary*, trans. J. Vriend (Grand Rapids: Eerdmans, 1997); Rodney A. Whitacre, *John* (Downers Grove, Ill.: InterVarsity, 1999); Andreas J. Köstenberger, *Encountering John: The Gospel in Historical, Literary, and Theological Perspective* (Grand Rapids: Baker, 1999); Craig S. Keener, *The Gospel of John: A Commentary*, 2 vols. (Peabody, Mass.: Hendrickson, 2003).

individual details and entire passages in the Fourth Gospel. Extraordinarily helpful is Keener's erudite tome, particularly because of his mastery of the primary background literature and inclusion of numerous cross-references to Jewish sources not available anywhere else. And the more parallels a given saying or deed attributed to Jesus has in pre-Christian Judaism, combined with Jesus' characteristic or distinctive challenges to conventional Israelite religion, the more likely we have authentic Jesus material at hand.

Evangelicals have also produced a number of shorter studies that helpfully summarize one or more areas of research that support the historicity of John. Stephen Barton discusses the compatibility of history and theology in the Fourth Gospel in broad strokes.[47] John Christopher Thomas points out numerous parallels between the exegetical arguments in select passages in John and the practices of Judaism discussed in those portions of the rabbinic literature that most likely reflect pre-70 conditions.[48] Moisés Silva and David Wenham have collected a number of the most salient arguments from recent scholarship in presentations on the "state of the discussion,"[49] with Wenham elaborating on his own recurring interest: the presence of parallels in the epistles that predated the written form of the Gospels, suggesting reliance on early oral tradition.[50]

Two additional books of recent vintage deserve mention in this context, even though they do not directly discuss issues of historicity or the historical Jesus in John. First, Martin Hengel's *The Johannine Question* is a monograph on the question of the authorship of the Fourth Gospel.[51] Though Hengel does not opt for John, the apostle and son of Zebedee, as author, he does argue vigorously for a different John (the ambiguous "presbyter" of Papias's testimony [see Eusebius, *Hist. eccl.* 3.39.3–4]) who was a disciple and close follower of the apostle of the same name. Indeed, for Hengel, this John the presbyter is the Beloved Disciple, a Palestinian Jew, an eyewitness of much of Jesus' ministry, and an old man writing to Ephesus at the end of the first century. In fact, "it would be conceivable that

47. Stephen Barton, "The Believer, the Historian, and the Fourth Gospel," *Theology* 96 (1993): 289–302.

48. John Christopher Thomas, "The Fourth Gospel and Rabbinic Judaism," *ZNW* 82 (1991): 159–82.

49. Moisés Silva, "Approaching the Fourth Gospel," *CTR* 3 (1988): 17–29; David Wenham, "The Enigma of the Fourth Gospel: Another Look," *TynBul* 48 (1997): 149–78; idem, "A Historical View of John's Gospel," *Them* 23 (1998): 5–21.

50. Wenham has helpfully combined much of his material, also treated in the studies cited, with other arguments to produce a short book, *John's Gospel: Good News for Today* (Leicester: Religious and Theological Students Fellowship, 1997). From a more centrist perspective, a recent study by Francis J. Moloney, "The Fourth Gospel and the Jesus of History" (*NTS* 46 [2000]: 42–58), also proves helpful, as do the programmatic remarks by Marianne Meye Thompson, "The Historical Jesus and the Johannine Christ," in *Exploring the Gospel of John*, ed. R. Alan Culpepper and C. Clifton Black (Louisville: Westminster John Knox, 1996), 21–42.

51. Martin Hengel, *The Johannine Question* (London: SCM; Philadelphia: Trinity, 1989); subsequently expanded as *Die johanneische Frage: Ein Lösungsversuch*, WUNT 67 (Tübingen: Mohr [Siebeck], 1993).

with the 'beloved disciple' 'John the elder' wanted to point more to the son of
Zebedee, who for him was an ideal, even *the* ideal disciple," so that the younger
John may have appealed to the older John as his teacher to "prepare for the 'im-
mortalizing' of the two persons in the one beloved disciple."[52] One can scarcely
come closer to affirming apostolic authorship without actually doing so! In either
case, however, the probability that the author of the Fourth Gospel had access
to considerable historical traditions about Jesus remains high.[53]

The second book is a collection of essays, edited by Richard Bauckham,
arguing that each of the four Gospels was not initially designed just for one
Christian community, but was intended to be widely disseminated within the
first-century Roman Empire.[54] Bauckham himself authors the chapter most
relevant for Johannine studies, defending the view that the Fourth Gospel
presupposes knowledge of at least Mark, among the Synoptics, on the part of
its audience.[55] It is not clear that Bauckham's essay has demonstrated John's
awareness of the written form of Mark, but it does make it highly probable
that knowledge of the core kerygma of the words and works of Jesus was both
detailed and widespread. Thus, we have come almost full circle to the views of
Sanday in 1905, but they are nuanced in such a way that takes into account the
massive evidence for *literary* independence of John from the Synoptics, while
also suggesting that John knew that he was choosing largely different material
from his predecessors but did not see his emphases as conflicting with theirs.

More Specialized Studies

At least as significant as the items treated in the previous section of this
essay are a whole host of more specialized studies on passages and topics in

52. Hengel, *Johannine Question*, 132, 130.

53. Cf. the updating of Hengel's arguments with respect to all four canonical Gospels in his *The
Four Gospels and the One Gospel of Jesus Christ* (London: SCM; Harrisburg, Pa.: Trinity, 2000). Even
if the author of the Fourth Gospel was merely a close follower of the apostle John, Alan Millard's
recent study *Reading and Writing in the Time of Jesus* (Sheffield: Sheffield Academic Press, 2000),
esp. 197–22, 223–29, advances arguments about the likelihood of some hearers in the audiences
of Jesus' longer discourses having the ability and desire to take shorthand notes of the outlines of
his speeches, which would have been carefully preserved side by side with the already conservative
oral tradition. So a case for the substantial historicity of John by no means depends on the case
for apostolic authorship. A survey by James H. Charlesworth, *The Beloved Disciple: Whose Witness
Validates the Gospel of John?* (Valley Forge, Pa.: Trinity, 1995), demonstrates the weakness of all
of the historic alternatives to apostolic authorship, but its relatively unique defense of Thomas as
author depends on having already rejected John the son of Zebedee as a candidate. Otherwise, all
of Charlesworth's arguments for Thomas actually support John the apostle even more strongly.

54. Richard Bauckham, ed., *The Gospels for All Christians: Rethinking the Gospel Audiences*
(Grand Rapids: Eerdmans, 1998).

55. Richard Bauckham, "John for Readers of Mark," in Bauckham, *The Gospels for All
Christians*, 147–71.

the Fourth Gospel that collectively allow us to proceed even further down the path of rehabilitating John for use in historical-Jesus research. All of these have appeared within the last thirty years of Johannine scholarship—the period of time on which this book is largely focused. A substantial majority of them have emerged since 1990.

A number of these studies have centered around individual pericopae or chapters in the Fourth Gospel. Richard Bauckham comprehensively surveys the rabbinic traditions about various men named Naqdimon from the Gurion family, demonstrating how the portrait of Nicodemus in John 3 (and elsewhere in the Fourth Gospel) corresponds to what we know of this family. They formed part of the Jewish ruling elite, were Pharisees and teachers of the law, and had vast material wealth. Bauckham plausibly suggests that the Nicodemus of the Gospel of John may have been the uncle of the Naqdimon ben Gurion who plays a prominent role in the later Jewish literature, and that the conversation recorded in John 3 is historically credible.[56] Teresa Okure treats John 4:1–42 from numerous perspectives in a detailed monograph and, along the way, includes cogent arguments for the substantial historicity of this encounter between Jesus and a Samaritan woman.[57]

J. C. O'Neill examines John 5:17–18 and related passages that involve some of the "highest" and seemingly aberrant claims by Jesus for himself in the Fourth Gospel. Careful linguistic and historical analysis leads him to conclude that

> Jesus is not being charged with being equal with God in all respects but with making himself equal with God in the one respect, in respect of claiming that he was the Messiah. That was a prerogative that the Father had reserved to himself. The Father, it was assumed, did have a Son, the Messiah. Human beings were allowed to speculate about whether John the Baptist or Jesus was that Messiah, but no human being was allowed to say that he was himself the Messiah. To do so would be to usurp the Father's prerogative and to arrogate to oneself equality with the Father in a prohibited respect.[58]

With Darrell Bock, in his important monograph on blasphemy and exaltation in pre–70 Judaism, we may need to add that it was not merely because Jesus "dared to make a messianic claim, when he needed to be silent, but because his messianic claim was perceived for clear reasons to be false and risky" (cf. *m. Sanh.* 11:5).[59] But this is still a kind of equality with God that stops well short of later Christian reflection about the second person of the Trinity, which

56. Richard Bauckham, "Nicodemus and the Gurion Family," *JTS* 47 (1996): 1–37.

57. Teresa Okure, *The Johannine Approach to Mission: A Contextual Study of John 4:1–42*, WUNT 2.31 (Tübingen: Mohr, 1988), esp. 188–91.

58. J. C. O'Neill, "'Making Himself Equal with God' (John 5:17–18): The Alleged Challenge to Jewish Monotheism in the Fourth Gospel," *IBS* 17 (1995): 50–61.

59. Darrell L. Bock, *Blasphemy and Exaltation in Judaism and the Final Examination of Jesus*, WUNT 2.106 (Tübingen: Mohr Siebeck, 1998), 25.

could not have developed within early first-century Jewish monotheism in the way that even the strongest claims attributed to Jesus in the Fourth Gospel could have.

Peder Borgen continues to build on his earlier full-scale treatment of John 6:25–59,[60] demonstrating the unity of Jesus' discourse on the bread of life and its close adherence to early Jewish midrashic form.[61] Borgen does not take the additional historical step of declaring it authentic, but he seems to have removed all the necessary obstacles from that path. Paul Anderson's monograph on John 6 advances the discussion further. On the one hand, he acknowledges that detailed homiletical and midrashic reflection on the original core teachings of Jesus have combined with issues in the Johannine community to create a complex mixture of tradition and redaction. On the other hand, he does not find any of this unfaithful to the teachings of the historical Jesus and identifies numerous signs of eyewitness testimony still remaining in the final form of John 6.[62]

A spate of recent studies has questioned Martyn's reconstruction of the historical background to John 9:22 and related texts. Already in 1981, Reuven Kimelman's analysis concluded that (1) the *birkat ha-minim* was directed against Jewish sectarians, not Gentile Christians; (2) later condemnations of *ha noṣrim* (= the Nazarenes?) focused solely on Jewish Christians; (3) no unambiguous evidence exists that Jews ever cursed Christians as part of the synagogue liturgy; (4) abundant evidence exists that Christians were welcome in the synagogue; (5) there was no one period of time when the *birkat ha-minim* became a watershed in the "parting of the ways" between Judaism and Christianity; and (6) there was no single, empire-wide edict causing irreparable separation between the two religions, but rather a long, gradual, and complex process involving numerous and varying local circumstances.[63] Recent studies have challenged some nuances of Kimelman's conclusions but overall have provided important support for the notion that John 9:22 is more historically credible in its putative context in the life of Jesus than in any end-of-first-century Greco-Roman setting.[64] One wonders how much of the rest of the

60. Peder Borgen, *Bread from Heaven: An Exegetical Study of the Concept of Manna in the Gospel of John and the Writings of Philo*, NovTSup 10 (Leiden: Brill, 1965).

61. Peder Borgen, "John 6: Tradition, Interpretation, and Composition," in de Boer, *From Jesus to John*, 268–91.

62. Paul N. Anderson, *The Christology of the Fourth Gospel: Its Unity and Disunity in the Light of John 6*, WUNT 2.78 (Tübingen: Mohr, 1996).

63. Reuven Kimelman, "*Birkat Ha-Minim* and the Lack of Evidence of an Anti-Christian Jewish Prayer in Late Antiquity," in *Jewish and Christian Self-Definition*, ed. E. P. Sanders et al., 3 vols. (Philadelphia: Fortress, 1980–82), 2:226–44.

64. See the survey of studies in Stephen Motyer, *Your Father the Devil? A New Approach to John and "the Jews"* (Carlisle: Paternoster, 1997), 92–94. Three important recent works in this vein are S. J. Joubert, "A Bone of Contention in Recent Scholarship: The 'Birkat Ha-Minim' and the Separation of Church and Synagogue in the First Century A.D.," *Neot* 27 (1993): 351–63; Pieter W. van der Horst, "The Birkat Ha-Minim in Recent Research," *ExpTim* 105 (1994):

facade of Martyn's two-level reading of the Fourth Gospel at the expense of John's historicity crumbles along with these findings.

John Christopher Thomas's monograph on John 13 not only provides wide-ranging insights into the historical background and meaning of the foot washing, but also demonstrates that it may be accepted as an authentic action of the historical Jesus with both soteriological and ecclesiological significance, as attributed to him in conversation with the disciples.[65] Ernst Bammel ably surveys the Jewish backgrounds to the farewell discourse in John 13–17.[66] The combination of similarities and differences that emerge makes it probable that Jesus did indeed utter something approximating this material on the last night of his life. Barry D. Smith advances the discussion of John's apparently conflicting chronology of the crucifixion in John 18–19 by showing that all the problematic texts in John, when properly exegeted, disclose the identical chronology as in the Synoptics.[67] And Grant R. Osborne demonstrates that John's distinctives in his two chapters on the resurrection combine historical and redactional concerns in complementary, rather than contradictory, fashion.[68]

In addition to studies that focus primarily or exclusively on one discrete segment of text within the Fourth Gospel, we may highlight several thematic studies. J. Augenstein has tackled the thorny question of John's use of expressions such as "your law" and "their law" that make it appear as if neither Jesus nor the author of the Fourth Gospel was Jewish (John 8:17; 10:34; 15:25; 18:31). He points out parallel OT language in words ascribed to Moses and Joshua when they spoke to the Israelites about "the Lord your God" (e.g., Deut. 2:30; 4:19, 21, 23, 24; 18:15; Josh. 1:11, 13, 15). The expressions are ad hominem, calling on the listeners to remember the teachings of their law (or their God), especially in contexts in which they are not observing it. It is not a disavowal of the authority of Torah (or Yahweh) by the speaker.[69]

Peter Ensor has devoted an entire volume to demonstrating that Jesus most likely spoke in language similar to that found in the Fourth Gospel about doing his Father's "work" (see esp. John 4:34; 5:17, 19–20; 9:3–4; 17:4).[70] Andreas Köstenberger investigates the theme of Jesus as rabbi, often held to be a post-70 anachronism, and again finds substantial historicity in John's

363–68; S. C. Mimouni, " 'La Birkat Ha-minim,' une priere juive contre les judeo chretiens," *RSR* 71 (1997): 275–98.

65. John Christopher Thomas, *Footwashing in John 13 and the Johannine Community,* JSNT-Sup 61 (Sheffield: JSOT Press, 1991).

66. Ernst Bammel, "The Farewell Discourse of the Evangelist John and Its Jewish Heritage," *TynBul* 44 (1993): 103–16.

67. Barry D. Smith, "The Chronology of the Last Supper," *WTJ* 53 (1991): 29–45.

68. Grant R. Osborne, *The Resurrection Narratives: A Redactional Study* (Grand Rapids: Baker, 1984), 147–92, 233–35, 246–66.

69. J. Augenstein, "Euer Gesetz—Ein Pronomen und die johanneische Haltung zum Gesetz," *ZNW* 88 (1997): 311–13.

70. Peter W. Ensor, *Jesus and His "Works": The Johannine Sayings in Historical Perspective,* WUNT 2.85 (Tübingen: Mohr [Siebeck], 1996).

portrait.[71] In a wide-ranging and iconoclastic work on the formation of the NT, Earle Ellis includes numerous examples of the longer discourses in John mirroring the specific *yelammedenu rabbenu* ("let our master teach us") form of rabbinic midrash, a form distinctive as well to some of the core parables of Jesus in the Synoptics widely held to be authentic. Ellis intersperses other observations germane to the authenticity of uniquely Johannine Jesus-sayings that suggest that we have only touched the tip of the iceberg in what could be done in this area.[72] And Adelbert Denaux revisits the frequently cited parallels between Jesus' distinctive teaching in John and Matt. 11:25–27//Luke 10:21–22. This so-called Johannine thunderbolt finds no fewer than fifty-one parallels scattered throughout the Fourth Gospel.[73] It is not at all improbable, therefore, to consider seriously the hypothesis that Jesus' style of teaching was more diverse than either of the two forms that most commonly set the Synoptics and John off from each other and that both traditions reflect large segments of authentic material.

Perhaps the most important of the recent thematic studies on John is Stephen Motyer's *Your Father the Devil? A New Approach to John and "the Jews."*[74] Taking its title from John 8:44, this work ranges widely throughout John to counter the repeated scholarly charges of anti-Semitism in the Fourth Gospel. It is precisely when the relevant texts are taken as historical and interpreted within their limited early first-century contexts that such charges can be refuted; hypotheses of their fictitious creation in light of church-synagogue tensions at the end of the first century, contra the critical consensus, actually make John's Gospel harder to exonerate.[75] Motyer also plausibly concludes that a text such as John 8:58 ("Before Abraham was, I am") "would *not* be heard as a claim to *be God*. It *would* be heard as a claim to be a divine agent, anointed with the name and power of God, and (in this case) active in the *genesis* of Abraham."[76] But that claim is intelligible within the diversity of pre-70 Judaism and the various "mutations" of monotheism that had already developed.[77]

71. Andreas J. Köstenberger, "Jesus as Rabbi in the Fourth Gospel," *BBR* 8 (1998): 97–128.

72. E. Earle Ellis, *The Making of the New Testament Documents,* BIS 39 (Leiden: Brill, 1999), esp. 154–83.

73. Adelbert Denaux, "The Q-Logion: Mt 11,27/Lk10,22 and the Gospel of John," in *John and the Synoptics,* ed. Adelbert Denaux, BETL 101 (Leuven: Leuven University Press, 1992), 163–99.

74. Carlisle: Paternoster, 1997.

75. See also Tommy D. Lea, "Who Killed the Lord? A Defense against the Charge of Anti-Semitism in John's Gospel," *CTR* 7 (1994): 103–23. More broadly, cf. idem, "The Reliability of History in John's Gospel," *JETS* 38 (1995): 387–402.

76. Motyer, *Your Father the Devil?* 209.

77. Cf. Larry W. Hurtado, *One God, One Lord: Early Christian Devotion and Ancient Jewish Monotheism* (Philadelphia: Fortress, 1988).

Conclusions

I have only scratched the surface in this short survey of the scholarship that could be discussed. In my *Historical Reliability of John's Gospel,* cited at the start of this essay, I walked my readers through a far broader spectrum of studies, both in an introduction to the Fourth Gospel more generally and in a passage-by-passage commentary on the evidence for the historical reliability of John's unique portrait of Jesus. Along the way, I highlighted the sizable amount of research that has already made probable John's substantial historicity. But without this extensive research being collected together in one place, few have been aware of it or of its cumulative force. I also have suggested that Tom Wright's nuanced criterion of double similarity and dissimilarity,[78] more or less identical to Gerd Theissen's four-part criterion of historical plausibility,[79] enables us to gain confidence in John's historicity at quite a few other junctures. None of this need deny John's distinctives, not least that most of his Gospel and not a little of Jesus' speech have been couched in John's distinctive idiom. Nor may we neglect the freedom that writing under the perceived inspiration of the Paraclete (John 14:26; 15:26; cf. 16:13) gave John to phrase matters. But we dare not overestimate this freedom. As Ben Witherington puts it in commenting on John 14:26,

> Thus the Spirit is seen as a source of continuing revelation for the disciples, but that revelation is seen as ultimately going back to the exalted Jesus and is not confused with the role of reminding the disciples what Jesus had said during his earthly ministry. The words of the exalted Jesus are basically *not* conveyed in the farewell discourses, they are only promised as something the Spirit *will* bring when the Spirit comes to the disciples.[80]

The door is therefore left wide open for doing what, with rare exceptions,[81] has not been done in the recent major studies of the historical Jesus, including those penned by evangelical authors.[82] That is to say, it is now possible judiciously to

---

78. N. T. Wright, *Jesus and the Victory of God* (London: SPCK; Minneapolis: Fortress, 1996), esp. 86.

79. In English, see Gerd Theissen and Annette Merz, *The Historical Jesus: A Comprehensive Guide* (London: SCM, 1997; reprint, Minneapolis: Fortress, 1998), 115–18; for elaboration in German, see Gerd Theissen and Dagmar Winter, *Die Kriterienfrage in der Jesusforschung: Vom Differenzkriterium zum Plausibilitätskriterium,* NTOA 34 (Freiburg: Universitätsverlag; Göttingen: Vandenhoeck & Ruprecht, 1998).

80. Witherington, *John's Wisdom,* 253.

81. Most notably, on occasion, in John P. Meier, *A Marginal Jew: Rethinking the Historical Jesus,* 3 vols., ABRL (New York: Doubleday, 1991–2001).

82. I am thinking of works such as E. P. Sanders, *Jesus and Judaism* (London: SCM; Philadelphia: Fortress, 1985); J. D. Crossan, *The Historical Jesus* (San Francisco: HarperSanFrancisco, 1991); Theissen and Merz, *The Historical Jesus.* As representative of evangelical works that focus almost exclusively on the Synoptics, we may mention Ben Witherington III, *The Christology*

incorporate elements from almost every major passage and theme in John into broader studies of the historical Jesus, integrating them with material already more widely accepted from the Synoptic Gospels. It remains to be seen who will be first to take up the challenge.

of Jesus (Minneapolis: Fortress, 1990); Scot McKnight, A New Vision for Israel: The Teachings of Jesus in National Context (Grand Rapids: Eerdmans, 1999); Wright, Jesus and the Victory of God. Even the otherwise excellent, more traditionally structured "life of Christ" by Robert H. Stein, Jesus the Messiah (Downers Grove, Ill.: InterVarsity, 1996), focuses almost entirely on Synoptic data. Contrast Craig L. Blomberg, Jesus and the Gospels: An Introduction and Survey (Nashville: Broadman & Holman; Leicester: Inter-Varsity, 1997).

Part 4

Earliest Christianity

12

Acts

Many Questions, Many Answers

Steve Walton

The year 1971 was a key date in the study of Acts; this was when the English translation of Ernst Haenchen's commentary was published,[1] and with hindsight, we now see that it marked the end of one era and the beginning of another. In this work, Haenchen's predominant concern is with Luke as a creative editor of the traditions about the earliest Christians; again and again he asks what Luke means by a story, using redaction-critical tools to answer that question, and combines this approach with considerable skepticism about the historical value of the stories in Acts. The impact of Haenchen's work meant that historical questions largely were not raised for another fifteen or more years, and the focus on Luke's theology remained central.

A year prior to Haenchen, I. Howard Marshall had published a seminal work on Luke's theology,[2] responding to the agenda set in the 1940s and 1950s by Haenchen, Conzelmann, and Dibelius, three giants in Acts scholarship.[3] Like

---

1. E. Haenchen, *The Acts of the Apostles: A Commentary,* trans. B. Noble et al. (Oxford: Blackwell; Philadelphia: Westminster, 1971; English translation of *Die Apostelgechichte,* KEK 3, 14th ed. [Göttingen: Vandenhoeck & Ruprecht, 1965]). Haenchen produced two further German editions of this commentary in 1968 and 1977.

2. I. H. Marshall, *Luke: Historian and Theologian* (Exeter: Paternoster; Grand Rapids: Zondervan, 1970).

3. Besides Haenchen's *Acts of the Apostles,* see H. Conzelmann, *The Theology of St. Luke* (London: Faber & Faber, 1960); idem, *Acts of the Apostles,* Hermeneia (Philadelphia: Fortress, 1987); M. Dibelius, *Studies in the Acts of the Apostles* (London: SCM, 1956).

these scholars, Marshall focuses on Luke's theological concerns, arguing that "salvation" should be seen as the theme of Luke-Acts. Unlike these scholars, Marshall holds that Luke's portrait of Jesus and the earliest churches is substantially historical, rightly asserting that the choice between theology and history, so central to the previous period of Acts scholarship, is a false dichotomy.[4]

Haenchen's and Marshall's work reflects the agenda of Acts studies since 1970. Almost all the major concerns of NT scholarship are relevant in studying Acts, one of the longest books of the NT: its varying text forms, its genre and purpose(s), the quest for sources, Luke's redactional activity and theological perspective, the historical basis of the events described, Luke's work as a narrator and storyteller, or the historical or theological compatibility of Acts and the Pauline Epistles. Thus, we must be selective in the topics we consider here.

We begin by noting several helpful surveys and outlining key recent approaches to Acts. We then will focus on three major topics: questions of genre and purpose, issues of history, and theological themes and emphases.

Surveys

Several helpful surveys cover Acts scholarship.[5] Two briefer, more recent surveys are especially valuable. Accessible and focused on theological questions is a volume by Mark Powell.[6] The outstanding work is that of Marshall, who both surveys the field comprehensively and makes a fine contribution of his own in his responses to the approaches and scholars he discusses.[7] For readers

4. Marshall later wrote a fine brief commentary that responded point by point to Haenchen: I. H. Marshall, *The Acts of the Apostles: An Introduction and Commentary,* TNTC (Leicester: Inter-Varsity; Grand Rapids: Eerdmans, 1980).

5. Pride of place among the older surveys must go to W. W. Gasque, *A History of the Criticism of the Acts of the Apostles* (Grand Rapids: Eerdmans, 1975); the 1988 edition adds, as an appendix, his valuable essay "A Fruitful Field: Recent Study of the Acts of the Apostles," *Int* 42 (1988): 117–31. Gasque works through the field in roughly chronological order, focuses more on historical questions than theological ones, and covers English, French, and German scholarship. The survey in Haenchen, *The Acts of the Apostles,* 14–50, is also valuable, works chronologically, and focuses more on German scholarship. Another very full and helpful survey is F. Bovon, *Luke the Theologian: Thirty-Three Years of Research (1950–1983),* trans. K. McKinney, Princeton Theological Monograph 12 (Allison Park, Pa.: Pickwick, 1987); this is an expanded translation of Bovon's *Luc le théologien: Vingt-cinq ans de rechcerches (1950–1975)* (Neuchâtel-Paris: Delachaux & Niestlé, 1978). Bovon studies major topics, in each case providing a fine chronological bibliography and then judicious and helpful discussion. Bibliographies include A. J. Mattill Jr. and M. B. Mattill, *A Classified Bibliography of the Literature on the Acts,* NTTS 7 (Leiden: Brill, 1966); W. E. Mills, *A Bibliography of the Periodical Literature on the Acts of the Apostles, 1962–1984,* NovTSup 58 (Leiden: Brill, 1986). Both are thorough and valuable.

6. M. A. Powell, *What Are They Saying about Acts?* (New York: Paulist Press, 1991); see also idem, "Luke's Second Volume: Three Basic Issues in Contemporary Studies of Acts," *TSR* 13 (1991): 69–81.

7. I. H. Marshall, *The Acts of the Apostles,* NTG (Sheffield: JSOT Press, 1992).

wishing for fuller discussion than this essay can provide, Marshall's work is highly recommended.[8]

New Approaches

The last thirty years have seen a number of innovations in NT scholarship, particularly in the study of narrative, the application of rhetorical study, and the use of social-scientific models. These trends are reflected in Acts research, which has been a laboratory for the development of newer methods.

Narrative Criticism

Luke Johnson's doctoral dissertation[9] marked the initiation of the "narrative turn" in NT scholarship in relation to Acts.[10] Johnson examined the literary function of possessions in Acts, seeking to understand how Luke perceived and thought theologically about their role by examining his literary presentation of them.[11]

Johnson's approach is now known as "narrative criticism"; it is the close relative of approaches developed in literary studies in other disciplines, building on the work of critics such as Booth and Chatman.[12] This approach focuses on the "final form" of the text; questions of sources and redaction are put aside, and scholars pay close attention to how the author tells the story, studying use of plot, characters, settings, and point of view.

Johnson notes the way that possessions perform particular functions in the narrative of Acts: they are used within an overall literary pattern of "prophet

8. See also J. B. Green and M. C. McKeever, *Luke-Acts and New Testament Historiography,* IBR Bibliographies 8 (Grand Rapids: Baker, 1994), a valuable annotated bibliography focused on questions of history and historiography in scholarship in English. German scholarship for 1974–82 is surveyed in two articles by E. Plümacher, "Acta-Forschung, 1974–1982 (Part 1)," *TRu* 48 (1983): 1–56; "Acta-Forschung, 1974–1982 (Forsetzung und Schluß)," *TRu* 49 (1984): 105–69.

9. Published as L. T. Johnson, *The Literary Function of Possessions in Luke-Acts,* SBLDS 39 (Missoula, Mont.: Scholars Press, 1977).

10. For a valuable general account of narrative criticism, see M. A. Powell, *What Is Narrative Criticism?* (Philadelphia: Fortress, 1991; London: SPCK, 1993). See also Powell, *What Are They Saying,* ch. 6. More briefly, see D. Wenham and S. Walton, *Exploring the New Testament,* vol. 1, *A Guide to the Gospels and Acts* (London: SPCK; Downers Grove, Ill.: InterVarsity, 2001), 84–88; S. S. Bartchy, "Narrative Criticism," *Dictionary of the Later New Testament and Its Developments,* ed. R. P. Martin and P. H. Davids (Downers Grove, Ill.: InterVarsity, 1997), 787–92.

11. Johnson, *Literary Function of Possessions,* 12–28, sketches his method; see also Johnson's fine commentary on Acts, *The Acts of the Apostles,* SP 5 (Collegeville, Minn.: Liturgical Press, 1992).

12. W. C. Booth, *The Rhetoric of Fiction* (Chicago: University of Chicago Press, 1961); S. Chatman, *Story and Discourse: Narrative Structure in Fiction and Film* (Ithaca, N.Y.: Cornell University Press, 1978).

and people," in which they display important features of the relationship of
the divine spokesman (Jesus or the apostles) and his followers; they appear
in situations that cause them to symbolize the authority of the Twelve, such
as in the placing of money at the apostles' feet (Acts 4:35, 37; 5:2);[13] and the
appropriate or inappropriate use of possessions shows the situation of people's
hearts (e.g., Judas, negatively, in 1:12–26, and the generosity of Barnabas in
4:36–37). Overall, then, Luke treats possessions metaphorically, as symbolizing key issues of human life, whether the nature of a person's attitudes, the
relationships between people, or the uneven power in such relationships.[14]

Johnson's work prepared the way for others to follow; particularly important
is Robert Tannehill,[15] who was the first to apply narrative criticism systematically to the whole of Acts.[16] Notable in Tannehill's work is a strong emphasis
on finding interconnections within the narrative of Luke-Acts. For example, in
discussing Paul's Miletus speech (Acts 20:18–35), Tannehill views the speech
as utilizing the widespread Lukan device of previews and reviews, as Paul looks
back over his past ministry (vv. 18b–21, 26–27, 31, 33–34) and speaks of events
yet to come (vv. 22–25, 29–30).[17] Tannehill also highlights the repetitions of
words within the speech, as well as noting links with Luke's Jesus.[18]

Of particular interest is the way Tannehill highlights how narrative-critical
study allows scholars to discuss what Luke's view is while leaving them free to
decide whether they agree with Luke or not. This allows dialogue about what
Luke says while reducing the danger of scholars simply reading their own views
into the NT texts. For example, Tannehill notes that Luke believes that Christians should seek to persuade Jewish people to become followers of Jesus, but
Tannehill is frank enough to say that he does not agree with Luke on this.[19]

Many others have followed,[20] including some fine studies of characterization. F. Scott Spencer provides a careful and thoughtful portrait of Philip that
models well how to do such a study,[21] and David Gooding provides a thoughtful

13. Johnson, *Literary Function of Possessions*, 200–207.
14. Ibid., 221.
15. R. C. Tannehill, *The Narrative Unity of Luke-Acts: A Literary Interpretation*, 2 vols., FF
(Minneapolis: Fortress, 1986–90), vol. 2, *The Acts of the Apostles*.
16. Johnson followed with his *Acts of the Apostles*.
17. Tannehill, *Narrative Unity of Luke-Acts*, 2:252.
18. Ibid., 2:255–61. On the parallels between Luke's portraits of Paul and Jesus, see S. Walton,
Leadership and Lifestyle: The Portrait of Paul in the Miletus Speech and 1 Thessalonians, SNTSMS
108 (Cambridge: Cambridge University Press, 2000), 99–136.
19. Tannehill, *Narrative Unity of Luke-Acts*, 2:3.
20. Good overviews are provided by W. S. Kurz, *Reading Luke-Acts: Dynamics of Biblical
Narrative* (Louisville: Westminster John Knox, 1993); and F. S. Spencer, "Acts and Modern
Literary Approaches," in *The Book of Acts in Its Ancient Literary Setting*, ed. B. W. Winter and
A. D. Clarke, BAFCS 1 (Carlisle: Paternoster; Grand Rapids: Eerdmans, 1993), 381–414.
21. F. S. Spencer, *The Portrait of Philip in Acts: A Study of Roles and Relations*, JSNTSup 67
(Sheffield: JSOT Press, 1992); see also Spencer's commentary, *Acts*, Readings: A New Biblical
Commentary (Sheffield: Sheffield Academic Press, 1997); J. A. Darr's careful study of character-

midlevel commentary that highlights narrative development, although some of his claims about the structure of Acts may be overstated.[22]

Rhetorical Criticism

Rhetorical critics focus on the argumentative structure of a work, aiming to identify how it seeks to persuade its readers, as well as what kind of persuasion is in view: deliberative (focusing on a decision to be taken about the future), judicial (focusing on a decision about the rightness or wrongness of a past set of events and actions), or epideictic (the broadest category, tending to highlight adherence to beliefs or values in the present and the future).[23] The roots of this approach are in the study of ancient rhetoric, the standard content of tertiary education in antiquity; scholars pursuing this approach believe that there is much to be gained by considering how the conventions of ancient speeches might engage with our NT texts, especially given that reading was invariably aloud in ancient cultures.[24]

Like narrative criticism, rhetorical criticism is a holistic approach to texts, concentrating on the text as an act of communication. It does not (as is sometimes asserted) necessarily assume that the NT authors had formal Greco-Roman rhetorical training, but rather postulates that the world of the NT was so permeated by rhetoric that unavoidably they would (consciously or unconsciously) speak and write in ways that reflected rhetoric's concerns and techniques. A benefit of this approach is that it can allow access to the author's mind as accurately as possible over a two-thousand-year gap, for it uses the conventions known to have been commonplace when Luke (in our case) wrote. The majority view among practitioners of this approach is that rhetorical criticism, like narrative criticism, adds another useful tool to the exegete's kit (not that it is the only valid approach).

In relation to Acts, the speeches have been natural targets for rhetorical criticism. Kennedy analyzes the Miletus speech (Acts 20:18–35), concluding

---

ization, which focuses on Luke's Gospel, *On Character Building: The Reader and the Rhetoric of Characterization in Luke-Acts* (Louisville: Westminster John Knox, 1992); and W. H. Shepherd Jr., *The Narrative Function of the Holy Spirit as a Character in Luke-Acts,* SBLDS 147 (Atlanta: Scholars Press, 1994).

22. D. W. Gooding, *True to the Faith: A Fresh Approach to the Acts of the Apostles* (London: Hodder & Stoughton; Grand Rapids: Gospel Folio, 1990); cf. Gooding's earlier work *According to Luke: A New Exposition of the Third Gospel* (Leicester: Inter-Varsity; Grand Rapids: Eerdmans, 1987).

23. For an introduction, see G. A. Kennedy, *New Testament Interpretation through Rhetorical Criticism* (Chapel Hill: University of North Carolina Press, 1984)—Kennedy discusses some Acts speeches in ch. 6; or, more briefly, S. Walton, "Rhetorical Criticism: An Introduction," *Them* 21 (1995–96): 4–9.

24. The Ethiopian eunuch is an example (Acts 8:28–30); cf. Aristotle, *Rhetoric* 3.5.6: "Generally speaking, that which is written should be easy to read or easy to utter, *which is the same thing*" (italics added). For bibliography, see Walton, "Rhetorical Criticism," 8 n. 52.

that it is a future-oriented form of epideictic speech seeking to persuade the Ephesian elders to view Paul's ministry positively and to imitate him.[25] Duane Watson identifies the same speech as an epideictic speech of farewell with the structure: *exordium* (introduction, seeking to gain the hearers' attention [vv. 18b–24]), *probatio* (main statement [vv. 25–31]), and *peroratio* (conclusion, aiming to rouse the audience's emotions [vv. 32–35]).[26] Ben Witherington argues, to the contrary, that the speech is deliberative, since its focus is the elders' future conduct, and identifies vv. 18–21 as *narratio* (telling the story of Paul's past conduct), vv. 22–25 as focusing on Paul's future, vv. 26–30 as applying Paul's example to the elders, and vv. 31–35 as *peroratio*.[27] As always in NT scholarship, debate exists among scholars as to the most appropriate application of the tool to particular texts.

Social-Scientific Methods

Social-scientific approaches also have risen to prominence since the 1970s, paying careful attention to the social and cultural setting(s) of early Christianity and using models and perspectives from modern social sciences.[28] When the Society of Biblical Literature set up its first study group on "The Social World of Early Christianity," four key tasks were outlined: (1) to describe the social facts of early Christianity and place it in its social setting; (2) to develop a social history of early Christianity; (3) to examine the social forces that led to the rise of Christianity and its institutions; (4) to consider the early Christian "symbolic universe," identifying how they saw the world and what structures and ideas supported that perspective.

Philip Esler has been prominent in applying such concerns to Luke-Acts in his doctoral work, published in 1987.[29] He seeks social and political concerns, which animate Luke's thinking, and regards apparently theological concerns as encoded versions of the political/social issues.[30] In particular, he regards the central issue that Luke is addressing as being "legitimation"—that is, providing

---

25. Kennedy, *New Testament Interpretation*, 133.

26. D. F. Watson, "Paul's Speech to the Ephesian Elders (Acts 20:17–38): Epideictic Rhetoric of Farewell," in *Persuasive Artistry: Studies in New Testament Rhetoric in Honour of George Kennedy*, ed. D. F. Watson, JSNTSup 50 (Sheffield: JSOT Press, 1991), 184–208.

27. B. Witherington III, *The Acts of the Apostles: A Socio-Rhetorical Commentary* (Carlisle: Paternoster; Grand Rapids: Eerdmans, 1998), 610–27.

28. For a valuable survey, see D. Tidball, *The Social Context of the New Testament* (Grand Rapids: Zondervan, 1984; Carlisle: Paternoster, 1997); first published in the United Kingdom as *An Introduction to the Sociology of the New Testament* (Exeter: Paternoster, 1983). D. Horrell, ed., *Social-Scientific Approaches to New Testament Interpretation* (Edinburgh: Clark, 1999), brings together a number of key essays about or using this approach.

29. P. F. Esler, *Community and Gospel in Luke-Acts: The Social and Political Motivations of Lucan Theology*, SNTSMS 57 (Cambridge: Cambridge University Press, 1987).

30. Ibid., 1–16; for a valuable summary, see Marshall, *The Acts of the Apostles* (1992), 41–42.

supporting justification for his readers' decision to become Christian believers from what he sees as a predominantly Jewish or "God-fearer" background.[31] Luke does this, according to Esler, by constructing a symbolic universe that provides a framework within which his readers can understand the world, and in particular that enables them to see why being Christian is better than being Jewish. In order to do this, Luke addresses some key areas: table fellowship, the law, the temple, the poor and the rich, and the Roman Empire.

Space here forbids full discussion of Esler's work,[32] but we can illustrate his approach by considering his discussion of table fellowship.[33] Esler finds it historically incredible that Peter would have eaten with Cornelius (Acts 10:48 implies this in its statement that Peter stayed with him "for several days") because of Peter's subsequent behavior in Antioch (Gal. 2:11–14).[34] Esler therefore asks what Luke's purpose can be in thus rewriting history, and argues that Luke uses these stories to address tensions within his community over table fellowship between Jewish and Gentile believers, because of criticism from Jewish believers and nonbelievers alike.[35]

The value of Esler's approach rests in his insistence that Luke's social setting had to have influenced the way he saw and presented his material. However, in the case of table fellowship, Esler underestimates how radical a shift was made by the earliest (Jewish) believers in being willing to eat with Gentiles. Because this change would have necessitated a radical rethinking of their understanding of the nature of God's covenant with his people, it is unlikely to have happened quickly; rather, the lengthy process of "reception" of this idea indicated in Acts, where the issue is only partially resolved even at the Jerusalem meeting (Acts 15), suggests that Luke was constrained by the actual events that took place in the way he told his story. Such a lengthy period of change makes it possible—indeed, probable—that Peter might act "inconsistently" (from a later perspective) by sometimes eating with Gentiles and sometimes withdrawing under pressure from more conservative Jewish believers (which is what Paul says happened in Antioch [Gal. 2:12]). A lengthy period of change also might well mean that in Luke's day such issues were still around, and this would give added relevance to Luke's retelling of these stories in Acts; but it need not mean that the stories were either generated or radically rewritten by Luke in response to the needs of his community.

31. Esler, *Community and Gospel in Luke-Acts*, 16–23.
32. Three valuable reviews offer fuller engagement: I. H. Marshall in *JTS* 39 (1988): 564–66; A. T. Kraabel in *JBL* 108 (1989): 160–63; M. M. B. Turner in *EvQ* 62 (1990): 365–68.
33. Esler, *Community and Gospel in Luke-Acts*, 71–109.
34. Ibid., 95–96.
35. Ibid., 105–9.

The Nature of Acts

Luke-Acts or Luke and Acts?

Until the 1990s, a wide consensus in scholarship held that Luke and Acts were two volumes of a single work, a consensus reflected in the use of the tag "Luke-Acts," coined by Henry Cadbury.[36] In 1993, Mikeal Parsons and Richard Pervo set out to challenge this view by reexamining the kind of unity that exists between Luke and Acts.[37] They have no quarrel with the assertion of shared authorship of the two books;[38] instead, they question whether Luke and Acts are united canonically (since there are no extant ancient canon lists that place them adjacently),[39] generically (since they are not from the same literary genre),[40] narratively (since there are differences),[41] and theologically (noting that Acts frequently can be subordinated to Luke because it is so much easier to do redaction criticism on Luke in relation to Mark than it is on Acts, where sources are no longer extant).[42]

However, Howard Marshall argues cogently that real unity does exist between the two books.[43] He points to the continuity suggested by the prologues, evidence that Luke's Gospel has been redacted in the light of material in Acts, and the ending of the Gospel, which implies that the Gospel is "part one." Further,[44] there are strong unifying theological themes to the two books: Jesus himself, the role of the apostles and witnesses, the kingdom and the Messiah, discipleship, and salvation for all people. More than that, the unifying themes are strongly focused in Acts 1–2, chapters that both form a "bridge" from Luke's Gospel to Acts and act as an "overture" to Acts by playing over its major themes: the fulfillment of Scripture; God's oversight of history; the teaching and example of Jesus; phenomena from the ministry of Jesus; the resurrection, exaltation, and authority of Jesus and the consequences that flow from those events; the Holy Spirit; and prayer.[45]

36. H. J. Cadbury, *The Making of Luke-Acts* (London: SPCK; New York: Macmillan, 1927).

37. M. C. Parsons and R. I. Pervo, *Rethinking the Unity of Luke and Acts* (Minneapolis: Fortress, 1993).

38. Ibid., 7–8, 116; cf. the key article, B. E. Beck, "The Common Authorship of Luke and Acts," *NTS* 23 (1977): 346–52, which decisively answers any linguistic doubts about common authorship.

39. Parsons and Pervo, *Unity of Luke and Acts*, 8–13, 116–19.

40. Ibid., 25–37; contra D. E. Aune, *The New Testament in Its Literary Environment* (Philadelphia: Westminster, 1987; Cambridge: Clarke, 1988), 77–157.

41. Parsons and Pervo, *Unity of Luke and Acts*, 48, 123 n. 21.

42. Ibid., 86.

43. I. H. Marshall, "Acts and the 'Former Treatise,'" in Winter and Clarke, *The Book of Acts,* 163–82.

44. See I. H. Marshall, "'Israel' and the Story of Salvation: One Theme in Two Parts," in *Jesus and the Heritage of Israel,* ed. D. P. Moessner (Harrisburg, Pa.: Trinity, 1999), 340–57.

45. See the discussion in S. Walton, "Where Does the Beginning of Acts End?" in *The Unity of Luke-Acts,* ed. J. Verheyden, BETL 142 (Leuven: Peeters, 1999), 448–67.

Genre, Audience, and Purpose(s)

The questions of genre, audience, and purpose(s) are closely linked, as a number of studies by Loveday Alexander and responses to her work demonstrate. Her doctoral work concluded that Luke's prefaces located his books among the "scientific" writers who wrote manuals of technical subjects.[46] This conclusion implies that the audience of Luke-Acts is not an elite, highborn group but people who, though educated, are not from the highest echelons of society.

Alexander has developed her work in a number of stimulating and helpful studies.[47] Others have made comparisons between Acts and the Greek historiographers, highlighting connections and parallels.[48] However, the Greek historians generally wrote about powerful figures in politics or war and expressed themselves in high-flown language, while Acts appears to fit neither of those features.

Richard Pervo has highlighted how Luke tells stories in ways that resemble some features of the Greek novels, and has argued that these parallels mean that the genre of Acts should be seen as ancient fiction.[49] Pervo certainly is right in affirming that Luke is a brilliant storyteller who can use narrative art with the best of ancient writers: he includes shipwreck, adventure, drama, and humor in his narrative. However, Pervo makes the error of assuming that to use narrative devices in this way is a feature found only in ancient fiction. The ancient historians, too, wrote in a pleasing way, in order to engage their audience: Lucian of Samosata, in the second century C.E., recommends that a historian's thinking should "have a touch of poetry . . . he will have need of a wind of poetry to fill his sails and help carry his ship along"; further, the historian should "give his audience what will interest and instruct them" (*How to Write History* 45, 53). Pervo thus is mistaken in arguing that the presence in Acts of generic features found in ancient fiction means that Acts is itself ancient fiction—the same features appear in the writings of ancient historians.

---

46. L. Alexander, *The Preface to Luke's Gospel: Literary Convention and Social Context in Luke 1:1–4 and Acts 1:1*, SNTSMS 78 (Cambridge: Cambridge University Press, 1993); more briefly, L. Alexander, "Luke's Preface in the Context of Greek Preface-Writing," *NovT* 28 (1986): 48–74.

47. Especially L. C. A. Alexander, "The Preface to Acts and the Historians," in *History, Literature, and Society in the Book of Acts*, ed. B. Witherington III (Cambridge: Cambridge University Press, 1996), 73–103; "Fact, Fiction and the Genre of Acts," *NTS* 44 (1998): 380–99; "Acts," in *The Oxford Bible Commentary*, ed. J. Barton and J. Muddiman (Oxford: Oxford University Press, 2001), 1028–61.

48. Notably, E. Plümacher, *Lukas als hellenistischer Schriftsteller: Studien zur Apostelgeschichte* (Göttingen: Vandenhoeck & Ruprecht, 1972); D. L. Balch, "Acts as Hellenistic Historiography," *SBLSP* (1985): 429–32—the latter replying to D. Schmidt, "The Historiography of Acts: Deuteronomistic or Hellenistic?" *SBLSP* (1985): 417–27.

49. R. I. Pervo, *Profit with Delight: The Literary Genre of the Acts of the Apostles* (Philadelphia: Fortress, 1987).

A number of scholars have considered parallels between Acts and Jewish historiography. Brian Rosner highlights numerous levels of connection between the OT history books' way of telling history and Acts.[50] The connections are linguistic, for Acts' language is in places strongly Septuagintal and thematic, particularly prophecy/fulfillment and the focus of Acts on Jerusalem. Luke uses scriptural models in composing stories in Acts, such as the conversion of Paul mirroring OT stories of God appearing and speaking with people. More broadly, Acts echoes OT literary techniques, especially from the Deuteronomic History: the use of set formulae (e.g., the series of notices of the church's growth in 6:7; 9:31; 12:24; 16:5; 19:20; 28:31), speeches that summarize and interpret the point that a story has reached (e.g., the prayer in 4:24–30), the periodization of history, and the focusing of the narrative on a few main characters (Peter, Stephen, Philip, and Paul). Most important, Acts shares the OT's theological understanding of history, which sees God as in control, carrying out his purposes. To see these connections suggests that at least part of the purpose of Acts is to explain both the continuity and discontinuity between the past actions of God and his present actions through Jesus and his followers.[51]

Both sets of cultural connections have strengths, and neither should be overplayed. Luke's strong emphasis that the work of God in Jesus and through his followers is in continuity with God's work in Scripture means that Acts would communicate well with those well-versed in the Jewish Scriptures—both Jews and God-fearers on the "fringe" of synagogues. But the fact that Acts tells stories that would "ring bells" with Greek and Roman hearers suggests that a significant section of Luke's audience might have that cultural heritage. At the intersection of these groups are the God-fearers, people who lived in both cultural "worlds," which has inclined some to see them as a key target audience for Luke-Acts,[52] although the range of material might also point to a considerably wider audience for Acts, spread around the Mediterranean basin—rather as Richard Bauckham has argued for the Gospels.[53]

Speeches

The speeches in Acts form some 20 to 30 percent of the book and therefore are highly significant. Scholarship since Dibelius[54] has commonly assumed

50. B. S. Rosner, "Acts and Biblical History," in Winter and Clarke, *The Book of Acts*, 65–82.

51. Ibid., 82.

52. E.g., J. Nolland, *Luke 1–9:20*, WBC 35A (Dallas: Word, 1989), xxxii–xxxiii; Witherington, *The Acts of the Apostles*, 63–65; J. B. Tyson, *Images of Judaism in Luke-Acts* (Columbia: University of South Carolina Press, 1992), 35–39.

53. R. Bauckham, ed., *The Gospels for All Christians* (Edinburgh: Clark; Grand Rapids: Eerdmans, 1997), esp. 9–48; cf. Esler, *Community and Gospel in Luke-Acts*, 221–23, postulating a very mixed community that Luke-Acts addresses.

54. Dibelius, *Studies in the Acts of the Apostles*, ch. 9.

that Luke's theology is principally to be found in the speeches, which are seen as Lukan creations.

A number of studies have begun to realign study of the speeches, including the work of Conrad Gempf.[55] Traditionally, the speeches have been considered as either fiction or history. On one side, Dibelius, Conzelmann, and Haenchen assert that the consistency of the theology of the speeches, which seems to be independent of the speaker, suggests that Luke has shaped the speeches to preach his theology. On the other side, scholars such as Bruce and Gasque have identified features in the speeches that suggest that they have a historical basis.[56]

Gempf proposes that this formulation of the issue is mistaken. He argues that a study of the ancient historians suggests that we should regard recorded speeches as records of *events* rather than either verbatim transcripts or works of fiction. Thus, when recording a speech, an ancient historian aimed at historical and literary appropriateness—that is, the speech recorded should be appropriate to the situation in which it appears and also appropriate to the book as a whole. Gempf compares the description of ancient battles, where the historian's concern was to record faithfully the event, its maneuvers, action, and results—but that would not necessitate a precise record of the individual actions of each combatant. Likewise, to record a spoken event faithfully would not require a verbatim record.[57] Thus, the writer sought to be faithful to the "speech-event" *and* to present it in a way that was accessible to a new audience who read the literary work.

Thus, first, the speeches should not be criticized as being "inaccurate" for failing to be verbatim reports. Second, where a speaker's views are in agreement with the views of the author reporting the speech, that need not imply that the author has simply created the speech—it only shows that the author has presented the speech appropriately for the overall character of the book. On the other hand, if a speech presents features known to be at variance with the author's approach, in form or content, then the author is likely to be recording faithfully. Third, the key issues in considering a speech's faithfulness are the signs of the situation in which it is located, and the style and beliefs of the speaker.[58] Thus, Gempf's approach has the possibility to recast the debate over the "historicity" of the speech in a more

55. C. H. Gempf, "Historical and Literary Appropriateness in the Mission Speeches of Paul in Acts" (Ph.D. diss., Aberdeen University, 1988); more briefly, "Public Speaking and Published Accounts," in Winter and Clarke, *The Book of Acts*, 259–303.

56. For example, F. F. Bruce, "The Speeches in Acts—Thirty Years After," in *Reconciliation and Hope: New Testament Essays on Atonement and Eschatology Presented to L. L. Morris on His 60th Birthday*, ed. R. J. Banks (Exeter: Paternoster, 1974), 53–68; W. W. Gasque, "The Speeches of Acts: Dibelius Reconsidered," in *New Dimensions in New Testament Study*, ed. R. N. Longenecker and M. C. Tenney (Grand Rapids: Zondervan, 1974), 232–50.

57. C. H. Gempf, "Public Speaking and Published Accounts," in Winter and Clarke, *The Book of Acts*, 262–64.

58. A key test case is Paul's Miletus speech (Acts 20:18–35), which is the only Pauline speech to believers, because it is the most "Pauline-letter-like" situation in Acts, and thus allows us to test

helpful, and more answerable, form. He has sketched how particular speeches might be studied using this approach, both in his doctoral dissertation and in a shorter article.[59] It remains for others to follow the trail he has blazed.

From a different but related angle, Bruce Winter examines Paul's defense speeches (Acts 24–26) against the backdrop of ancient speechmaking and shows that these speeches fit the style of rhetoric required in such a court setting.[60] Furthermore, speeches in those settings were regularly recorded in writing—we have over 250 examples of such court proceedings extant—so it is possible that Luke had access to such material in composing his record of this event. Winter applies his research to the speeches in Acts 24 and 26, showing that the standard features described in the rhetorical handbooks for such speeches are present: *exordium, narratio, confirmatio,* sometimes *refutatio,* and *peroratio.* He argues persuasively that Luke's composition here is likely utilizing official court records. Acts 23:26–30 provides a copy of an official letter, and this may well signal that Luke has at other points used official sources. Winter's careful research into the ancient sources opens up new possibilities that have yet to be fully developed by scholarship on the key passages in Acts.[61]

History

Debate over the historical value of Acts was moved off the scholarly agenda for a generation by Dibelius, Conzelmann, and Haenchen—discussion focused instead on Luke's theology, the assumption being that relatively little of historical value could be found in Acts. Recent times, however, have seen a revival of discussion of historical questions.

Historicity in General Terms

It was rather surprising when the debate over the historicity of Acts was reopened by Gerd Lüdemann, a scholar known for his historical skepticism.[62]

---

the assertion that Luke's portrait of Paul is at variance with that found in the Pauline letters. See the discussion of the Miletus speech, showing that it is very close to 1 Thessalonians (an undisputed Pauline letter) in language and thought, in Walton, *Leadership and Lifestyle,* esp. chs. 3, 5.

59. Besides Gempf's works cited above, see his article "Athens, Paul at," in *Dictionary of Paul and His Letters,* ed. G. F. Hawthorne, R. P. Martin, and D. G. Reid (Downers Grove, Ill.: InterVarsity, 1993), 51–54.

60. B. W. Winter, "Official Proceedings and the Forensic Speeches in Acts 24–26," in Winter and Clarke, *The Book of Acts,* 305–36; "The Importance of the *Captatio Benevolentiae* in the Speeches of Tertullus and Paul in Acts 24:1–21," *JTS* 42 (1991): 505–31.

61. Witherington, *The Acts of the Apostles,* begins the task of relating the forensic speeches to this framework.

62. G. Lüdemann, *Early Christianity according to the Traditions in Acts: A Commentary,* trans. J. Bowden (London: SCM, 1989); English translation of *Das frühe Christentum nach den Traditionen der Apostelgeschichte: Ein Kommentar* (Göttingen: Vandenhoeck & Ruprecht, 1987).

Lüdemann combs through Acts, seeking to distinguish tradition from redaction, and history from both, generally concluding that there is some historical core to stories that have been elaborated by Luke. This certainly is an advance on the work of Haenchen and his colleagues. Others have addressed the question, coming to conclusions similar to those of Lüdemann, but usually seeing a more substantial historical core to events.[63]

Historical Setting in Specifics

Our knowledge about the ancient world as it touches Acts has grown considerably in the last thirty years, not least because of the important series The Book of Acts in Its First Century Setting.[64] The valuable individual essays collected in the earlier volumes of the series are supplemented by the fine and substantial work of Irina Levinskaya and Brian Rapske in their individual volumes.[65]

In addition, Colin Hemer's work is highly significant.[66] He engages with a wide range of issues concerning history and Acts, and in particular shows in place after place that the "world" that Luke constructs in Acts fits well with what we know from ancient sources[67]—not least epigraphy, where Hemer adds substantially to our knowledge. This leads him to a careful engagement with chronological issues, arguing that the data of Acts and Galatians can best be fitted together by assuming that the visit to Jerusalem described in Gal. 2:1–10 is that found in Acts 11:29–30.[68] He shows that it is possible to reconstruct a Pauline chronology that takes the data of Acts seriously. He then considers questions of authorship, sources, and date, concluding that the traditional

63. Notably, M. Hengel, *Acts and the History of Earliest Christianity* (London: SCM; Philadelphia: Fortress, 1979); C. K. Barrett, "The Historicity of Acts," *JTS*, n.s., 50 (1999): 515–34; J. D. G. Dunn, *The Acts of the Apostles,* Epworth Commentaries (London: Epworth; Valley Forge, Pa.: Trinity, 1996), xv–xix.

64. Published jointly by Eerdmans and Paternoster, and edited by B. W. Winter, with I. H. Marshall and D. Gill, the series has now seen five of its six projected volumes published.

65. I. Levinskaya, *The Book of Acts in Its Diaspora Setting,* BAFCS 5 (Grand Rapids: Eerdmans; Carlisle: Paternoster, 1996); B. M. Rapske, *The Book of Acts and Paul in Roman Custody,* BAFCS 3 (Grand Rapids: Eerdmans; Carlisle: Paternoster, 1994).

66. C. J. Hemer, *The Book of Acts in the Setting of Hellenistic History,* WUNT 49 (Tübingen: Mohr Siebeck, 1989), and a string of valuable articles, sadly cut short by Dr. Hemer's untimely death. For a summary of his major book, see W. W. Gasque, "The Historical Value of Acts," *TynBul* 40 (1989): 136–57.

67. Hemer, *The Book of Acts,* esp. chs. 4–5.

68. Ibid., ch. 7; more briefly, see also C. J. Hemer, "Acts and Galatians Reconsidered," *Them* 2 (1977): 81–88; D. Wenham, "Acts and the Pauline Corpus II: The Evidence of Parallels," in Winter and Clarke, *The Book of Acts,* 215–58. For other views on Pauline chronology that also take the data of Acts as significant, see L. C. A. Alexander, "Chronology of Paul," in Hawthorne, Martin, and Reid, *Dictionary of Paul and His Letters,* 115–23; R. Riesner, *Paul's Early Period: Chronology, Mission Strategy, Theology* (Grand Rapids: Eerdmans, 1998). For views that are more skeptical of the historical value of Acts, see G. Lüdemann, *Paul, Apostle to the Gentiles: Studies in Chronology* (London: SCM, 1984); R. Jewett, *Dating Paul's Life* (London: SCM, 1979).

identification of Luke as the travel companion of Paul is the most plausible solution, and that Luke most probably wrote his "double work" in the early 60s, during the period of Paul's imprisonment in Caesarea. While Hemer's work has far from closed the debate over historicity, he has provided data with which all subsequent scholarship must engage and has put the scholarly community in his debt.

The Portrait of Paul in Acts

Since Philipp Vielhauer's key essay arguing that Luke's Paul is theologically at considerable variance to the Paul of the Epistles,[69] much debate has taken place about Luke's portrait of Paul. A. J. Mattill provided a clear "state of the art" summary in 1978,[70] and the broad contours remain: three main groupings can be identified.[71]

The first group identifies the portraits of Paul in Acts and the Epistles as consistent in matters of history, the treatment of the Torah, the Gentile mission, God's call, and flexibility in different cultural/religious contexts.[72] The second group sees the portraits as different but compatible.[73] Differences between the two portraits are those that naturally would arise between a self-portrait and one done by a close friend and associate: either portrait alone would be lopsided, for both fill in gaps in the other. The third group regards the authentic Pauline Epistles as presenting the "real" Paul, and the portrait in Acts as having been drawn from some distance in both time and theology.[74] Luke

---

69. P. Vielhauer, "On the Paulinism of Acts," in *Studies in Luke-Acts,* ed. L. E. Keck and J. L. Martyn (Nashville: Abingdon, 1966; London: SPCK, 1968); English translation of "Zum Paulinismus der Apostelgeschichte" (1950). For fuller analysis of this debate, see Walton, *Leadership and Lifestyle,* 2–12.

70. A. J. Mattill Jr., "The Value of Acts as a Source for the Study of Paul," in *Perspectives on Luke-Acts,* ed. C. H. Talbert (Danville, Va.: Association of Baptist Professors of Religion; Edinburgh: Clark, 1978), 76–98.

71. Mattill adds a fourth "group," but this is comprised of one scholar, W. C. van Manen, who regards all of the Pauline Epistles as pseudepigraphical—a position some way from the mainstream of scholarship; see Mattill, "The Value of Acts," 95–97; W. C. van Manen, "Paul," in *Encyclopaedia Biblica,* ed. T. K. Cheyne and J. Sutherland, 4 vols. (New York: Macmillan, 1889–1903), 3:3603–6, 3620–38.

72. For example, F. F. Bruce, *The Acts of the Apostles,* 2nd ed. (London: Tyndale; Grand Rapids: Eerdmans, 1952); Gasque, *Criticism of the Acts of the Apostles.*

73. For example, S. E. Porter, *The Paul of Acts: Essays in Literary Criticism, Rhetoric and Theology,* WUNT 115 (Tübingen: Mohr Siebeck, 1999), esp. ch. 9; the later F. F. Bruce, such as "Is the Paul of Acts the Real Paul?" *BJRL* 58 (1975–76): 282–305; Hemer, *The Book of Acts,* 244–47; J. Jervell, *The Unknown Paul* (Minneapolis: Augsburg, 1984); A. J. Mattill Jr., "The Purpose of Acts: Schneckenburger Reconsidered," in *Apostolic History and the Gospel: Biblical and Historical Essays Presented to F. F. Bruce on His Sixtieth Birthday,* ed. W. W. Gasque and R. P. Martin (Exeter: Paternoster, 1970), 108–22.

74. For example, Vielhauer, "On the Paulinism of Acts"; Haenchen, *The Acts of the Apostles;* Conzelmann, *Acts of the Apostles.*

writes to "edify," and his book generally is to be seen as unhistorical except in the broadest terms.

John Lentz regards the portrait of Paul in Acts as historically incredible because it presents him as simultaneously being a Jew, a Roman citizen, and a citizen of Tarsus.[75] Lentz argues at length that there would have been glaring incompatibilities, such as the requirements of participation in non-Jewish worship for Tarsian citizens, by looking for contemporary (or nearly contemporary) evidence of what the three commitments would involve. However, Luke's readers (and perhaps Luke himself) would not have been aware of such inconsistencies, in Lentz's view, presumably because Lentz assigns a late date to Luke-Acts.

Luke's purpose in portraying Paul as a person of high social status and moral virtue was to evangelize the world of the social elite. He did this, Lentz claims, by showing that the church could attract those of high standing and by asserting that Christianity offered the believer a new social status that would be recognized by outsiders.

Lentz's case is built up first by examining what is meant by social status and moral virtue in classical authors and justifying the use of modern categories of social stratification. He then seeks to demonstrate that the portrayal of Paul as Greek, Roman, and Pharisee is flawed, before going on to show how Luke presents Paul as a morally virtuous person. The longest section of the book is an examination of Paul's trials (Acts 22–26) and a consideration of his appeal to Caesar (Acts 25), in both of which Lentz is highly critical of Luke's accuracy because of alleged inconsistencies with Roman law.

Four points may be made in general response.[76] First, Lentz often argues from general principles of consistency from his twentieth-century perspective, whereas Paul himself seems to have been a highly flexible person (e.g., 1 Cor. 9:19–23).

Second, Lentz's use of sources is questionable: he makes extensive use of the sixth-century C.E. *Digest* of Justinian as a source for first-century Roman law, but is doubtful of using Acts, which is acknowledged to be a first-century work, as reliable for the existence of the right of appeal to Caesar (for which it is the only first-century literary evidence[77]). Good scholarship requires that contemporary material should be regarded as more significant.

75. J. C. Lentz Jr., *Luke's Portrait of Paul*, SNTSMS 77 (Cambridge: Cambridge University Press, 1993).

76. More fully, see Rapske, *Paul in Roman Custody*, and his review of Lentz, *Luke's Portrait of Paul*, in *EvQ* 66 (1994): 347–53.

77. Although, note Rapske's discussion (*Paul in Roman Custody*, 48–51) of numismatic evidence for the right of appeal, and A. N. Sherwin-White, "The Roman Citizenship: A Survey of Its Development into a World Franchise," in *ANRW* 1.2:23–58.

Third, the focus on Acts 22–26 (although not exclusive) is in danger of missing vital indicators elsewhere in Acts. For example, the absence of Paul's speech to the Ephesian elders (20:18–35) is puzzling if Lentz's concern is the whole portrait of Paul in Acts.

Fourth, the dismissal or marginalization of other scholarship is disappointing. Marshall and Bruce figure in the footnotes, but often simply are dismissed without argument. Lentz's implication that such scholars have already made up their minds is clear: he appears not to reckon with the possibility that his presuppositions might affect his reading of the evidence.

By contrast, Rapske has shown how much study of ancient sources illuminates Luke's portrayal of Paul's imprisonments.[78] His fine monograph presents the ancient evidence carefully and demonstrates that Luke's portrait of Paul's conditions in imprisonment is, if anything, somewhat restrained and underdrawn. He considers the Roman legal processes, the impact of Roman citizenship for those facing accusation or trial, and then examines the Acts accounts of Paul's imprisonment in the light of this background. He goes on to examine what we know of ancient prison conditions in the Greco-Roman world and highlights the importance for prisoners of having helpers who brought them food, clothing, and provided simple services such as washing. Rapske's work suggests how first-century readers would perceive Paul as a prisoner: a person of low status and shame, contrary to Lentz's claim that Luke's Paul was one of high social standing and honor. Here is another example of study of the ancient context enabling us to read Acts better.

Theology

Finally, we come to theology. In some respects the period since Haenchen's commentary in English has been fruitful, but in others, disappointing. As always, a position presented has provoked responses—and frequently it is the responses that have taken scholarship forward. I will note some valuable surveys before sketching debate in four areas.

Surveys/Collections

Five useful surveys or collections of essays have appeared in recent times. Joseph Fitzmyer surveys the field of Lukan theology and provides a useful engagement with a wide range of issues.[79] François Bovon provides a wonderful resource of digested studies during 1950–83.[80] Howard Kee and Jacob Jervell

---

78. Rapske, *Paul in Roman Custody*.

79. J. A. Fitzmyer, *Luke the Theologian* (London: Chapman; New York: Paulist Press, 1989).

80. Bovon, *Luke the Theologian*.

have produced helpful surveys of the theology of Acts.[81] Most recent is Howard Marshall and David Peterson's *Witness to the Gospel,*[82] which contains essays on most major theological questions concerning Acts.

Delay of the Parousia

Since Conzelmann, much of scholarship has taken it as a given that Luke is writing to respond to the "delay of the parousia."[83] Thus, he writes in the 80s or 90s, at a time when the imminent expectation of the end has died down and Christians are coming to terms with a longer "salvation history." Marshall critiques this position.[84] First, the evidence suggests that the focus of the earliest church's life was the death and resurrection of Jesus rather than his parousia. Second, the evidence is that Paul was aware of a "waiting" period before the end (e.g., 1 Thess. 1:10; 4:13–5:11, from an acknowledged early letter), and thus the issue of the "delay" should not be located with Luke alone—there was recognition of it earlier and elsewhere. Third, considerable continuity exists between the theology of the Spirit and of mission in Paul and Luke-Acts, and thus Luke's concerns are not new in his later period in response to a "delay." Indeed, to speak of "delay" is to suggest that the coming of Christ is "late," whereas the major emphasis of Luke, in common with other NT authors, is that the timing of the parousia is unpredictable (e.g., Acts 1:7).[85]

Work of the Spirit

A significant debate about Luke's theology of the Spirit has developed among scholars engaging with issues raised by the Pentecostal and charismatic movements, focused increasingly on the significance of the gift of the Spirit. The standard Pentecostal position is that Luke presents the gift of the Spirit exclusively as power for witness, a view argued by Robert Menzies.[86] Menzies relates

81. H. C. Kee, *Good News to the Ends of the Earth: The Theology of Acts* (London: SCM, 1990); J. Jervell, *The Theology of the Acts of the Apostles,* NTT (Cambridge: Cambridge University Press, 1996).

82. I. H. Marshall and D. Peterson, eds., *Witness to the Gospel: The Theology of Acts* (Grand Rapids: Eerdmans, 1998).

83. See the statement in C. K. Barrett, *A Critical and Exegetical Commentary on the Acts of the Apostles,* 2 vols., ICC (Edinburgh: Clark, 1994, 1998), 2:lxxxii–lxxxiii.

84. Marshall, *Luke: Historian and Theologian,* 77–88; idem, *The Acts of the Apostles* (1980), 48–55; see also D. E. Aune, "The Significance of the Delay of the Parousia for Early Christianity," in *Current Issues in Biblical and Patristic Interpretation,* ed. G. F. Hawthorne (Grand Rapids: Eerdmans, 1975), 87–109.

85. See the judicious discussion in Witherington, *The Acts of the Apostles,* 184–86.

86. R. P. Menzies, *Empowered for Witness: The Spirit in Luke-Acts,* JPTSup 6 (Sheffield: Sheffield Academic Press, 1994), a slightly revised edition of his published doctoral thesis, *The Development of Early Christian Pneumatology with Special Reference to Luke-Acts,* JSNTSup 54

the Spirit in Luke-Acts to the Jewish expectation of the "Spirit of prophecy," whose activity is seen typically in speech or knowledge gifts such as prophecy, invasive praise inspired by the Spirit, and defense and proclamation of the gospel. Menzies maintains that whenever the Spirit's activity is found in Luke-Acts, this pattern is to be seen. This gift of the Spirit as a *donum superadditum,* or "second grace," is to be distinguished from the Pauline understanding of the Spirit as necessary for salvation (e.g., Rom. 8:9), performing miracles (e.g., Gal. 3:5), and transforming believers (e.g., 2 Cor. 3:18). Menzies argues that Luke presents a strongly Jewish understanding of the Spirit, and that Paul is the real theological innovator in his understanding of the Spirit's work as necessary for salvation. This argument leads naturally to the Pentecostal view that there is an experience of the Spirit that is both distinct from the experience of salvation and necessary for Christian witness.

Menzies's argument comes under fire from two directions. James Dunn (initially writing prior to Menzies, but later engaging with Menzies's writings) argues that Luke does present the Spirit as soteriologically necessary.[87] He argues that key passages in Acts present the Spirit as bringing new members into the believing community; the Samaria episode is a crucial example (Acts 8:4–24), for there is no evidence of witness by the Samaritan converts—rather, it is Peter and John who proclaim the gospel in the other Samaritan villages (8:25).

Max Turner, on the other hand, critiques Menzies's reading both of the Jewish sources and of Luke-Acts.[88] While accepting that the major emphasis of Jewish and Lukan understanding of the Spirit is power for witness, Turner points to material in both sources that shows the Spirit performing miracles, actually bringing people into the salvation community, and continuing to transform them ethically once they are within the community. In the Jewish sources, the Qumran hymns, the Septuagint, and the Targumim are central to his argument, providing evidence of such activities by the Spirit.[89] In Luke-Acts, Turner argues, the Spirit is seen as the power of Israel's restoration, bringing to reality the promises of God concerning a messiah born of the Spirit and equipped by the Spirit for his task (Luke 1:35; 3:21–22; 4:1, 14, 18),[90] and

(Sheffield: JSOT Press, 1991); see also R. Stronstad, *The Prophethood of All Believers: A Study in Luke's Charismatic Theology,* JPTSup 16 (Sheffield: Sheffield Academic Press, 1999).

87. J. D. G. Dunn, *Baptism in the Holy Spirit* (London: SCM; Philadelphia: Westminster, 1970), esp. chs. 2–9; for engagement with Menzies, see idem, "Baptism in the Spirit: A Response to Pentecostal Scholarship on Luke-Acts," *JPT* 3 (1993): 3–27; and responses: R. P. Menzies, "Luke and the Spirit: A Reply to James Dunn," *JPT* 4 (1994): 115–38; J. B. Shelton, "A Reply to James D. G. Dunn's 'Baptism in the Spirit: A Response to Pentecostal Scholarship on Luke-Acts,'" *JPT* 4 (1994): 139–43.

88. M. Turner, *Power from on High: The Spirit in Israel's Restoration and Witness in Luke-Acts,* JPTSup 9 (Sheffield: Sheffield Academic Press, 1996); more briefly, M. Turner, "The 'Spirit of Prophecy' as the Power of Israel's Restoration and Witness," in Marshall and Peterson, *Witness to the Gospel,* 327–48.

89. Turner, "Spirit of Prophecy," 335–37; *Power from on High,* chs. 4–5.

90. Turner, "Spirit of Prophecy," 336–37; *Power from on High,* chs. 6–9; cf. D. W. Pao, *Acts and the Isaianic New Exodus,* WUNT 2.130 (Tübingen: Mohr Siebeck, 2000; reprint, Grand Rapids: Baker, 2002).

a renewed life of the community of those who believe in him (e.g., in the Pentecost account there are echoes of the Sinai gift of the Torah, and Jesus is seen as the prophet like Moses).[91]

Luke and Judaism

Turner's understanding of the nature of the gift of the Spirit leads into discussion of the status of Judaism in Acts, a debate with special sharpness and relevance because of the Holocaust/Shoah in Nazi Germany. Joseph Tyson provides a valuable overview of the debate in an edited collection and his own survey of the different positions.[92] Three scholars illustrate the issues well.

Jack T. Sanders argues that Luke is anti-Semitic, claiming that Luke holds the Jewish people responsible for the death of Jesus.[93] He proposes that Luke consistently presents the Jewish leaders, excepting the Pharisees, as opposed to the gospel and to Jesus. The city of Jerusalem itself is the acme of opposition to God and his purposes. Thus, the Acts speeches, especially those to Jewish audiences, condemn the Jews wholesale.

By contrast, Jacob Jervell sees the place of Jewish people and Jewish issues as very much at the heart of Luke's theology and perspective.[94] Jervell highlights the evidence of "mass conversions" of Jews running through Acts (2:41; 4:4; 5:14; 6:1, 7; 9:42; 12:24; 13:43; 14:1; 17:10–12; 19:20; 21:20). He further argues that mission to Gentiles is not to "pure" (i.e., pagan) Gentiles, but only to God-fearers; he cites Acts 11:21, 24; 13:43; 14:1; 17:4, 12; 18:8, 10 as having this sense.[95] Thus by "Israel," Luke refers to Jews who believe in Jesus, not to ethnic Israel; the church's mission produces a major division in ethnic Israel between those who are now the true people of God and those who reject Jesus. Jervell regards the end of Acts as marking the end of the mission to ethnic Israel, and sees Acts 28:28 as a final turning to "pure" Gentiles. This is a very different view from the earlier consensus that mission to the Gentiles begins when the Jews reject the gospel.[96]

91. Turner, "Spirit of Prophecy," 345–46; *Power from on High,* ch. 10.

92. J. B. Tyson, ed., *Luke-Acts and the Jewish People: Eight Critical Perspectives* (Minneapolis: Augsburg, 1988); *Luke, Judaism, and the Scholars: Critical Approaches to Luke-Acts* (Columbia: University of South Carolina Press, 1999); see also Tyson, *Images of Judaism in Luke-Acts.*

93. J. T. Sanders, *The Jews in Luke-Acts* (London: SCM, 1987); summarized in Tyson, *Luke, Judaism, and the Scholars,* 113–22.

94. J. Jervell, *Luke and the People of God* (Minneapolis: Augsburg, 1972); idem, *Theology,* esp. ch. 3; similar is R. L. Brawley, *Luke-Acts and the Jews: Conflict, Apology, and Conciliation,* SBLMS 33 (Atlanta: Scholars Press, 1987); see the summaries in Tyson, *Luke, Judaism, and the Scholars,* 91–109, 122–27.

95. J. Jervell, "The Church of Jews and Godfearers," in *Luke-Acts and the Jewish People: Eight Critical Perspectives,* ed. J. B. Tyson (Minneapolis: Augsburg, 1988), 11–20.

96. See Tyson, *Luke, Judaism, and the Scholars,* 66–90, on Haenchen and Conzelmann, who represent the earlier consensus.

Jon Weatherly makes a less noticed but important contribution to the debate by challenging Sanders's analysis at one of its most significant points: the question of whom Luke regards as responsible for the death of Jesus.[97] Sanders asserts that Luke regards the Jewish people as a whole as responsible,[98] citing the speeches in Acts in support. However, Weatherly notes that those responsible for the death of Jesus are asserted to be the Jews *of Jerusalem*—and their leaders in particular—rather than all Jews.[99] Thus, in Jerusalem alone "you" are held to be responsible for the death of Jesus (e.g., Acts 2:23; 3:14; 4:10), whereas in the Diaspora it is "they" who are responsible—that is, the Jews of Jerusalem (e.g., Acts 13:27–29). Weatherly's argument makes a significant contribution to answering the claim that Luke is anti-Semitic.

The Church and the Roman Empire

Finally, the last thirty years have seen fresh debate on the relationship of the church and the Roman Empire in Acts.[100] The older consensus was that Luke was presenting an apologetic for Christianity to the Roman Empire, aiming to convince Roman officials that Christianity is politically harmless.[101] In particular, many held that Luke is seeking the same freedoms for Christianity as a *religio licita* (a "legally recognized" religion) that Judaism enjoys. This consensus has come under considerable fire during our period, with several alternative proposals being offered.

The opposite view, that Luke is offering an apologetic to the church on behalf of the empire, is Paul Walaskay's claim.[102] He points to key features of Luke-Acts that do not fit the consensus view[103]—notably, that in Acts Jesus is constantly referred to as "Lord," a title hardly compatible with Caesar's claim to be Lord. Further, Luke does not aggressively attack Roman power

---

97. J. A. Weatherly, *Jewish Responsibility for the Death of Jesus in Luke-Acts,* JSNTSup 106 (Sheffield: Sheffield Academic Press, 1994); see also his review of Sanders's *Jews in Luke-Acts* in *TynBul* 40 (1989): 107–17.

98. Sanders, *The Jews in Luke-Acts,* ch. 3.

99. Weatherly, *Death of Jesus in Luke-Acts,* ch. 2.

100. For a fuller account, see S. Walton, "The State They Were In: Luke's View of the Roman Empire," in *Rome in the Bible and the Early Church,* ed. P. Oakes (Carlisle: Paternoster; Grand Rapids: Baker Academic, 2002), 1–41.

101. B. S. Easton, *Early Christianity: The Purpose of Acts and Other Papers* (Greenwich, Conn.: Seabury, 1954), 42–57; Cadbury, *The Making of Luke-Acts,* 301–15; Conzelmann, *The Theology of St. Luke,* 137–49; F. F. Bruce, *The Book of Acts,* rev. ed., NICNT (Grand Rapids: Eerdmans, 1988), 8–13.

102. P. W. Walaskay, *"And So We Came to Rome": The Political Perspective of St. Luke,* SNTSMS 49 (Cambridge: Cambridge University Press, 1983); similar, although more nuanced, is V. K. Robbins, "Luke-Acts: A Mixed Population Seeks a Home in the Roman Empire," in *Images of Empire,* ed. L. Alexander, JSOTSup 122 (Sheffield: JSOT Press, 1991), 202–21.

103. Walaskay, *We Came to Rome,* 15–37.

in the way that other Second Temple Jewish writings do (e.g., 4 Ezra, *Sibylline Oracles*, and Revelation). Instead, Luke places the birth of Jesus and the growth of the Christian movement within the empire's history (e.g., Luke 2:1–5; 3:10–14). The trials of Jesus and Paul, Walaskay argues, are both presented as showing Rome and its representatives to be dealing justly with the accused.

Esler's reconstruction of Luke's community as including Roman soldiers or administrators leads him to the view that Luke is offering legitimation of his readers' Christian faith, including the assurance that faith in Christ is compatible with loyalty to Rome.[104] Thus, Luke stresses the antiquity of Christianity, not least by linking it with Israelite ancestors (e.g., Acts 3:13; 5:30; 15:10; 22:14; 26:6; 28:25), and includes Romans among his conversion stories (e.g., Acts 10:1–11:18; 13:6–12; 18:7). Esler's procedure involves "mirror-reading" the text to identify its audience, and this method is fraught with problems because it involves the assumption that significant features of the text must reflect significant features of Luke's audience—an assumption that only need be stated to see its dangers.[105]

Richard Cassidy offers a stronger proposal in coming to terms with the mixed message that comes through Luke-Acts concerning the empire.[106] Paul's presence in cities frequently is a cause of public disorder, and Paul, although generally cooperative with Roman officials, is far from unquestioning in his loyalty (e.g., Acts 24:25; 25:10–11; 28:19). Cassidy proposes that Luke's presentation of the empire combines three elements: Luke wishes to (1) express his faith in Jesus to his readers; (2) provide guidance to his fellow believers on how to live under Roman rule; and (3) provide guidance and perspective for Christians on how to react when on trial before the authorities.[107]

Prospect

The last thirty years have been a fruitful period in Acts scholarship. Many positions from the earlier consensus have been reviewed and challenged, and a new consensus is yet to emerge. The number and variety of commentaries

---

104. Esler, *Community and Gospel in Luke-Acts*, 201–19; similar are Witherington, *The Acts of the Apostles*, 810–11; H. K. Bond, *Pontius Pilate in History and Interpretation*, SNTSMS 100 (Cambridge: Cambridge University Press, 1998), 161–62.

105. See J. M. G. Barclay, "Mirror-reading a Polemical Letter: Galatians as a Test Case," *JSNT* 31 (1987): 73–93.

106. R. J. Cassidy, *Society and Politics in the Acts of the Apostles* (Maryknoll, N.Y.: Orbis, 1987), esp. 145–70.

107. For a summary, see ibid., 160. My own proposal is related. I suggest that Luke is presenting a variety of scenarios for the empire's attitude toward Christians and offering guidance on how to respond in these situations (Walton, "The State They Were In," 33–35).

that have appeared recently,[108] or are soon to appear,[109] suggests that debate will go on, generating greater understanding of this very challenging and relevant NT book.

108. Notable works of the last ten years include R. W. Wall, "The Acts of the Apostles," in *The New Interpreter's Bible,* ed. L. E. Keck, vol. 10 (Nashville: Abingdon, 2002), 1–368; Witherington, *The Acts of the Apostles;* J. Jervell, *Die Apostelgeschichte,* 17th ed., KEK 3 (Göttingen: Vandenhoeck & Ruprecht, 1998); P. W. Walaskay, *Acts,* Westminster Bible Companions (Louisville: Westminster John Knox, 1998); J. A. Fitzmyer, *The Acts of the Apostles: A New Translation and Commentary,* AB 31 (New York: Doubleday, 1998); Spencer, *Acts;* Dunn, *The Acts of the Apostles;* Barrett, *Commentary on the Acts of the Apostles;* Johnson, *The Acts of the Apostles.*

109. Including work by Loveday Alexander, Beverly Gaventa, Stanley Porter, Joel Green, and the present author.

13

James, Jesus' Brother

Bruce Chilton

Interest in Jesus' brother Ya'aqov, anglicized as "James," is flourishing. Among recent contributions, one might mention a presentation of texts and analysis by Wilhelm Pratscher,[1] a semipopular treatment by Pierre-Antoine Bernheim,[2] and a careful, innovative contribution from Richard Bauckham.[3] These books represent vigorous attempts to recover a critical portrait of James. They all respond, directly and indirectly, to the controversial thesis of Robert H. Eisenman, who has argued over a number of years that James is to be identified with the "righteous teacher" of Qumran.[4] Among the many and vehement responses to that thesis, perhaps the most mature and effective is that of John Painter.[5]

Recovery of interest in James is a useful corrective in both historical and theological terms, in that his place within primitive Christianity had been all but eclipsed by the influence of Paulinism in its many forms. The vehemence of response to Eisenman's thesis, quite apart from the specific questions it raises (exegetical, historical, and even archaeological), might best be explained on

1. Wilhelm Pratscher, *Der Herrenbruder Jakobus und die Jakobustraditionen*, FRLANT 139 (Göttingen: Vandenhoeck & Ruprecht, 1987).

2. Pierre-Antoine Bernheim, *James, Brother of Jesus*, trans. J. Bowden (London: SCM, 1997); cf. idem, *Jacques, Frère de Jésus* (Paris: Nôesis, 1996).

3. Richard Bauckham, *James: Wisdom of James, Disciple of Jesus the Sage*, New Testament Readings (London and New York: Routledge, 1999).

4. Among Eisenman's many publications, see especially *James the Brother of Jesus: The Key to Unlocking the Secrets of Early Christianity and the Dead Sea Scrolls* (New York: Viking, 1996).

5. John Painter, *Just James: The Brother of Jesus in History and Tradition* (Columbia: University of South Carolina Press, 1997).

theological grounds. A silent James is, after all, more easily accommodated to the picture of a smooth transition between Jesus and Paul than is a James who (as in Eisenman's reconstruction) substantially contradicts both Paul and Jesus.

Within this debate, a well-defined set of issues has been perennially in play:[6]

Was James really Jesus' brother?

Was James sympathetic to Jesus prior to the resurrection?

Did James require circumcision of males along with baptism for initiation into the Jesus movement?

Was there any substantial place for non-Jews within James's understanding of the covenant with Abraham, Isaac, and Jacob?

Did James oppose a Pauline teaching of salvation by grace and insist upon obedience to the Torah?

Was James the most prominent person in the Jesus movement between the resurrection and his own death?

None of the treatments already cited here fails to take a stand on each of these issues, and for the most part each issue is also responsibly engaged in those and other discussions. Of the six questions presented here, only one is easily dismissed on the basis of the evidence at hand. But even that, the third question—and the old canard that James required circumcision of all believers—continues to exert so great an influence in popular and scholarly discussion that it should be addressed here.

In what follows, we will work through the six questions to a conclusion, reviewing major primary sources as we proceed, and articulating what I take to be coherent assessments of the secondary literature in the positions that are staked out. The basis of my evaluation has largely been developed during meetings of "the Consultation on James," which I have chaired on behalf of the Institute of Advanced Theology. But the Consultation itself speaks through its own publications,[7] and often it expresses ranges of agreement and disagreement rather than set findings (in the manner, say, of "the Jesus Seminar"), so that my judgments expressed here are not attributable to other members of the Consultation.

None of the primary documents at issue is claimed by most scholars to have come directly from James himself. His views are attested even more indirectly than are his brother's. But the case of Jesus sheds light by way of analogy on

6. For a typical presentation, see the table of contents in Bernheim, *James, Brother of Jesus.*

7. See B. D. Chilton and C. A. Evans, eds., *James the Just and Christian Origins,* NovTSup 98 (Leiden: Brill, 1999), in which I first posed these questions without answering them (p. 4); and B. D. Chilton and J. Neusner, eds., *The Brother of Jesus: James the Just and His Mission* (Louisville: Westminster John Knox, 2001).

James: although a Jesus of history is not "in" our sources, there is, no doubt, a Jesus of literary history behind them.

That is, the Gospels (as well as other documents) refer back to Jesus as their point of generation, and we may infer what practices Jesus engaged in, what beliefs he adhered to, so as to produce the accounts concerning him in the communities of followers that produced the documents. The framing world of those practices and beliefs in the formative period of the NT (whether in the case of Jesus or his followers) was Judaism. Practices and beliefs are attested in the documents manifestly, whether or not their attribution to Jesus is accepted, and that is a suitable point of departure for the genuinely critical question of Jesus. That question cannot be formulated as, What did Jesus really say and really do? Rather, the critical question is, What role did Jesus play in the evolution of practices and beliefs in his name?[8]

That generative question may be broadened, of course, to apply not only to Jesus and the Gospels, but also to primitive Christianity and the NT.[9] In the present case, that involves specifying the practices and beliefs that attach to James within the sources and seeking to understand his place within them. Not every practice, not every belief, may be assumed to be correctly attributed to James, but the various streams of tradition that the documents represent do come together to constitute stable associations of practices and beliefs with James. The nodal issues of practices and beliefs, not "facts," represent our point of departure.

Was James Really Jesus' Brother?

The point of departure for considering this question is Mark 6:3 (cf. Matt. 13:55–56), where James is actually named as Jesus' brother, along with four other men; at least two, unnamed and unenumerated, sisters are also mentioned. Until recently, Roman Catholic opinion has been dominated by the position of St. Jerome (in his controversial work *Against Helvidius*), who argued that although "brothers" and "sisters" are the terms used in Greek, the reference is actually to cousins. Dispute has focused on the issue of whether that view can be sustained linguistically, and on the whole the finding has been negative. Before Jerome, Helvidius himself had maintained during the fourth century that the brothers and sisters were just what their name implies—siblings of Jesus; although he had been born of a virgin, their father was Joseph and their

8. For development of this perspective, see B. D. Chilton, *The Temple of Jesus: His Sacrificial Program within a Cultural History of Sacrifice* (University Park: Pennsylvania State University Press, 1992); *Pure Kingdom: Jesus' Vision of God* (Grand Rapids: Eerdmans; London: SPCK, 1996); *Rabbi Jesus: An Intimate Biography* (New York: Doubleday, 2000).

9. See Bruce Chilton and Jacob Neusner, *Judaism in the New Testament: Practices and Beliefs* (London and New York: Routledge, 1995).

mother was Mary. That view clearly played havoc with the emerging doctrine of Mary's virginity after Jesus' birth, and that issue occupied the center of attention. In a recent work that received the imprimatur, John P. Meier has endorsed the Helvidian theory, to some extent on the basis of support from second-century church fathers.[10] During that century, a group referred to as the Ebionites even denied Jesus' virgin birth in the technical sense; his "brothers" and "sisters" were implicitly that in the full sense of those words (see Irenaeus, *Against Heresies* 1.26.1–2).

Richard Bauckham has given new currency to the view of Jesus' relationship to James developed by Epiphanius during the fourth century (*Panarion* 1.29.3–4; 2.66.19; 3.78.7, 9, 13), and supported by the second-century *Protevangelium of James* (9:2) and perhaps the *Gospel of Peter* (according to Origen's *Commentary on Matthew* 10:17).[11] On this view, Mary was Jesus' mother, not James's, since Joseph had a wife prior to his marriage to Mary. Joseph's relatively advanced age is traditionally held to account for his early departure from the narrative scene of the Gospels, and that reasonable inference lends support to this theory, while James's emphasis on the Davidic identity of the church (see Acts 15:16) is easily accommodated on this view. James's seniority relative to Jesus might be reflected in the parable of the prodigal (Luke 15:11–32). The story about those with Jesus seizing him in response to his exorcisms (Mark 3:21; cf. 3:31–35) reflects the kind of almost parental concern that an older brother might feel for a younger brother.

Another, more pragmatic, consideration provides support for Epiphanius's theory,[12] although in a modified form. As we noted, Joseph disappears from the scene of the Gospels from the time Jesus was about twelve years old.[13] His death at that time has been the traditional surmise, and such a chronology has implications for understanding Jesus' relationships with his siblings. On the Helvidian view, Mary must have given birth to at least seven children in twelve years (Jesus, his brothers, and two or more sisters). Assuming that not every child she gave birth to survived infancy, more than seven labors would be required during that period—all this within a culture that confined women after childbirth and prohibited intercourse with a woman having a flow of blood, and despite the acknowledged prophylactic effect of lactation and Joseph's age.

---

10. John P. Meier, *A Marginal Jew: Rethinking the Historical Jesus,* 3 vols., ABRL (New York: Doubleday, 1991–2001), 1:332.

11. See Richard Bauckham, "The Brothers and Sisters of Jesus: An Epiphanian Response to John P. Meier," *CBQ* 56 (1994): 686–700.

12. Discussion of this issue typically has adjudicated among the Helvidian, Epiphanian, and Hieronymian theories, as a result of the typology of J. B. Lightfoot, *Saint Paul's Epistle to the Galatians* (London: Macmillan, 1865).

13. For a study of the issue of doubtful paternity in Judaism during this period and later, see Meir Bar-Ilan, "The Attitude toward *Mamzerim* in Jewish Society in Late Antiquity," *Jewish History* 14 (2000): 125–70.

Although the consideration of a likely rate of fertility provides some support to the Epiphanian theory, in its unadulterated form it strains credulity
in its own way. A widower with at least six children already in tow is perhaps
not the best candidate for marriage with a young bride. A modified form of
the theory (a hybrid with Helvidius's suggestion) makes James and Joses the
products of Joseph's previous marriage, and Jesus, Simon, and Judah the sons
of Joseph with Mary. The latter three sons have names notably associated with
a zealous regard for the honor of Israel, and may reflect the taste of a common
mother. Absent their names, or even a count of how many were involved, no
such assignment of marriages can be attempted for Jesus' sisters.

On the Helvidian view, James was Jesus' younger and full brother in a family quickly produced, whose siblings were close in age. On the Epiphanian
view, James was older and was Jesus' half brother. It seems to me that suitably
modified, the view of Epiphanius provides the more plausible finding.

Was James Sympathetic to Jesus Prior to the Resurrection?

The Gospels, when they refer to James at all, do so with no great sympathy.[14] He is listed at the head of Jesus' brothers in the Synoptic Gospels, but
in a statement of a crowd in Nazareth that is skeptical that one whose family
they know can be responsible for wonders (Mark 6:1–6; Matt. 13:53–58). In
John, he is presumably included among the unnamed brothers who argued
with Jesus about his refusal to go to Jerusalem for a feast (John 7:2–10), and
James is also referred to anonymously in the Synoptics as being among the
brothers whom, even with his mother, Jesus refused to interrupt his teaching
in order to greet (Mark 3:31–35; Matt. 12:46–50; Luke 8:19–21). The most
plausible inference is that Jesus and James were somehow at odds during this
period, but personal animosity is scarcely provable. The real breaking point
with everyone at Nazareth came at the attempted stoning there (Luke 4:16–30),
which seems to have made Jesus negative about his own family.

On the other hand, James is recognized within the earliest list of those to
whom the risen Jesus appeared (1 Cor. 15:7), and—closely associated with the
temple—he quickly emerged as the dominant figure in the Jesus movement.[15]
Taken together, these two data suggest that by the end of Jesus' life, during his
last pilgrimage to Jerusalem, James and his brother had reconciled. Aside from
Paul's reference to James in his list of witnesses to the resurrection, the NT
does not record an actual appearance to James, but the noncanonical *Gospel
of the Hebrews* does. There, Jesus assures his brother that "the Son of Man has

14. This is a point of departure for Robert Eisenman, *James the Just in the Habakkuk Pesher,*
SPB 35 (Leiden: Brill, 1986).

15. In contrast to Eisenman, this is the point of departure for Ethelbert Stauffer, "The Caliphate
of James," *JHC* 4 (1997): 120–43 (from his German article in *ZRGG* 4 [1952]: 193–214).

been raised from among those who sleep" (cited by Jerome, *De viris illustribus* 2). This vision occurs after James had fasted in consequence of his brother's death. The authority of James, it seems, was a key force in the complete identification between Jesus and the figure of "one like a son of man" in Dan. 7 (see also Hegesippus, as cited by Eusebius, *Hist. eccl.* 2.23.1–18)—an angelic figure in the heavenly court—after the resurrection.

Did James Require Circumcision of Males along with Baptism for Initiation into the Jesus Movement?

Acts attributes to James (and to James alone) the power to decide whether non-Jewish male converts in Antioch needed to undergo circumcision. He determines that they do not need to do so.[16] Under the influence of the thesis of F. C. Baur, it is sometimes assumed that James required circumcision of all such converts,[17] but that requirement is attributed to Christian Pharisees in Acts (15:5), not to James. Nonetheless, James does proceed to command non-Jewish Christians to observe certain requirements of purity (so Acts 15:1–35). That may explain why emissaries from James make their appearance as villains in Paul's description of a major controversy at Antioch. They insisted on a separate meal fellowship of Jews and non-Jews, while Paul, with more than equal insistence (but apparently little or no success), argued for the unity of Jewish and non-Jewish fellowship within the church (Gal. 1:18–2:21). How precisely James came to such a position of prominence is not explained in Acts; his apostolic status was, no doubt, assured by the risen Jesus' appearance to him.

Like Josephus (*Ant.* 20.197–203), Hegesippus (in concert with Clement, Eusebius reports) portrays James as being killed by Ananus at the temple. In addition, Hegesippus describes James in terms that emphasize his purity in such a way that, as in Acts, his association with the Nazirite vow is evident (cf. Acts 21:17–36). James's capacity to win the reverence of many Jews in Jerusalem (not only his brother's followers) derives from this practice and from his encouragement of others in the practice. The fact is frequently overlooked, but needs to be emphasized, that the Mishnah envisages the Nazirite practice for slaves, as well as Israelites, both male and female (see *m. Naz.* 9:1).[18] James's focus was purity in the temple under the aegis of his risen brother, the Son of Man, but there is no trace of his requiring

16. See Richard Bauckham, "James and the Jerusalem Church," in *The Book of Acts in Its Palestinian Setting*, ed. R. Bauckham, BAFCS 4 (Grand Rapids: Eerdmans, 1995), 415–80.

17. On the influence of the "Tübingen School," see Ernst Haenchen, *The Acts of the Apostles: A Commentary*, trans. B. Noble et al. (Philadelphia: Westminster, 1971), 15–24. In view of Professor Hengel's association with Tübingen during the intervening period, we may have to think again about this designation!

18. For the roots of the practice, see Eliezer Diamond, "An Israelite Self-Offering in the Priestly Code: A New Perspective on the Nazirite," *JQR* 88 (1997): 1–18.

circumcision of Gentiles. It needs to be kept in mind that Jesus himself had expelled traders from the temple, not as some indiscriminate protest about commercialism, but as part of Zechariah's prophecy (see Zech. 14) of a day when all the peoples of the earth would be able to offer sacrifice to the Lord without the intervention of middlemen. James's Nazirite practice realized that prophecy in his brother's name.

Josephus reports that James was killed in the temple in 62 C.E. at the instigation of the high priest Ananus during the interregnum of the Roman governors Festus and Albinus (*Ant.* 20.197–203). Hegesippus gives a more circumstantial, less politically informed, account of the martyrdom. James is set up on a parapet of the temple, being known and addressed by his opponents by the titles "Righteous and *Oblias*," Hegesippus reports. The second title has caused understandable puzzlement (especially when Hegesippus's rendering of the term as "bulwark" is accepted),[19] but it is easily related to the Aramaic term *ʾăbēl,* which means "to mourn." Recent finds in the vicinity of the Dead Sea (not only near Qumran) have greatly enhanced our understanding of Aramaic as spoken in the time of Jesus and his followers. The use of the term is attested there.[20] James probably was known as "mourner."

A minor tractate of the Talmud lays down the rule that a mourner (*ʾăbēl*) "is under the prohibition to bathe, anoint [the body], put on sandals and cohabit" (*Sem.* 4:1). This largely corresponds to the requirements of a Nazirite vow and to Hegesippus's description of James's practice; for Jesus himself to have called his brother "mourner" would fit in with his practice of giving his followers nicknames. A tight association with the temple on James's part is attested throughout and from an early period, but not a universal requirement of circumcision.

Was There Any Substantial Place for Non-Jews within James's Understanding of the Covenant with Abraham, Isaac, and Jacob?

Hegesippus's account of James's prominence is confirmed by Clement, who portrays James as the first elected bishop in Jerusalem (also cited by Eusebius, *Hist. eccl.* 2.1.1–6), and by the pseudo-Clementine *Recognitions,* which makes James into an almost papal figure, providing the correct paradigm of preaching to Gentiles. Paul is so much the butt of this presentation that *Recognitions* (1.43–71) even relates that Saul, prior to his conversion to Christianity, physically assaulted James in the temple. Martin Hengel refers

19. As a matter of fact, Hegesippus accepts that this signification is Greek; James seems to be so named here because after his death the seige of Jerusalem was successful.

20. See Joseph A. Fitzmyer and Daniel J. Harrington, *A Manual of Palestinian Aramaic Texts,* BibOr 34 (Rome: Biblical Institute, 1978).

to this presentation as an apostolic novel (*Apostelroman*), deeply influenced by the perspective of the Ebionites, and probably to be dated within the third and fourth centuries.[21]

Yet even in Acts 15, the use of Scripture attributed to James, like the argument itself, is quite unlike Paul's. James claims that Peter's baptism of non-Jews is to be accepted because "the words of the prophets agree, just as it is written" (Acts 15:15), and he goes on to cite from the Book of Amos. The passage cited will concern us in a moment; the form of James's interpretation is an immediate indication of a substantial difference from Paul. As James has it, there is actual agreement between Simeon and the words of the prophets, as two people might agree: nowhere else in the NT is the verb *symphōnein* used with respect to Scripture. The continuity of Christian experience with Scripture is marked as a greater concern than within Paul's interpretation, and James expects that continuity to be verbal, a matter of agreement with the prophets' words, not merely with possible ways of looking at what they mean.

The citation from Amos (9:11–12, from the LXX, the Bible of Luke-Acts) comports well with James's concern that the position of the church agree with the principal vocabulary of the prophets (Acts 15:16–17):

> After this I will come back and restore the tent of David which has fallen, and rebuild its ruins and set it up anew, that the rest of men may seek the Lord, and all the Gentiles upon whom my name is called.

In the argument of James as represented here, what the belief of Gentiles achieves is not the redefinition of Israel (as in Paul's thought), but the restoration of the house of David, with Gentile recognition of the Torah as it impinged on them.[22] The argument is possible because a Davidic genealogy of Jesus—and, therefore, of his brother James—is assumed.[23]

---

21. See "Jakobus der Herrenbruder—der erste 'Papst'?" in *Glaube und Eschatologie: Festschrift für Werner Georg Kümmel zum 80. Geburtstag,* ed. E. Grässer and O. Merk (Tübingen: Mohr, 1985), 71–104, 81. The ordering of Peter under James clearly is a part of that perspective, as Hengel shows, and much earlier Joseph Lightfoot found that the alleged correspondence between Clement and James was a later addition to the pseudo-Clementine corpus (see J. B. Lightfoot, *The Apostolic Fathers,* 5 vols. [London: Macmillan, 1890], 1:414–20). But even if the Pseudo-Clementines are taken at face value, they undermine Eisenman's view (or the view of the Tübingen School, which, as Hengel points out, is the source of such contentions): they portray James as the standard for how Hellenistic Christians are to teach (see *Recognitions* 11.35.3).

22. See Markus Bockmuehl, "The Noachide Commandments and New Testament Ethics," in *Jewish Law in Gentile Churches: Halakhah and the Beginning of Christian Public Ethics* (Edinburgh: Clark, 2000), 145–73.

23. See Ethelbert Stauffer, *Jesus and His Story,* trans. R. Winston and C. Winston (New York: Knopf, 1960), 13–15.

Did James Oppose a Pauline Teaching of Salvation by Grace and Insist on Obedience to the Torah?

It is true that the Epistle of James sets out an elaborate argument—including a reading of Gen. 22 that seems to contradict Paul's—to the effect that faith without works is dead (cf. James 2:14–26 and Rom. 4). But the epistle does not set out Paul's position in anything like detail; as Peter Davids has remarked, "There is no sense of the Pauline tension between faith and Torah piety, for James' community is in a different context."[24] Paul surely is the most prominent explorer of that tension, but his position is subtler than what is refuted in the Epistle of James.[25] That is no surprise, since Paul himself had to correct antinomian readings of his own views among those sympathetic to him (see 1 Cor. 5–6). The Pastoral Epistles and 2 Pet. 3:15–16 suggest that this difficulty grew over time.

The dating of the Epistle of James, and particularly the question whether it was written before or after the destruction of the temple in 70 C.E., continues to cause controversy.[26] But the sense of social crisis reflected in the epistle is unmistakable, as well as its urgent expectation of Jesus' parousia (James 5:7–8; cf. 2 Pet. 3:4, 12). But if we think back to Hegesippus's description of James's ethos, that is not surprising. With the threat to the very possibility of sacrificial worship in the temple (whether after its destruction or in the turbulent conditions that preceded that trauma), a fundamental aspect of James's position was compromised, an aspect with which Paul himself could agree (as Acts 21:16–36 and Rom. 15:16 suggest). What remained was Jesus' identity as the Son of Man, and the challenge to James's theology (before or after his own death) was to maintain and even enhance that identity as worship in the temple became increasingly problematic. In that context, whether James happened to have agreed with Paul in a doctrine that Paul had articulated in quite a different context appears to be a secondary concern.

Was James the Most Prominent Person in the Jesus Movement between the Resurrection and His Own Death?

It is telling that Jerome, in his attempt to draw together the material relating to James, cites the *Gospel of the Hebrews* alongside the NT, Hegesippus, and Josephus. The conflation attests the fragmentary nature of the references, as well

24. See Peter Davids, "James's Message: The Literary Record," in Chilton and Neusner, *The Brother of Jesus,* 66–87.

25. In this regard, see George B. Caird, *New Testament Theology,* completed and edited by L. D. Hurst (Clarendon: Oxford, 1994), 190.

26. See Wiard Popkes, *Der Brief des Jakobus,* THKNT 14 (Leipzig: Evangelische Verlagsanstalt, 2001).

as the appearance they give of having been spun out of one another or out of cognate traditions. Although use of these sources is unavoidable as the necessary point of departure for any discussion of James, they all shape James into an image that comports with their own programs. The James of the Gospels is kept at bay so as not to deflect attention from Jesus until the resurrection, when James implicitly or explicitly (in the case of Paul and the *Gospel of the Hebrews*) becomes an important witness; the James of Acts reconciles the church within a stance that leads on to the position of Paul; Paul's James divides the church; Josephus relates James's death to illustrate the bloody-mindedness of Ananus the high priest, while Hegesippus does so to illustrate the righteousness of James and his community; Clement makes James the transitional figure of the apostolic tradition, and the Pseudo-Clementine *Recognitions* use and enhance that standing in order to attack the figure of Paul.

All the way through, James is deployed in these sources to assert what is held to be an authoritative construction of the Jesus movement.[27] Accordingly, he is marginalized (in the Gospels), appealed to as an authoritative witness (in Acts and Paul), criticized (in Paul),[28] portrayed as a victim (by Josephus) or a hero (by Hegesippus), hailed as both a source of unity (by Clement and in the tradition of Acts) and the trump card to use against Paul (in the *Recognitions*). Everything that makes the figure of "the historical Jesus" in a historicist understanding problematic makes "the historical James" in that sense out of the question.

James's devotion to the temple and to his brother as the Danielic Son of Man after the resurrection made him the most prominent Christian leader in Jerusalem. The practice of the Nazirite vow was his distinguishing feature, and his belief in his brother as the gate of heaven, the heavenly portal above the temple, made him a figure to be revered and reviled in Judaism, depending upon one's evaluation of Jesus. Among Christians, he promulgated his understanding of the establishment of the house of David by means of an interpretation reminiscent of the Essenes, although he insisted that baptized, uncircumcised non-Jews had an ancillary role. As the bishop or overseer (*mebaqqer*, in the Dead Sea Scrolls) of his community, he exercised a function that entered the Greek language as *episkopos*, and the influence of his circle is attested in the NT and later literature (including the *Gospel of Thomas,* the *Apocryphon of James,* the *Protevangelium of James,* the *First* and *Second Apocalypse of James,* the *Gospel of Peter,* the *Apocalypse of Peter,* the *Kerygma Petrou,* the *Acts of Peter,* the *Letter of Peter to Philip,* and the *Acts of Peter* (ca. 200 C.E. or later).

Once James's distinctive importance has been recognized, it is natural to ask, How great was his influence upon the earliest phase of primitive Christian

27. See Kenneth L. Carroll, "The Place of James in the Early Church," *BJRL* 44 (1961): 49–67.

28. See Walter Schmithals, *Paulus und Jakobus,* FRLANT 85 (Göttingen: Vandenhoeck & Ruprecht, 1963).

and early Christian literature? It has been argued, for example, that passages within the Synoptic Gospels might well bear the stamp of James's perspective. Within the narrative of Jesus' passion in the Synoptics, only one passage makes the Last Supper correspond to the Passover (Matt. 26:17–20//Mark 14:12–17//Luke 22:7–14), and that presentation conflicts with the Johannine and Pauline presentations. That would limit participation in the meal and in its commemoration to those circumcised, in the case of males (see Exod. 12:48), a move that would accord with James's Israelite construction of the church's leadership.[29] Similarly, the teaching attributed to Jesus with regard to vowing property as *qorbana,* a gift to the temple, manifests an interest in, and a familiarity with, cultic institutions, as well as a style of exegesis associated with the *pesharim* of Qumran, which better accords with James than with Jesus (Matt. 15:1–20//Mark 7:1–23).[30] Lastly, the story of the demons and the swine of Gergesa, with its emphasis on the impurity of non-Jews (Romans especially) (Matt. 8:28–34//Mark 5:1–20//Luke 8:26–39) has been linked with a Jacobean cycle of tradition, and the secret knowledge of the demons that Jesus was *Nazarenos,* a Nazirite, is plausibly linked to the same cycle.[31]

Conclusion

Within the terms of reference of early Judaism and primitive Christianity, no single issue can compare in importance to that of the temple. The Nazirite practice attributed to James and those in contact with him provides a highly focused degree of devotion to the temple. As usually presented, of course, the social history of primitive Christianity and early Christianity has been Hellenistic in orientation. That is perfectly natural, given the actual provenience and language of the NT and the bulk of the corpus of Christianity in late antiquity. Still, social histories such as those by Wayne Meeks,[32] Abraham Malherbe,[33] and Dennis Smith and Hal Taussig[34] have tended not to engage the sources of Judaism, and especially the Judaism of Aramaic and Hebrew sources, with the same vigor that has been applied to the Hellenistic dimension of analysis. That is perfectly understandable, given the particular documents that they have dealt with and the specific questions that they applied to those documents.

29. See Bruce Chilton, *A Feast of Meanings: Eucharistic Theologies from Jesus through Johannine Circles,* NovTSup 72 (Leiden: Brill, 1994), 93–108.

30. See Bruce Chilton, "A Generative Exegesis of Mark 7:1–23," *JHC* 3 (1996): 18–37.

31. See Jacob Neusner and Bruce Chilton, *The Body of Faith: Israel and the Church,* Christianity and Judaism, the Formative Categories (Valley Forge, Pa.: Trinity, 1996), 98–101.

32. Wayne Meeks, *The First Urban Christians: The Social World of the Apostle Paul* (New Haven: Yale University Press, 1983).

33. Abraham Malherbe, *Social Aspects of Early Christianity* (Philadelphia: Fortress, 1983).

34. Dennis Smith and Hal Taussig, *Many Tables: The Eucharist in the New Testament and Liturgy Today* (Philadelphia: Trinity; London: SCM, 1990).

But a figure such as James will simply remain a cipher, and in all probability a cipher for some form of Paulinism or another, unless he is located within the milieu that not only produced him, but also was embraced as a consciously chosen locus of devotion and activity. Many teachers associated with the Jesus movement managed at least partially to avoid the temple altogether; James is found virtually *only* there after the resurrection.

The specificity of that location raises the issue of James's relation to other forms of Christianity, to other forms of Judaism, and especially to those responsible for the operation of the temple. Here the analysis of James in socially historical terms comes closest to classic history in its specificity.

Whether in the key of an emphasis on the "social" or the "historical" within socially historical analysis, what emerges from our consideration is a distinctive cultic focus upon the validation of the covenant with Israel, which blesses all nations on the authority of Jesus, understood in his resurrection to be identifiable with the "one like a son of man" of Dan. 7.

14

Matthew

Christian Judaism or Jewish Christianity?

Donald A. Hagner

One of the virtually firm conclusions in Matthean studies is that the Gospel was written to Jews who had come to faith in Jesus as the Messiah. The key element supporting this conclusion is the statement, unique to Matthew, that Jesus came not to "abolish the law," but to "fulfill" it, and that "not one letter, not one stroke of a letter, will pass from the law until all is accomplished" (Matt. 5:17–18). In addition to this concern with faithfulness to the law, however, there are many other marks of Matthew's Jewishness: the extensive quotation of the OT, especially the distinctive eleven quotations introduced with the fulfillment formula "this happened to fulfill the words spoken by the prophet"; rabbinic-like patterns of argument, as in the antitheses of the Sermon on the Mount (5:21–48) and in the discussion of divorce (19:3–9); the repeated stress on righteousness; the preference for the language "kingdom of heaven" rather than "kingdom of God"; Matthew's omission of Mark's description of the practice of the Pharisees (cf. Mark 7:3–4 with Matt. 15:2); Matthew's omission of Mark's editorial comment "Thus he declared all foods clean" (cf. Mark 7:19 with Matt. 15:17); the reference to the limitation of Jesus and his disciples' mission to Israel (10:5–6; 15:24); the statement concerning the Pharisees sitting "in Moses' seat" (23:2); the mention of the Sabbath in

24:20; the explicit response to the Jewish allegation that the body of Jesus had been stolen (28:11–15).

This evidence, and more like it, has led almost all Matthean scholars to the conclusion that the author of Matthew was a Jew who wrote to a Jewish-Christian community (or communities) consisting of mainly, if not exclusively, Jewish believers in Jesus.[1] Pushing this conclusion to its extreme, however, several scholars recently have argued that Matthew's community is best understood not as a Christian community, but rather as a sect within Judaism. They contend that Matthew's community should be regarded not as representing a Jewish Christianity, but rather a Christian Judaism. At first glance, this may seem to be only a subtle and unimportant ter-minological difference. The question comes down to which word should serve as the determining noun and which the modifying adjective. The noun denotes that which is of primary significance; the adjective, second-ary significance. That is, do we have in Matthew basically a Judaism with a Christian overlay, so to speak, or basically a Christianity that has Jewish characteristics? Is Matthew's community best regarded as a sect of Second Temple Judaism? Or does that community affirm things that of necessity separate it from Judaism? As we will see, the conclusion of this matter is very important. It impacts the understanding of the Gospel of Matthew in important ways and also has significant ramifications for our understanding of early Christianity.

We will focus here on the three leading advocates of the view that Matthew's community is a Christian form of Judaism: J. Andrew Overman,[2] Anthony J. Saldarini,[3] and David C. Sim.[4] Although there are, of course, differences among these three authors, their views are similar enough for us to treat them together in this essay. I will present their main arguments and conclusions, arguing along the way that their viewpoint is inadequate and does not do justice to the full content of the Gospel of Matthew.

1. Exceptions can be found in K. W. Clark, "The Gentile Bias in Matthew," *JBL* 66 (1947): 165–72; P. Nepper-Christensen, *Das Matthäusevangelium: Ein judenchristliches Evangelium?* (Aarhus: Universitetsforlaget, 1954), although in later years he disavowed this conclusion. More recently, John P. Meier has also argued for a Gentile author. See his article "Matthew, Gospel of," *ABD* 4:622–41.

2. J. Andrew Overman, *Matthew's Gospel and Formative Judaism: The Social World of the Matthean Community* (Minneapolis: Fortress, 1990); *Church and Community in Crisis: The Gospel according to Matthew,* The New Testament in Context (Valley Forge, Pa.: Trinity, 1996).

3. Anthony J. Saldarini, *Matthew's Christian-Jewish Community* (Chicago: University of Chicago Press, 1994); "The Gospel of Matthew and Jewish-Christian Conflict," in *Social History of the Matthean Community: Cross-Disciplinary Approaches,* ed. David L. Balch (Minneapolis: Fortress, 1991), 38–61.

4. David C. Sim, *The Gospel of Matthew and Christian Judaism: The History and Social Setting of the Matthean Community* (Edinburgh: Clark, 1998); "Christianity and Ethnicity in the Gospel of Matthew," in *Ethnicity and the Bible,* ed. Mark G. Brett, BIS 19 (Leiden: Brill, 1996), 171–95; "The Gospel of Matthew and the Gentiles," *JSNT* 57 (1995): 19–48.

Matthew and First-Century Judaism

One of the established conclusions of recent study of Second Temple Judaism is that it was marked by great diversity of viewpoint, ranging from such manifestations of Judaism as that found in the Qumran community to that of the Sadducean establishment. The old idea of a more or less uniform "normative" or standard Judaism that supposedly existed in the first century has had to give way to the realization that the first century, at least until 70 C.E., was characterized by much diversity.[5] Even of the situation from 70 onward, scholars now prefer to talk of "formative" Judaism—that is, Judaism in the process of formation—until we reach the relative stability represented by the production of the Mishnah, ca. 200. Many, if not most, first-century Jewish sects regarded themselves as the righteous remnant of Israel, as representing the true Israel, and as following the true interpretation of the law of Moses. Each in its own way was hostile toward the temple establishment and was in competition against the other sects for leadership in Israel. At first glance, it may seem to the reader that Matthew's community fits such descriptors well.

A vivid parallel to Christianity can be seen in, for example, the Qumran community. Here is a Jewish sect that believed it was in the last days, that it was the community of the new covenant, the manifestation of the righteous remnant of Israel and thus itself the true Israel. This separatist community saw itself as having been prophesied in the Scriptures, and it used a method of scriptural interpretation (called *pesher*—i.e., "this is that which was prophesied") that is very much like the interpretive method used by NT authors. Their founder and leader, called the Teacher of Righteousness, taught the community the meaning of the Scriptures, and he ended up being put to death. The community's piety and ethical teaching were similar to that of the NT: they shared their property (cf. Acts 4:34–35); they regularly partook of a sacred meal not unlike the Lord's Supper. There were, to be sure, differences with Christianity, as in, for example, their concern for the restoration of the Zadokite priesthood, as well as their preoccupation with matters of ritual purity and proper calendar. A key difference, however, to which we will return in this essay, is that whereas the new covenanters of Qumran looked for the imminent coming of two messiahs (a priestly messiah of the line of Aaron, and a royal messiah of the line of David), Matthew's community, together with all the Christians of the NT, believed that the Messiah, Jesus, had already come.

Overman, Saldarini, and Sim argue that Matthew's community, not unlike the Qumran covenanters, reflects a perspective that can be placed on the spectrum of first-century Jewish sects. According to Overman, followed by Sim, a Jewish "sect" has three defining characteristics: (1) it thinks in the dualistic terms of insiders and outsiders, expressed in language such as the "righteous" and the "lawless"; (2) it is hostile toward the Jewish leadership; and (3) it is

5. See Saldarini, *Matthew's Christian-Jewish Community,* 13–18.

committed to the centrality of the law.[6] Matthew fits the first two of these criteria, but we must look more closely at the third, the question of the law.

The Law in Matthew

Unquestionably, the strongest plank in our authors' argument is Matthew's well-known emphasis on the continuing validity of the law. The famous words are found only in Matthew (5:17–20):

> Do not think that I have come to abolish the law or the prophets; I have come not to abolish but to fulfill. For truly I tell you, until heaven and earth pass away, not one letter, not one stroke of a letter, will pass away from the law until all is accomplished. Therefore, whoever breaks one of the least of these commandments, and teaches others to do the same, will be called the least in the kingdom of heaven; but whoever does them and teaches them will be called great in the kingdom of heaven. For I tell you, unless your righteousness exceeds that of the scribes and Pharisees, you will never enter the kingdom of heaven. (NRSV)

What conclusion is to be drawn concerning the identity of Matthew's community from this passage? According to Overman, during the first century "the law became perhaps *the* central means by which . . . sectarian communities attempted to establish the truth of their claims and discredit the claims and position of their opponents."[7] Thus, Matt. 5:17–20 qualifies Matthew's community to be considered as a sect within Judaism.

It is clear, and disputed by very few, that Matthew holds the law in high regard. This can hardly be regarded as surprising. It is not difficult to believe that all Jewish Christians, believing that their Christian faith was the fulfillment of the promises of Scripture, held the law in high regard. It should be pointed out that for all of the differences between the two, this is no less true of Paul than of Matthew.[8] Jesus has, in effect, become the rabbi of the Jewish Christians and shows to them the correct meaning of Torah.

One of the distinctive ways Matthew thus presents Jesus is as the definitive interpreter of the law. The meaning of "fulfill" (*plērōsai*) in 5:17 is "to bring to its intended meaning."[9] The Sermon on the Mount is virtually an exposition of the righteousness of the law. Jesus is the teacher of the law par excellence: "You are not to be called rabbi, for you have one teacher (*didaskalos*). . . . Nor

---

6. Overman, *Matthew's Gospel and Formative Judaism*, 16–30; Sim, *Gospel of Matthew and Christian Judaism*, 109–13.

7. Overman, *Matthew's Gospel and Formative Judaism*, 30. Cf. Saldarini, *Matthew's Christian-Jewish Community*, 124.

8. See D. A. Hagner, "Balancing the Old and the New: The Law of Moses in Matthew and Paul," *Int* 51 (1997): 20–30.

9. See D. A. Hagner, *Matthew*, 2 vols., WBC 33A–B (Dallas: Word, 1993–95), 1:102–10.

be called masters, for you have one master (*kathēgētēs*), the Christ" (23:8–10).[10] Jesus alone brings the correct, authoritative understanding of Torah and can do so because he is the promised Messiah. Law is an important issue in the Gospel, without question.

Nevertheless, Sim overstates the matter when he writes, "The Mosaic law occupies a central place in the Gospel of Matthew."[11] On the contrary, it is Jesus the Messiah, not the law, who is at the center of Matthew. This is clear throughout the Gospel. The unparalleled authority of Jesus is apparent wherever the meaning of the law is in question. The reaction of those who heard Jesus is revealing: "The crowds were astonished at his teaching, for he taught them as one who had authority, and not as their scribes" (7:28; cf. 13:54; 22:33).

The interpretation of the law by Jesus according to Matthew has a new and radical character about it that lifts it to a different level from that of contemporary teachers of the law. Jesus, indeed, has an incomparable authority that transcends that of Torah. The very fact that the statement of 5:17 must begin with a cautionary note, "Do not think that I have come to abolish the law," hints at this fact. It is also suggested by the antitheses of 5:21–48. Even if the latter are finally to be understood as exposition of the Torah, Jesus' teaching transcends the law at the level of the letter of the text. Thus, for example, in the fourth antithesis (5:33–37), when Jesus denies the propriety of taking oaths, he disallows what the Torah allows. And in the fifth antithesis (5:38–42) he disallows the taking of vengeance, while the Torah allows and regulates it. In short, Jesus possesses an astonishing authority. Consonant with this is the repeated formula "You have heard it said . . . but I say to you. . . ." What is remarkable here is the emphatic "but I say to you," where we might have expected "but Torah (or Moses) says."[12] Similarly, Jesus invites his hearers to come to him, to take his yoke upon them and to learn of him. It is the yoke of Jesus, not the yoke of Torah, that is in view, and Jesus says, "My yoke is easy" (11:28–30).

This sovereign interpretation of the law by Jesus can be seen in other places in Matthew. He interprets the Sabbath law with exceptional freedom and concludes that he, "the Son of Man," is "lord of the sabbath" (12:8).[13] And

10. On this, see S. Byrskog, *Jesus the Only Teacher: Didactic Authority and Transmission in Ancient Israel, Ancient Judaism and the Matthean Community,* ConBNT 24 (Stockholm: Almqvist & Wiksell, 1994).

11. Sim, *Gospel of Matthew and Christian Judaism,* 123. The section heading is "The Centrality of the Law."

12. Jewish scholar Jacob Neusner has expressed the revolutionary character of this formulation in these words: "Torah does not prepare me for a message contrasting what the Torah has said with what 'I' say, nor does the Torah help me to understand a message framed in such a way that the very source of the teaching that has been said, the Torah itself, is sidestepped" (*A Rabbi Talks with Jesus: An Intermillennial, Interfaith Exchange* [New York: Doubleday, 1993], 33–34).

13. Matthew does omit the logion of Mark 2:27: "The sabbath was made for man, not man for the sabbath." This may be too radical for Matthew's readers (so Overman, *Church and*

although Matthew will not draw the implication that Mark draws from it, he nevertheless does record the statement of Jesus that "not what goes into the mouth defiles a person, but what comes out of the mouth, this defiles a person" (15:11), thereby in principle undercutting the dietary law.[14] In these instances, of course, it is not a matter of Jesus being disloyal to the law of Moses; rather, it is much more a matter of an incomparable, authoritative interpretation of the law that relativizes the law in the presence of the Messiah,[15] who alone can bring it to its definitive interpretation.

No one can doubt that Torah is one of the pillars of Judaism and that faithful obedience to the commands of Torah is of central importance to Jewish identity. Similarly, it is clear that obedience to the law remains important for Matthew. What is of crucial significance, however, is that it is not the law in itself that is the center of Matthew's concern, but the law only as mediated through the teaching of Jesus. The focus constantly shifts to Jesus. Where one might have expected a reference to Torah, Jesus says, "Where two or three are gathered in my name, there am I in the midst of them" (18:20).[16] It is finally the words of Jesus that are of ultimate authority: "Heaven and earth will pass away, but my words will not pass away" (24:35). At the end of the Gospel, Jesus calls his disciples to teach new disciples "to observe all that I have commanded you" (28:20). They are finally called to obey not Torah, but Jesus.[17]

Thus, an important shift occurs in Matthew that explains the newness of its perspective on the law. To be sure, the law remains significant for these Jewish Christians, but only as it is taken up in the teaching of Jesus. It is hardly the case, however, that Matthew's words in 5:17–20 necessitate the conclusion that his community is to be regarded as a sect of Judaism.[18]

Community in Crisis, 177). Nevertheless, it is remarkable that Matthew does keep the statement that Jesus is lord of the Sabbath.

14. The Jesus of Mark and Luke (and Paul, too, for that matter [1 Cor. 7:10–11]) allows no exception to the prohibition of divorce (Mark 10:11; Luke 16:18). Matthew, however, adds the exception clause "except for sexual immorality [*porneia*]" (Matt. 5:32; 19:9), thus lessening the absolute prohibition, presumably for the sake of his Jewish readers. In so doing, Jesus takes the Shammaite position, or the narrow interpretation, on Deut. 24:1, against the broader interpretation of the Hillelites. See Hagner, *Matthew,* 1:123; 2:547–51.

15. Neusner finds himself saying to the Jesus of Matthew, "I really don't see how your teachings and the Torah's teachings come together. That isn't because things you say don't appeal to the Torah; some of them do. It's because most of what you say and most of what the Torah says scarcely intersect" (*A Rabbi Talks with Jesus,* 134).

16. In the Mishnah (*ʾAbot* 3:2) a similar statement occurs: "If two sit together and words of the Law [are spoken] between them, the Divine Presence [= the Shekinah] rests between them."

17. Klyne Snodgrass attempts to avoid an either/or situation by arguing that Matthew puts his emphasis on both Christ and Torah ("Matthew and the Law," in *Treasures New and Old: Contributions to Matthean Studies,* ed. D. R. Bauer and M. A. Powell, SBLSymS 1 [Atlanta: Scholars Press, 1996], 126). In my opinion, it is better to say that Christ is the center of Matthew, and that Torah is *in effect* preserved only through Christ's teaching.

18. So, too, in an insightful article, Douglas R. A. Hare: "Those few verses that seem to require strict conformity with the ritual requirements of the Torah can be understood in a very different

Matthew's Christology

One of the most striking features of the Gospel of Matthew is its exalted Christology.[19] Jesus is the Messiah, but not merely a human messiah. He is the Son of God,[20] but not like others who have been called "sons of God." He is uniquely the Son of God, enjoying a relationship with the Father that is unparalleled in its intimacy.[21] In three special instances he is confessed to be the Son of God (14:33; 16:16; 27:54). To be noted also are the words of revelation in 3:17 and 17:5: "This is my beloved Son, with whom I am well pleased." For Matthew, Jesus is Emmanuel (1:23), meaning "God with us"—now not only in the sense of one who represents God, but directly, as one who *is* God with us.[22]

As the Messiah, Jesus is obviously the Son of David, who brings the Davidic covenant to its fulfillment (e.g., 1:1; 9:27; 15:22; 20:30–31; 21:9). At the same time, however, Jesus is more than David's son: he is also David's Lord. This point is made clear by means of the quotation of Ps. 110:1 in 22:42–45. For Matthew, it is David's *kyrios* who is invited to sit at God's right hand, where the risen Jesus now sits. This calls to mind the many references to Jesus as *kyrios* in the Gospel (e.g., 7:21–22; 8:25; 14:28, 30; 26:22). Although in certain contexts the word can be merely a term of respect, like our word "sir," for Matthew and his community *kyrios* identifies Jesus as sovereign "Lord," or ruler, who functions as deity. The word *kyrios* in Matthew is reserved for use by disciples or potential disciples and is never used by Jesus' opponents to refer to him (they usually refer to Jesus as "teacher" or "rabbi").

Matthew also presents Jesus as the divine Son of Man, who at the end of the age will act as judge of the nations: "When the Son of Man comes in his glory, and all the angels with him, then he will sit on his glorious throne. Before him will be gathered all the nations, and he will separate them one from another as a shepherd separates the sheep from the goats" (25:31–32; cf. 16:27–28).

In keeping with this exalted view of Jesus are the remarkable words of 11:27: "All things have been delivered to me by my Father; and no one knows the Son

---

way; they do not validate the hypothesis [that Matthew was written for a law-observant Jewish sect]" ("How Jewish Is the Gospel of Matthew?" *CBQ* 62 [2000]: 277). Hare also concludes that "for Matthean Christians Jesus has replaced Torah as the key to a right relationship with the God of Israel" (277).

19. See Birger Gerhardsson, "The Christology of Matthew," in *Who Do You Say That I Am? Essays on Christology*, ed. Mark Allan Powell and David R. Bauer (Louisville: Westminster John Knox, 1999), 14–32; Christopher Tuckett, *Christology and the New Testament: Jesus and His Earliest Followers* (Louisville: Westminster John Knox, 2001), 119–32.

20. This is the main christological title for Matthew. See J. D. Kingsbury, *Matthew: Structure, Christology, Kingdom* (Philadelphia: Fortress, 1975), 40–83.

21. See D. J. Verseput, "The Role and Meaning of the 'Son of God' Title in Matthew's Gospel," *NTS* 33 (1987): 532–56.

22. See David Kupp, *Matthew's Emmanuel: Divine Presence and God's People in the First Gospel*, SNTSMS 90 (Cambridge: Cambridge University Press, 1996).

except the Father, and no one knows the Father except the Son and anyone to whom the Son chooses to reveal him." We may compare these words with the words of the risen Jesus at the end of the Gospel: "All authority in heaven and on earth has been given to me" (28:18). It is thus in "the name of the Father and of the Son and of the Holy Spirit" that the disciples are to baptize their converts (28:19). This Jesus furthermore promises to be with them "always, to the close of the age" (28:20).

Surely, we encounter in Matthew one of the highest Christologies of the NT. Matthew's Christology is also evident not only in the titles given to Jesus and the direct statements made concerning him, but also indirectly in numerous other ways. We have, for example, seen this in the absolutely authoritative way in which he relates to the law. It also is evident in his encounter with the realm of evil (seen in the exorcisms), his miraculous healings, the raising of the dead, the so-called nature miracles (e.g., stilling the storm, walking on the water, multiplying the loaves and fishes), and the central, mediatorial position he assigns himself in the relationship between humanity and God: "So everyone who acknowledges me before others, I also will acknowledge before my Father who is in heaven; but whoever denies me before others, I also will deny before my Father who is in heaven" (10:32). Further, to receive Jesus is to receive God (10:40). To be persecuted for the sake of righteousness is to be persecuted for Jesus' sake (5:10–11).

In short, Jesus is an exalted figure in Matthew far beyond any others who have been sent from God in the history of Israel—someone "greater than Solomon" (12:42), indeed, someone even "greater than the temple" (12:6). He is the one who is "God with us" (1:23) and whose name alone, as Son, can formulaically be put together with God and the Holy Spirit (28:19).[23]

In Matthew, then, Jesus Christ is at the very center of the story. All revolves around him. Saldarini has to admit as much: "Matthew hopes to unite all within a Jesus-centered Israel."[24] Likewise, Overman refers to Matthew's community as standing "within Jesus-centered Judaism."[25] At least from a later perspective, this sounds rather like an oxymoron. Saldarini admits the shift in Matthew: "As a consequence of this focus on Jesus as central authority and symbol, Torah becomes subordinate to both Jesus and his interpretation of its provisions, as articulated in a unique way by Matthew."[26]

---

23. In light of all of this, Saldarini's comment is misleading: "Though Christology quickly became a problem for Jewish believers-in-Jesus, when Matthew wrote, there was no articulated and theologically sophisticated set of claims for Jesus that could be called a Christology, with all the Trinitarian overtones that term implies" (*Matthew's Christian-Jewish Community*, 286 n. 7). Granted, we are not at Nicaea or Chalcedon, but Matthew does articulate a high Christology, even with an implied Trinity at the end of his Gospel.

24. Ibid., 202.

25. Overman, *Church and Community in Crisis*, 20.

26. Saldarini, "Matthew and Jewish-Christian Conflict," 50.

But above all what defines first-century Israel, and indeed later Israel too, is that it is Torah-centered. Can there be a Jesus-centered Israel that has not departed from the very essence of Judaism? In Matthew, Christ has taken the place of Torah.[27] Where this has happened, one may wonder how Matthew's community can fairly be described as a sect within Judaism, despite that community's own distinctive way of loyalty to the Torah. Robert Gundry has put it effectively in a response to Saldarini (and Alan F. Segal): "This high Christology of Matthew and its fundamental difference from anything known to Judaism, including the two powers doctrine, is almost bound to have fixed a great gulf between Matthew's community and Judaism."[28] David Kupp, too, in his study of Matthew's Christology, concludes that Christology is a dividing point: "It is probably not excessive to claim . . . that this christological development functioned as a clear parameter between Matthew's communities and his Jewish counterparts."[29]

The Mission of Jesus

We must examine more closely the mission of Jesus and his disciples. Jesus came not primarily to teach or expound Torah, but to proclaim the imminent arrival of the kingdom of God. At a major turning point early in Matthew's narrative, Jesus begins his ministry echoing the words of John the Baptist (3:2): "Repent, for the kingdom of heaven is at hand" (4:17). His disciples are sent out with the same proclamation in 10:7. It is crucial to notice here that what is in view is nothing less than a turning of the ages, a shift of the aeons, a new time frame in salvation history. This fact alone makes the description of Jesus as a "reformer of Judaism" totally inadequate.

The new reality of the dawning kingdom depends mysteriously on the cross. Thus, from the Jewish perspective this messiah comes to do the strangest work of all: to die on the cross. At the beginning of the story Matthew notes that Jesus "will save his people from their sins" (1:21). In 20:28, Jesus says that "the Son of Man came not to be served but to serve, and to give his life as a ransom for many." The death of Jesus, in fulfillment of the Scriptures (e.g., 26:54, 56), is at the center of the purpose of Jesus, for only in this way can

27. Jacob Neusner, reflecting the standard Jewish viewpoint, refers to "that other position, the one of Torah, that Jews have affirmed in the nearly two thousand years since they went their own way and chose not to follow Jesus at all. This I say without apology, without deceit or guile. What I do is simply reaffirm the Torah of Sinai over and against Matthew's Jesus Christ" (*A Rabbi Talks with Jesus*, 15). Neusner describes Matthew's view of Jesus as one who is "a wholly supernatural figure—and no one can encounter Matthew's Jesus without concurring that before us in the evangelist's mind is God incarnate" (14).

28. Robert Gundry, "A Responsive Evaluation of the Social History of the Matthean Community in Roman Syria," in Balch, *Social History of the Matthean Community*, 64.

29. Kupp, *Matthew's Emmanuel*, 221.

the kingdom become a reality. Thus, anticipating his death, Jesus says to the disciples, "This is my blood of the covenant, which is poured out for many for the forgiveness of sins" (26:28).

We encounter in Matthew an agenda for Jesus that far transcends the interpretation of the Torah. For this reason, despite its partial truth, this statement by Saldarini is hardly correct: "Faithful adherence to an interpretation of all the commandments that stresses justice and mercy is *the core of Jesus' message* and of the Matthean way of life."[30] The same must be said of Saldarini's reference to "Matthew's version of a reformed Judaism" and his statement that "Israel, its destiny and Jesus' mission to reform Israel and instruct it in God's will is central to the Matthean narrative and to Matthew's world view."[31]

That Jesus teaches the righteousness of the Torah, through his authoritative interpretation of it, can hardly be questioned. The great difference is that this activity is, by comparison, distinctly subordinate to his main purpose. Preoccupation with the Torah, the identifying characteristic of Judaism, necessarily gives way to the proclamation of the kingdom, the sacrifice on the cross, and the creation of a new people of God, consisting now of Jews and Gentiles. To these last matters we now turn.

The Gentiles in Matthew

Those who regard Matthew's community as a sect within Judaism point to well-known passages in the Gospel where the Gentiles are excluded from the interest of both Jesus and the disciples. In 10:5–6, as Jesus sends out the disciples on their preaching ministry, he charges them with these words: "Go nowhere among the Gentiles, and enter no town of the Samaritans, but go rather to the lost sheep of the house of Israel." Similarly, in 15:24, Jesus' refusal to heal the daughter of the Canaanite woman is explained with the words "I was sent only to the lost sheep of the house of Israel." This restriction of concern to Israel is, however, clearly limited to a specific time frame: prior to the death and resurrection of Jesus. There are clear markers in Matthew that the proclamation of the gospel to the Gentiles was subsequently to take place. Thus in 24:14, Jesus says, "And this gospel of the kingdom will be preached throughout the whole world [*en holē tē oikoumenē*], as a testimony to all nations [*pasin tois ethnesin*]." And at the end of the Gospel, Jesus commands his disciples, "Go therefore and make disciples of all nations [*panta ta ethnē*]"

---

30. Saldarini, *Matthew's Christian-Jewish Community*, 163 (italics added). Saldarini knows that the goal of Jesus is "preeminently" his death (166), but in his portrayal of Jesus this seems subordinate to Jesus as a teacher and reformer of Judaism (see esp. 177–79).

31. Ibid., 83. It also can be misleading when Saldarini, speaking of Matthew, writes, "The author presents Jesus as an informed, observant Jew who protests certain practices and interpretations and proposes certain reforms of attitude and practice in order to promote greater fidelity to God and God's teaching in the Bible" (126).

(28:19). And they are to go, not circumcising converts into the community of Israel, but baptizing them into a new community "in the name of the Father and of the Son and of the Holy Spirit."

But why did Matthew bother to include the restrictive sayings at all, when by the time he wrote, the Gentile mission had long been flourishing and the restrictions were so obviously anachronistic? The reason is not simply that they were part of the tradition available to him, but rather that they made clear a point that was important to him and his Jewish Christian readers: Jesus brought the kingdom in the first place to Israel as a matter of covenant faithfulness. Israel thus still retained its priority in salvation history. Christianity was not to be thought of as a Gentile religion, nor was it in any sense disloyal to God's purposes for Israel; it was, instead, their fulfillment.

In addition to this striking material in Matthew that points exclusively to Israel, however, there is plenty of evidence that the Gentiles are part of the story too.[32] In the opening words of the Gospel, Jesus is introduced not only as the Son of David, with its nationalistic tonality, but also as the Son of Abraham, with its allusion to the Abrahamic covenant's promise of blessing to the nations. In the story of the visit of the magi in 2:1–12, the universal horizons of the story are also implied. More impressive along this line is the narrative concerning the Roman centurion in 8:5–13, in which Jesus remarks concerning this Gentile, "Truly, I say to you, not even in Israel have I found such faith" (cf. the acclamation of the faith of the Canaanite woman in 15:28), adding, "I tell you, many will come from east and west and sit at table with Abraham, Isaac, and Jacob in the kingdom of heaven" (8:10–11).

The formula quotation of Isa. 42:1–4, 9 in Matt. 12:18–21 contains the statement that the servant will "proclaim justice to the Gentiles," and Matthew prolongs the quotation in order to be able to include the final words "and in his name will the Gentiles hope." The parable of the vineyard concludes with the words "Therefore I tell you, the kingdom of God will be taken away from you and given to a nation producing the fruits of it" (21:43), referring to new tenants who will occupy the vineyard: the Gentiles. Likewise, the parable in 22:1–10 concludes with an implicit reference to the Gentiles in the words "The wedding is ready, but those invited were not worthy. Go therefore to the thoroughfares, and invite to the marriage feast as many as you find" (22:8–9). And at the death of Jesus it is the Gentile Roman guards who draw the correct conclusion concerning the identity of Jesus when they say, "Truly this was the Son of God" (27:54), thereby anticipating the effective evangelization of the Gentiles.

There are, of course, also negative references to the Gentiles in Matthew (e.g., 5:47; 6:7, 32; 18:17), as pointed out by David Sim.[33] But given the posi-

---

32. For a fuller treatment supporting the view argued here, see Donald Senior, "Between Two Worlds: Gentiles and Jewish Christians in Matthew's Gospel," *CBQ* 61 (1999): 1–23, esp. 14–16.

33. Sim, "Matthew and the Gentiles." Cf. idem, *Gospel of Matthew and Christian Judaism*, 215–56.

tive material about the Gentiles reviewed above, there is hardly any reason for taking these as indicative of an anti-Gentile bias in the Gospel,[34] as does Sim. They may be understood as relatively innocent data that simply reflect the traditional ways that Jesus and Jews, and indeed Christian Jews too, would customarily speak of pagan Gentiles.[35]

In light of the positive passages about the faith of Gentiles, it is also very difficult to agree with Sim's peculiar conclusion that Matthew's community was interested only in a Jewish mission and had no interest in evangelizing the Gentiles.[36] Not only does Jesus indicate the future mission to the Gentiles in 24:14, but also he commissions his disciples to make disciples of all nations in 28:19. Not to engage in the Gentile mission would, in effect, have made Matthew's community disobedient to the command of their Lord![37]

The Jews in Matthew

One of the well-known and striking characteristics of the very Jewish Gospel of Matthew is its apparent hostility toward the Jews. Some infamous passages immediately come to mind. First is the blistering tirade against the scribes and Pharisees in Matt. 23, where the repeated refrain "Woe to you, scribes and Pharisees, hypocrites" occurs six times. Throughout the Matthean narrative the Pharisees are referred to negatively (e.g., 3:7; 9:34; 22:15). According to 12:14, "The Pharisees went out and took counsel against him, how to destroy him" (cf. 12:24). The author makes a concerted effort to separate himself and his community from the (non-Christian) Jews. In 28:15, when he tells the story of the soldiers being bribed to report that the disciples stole the body of Jesus, he writes, "And this story has been spread among (the) Jews to this day." Similarly, he refers several times to "their synagogues" (4:23; 9:35; 10:17; 12:9; 13:54; cf. "your synagogues" in 23:34). There is also the horrific 27:25, where the Jewish crowd brashly assumes culpability for the death of Jesus: "His blood be upon us and on our children." All of this leads to a strong sense of the separation between Matthew's community and the Jewish synagogue and people.

34. A comparison of the two sets of passages indicates that the positive are of much more consequence for Matthew, while the negative are incidental to his perspective.

35. Senior refers to these statements as "stereotypical and stock judgments" ("Between Two Worlds," 11).

36. Sim, *Gospel of Matthew and Christian Judaism*, 236–47.

37. W. G. Thompson observes, Matthew's community "must, in a word, choose to become universalist rather than remain sectarian, since only in so doing would they become in fact the true Israel, by carrying out the mission of their risen Lord" (E. A. LaVerdiere and W. G. Thompson, "New Testament Communities in Transition: A Study of Matthew and Luke," *TS* 37 [1976]: 595). Except for his later dating of Matthew, Thompson's view is close to that argued in the present essay: "Matthew needed to show his community that they were no longer a sectarian group within Judaism but had become an independent movement separate from Jamnia Pharisaism and rooted in Jesus Christ" (576).

Furthermore, there are the well-known and remarkable statements about the rejection of the Jews. We have already noted the anticipation of the future Gentile mission in 8:10–11. But those verses are followed by these words in 8:12: "The sons of the kingdom will be thrown into the outer darkness; there they will weep and gnash their teeth." In the context, the "sons of the kingdom" are the Jews who, in contrast to the Gentiles, do not believe in Jesus or the gospel.

Perhaps the most dramatic text along this line is the parable of the rented vineyard (21:33–43). When the recalcitrant tenants of the vineyard—from the parallels to Isa. 5, clearly Israel—take the son (unmistakably Jesus as the Son of God), cast him out of the vineyard, and kill him, the listeners pronounce the right verdict: "He will put those wretches to a miserable death, and let out the vineyard to other tenants who will give him the fruits in their seasons" (21:41). This conclusion is reaffirmed by Jesus: "Therefore I tell you, the kingdom of God will be taken away from you and given to a nation producing the fruits of it" (21:43).

This parable is the second of three that proceed along a similar line. In the first, the parable of the two sons (21:28–32), Jesus concludes, "Truly I say to you, the tax collectors and the harlots go into the kingdom of God before you. For John came to you in the way of righteousness, and you did not believe him, but the tax collectors and the harlots believed him; and even when you saw it, you did not afterward repent and believe him" (21:31–32). In the third, the parable of the marriage feast (22:1–14), when those invited "would not come," the invitation is broadened: "The wedding is ready, but those invited were not worthy. Go therefore to the thoroughfares, and invite to the marriage feast as many as you find" (22:8–9). Here at the eschatological announcement of the kingdom, those initially invited, the unresponsive Jews, will give way to others, the Gentiles.

We should note that this traditional reading of the material surveyed in this section has been challenged in recent years by a number of scholars. Understandably, there is a growing desire to rid Matthew of its so-called anti-Judaism and hence of its anti-Semitic potential.[38] The common conclusion in this approach is that it is the Jewish leaders—the chief priests, the elders, the Sadducees, the scribes, and particularly the Pharisees—not the Jews as a people, who fall under Matthew's criticism. This is, of course, partially, even mainly, correct. The Jewish leaders obviously do bear a large responsibility. Nevertheless, such an explanation hardly works in every instance. The people

38. See J. D. G. Dunn, "The Question of Anti-semitism in the New Testament Writings of the Period," in *Jews and Christians: The Parting of the Ways, A.D. 70 to 135*, ed. J. D. G. Dunn, WUNT 66 (Tübingen: Mohr Siebeck, 1992; reprint, Grand Rapids: Eerdmans, 1999), 177–211, esp. 203–10; cf. idem, *The Partings of the Ways: Between Christianity and Judaism and Their Significance for the Character of Christianity* (London: SCM; Philadelphia: Trinity, 1991), 151–56.

as a whole[39]—that is, those who have rejected Jesus—and not just the leaders, are in view in important passages such as 8:12 ("the sons of the kingdom") and 27:25 ("all the people"), as well as in 28:15 (where Matthew distinguishes his community from "Jews").[40] Furthermore, although the parable of 21:33–43 is spoken to the chief priests and the Pharisees (21:45; cf. 21:23, where "elders" occurs rather than "Pharisees") and thus the kingdom obviously is taken away from them (21:43), the kingdom is given not to new leaders but to a new "nation" (*ethnos*). But where the kingdom is given to a new nation, the church, there are unmistakable implications for the nation of Israel.[41]

The Break with the Synagogue

A key question raised by the matters reviewed thus far is when the church broke away from the synagogue. Matthean scholarship traditionally has given much attention to Yavneh (Jamnia) in this connection. Yavneh, near Ashdod, is where Yoḥanan ben Zakkai and other Jewish leaders began to reconsolidate Judaism after the destruction of Jerusalem and the temple. It often has been argued that in the 80s at Yavneh an addition in the form of a curse upon the "heretics" (*minim*) was made to the synagogue liturgy for the purpose of driving Jewish believers in Jesus out of the synagogue.[42] Recent scholarship has emphasized, however, that we know very little for certain about activities of the academy of Yavneh.[43] It is not surprising that those in view here who

39. In his study of anti-Judaic aspects of the Passion Narrative in Matthew, Erwin Buck regards it as "clear that Matthew does not simply intend to shift the responsibility for the suffering of Jesus onto the Jewish leaders and away from the Jewish people. His focus on the elders as 'elders *of the people*' is calculated to draw the Jewish *people* into the limelight as well" ("Anti-Judaic Sentiments in the Passion Narrative according to Matthew," in *Anti-Judaism in Early Christianity*, vol. 1, *Paul and the Gospels,* ed. Peter Richardson with David Granskou [Waterloo, Ont.: Wilfrid Laurier University Press, 1986], 171).

40. Overman manages to turn this verse on its head, taking it to mean "This rumor has circulated among all of us [*Ioudaiois*] to this day" (*Church and Community in Crisis,* 401). More to the point is Peter J. Tomson, who concludes that this text contains "an unmistakably negative message" that "testifies to an estrangement from the Jews" (*"If This Be from Heaven . . ."*: *Jesus and the New Testament Authors in Their Relationship to Judaism,* The Biblical Seminar 76 [Sheffield: Sheffield Academic Press, 2001], 279).

41. See Scot McKnight, "A Loyal Critic: Matthew's Polemic with Judaism in Theological Perspective," in *Anti-Semitism and Early Christianity: Issues of Polemic and Faith,* ed. C. A. Evans and D. A. Hagner (Minneapolis: Fortress, 1993), 75. Tomson concludes, "We are thus left with the paradoxical conclusion that Matthew with its strong Jewish-Christian colouring simultaneously contains a turning towards the non-Jews with an anti-Jewish tenor" (*"If This Be from Heaven,"* 284). Tomson attributes this to a fourth and final layer of redaction produced by an unknown Gentile church (407).

42. Cf. Justin Martyr: "In your synagogues you curse all who have become Christians" (*Dial.* 96; cf. 16).

43. See J. P. Lewis, "Jamnia (Jabneh), Council of," *ABD* 3:634–37. Cf. Graham N. Stanton, *A Gospel for a New People: Studies in Matthew* (Edinburgh: Clark, 1992), 142–45.

maintain that Matthew's community was a sect within Judaism do not appeal to Yavneh to support their argument.[44]

Even if the so-called Benediction of the Heretics did come into being in the 80s, it probably was not of the determinative importance that often has been assigned to it. The inference sometimes has been drawn that up until the introduction of this liturgical element there was no Jewish hostility toward Jews who believed in Jesus, and that the latter were able to remain comfortably in the synagogue. This hardly seems to have been the case. Instead, evidence points to Jewish hostility against Jewish believers in Jesus practically from the beginning. This no doubt varied from place to place and time to time, but gradually increased over the years, coming to something of a head after the events of 70, and further escalating from that time.[45] Thus, William Horbury concludes that the benediction "was not decisive on its own for the separation of church and synagogue, but it gave solemn liturgical expression to a separation effected in the second half of the first century through the larger group of measures to which it belongs."[46]

If this is true, then we hardly need to date Matthew as later, after the Yavneh decision, as perhaps a majority of Matthean scholars do. Nothing about the tensions in the Gospel or about the developed state of Matthew's Christian perspective requires a date in the 80s. It should also be emphasized here that we have no hard evidence about when or to whom Matthew was written. We depend necessarily on conclusions that are merely inferential in nature. This bears repeating, especially given the unwarranted confidence of some in concluding that Matthew writes in response to developments at Yavneh.[47]

44. See Sim, *Gospel of Matthew and Christian Judaism,* 150–51.

45. For a fuller discussion, see D. A. Hagner, "The *Sitz im Leben* of the Gospel of Matthew," in Bauer and Powell, *Treasures New and Old,* 27–68, esp. 32–45.

46. Horbury, "The Benediction of the Minim and Early Jewish-Christian Controversy," *JTS* 33 (1982): 19–61. Likewise, R. Kimelman: "Thus *birkhat ha-minim* does not reflect a watershed in the history of the relationship between Jews and Christians in the first centuries of our era. . . . Apparently there never was a single edict which caused the so-called irreparable separation between Judaism and Christianity. The separation was rather the result of a long process dependent upon local situations" ("*Birkhat Ha-Minim* and the Lack of Evidence for an Anti-Christian Jewish Prayer in Late Antiquity," in *Jewish and Christian Self-Definition,* ed. E. P. Sanders et al., 3 vols. [Philadelphia: Fortress, 1980–82], 2:244).

47. Stanton makes the same point, though he still thinks the Yavneh connection is "a strong probability" (*Gospel for a New People,* 145). Early representatives of the view that Yavneh is the background against which to read Matthew are G. D. Kilpatrick, *The Origins of the Gospel of St. Matthew* (Oxford: Clarendon, 1946), and especially W. D. Davies, *The Setting of the Sermon on the Mount* (Cambridge: Cambridge University Press, 1966). Kilpatrick held to the curious conclusion that Matthew is a document "whose thought is of the same kind as that of the Talmud" (105). More convincing is Krister Stendahl's statement that in Matthew we encounter an "interest in ethics rather than *halakha*" (*The School of St. Matthew and Its Use of the Old Testament* [Philadelphia: Fortress, 1968], xiii. I owe this reference to Stanton, 121–22). Ulrich Luz rejects outright the notion that Matthew is a Christian answer to Yavneh (*Matthew: A Commentary,* vol. 1, *Matthew 1–7,* trans. Wilhelm C. Linss [Minneapolis: Augsburg, 1989], 88).

There is, therefore, no specific date to which we can appeal for the breaking away of Jewish-Christian groups from the synagogues, and for the movement of Matthew's community and the change of perspective from an intramural one to an extramural one. My argument is that for all its Jewishness, Matthew indicates in a variety of ways that its community of necessity has had to break with the synagogue. The new things that the community affirmed were so incompatible with Judaism's orientation that its members could not have remained within Judaism, even in its formative state with the wide tolerance of diversity. This does not mean, however, that they were no longer interested in the Jews, no longer interested in evangelizing them, or no longer interested in defending their perspective against Jewish criticisms of it. Nor does it mean that their Christian faith was not Jewish in character. Even after the break, Jewish Christians would have been concerned about what was happening in the synagogues and would almost of necessity have been in continuing dialogue with Jews.

Matthew's community is, in short, a new community. Implicitly it claims to be the new and true Israel. Saldarini's comment that Matthew "has no name for his group"[48] overlooks the actual constitution of this new group, called by Matthew (the only Gospel to do so) the *ekklēsia* in 16:18 (cf. 18:17). To be sure, this reflects the idea of the *qāhāl* as the "congregation of Israel" or "community of YHWH." But now we confront the establishment of a new community[49] of the Messiah: "*my* church," to be built upon the rock of Peter and the other disciples by implication. Benno Przybylski puts it vividly: "It is clear that the relationship between the synagogue and the church is one of opposition. Christians do not belong to the synagogue but to the church. The schism between members of the synagogue and church is complete in the Matthean community."[50] It is indeed the sheer extent of the newness one encounters in Matthew that seems to prohibit the conclusion that Matthew's community be considered as a sect *within* Judaism. We have already encountered examples of that newness, but now we turn to look at that newness more systematically.

Newness in Matthew

Certainly one of the most remarkable things about the Gospel of Matthew—indeed, it is what gives rise to the question addressed in this

---

48. Saldarini, "Matthew and Jewish-Christian Conflict," 41–42.

49. See the discussion of this point in G. Stanton, "Revisiting Matthew's Communities," in *SBLSP* 33 (1994): 16–18.

50. Benno Przybylski, "The Setting of Matthean Anti-Judaism," in Richardson and Granskou, *Paul and the Gospels,* 195. Cf. Gundry: "So we have not just a reforming sect within the people of God, Israel . . . but a distinctly new people whose church-assembly differs from the synagogue-gatherings of Jews" ("Social History of the Matthean Community," 64).

essay—is the unusual combination of old and new. In a striking verse that many have taken to be Matthew's self-description, Jesus, at the end of the parable discourse, says, "Therefore every scribe who has been trained for the kingdom of heaven is like a householder who brings out of his treasure box new things [*kaina*] and old things [*palaia*]" (13:52).[51] Because of their importance, the evangelist first mentions the "new things," and only then the "old things." By the latter the evangelist must have in mind the Torah and the prophets, as well as the promises to, and thus the hope of, Israel. The old things speak of continuity—the very things that are stressed by the advocates of the idea that Matthew's community is a sect within Judaism. The new things, however, speak of discontinuity—matters that should not be underestimated.

What are the new things that Matthew may have in mind? I have already referred to much of this material, so here I can be relatively brief. Perhaps the most overwhelmingly new thing is the assertion that the expected messiah and the kingdom of God had come, and thus that the Scriptures had been fulfilled. "Truly, I say to you, many prophets and righteous people longed to see what you see, and did not see it, and to hear what you hear, and did not hear it" (13:17). The time of fulfillment has come; the eschatological age itself has begun. It is not merely that the kingdom has "drawn near [*ēngiken*]" (3:2; 4:17; 10:7), for Jesus says, "If I cast out demons through the Spirit of God, then the kingdom of God has come [*ephthasen*] upon you" (12:28). But the kingdom has come without overwhelming the present order. It is present in the form of a mystery yet to be made plain to all, like an apparently insignificant mustard seed, unseen leaven in dough, hidden treasure, or a small pearl worth all (13:31–33, 44–46). Surprisingly, despite the coming of the kingdom, the judgment of the wicked is delayed until some future time (13:24–30, 36–43, 47–50). Thus, the present evil age strangely coexists with the presence of the eschatological kingdom.

Certainly of greatest importance among the new things that this evangelist concerns himself with is the exalted character of the person of Jesus. God's Messiah, as we have seen, is not merely an anointed human being, however special. In Matthew's Christology, Jesus uniquely is "God with us," one who manifests deity, without compromising Matthew's monotheism. With this high Christology, again as we have seen, comes a new discipleship, oriented to Jesus and his teaching rather than to the Torah. This is above all the astounding new fact that requires a radical transformation of perspective and priorities. There is, furthermore, the radical and perfectionist character of the righteousness to which Jesus calls his disciples, something that is inseparable from the announcement of the gift and grace of the kingdom.

---

51. For a fuller discussion, see D. A. Hagner, "New Things from the Scribe's Treasure Box (Matt. 13:52)," *ExpTim* 109 (1998): 329–34, upon which this section is largely dependent.

That Matthew's Messiah must die as a sacrifice to make atonement for sins (1:21; 20:28) is both new and scandalous to the Jewish perspective, as the initial reactions of the disciples and Paul make clear. The death of the Messiah is, for Matthew, fulfillment of Scripture and the will of God (26:31, 39, 42, 54, 56). Matthew's account of the Last Supper has Jesus refer to the cup as containing "my blood of the covenant, which is poured out for many for the forgiveness of sins" (26:28). Matthew here follows Mark closely but does not have the word "new" before "covenant."[52] Nevertheless, that this is the blood of a new sacrifice readily suggests a new covenant that consummates earlier ones as well as simultaneously renders obsolete the temple and its sacrifices (the end of which Jesus prophesies in 24:2, 15). Such a conclusion is further reinforced by the reality of the new community established by Jesus, the *ekklēsia*.

The church—the community centered upon Jesus, his death and resurrection—is the community of fulfillment that formally stands in the place of Judaism. It is, in effect, the new, true Israel, in which the Gentiles too will find their rightful place. The Jews, of course, are still very much in the picture, but now by taking their place along with the Gentiles in a new entity that transcends Israel, the new reality of the church. In this way, Israel's servant role as a light to the nations finds its fulfillment.

Matthew has addressed the issue of old and new in the metaphors of an unshrunk patch of cloth used to repair an old garment and of new wine and old wineskins (9:16–17). The question concerns the incompatibility of the new and the old. One cannot simply append the new to the old. Christianity is not simply the addition of something new to Judaism. Its newness is too great for that. Old wineskins cannot contain new wine; new wine requires new wineskins. The new reality of the kingdom, with all the newness that it entails, cannot leave things as they were, or only slightly altered. At the end of this passage Matthew adds a few words to the material derived from his Markan source that reflect Matthew's unique perspective on these matters. One must put new wine into new wineskins. But only Matthew adds the words "and so both are preserved" (9:17). What has come is definitely new, but at the same time, in a sense the old is preserved as well—granted, not in the form of the old skins, but in the form of new skins. If we take the new wine as being the proclamation of the gospel of the kingdom by Jesus, then the old skins may stand for the formal elements of Judaism, while the new skins may reflect the new forms coming into existence in the church. The point seems to be that the righteousness of the Torah is preserved by the gospel—now, however, not in the form of Torah-obedience, but rather in the form of obedience to the teaching of Jesus, which Matthew, as we have seen, regards as the true interpretation of Torah. In this novel way both gospel and law are preserved. The

---

52. Although the majority of late MSS (but also A, C, D) do have *kainēs*, "new," probably by harmonization with Luke 22:20, the word is lacking in the earliest and best MSS (e.g., 𝔓37, ℵ, B).

new is analogous to, and takes up the righteousness of, Torah, albeit in a new and revolutionary way.

Conclusion

The Gospel of Matthew is, undoubtedly, an exceptionally Jewish document. Overman, Saldarini, and Sim have effectively brought us a new appreciation of this fact. Sim, however, like Saldarini and Overman, overstates the case when he says, "The religion of the Matthean community was not Christianity but Judaism."[53] The appeal to Matt. 5:17–20 and the exclusivist sayings will not bear the weight of the hypothesis.

There is plenty of continuity with Judaism in Matthew, but that does not mean that Matthew's community is properly regarded as a Jewish sect. As I have tried to show, there is far too much newness in Matthew to sustain such a conclusion. The differences are far too significant to be described as mere "deviance" from other Jewish groups. To my mind, Overman, Saldarini, and Sim seriously underestimate the degree, character, and significance of the newness. Matthew reflects a new community with a new focus of a revolutionary kind that puts it in strong contrast with all other contemporary Jewish communities. This conclusion, as we have seen, rests not on any single item, but rather upon a cumulative argument. An eschatological turning point has been reached, and this involves a radical reorientation of previous perspectives. I hasten to add that in no way does a recognition of this provide the slightest justification for anti-Semitism.

Of course, Matthew would not have thought of Christianity as a new religion. Such a conclusion would be anathema to any Jewish Christian, including Paul. For Matthew, Jewish Christianity is the perfection and fulfillment of Judaism. It is important to note that a thoroughly Jewish Christianity is still Christianity and not Judaism. Matthew's community—so too Paul!—regarded itself as being in its own way faithful to the Mosaic law, as it followed the teaching of Jesus. And it is, of course, true that these Christians never stopped thinking of themselves as Jews.

Matthew, in short, represents not Judaism without Christianity, nor Christianity without Judaism, nor an indiscriminate blend of the two. Because of the "new things" affirmed by Matthew's community, it is best described not as a Christian form of Judaism, but as a Jewish form of Christianity. Matthew's full Jewishness need not be taken as indicating a non-Christian community. As G. D. Kilpatrick astutely observed many years ago, "The fact that Mat-

---

53. Sim, *Gospel of Matthew and Christian Judaism,* 163. He adds, "To suggest otherwise and place Matthew in the same category as Paul and the Hellenists involves a complete misrepresentation of the evangelist's position." Why the admission that Matthew's community was genuinely Christian must place Matthew with Paul and the Hellenists is unclear to me.

thew is the New Testament book closest to Rabbinical Judaism . . . *does not weaken its Christian character.*"[54] There is no reason why the full Jewishness of the Gospel of Matthew cannot be given its due emphasis without denying the fully Christian identity of its community.

54. Kilpatrick, *Origins of the Gospel,* 101 (italics added).

15

Paul

Life and Letters

Bruce N. Fisk

It would be difficult to decide whether the apostle Paul was less or more contro-versial in his day than in our own. It might be a tie. As in the first century, so in the twenty-first, Paul still draws admirers and raises hackles; he musters respect and garners ridicule; he fosters community and provokes dissent. The quest for the historical Paul has never been more vigorous, more variegated, nor, arguably, more bewildering. This report on the current state of that quest proceeds along the following lines: (1) the struggle to establish a Pauline corpus; (2) develop-ment and contingency in Paul's thought; (3) Paul and politics; (4) the Paul of Acts and the Paul of Paul; (5) Paul's Jewish and Hellenistic cultural contexts; (6) Paul's knowledge of Jesus; (7) Pauline communities and contemporary models; (8) Paul's letters and their first recipients.

Border Skirmish: The Struggle to Establish a Pauline Corpus

It has become customary to distinguish three tiers within the Pauline corpus:

- *Undisputed:* Romans, 1 and 2 Corinthians, Galatians, Philippians, 1 Thes-salonians, Philemon

- *Deutero-Pauline:* Ephesians, Colossians, 2 Thessalonians
- *Pseudonymous:* 1 and 2 Timothy, Titus

Because of their remarkable affinity in vocabulary, syntax, and content, the authenticity of the "undisputed" letters is seldom challenged.[1] Likewise, the non-Pauline authorship of the remainder is taken by many to be an assured result of modern scholarship.[2] Has the church too hastily attributed to Paul the work of his earliest interpreters? Has the academy too eagerly demoted to secondary status letters that genuinely derive from the apostle himself? Might some letters represent the work of a Pauline disciple or "school"? Should we seek to distinguish historical Paul from canonical Paul? We begin with the debate concerning the authorship of Ephesians and Colossians, followed by a more sustained discussion of the Pastorals.[3]

1. Scholars prepared to dispute the "undisputed" letters, either by positing substantial interpolations or wholesale post-Pauline redaction, include W. Schmithals, *Die Briefe des Paulus in ihrer ursprünglichen Form* (Zürich: Theologischer Verlag, 1984); L. E. Keck, *Paul and His Letters* (Philadelphia: Fortress, 1988), 16–19; D. J. Doughty, "Pauline Paradigms and Pauline Authenticity," *JHC* 1 (1994): 95–128. But theories of post-Pauline redaction have failed to win widespread approval, except perhaps in the case of 2 Corinthians, which often is taken to be a composite of at least two distinct letters. In the absence of explicit testimony or manuscript evidence, all such partition and redaction theories must bear the burden of proof. An even more radical approach—one that disputes Pauline authorship across the board (and sometimes even Paul's historical existence)—was championed by nineteenth-century Dutch Radical Critics, under the influence of Bruno Bauer (1809–82), whose work has been getting a new lease on life through the *Journal of Higher Criticism.*

2. Witness the conclusions drawn by various contributors to the *Anchor Bible Dictionary,* ed. D. N. Freedman, 6 vols. (New York: Doubleday, 1992), one of the better cross-sections of critical biblical scholarship currently available (see, e.g., V. P. Furnish on Colossians and Ephesians, H. D. Betz on Paul, and J. H. Charlesworth on pseudonymity). Research into the phenomenon of pseudonymity has broadened in recent years. Among the more important studies of Jewish and Greek pseudonymity are W. Speyer, *Die literarische Fälschung im heidnischen und christlichen Altertum,* Handbuch der Altertumswissenschaft 1.2 (Munich: Beck, 1971); D. G. Meade, *Pseudonymity and Canon: An Investigation into the Relationship of Authorship and Authority in Jewish and Earliest Christian Tradition,* WUNT 39 (Tübingen: Mohr Siebeck, 1986); L. S. Donelson, *Pseudepigraphy and Ethical Argument in the Pastoral Epistles,* HUT 22 (Tübingen: Mohr Siebeck, 1986), 7–66; N. Brox, ed., *Pseudepigraphie in der heidnischen und jüdisch-christlichen Antike,* Wege der Forschung 484 (Darmstadt: Wissenschaftliche Buchgesellschaft, 1977); N. Brox, *Falsche Verfasserangaben: Zur Erklärung der frühchristlichen Pseudepigraphie,* SBS 79 (Stuttgart: Katholisches Bibelwerk, 1975); B. M. Metzger, "Literary Forgeries and Canonical Pseudepigrapha," *JBL* 91 (1972): 1–24; K. Aland, "The Problem of Anonymity and Pseudonymity in Christian Literature of the First Two Centuries," *JTS* 12 (1961): 39–49.

3. The authorship of 2 Thessalonians was disputed already in 1801 (by J. E. C. Schmidt), in 1839 (by F. H. Kern), in 1845 and 1855 (by F. C. Baur), and, most notably, in 1903 (by W. Wrede). More recently, W. Trilling, *Untersuchungen zum zweiten Thessalonicherbrief,* ETS 27 (Leipzig: St. Benno, 1972), further challenged the letter's authenticity, as have published dissertations by G. S. Holland, *The Tradition That You Received from Us: 2 Thessalonians in the Pauline Tradition,* HUT 24 (Tübingen: Mohr Siebeck, 1988), and F. W. Hughes, *Early Christian Rhetoric and 2 Thessalonians,* JSNTSup 30 (Sheffield: JSOT, 1989). For a concise defense of the

Ephesians and Colossians

It was primarily the weight of F. C. Baur's influence, extending long past his death in 1860, that unsettled scholarly confidence in the Pauline authorship of Ephesians. That Ephesians employed gnostic terms and ideas was patently clear to Baur, whose creative analysis persuaded R. Bultmann, E. Käsemann, H. Conzelmann, and others. More recently, however, the argument for a fully developed gnostic background for Ephesians has fallen on hard times, and the authorship debate has taken turns decidedly literary and theological. The argument from literary style draws attention to pleonastic elements (e.g., prepositions, participles), the use of the genitive, the length of many sentences, and the letter's elevated diction, particularly in the first three chapters. Do these distinctive features point away from Paul, or can they be explained by appealing to a circular-letter hypothesis (which might call for variations in style) or to the letter's epideictic rhetorical mode? The argument from theology identifies central themes in Ephesians—specifically its cosmic Christology (e.g., 1:3–4, 9–10, 20–23; 2:6; 4:8–10), realized eschatology (e.g., 1:3, 20–22; 2:2–8; 6:17), and developed ecclesiology (e.g., 1:23; 2:19–22; 4:16; 5:23)—themes that arguably represent not merely a natural development of, but rather a notable departure from, the theology of Paul as it is reflected in the seven undisputed letters.[4] In light of all this, and in the face of so many parallels—verbal, structural, and thematic—between Ephesians and Colossians, a strong case can be made that the author of Ephesians was interpreting and updating Paul's gospel, creating what A. T. Lincoln has called an "actualization of authoritative tradition."[5] There are, of course, other ways to explain the differences between Ephesians and the undisputed letters. Perhaps it is enough to say that the letter reflects the apostle's own thoughts, albeit distilled and aged during the years of Paul's Gentile mission. For G. B. Caird, followed by F. F. Bruce, if the epistle is not by Paul, it remains "a mas-

letter's pseudonymity, based largely upon its eschatology, see B. D. Ehrman, *The New Testament: A Historical Introduction to the Early Christian Writings* (New York: Oxford University Press, 1997), 344–46. In support of Pauline authorship, I. H. Marshall's slim commentary, published in 1983 (*1 and 2 Thessalonians*, NCB [Grand Rapids: Eerdmans], 28–45), offers point-for-point responses to Trilling. Today, some scholars (e.g., H. C. Kee, *Understanding the New Testament*, 5th ed. [Englewood Cliffs, N.J.: Prentice-Hall, 1993], 224) find the evidence to be "ambiguous," though many others (e.g., J. D. G. Dunn, *The Theology of Paul the Apostle* [Grand Rapids: Eerdmans, 1998], 13, 298) still count the letter among the Paulines.

4. See, for example, J. C. Beker, *Paul the Apostle: The Triumph of God in Life and Thought* (Philadelphia: Fortress, 1980), 163, on the apparent collapse of the apocalyptic future in Colossians and Ephesians.

5. A. T. Lincoln, *Ephesians*, WBC 42 (Waco, Tex.: Word, 1990), lviii. For a convenient summary of scholarship in support of Ephesian dependence upon Colossians, see V. P. Furnish, "Ephesians, Epistle to the," *ABD* 2:536–37. The view that Colossians borrows from Ephesians, defended by E. T. Mayerhoff (1838) and J. Coutts (1958), is now all but extinct.

terly summary of Paul's theology by a disciple who was capable of thinking Paul's thoughts after him."[6]

Challenges to Pauline authorship of Colossians have tended, in recent years,[7] to focus on five points: the letter's distinctive language and style, certain theological idiosyncrasies,[8] the letter's portrait of Paul, affinities between Colossians and Philemon,[9] and, more generally, the widespread phenomenon of pseudonymity.[10] A majority of scholars, perhaps 60 percent,[11] now treat

6. G. B. Caird, *The Apostolic Age* (London: 1955), 133, cited in F. F. Bruce, *Paul: Apostle of the Heart Set Free* (Grand Rapids: Eerdmans, 1977), 424. Bruce's title for his chapter on Ephesians is telling: "The Quintessence of Paulinism." Similarly, L. T. Johnson, *The Writings of the New Testament: An Interpretation* (Philadelphia: Fortress, 1986), 372: "If not written by Paul or under his direct supervision, Ephesians is the work of Paul's best disciple, one whose religious perceptions and theological vision are not inferior to Paul's own. In Ephesians we find a masterly statement on the work of God in the world and church, expressed not by the passion of polemic or the logic of argumentation but by prayerful meditation." More speculatively, D. Trobisch, *Paul's Letter Collection: Tracing the Origins* (Minneapolis: Fortress, 1994), 53 (cf. 54 n. 22), puts forth the bold thesis that Ephesians represents "the beginning of an appendix" to Paul's own collection of the *Hauptbriefe*.

7. Already in 1838, E. T. Mayerhoff had weighed in against the Pauline authorship of Colossians, maintaining that the letter was dependent upon Ephesians, contained sub-Pauline ideas, and reflected the second-century campaign against gnosticism. J. B. Polhill, "The Relationship between Ephesians and Colossians," *RevExp* 70 (1973): 439–50, chronicles the debate over the relationship between Colossians and Ephesians up until 1970. For more recent discussion, see the summary by R. F. Collins, *Letters That Paul Did Not Write* (Wilmington, Del.: Glazier, 1988).

8. For example, the emphasis upon forgiveness of sins (1:13–14; 2:13; 3:13), realized eschatology (1:5, 23, 27; 2:12–13; 3:1), and Christ's headship over the church and even the cosmos (1:18; 2:10, 19). On theological "inconsistency" in Colossians, see E. Lohse, "Pauline Theology in the Letter to the Colossians," *NTS* 15 (1969): 211–20. See also below, n. 42.

9. This sort of evidence is hardly conclusive. Did a later author strive to lend Colossians a Pauline aura, or are these parallels clear signs of authenticity? As Bo Reicke (*Re-examining Paul's Letters: The History of the Pauline Correspondence*, ed. D. P. Moessner and I. Reicke [Harrisburg, Pa.: Trinity, 2001], 75) points out, the latter seems more plausible: "It is highly improbable that a so-called deutero-Paulinist would have taken the names from a private note to Philemon and used them to secure historical credibility for a later composition that was meant to impress Christians in Phrygia."

10. R. E. Brown (*An Introduction to the New Testament* [New York: Doubleday, 1997], 610) envisions two subtypes of pseudonymity: (1) texts written during Paul's lifetime, or soon after his death, by someone passing on what Paul himself wanted to say; and (2) texts written several decades later by someone writing in Paul's name, addressing a situation that had not arisen during Paul's life. On the first scenario, if Paul himself did not write Colossians, its writer may have been Timothy, who was "designated as a co-sender" who could "speak authoritatively for Paul" (615). On this view, Timothy would be more like a scribe, and it might then be unhelpful to call Colossians pseudonymous. For a list of seven subtypes of pseudonymity, see J. H. Charlesworth, "Pseudonymity and Pseudepigraphy," *ABD* 5:540–41.

11. According to R. E. Brown. Representatives would include E. Lohse (*Colossians and Philemon*, Hermeneia [Philadelphia: Fortress, 1971]); E. Schweizer (*The Letter to the Colossians: A Commentary* [Minneapolis: Augsburg, 1982; in German, EKKNT 12, 1976]); J. Gnilka (*Der Kolosserbrief*, HTKNT 10 [Freiburg: Herder, 1980]); N. Perrin and D. C. Duling (*The New Testament: An Introduction*, 2nd ed. [San Diego: Harcourt Brace Jovanovich, 1982]). E. P. Sanders's challenge to Pauline authorship, "Literary Dependence in Colossians," *JBL* 85 (1996): 28–45,

Colossians as deutero-Pauline, although a vocal minority continue to defend the traditional view.[12] Whether or not Tychicus (Col. 4:7) enjoyed sufficient editorial license to account for the numerous stylistic differences[13] will, no doubt, continue to be a matter of speculation.

The Pastoral Epistles

Debate about the authenticity of the Pastorals[14] goes back at least to F. Schleiermacher (1807) and F. C. Baur (1835). Within contemporary biblical scholarship, the weight of the majority counts heavily against Pauline authorship. The following talking points surface with regularity:

- *Language and Style:* The proportion of words rare or unique in the established Pauline corpus is high; certain stylistic and rhetorical features set the Pastorals apart from the undisputed letters.[15] Would a single author,

---

was based upon similarities between Colossians and 1 Thessalonians, 1 Corinthians, and Philippians. R. Collins (*Letters That Paul Did Not Write,* 206) sees the writer idealizing Paul as saint and martyr. R. E. Brown himself (*Introduction to the New Testament,* 614–17) tentatively posits the existence of an active Pauline school in Ephesus in the 80s.

12. See, for example, P. T. O'Brien, *Colossians, Philemon,* WBC 44 (Waco, Tex.: Word, 1982), xli–xlix; and W. G. Kümmel, *Introduction to the New Testament,* trans. H. C. Kee, rev. ed. (Nashville: Abingdon, 1975), 340–46. L. Johnson (*The Writings of the New Testament,* 357–59) finds no substantial difference between the eschatology of Col. 2:12–13; 3:1 and Rom. 6:1–14. D. A. Carson, D. J. Moo, and L. Morris (*An Introduction to the New Testament* [Grand Rapids: Zondervan, 1992], 331–34) can imagine Paul to have been more than capable of adopting new vocabulary and concepts in response to a new situation. For Bo Reicke (*Re-examining Paul's Letters,* 76–78), Pauline authorship is virtually assured, as the earthquake of 61 C.E. that leveled Laodicea (Tacitus, *Ann.* 14.27.1), and probably also Colossae, makes a post-70 pseudepigraph highly unlikely.

13. So, tentatively, B. Witherington III, *The Paul Quest: The Renewed Search for the Jew of Tarsus* (Downers Grove, Ill.: InterVarsity, 1998), 110.

14. Lexical and stylistic similarities among these three epistles have led most scholars to treat them as a unit, though recently several scholars have shown the value of examining evidence from a single letter on its own terms. D. A. Hagner, for example, in "Titus as a Pauline Letter," *SBLSP* 37, part 2 (1998): 546–58, assesses the evidence for the Pauline authorship of Titus independently of the other two. Hagner finds that Paul could have readily written "a different kind of letter when new circumstances required it of him" (549), and that an amanuensis such as Luke or Tychichus would explain "some of the more Greco-Roman aspects of the letter" (556). More commonly, however, the Pastoral Epistle whose style and substance is said to resemble most closely the authentic Paulines is 2 Timothy. See, for example, Johnson, *Writings of the New Testament,* 381–89; J. Murphy-O'Connor, *Paul: A Critical Life* (Oxford: Oxford University Press, 1996), 356–59; G. D. Fee, "Toward a Theology of 2 Timothy—from a Pauline Perspective," *SBLSP* 36 (1997): 732–49. On the pitfalls of treating the three Pastorals as a group in isolation from the other epistles, see Carson, Moo, and Morris, *Introduction to the New Testament,* 359–60.

15. To cite a single example, observe their shared use of the otherwise non-Pauline expression "a faithful saying" (1 Tim. 1:15; 4:9; 2 Tim. 2:11; Titus 3:8). For a review of the data, see K. J. Neumann, *The Authenticity of the Pauline Epistles in the Light of Stylostatistical Analysis,*

over time, alter his vocabulary and style so dramatically? And how much freedom can Paul give a secretary before Pauline authorship becomes mere apostolic blessing?

- *Church Order:* The church hierarchy presupposed in the Pastorals seems more elaborate than what is found in the Pauline churches; a charismatic community has evolved into the household of God; egalitarianism apparently has given way to episcopal hierarchy. Complicating matters, however, is the fact that the three Pastorals are not uniformly concerned with matters of church order. Nor do all scholars agree that corresponding references in the undisputed letters describe a state of affairs that is qualitatively different.[16]
- *Recipients:* Close associates of Paul, such as Timothy and Titus, would not need many of the instructions that the Pastorals contain. Do these epistles indirectly target entire congregations?[17] Might the author have employed the names "Timothy" and "Titus" to represent the actual recipients: church leaders of a later generation?[18]
- *Opponents:* The Pastorals appear to address a post-Pauline form of Christian gnosticism or asceticism (1 Tim. 4:3, 8; 6:20; 2 Tim. 2:17–18). How do the false teachers portrayed in the Pastorals compare with those described in Galatians, Colossians, and the Corinthian correspondence?[19]
- *Historical Setting:* Historical and geographical details in the Pastorals (esp. 2 Tim. 4:9–21) do not fit easily into the career of Paul outlined in Acts and implied by the other epistles. Was Paul released from the imprisonment described in Acts 28, after which he traveled and wrote before being rearrested and executed (cf. *1 Clem.* 5:7)?[20] Is the chronology set out by

SBLDS 120 (Atlanta: Scholars Press, 1990); D. Guthrie, *The Pastoral Epistles*, 2nd ed., TNTC (Leicester: Inter-Varsity, 1990), 224–40.

16. See, for example, Johnson, *Writings of the New Testament*, 385–86; S. E. Porter, "Pauline Authorship and the Pastoral Epistles: Implications for Canon," *BBR* 5 (1995): 110–11.

17. According to J. T. Reed ("'To Timothy or Not': A Discourse Analysis of 1 Timothy," in S. E. Porter and D. A. Carson, eds., *Biblical Greek Language and Linguistics: Open Questions in Current Research*, JSNTSup 80 [Sheffield: Sheffield Academic Press, 1993], 90–118), however, the rhetorical focus of 1 Timothy is indeed on Timothy himself.

18. See Meade, *Pseudonymity and Canon,* 127–30, on the "double pseudonymity" (i.e., both author and recipient) of the Pastorals.

19. See P. H. Towner, "Gnosis and Realized Eschatology in Ephesus (of the Pastoral Epistles) and the Corinthian Enthusiasm," *JSNT* 31 (1987): 95–124; *The Goal of Our Instruction: The Structure of Theology and Ethics in the Pastorals,* JSNTSup 34 (Sheffield: Sheffield Academic Press, 1989), 9–45. The notion of "over-realized eschatology" in Corinth, however, on which aspects of Towner's model depend heavily, has recently been shown to be problematic. See, for example, B. W. Winter, *After Paul Left Corinth: The Influence of Secular Ethics and Social Change* (Grand Rapids: Eerdmans, 2001), 25–26; R. B. Hays, "The Conversion of the Imagination: Scripture and Eschatology in 1 Corinthians," *NTS* 45 (1999): 391–412, 396–97, 399, 407–9.

20. So, for example, E. E. Ellis, "Pastoral Letters" in *Dictionary of Paul and His Letters,* ed. G. F. Hawthorne, R. P. Martin, and D. G. Reid (Downers Grove, Ill.: InterVarsity, 1993), 661;

Acts and the other epistles simply too fragmentary to warrant excluding the Pastorals as an additional source for Paul's life?[21]

- *Picture of Paul:* The Pastorals portray Paul as the soon-to-be martyred saint, as a legendary but lonely hero, as the guardian of the truth.[22] Is this portrait of Paul incompatible with the composite sketch we find in the undisputed epistles? And what of the uncomplimentary elements of the portrait (e.g., 1 Tim. 1:15)? Are personal details evidence of authenticity, or are they telltale signs of pseudonymity?[23]

Although this evidence is less than "overwhelming,"[24] many have found it persuasive, including now senior British evangelical I. Howard Marshall,[25] for whom the cumulative effect of these sorts of arguments casts "very strong doubts on the traditional evangelical defense of direct Pauline authorship."[26] If Marshall is right, and strong doubts are in order, at least three alternative proposals have a measure of plausibility:

1. *Delegate:* Paul empowered a secretary or delegate to write on his behalf and during his lifetime.[27]

R. H. Gundry, *A Survey of the New Testament,* 3rd ed. (Grand Rapids: Zondervan, 1994), 412–13. It must be admitted, however, that the two-imprisonment hypothesis, however plausible, is also fragile. Not only the external testimony (e.g., *1 Clem.* 5:1–7; *Acts Pet.* 1–3, 40; Muratorian Canon), but also various clues within the NT (e.g., Phil. 1:19, 25; 2:24; Rom. 15:24, 28; Acts 1:8; 13:47; 28:30–31) are less than decisive. See the cautious assessment of the evidence by Bruce, *Paul: Apostle of the Heart Set Free,* 441–55.

21. So, Porter, "Pauline Authorship," 107–8; tentatively, Johnson, *The Writings of the New Testament,* 383.

22. Note especially S. G. Wilson (*Luke and the Pastoral Epistles* [London: SPCK, 1979], 107–24), who finds this portrait of Paul to correspond closely, in many respects, to what we find in Acts.

23. The first view is widespread among defenders of authenticity. For the second alternative, see F. Young, *The Theology of the Pastoral Letters* (Cambridge: Cambridge University Press, 1994); J.-D. Kaestli, "Luke-Acts and the Pastoral Epistles: The Thesis of a Common Authorship," in *Luke's Literary Achievement: Collected Essays,* ed. C. M. Tuckett, JSNTSup 116 (Sheffield: Sheffield Academic Press, 1995), 110–26, 115–16. For Meade (*Pseudonymity and Canon,* 122–23), the emphasis placed on Paul's apostolic authority, along with a parallel emphasis upon tradition, "provides the hermeneutical key for the pseudepigraphal techniques used."

24. Contra S. L. Harris, *The New Testament: A Student's Introduction,* 4th ed. (Boston: McGraw-Hill, 2002), 366.

25. Marshall recently coauthored a major critical commentary on the Pastorals: I. H. Marshall and P. H. Towner, *A Critical and Exegetical Commentary on the Pastoral Epistles,* ICC (Edinburgh: Clark, 1999).

26. I. H. Marshall, "Prospects for the Pastoral Epistles," in *Doing Theology for the People of God,* ed. D. Lewis and A. McGrath (Downers Grove, Ill.: InterVarsity, 1996), 137–55. There follows, for Marshall, an important corollary: some evangelical scholars may be "defending the impossible."

27. The most commonly proposed candidate for the job is Luke. See, for example, A. Feuillet, "La doctrine des Epîtres Pastorales et leurs affinités avec l'œuvre lucanienne," *RThom* 78 (1978):

2. *Fragments:* Genuine Pauline fragments have been edited after Paul's death into a series of quasi-Pauline epistles. Authentic fragments could include 2 Tim. 1:16–18; 3:10–11; 4:1–2a, 5b–22; Titus 3:12–15.[28]

3. *Pseudonymity:* The letters were written by an unknown author or school[29] not long after Paul's death, in order to preserve and interpret, or perhaps to domesticate, Paul's teachings for a new context.[30] On this view, Pauline attribution should be understood as the author's claim to be faithfully preserving Pauline tradition.

Not surprisingly, a number of Marshall's fellow evangelicals would demur. For Earle Ellis, "The role of the secretary . . . and the use of preformed traditions . . . in the composition of the Pastorals cut the ground from under the pseudepigraphal hypothesis with its mistaken nineteenth-century assumptions about the nature of authorship."[31] More restrained are D. A. Carson, D. J. Moo, and L. Morris: "The difficulty is not the idea of pseudonymity but the lack of *evidence* that the New Testament Christians gave any countenance to the idea."[32]

181–225; more tentatively, Ben Witherington III, who is open to the idea that Luke penned the Pastorals "in his own style and on Paul's behalf" near the end of, or very shortly after, Paul's life (*The Paul Quest,* 112, cf. 10). This view is not to be confused with the third view, which posits pseudonymous authorship, perhaps by Luke, some time after Paul's death. On this distinction, see J.-D. Kaestli, "Luke-Acts and the Pastoral Epistles," 112–13.

28. The fragmentary hypothesis was developed in detail by P. N. Harrison, *The Problem of the Pastorals* (London: Oxford University Press, 1921), and modified in *Paulines and Pastorals* (London: Villiers, 1964), 106–28; similarly, A. T. Hanson, *The Pastoral Letters,* CBC (New York: Cambridge University, 1966), though retracted in *The Pastoral Epistles,* NCB (Grand Rapids: Eerdmans, 1982), 5–11. More recently, J. D. Miller (*The Pastoral Letters as Composite Documents,* SNTMS 93 [Cambridge: Cambridge University Press, 1997]) argues that a Pauline school used fragments of authentic tradition. The failure of this theory to garner broader support is no doubt related to the absence of incontrovertible evidence—whether textual or redactional—in the letters themselves.

29. The evidence does not allow us confidently to identify their author(s). The case for Lukan authorship of the Pastorals, as made by Wilson, *Luke and the Pastoral Epistles,* is surprisingly strong but certainly not airtight, as Kaestli, "Luke-Acts and the Pastoral Epistles," has shown. The parallels to Luke are not, finally, more substantial than those to the undisputed Paulines. Kaestli's own view, that Luke-Acts may have influenced the composition of the Pastorals, merits careful scrutiny.

30. Marshall's own proposal, which has much to commend it, belongs here, although he rejects the designation "pseudonymity" (which he takes to imply deception): "We can thus propose a general scenario in which the tendencies that can be detected in Paul's lifetime and especially toward the end of it continued and required the same kind of response as he would have given. In this situation somebody produced letters written in the name of Paul, addressed to his immediate helpers and with the implicit rubric: 'These letters represent the kind of thing that I think that Paul would have to say to our churches today if he were still alive'" ("Prospects for the Pastoral Epistles," 151). Similarly, Meade, *Pseudonymity and Canon,* 139: "In the Pastorals, attribution is primarily an assertion of authoritative tradition, not of literary origins."

31. Ellis, "Pastoral Letters," 661.

32. Carson, Moo, and Morris, *Introduction to the New Testament,* 370. Similarly, Porter, "Pauline Authorship," 113–16.

The claim that pseudonymity almost inevitably entails deception understandably gives many conservatives pause.[33] In any case, the irony of the contemporary debate is captured nicely by Bo Reicke:

> Conservative theologians risk being accused of unorthodoxy if they do not believe that every Pauline letter is genuine, whereas liberal theologians fear being accused of unorthodoxy if they do not believe that certain Pauline letters are spurious.[34]

Reicke's own project, published now some fourteen years after his death in 1987, labors bravely to fit all thirteen Epistles into a single decade of Paul's life: 51–61 C.E. A model of critical inquiry and lucidity, Reicke's analysis incorporates four observations about Paul's circumstances:

1. Paul adapted his addresses to his audiences.
2. Many of Paul's letters have not survived.
3. Paul's colleagues contributed substantially to the ideas and wording of his letters.
4. Paul normally dictated to secretaries, whose literary styles left their mark on his corpus.[35]

Reicke contends that when these elements are given their due, many of the arguments mounted against authenticity seem anachronistic and narrow minded. For example,

> the very practice of dictation implies that disconnections, interpolations, and fluctuations may, for psychological reasons, have emerged in the original composition and are not necessarily the result of scribal errors or deliberate changes of a later hand.[36]

33. Porter, "Pauline Authorship," 118–23. Cf. Ehrman's equation (*The New Testament,* 341–44) of "pseudonymity" with "forgery."

34. Reicke, *Re-examining Paul's Letters,* 32.

35. Ibid.

36. Ibid., 31. On Paul's use of secretaries and coauthors, see E. R. Richards, *The Secretary in the Letters of Paul,* WUNT 2.42 (Tübingen: Mohr, 1991), 153–98; J. Murphy-O'Connor, *Paul the Letter-Writer: His World, His Options, His Skills,* GNS 41 (Collegeville, Minn.: Liturgical Press, 1995). The following table, adapted from Richards (190), sets forth the principal data:

Table 15.1 Cosenders and Secretaries in Paul's Letters

	Cosender	Evidence of secretary/ author's hand	Postscripts
Romans		16:22	
1 Corinthians	Sosthenes	16:21	16:22–24
2 Corinthians	Timothy		chs. 10–13 (?)
Galatians	"all the brethren with me" (?)	6:11	6:12–18

Continued

Perhaps the wisest course, given the daunting challenges of identifying fully the boundaries of Paul's thought,[37] of sorting out Pauline chronology (with or without the help of Acts), and of puzzling out the influences of his colleagues and the varieties of pseudonymity, is simply to leave the authorship question open. The literary turn in recent biblical criticism has, in any case, deflected the attention of many scholars away from questions of authorship and toward the text itself—its theology, rhetoric, and reception.[38] Whether or not all parties will manage to proceed cautiously, wary of the prejudicial effects of ideological and apologetic agenda,[39] one can hope that these Epistles would continue to be studied fruitfully in their social, theological, canonical, and ecclesial contexts, even without final resolution of the authorship question.[40]

Quest for Coherency: Development and Contingency in Paul's Thought

Particularly since the work of E. P. Sanders and Heikki Räisänen, words such as "unsystematic," "inconsistent," and even "incoherent" have become com-

Table 15.1 continued	Cosender	Evidence of secretary/ author's hand	Postscripts
Philippians	Timothy		
1 Thessalonians	Silvanus, Timothy		5:27–28 (?)
Philemon	Timothy	19	20–25
Colossians	Timothy	4:18a	4:18b
2 Thessalonians	Silvanus, Timothy	3:17	3:17–18

37. Raymond Brown (*Introduction to the New Testament*, 613) calls (in an analogous discussion of Colossians) for a measure of humility in this regard. E. E. Ellis ("The Pastorals and Paul," *ExpTim* 104 [1992–93]: 46) is more adamant: the Paul of those who deny that he could have written the Pastorals is simply "too small."

38. See, for example, J. W. Aageson, "2 Timothy and Its Theology: In Search of a Theological Pattern," *SBLSP* 36 (1997): 692–714; J. L. Sumney, "A Reading of the Theology of 1 Timothy without Authorial Presuppositions" (paper presented to the Theology of the Disputed Paulines Group at the annual meeting of the Society of Biblical Literature, New Orleans, November 1996).

39. See the three "tendencies" in the authorship debate highlighted by Johnson (*The Writings of the New Testament*, 381–82), who offers his own assessment: "In each letter there is . . . just enough divergence from any reader's instinctive perception of what is Pauline that even those most sympathetic to [the Pastorals'] authenticity must wonder at this blend of the familiar and the strange so erratically distributed over three documents" (382).

40. Cf. Aageson, "2 Timothy and Its Theology," 713–14. Even among scholars affirming their Pauline authorship, the Pastorals tend to fill a secondary role as de facto commentary on the undisputed letters. For a canonical approach to the Pastorals—one allowing for their pseudonymity—see the brief article by R. W. Wall, "Pauline Authorship and the Pastoral Epistles: A Response to S. E. Porter," *BBR* 5 (1995): 125–28, to which Porter responds in "Pauline Authorship and the Pastoral Epistles: A Response to R. W. Wall's Response," *BBR* 6 (1996): 133–38.

monplace in scholarly discourse about Paul.[41] How much thematic variation can we allow before abandoning the notion of a unified literary corpus?[42] Does Paul's "remarkable malleability" ever merit the charge of inconsistency?[43] N. T. Wright, in recent dialogue with the Pauline Theology Group of the Society of Biblical Literature, neatly sketches the various options available:

> An apparent inconsistency in Plato, say, is a cause for scholarly questioning. Did he *change his mind?* Was he aware of the problem? Is there a *third passage that reconciles the two?* Are we forcing his ideas into the wrong mold? This problem increases when the text in question forms part of a corpus regarded by some as in some sense authoritative—which is still the case among many Pauline scholars, including some who expose his apparent inconsistencies. Do we set up a scheme of *textual surgery?* Or postulate *development of thought?* Or *situation ethics?* Or suggest using *Sachkritik?* Or do we carefully expound the passages in question so that *one set is allowed to dominate* and the others apparently made to harmonize with it? Or should we have part of the cake and eat the other part, dividing it up into *"coherence" and "contingency"?* Or should we simply give up and say that *Paul contradicts himself* on major matters, that the impression of profundity is simply the result of this confusion, and that many of his arguments are not real arguments but psychologically explicable *secondary rationalizations?*[44]

41. E. P. Sanders, *Paul, the Law, and the Jewish People* (Philadelphia: Fortress, 1983); H. Räisänen, *Paul and the Law* (Tübingen: Mohr, 1983).

42. The following points illustrate the sort of theological diversity commonly detected in Paul:

- Contrast the pro-Mosaic law stance in Rom. 3:31 with Eph. 2:15.
- Contrast a (subtle) opposition to slavery (1 Cor. 7:21; Gal. 3:28; Philemon) with an emphasis on social order and dutiful submission (Col. 3:22–4:1; Eph. 6:5–9; 1 Tim. 6:1–2).
- Contrast the use of *ekklēsia* (church) almost exclusively for specific, local Christian communities in 1 Thessalonians, Galatians, 1 and 2 Corinthians, and Romans with its reference to an abstract, universal body over which Christ reigns as the supreme head in Col. 1:18, 24.
- Contrast a future-oriented eschatology (Phil. 3:11–12, 20–21) with something less urgent and more realized (Eph. 2:5–6; Col. 1:13; 2:12; 3:1).
- Contrast the (assumed) verbal participation of women in the assembly (1 Cor. 11:2–16) with prohibitions of such practice (1 Tim. 2:11–15).
- Contrast the view that deceased believers "slept" as disembodied souls until the parousia (1 Thess. 4:17; 1 Cor. 15) with the idea that they communed, consciously, with Christ (2 Cor. 5:8; Phil. 1:23).

Each of these points merits careful scrutiny on its own terms. Here I observe only that such diversity has encouraged a majority of Pauline scholars to affirm the pseudonymity of at least some epistles, while a sizable minority detect but one hand—the apostle, responding to a bewildering array of pastoral concerns, and to crises ecclesial, personal, and political.

43. The cited phrase comes from J. L. Martyn (*Galatians: A New Translation with Introduction and Commentary*, AB 33A [New York: Doubleday, 1997], 523), who reads Galatians, against the current vogue, as an integrated, theologically coherent whole.

44. N. T. Wright, "Putting Paul Together Again: Toward a Synthesis of Pauline Theology (1 and 2 Thessalonians, Philippians, and Philemon)," in *Pauline Theology*, ed. J. M. Bassler et al., 3 vols. (Minneapolis: Fortress, 1991–97), 1:186–87 (italics added).

Among the options that Wright catalogs (and apparently rejects) is the notion that we can detect "development" in Paul's thought—that we can plot Paul's ideas along something of a chronological trajectory. More than a few scholars have labored bravely toward this end. C. H. Dodd, back in 1935, thought that the "futurist eschatology" of Paul's early years gave way, in time, to "Christ-mysticism." Closer to our era, Lucien Cerfaux outlined how Paul's view of the "intermediate state" evolved over time, culminating in 2 Cor. 4:7–5:10 and Phil. 1:19–26. In 1975, John Drane proposed to make sense of Paul's diverse statements on the law by having him evolve from "libertine" (in Galatians) to "legalist" (in 1 Corinthians) and finally to something of a mature synthesis of the two (Romans). On the same topic, a decade later, Hans Hübner traced a two-stage development from rejection (Galatians) to rehabilitation (Romans) of the Mosaic law. That same year, Gerd Lüdemann sought to show that Paul's doctrine of the resurrection evolved from "realistic" in 1 Thessalonians to "dualistic" in 1 Corinthians, in part because death was becoming increasingly common for Christians in the (on Lüdemann's framework) decade between the two letters. And Calvin Roetzel recently has traced Paul's "theologizing" from 1 Thessalonians in the early 50s to 1 Corinthians in the mid-50s to Romans a few years later.[45] Such proposals are not without problems, for neither the relative dating of the letters nor their historical circumstances are sufficiently established for us to trace theological development with any confidence.[46] But even if attempts to trace development are invariably speculative, the possibility of genuine, even substantial, development in Paul's thought can hardly be ruled out, which suggests the need for criteria against which the content of disputed epistles and putative interpolations might be measured. To the extent that scholars find "development" a useful category for sorting out Paul's ideas, some will understandably want to argue that the Pastorals represent simply the latest developments of Paul's theology—snapshots of Paul's pastoral reflection in the final stages of his life.[47]

45. C. H. Dodd, *The Apostolic Preaching and Its Developments* (New York: Harper & Row, 1964), 63; L. Cerfaux, *The Christian in the Theology of St. Paul* (London: Chapman, 1967); J. W. Drane, *Paul, Libertine or Legalist? A Study in the Theology of the Major Pauline Epistles* (London: SPCK, 1975); H. Hübner, *Law in Paul's Thought* (Edinburgh: Clark, 1984); G. Lüdemann, *Paul, Apostle to the Gentiles: Studies in Chronology,* trans. F. S. Jones (Philadelphia: Fortress, 1984), 201–61; C. J. Roetzel, *Paul: The Man and the Myth* (Minneapolis: Fortress, 1999), 93–134. Similarly, H. D. Betz ("Paul," *ABD* 5:196–99) finds three stages of development: "earlier phases" (1 Thessalonians, Galatians, Philippians), the "crisis at Corinth," and the "later Paul" (Romans).

46. Cf. E. P. Sanders, *Paul and Palestinian Judaism* (Philadelphia: Fortress, 1977), 432 (see esp. n. 9); Dunn, *Theology of Paul,* 21. See also critiques by J. C. Beker, "Recasting Pauline Theology: The Coherence-Contingency Scheme as Interpretive Model," in Bassler et al., *Pauline Theology,* 1:15–24, 21–23; P. J. Achtemeier, "Finding the Way to Paul's Theology: A Response to J. Christiaan Beker and J. Paul Sampley," in Bassler et al., *Pauline Theology,* 1:25–36, 27; Räisänen, *Paul and the Law,* 7–10; earlier, V. P. Furnish, "Development in Paul's Thought," *JAAR* 38 (1970): 289–303.

47. Thus, Witherington (*The Paul Quest,* 113) claims to have found "nothing Paul might not have said as his life came to a close."

Also making Wright's "top-ten list" of solutions to the problem of Pauline coherency is the model developed by J. Christiaan Beker, according to which Paul's hermeneutic "consists in the constant interaction between the coherent center of the gospel and its contingent interpretation."[48] If Beker is right—and there are good reasons to think that he is—then any attempt to extract a pure "theology of Paul" from its diverse applications in real life is misguided. As Richard Hays explains, "Paul's statements and exhortations are always in fact *interpretations* of a body of traditions or beliefs, spoken as 'a word on target' for a particular situation."[49] Most applications of Beker's model have focused on the undisputed letters. Indeed, Beker contends that the Pastorals are simply too coherent, on the one hand, and too detached from historical contingencies, on the other hand, to fit the paradigm.[50] But not all agree. Donald Hagner, for example, recently has shown how the theology, ethics, and exhortations of Titus are thoroughly integrated, suggesting (to him, at least) that the contingent circumstances of the Pastorals, combined with Paul's "chameleon-like" tendencies, may be more than enough to explain the striking differences.[51]

Interpretation or Domestication? Paul, Deutero-Paul, and Politics

The disjunction between Paul and deutero-Paul has been particularly productive for certain feminist, postcolonial, and liberationist scholars interested in the social struggles going on behind the text and concerned to expose centuries of oppression and domination perpetrated in the name of Pauline Christianity. Especially noteworthy here is Neil Elliott's *Liberating Paul: The Justice of God and the Politics of the Apostle,* which chronicles carefully what Elliott calls "the canonical betrayal of the Apostle" on matters of social class, gender, race, and the use of power.[52] For Elliott, the authentic voice of the apostle was suppressed, and his message grossly distorted, when his letters took their place within a

48. Beker, *Paul the Apostle,* 11. Similarly, Beker observes that Paul is "able to make the gospel a word on target for the particular needs of his churches without either compromising its basic content or reducing it to a petrified conceptuality" (12). Likewise, Dunn, *Theology of Paul,* 21: "It was the dynamic character of Paul's theology which made one of the lasting impressions of the ten-year-long discussions in the SBL Pauline Theology group—the sense that Paul's theology was an 'activity,' was always interactive, the sense that Paul was never simply theologian per se, but was always at one and the same time Paul the theologian, missionary, and pastor, or, in a word, Paul the apostle" (cf. 23). For a recent and rather elegant treatment of Paul along these lines, see Roetzel, *Paul: The Man and the Myth,* 93–134.

49. R. B. Hays, "Crucified with Christ: A Synthesis of the Theology of 1 and 2 Thessalonians, Philemon, Philippians, and Galatians," in Bassler et al., *Pauline Theology,* 1:229.

50. J. C. Beker, *Heirs of Paul: Paul's Legacy in the New Testament and in the Church Today* (Minneapolis: Fortress, 1991), 46.

51. Hagner, "Titus as a Pauline Letter," 548.

52. N. Elliott, *Liberating Paul: The Justice of God and the Politics of the Apostle* (Maryknoll, N.Y.: Orbis, 1994). The cited phrase is the title of ch. 2 (p. 25).

larger NT canon. The hermeneutical payoff, it turns out, is substantial: the popular image of Paul as a social conservative who accepted systemic injustice and social inequity is due in large part to the assimilation of Paul's thought to the pseudo-Pauline *Haustafeln*. Indeed, it appears to Elliott that the deutero-Pauline letters arose in the first place precisely "to manage, or hijack, the authority of Paul's legacy." Far from being faithful and sympathetic extensions of the apostolic kerygma, they are instead perverse and contaminating distortions of it.[53] Needless to say, such language is rather jarring to those committed to the authority of a canon that includes Ephesians and the Pastorals. The question of the starting point suggests itself. Did Elliott recover a more liberating Paul only after he established an authentic Pauline corpus by other means? Or did he begin with a particular construction of Paul, measured against which certain nonconformist texts were declared to be inauthentic? Elliott's study is, in any case, a powerful challenge—one well worth facing—to all inclined to hear in Paul "the unbaptized voice of a sanctified status quo, of shameless patriarchy, of the Church Militant and Militarized."[54]

Portraits of an Apostle: The Paul of Acts and the Paul of Paul

Alongside his Epistles, our other major source for understanding Paul is the Book of Acts.[55] Most agree that the author of Acts, whom I will call Luke, did in fact intend to write history,[56] and yet it is axiomatic among Pauline scholars, at least since F. C. Baur, that historical reconstructions of Paul must give priority to his letters. Indeed, for Gerd Lüdemann, the only responsible approach is first to construct a framework based solely on Paul's (undisputed)

53. See N. Elliott, "Paul and the Politics of Empire: Problems and Prospects," in R. A. Horsley, ed., *Paul and Politics: Ekklesia, Israel, Imperium, Interpretation* (Harrisburg, Pa.: Trinity, 2000), 26–27; and esp. idem, *Liberating Paul*, 25–54. Also on Elliott's list of sub-Pauline contaminations are 1 Cor. 14:34–35 (on women) and 1 Thess. 2:14–16 (on the Jews)—two admittedly difficult texts around which controversy continues to swirl.

54. Elliott, *Liberating Paul*, 17.

55. See also 2 Pet. 3:15–16; *1 Clem.* 47. For an additional, though not entirely independent source, see the *Acts of Paul* (late second century), which includes the problematic *3 Corinthians*, available in W. Schneemelcher, ed., *New Testament Apocrypha*, 2 vols. (Louisville: Westminster John Knox, 1989), 2:213–70.

56. This is not the place to explore the broader question of Luke's general trustworthiness as a historian. Acts has been compared and contrasted with Jewish historical works of the Hellenistic period (e.g., 1 and 2 Maccabees), and with Greek and Roman histories (e.g., Thucydides, Livy, Josephus). For important contributions to the discussion, see Bertil Gärtner, *The Areopagus Speech and Natural Revelation*, ASNU 21 (Uppsala: Gleerup, 1955), 7–36; F. F. Bruce, "The Acts of the Apostles: Historical Record or Theological Reconstruction?" in *ANRW* 2.25.3:2570–603; W. C. van Unnik, "Luke-Acts, a Storm Center in Contemporary Scholarship," in *Studies in Luke-Acts*, ed. L. E. Keck and J. L. Martyn (Philadelphia: Fortress, 1980), 15–32; C. J. Hemer, *The Book of Acts in the Setting of Hellenistic History* (Tübingen: Mohr, 1989); for a convenient summary, see M. A. Powell, *What Are They Saying about Acts?* (New York: Paulist Press, 1991), 80–95.

letters, and only then attempt to integrate the traditions of Acts.[57] There are, however, voices prepared to challenge critical orthodoxy on this point and to take Luke's portrait of Paul seriously on its own terms.[58]

For us, the critical question concerns the extent to which Acts should be allowed to add details to the rather sketchy portrait of Paul's life provided by his own correspondence. Was the author of Acts (who presumably composed his narrative not long after composing the third Gospel) Luke, the physician and traveling companion of Paul? Predictably, the academy is divided and probably will remain so, especially since Acts is formally anonymous.[59] Authorial identity aside, can Acts be trusted as a witness to the "historical" Paul? Scholars have long observed differences between the portraits of Paul in Acts and the letters, and these differences are routinely thought to signal Luke's nonhistorical, or quasi-historical, agenda.[60] In Acts, we meet Paul the orator and persuasive rhetorician (Acts 13, 14, 17, 22, 24, 26); Paul's letters depict him as a correspondent whose attempts at face-to-face persuasion do not always meet with success (2 Cor. 10:10; 11:6). In Acts, Paul is a wonder worker—a side of Paul almost completely hidden in the Epistles (Rom. 15:18–19; 2 Cor. 12:12). The Paul of Acts is embattled but triumphant, a towering figure with

57. Lüdemann, *Paul, Apostle to the Gentiles,* 21, 23, 44, and passim. Cf. the approaches of K. P. Donfried, "Chronology," *ABD* 1:1016–22; L. C. A. Alexander, "Chronology of Paul," in Hawthorne, Martin, and Reid, *Dictionary of Paul and His Letters,* 115–23. Intriguingly, much of Lüdemann's letters-only chronology finds confirmation in the traditions incorporated into Acts, although Lüdemann often finds the Lukan sequence problematic. For Lüdemann's attempt to separate Lukan redaction from the pre-Lukan traditions, see idem, *Early Christianity according to the Traditions in Acts: A Commentary* (Minneapolis: Fortress, 1989).

58. Leading the effort to recover Acts as an essentially reliable historical source for Paul's life has been Martin Hengel of Tübingen, whose contributions include *Acts and the History of Early Christianity,* trans. J. Bowden (Philadelphia: Fortress, 1979); *Between Jesus and Paul,* trans. J. Bowden (Philadelphia: Fortress, 1983); *The Pre-Christian Paul* (Philadelphia: Trinity, 1991); and M. Hengel and A. M. Schwemer, *Paul between Damascus and Antioch: The Unknown Years,* trans. J. Bowden (Louisville: Westminster John Knox, 1997). See also J. Jervell, *The Unknown Paul: Essays on Luke-Acts and Early Christian History* (Minneapolis: Augsburg, 1984), 13–25, 52–95; idem, "Paul in the Acts of the Apostles: Tradition, History, Theology," in *Les Actes des Apôtres: Traditions, rédaction, théologie,* ed. J. Kremer, BETL 48 (Gembloux: Duculot, 1979), 297–306; Hemer, *Book of Acts;* D. Wenham, "Acts and the Pauline Corpus, II: The Evidence of Parallels," in *The Book of Acts in Its Ancient Literary Setting,* ed. B. W. Winter and A. D. Clarke, BAFCS 1 (Grand Rapids: Eerdmans, 1993), 215–58; F. F. Bruce, "Paul in Acts and Letters," in Hawthorne, Martin, and Reid, *Dictionary of Paul and His Letters,* 679–92; Reicke, *Re-examining Paul's Letters.*

59. Arguing for the traditional view that Paul's companion composed Acts are Hengel and Schwemer, *Paul between Damascus and Antioch,* 7, 18–19. Influential arguments to the contrary were presented some time ago by P. Vielhauer, "On the 'Paulinism' of Acts," now available in Keck and Martyn, *Studies in Luke-Acts,* 33–50 (German original, 1951); and by Kümmel, *Introduction to the New Testament,* 174–85. For a summary, see Ehrman, *The New Testament,* 137–39.

60. Scholars' reluctance to give substantial weight to the narrative of Acts in their reconstruction of the "historical" Paul is testimony to the influence of Ernst Haenchen, Martin Dibelius, and John Knox.

no true rivals. By contrast, the Paul of Paul is frequently on the defensive and locked in combat with opponents at almost every turn.[61]

On the other hand, given the time span between their composition, the absence of any literary dependence,[62] and the differing agenda of the authors, the many agreements between Acts 9–15 and Paul's letters are striking. Both Pauls begin as zealous Pharisees who vigorously oppose the earliest Christians, and both undergo a dramatic transformation resulting in a God-ordained mission to the Gentiles. Both do manual labor so as not to require financial support, and both adapt their behavior to accommodate alternately Jews or Gentiles. The fact that the Lukan Paul routinely advances his Gentile mission by first visiting Jewish synagogues is likewise wholly consistent with Paul's remark in Rom. 1:16.[63]

It is one thing, however, to affirm the broad compatibility of Paul and Acts, and quite another to puzzle out the details. Since Paul left so few chronological indicators in his letters (see, e.g., Gal. 1:18; 2:1; 2 Cor. 11:32–33), any effort to establish a firm timeline of major events requires large amounts of guesswork. As a test case, we consider the relationship between Acts 9–15 and Paul's autobiographical account in Gal. 1–2. Several questions, all of them seemingly elementary, remain unresolved.

1. In what year was Paul "converted"?[64] A consensus has been building toward the year 30 C.E. for the crucifixion of Jesus.[65] Dates for Paul's

---

61. On these portraits, see S. E. Porter, *The Paul of Acts: Essays in Literary Criticism, Rhetoric and Theology* (Tübingen: Mohr Siebeck, 1999), 100–101; Powell, *What Are They Saying about Acts?* 34–35; E. Haenchen, *The Acts of the Apostles: A Commentary*, trans. B. Noble et al. (Philadelphia: Westminster, 1971), 112–16.

62. See Lüdemann, *Early Christianity*, 7–9.

63. See Bruce, "Paul in Acts and Letters," 680–81. The principal biographical references in Paul are Rom. 1:1–17; 9:1–5; 15:14–33; 1 Cor. 9:1–23; Gal. 1:10–2:18, 34; Phil. 3:2–11. For a continuous narrative of Paul's early years, integrating Acts and Paul's letters, see Hengel and Schwemer, *Paul between Damascus and Antioch.* On the relationship between Acts and Gal. 2, see M. Silva, *Explorations in Exegetical Method: Galatians as a Test Case* (Grand Rapids: Baker, 1996), 129–39. These sorts of correspondences between Acts and (all thirteen of) Paul's letters feature prominently in the historical reconstruction by Reicke, *Re-examining Paul's Letters.*

64. The quotation marks signal scholarly reluctance, under the gaze of K. Stendahl, to apply the term "converted" to Paul. See below, n. 72, and Roetzel, *Paul: The Man and the Myth*, 45.

65. See R. Riesner, *Paul's Early Period: Chronology, Mission Strategy, Theology*, trans. D. Stott (Grand Rapids: Eerdmans, 1998; in German, 1994), 52–58; Hengel and Schwemer, *Paul between Damascus and Antioch*, 26. But the year 33 C.E. is also popular, with support from B. Reicke, *The New Testament Era: The World of the Bible from 500 B.C. to A.D. 100*, trans. David E. Green (London: Black, 1968), 3–6; L. C. A. Alexander, "Chronology of Paul," in Hawthorne, Martin, and Reid, *Dictionary of Paul and His Letters*, 116; H. Hoehner, "Chronology," in *Dictionary of Jesus and the Gospels*, J. B. Green, S. McKnight, and I. H. Marshall, eds. (Downers Grove, Ill.: InterVarsity, 1992), 119–22; R. Jewett, *A Chronology of Paul's Life* (Philadelphia: Fortress, 1979), 28.

conversion typically fall within a few years of Jesus' death, but so far there is no widespread agreement.[66]

2. How many times did Paul travel to Jerusalem? More specifically, does Gal. 2:1 correspond to the famine-relief visit of Acts 11:27–30 or to the Jerusalem council of Acts 15? It is commonly assumed that Paul's *narratio* in Gal. 1–2 purports to include all of Paul's trips to Jerusalem prior to the letter's composition, in which case the number of trips is two: first "after three years" (1:18), and then again "after fourteen years" (2:1). Acts, however, describes three trips to the city in the early years of Paul's ministry: one from Damascus (9:26–30), and two from Antioch (11:27–30 and 12:25; 15:1–4). Several solutions merit careful review:

- The author of Acts has intruded an extra (or, out-of-sequence) journey to Jerusalem, indicating that he had no, or limited, personal knowledge of Paul's life.[67]
- Gal. 1:18 corresponds to Acts 9:26–30, and Gal. 2:1 to Acts 11:27–30. Paul composed Galatians prior to his participation in the Jerusalem council (Acts 15). This is said to explain the absence of any reference to the Jerusalem decree (Acts 15:28–29), a decree having obvious bearing on the circumcision controversy in Galatia. But it requires a fourteen-year lapse (Gal. 2:1) between Acts 9 and 11, and it ignores obvious differences between the descriptions of the two visits.
- The famine-relief visit of Acts 11 is out of sequence—note the vague time references in 11:27–28—and may have occurred after the death of Herod Agrippa I (Acts 12:20–23) in 44 C.E., some time during the reign of Claudius (41–54 C.E.). Some suggest that it is Luke's equivalent to Paul's collection.[68]
- Paul felt no obligation to mention the famine-relief visit;[69] Gal. 2:1–10 corresponds to the council of Acts 15. The striking similarities between the two accounts, and the (arguably) resolvable differences, render it implausible that we have two separate events in view.[70]

66. Thus Lüdemann (*Paul, Apostle to the Gentiles*) suggests either 30 or 33 C.E.; Riesner (*Paul's Early Period*) settles on 31/32 C.E.; Hengel and Schwemer (*Paul between Damascus and Antioch*), along with Carson, Moo, and Morris (*Introduction to the New Testament*), prefer 33 C.E.; L. C. A. Alexander opts for slightly later, 34/35 C.E. For the best survey of the evidence, see Riesner, *Paul's Early Period*, 59–74.

67. So Lüdemann, *Early Christianity*, 5–7.

68. See Alexander, "Chronology of Paul," 120–22.

69. The notion that Paul would feel obliged to mention all his visits assumes that chs. 1 and 2 form a single, sustained response to Paul's opponents. But see Silva, *Explorations in Exegetical Method*, 99–100, 136–38, for problems with this view.

70. See ibid., 129–39, for a review of the issues. Cf. Reicke, *Re-examining Paul's Letters*, 16–25. Silva's proposal—Galatians is late (i.e., written after the Jerusalem council) but addressed

Table 15.2 Comparison of Galatians 2:1–10 and Acts 15:1–32

Similarities	Differences	
	Galatians	Acts
The key locations are Jerusalem and Antioch.	Paul went to Jerusalem from Antioch "in response to a revelation" (2:2).	Paul was appointed to go to Jerusalem by the church in Antioch (15:2).
Paul, Barnabas, and others represent Antioch (Gal. 2:1 mentions Titus; Acts 15:2 has "some of the others").	Titus accompanied Paul and Barnabas (2:1, 3).	No mention of Titus (15:2).
Another group seeks to impose circumcision on Gentile converts (Gal. 2:4; Acts 15:1, 5).	Paul calls them "false brethren" (*pseudadelphoi*) (2:4).	"Some from the sect of the Pharisees who had believed" (Acts 15:5).
Paul presents his gospel to the leaders (Gal. 2:2, 6–10; Acts 15:4, 12).	The leaders in Jerusalem mentioned are James, Cephas (Peter), and John (2:9).	Peter, James, Judas, and Silas mentioned, but not John (15:7, 13, 22, 27, 32).
The event is marked by heated conflict (Gal. 2:4–5; Acts 15:2, 6, 10, 24).		
Paul and Barnabas are affirmed (Gal. 2:7–9; Acts 15:4, 25–26).		
Circumcision is not imposed on the Gentiles (Gal. 2:3, 5, 7–9; Acts 15:19, 28).	No mention of a formal decree.	The formal, written decision is emphasized (15:23, 30).

3. Was Galatians addressed to believers in the regions described in Acts 14:1, 8, 20 (the "South Galatian" theory), or in the region that may be in view in Acts 16:6 (the "North Galatian" theory)? Contrary to popular impressions, the burden of these questions is more chronological than geographical. Whereas the North Galatian theory requires a late (i.e., post–Jerusalem council) date for the letter, the South Galatian theory allows for, but certainly does not require, an early (i.e., pre–Jerusalem council) date. Hence, if the South Galatian theory prevails—as seems likely—we must still decide whether Paul composed Galatians before or after the Jerusalem council of Acts 15 and interpret the epistle accordingly.

---

to the churches in southern Galatia—avoids most of the usual pitfalls, but it still must explain Paul's failure to mention the decree.

Both Jew and Greek: Paul in Cultural Context

Hellenistic Judaism

Increasingly during the last twenty-five years, "post-Holocaust" Pauline scholarship has sought to reclaim Paul from earlier, sometimes anti-Semitic, attempts to de-Judaize him.[71] Pointing the way were scholars such as Krister Stendahl, Harvard professor and bishop of Stockholm, whose questions in the early 1960s forced scholars to reconsider the relationship of Paul to his Jewish heritage.[72] And E. P. Sanders turned more than a few heads when, in the following decade, he unleashed his *Paul and Palestinian Judaism* and announced that Paul, far from misunderstanding the Judaism of his day or attacking a Hellenized distortion of it, was in substantial agreement with the common Jewish understanding of both Mosaic law and divine grace.[73]

But what sort of Jew was Paul? What are we to make of Paul's fervent claims to be an Israelite, a Hebrew, and a Pharisee (Rom. 11:1; 2 Cor. 11:22; Phil.

---

71. It was Rudolf Bultmann's Paul who happily discarded his Jewishness in order to translate his gospel into language and categories amenable to the Gentile world of his day. Notable among the many self-consciously "post-Holocaust" works on Paul would be R. R. Ruether, *Faith and Fratricide* (New York: Seabury, 1974); L. Gaston, *Paul and the Torah* (Vancouver: University of British Columbia Press, 1987); S. Hall III, *Christian Anti-Semitism and Paul's Theology* (Minneapolis: Fortress, 1993).

72. K. Stendahl, *Paul among Jews and Gentiles* (Philadelphia: Fortress, 1976 [based, in part, on lectures delivered at Austin Presbyterian Seminary and Colgate Rochester Divinity School in 1963–64]), asked whether Paul was converted (away from his Jewish faith) or called (within it)? That is, did Paul abandon his Jewish faith to become a Christian? For Stendahl, the answer was clear: the "pre-Christian" Paul sensed no deficiency in his ancestral religion, nor was his conscience particularly troubled by moral failure. Hence, "the usual conversion model of Paul the Jew who gives up his former faith to become a Christian is not the model of Paul but of ours. Rather, his call brings him to a new understanding of his mission, a new understanding of the law which is otherwise an obstacle to the Gentiles. His ministry is based on the specific conviction that the Gentiles will become part of the people of God without having to pass through the law. This is Paul's secret revelation and knowledge" (ibid., 9). But Stendahl's sharp conversion-versus-calling dichotomy almost certainly was overstated. See, for example, B. R. Gaventa, *From Darkness to Light: Aspects of Conversion in the New Testament* (Philadelphia: Fortress, 1986); A. F. Segal, *Paul the Convert: The Apostolate and Apostasy of Saul the Pharisee* (New Haven: Yale University Press, 1990), 3–183; T. L. Donaldson, *Paul and the Gentiles: Remapping the Apostle's Convictional World* (Philadelphia: Fortress, 1997), 17.

73. Sanders, *Paul and Palestinian Judaism,* 517–18, 548. See also idem, *Paul, the Law, and the Jewish People;* and idem, *Paul* (Oxford: Oxford University Press, 1991). It lies well beyond the scope of this essay to chart the numerous responses to Sanders's "new perspective," except to acknowledge the rising wave of critical responses: D. A. Carson, P. T. O'Brien, and M. Seifrid, eds., *Justification and Variegated Nomism,* vol. 1, *The Complexities of Second Temple Judaism* (Grand Rapids: Baker, 2001); A. A. Das, *Paul, the Law, and the Covenant* (Peabody, Mass.: Hendrickson, 2001); Peter Stuhlmacher, *Revisiting Paul's Doctrine of Justification: A Challenge to the New Perspective* (Downers Grove, Ill.: InterVarsity, 2001); M. A. Seifrid, *Christ, Our Righteousness: Paul's Theology of Justification,* NSBT 9 (Downers Grove, Ill.: InterVarsity, 2001); responding more to J. D. G. Dunn than to E. P. Sanders, S. Kim, *Paul and the New Perspective: Second Thoughts on the Origin of Paul's Gospel* (Grand Rapids: Eerdmans, 2002).

3:5)? And why are such self-descriptions principally restricted to polemical contexts? Although we know very little about Pharisaic practices in the first-century Diaspora,[74] and much that we know about pre-70 C.E. Palestinian Pharisaism comes from later periods, it is nevertheless possible to construct a reasonably detailed profile of Paul's Jewish identity, based on his letters and, with a measure of reserve, on descriptions in Acts.

- Paul was a Pharisee (Phil. 3:5; Acts 23:6)[75] and thus embraced certain oral traditions beyond the written Torah (Gal. 1:14; Phil. 3:4–6).[76]
- Paul's thought was shaped by Jewish apocalypticism and its affirmation of a future resurrection of the dead (1 Thess. 4:16; 1 Cor. 15; Phil. 3:21; Acts 17:3, 18).[77]
- Paul was marked by a religious zeal that propelled both his animosity toward Christians (Gal. 1:13–14, 23; 1 Cor. 15:9–10; Phil. 3:6; Acts 9:1–2; 22:3–5) and, subsequently, his Christian mission (1 Cor. 9:16, 23).[78]

74. See especially Hengel, *The Pre-Christian Paul,* 29–34.

75. It is doubtful, however, that we can confidently assign Paul to one or another known branch within first-century Pharisaism. N. T. Wright's suggestion (*The New Testament and the People of God* [Minneapolis: Fortress, 1992], 192, 202; *What Saint Paul Really Said* [Grand Rapids: Eerdmans, 1997], 25–35; "Paul, Arabia, and Elijah," *JBL* 115 [1996]: 683–92, 686, 690–91) that Paul's loyalties lay with the Shammaite wing of the movement has not won wide approval, in part because it is unclear how much of the Hillel/Shammai polarity in rabbinic literature corresponds to historical reality in pre–70 C.E. Judea. Moreover, Acts presents a Paul influenced by Gamaliel, whose tolerance is well known (Acts 5:33–39), and authorized by the high priest, a Sadducee (Acts 5:17; 9:1–2). See Hengel and Schwemer, *Paul between Damascus and Antioch,* 119; L. T. Johnson, "Which Paul?" *First Things* 80 (1998): 58–60; B. Chilton, "The Mystery of Paul: Three New Books Explore the Man Who Shaped Christianity," *BRev* 14 (1998): 41.

76. According to Acts 22:3, his teacher in Jerusalem was the esteemed Gamaliel I, though Luke may have inferred this from two facts: Paul's zealous Pharisaism and Gamaliel's leadership role in the party. Cf. Sanders, *Paul,* 8. On Pharisaic oral law, see E. P. Sanders, *Judaism: Practice and Belief, 63 B.C.E.–66 C.E.* (Philadelphia: Trinity, 1992), 421–24; *Jewish Law from Jesus to the Mishnah: Five Studies* (Philadelphia: Trinity, 1990), 97–130, in which Sanders makes the case that the Pharisees of Paul's day did not accord their oral traditions the same status as biblical law.

77. On this point, Paul stands in agreement not only with other Pharisees, but also with most Jews (excluding the Sadducees). See further Sanders, *Judaism,* 298–301.

78. The reason(s) behind Paul's persecution of the early church are not entirely clear (cf. Gal. 1:13; 1 Cor. 15:9; cf. 1 Tim. 1:13; Acts 8:1–3; 9:21; 22:4–5; 26:9–11). Was it to stamp out apostasy before it spread? Did he fear Roman reprisal? Was it zeal for Torah, temple, and Jewish purity? See C. Roetzel, *Paul: The Man and the Myth,* 38–42; R. A. Horsley and N. A. Silberman, *The Message of the Kingdom: How Jesus and Paul Ignited a Revolution and Transformed the Ancient World* (Minneapolis: Fortress, 1997), 120–23; J. D. G. Dunn, "Paul's Conversion—A Light to Twentieth Century Disputes," in *Evangelium, Schriftauslegung, Kirche,* ed. J. Ådna, S. J. Hafemann, and O. Hofius (Göttingen: Vandenhoeck & Ruprecht, 1997), 77–93; Seifrid, *Christ, Our Righteousness,* 13–24. Cf. P. Fredriksen, *From Jesus to Christ: The Origins of the New Testament Images of Jesus,* 2nd ed. (New Haven: Yale University Press, 2000).

- Paul's abrupt shift from persecutor of Christians to Christian preacher is best understood within the framework of Israel's prophetic-call tradition.[79]
- As a follower of Jesus Christ, Paul continued to embrace his Jewish heritage (Rom. 3:1–4; 11:1; 2 Cor. 11:22; Gal. 1:14; 2:15; Phil. 3:4–6) and sought to evangelize Jews as well as Gentiles (Rom. 1:16; 9:1–5; 11:1–36), yet Paul's principal identity was no longer ethnic (1 Cor. 9:20–23; Gal. 6:15; Rom. 2:29; Phil. 3:3).

In some circles, rehabilitating Paul the rabbi has sometimes meant denying Paul the Hellenist and ignoring certain aspects of Greco-Roman culture crucial for understanding Paul's thought-world. But the Judaism of Paul's day did not divide neatly into Hellenistic (Diaspora) and Palestinian (Pharisaic), as if Jews in the homeland remained unified and pure and had managed to avoid entirely the impact of three centuries of Hellenization. Indeed, as Daniel Boyarin observes, it was "precisely that pure Jewish cultural world that Paul grew up in [that] was thoroughly Hellenized and platonized."[80] Whether Paul came of age, then, in Palestine or the Diaspora, his was a Hellenistic Judaism through and through.[81]

It is possible, conversely, to overstate the significance of Paul's Hellenistic milieu, as is the case with two of the more imaginative characterizations of Paul to come along in a while. Hyam Maccoby's *The Mythmaker: Paul and the Invention of Christianity*[82] introduces us to a Paul who was not actually born a Jew—on this point, it turns out, Paul's letters tell lies. Rather, Paul

79. For a concise summary of the biblical data, see Sanders, *Paul,* 9–10. On Paul's prophetic "call," see especially Stendahl, *Paul Among Jews and Gentiles,* 7–23; but also Roetzel, *Paul: The Man and the Myth,* 44–46; S. Kim, *The Origin of Paul's Gospel* (Grand Rapids: Eerdmans, 1981), 56–66, 91–99; idem, *Paul and the New Perspective,* 241–53; B. J. Malina and J. H. Neyrey, *Portraits of Paul: An Archaeology of Ancient Personality* (Louisville: Westminster John Knox, 1996), 211–18.

80. D. Boyarin, *A Radical Jew: Paul and the Politics of Identity* (Berkeley: University of California Press, 1994), 267–68 n. 30. By "platonized," Boyarin has in mind particularly "the adoption of a dualist philosophy in which the phenomenal world was understood to be the representation in matter of a spiritual or ideal entity which corresponded to it."

81. Cf. Segal, *Paul the Convert,* 84; W. D. Davies, *Paul and Rabbinic Judaism,* 4th ed. (Philadelphia: Fortress, 1980), 320; S. Neill and T. Wright, *The Interpretation of the New Testament: 1861–1986,* 2nd ed. (New York: Oxford University Press, 1988), 370, 375–76. Contrast the forced dichotomy between "Greek" and "Jewish" in the portrait of Paul presented by C. J. den Heyer, *Paul: A Man of Two Worlds,* trans. J. Bowden (Philadelphia: Trinity, 2000). For an exemplary study of Paul as a first-century Hellenist, see Malina and Neyrey, *Portraits of Paul.* Malina and Neyrey identify Paul, along with his Mediterranean contemporaries, as collectivists for whom "a person's social standing, social identification, and social worth derived from one's group orientation in terms of generation, geography, and gender" (202). Rarely has Paul's oddness (vis-à-vis modern Western individualists) been more clearly exposed.

82. Hyam Maccoby, *The Mythmaker: Paul and the Invention of Christianity* (New York: Harper & Row, 1986).

journeyed from Tarsus to Jerusalem in order to convert officially to Judaism. When things did not proceed as planned, an anguished Paul compensated by inventing his own gnostic[83] and inherently anti-Semitic religion (to the understandable dismay of Jesus' disciples), no longer about a Jewish prophet but now about a divine visitor who arrived to impart saving knowledge and to rescue humanity from darkness. For obvious reasons, Maccoby's thesis has failed to persuade.[84]

For a second portrait we turn to journalist of note and award-winning novelist A. N. Wilson. For Wilson, the primary fund for Paul's theological reflection was the paganism of his hometown, Tarsus. It was, in particular, the Mithras cult with its worship of the demigod Herakles, and its gospel of divine life through bull's blood, that enabled Paul to invent the Christian Eucharist and to "draw out a mythological and archetypical significance from the death of a Jewish hero, Jesus of Nazareth."[85] Wilson rejects Maccoby's non-Jewish Paul, but in his place he offers a non-Pharisaic Paul (employed early on, it turns out, among the temple police) who was profoundly shaped by pagan cultic ritual, and who deserves credit for inventing Christianity or, more accurately, a Christ cult. To his credit, Wilson, like H. J. Schoeps before him,[86] takes seriously the influence of the Diaspora on Paul's thought and the impact of both Judaism and Hellenism on his theological formation, but as with Maccoby's gnostic Paul, Wilson's portrait of a cultic Paul has won few adherents, not least because of its selective appeal to the evidence, its privileging of Acts (or bits of it) over Paul's own correspondence, and its indulgence in fanciful speculation.[87]

---

83. In his sequel, *Paul and Hellenism* (Philadelphia: Trinity, 1991), Maccoby gives more attention (especially in chs. 3 and 4) to Hellenistic mystery religions as the source of Pauline soteriology (dying and rising gods, vicarious sacrifice, etc.) and theology of the Eucharist.

84. For starters, evidence that a bona fide gnosticism left its imprint on Paul's thought is lacking. The crucial data derive from a later era (e.g., Epiphanius [fourth century]). See the assessment by J. L. Martyn, *Theological Issues in the Letters of Paul* (Nashville: Abingdon, 1997), 70–75.

85. A. N. Wilson, *Paul: The Mind of the Apostle* (New York: Norton, 1997), 27 (cf. 71). For more rigorous attempts to show parallels between Paul and the Hellenistic cults (including the Mithraic mysteries), see H. D. Betz, "The Mithras Inscriptions of Santa Prisca and the New Testament," *NovT* 10 (1968): 62–80; idem, "Transferring a Ritual: Paul's Interpretation of Baptism in Romans 6," in *Paul in His Hellenistic Context*, ed. T. Engberg-Pedersen (Minneapolis: Fortress, 1995), 84–118; G. Lease, "Mithraism and Christianity: Borrowings and Transformations," in *ANRW* 2.23.2:1306–32. Early proponents of this approach, from the *Religionsgeschichtliche Schule*, include Richard Reitzenstein (1910), Alfred Loisy (1911–12), Wilhelm Bousset (1913), and Rudolf Bultmann (1949).

86. H. J. Schoeps, *Paul: The Theology of the Apostle in the Light of Jewish Religious History* (Philadelphia: Westminster, 1961). Schoeps contended that Paul's theological critique of the law targeted a secondary, Hellenized form of Judaism rather than the pure religion as it was practiced in Palestine. For a handy summary of Schoeps's take on Paul, see S. Westerholm, *Israel's Law and the Church's Faith: Paul and His Recent Interpreters* (Grand Rapids: Eerdmans, 1988), 39–46.

87. See the critiques by Wright, *What Saint Paul Really Said*, 167–78; Johnson, "Which Paul?" 58–60.

Other assessments of Paul's Hellenistic milieu have been more successful, if still controversial. In 1994, talmudic scholar and latecomer to NT studies Daniel Boyarin published *A Radical Jew: Paul and the Politics of Identity*.[88] Crucial to Boyarin's construction of Paul is the notion that he was, even as a follower of Jesus, both thoroughly Jewish and simultaneously embedded in Hellenistic modes of thought. More narrowly, Paul was deeply influenced by the Neoplatonic dualism of his day, by the Greek ideal of unity, and by his conviction that Christ came to save all, Gentile and Jew alike. This, says Boyarin, along with universalistic tendencies drawn from his Israelite religion as reinterpreted in a Hellenistic context, compelled Paul to offer a thoroughgoing cultural critique of Jewish exclusivism and ethnocentrism. Not surprisingly, many have resisted Boyarin's construal of Paul as someone energized by a "platonic hermeneutic" that elevated the spiritual and universal to the detriment of the physical and historical.

Research into Hellenistic aspects of Paul's world continues to bear fruit. For Bruce Winter (following the lead of J. Munck and G. W. Bowersock), Paul has emerged as an important witness to the early stages of the Second Sophistic, insofar as Paul's missionary strategy in Corinth was deliberately antisophistic (1 Cor. 1:17; 2:1–5; 2 Cor. 10:10). If Winter is right, Paul's opponents in that community (cf. 2 Cor. 10–13) resented his refusal to adopt the public tactics and elitist values of the sophists.[89] For G. W. Peterman, Paul's letter to the Philippians implicitly challenges Greco-Roman ideas about gift and obligation in order to redefine sharing within the Christian community.[90] More controversially, Mark Given has argued, on the basis of Paul's own rhetorical self-awareness and his opponents' charges, that Paul's speech was disingenuous, that the apostle's missionary strategy (enunciated in 1 Cor. 9:19–23) deliberately deployed the sophistic arts (ambiguity, cunning, and deception) to persuade his benighted

88. Daniel Boyarin, *A Radical Jew: Paul and the Politics of Identity*, Contraversions 1 (Berkeley: University of California Press, 1994). Boyarin describes himself as "a talmudist and postmodern Jewish cultural critic" and "a practicing Jewish, non-Christian, critical but sympathetic reader of Paul." Boyarin's intuition (following Segal, *Paul the Convert*, 48) is surely sound: "Paul's letters may be more important to the history of Judaism than the rabbinic texts are to the interpretation of Christian Scriptures" (see Boyarin's introduction).

89. B. W. Winter, *Philo and Paul among the Sophists: Alexandrian and Corinthian Reponses to a Julio-Claudian Movement*, 2nd ed. (Grand Rapids: Eerdmans, 2002). This volume represents a second revision of Winter's 1988 dissertation, which proposed an alternative to the gnostic hypothesis advanced by W. Schmithals, *Gnosticism in Corinth: An Investigation of the Letters to the Corinthians*, trans. J. E. Steely, 3rd ed. (Nashville: Abingdon, 1971). See also J. Munck, *Paul and the Salvation of Mankind* (Atlanta: John Knox, 1959); G. W. Bowersock, *Greek Sophists in the Roman Empire* (Oxford: Clarendon, 1969).

90. G. W. Peterman, *Paul's Gift from Philippi: Conventions of Gift Exchange and Christian Giving*, SNTSMS 92 (Cambridge: Cambridge University Press, 1997). In addition to Philippians, Peterman also considers 1 and 2 Corinthians, Rom. 15:25–31, Philem. 17–19, 1 Tim. 5:4, and Rom. 5:7. Behind Peterman stands the work of P. Marshall, *Enmity in Corinth: Social Conventions in Paul's Relations with the Corinthians*, WUNT 2.23 (Tübingen: Mohr Siebeck, 1987).

readers of a truth that they might not otherwise recognize.[91] Also contested is Troels Engberg-Pedersen's claim to have identified a foundational correspondence between the anthropology and ethics of Paul and their counterparts in Stoicism.[92] Not content to flag surface parallels and similar moral topoi, Engberg-Pedersen labors to show that Paul's understanding of conversion, of moral transformation, of community formation, and of corporate identity so resonates with Stoicism that we might have to consider historical influence.[93]

Hometown, Education, and Citizenship

Notwithstanding the vibrant interest in Paul's Hellenistic context reflected in these sorts of studies, no consensus yet attaches to certain rudimentary questions. Where, for example, did Paul come of age? In what city was Paul's mind shaped and his theological imagination fueled? A generation ago, W. C. van Unnik argued, against the grain of scholarly opinion, in support of Luke's claim (Acts 22:3) that Paul was not a child of the Diaspora: Paul may have been born in Tarsus, but he was raised in Jerusalem at the feet of Gamaliel, in the very center of Judaism.[94] On this view, the primary influences on Paul's thought came from Pharisaic Judaism rather than the broader Hellenistic culture. Since van Unnik, however, many have been inclined to question Luke's account. Particularly influential was Ernst Haenchen, who, along with Rudolf Bultmann, found Gal. 1:22—"I was still unknown by sight to the churches of Judea"—difficult to square with the notion that Paul had been a long-term resident of the region's chief city.[95] For Haenchen and many since, Luke's theological interest in Jerusalem was reason enough for him to situate Paul, his hero, there. Between van Unnik and Haenchen stands Martin Hengel, for whom Paul's solid grasp of Greek[96] and regular

91. M. D. Given, *Paul's True Rhetoric: Ambiguity, Cunning, and Deception in Greece and Rome* (Harrisburg, Pa.: Trinity, 2001).

92. T. Engberg-Pedersen, *Paul and the Stoics* (Louisville: Westminster John Knox, 2000).

93. Engberg-Pedersen, *Paul and the Stoics,* 103. For the sort of older comparative work between Pauline Christianity and Stoicism that Engberg-Pedersen deems insufficient, see J. B. Lightfoot's classic essay "St. Paul and Seneca," in *St. Paul's Epistle to the Philippians* (1868; reprint, Grand Rapids: Zondervan, 1953), 270–328.

94. W. C. van Unnik, *Tarsus or Jerusalem, the City of Paul's Youth,* trans. G. Ogg (London: Epworth, 1962). Van Unnik also takes Acts 26:4–5 to imply that Paul had been known in Jerusalem for a long time. E. R. Richards (*Secretary in the Letters of Paul,* 144–53) agrees that Paul was raised and trained in Jerusalem, but avoids van Unnik's error of dichotomizing between a Jewish Jerusalem and a Hellenized Diaspora.

95. E. Haenchen, *Die Apostelgeschichte* (Göttingen: Vandenhoeck & Ruprecht, 1963). For van Unnik (*Tarsus or Jerusalem,* 52), however, this argument fails to take into account "the realities of everyday life." That is, "It can hardly be assumed that in a city like Jerusalem everyone would know definitely all the pupils of the rabbis."

96. It is not clear whether Paul's first language was Greek or whether he spoke Aramaic or even Hebrew in the home (as Phil. 3:5 might suggest; cf. 2 Cor. 11:22) (see R. N. Longenecker,

use of the LXX signals that the cosmopolitan city of Tarsus must also have played an important, if only secondary, role in Paul's formation.[97] Bristling against the thesis of Hans Böhlig that Greco-Roman mystery religions left a deep impression on Paul's thought, Hengel doubts whether the Tarsus of Paul's day saw any actual worship of mystery gods at all, and he rejects the portrait of Paul as a highly trained rhetor. In Hengel's assessment, pagan influences on Paul and his fellow Jews were far more likely to come from Stoic philosophy and rhetoric:

> In reality, Paul's language and "elements of education" do not go beyond what he could have learned within the Greek-speaking synagogues and in conversation with learned non-Jews, whom he did not avoid. . . . Here, Tarsus need not stand at the centre, as the place where he was educated; Jerusalem . . . would have been enough.[98]

These remarks of Hengel raise the broader question of Paul's access to education.[99] Since we have almost no direct knowledge of Paul's schooling (Gal. 1:14; cf. Acts 22:3), scholars have been forced to reason backward from various clues in his letters. It is clear, for example, that Paul could read and write Greek, was thoroughly versed in the Greek Bible, and was comfortable

---

Paul, Apostle of Liberty [Grand Rapids: Baker, 1976], 22, 32, 274). He was probably bilingual or even trilingual. What is clear is that Paul was thoroughly fluent in Greek and thoroughly at home in the Greek OT. See Hengel, *The Pre-Christian Paul*, 34–37; Roetzel, *Paul: The Man and the Myth*, 11–12; R. Stegner, "Jew, Paul the," in Hawthorne, Martin, and Reid, *Dictionary of Paul and His Letters*, 504.

97. Hengel, *The Pre-Christian Paul*, 37–39. The prevailing view, that Paul habitually drew upon a Greek translation of Scripture (similar to the LXX), rather than directly from Hebrew, remains secure, notwithstanding the recent challenge by T. H. Lim (*Holy Scripture in the Qumran Commentaries and Pauline Letters* [Oxford: Clarendon, 1997]), who argues (unsuccessfully) that Paul would have regularly consulted biblical texts in Hebrew, Aramaic, and Greek. On Paul's relationship to the LXX, see C. D. Stanley, *Paul and the Language of Scripture: Citation Technique in the Pauline Epistles and Contemporary Literature*, SNTSMS 69 (Cambridge: Cambridge University Press, 1992); D.-A. Koch, *Die Schrift als Zeuge des Evangeliums: Untersuchungen zur Verwendung und zum Verständnis der Schrift bei Paulus*, BHT 69 (Tübingen: Mohr Siebeck, 1986); J. R. Wagner, *Heralds of the Good News: Isaiah and Paul "in Concert" in the Letter to the Romans*, NovTSup 101 (Brill: Leiden, 2002); K. H. Jobes and M. Silva, *Invitation to the Septuagint* (Grand Rapids: Baker, 2000), 183–205.

98. Hengel and Schwemer, *Paul between Damascus and Antioch*, 170–71. On 171, Hengel continues, "The striking thing about Paul and the whole of earliest Christianity is that we do not find a deeper philosophical-oratorical education and a style corresponding to what we meet in Philo, Justus of Tiberias or Josephus. Luke and the author of Hebrews are exceptions here. . . . The significance of the rhetoric of the schools on Paul is much exaggerated today, following a fashionable trend." Cf. Winter, *Philo and Paul*, 246–52. In support of the notion that Paul had at least some rhetorical training, see D. Martin, *The Corinthian Body* (New Haven: Yale University Press, 1996), 38–68.

99. Representative discussions of Paul's education include Hengel, *The Pre-Christian Paul*, 18–62; Murphy-O'Connor, *Paul: A Critical Life*, 47; Roetzel, *Paul: The Man and the Myth*, 22–24; Witherington, *The Paul Quest*, 89–98.

in the role of interpreter.[100] All of this suggests a thoroughly Jewish education involving extended exposure to Israel's sacred texts, postbiblical traditions, and intepretive approaches. At the same time, when we closely examine the shape of Paul's arguments, we find not only traditional Jewish elements, but also clear signs of Hellenistic influence. The flourishing discipline of rhetorical criticism, inspired largely by the seminal work of Hans Dieter Betz, has highlighted numerous parallels, in style and argumentation, between Paul and contemporary Greco-Roman rhetoric.[101]

The question of Paul's Roman citizenship (*civitas Romana*) is also a matter of some dispute. Although the author of Acts makes a point of affirming Paul's elevated status in the empire and its accompanying privileges (see Acts 16:37–38; 21:39; 22:25–29; 25:10–12; cf. 28:16), some have characterized

---

100. For Paul in the act of interpreting Scripture, see especially Rom. 9:6–29 and 1 Cor. 10:1–13. On Paul's interpretation of Scripture, a good place to start is R. B. Hays, *Echoes of Scripture in the Letters of Paul* (New Haven: Yale University Press, 1989). See also Koch, *Die Schrift als Zeuge des Evangeliums,* 98–101; D. M. Smith, "The Pauline Literature," in D. A. Carson and H. G. M. Williamson, eds., *It Is Written: Scripture Citing Scripture* (Cambridge: Cambridge University Press, 1988), 265–91; Wagner, *Heralds of the Good News.*

101. See esp. H. D. Betz, *Galatians: A Commentary on Paul's Letter to the Churches in Galatia,* Hermeneia (Philadelphia: Fortress, 1979); *2 Corinthians 8 and 9: A Commentary on Two Administrative Letters of the Apostle Paul,* Hermeneia (Philadelphia: Fortress, 1985); *Der Apostel Paulus und die sokratische Tradition: Eine exegetische Untersuchung zu seiner "Apologie" 2 Korinther 10–13,* BHT 45 (Tübingen: Mohr, 1972). See also A. J. Malherbe, *Paul and the Popular Philosophers* (Minneapolis: Augsburg Fortress, 1989); M. M. Mitchell, *Paul and the Rhetoric of Reconciliation: An Exegetical Investigation of the Language and Composition of 1 Corinthians* (Louisville: Westminster John Knox, 1991); S. K. Stowers, *Letter Writing in Greco-Roman Antiquity* (Philadelphia: Westminster, 1986); R. D. Anderson, *Ancient Rhetorical Theory and Paul* (Kampen: Kok Pharos, 1996; Leuven: Peeters, 1999); D. Watson, "Rhetorical Criticism of the Pauline Epistles Since 1975," *CurBS* 3 (1995): 219–48; G. A. Kennedy, *New Testament Interpretation through Rhetorical Criticism* (Chapel Hill: University of North Carolina Press, 1984). On Pauline rhetoric in Romans alone, see the essays by D. E. Aune, K. P. Donfried, W. Wuellner, and others in *The Romans Debate: Revised and Expanded Edition,* ed. K. P. Donfried (Edinburgh: Clark, 1991); J. D. Kim, *God, Israel, and the Gentiles: Rhetoric and Situation in Romans 9–11,* SBLDS 176 (Atlanta: Society of Biblical Literature, 2000); S. K. Stowers, *A Reading of Romans: Justice, Jews, and Gentiles* (New Haven: Yale University Press, 1994); D. A. Campbell, *The Rhetoric of Righteousness in Romans 3:21–26,* JSNTSup 65 (Sheffield: Sheffield Academic Press, 1992); E. A. Castelli, *Imitating Paul: A Discourse of Power* (Louisville: Westminster, 1991); N. Elliott, *The Rhetoric of Romans: Argumentative Constraint and Strategy and Paul's Dialogue with Judaism,* JSNTSup 45 (Sheffield: JSOT Press, 1990). Beyond Romans, I will mention only the important collection of essays from the Seminar on the Thessalonian Correspondence (which met under the auspices of the Society for New Testament Studies from 1995 to 1997) applying rhetorical criticism to the Thessalonian correspondence: K. P. Donfried and J. Buetler, eds., *The Thessalonians Debate: Methodological Discord or Methodological Synthesis?* (Grand Rapids: Eerdmans, 2000). For introductions to the discipline, see B. Mack, *Rhetoric and the New Testament* (Minneapolis: Fortress, 1990); D. L. Stamps, "Rhetorical Criticism of the New Testament: Ancient and Modern Evaluation of Argumentation," in *Approaches to New Testament Study,* ed. S. E. Porter and D. Tombs, JSNTSup 120 (Sheffield: Sheffield Academic Press, 1995), 77–128.

Luke's portrait as "legendary" or "too good to be true."[102] A case against Paul's Roman citizenship might include the following points:[103]

1. It seems to have been rare for Rome to grant citizenship to Jews in the eastern provinces, and in those cases probably only to those who were rich, influential, and culturally Roman.[104]
2. Paul's Jewish piety and zeal (cf. Phil. 3:6; Gal. 1:14) make it unlikely that his family would have participated in the civic cult, in Greco-Roman religious festivals, and in the gymnasium—practices expected of Roman citizens.[105]
3. Nowhere in his letters does Paul appeal to his Roman citizenship, even when such an appeal might have been very effective (Phil. 3:20; 1 Cor. 4:13; Romans).[106]
4. For Luke to portray Paul as a loyal and respectable citizen of the empire clearly advances Luke's own political and theological agenda.[107]

On the other hand, a limited number of first-century Jews did indeed enjoy Roman citizenship. Moreover, one might imagine Paul feeling a measure of ambivalence about his privileged status and choosing to remain silent on this point lest he gain converts for the wrong reasons. Luke, in any case, must be allowed to use reliable historical information to advance his cause.[108] Moreover, the

102. Respectively, C. K. Barrett, *Paul: An Introduction to His Thought* (Louisville: Westminster John Knox, 1994), 161; J. C. Lentz, *Luke's Portrait of Paul* (Cambridge: Cambridge University Press, 1993), 171.

103. Cf. Roetzel, *Paul: The Man and the Myth*, 19–22; W. Stegmann, "War der Apostel Paulus ein römischer Bürger?" *ZNW* 78 (1987): 200–229.

104. See, however, Riesner (*Paul's Early Period*, 148–49), who is not persuaded that Paul's manual trade (whether tentmaker or leather-worker) conclusively proves lowly origins, and who points to evidence for Jewish citizens in Asia Minor. See also the appeal of Witherington (*The Paul Quest*, 69–73) to G. H. R. Horsley, *NewDocs* 4:311, and B. Rapske, *The Book of Acts and Paul in Roman Custody*, BAFCS 3 (Grand Rapids: Eerdmans, 1994), 89–90. On Paul's status as tradesperson, and its negative implications for Paul's status, see R. F. Hock, *The Social Context of Paul's Ministry: Tentmaking and Apostleship* (Philadelphia: Fortress, 1980). On Paul's status and trade, see also A. C. Thiselton, *The First Epistle to the Corinthians: A Commentary on the Greek Text*, NIGTC (Grand Rapids: Eerdmans, 2000), 23–29.

105. Riesner (*Paul's Early Period*, 151) counts this as "the most weighty critical question." The evidence of Philo (*Legat.* 155–57), however, confirms the presence of Jewish citizens in Rome, whose religious scruples were respected.

106. Against Riesner (*Paul's Early Period*, 156), who finds no reason why Paul would have wanted to mention his citizenship in his letters.

107. Similarly, H. Conzelmann, *Acts of the Apostles*, trans. J. Limburg, A. T. Kraabel, and D. Juel (Philadelphia: Fortress, 1987). Paul's appeals to his citizenship in Acts are disputed by, for example, H. Koester, *Introduction to the New Testament*, 2 vols., FF (Philadelphia: Fortress, 1982), 2:98–99, on the grounds that Roman citizens could avoid the very punishments that Paul claims to have received (2 Cor. 11:23–25).

108. See Witherington (*The Paul Quest*, 71), who suspects that Paul was selective and opportunistic in his use of his citizenship: "It is unlikely that Paul would have been pleased if some-

suggestion merits consideration that when Luke called Paul a "citizen" (*politēs*), he was signaling Paul's membership in a *politeuma* (association, community, colony) along with other Diaspora Jews (cf. Phil. 3:20). To a lesser degree than Roman citizenship, affiliation with such *politeumata* brought certain privileges relating to, for example, taxation and self-government.[109]

Strangers or Allies? Paul's Knowledge of Jesus

Two issues—one historical and the other theological—must be carefully distinguished. On the historical front, we want to know how much Paul knew of Jesus, his teachings and his life, and how he came to know it. Theologically, the question concerns the extent to which the teachings of Jesus and of Paul are compatible. Although the second of these has more wide-ranging consequences, this essay must be content with the first. It is initially surprising that the same Paul who calls himself Christ's slave, and who can reduce his message to the phrase "Christ crucified" (1 Cor. 1:23), makes such limited use of Jesus' teachings and refers so rarely to the events of Jesus' life. Alternatively, it may be equally stunning that one who never met, let alone followed, the earthly Jesus could be so preoccupied with his death, resurrection, and imminent return.

If Paul were our only source for knowledge about the historical Jesus, we would not know that Jesus came from Galilee and was the son of Mary (but see Gal. 4:4), nor that he was baptized, taught in parables, and performed miracles, nor that he ate with sinners and confronted Pharisees, nor that he entered Jerusalem and overturned tables in the temple. The silence in Paul's letters may be misleading, however, for, as Calvin Roetzel observes, "We must assume that when Paul preached he told the story of Jesus, and when he wrote occasional letters to the churches there was no need to retell the story; he had to apply and interpret it for each new situation."[110] Speculation about the relatively few explicit references to the life of Jesus in Paul's letters has tended to pursue three options:[111]

---

one became a Christian adherent because of having heard the gospel from Paul the high-status Roman citizen and seeking to follow a teacher of high social status. Paul wanted the claims of the gospel to stand on their own merits. No offense but the cross itself, no inducement but its compellingly persuasive message."

109. See Roetzel, *Paul: The Man and the Myth*, 21–22, 42, along with the earlier studies of M. Smallwood, ed., *Philonis Alexandrini Legatio ad Gaium*, 2nd ed. (Leiden: Brill, 1970); and S. Applebaum, "The Legal Status of the Jewish Communities in the Diaspora," in *The Jewish People in the First Century: Historical Geography, Political History, Social, Cultural and Religious Life and Institutions*, ed. S. Safrai and M. Stern, 2 vols., CRINT 1.1 (Philadelphia: Fortress, 1974), 1:453.

110. Roetzel, *Paul: The Man and the Myth*, 95. Cf. idem, *The Letters of Paul: Conversations in Context*, 4th ed. (Louisville: Westminster John Knox, 1998), 72–74.

111. Similarly Ehrman, *The New Testament*, 332–35.

1. Paul's knowledge of Jesus traditions was extensive; he addressed his letters to converts who were already familiar with Jesus' teachings, so Paul had no reason to include them. This option needs to explain why Paul chooses not to buttress his own views by appealing to Jesus' teachings. Why would Paul, when he readily summarizes his own preaching among them and frequently quotes Scriptures that presumably they already knew, exclude Jesus' teachings?

2. Paul's knowledge of Jesus traditions was extensive, but he found little of it relevant to his own mission and his message about the cross and resurrection (cf. 1 Cor. 2:2). This view makes one wonder why Paul, on occasion, does appeal to Jesus' teachings.

3. Paul's knowledge of Jesus traditions was minimal. He probably gained some knowledge from Jesus' apostles and family, but he did not draw heavily from these sources for his thought. This view needs to explain the wide-ranging diversity (and, by some accounts, frequency) of Paul's appeals to Jesus traditions.

The following table highlights key points of contact between Paul's letters and the dominical traditions preserved in the Gospels:

Table 15.3 References to Jesus' Teachings in Paul

A. Explicit References and Clear Allusions

Dominical Teaching	Pauline Introductory Formula	Pauline Reference	Gospel Parallels
Husbands and wives should not separate.	"I give this instruction, not I but the Lord. . . ."	1 Cor. 7:10–11	Matt. 5:31–32 & Luke 16:18; Mark 10:11–12 & Matt. 19:3–12
The laborer is worthy of payment.	"So also the Lord commanded those who proclaim the gospel. . . ."	1 Cor. 9:14	Matt. 10:10; Luke 10:7
"This is my body, which is given for you. Do this in remembrance of me." (Luke)	"For I received from the Lord what I also handed on to you. . . ."	1 Cor. 11:23–24	Matt. 26:26; Mark 14:22; Luke 22:19
"This cup that is poured out for you is the new covenant in my blood." (Luke)		1 Cor. 11:25	Matt. 26:27; Mark 14:24; Luke 22:20
The Lord will descend with angel and trumpet, and the dead will rise.[112]	"For this we say to you by a word of the Lord. . . ."	1 Thess. 4:15–17	Matt. 24:30–31; cf. Mark 13; Luke 21

112. In defense of a common eschatological tradition shared by both Paul and the Synoptic evangelists is A. J. McNicol, *Jesus' Directions for the Future: A Source and Redaction-History*

| Address to prophets | "The things I write to you are the Lord's commandment." | 1 Cor. 14:37 | Mark 10:2–12 Matt. 5:31–32 |

B. Echoes and Parallels

Dominical Teaching	Pauline Reference	Gospel Parallels
Faith that moves mountains	1 Cor. 13:2	Matt. 17:20 & Luke 17:6; Matt. 21:21 & Mark 11:23
Bless those who curse you	1 Cor. 4:12; Rom. 12:14	Luke 6:28; cf. Matt. 5:44
Turn the other cheek	1 Thess. 5:15; Rom. 12:17	Luke 6:29 & Matt. 5:39–40
Live at peace	Rom. 12:18	Mark 9:50; cf. Matt. 5:9
Love your enemies	Rom. 12:19–21	Luke 6:27, 35a & Matt. 5:44
Render unto Caesar	Rom. 13:7	Matt. 22:15–22
Do not judge	Rom. 14:13	Matt. 7:1 & Luke 6:37
Suspension of food laws	Rom. 14:14	Mark 7:14–23; Matt. 15:15–20
Coming day will surprise	1 Thess. 5:2	Luke 12:39–40 & Matt. 24:43–44
Be at peace with one another	1 Thess. 5:13	Mark 9:50

Scholarly interest in tracing lines of historical continuity and discontinuity between Jesus and Paul is on the rise.[113] In 1971, D. L. Dungan argued that

---

Study of the Use of the Eschatological Traditions in Paul and in the Synoptic Accounts of Jesus' Last Eschatological Discourse, New Gospel Studies 9 (Macon, Ga.: Mercer University Press, 1996). Notwithstanding his preference for the Griesbach hypothesis (Matthean priority), McNicol's identification of Synoptic/Pauline parallels is persuasive.

113. Important studies include J. M. G. Barclay, "Jesus and Paul," in Hawthorne, Martin, and Reid, *Dictionary of Paul and His Letters;* R. Bultmann, "The Significance of the Historical Jesus for the Theology of Paul," in *Faith and Understanding: Collected Essays* (London: SCM, 1969), 220–46; J. W. Drane, "Patterns of Evangelization in Paul and Jesus: A Way Forward in the Jesus-Paul Debate?" in *Jesus of Nazareth: Lord and Christ,* ed. J. B. Green and M. Turner (Grand Rapids: Eerdmans, 1994), 281–96; J. D. G. Dunn, "Jesus Tradition in Paul," in *Studying the Historical Jesus: Evaluations of the State of Current Research,* ed. B. Chilton and C. A. Evans, NTTS 19 (Leiden: Brill, 1998), 155–78; idem, "Paul's Knowledge of the Jesus Tradition: The Evidence of Romans," in *Christus Bezeugen,* ed. K. Kertelge, T. Holtz, and C.-P. März, ETS 59 (Leipzig: St. Benno, 1988), 193–207; J. W. Fraser, *Jesus and Paul* (Appleford: Marcham, 1974); V. P. Furnish, *Jesus according to Paul* (Cambridge: Cambridge University Press, 1993); idem, "The Jesus-Paul Debate: From Baur to Bultmann," in *Paul and Jesus: Collected Essays,* ed. A. J. M. Wedderburn, JSNTSup 37 (Sheffield: JSOT Press, 1989), 17–50; T. Holtz, "Paul and the Oral Gospel Tradition," in *Jesus and the Oral Gospel Tradition,* ed. H. Wansborough, JSNTSup 64 (Sheffield: Sheffield Academic Press, 1991), 380–93; J. C. Hurd, "'The Jesus Whom Paul Preaches' (Acts 19:13)," in *From Jesus to Paul,* ed. P. Richardson and J. C. Hurd (Waterloo, Ont.: Wilfrid Laurier University Press, 1984), 73–89; H. Maccoby, *The Mythmaker: Paul and the Invention of Christianity* (London: Weidenfeld & Nicholson, 1986); H.-W. Kuhn, "Der irdische Jesus bei Paulus als traditionsgeschichtliches und theologisches Problem," *ZTK* 67 (1970): 295–320; F. Neirynck, "Paul and the Sayings of

Paul's allusive use of Jesus' teachings in the Corinthian correspondence suggests that that congregation had already been taught Jesus traditions.[114] More ambitiously, evangelical scholars Seyoon Kim and David Wenham have sought to show that the lines of influence and continuity between Jesus and Paul were more substantial than often is acknowledged.[115] Not only do Kim and Wenham assess Paul's knowledge of traditions about Jesus—a tricky enterprise, given how few explicit Jesus-citations Paul includes—but both authors (Wenham especially) also compare the theology of Jesus and Paul on a range of topics: the kingdom of God, Jesus' identity, Jesus' death, the mission and nature of the church, ethics, and eschatology, this being an even trickier maneuver because Jesus left us no literary corpus. And both find Paul's theological understanding rather close to, and certainly compatible with, Jesus' teaching.

Establishing direct lines of influence and dependence is always rather precarious; some alleged parallels might derive from a shared cultural milieu or from Paul's knowledge of early Christian traditions rather than directly from Jesus himself. And Wenham may be inclined to underestimate some of the differences.[116] But even if these sorts of studies have shown that Paul knew of, and drew upon, a sizable collection of Jesus' sayings, Paul's reluctance to acknowledge a debt to his Lord's teachings remains something of a puzzle. As a source for his ethical reflection Paul seems more inclined to acknowledge

---

Jesus," in *L'Apôtre Paul: Personnalité, style et conception du ministère*, ed. A. Vanhoye, BETL 73 (Leuven: Leuven University Press, 1986), 265–321; P. Richardson and P. Gooch, "Logia of Jesus in 1 Corinthians," in *The Jesus Tradition outside the Gospels*, ed. D. Wenham, Gospel Perspectives 5 (Sheffield: JSOT Press, 1985), 39–62; H. N. Ridderbos, *Paul and Jesus* (Philadelphia: Presbyterian & Reformed, 1958); A. Schlatter, *Jesus und Paulus: Eine Vorlesung und einige Aufsätze* (Stuttgart: Calwer, 1961); C. H. H. Scobie, "Jesus or Paul? The Origin of the Universal Mission of the Christian Church," in Richardson and Hurd, *From Jesus to Paul*, 47–60; D. P. Stanley, "Pauline Allusions to the Sayings of Jesus," *CBQ* 23 (1961): 26–39; P. Stuhlmacher, "Jesustradition im Römerbrief?" *TBei* 14 (1983): 240–50; C. M. Tuckett, "1 Corinthians and Q," *JBL* 102 (1983): 607–18; N. Walter, "Paul and the Early Christian Jesus-Tradition," in Wedderburn, *Paul and Jesus*, 51–80; A. J. M. Wedderburn, "Paul and Jesus: The Problem of Continuity," in Wedderburn, *Paul and Jesus*, 99–115; D. Wenham, "Paul's Use of the Jesus Tradition: Three Samples," in Wenham, *The Jesus Tradition*, 7–37; idem, "The Story of Jesus Known to Paul," in Green and Turner, *Jesus of Nazareth*, 297–311; S. G. Wilson, "From Jesus to Paul: The Contours and Consequences of a Debate," in Richardson and Hurd, *From Jesus to Paul*, 1–21; Witherington, *Jesus, Paul, and the End of the World* (Downers Grove, Ill.: InterVarsity, 1992).

114. D. L. Dungan, *The Sayings of Jesus in the Churches of Paul* (Oxford: Blackwell, 1971).

115. S. Kim, "Jesus, Sayings of," in Hawthorne, Martin, and Reid, *Dictionary of Paul and His Letters*, 474–92; D. Wenham, *Paul: Follower of Jesus or Founder of Christianity?* (Grand Rapids: Eerdmans, 1995). Cf. Roetzel, *Paul: The Man and the Myth*, 95–96. Kim's article now appears as ch. 8 in S. Kim, *Paul and the New Perspective: Second Thoughts on the Origin of Paul's Gospel* (Grand Rapids: Eerdmans, 2002), 259–92.

116. So Morna Hooker in her review of *Paul*, by D. Wenham, *RBL*, June 26, 2000 (online: http://www.bookreviews.org/pdf/2245_1403.pdf). Among the points of contrast (see Ehrman, *The New Testament*, 336), we note that Jesus' teaching focused on repentance, on conforming to God's will, and on the end of time, whereas Paul's kerygma announced Jesus' death on the cross and his vindication at the resurrection.

Scripture, albeit reinterpreted in the light of Christ crucified and risen, and the new community gathered in his name. Paul, it appears, did not "read" the life of Jesus and the Scriptures of Israel independently, but rather together, as mutually interpreting and mutually transforming.[117]

Strangely Familiar: The Shaping of Paul's Communities

One of many interdisciplinary partnerships to form in recent decades, the social-scientific approach to NT studies has encouraged rigorous analysis of the social forces and structures at work in the earliest Roman-era churches.[118] Wayne Meeks was among the first to compare systematically Paul's communities with a range of contemporary groups and organizations: the Roman household, the voluntary association, the synagogue, and the philosophical or rhetorical school. To Meeks's list we might want to add the secret societies that guarded the ancient mysteries.[119]

Various scholars have defended one or another of these groups as the best model for understanding the formation and identity of Paul's churches. Already in 1975, John Gager found the structure of the Diaspora synagogue helpful in explaining early Christian use of Scripture, leadership, liturgy, and social order. More recently, both James Burtchaell and Judith Lieu have flagged the importance of the Jewish synagogue in the formation of Paul's churches. For Burtchaell, the relevant continuity concerns the officers presiding over the liturgy; for Lieu, the synagogal matrix of the early church was what encouraged the conversion of many Gentile "God-fearers" to Christianity.[120] Along these lines, the provocative thesis of Mark Nanos, that Romans addresses (predominantly Gentile) Christians who continued to move in (predominantly

---

117. Similarly Hays, *Echoes of Scripture,* 157, 168, and passim.

118. Emerging almost simultaneously in the early 1980s were three seminal studies in social-scientific criticism: G. Theissen, *The Social Setting of Pauline Christianity: Essays on Corinth* (Philadelphia: Fortress, 1982); W. A. Meeks, *The First Urban Christians: The Social World of the Apostle Paul* (New Haven: Yale University Press, 1983); A. J. Malherbe, *The Social Aspects of Early Christianity,* 2nd rev. ed. (Philadelphia: Fortress, 1983). For a survey of subsequent developments, see C. Osiek, *What Are They Saying about the Social Setting of the New Testament?* 2nd ed. (New York: Paulist Press, 1992).

119. See R. S. Ascough, *What Are They Saying about the Formation of Pauline Churches?* (New York: Paulist Press, 1998).

120. J. G. Gager, *Kingdom and Community: The Social World of Early Christianity* (Englewood Cliffs, N.J.: Prentice-Hall, 1975); J. T. Burtchaell, *From Synagogue to Church: Public Services and Offices in the Earliest Christian Communities* (New York: Cambridge University Press, 1992); J. M. Lieu, "Do God-Fearers Make Good Christians?" in *Crossing the Boundaries,* ed. S. E. Porter, P. Joyce, and D. E. Orton, BIS 8 (Leiden: Brill, 1994), 329–45. For recent debate regarding the category of "God-fearers" (cf. Acts 10, 13, 16–18) within first-century Judaism, see J. A. Overman and R. S. MacLennan, eds., *Diaspora Jews and Judaism,* SFSHJ 41 (Atlanta: Scholars Press, 1992).

non-Christian) Jewish synagogal circles, can stand only if the influence of the synagogue and its leadership on the Roman church continued for some time after the gospel took root.[121]

The idea that Paul conceived of Christianity in terms of the philosophical schools was developed by E. A. Judge, who compared Paul's followers to scholastic societies and Paul to a traveling sophist whose lectures contributed to the already lively discourse of the public square.[122] Around the same time, Hans Conzelmann was suggesting that we should think of Paul establishing an "actual school," most likely in Ephesus, to train collaborators and to advance the movement.[123] More recently, and more persuasively, Stanley Stowers, a former student of Malherbe, has argued that the diatribal, pedagogical style of Romans suggests that Paul modeled his communities after the mentor-student relationship of the philosophical schools.[124] Meanwhile, David Aune and Anthony J. Guerra have classified Romans (or its central section) as a protreptic letter designed to commend to Paul's readers—soon to be his "school" at Rome—the Christian life.[125] Loveday Alexander is likewise convinced of the aptness of the philosophical school model for explaining certain features of the earliest Pauline groups, and, most recently, Troels Engberg-Pedersen has built a case for viewing Paul's community formation in, for example, Philippi, as modeled after Stoic thought: "Paul is speaking and acting as a teacher in relation to his pupils in the way of the Stoic sage."[126]

The voluntary association has long been a favorite analogy for the early church. In recent times, essays by John S. Kloppenborg, Bradley H. McLean, and Wendy Cotter in the 1993 Festschrift for John C. Hurd make the case, and a monograph by Thomas Schmeller examines the Corinthian community in light of the voluntary association, focusing especially on matters of hierarchy,

---

121. M. Nanos, "The Jewish Context of the Gentile Audience Addressed in Paul's Letter to the Romans," *CBQ* 61 (1999): 283–304; *The Mystery of Romans: The Jewish Context of Paul's Letter* (Minneapolis: Fortress, 1996), 75, 84, 85–165. Nanos's proposal thus moves beyond the consensus view, illustrated by J. D. G. Dunn (*Romans*, 2 vols., WBC 38A–B [Dallas: Word, 1988], 1:liii), that the Roman Christians "were not yet clearly distinguished from the wider Jewish community."

122. E. A. Judge, "The Earliest Christians as a Scholastic Community," *JRH* 111 (1960): 4–15. See also idem, *The Social Pattern of Christian Groups in the First Century: Some Prolegomena to the Study of New Testament Ideas of Social Obligation* (London: Tyndale, 1960).

123. Hans Conzelmann, "Luke's Place in the Development of Early Christianity," in Keck and Martyn, *Studies in Luke-Acts*, 298–316. For Conzelmann, this goes a long way to explaining the emergence of the deutero-Pauline literature.

124. S. K. Stowers, *The Diatribe and Paul's Letter to the Romans*, SBLDS 57 (Chico, Calif.: Scholars Press, 1981). See also Stowers's essay "The Diatribe," in *Greco-Roman Literature and the New Testament: Selected Forms and Genres*, ed. D. E. Aune, SBLSBS 21 (Atlanta: Scholars Press, 1988), 71–83.

125. D. E. Aune, "Romans as a *Logos Protreptikos*," in Donfried, *The Romans Debate*, 278–96; A. J. Guerra, *Romans and the Apologetic Tradition: The Purpose, Genre and Audience of Paul's Letter*, SNTSMS 81 (Cambridge: Cambridge University Press, 1995).

126. Engberg-Pedersen, *Paul and the Stoics*, 107.

patronage, and egalitarianism.[127] The table below highlights major points of similarity and difference, some of which remain in dispute, between the Pauline communities and various other groups.

Table 15.4 Pauline Communities versus Other Groups:
Similarities and Differences

	Points of Similarity	Points of Difference
Household	• met in homes • household conversion to new way of life • used as metaphor for entire church	• no parallel rituals • cannot explain authority of a leader who is not also the paterfamilias • cannot explain ties between house churches
Voluntary Association	• voluntary membership • depended on wealthy patrons • enjoyed common meals • crossed gender and class barriers • provided setting for rituals, practices, celebrations • made arrangements for burial • conditions for, and expectations of, membership	• church demanded primary loyalty • church more inclusive, open, heterogeneous, egalitarian • few shared terms (e.g., *episkopos, diakonos, ekklēsia*) • church met more frequently • church known for proselytizing • association more local
Synagogue	• *ekklēsia* in LXX used of Israel • sometimes met in private homes (less so in the cities of Pauline communities) • liturgy: Scripture reading and interpretation; prayers; meals • rituals: washing (cf. baptism), Passover (cf. communion), circumcision • dispute settlement • moral reference point/framework: OT	• few shared terms; *archontes, archisynagōgos, synagōgē* not used by Paul • church patrons not called "father" or "mother" • women's role greater in Pauline communities • church not defined ethnically • circumcision not required in Pauline communities
Ancient Mysteries	• membership was voluntary • promised salvation to adherents • initiation ritual involving dying and rising with the god (disputed) • sacred meal shared among adherents	• little or no shared terminology • mysteries apparently did not demand exclusive loyalty • mysteries were not missionary/evangelistic
Philosophical or Rhetorical School	• teaching was central • moral exhortation in meetings, letters • some held possessions in common and shared standards of behavior • emphasis on unity around the teachings of the founder	• schools had no rituals or initiatory rites analogous to baptism, communion, common meal • church did not have public or private sacrifices, festivals, processions

127. See B. H. McLean, ed., *Origins and Method: Towards a New Understanding of Judaism and Christianity,* JSNTSup 86 (Sheffield: JSOT Press, 1993); relevant essays in that volume include J. S. Kloppenborg, "Edwin Hatch, Churches and Collegia," 212–38; B. H. McLean,

Our knowledge of these groups is growing, and many points of convergence between Paul's churches and other social groups have proven immensely illuminating. However, several cautionary notes should be given. First, Meeks's findings, corroborated now by Ascough, bear repeating:

> None of the . . . models . . . captures the whole of the Pauline *ekklesia*, although all offer significant analogies. At the least, the household remains the basic context within which most if not all the local Pauline groups established themselves, and the manifold life of voluntary associations, the special adaptation of the synagogue to urban life, and the organization of instruction and exhortation in philosophical schools all provide examples of groups solving certain problems that the Christians, too, had to face.[128]

Second, the better studies tend to emphasize analogical correlations between the church and other social groups rather than genealogical ones. It is safer to highlight similarities than to attempt to prove lines of dependence and pedigree. Third, the value of such comparative studies is by no means limited to points of similarity; the unique dimensions of the early church (e.g., its missionary zeal) emerge all the more clearly. Fourth, it is irresponsible to assume that all of Paul's churches took shape in the same way or to impose the essential features of one community (typically Corinth), without warrant, on all the others.[129] And finally, whatever other cultural forces helped shape the earliest Pauline communities, we surely must include Paul's letters themselves. Even his opponents had to agree that Paul's correspondence was, in essence, one protracted, ambitious effort in community formation, and further, that Paul's primary context for his own ethical reflection was the Christian community itself.[130]

"The Agrippinilla Inscription: Religious Associations and Early Church Formation," 239–70; W. Cotter, "Our Politeuma Is in Heaven: The Meaning of Phil. 3:17–21," 92–104. See also T. Schmeller, *Hierarchie und Egalität: Eine sozialgeschichtliche Untersuchung paulinisher Gemeinden und griechisch-römischer Vereine*, SBS 162 (Stuttgart: Katholisches Bibelwerk, 1995); and J. S. Kloppenborg and S. G. Wilson, eds., *Voluntary Associations in the Graeco-Roman World* (New York: Routledge, 1996).

128. Meeks, *The First Urban Christians*, 84. See also idem, "Breaking Away: Three New Testament Pictures of Christianity's Separation from the Jewish Communities," in *"To See Ourselves as Others See Us": Christians, Jews, "Others" in Late Antiquity*, ed. J. Neusner and E. S. Frerichs (Chico, Calif.: Scholars Press, 1985), 93–115, in which he emphasizes the role of the household in the formation of Pauline groups (and downplays the influence of the Diaspora synagogue). Likewise, for R. Ascough, "Households were often the basic cells of church formation and a vital factor in the church's development," but "no one model is adequate in and of itself for explaining all aspects of Paul's Christian communities" (*Formation of Pauline Churches*, 9, 95).

129. On this point, see Ascough, *Formation of Pauline Churches*, 95–99; also J. Z. Smith, *Drudgery Divine: On the Comparison of Early Christianities and the Religions of Late Antiquity* (Chicago: University of Chicago Press, 1990).

130. On the letters as means of community formation, see R. B. Hays, "Ecclesiology and Ethics in 1 Corinthians," *Ex Auditu* 10 (1994): 31–43; idem, *The Moral Vision of the New Testa-*

Words on Target: Paul's Letters and Their First Recipients

It remains to consider the setting and occasion of the undisputed letters within Paul's career. As the following table demonstrates, a consensus has yet to emerge on the relative dating of Paul's Epistles:[131]

Table 15.5 Proposed Dates for Paul's Letters

Year	F. F. Bruce (1977)	R. A. Jewett (1979)	G. Lüdemann (1984)	B. Reicke (1987/2001)	K. Donfried (1992)	B. Witherington (1998)	C. Roetzel (1999)
41			1 Thess.				
46							
47			Jerusalem Council		1 Thess. (between 36 and 50)		Jerusalem Council
48	Galatians?	1–2 Thess.					
49	Jerusalem Council	Jerusalem Council	1 Cor.	Jerusalem Council		Galatians	
50	1–2 Thess.		2 Cor. 1–9, 2 Cor. 10–13, Galatians		Jerusalem Council	Jerusalem Council	1 Thess.
51			Romans			1–2 Thess.	
52				2 Thess.	Galatians,		Galatians
53		Galatians		1 Thess.	Philippians,	1 Cor.	
54					Philemon, 1 Cor.,		1 Cor.
55	1–2 Cor.	Philippians, 1–2 Cor.		Galatians	2 Cor.	2 Cor.	2 Cor. 10–13, Philippians, Philemon
56		Philemon, Colossians		1 Cor., 1 Timothy	Romans	Romans	2 Cor. 1–9, Romans
57	Romans	Romans		2 Cor.			
58				Romans, Titus			

---

ment: A Contemporary Introduction to New Testament Ethics (San Francisco: HarperSanFrancisco, 1996), 18–72; R. Banks, *Paul's Idea of Community: The Early House Churches in Their Historical Setting* (Grand Rapids: Eerdmans, 1980); J. P. Sampley, *Walking between the Times: Paul's Moral Reasoning* (Minneapolis: Fortress, 1991).

131. See F. F. Bruce, *Paul: Apostle of the Heart Set Free*, 475; R. A. Jewett, *A Chronology of Paul's Life* (Philadelphia: Fortress, 1979); Lüdemann, *Paul: Apostle to the Gentiles*, 262–63; Reicke, *Re-examining Paul's Letters* (published in 2001, after Reicke's death in 1987); K. P. Donfried, "Chronology: New Testament," *ABD* 1:1016–22; Witherington, *The Paul Quest*, 304–31; Roetzel, *Paul: The Man and the Myth*, 182–83. Lüdemann offers an alternative chronology (based on a later date for the crucifixion), arrived at by adding three years to each of these dates. In some cases, uncertainty has prompted scholars to posit a range of several years for a letter's composition. Where this could be shown only with difficulty, the table here indicates the earliest proposed date.

Year	F. F. Bruce (1977)	R. A. Jewett (1979)	G. Lüdemann (1984)	B. Reicke (1987/2001)	K. Donfried (1992)	B. Witherington (1998)	C. Roetzel (1999)
59				Philemon, Colossians, Ephesians			
60	Ephesians, Colossians, Philippians, Philemon?			2 Timothy		Colossians, Philemon, Philippians, Ephesians?	
61							
62				Philippians			
65	1–2 Timothy, Titus?					1–2 Timothy, Titus (as late as 68)	

Surprisingly few fixed points constrain the chronology debate. One must consider Claudius's expulsion of the Jews from Rome (49 C.E.?),[132] as well as Gallio's appointment to proconsul over Achaia (51–52 C.E.).[133] Beyond this, however, we must muddle through with evidence internal to Paul's letters and Acts—the sequence of events in Gal. 1 and 2; Paul's trial catalogs in 2 Cor. 6, 11, and 12, including his escape from Damascus during the rule of Aretas (2 Cor. 11:32–33); allusions to Paul's fundraising; linguistic variation—evidence that frequently is tolerant of diverse interpretations. Fortunately, work can proceed on the occasion, social context, and reception of specific letters even if little agreement surrounds their relative placement and date. Space constraints allow us to consider only a pair of the more long-standing, yet still lively, debates.

The Romans Debate

Paul's own testimony in Romans makes it clear that he had not yet been to Rome (15:22–23; 1:8–15), that he hoped to solicit from the churches in Rome support for his mission to Spain (15:24, 28b, 32), and that en route from Corinth to Rome and parts west he planned to visit Jerusalem, bearing his precious collection for the poor (15:25–32; cf. Gal. 2:10). Paul's request for prayer (15:30–31) signals his fear that this collection might not meet with approval, apparently because certain opponents in Jerusalem were questioning the legitimacy of his Gentile mission (15:31). This much seems clear. But why such a lengthy treatise on the gospel (1:16), divine righteousness (1:17; 3:5, 21), justification (5:1), the law (7:1–8:4), Israel (9:1–11:36), and more? Did he seek only to "remind" an established church of what lay at the heart of his message (15:15)? To borrow a question from J. P. Sampley, "Why is Romans so long?"[134]

132. See below, n. 136.
133. According to Acts 18:12–17, Paul appeared before Gallio in Corinth, thus fixing the date of Paul's second journey.
134. J. P. Sampley, "Romans in a Different Light," in Bassler et al., *Pauline Theology,* 3:117.

Recent years have witnessed a growing inclination among scholars to read Romans in light of the political and religious climate in the capital.[135] According to the prevailing wisdom, Claudius's expulsion of Jews from Rome, evidently in 49 C.E.,[136] left behind a predominantly Gentile church that grew increasingly dismissive of (or hostile toward) the residual Jewish population (cf. 11:13–24). When Jews such as Priscilla and Aquila returned home (16:3–5; 1 Cor. 16:19; Acts 18:2) some time after Nero's rise to power in 54 C.E., their reception was chilly at best. Meanwhile law-free Gentile Christianity was arousing the suspicions of at least some returning Jewish believers. Against this view, however, it must be noted (1) that the timing and extent of the expulsion remain in dispute; (2) that it is not entirely clear that the weak and the strong of Rom. 14:1–15:13 can be neatly equated with Jewish and Gentile Christians, respectively;[137] and (3) that this proposal, in any case, struggles to account for the rest of the letter.

Almost certainly, Paul's reasons for Romans were complex. A. J. M. Wedderburn quite reasonably imagines Paul addressing a spectrum of (largely) Gentile believers, ranging from Judaizers, for whom Paul's law-free gospel and Gentile collection smacked of antinomianism, to triumphalist Gentile believers, who despised all things Jewish and denied the church's spiritual debt

135. Such views stand out against the earlier tendency to read Romans as an abstract summation of Paul's theology. Note especially Günther Bornkamm, whose 1963 article "The Letter to the Romans as Paul's Last Will and Testament" is now available in Donfried, *The Romans Debate*, 16–28; sympathetic to Bornkamm's position is H. D. Betz, "Paul," *ABD* 5:198. Similarly, Jacob Jervell argued in 1971 ("The Letter to Jerusalem," also now in Donfried, *The Romans Debate*, 53–64) that Romans provides us with the text of a speech that Paul planned to deliver, along with his collection, in Jerusalem.

136. This date for the expulsion is by no means uncontested. Three sources attest to the event: Acts 18:2; Suetonius, *Claudius* 25.4 (second century); and Orosius, *Historiarum adversum paganos libri* 7.6.15–16 (fifth century). Suetonius does not date the expulsion, and although Orosius claims Josephus as his authority, no such reference in Josephus survives. For a helpful assessment of the evidence (defending the year 49 C.E.), see F. F. Bruce, "The Romans Debate—Continued," in Donfried, *The Romans Debate*, 177–81. G. Lüdemann (*Paul, Apostle to the Gentiles*, 6–7) wants to equate the expulsion with the ban imposed by Claudius in 41 C.E. and described by Dio Cassius (*Historiae Romanae* 60.6.6). Arguing against harmonizing our three references, and thus against the value of the edict of Claudius for illuminating the occasion of Romans, are D. Slingerland, "Suetonius *Claudius* 25.4, Acts 18, and Paulus Orosius's *Historiarum adversum paganos libri VII*: Dating the Claudian Expulsion(s) of Roman Jews," *JQR* 83 (1992): 127–44; M. Nanos, *The Mystery of Romans*, 372–87.

137. M. Reasoner (*The Strong and the Weak: Romans 14:1–15:13 in Context*, SNTSMS 103 [Cambridge: Cambridge University Press, 1999]) detects in Paul's "strong/weak" language a reference to degrees of status and honor in Roman society (though he does find the strong to be predominantly Gentile Christians, and the weak to be predominantly scrupulous Jewish Christians). See also idem, "The Theology of Romans 12:1–15:13," in Bassler et al., *Pauline Theology*, 3:288–90, 297–98. Alternatively, M. Nanos (*The Mystery of Romans*, 143) identifies the weak with "Jews who do not yet believe in Jesus as the Christ of Israel or Savior of the nations: they are the non-Christian Jews in Rome." Cf. idem, "Jewish Context of the Gentile Audience," 283–304.

to Israel.[138] Similarly, N. T. Wright argues not only that the letter addresses problems internal to the Roman church, but also that Paul wrote to insure that a predominantly Gentile congregation would embrace his missionary strategy and message:

> In making Rome his new base, there was always the danger . . . that local anti-Jewish sentiment would lead Gentile Christians not only to isolate Jews within the Christian fellowship but also to marginalize a mission that included Jews. Paul, therefore, wanted to insist that the gospel was "for the Jew first and also, equally, for the Greek."[139]

Perhaps the lesson of the Romans debate is that historical reality is almost always messier (and more interesting) than any scholarly reconstruction.

The Corinthian Correspondence and Paul's Opponents

Scholarly fascination with Paul's opponents dates back at least to F. C. Baur, who argued (unsuccessfully, it turns out) that early Christianity was forged in the heat of a battle between Peter's pro-law, Jerusalem-based forces and Paul's law-free Diaspora camp.[140] More recent proposals have been much less sweeping, but most would have to grant Baur's point that the earliest Christians were a raucous, divided lot, and that Paul's gospel and his apostleship often were sharply contested.[141] Along with Galatians, the Corinthian correspondence affords perhaps our best window on Paul's sparring partners and on the lost world they represent. Many have set out to rehearse (with varying degrees of confidence and specificity) the details of Paul's often-stormy relationship with the Corinthian community. One such rehearsal runs as follows:[142]

138. A. J. M. Wedderburn, "The Purpose and Occasion of Romans Again," in Donfried, *The Romans Debate*, 200–202. Cf. D. J. Moo, *The Epistle to the Romans*, NICNT (Grand Rapids: Eerdmans, 1996); T. R. Schreiner, *Romans*, BECNT (Grand Rapids: Baker, 1998), 15–23; Dunn, *Romans*, 1:lv–lviii.

139. N. T. Wright, "Romans and the Theology of Paul," in Bassler et al., *Pauline Theology*, 3:35. To this Wright now adds a broader, political dimension to Paul's agenda in Romans: "Paul's declaration that the gospel of King Jesus reveals God's *dikaiosynē* must also be read as a deliberate laying down of a challenge to the imperial pretension" ("Paul's Gospel and Caesar's Empire," in Horsley, *Paul and Politics*, 172).

140. Appearing in 1835, in *Tübinger Zeitschrift für Theologie*, was Baur's seminal essay, "The Christ-party in the Corinthians Church, the Opposition of Petrine and Pauline Christianity in the Primitive Church, the Apostle Peter in Rome." Baur, of course, did not initiate the "opponents" debate, but he was the first to make it the Archimedean point of early Christianity. For developments before and after Baur, see E. E. Ellis, "Paul and His Opponents: Trends in the Research," in *Prophecy and Hermeneutic in Early Christianity* (Grand Rapids: Eerdmans, 1978), 80–115.

141. Dieter Georgi (*The Opponents of Paul in 2 Corinthians* [Philadelphia: Fortress, 1986], 2) puts it nicely: "The problem stated by Baur is still with us today despite obituaries and furious rampages to the contrary."

142. In addition to the standard commentaries and introductions, see J. M. Gilchrist, "Paul and the Corinthians: The Sequence of Letters and Visits," *JSNT* 34 (1988): 47–69.

1. Along with Silvanus and Timothy (2 Cor. 1:19), Paul spends one and a half years preaching in Corinth (50–52 C.E.) and founding the church (Acts 18:1–18). According to Acts 18:12, this visit overlapped with Gallio's term as provincial governor (from July 51 to June 52).[143] Paul receives some external funding during this period (Phil. 4:14–16) to supplement his own income (1 Cor. 9:3–18), but none from the Corinthians themselves (1 Cor. 9:12, 15–18; 2 Cor. 11:7–9).

2. Paul sends the church his (now lost) "previous letter," which was, in part, misunderstood or disregarded (1 Cor. 5:9–13).[144]

3. Members of Chloe's household[145] come to Paul with information about problems at Corinth (1 Cor. 1:11–12; 5:1–2; 11:18).

4. A delegation including Stephanus, Fortunatus, and Achaicus subsequently arrives in Ephesus, carrying news, a gift (1 Cor. 16:17), and a letter from the church containing questions and/or counterarguments[146] to which Paul must respond (1 Cor. 7:1).

5. Paul writes 1 Corinthians from Ephesus, likely between 53 and 56 C.E. (1 Cor. 16:5–9; Acts 19:1–41 [v. 22]; 20:1–3). Timothy may have delivered the letter (1 Cor. 16:10; Acts 19:22), or Titus, or perhaps (since 1 Cor. 16:17–18 sounds like a letter of commendation) the trio of Stephanas, Fortunatus, and Achaicus carried it on their return trip.

6. If Timothy did not actually accompany 1 Corinthians, he was to arrive shortly thereafter to strengthen Paul's position in the church (1 Cor. 4:17; 16:10–11) against pockets of opposition (1 Cor. 4:18).

7. Paul travels to Corinth for a brief, "sorrowful" visit (2 Cor. 2:1–2, 12:21), and then returns to Ephesus, apparently in distress.

8. Paul intends to return after a time in Macedonia (2 Cor. 1:16), but a change in plans gives opponents further reason to question his credibility (2 Cor. 1:15–2:1).

---

143. Few have followed G. Lüdemann, who disputes the historicity of the trial before Gallio (*Paul, Apostle to the Gentiles,* 160), in dating Paul's first visit to Corinth as early as 41 C.E.

144. Against J. C. Hurd and W. Schmithals, V. P. Furnish (*2 Corinthians,* AB 32A [New York: Doubleday, 1984], 27, 371–83) has shown how unlikely it is that 2 Cor. 6:14–7:1 preserves part of this lost letter.

145. According to G. Theissen (*Social Setting of Pauline Christianity,* 92–94), "Chloe's people" probably are slaves or dependent workers—actual family members would take their father's name even if Chloe was a widow—and thus lower-class members of the church at Corinth who briefly connected with Paul while on business in Ephesus. Alternatively, G. D. Fee (*The First Epistle to the Corinthians,* NICNT [Grand Rapids: Eerdmans, 1987]) suggests that they were agents of a wealthy Asian businesswoman, but not from the Corinthian church, since neither Paul nor the Corinthian church could assume that members would be impartial witnesses to the problem. See also J. Hurd, *The Origin of 1 Corinthians* (1965; reprint, Macon, Ga.: Mercer University Press, 1983), 48.

146. Fee (*First Epistle to the Corinthians,* 6–11) argues that the Corinthians' letter to Paul took "considerable exception" to Paul on several points.

9. Instead of a visit (2 Cor. 1:23; 2:1), Paul unleashes his "tearful" or "severe" letter—perhaps 2 Cor. 10–13[147]—as a counterattack on his opponents (2 Cor. 2:4; 7:8).

10. Titus reports to Paul, now in Macedonia, that the letter has done its work (2 Cor. 7:6–16).

11. Paul composes the more conciliatory 2 Cor. 1–9.[148]

12. Paul sends this letter with Titus and other delegates, who arrive to gather the collection (2 Cor. 8:6, 16–24; 9:3–4; 12:17–18).

13. A fresh round of opponents, dubbed by Paul "false apostles," arrive in Corinth and create a stir (2 Cor. 10:2, 10–12; 11:4–18, 22–23).[149]

14. Paul pens 2 Cor. 10–13 as a counterblast to these rival apostles.[150]

15. En route to Jerusalem with the collection, Paul reaches Corinth fully intending, if need be, to confront his opponents (2 Cor. 10:2, 11; 12:14; Acts 20:2–3).

The task of comparing and correlating "opponents" across the Pauline corpus and around the Mediterranean lies well beyond the scope of this essay. One might wonder, for example, whether the group that Paul accused of advancing "another gospel" in Corinth (*euangelion heteron* [2 Cor. 11:4]) knew those who preached "another gospel" in Galatia (*heteron euangelion* [Gal. 1:6–10]). Would it help, we would like to know, if we read 2 Corin-

147. This "severe" letter traditionally has been associated with 1 Corinthians and the accompanying crisis with the flagrant offender of 1 Cor. 5:1–5 (cf. 2 Cor. 2:5–11; 7:12). Scholars today, however, are more inclined to identify this letter with 2 Cor. 10–13 or (more plausibly) to declare it lost. Defending the first option is D. G. Horrell, *The Social Ethos of the Corinthian Correspondence: Interests and Ideology from 1 Corinthians to 1 Clement* (Edinburgh: Clark, 1996); H. D. Betz, "Corinthians, Second Epistle to the," *ABD* 1:1149; Georgi, *Opponents of Paul,* 9–14; B. L. Mack, *Who Wrote the New Testament? The Making of the Christian Myth* (San Francisco: HarperSanFrancisco, 1995), 127; Ehrman, *The New Testament,* 302. Opting for the latter is R. P. Martin, *2 Corinthians,* WBC 40 (Waco, Tex.: Word, 1986), xlvii–l.

148. See below, point 14 and the accompanying note. Partition theories such as this that lack support in the manuscript tradition are notoriously speculative.

149. On their newcomer status, see P. W. Barnett, "Opponents of Paul," in Hawthorne, Martin, and Reid, *Dictionary of Paul and His Letters,* 647.

150. The notion that chs. 10–13 serve as a separately addressed sequel to chs. 1–9, while speculative, goes a long way toward explaining the stark contrast in tone and contrast between the two units, while avoiding more complex (and even more speculative) theories of partition, such as the six-part division proposed by both W. Schmithals, *Gnosticism in Corinth,* 96–101, and H. D. Betz, conveniently summarized in "Corinthians, Second Epistle to the," *ABD* 1:1149–50. Advocating the sequel model are Martin, *2 Corinthians,* xxxiv, 298; V. P. Furnish, *2 Corinthians,* 35–41; F. F. Bruce, *1 and 2 Corinthians,* NCB (Grand Rapids: Eerdmans, 1971), 166–70. For weighty challenges to such partition theories, see Kümmel, *Introduction to the New Testament,* 290–91; the rhetorical analyses of F. Young and D. F. Ford, *Meaning and Truth in 2 Corinthians* (Grand Rapids: Eerdmans, 1987), 27–59; Witherington, *Conflict and Community in Corinth: A Socio-Rhetorical Commentary on 1 and 2 Corinthians* (Grand Rapids: Eerdmans, 1995), 331–39, 350–51.

thians through the lens of the Judaizing controversies of Galatians and Acts 15?[151] Early work on the problem of Paul's Corinthian "opponents" tended to lump them together as a united front of, say, Judaizers (F. C. Baur) or "Gnostic pneumatics" (R. Bultmann, W. Schmithals) or Hellenistic Jewish "divine men" missionaries (D. Georgi, H. D. Betz). But the drift has been away from a one-size-fits-all "opponent" toward a more complex and nuanced understanding of Corinthian social reality.[152] The "false apostles" of 2 Cor. 10–13 appear to have been itinerant Jewish-Christian teachers (2 Cor. 11:22), perhaps from Jerusalem (2 Cor. 11:4–5), who laid claim to pneumatic powers, scored full points for appearance and public oratory (2 Cor. 10:10; 11:6), embodied the sophistic boasting tradition (2 Cor. 10:14–18; 11:18, 30; 12:1, 5–6, 9), and ridiculed Paul for his public persona and fiscal policies (2 Cor. 12:13–18). Evidently, these orators, along with their admirers, took strong issue with Paul's frontal attack on sophistry as spelled out in 1 Cor. 1–4:

> By borrowing key rhetorical categories from that critique they mounted a major attack against him by highlighting Paul's inherent deficiencies as a public speaker in order to justify their own ministry in the church and to repulse any attempts by Paul to re-establish the authority lost during the humiliating visit to Corinth which followed the writing of 1 Corinthians.[153]

Chief among Paul's concerns, then, in penning the Corinthian correspondence was the seductive lure of sophistic rhetoric, with its agenda of self-promotion, its offer of public recognition, and its knack for producing factions.[154] It appears not only that a number of Paul's opponents were grounded in this

151. The same challenge faces interpreters of Philippians and Colossians. The opponents in Phil. 3 alone have been identified in at least eighteen different ways. See the catalog in J. J. Gunther, *St. Paul's Opponents and Their Background: A Study of Apocalyptic and Jewish Sectarian Teachings,* NovTSup 35 (Leiden: Brill, 1973). Should we compare those "whose end is destruction" (Phil 3:19) with those "whose end shall be according to their deeds" (2 Cor. 11:15)? On the identity of Paul's opponents generally, see J. L. Sumney, *Identifying Paul's Opponents,* JSNTSup 40 (Sheffield: JSOT Press, 1990); idem, *"Servants of Satan," "False Brothers" and Other Opponents of Paul,* JSNTSup 188 (Sheffield: Sheffield Academic Press, 1999); Barnett, "Opponents of Paul"; Ellis, "Paul and His Opponents"; Gunther, *St. Paul's Opponents and Their Background.*

152. See H. D. Betz, "Corinthians, Second Epistle to the," 1152; Witherington, *Conflict and Community in Corinth,* 346–47; Ellis, "Paul and His Opponents," 103; Sumney, *Identifying Paul's Opponents;* R. P. Martin, "The Opponents of Paul in 2 Corinthians: An Old Issue Revisited," in *Tradition and Interpretation in the New Testament,* ed. G. F. Hawthorne and O. Betz (Grand Rapids: Eerdmans, 1987), 279–87.

153. Winter, *Philo and Paul,* 203; cf. 229.

154. Those following this general line of interpretation, in addition to Winter, include Thiselton, *First Epistle to the Corinthians;* Witherington, *Conflict and Community in Corinth,* 347–50; S. M. Pogoloff, *Logos and Sophia: The Rhetorical Situation of 1 Corinthians,* SBLDS 134 (Atlanta: Scholars Press, 1992); R. B. Hays, "The Conversion of the Imagination"; idem, *First Corinthians* (Louisville: John Knox, 1997); Fee, *First Epistle to the Corinthians.*

philosophical tradition, but also that by the time Paul wrote 2 Cor. 10–13, their campaign had gained momentum:

> Here now were not just congregational members who were wise by the standards of this age but rhetorically trained teachers who refused to join in becoming fools in order to become wise as Christians.[155]

The trick, for Paul, was to stand strong against professional orators and soap-box debaters without betraying the weakness of the message he was called to proclaim, and without collapsing under the "daily pressure" he felt for "all the churches" (2 Cor. 11:28).

---

155. Winter, *Philo and Paul*, 237. On the sophistic boasting tradition, see 232–34.

16

Paul's Theology

James D. G. Dunn

There are several ways of reviewing Paul's theology and the debates about it, especially those that have stimulated the last thirty to forty years of Pauline scholarship. One is to proceed through Paul's theology in a systematic fashion, theme by theme, noting what have been the key issues and contributions under each heading. That is one way of describing what I attempted to do in my last full-scale foray into the subject, and those who want to pursue that approach should still find it of value.[1] The present objective could be served by a brief summary of that larger exercise; but for those already familiar with the 1998 volume, such a summary would be both insufficient and repetitive.

Another possibility is to proceed letter by letter: Paul's theology understood as the theology of each Pauline letter. There are those, indeed, who think that this is the only realistic way to construct a "theology of Paul."[2] A decade-long seminar at the annual meeting of the Society of Biblical Literature attempted a fresh approach to the subject in just these terms. It turned away from older questions—whether we can speak of a center or core of Paul's theology or a discernible development through his letters—and focused instead on the theology of each letter in turn, hoping thereby to build up some kind of cumulative picture.[3] The trouble was that the process

---

1. J. D. G. Dunn, *The Theology of Paul the Apostle* (Grand Rapids: Eerdmans, 1998).
2. The most pertinent critiques of the enterprise undertaken in my *Theology of Paul the Apostle* have been those written from that perspective.
3. Papers published in *Pauline Theology*, 4 vols: vol. 1, *Thessalonians, Philippians, Galatians, Philemon*, ed. J. M. Bassler (Minneapolis: Fortress, 1991); vol. 2, *1 and 2 Corinthians*, ed. D. M.

soon found itself becoming bogged down in disagreements as to whether individual letters were sufficiently complete in themselves to enable us to draw out a coherent theology of each letter, or whether allusions and passing references in one letter depended in varying degrees on illumination from other letters; whether, in communication terms, the letter writer depended on his audience's fuller knowledge to fill out such allusions; whether, in the terms used by J. C. Beker, individual letters were best read as the contingent expressions of a fuller coherent theology.[4] So, there are major problems with that second approach. And anyway, the enterprise so conceived would overlap too much with the contribution by Bruce Fisk.[5] A different way of proceeding is called for.

A third possibility is to proceed chronologically through the last half century, reviewing the contributions of the main participants in the discussion of Paul's theology year by year. The problem then would be that unless the contributions were grouped by subject, the review would jump about all over the place and probably prove disorienting for the reader. Alternatively, if the contributions were grouped by subject or by letter, the result would be very similar to the first and second approaches, already discounted.

Instead, I will follow a different approach, suggested in the first chapter of my *Theology of Paul the Apostle,* where I briefly offer two ways of conceptualizing Paul's theology.[6] One draws on the current popularity of narrative theology, particularly as brought to the attention of Pauline scholars by Richard Hays,[7] and envisages Paul's theology in terms of the different stories involved in that theology: the stories within which he himself was living, as Jew, as Christian, as apostle. Alternatively, we can speak of the different levels of Paul's theology: the deep substructures where Paul's assumptions were rooted and that usually have to be deduced or dug out because they are not often expressed explicitly; the transformative levels from which his distinctive Christian insights grew; and the surface (but not superficial!) levels where Paul was dealing with the issues and problems that confronted the churches to which he wrote.

Hay (Minneapolis: Fortress, 1993); vol. 3, *Romans,* ed. D. M. Hay and E. E. Johnson (Minneapolis: Fortress, 1995); vol. 4, *Looking Back, Pressing On,* ed. D. M. Hay and E. E. Johnson (Atlanta: Scholars Press, 1997).

4. J. C. Beker, *Paul the Apostle: The Triumph of God in Life and Thought* (Philadelphia: Fortress, 1980).

5. See chapter 15 of the present volume.

6. Dunn, *Theology of Paul the Apostle,* 17–19.

7. R. B. Hays, *The Faith of Jesus Christ: An Investigation of the Narrative Substructure of Galatians 3:1–4:11,* SBLDS 56 (Chico, Calif.: Scholars Press, 1983; reprint, Grand Rapids: Eerdmans, 2002). See also N. T. Wright, *The Climax of the Covenant: Christ and Law in Pauline Theology* (Edinburgh: Clark, 1991); B. Witherington III, *Paul's Narrative Thought World* (Louisville: Westminster John Knox, 1994); B. W. Longenecker, ed., *Narrative Dynamics in Paul: A Critical Assessment* (Louisville: Westminster John Knox, 2002).

Neither image (story or level) is entirely satisfactory. "Story" implies, perhaps imposes, a narrative continuity (beginning and end, linked by a coherent plot) on convictions and concepts that may have been more disparate. Was the "story" seen as such by Paul, or is it the creation of the modern commentator?[8] And the imagery of "levels" could encourage a too-static conception of Paul's theology. So it is important that the images do not become allegories or permit consideration only of what fits each image. The point of evoking these images is simply to enable a fuller appreciation of the dynamic of Paul's theology—that is, his *theologizing*—as the different stories of which he was part interacted with one another, as his thinking and teaching in effect constantly moved between the different levels.

These two ways of looking at Paul's theology overlap sufficiently and offer a fresh and coherent way of reviewing Paul's theology and the contemporary debates about it. It will be simplest and make best sense to speak of five stories or levels and to examine them in turn: (1) the story of God and creation—the deepest axiomatic level of Paul's theology; (2) the story of Israel—the second level, where inherited presuppositions came under greatest strain from the revelation experienced by Paul; (3) the story of Jesus—the third level and source of the transformation of Saul the Pharisee into Paul the apostle; (4) the story of Paul—the transformative level, from his conversion onward; (5) the story of Paul's churches—the surface level, at which the interaction between Paul and his churches is most immediately accessible through the letters Paul wrote to these churches.

It is worth repeating, so important is the point, that none of these stories stands on its own. It is the interaction between them that makes Paul's theology so fascinating, puzzling, and frustrating by turns, and that has provided the grist to the mills of ongoing debate. It is the dissonance between the stories that raises the question of the coherence or inconsistency of Paul's theology. Alternatively expressed, it is the grinding of the different levels against each other that has caused the earthquakes both in Paul's theology itself and in modern attempts to come to grips with that theology. By clarifying each story, each level, as it comes to expression, explicitly or implicitly, in Paul's theology, we should be able to enter more fully into Paul's theology (and theologizing) and to understand better why modern attempts to understand his theology have proved so controversial.

The Story of God and Creation

Here is the most axiomatic dimension of Paul's theology. This also means, using the imagery of levels, that it is the most fundamental—that is, founda-

---

8. There is an analogous danger of imposing a "grand narrative" on the Jesus tradition, noted by H. Moxnes, "The Historical Jesus: From Master Narrative to Cultural Context," *BTB* 28 (1998): 135–49.

tional—level of his theology. This further means that it is the most hidden and overlooked feature of Paul's theology—so axiomatic as not requiring to be made explicit.

Here at once we see the danger of working only at the level of Paul's explicit teaching. As in all dialogue, beliefs and perceptions that were shared between the dialogue partners did not need to be articulated, but could be taken for granted by them. But for anyone listening in to that dialogue, so much of the dialogue will be meaningless or misunderstood unless the listener is also aware of these taken-for-granteds presupposed by the dialogue partners. This was a danger highlighted by that very perceptive Scandinavian NT scholar Nils Dahl when in a 1975 essay he drew attention to "the neglected factor in New Testament theology."[9] Dahl was reacting against the previous generation's claim that in effect, early Christian theology was almost exclusively Christology. It is a danger that contemporary evangelicals also need to heed lest a focus on Christ and Christology obscure too much the more foundational "*theo*-logy" level of Paul's theology.[10]

The image of story works well in this case, for it imposes no strain upon the data to envisage the whole as a connected narrative: beginning with God and his creation, and ending with the climax of final judgment, with the connecting plot understood in terms of God's overarching will or purpose—in the overused wordplay, "history as His story." The taken-for-granted character of Paul's theology at this point is clear. The fullest and most carefully contrived statement of Paul's gospel begins with the axiom of God as creator; Paul's theology as story begins with "the creation of the world" (Rom. 1:20, 25). Similarly, he has no doubt that the story climaxes with God as judge and final judgment; the long exposition on the point is clearly constructed around key unquestionable axioms (Rom. 2:6, 13), and disturbing corollaries are dismissed with an "Of course, how could it be otherwise?" assertion ("How then could God judge the world?" [Rom. 3:6]). Equally axiomatic is the assumption that the sum and substance of a right relation with God and right living can be expressed in terms of knowing God (Rom. 1:21, 28; 1 Cor. 1:21; Gal. 4:9) and doing his will (e.g., Rom. 1:10; 2:18; 12:2; 15:32; 1 Cor. 1:1). Typical of Paul's theology is the way he concludes his most intensive and agonizing sequence

---

9. N. A. Dahl, "The Neglected Factor in New Testament Theology," reprinted in *Jesus the Christ: The Historical Origins of Christological Doctrine,* ed. D. H. Juel (Minneapolis: Fortress, 1991), 153–63; note also L. Morris, *New Testament Theology* (Grand Rapids: Zondervan, 1986), 25–38.

10. The early charismatic movement needed similarly to be pulled up short at this point by T. A. Smail, *The Forgotten Father* (London: Hodder & Stoughton, 1980). One notable attempt to study the theology of Paul and Romans is L. Morris, "The Theme of Romans," in *Apostolic History and the Gospel,* ed. W. W. Gasque and R. P. Martin (Grand Rapids: Eerdmans, 1970), 249–63; see also idem, "The Apostle Paul and His God," in *God Who Is Rich in Mercy,* ed. P. T. O'Brien and D. G. Peterson (Homebush West, N.S.W.: Lancer, 1986), 165–78.

of theologizing by simply praising God for his "unsearchable judgments" and "inscrutable ways" (Rom. 11:33–36).

None of this has caused much if any controversy in the past generation.[11] The trouble has been that Paul's *theo*-logy has been so much taken for granted and neglected that it has not been allowed to interact within the contemporary reconstructions of Paul's theology. In particular, the fact that the story of salvation plays out within this more foundational story has not been taken seriously enough. As we will see below in "The Story of Israel" and "The Story of Paul," the heavy Protestant emphasis on justification by faith has given too little weight to the fact that Paul's theology of justification (= acquittal) is drawn from the imagery of final judgment and is incomplete without reference to final acquittal (= justification). Likewise, the insight that the most fundamental concern in ethics is to do the will of God has been given too little play in discussions about Paul and the law.

Almost equally passé have been the earlier debates about Paul's anthropology: whether the chief influence on it is from the side of Hebrew or Greek conceptuality[12]—the former having won the day. On the other hand, it should be noted that the history-of-religions (Hermann Gunkel) perception that S/spirit in Paul has to be understood in terms of the experience of power was an important (and unsung) precursor of the Pentecostal and charismatic movement's rediscovery of the experience of the Spirit.[13] The only significant controversy in relation to Paul's anthropology has been whether one of Paul's key terms, "body," means "physical body"[14] or something more like "embodiment" in different environments.[15] The debate is felt keenly in evangelical circles because it affects the way that the "resurrection body" is conceptualized (1 Cor. 15:44–50)—whether as a resurrection of physical flesh or as a different kind of embodiment ("spiritual body").[16]

11. The earlier discussion about "the wrath of God" (C. H. Dodd, *The Epistle of Paul to the Romans*, MNTC [London: Hodder & Stoughton, 1932], 20–24; A. T. Hanson, *The Wrath of the Lamb* [London: SPCK, 1957]; more recently, S. H. Travis, *Christ and the Judgment of God: Divine Retribution in the New Testament* [Basingstoke: Marshall, 1986]) has not been a factor of major significance in the contemporary generation of Pauline scholarship.

12. See W. D. Stacey, *The Pauline View of Man in Relation to Its Judaic and Hellenistic Background* (London: Macmillan, 1956); R. Jewett, *Paul's Anthropological Terms: A Study of Their Use in Conflict Settings*, AGJU 10 (Leiden: Brill, 1971).

13. See J. D. G. Dunn, *Jesus and the Spirit: A Study of the Religious and Charismatic Experience of Jesus and the First Christians* (London: SCM, 1975); G. D. Fee, *God's Empowering Presence: The Holy Spirit in the Letters of Paul* (Peabody, Mass.: Hendrickson, 1994).

14. R. H. Gundry, *Sōma in Biblical Theology: With Emphasis on Pauline Anthropology*, SNTSMS 29 (Cambridge: Cambridge University, 1976).

15. Dunn, *Theology of Paul the Apostle*, 55–61.

16. Cf. the discussions in A. C. Thiselton, *1 Corinthians*, NIGTC (Grand Rapids: Eerdmans, 2000), 1276–81; J. D. G. Dunn, "'How Are the Dead Raised? With What Body Do They Come?' Reflections on 1 Corinthians 15," *SwJT* 45 (2002–3): 4–18; M. J. Harris, *Raised Immortal: Resurrection and Immortality in the New Testament* (Grand Rapids: Eerdmans, 1983); idem, *From Grave to Glory: Resurrection in the New Testament* (Grand Rapids: Zondervan, 1990).

Also producing some controversy has been the question about other actors in the grand narrative of creation to final judgment. That Paul does speak of Satan and "the god of this age" is clear (e.g., 1 Cor. 5:5; 2 Cor. 4:4), but his sole reference to "demons" (1 Cor. 10:20–21) seems simply to echo Deut. 32:17, 21 without further reflection. And the reference to "so-called gods" (1 Cor. 8:5–6; 2 Thess. 2:4) and "beings that by nature are no gods" (Gal. 4:8) leaves the issue somewhat confused. Walter Wink has capitalized on this ambiguity to argue that "principalities and powers" are best interpreted as "the inner and outer aspects of any given manifestation of power," referring particularly to corporate structures and political systems.[17] Here the debate needs to focus on the existential reality of oppressive power(s) without becoming distracted too much by issues of conceptuality. Paul's confidence was that such powers had been overcome and were no barrier to relationship with God (Rom. 8:38–39). Presumably significant is the fact that the principal oppressive powers of which he speaks are sin (repeatedly personified in Rom. 5:12–8:3) and death (almost as prominent in the same chapters); and certainly it is notable that the last of the "authorities and powers" to be destroyed, "the last enemy," is death (1 Cor. 15:24–26).[18]

The most lively discussion regarding this level of Paul's theology has been about Paul's use of the creation and fall stories of Gen. 2–3—that is, Paul's "Adam theology." That Paul did conceive of the human condition, particularly subjection to death, as a consequence of Adam's sin is not in dispute; nor is the fact that Paul could sum up the whole story of humankind in terms of the two men, Adam and Christ (Rom. 5:12–21; 1 Cor. 15:21–22). On the other hand, the ambiguity as to whether death is a natural consequence of physical existence (i.e., of creation) or a consequence of sin (the fall) remains unresolved (Rom. 5:13). Likewise open is the question of whether Paul thought of Adam as what we would call a historical individual (as Rom. 5:12–14 seems to imply), or as a way of speaking of the universal experience of human desire and consequent vulnerability to temptation (as in Rom. 7:7–11). And the clear echo of Gen. 3:17–18 in Rom. 8:19–22, with its implications of creation caught up in the human fall and the promise that creation will share in the

17. W. Wink's trilogy *The Powers* (Minneapolis: Fortress, 1984, 1986, 1992); the reference here is to vol. 1, *Naming the Powers*, 5. The thesis of W. A. Carr (*Angels and Principalities*, SNTSMS 42 [Cambridge: Cambridge University, 1981]) that the powers were not conceived by Paul as evil or hostile has won little or no support.

18. Dunn, *Theology of Paul the Apostle*, 317–459. The older idea that Paul regarded "flesh" also as an oppressive power, as in R. Bultmann (*The Theology of the New Testament*, 2 vols. [London: SCM, 1952], 1:245), has largely been abandoned in favor of the view that flesh denotes the weakness of the human condition and vulnerability to the power of sin (exploiting human appetites/desires). But the protest by, for example, C. K. Barrett (*Paul: An Introduction to His Thought* [London: Chapman; Louisville: Westminster John Knox, 1994], 69), that *sarx* is an important technical term in Paul that should be retained as "flesh" and not distorted by translations (!) such as "sinful nature," needs to be paid more heed.

final liberation, has still to be adequately exploited in terms of its ecological ramifications.

The controversy has focused rather on the extent and significance of Paul's Adam theology. Does he draw on it in Rom. 1:18–25, and is it implicit in passages such as Rom. 8:3 and Gal. 4:4–5, as Morna Hooker in particular has argued?[19] And is it the key to interpreting the famous *carmen Christi* of Phil. 2:6–11, as I, among others, have argued?[20] Here we begin to see that two of Paul's stories interact, as Paul himself clearly envisaged (Rom. 5:14; 1 Cor. 15:21–22), raising the question of whether Paul was reading the story of Christ through that of Adam, or vice versa.[21] The question is as fundamental for our appreciation of Paul's theology as both stories are for Paul's theology itself. Does the substructure of Paul's theology remain unchanged by the upper levels built upon it? Does the story of God and creation remain constant whatever the other stories say? Or does the story of Christ in effect replace the earlier stories and become the prism through which the light of these earlier stories is refracted? Such questions will be clarified as we proceed through the other stories/levels, but they can never be finally resolved.

The Story of Israel

Almost equally foundational for Paul's theology is the particularization of the first level/story in reference to Israel. Paul, we know, was brought up as a Jew, indeed as a very devout Jew. Although born in the western Diaspora (according to Acts 22:3), he inherited a strongly nationalistic identity as "a Hebrew of the Hebrews" (Phil. 3:5). His "higher education" was as a Pharisee (Phil. 3:5), which must mean that he received it in Jerusalem,[22] and his zeal for the ancestral traditions outstripped that of his contemporaries (Gal. 1:14). We can be confident, then, that Paul's pre-Christian faith would have fully reflected the character of Second Temple Judaism in the early decades of the common era. The story of Israel current at that time would have been one that Paul fervently embraced as his own. That this story came into conflict in at least some degree with the story of Jesus is unquestionable and provides the basic dynamic of Paul's theology. But what the conflict was, and the extent to which it reshaped Paul's story of Israel, has been one of the major controversies of the last quarter century in Pauline scholarship.

19. M. D. Hooker, "Adam in Romans 1," *NTS* 6 (1959–60), 297–306; also *From Adam to Christ: Essays on Paul* (Cambridge: Cambridge University Press, 1990).

20. Dunn, *Theology of Paul the Apostle,* 281–88.

21. The latter is advocated by R. Scroggs, *The Last Adam: A Study in Pauline Anthropology* (Philadelphia: Fortress, 1966).

22. M. Hengel, *The Pre-Christian Paul* (London: SCM, 1991).

The outlines of the story of Israel are clear. God had chosen Israel to be his special people. In fulfillment of his promises to the patriarchs, his covenant with Abraham, he had multiplied Abraham's descendants, delivered them from slavery in Egypt, and given them the promised land as their heritage. To direct them in their living as his people, God had also given them the Torah/law. Paul, as a devout Jew and still as a believer in Jesus Messiah, had taken all this for granted—as the many echoes of these themes in his letters indicates (particularly Rom. 4 and Gal. 3–4).

There are two interesting points where the story of Israel overlapped with the story of God and creation. One is what appears to be a deliberate echo of the Gen. 2 story in the visions of Dan. 7. There appears first the beastlike being, then the manlike being, and then the latter is given dominion over the former. The implication for those familiar with Gen. 2 is that Israel ("the saints of the Most High") as the crown of creation (the "one like a son of man") will be given dominion over the other nations (the beastlike creatures). This is a rereading of the story of creation that the first Christians were already subverting in turn by reading the "one like a son of man" as Jesus.

The other point is the fact that Israel's own prophets are remembered particularly for their denunciations of Israel's unfaithfulness. Israel's covenant consciousness included the shame of the sins of the golden calf and of Baal Peor (Exod. 32; Num. 25), which were deeply etched into Israel's story. It is noteworthy how Paul echoes this line of self-criticism and does so by linking the memory of these failures with that of Adam; Israel's story also included a fall, like that of the first story. The point is evident in the indictment of Rom. 1, with its echo of Jer. 2:5–6 and Ps. 106:20 (Rom. 1:21, 23), as well as in Rom. 7:7–13, whose "I" reflects the experience not only of Adam (the most common view), but also of Israel—as Douglas Moo has observed.[23] Paul was not the first Jew to find Israel guilty before God, along with the rest of the world (Rom. 3:19).

The other most striking tension in Israel's own telling of its story (Israel's Scriptures) was in relation to the Gentiles. We have already noted that if God is one—the basic Jewish creed (Deut. 6:4), which Paul continued to assert (Rom. 3:30; 1 Cor. 8:6; Gal. 3:20)—then what does that say about the gods of other nations? More to the point, how could the one God be conceived as the God of Israel alone, and not also of the (other) nations (Gentiles)? Paul was not the first to wrestle with such issues. As Amos poses the question, If God brought Israel out of the land of Egypt, did he not also bring out the Philistines from Caphtor and the Syrians from Kir (Amos 9:7)? And the Book of Jonah was a standing rebuke to those who assumed that God would have no concern for other nations, including Israel's historic enemies. The tension is reflected in two Pauline passages. In Rom. 3:29–30, Paul presses the logic of affirming that God is one: consequently, he must be the God of Gentiles

---

23. D. J. Moo, "Israel and Paul in Romans 7:7–12," *NTS* 32 (1986): 122–35.

too; as Dahl again observed, Jewish monotheism implied universalism rather than particularism.[24] But Eph. 2:12 looks at the same issue in terms of Israel's privileged status before God: the other nations (Gentiles) were strangers to that covenant favor, "having no hope and without God in the world." As we will see below ("The Story of Paul"), Paul's own story tried to exploit that tension to explain and justify his calling as apostle to the Gentiles.

Here it is important to recognize that Paul continued to affirm his own identity as an Israelite and Israel's identity as the people called by God (Rom. 9–11). In Paul's understanding, that call was irrevocable (11:29). As most commentators on Romans have recognized, a fundamental axiom for Paul was the faithfulness of God[25]—that is, his faithfulness to Israel, within the story of his faithfulness to his creation. Still, for Paul, as a Christian, the basic outline of the story of Israel was nonnegotiable, even if it had to be qualified, or better clarified, by the reminder that God's righteousness denotes his obligation to creation and not just to Israel. Even though the attempt has been made to read Rom. 9–11 in terms of individuals rather than peoples,[26] it is clear enough that the chief concern for Paul was to affirm that the corporate entity Israel is still at the heart of God's purpose of salvation (11:25–26). The fresh element introduced by Paul was the attempt to redefine Israel in terms of divine call rather than physical descent or "works" (9:6–12), so that "Israel" could be (re)conceived as including Gentiles (9:24; 11:17–24), and therefore as able to embody a universal hope (11:32). A striking feature of this passionate exposition is the extent to which he expresses that hope in traditional Jewish terms (a deliverer who will come from Zion [11:26]), even though the gospel seemed to cast them in the role of enemies in the meantime (11:28).[27]

Here again, so much of this is at the presuppositional level that it rarely has been brought to the surface or occasioned much controversy. It is true that 1 Thess. 2:14–16 has caused considerable puzzlement, and even provided reason for some to accuse Paul (or an interpolator) of anti-Judaism, the precursor of anti-Semitism.[28] But that probably is an overreaction to a piece of passionate polemic; in any overall assessment of Paul's reaction to his native Judaism and retelling of the story of Israel, the much fuller exposition of Rom. 9–11 must

24. N. A. Dahl, "The One God of Jews and Gentiles (Romans 3:29–30)," in *Studies in Paul* (Minneapolis: Augsburg, 1977), 178–91.

25. Particularly Rom. 3:1–3; 9:6; 11:25–32. See W. S. Campbell, *Paul's Gospel in an Intercultural Context: Jew and Gentile in the Letter to the Romans,* Studien zur interkulturellen Geschichte des Christentums 69 (Frankfurt: Lang, 1992).

26. J. Piper, *The Justification of God: An Exegetical and Theological Study of Romans 9:1–23* (Grand Rapids: Baker, 1983).

27. On the issue of whether Paul thought in terms of two covenants or one at this point, see Dunn, *Theology of Paul the Apostle,* 528 n. 138; and further, "Two Covenants or One? The Interdependence of Jewish and Christian Identity," in *Geschichte—Tradition—Reflexion,* ed. H. Cancik, H. Lichtenberger, and P. Schäfer, 3 vols. (Tübingen: Mohr, 1996), 3:97–122.

28. See C. J. Schlueter, *Filling Up the Measure: Polemical Hyperbole in 1 Thessalonians 2:14–16,* JSNTSup 98 (Sheffield: JSOT Press, 1994).

be given pride of place as the maturest expression of his theology of Israel. Here, however, it is worth noting that the switch from a traditional anti-Semitism in Christian theology to a stronger support for the state of Israel established in 1948, not least in the light of Rom. 9–11, includes a fundamentalist Christian support for the political platform in Israel that lays claim to the west bank of the river Jordan on the basis of the land promised to Abraham. That is not in line with the theology of Paul, who stands more in the tradition of the prophet Amos and the Book of Jonah, and who, as we will see, argues by implication that the promise to Abraham has been misunderstood within Judaism's dominant traditions.

The main controversy with regard to the function of this story in Paul's theology has been over the Torah, the law of Moses. The traditional, particularly Protestant, view had been that the Judaism against which Paul reacted was a legalistic religion, obsessed by the idea of earning salvation by the performance of "good works." Paul, however, had come to the realization that salvation could never be earned by human effort, and he propounded instead the gospel of justification by faith and faith alone. For many years such a characterization of Judaism had caused puzzlement to Jewish and Christian scholars familiar with Judaism. But it was not until E. P. Sanders protested with polemical vehemence that the protests were really heard.[29]

Sanders observed that the starting point for Judaism's self-understanding as the people of God (both Second Temple Judaism and rabbinic Judaism) was the covenant made by God with Israel; nowhere in Jewish writings was the covenant regarded as an achievement of human merit. And although Jews had the responsibility to maintain their covenant standing by obedience to the law, the repeated emphasis on repentance and the centrality of a sacrificial system that provided atonement for the repentant within Israel's pattern of religion meant that the characterization of that religion as legalistic and merit-based was misconceived, unjustified, and prejudicial. Sanders coined the phrase "covenantal nomism" to embrace both aspects—the divine initiative of God's choice of a "not people" (covenant), and the response of obedience required from that people (law/nomism).

Sanders's call for this radical reconsideration of Judaism's "pattern of religion" was hailed in 1983 as "the new perspective on Paul."[30] In reality it was a new perspective on Paul's Judaism, but it called for a radical reconsideration of what it was in his ancestral religion that Paul objected to. For if Judaism was based on the divine initiative and grace of election, and if it did not demand perfection of obedience but provided atonement for sin, then what was there to object to? Sanders's own solution was that Paul's encounter with Christ had provided a solution, from which Paul had deduced that Judaism was the plight from

29. E. P. Sanders, *Paul and Palestinian Judaism* (London: SCM, 1977).

30. J. D. G. Dunn, "The New Perspective on Paul," reprinted in *Jesus, Paul, and the Law: Studies in Mark and Galatians* (London: SPCK, 1990), 183–214.

which he had been saved;[31] and otherwise, Sanders could not see how Paul's treatment of the law could be saved from confusion and inconsistency.[32]

In response, I have argued that the new perspective sheds light on Paul's theology by allowing us to see that its polemical thrust was directed not against the idea of achieving God's acceptance by the merit of personal achievement (good works), but against the Jewish intention to safeguard the privilege of covenant status from being dissipated or contaminated by non-Jews.[33] Paul was reacting primarily against the exclusivism that he himself had previously fought to maintain.[34] In other words, it is the troubling converse of the doctrine of election to which he objected. That is, what troubled Paul was not so much the problematic implications of covenant theology for those outside the covenant, as already noted, but rather the corollary that the law functioned not only as a directory for Israel's conduct but also as a marker (particularly circumcision and laws of clean and unclean) that distinguished Israel from the other nations and required them to keep separate from other nations (holy to God) and, consequently, also served as a boundary between Israel and the other nations. This separatist attitude is reflected in Rom. 2:17–20 and 3:29–30 and contested in Gal. 2:12–16.[35] This was the function of the law to which Paul objected: the law as Israel's protector and tutor; from Paul's Christian perspective, that function had been valid for a time, but its time was now past (Gal. 3:19–4:11).[36]

At this point it is insightful to note how Paul was able to draw together his anthropology (from the first story) and his critique of traditional Judaism as reflected in the attempts of Christian-Jewish missionaries to reconvert Paul's converts. For Judaism had always emphasized the importance of circumcision "in the flesh" as Israel's most distinctive single identity marker (Gen. 17:11–14). It was this that had given Paul the Pharisee his "confidence in the flesh" (Phil. 3:3–4)—that is, not his confidence in his ability to keep the law, as Bultmann had supposed,[37] but confidence in his ethnic identity as a member of the covenant people. And it was the thought that the Jewish missionaries would be able to glory in the flesh of his converts, when the latter accepted

31. Critiqued by F. Thielman, *From Plight to Solution: A Jewish Framework for Understanding Paul's View of the Law in Romans and Galatians*, NovTSup 61 (Leiden: Brill, 1989).

32. E. P. Sanders, *Paul, the Law, and the Jewish People* (Philadelphia: Fortress, 1983); similarly, H. Räisänen, *Paul and the Law*, WUNT 29 (Tübingen: Mohr Siebeck, 1983). Critiqued by T. R. Schreiner, *The Law and Its Fulfillment: A Pauline Theology of the Law* (Grand Rapids: Baker, 1993), 87–90, 136–37.

33. Dunn, *Theology of Paul the Apostle*, 334–89 (see also below, "The Story of Paul").

34. See n. 67, below.

35. The attitude is archetypally expressed in the laws of clean and unclean, whose very function was to mark Israel's separateness from the nations (Lev. 20:24–26), and archetypally addressed among the first Christians in Acts 10–11 (cf. 10:14 and 11:2–3 with 10:28, 34–35, and 11:9–12).

36. Dunn, *Theology of Paul the Apostle*, 128–61.

37. Bultmann, *Theology of the New Testament*, 1:242–43.

circumcision and submerged their identity in fleshly Israel, that most irritated Paul (Gal. 6:12–13).[38]

The "new perspective" on Paul's Judaism has provoked a vigorous response, particularly from Lutheran scholars who perceive their defining doctrine of justification by faith to be somehow under threat. For example, Stephen Westerholm has insisted that Rom. 4:4–5 must be directed against Jewish belief in "works righteousness," and therefore it proves that there were Jews at the time of Paul who so taught.[39] Tübingen has produced a triple counterblast. Friedrich Avemarie has observed that the rabbinic evidence is more mixed and argues that Sanders has pushed the covenant side of his "covenantal nomism" too hard.[40] And Peter Stuhlmacher and Seyoon Kim have reacted with still more vigor: "the new perspective" is not "the true perspective on Paul"; the Reformation doctrine of justification is to be reaffirmed.[41] Simon Gathercole in turn has drawn attention to Second Temple Jewish texts that make salvation dependent on Torah-obedience.[42] One key issue that has emerged is the need to clarify how the present and future tenses of justification hold together, how justification by faith and not works correlates with final judgment "according to works" both in Israel's story and in Paul's gospel. A lively debate is thus under way and will run well into the twenty-first century. We will have to return to it here when considering how the stories still to be examined interact with the first two.

The Story of Christ

It is, of course, the story of Christ that threw Paul's two earlier stories into confusion and caused him to reconfigure them in greater or lesser degree. His initial encounter with that story is not reported, but as a young Pharisee training in Jerusalem, presumably in the 20s, he must have known of Jesus' mission in Galilee and may even have heard him in Jerusalem during the late 20s. How he reacted to Jesus, or to the reports he heard about Jesus, then or later, we cannot say. The one hint that we have is the probable reflection in 1 Cor. 1:23 and Gal. 3:13 of his earlier reaction to the message of a crucified

---

38. Dunn, *Theology of Paul the Apostle*, 68–70.

39. S. Westerholm, *Israel's Law and the Church's Faith: Paul and His Recent Interpreters* (Grand Rapids: Eerdmans, 1988). See also Schreiner, *The Law and Its Fulfillment*, 41–71, 93–121.

40. F. Avemarie, *Tora und Leben: Untersuchungen zur Heilsbedeutung der Tora in der frühen rabbinischen Literatur*, TSAJ 55 (Tübingen: Mohr Siebeck, 1996); "Erwählung und Vergeltung," *NTS* 45 (1999): 108–26.

41. P. Stuhlmacher, *Revisiting Paul's Doctrine of Justification: A Challenge to the New Perspective* (Downers Grove, Ill.: InterVarsity, 2001); S. Kim, *Paul and the New Perspective: Second Thoughts on the Origin of Paul's Gospel*, WUNT 140 (Tübingen: Mohr Siebeck, 2002).

42. S. J. Gathercole, *After the New Perspective: Works, Justification, and Boasting in Early Judaism and Romans 1–5* (Grand Rapids: Eerdmans, 2002).

messiah: how could a crucified man, cursed by God, be regarded as Israel's messiah?[43]

That the crucified Jesus was indeed God's Messiah (Christ) must have been a conviction borne upon Paul in his conversion. Paul speaks of his conversion in other terms, but his previous (implied) revulsion at the cross evidently rebounded in the crucified Christ becoming the central feature of his proclamation as a missionary (1 Cor. 1:23; 2:2; 2 Cor. 5:14–15, 18–21; Gal. 3:1).

The resultant centrality of the death of Jesus to Paul's theology is hardly open to dispute, but it evidently belonged so much to the common ground between Paul and his readers that he found it unnecessary to expound its significance at great length. What we have are summary statements, perhaps already functioning as creedal formulae to express a fundamental element in Christian faith (e.g., Rom. 1:3–4; 3:21–26; 4:25).[44] These include a variety of metaphors used by Paul to document the significance of the cross. It was a sin-offering (Rom. 8:3), a means of dealing with sin (2 Cor. 5:21), and a means of atonement (Rom. 3:25). It was an act of redemption, like the liberation of Israel from Egypt, or the manumission of a slave (Rom. 3:24; 1 Cor. 7:21–23). It was an act of reconciliation, God reconciling the world to himself (2 Cor. 5:18–20; Col. 1:20). Despite appearances to the contrary, it actually constituted victory over the hostile powers (Col. 2:15).

The controversies arise over the significance of these images. Which of them is central?[45] How far can the metaphor (sacrifice, buying back) be pressed?[46] In particular, does the concept of Jesus' death as *hilastērion* envisage Jesus as the "mercy seat" or as the atoning event that took place there,[47] as expiation or propitiation?[48] A more recent debate, also sparked by Richard Hays, has focused on the phrase "the faith of Jesus" (*pistis Christou,* as in Rom. 3:22, 26; Gal. 2:16; 3:22). Traditionally, this has been taken as an objective genitive (the Greek is indeterminative on the point), to signify "faith in Jesus." But Hays and a galaxy of followers argue that it should be taken as a reference to Jesus' own faith, "the faith(fulness) of Jesus," and read as equivalent to "the obedience of Christ" (cf. Rom. 5:19).[49] The effect is

---

43. See Hengel, *The Pre-Christian Paul,* 64, 83–84.

44. See the details in Dunn, *Theology of Paul the Apostle,* 174–75.

45. The choice of R. P. Martin is clear: *Reconciliation: A Study of Paul's Theology* (London: Marshall, Morgan & Scott; Atlanta: John Knox, 1981).

46. It was the language of sacrifice that proved most unacceptable to, for example, G. Friedrich, *Die Verkündigung des Todes Jesu im Neuen Testament,* Biblisch-theologische Studien 6 (Neukirchen-Vluyn: Neukirchener, 1982).

47. For example, P. Stuhlmacher (*Reconciliation, Law, and Righteousness: Essays in Biblical Theology* [Philadelphia: Fortress, 1986], 96–103) presses the most obvious sense of "place of atonement," though it is not hard to see how the one sense could merge into the other.

48. The old debate between C. H. Dodd, *The Bible and the Greeks* (London: Hodder & Stoughton, 1935), 82–95 (expiation), and L. Morris, *The Apostolic Preaching of the Cross,* 3rd ed. (1st ed., 1955; Grand Rapids: Eerdmans; London: Tyndale, 1965), 144–213 (propitiation).

49. R. B. Hays, *The Faith of Jesus Christ;* M. D. Hooker, *"Pistis Christou,"* in *From Adam to Christ,* 165–86.

to remove the phrase from Paul's own story (his own discovery of justification by faith) and to accord it a place in the story of Jesus as its primary locus. However, whether this reallocation of the phrase *pistis Christou* does sufficient justice to the importance of the call for "faith" in Paul's gospel and to his exposition of the key text Gen. 15:6 in Gal. 3:6–9 and Rom. 4 is an open question.[50]

If Paul's gospel focuses (by implication) so intensively on the death of Jesus, what about the earlier phase of the story of Jesus? Paul's seeming lack of interest in the "historical Jesus" is notorious, and it has given substance to the older claim of Bultmann that the kerygma depended exclusively on the proclamation of Jesus' death and resurrection.[51] But the argument assumed too readily that absence of explicit mention of Jesus' life and teaching implied ignorance and disregard, without asking whether it was necessary to the dialogue of these letters that such explicit mention should be made.[52] Here it is also important to note how Paul, in effect, integrates the two earlier stories into the story of Christ. His reading of Christ as the last Adam (1 Cor. 15:45) carries the implication that Christ in some measure recapitulated the story of Adam (as Irenaeus saw), thus turning the disaster of human existence subject to death into the triumph of God's design for humanity completed in Christ's resurrection (Phil. 2:6–11). And his insistence that Jesus was "born under the law" (Gal. 4:4) and "became a servant of circumcision" (Rom. 15:8) has the same effect: to indicate that Jesus recapitulated the story of Israel in order to redeem Israel (Gal. 4:5). So, of course, Jesus' life was important for Paul, and N. T. Wright pushes the point still further in arguing that Jesus as Messiah represents Israel: "the last Adam is the eschatological Israel."[53]

More controversial have been the almost equally scarce allusions to Christ's preexistence. The debate is not, or should not be, *whether* Paul used the language of preexistence when speaking of Christ. That is not in contention (particularly 1 Cor. 8:6; Col. 1:15); though if Phil. 2:6–11 uses the Adam story as its template, the question remains whether Paul could have been thinking in terms of mythic history (the time of Adam as prehistory) or of incarnation as the counterpoise to Adam's fall.[54] The debate is rather about the *significance* of the language. If Paul was deliberately echoing the language used of divine Wisdom, her role in creation, as most agree, then the debate depends on how Wisdom was conceptualized: was she a being distinct from the one God, or rather a way of speaking (by personification) about God's wise dealings with

50. See the debate between Hays and Dunn (with further bibliography) in Hay and Johnson, *Looking Back, Pressing On*, 35–81.

51. Various aspects are discussed in A. J. M. Wedderburn, ed., *Paul and Jesus: Collected Essays*, JSNTSup 37 (Sheffield: JSOT Press, 1989).

52. Contrast D. Wenham, *Paul: Follower of Jesus or Founder of Christianity?* (Grand Rapids: Eerdmans, 1995); Dunn, *Theology of Paul the Apostle*, 183–95.

53. Wright, *Climax of the Covenant*, 34–35.

54. See the discussion in R. P. Martin and B. J. Dodd, eds., *Where Christology Began: Essays on Philippians 2* (Louisville: Westminster John Knox, 1998).

his creation and his people? In identifying Christ, in effect, with God's wisdom, was Paul doing anything different in kind from Sirach's identification of the Torah with God's wisdom (Sir. 24:23)?[55]

But if the story of Jesus leading up to the cross is not given particular prominence in Paul's theology, the same certainly cannot be said of the sequel to the cross. No one can realistically dispute that the resurrection of Christ was central to Paul's gospel; 1 Cor. 15:3–8, 14, 17 should be sufficient proof of the point. Nor is it open to doubt that, for Paul, Jesus' exaltation to the right hand of God and designation as "Lord" (Ps. 110:1) was equally central. In the Pauline Epistles, the title "Lord" (*kyrios*) is used of Jesus well over two hundred times; texts such as Rom. 10:9 (an early baptismal confession?) and Phil. 2:11 are again sufficient to make the point.

Controversy begins over the significance of the title *kyrios*. There are texts using *kyrios* of God (Yahweh) that Paul refers to Christ: notably, Rom. 10:13 (Joel 2:32) and Phil. 2:10–11 (the insistently monotheistic Isa. 45:23). Should we conclude, then, that Paul identified Jesus with/as Yahweh?[56] Or does it simply mean that Paul conceived of God sharing his lordship with Christ, as Ps. 110:1 implies (1 Cor. 15:24–28)? Pressing the same issue, did Paul speak of Jesus as "god/God"? The debate here focuses on Rom. 9:5 and the possibility of reading it two ways.[57] Larry Hurtado has argued that already in Paul we see the decisive mutation in Jewish monotheism (to a form of binitarianism) occasioned by the devotion offered to Christ in earliest Christian worship.[58] Others prefer to speak in terms of Jewish monotheism reconfigured as "christological monotheism."[59] That the story of Christ has already begun the transformation of monotheism, which reaches its most profound expression in the historic creeds, is clear, though greater caution is necessary than often is recognized in assessing the stage in that process that Paul himself had reached, as distinguished from the stimulus that his writing brought to the process.[60]

In many ways more challenging are recent contributions by J. L. Martyn.[61] This is so not simply because he challenges the whole logic of narrative

---

55. See K.-J. Kuschel, *Born before All Time? The Dispute over Christ's Origin* (London: SCM, 1992); Dunn, *Theology of Paul the Apostle,* 266–93.

56. D. B. Capes, *Old Testament Yahweh Texts in Paul's Christology,* WUNT 2.47 (Tübingen: Mohr Siebeck, 1992).

57. See M. J. Harris, *Jesus as God: The New Testament Use of Theos in Reference to Jesus* (Grand Rapids: Baker, 1992).

58. L. W. Hurtado, *One God, One Lord: Early Christian Devotion and Ancient Jewish Monotheism* (Philadelphia: Fortress, 1988; Edinburgh: Clark, 1998); "Pre-70 C.E. Jewish Opposition to Christ-Devotion," *JTS* 50 (1999): 35–58; *At the Origins of Christian Worship: The Context and Character of Earliest Christian Devotion* (Grand Rapids: Eerdmans, 1999).

59. C. C. Newman, J. R. Davila, and G. S. Lewis, eds., *The Jewish Roots of Christological Monotheism,* JSJSup 63 (Leiden: Brill, 1999).

60. Dunn, *Theology of Paul the Apostle,* 244–60.

61. J. L. Martyn, *Galatians,* AB 33A (New York: Doubleday, 1997); *Theological Issues in the Letters of Paul* (Edinburgh: Clark, 1997).

theology, with its imagery of a continuous narrative—that would merely call into question what thus far has proved to be a useful analytic tool—but because he questions the whole perception of a continuity of divine purpose through Israel to Christ. This, he argues, is the way the *opponents* of Paul in Galatia conceived of the gospel, which was why they could press the logic of circumcision so hard (Gen. 17:9–14). But the apocalyptic character of the gospel (Gal. 1:12) puts law and gospel in antithesis (4:21–5:1); the gospel is about a new age, a new creation (1:4; 6:15); the vertical has disrupted the horizontal (3:23–26); Paul's gospel works on a quite different plane. Martyn's contribution offers a challenge to historical descriptions of Paul's theology similar to that offered by Barth's *Römerbrief* some eighty years ago. Likewise, it is open to the equivalent critique of overstatement: however confrontational Paul's letter to the Galatians, it still worked with the concept of "inheritance" (as in Gal. 4:1–7), a key element in the story of Israel and one that undergirded the more measured exposition of the gospel, including Israel and the gospel in Rom. 4 and 9–11. But the issues here are best clarified in terms of the fourth story constituting Paul's theology.

The Story of Paul

The story of Paul, insofar as it forms a central strand of Paul's theology, is primarily the story of Paul's conversion and its aftermath, since these events seem to have decisively shaped the most enduringly distinctive elements of his theology—particularly his focus on Christ, his attitude toward the law, and his teaching on justification. Galatians 1–2 features the most explicitly narrative format in all of Paul's theologizing as he attempted to explain and defend the key features of his gospel by telling his own story.[62]

The significance of Paul's conversion is among the most debated topics in Pauline studies. That he had been a persecutor of the church is not in doubt (1 Cor. 15:9; Gal. 1:13, 23; Phil. 3:6); nor that he was converted while acting out that persecuting zeal, as these same passages imply, and as Acts 9, 22, and 26 state explicitly. But why had he attempted so violently to "destroy the church"? The issue is important because the most obvious way of understanding Paul's conversion is literally as a "turning around" to follow the very way that he had been attempting to destroy.

That Paul was converted to belief in Jesus as Messiah and Lord almost goes without saying. Paul does not actually say so, but if the implications drawn earlier from 1 Cor. 1:23 and Gal. 3:13 are sound, then Paul, in recognizing that the one who encountered him on the Damascus road was

---

62. See H. D. Betz, *A Commentary on Paul's Letter to the Churches in Galatia*, Hermeneia (Philadelphia: Fortress, 1979), on Gal. 1:12–2:14 (= the Narratio); B. R. Gaventa, "Galatians 1 and 2: Autobiography as Paradigm," *NovT* 28 (1986): 309–26.

indeed the Jesus who had been crucified, must have concluded that God had raised and exalted this Jesus and thus given divine confirmation to the very confession that Paul had hitherto attempted to extirpate. The disputed question is whether the Damascus road encounter itself provided a fuller stimulus to his Christology: whether, as Kim in particular argues, Paul had a kind of mystical experience in which he saw Jesus as the glory of God—an experience that provided the basis for his Wisdom Christology.[63] The probable allusion to his own conversion in 2 Cor. 4:4–6 could be so interpreted.

Was his persecuting passion the result of "zeal for the law" (Gal. 1:13–14; Phil. 3:6)? Then he could have been objecting violently to disregard for the law among early Christian Jews. The Hellenists, who provoked Saul to hostile repression, according to Acts 8:1–3, are the obvious candidates—especially as the accusation against Stephen was put in terms of "changing the customs that Moses delivered" to Israel (Acts 6:14). Thus, it could be argued, as does Stuhlmacher, that the antagonism to the law that is usually seen as a principal feature of Paul's theology can be traced right back to the about-face on the Damascus road.[64] The difficulty in this case is that Paul was not as antagonistic toward the law as the reference to "the end of the law" (Rom. 10:4) is usually taken to imply—certainly not the law as a whole. His antagonism was directed more specifically to particular functions of the law, notably his fellow Jews' failure to recognize that its role as a "dividing wall" between Jew and Gentile (Eph. 2:14) was at an end, and to recognize its role as sin's cat's-paw to entice self-destructive desire (Rom. 7:7–12).[65]

If it was a more restrictive role for the law that Paul was objecting to, then the most obvious candidate is the role of the law in requiring Israel to maintain itself separate from other nations. It probably was "zeal" to maintain such separation that had motivated Paul's previous persecution. "Zeal" was the characteristic motivation of those earlier in Israel's history who had determined to prevent any disregard for, or crossing of, the boundaries between Israel and the nations that might threaten Israel's holiness (note Jdt. 9:2–4; Jub. 30),[66] and it was this same "zeal" that obviously explains the violence of Paul's persecution

63. S. Kim, *The Origin of Paul's Gospel*, WUNT 2.4 (Tübingen: Mohr Siebeck, 1981), 137–268; cf. A. F. Segal, *Paul the Convert: The Apostolate and Apostasy of Saul the Pharisee* (New Haven: Yale University Press, 1990), 34–71; C. C. Newman, *Paul's Glory Christology: Tradition and Rhetoric*, NovTSup 69 (Leiden: Brill, 1992).

64. P. Stuhlmacher, "'The End of the Law': On the Origin and Beginnings of Pauline Theology," in *Reconciliation, Law, and Righteousness*, 134–54.

65. It should occasion little surprise that I found it necessary to spread my discussion of Paul and the law across no less than three different chapters in *Theology of Paul the Apostle*, 128–61, 334–89, 625–69.

66. The archetypal hero of such zeal was Phinehas (Num. 25:6–13; Sir. 45:23–24; 1 Macc. 2:54; 4 Macc. 18:12; Pseudo-Philo, *Bib. Ant.*, 46–48); see further Dunn, *Theology of Paul the Apostle*, 350–53.

(Phil. 3:6).[67] And from the sequence in Gal. 1:13–16, it certainly seems that what Paul converted to was the very openness to the Gentiles (Gal. 1:16) that he hitherto had abominated. Paul is clear that the resurrection appearance on the Damascus road is what constituted him as an apostle (1 Cor. 9:1; 15:8–9; Gal. 1:1, 12); and Paul never seems to have been in doubt that his apostleship was "to the Gentiles" (Gal. 2:7–9; Rom. 11:13).

A closely correlated question is whether Paul saw what happened to him on the Damascus road as a "conversion" or rather as a call.[68] He never speaks of it in terms of a conversion as such; and certainly he regarded it as a call, as the echoes of Jer. 1:5 and Isa. 49:1–6 in Gal. 1:15–16 clearly imply. The issue is not simply a matter of semantics, for what is actually at stake is Paul's understanding of the relation between the movement to which he thereby committed himself and his ancestral Judaism. He certainly did not regard himself as having converted from one religion to another; the movement to be subsequently known as "Christianity" was not yet distinct from its parent Judaism. To be sure, Paul implies that he had left "Judaism," but he evidently means what we today would more precisely describe as "Pharisaic Judaism." So if we are to speak of it as a conversion—and it remains the classic example of a sudden conversion—then it was a conversion within Second Temple Judaism, from one "sect" of Second Temple Judaism to another (Pharisees to Nazarenes).[69]

The importance of this for Paul's theology is that he should not be lightly characterized as a turncoat, an "apostate" from Judaism, and so neither should the gospel that he preached (Christianity) be described as apostasy from the heritage to which he (it) was heir.[70] On the contrary, Paul regarded the gospel as the continuation, enactment, and fulfillment of the promise to Abraham that in him "all the nations will be blessed" (Gal. 3:8; Gen. 12:3). And so also the movement of which he thus became an apostle is not to be regarded as a separate religion. There is no thought in Paul's theology of "the church" versus Israel. On the contrary, the church is able to be the church of God precisely by being incorporated/grafted into the olive tree that is Israel (Rom. 11:17–24). The implications for Christianity's self-understanding, and against the subsequent emphasis in Christian theology that Christianity had "superseded" Israel, are far-reaching.[71]

67. The point is given insufficient recognition by Hengel, *Pre-Christian Paul*, 84, and T. L. Donaldson, "Zealot and Convert: The Origin of Paul's Christ-Torah Antithesis," *CBQ* 51 (1989): 655–82.

68. See K. Stendahl, *Paul among Jews and Gentiles; and Other Essays* (Philadelphia: Fortress, 1976).

69. Segal, *Paul the Convert*, xii–xiv, 6–7.

70. Despite the subtitle, *The Apostolate and the Apostasy of Saul the Pharisee*, of Segal's *Paul the Convert*.

71. See W. D. Davies, "Paul and the People of Israel," *NTS* 24 (1977–78): 4–38; M. Barth, *The People of God*, JSNTSup 5 (Sheffield: JSOT Press, 1983); P. von der Osten-Sacken, *Christian-Jewish Dialogue: Theological Foundations*, trans. M. Kohl (Philadelphia: Fortress, 1986).

Thereby Paul grasped the nettle that has stung all attempts to extract a consistent theology of the (other) nations from the OT. Even the classic solution of Deut. 32:8–9—that God had allotted each nation its guardian angel (god) but kept Israel for himself—no longer was adequate. For apart from anything else, there remained the complete lack of agreement as to the fate of the Gentiles—whether destruction, or enslavement, or conversion.[72] Paul, it would appear, went beyond the most positive hope—the eschatological pilgrimage of the Gentiles to Zion—and concluded that his call was to take the good news in mission to the Gentiles. The success of this fundamental theological insight was ensured by the willingness of the Jerusalem apostles (James included) to recognize its validity (Gal. 2:7–9). Thereby ensured also was the character of the Christian gospel as outreach, as missionary theology.[73]

A related question is how quickly these distinctive ideas came to him. Seyoon Kim thinks that most of the key features of Paul's theology can be traced back in one degree or other to the Damascus road experience.[74] And certainly Paul seems to imply, as we have seen, that he experienced the Damascus road encounter as a call to go to the Gentiles (as also Acts 9:15; 26:17–20). But that he immediately did so (in Arabia? [Gal. 1:17]) is questionable; he speaks of his preaching only subsequently (Gal. 1:23). And the fact that Paul puts so much stress on the Jerusalem conference and the subsequent Antioch incident in Gal. 2:1–14 strongly suggests that these events were critical for Paul in the shaping of his theology, of "the truth of the gospel" as he came to grasp it with increasing sharpness. Certainly it must be significant that such a major confrontation took place in Antioch (2:14) so soon after the amicable agreement in Jerusalem (2:9). And part of the significance presumably is that certain issues had not been sufficiently grasped or clarified at the former meeting. It was in responding to a new crisis and challenge to his gospel that Paul probably achieved the most sharply distinctive and most profound expression of his gospel: Gal. 2:15–17.

Here we come to one of the most troublesome of recent disputes regarding Paul's theology in evangelical circles. For the logic of the exposition thus far is that this profoundest expression of Paul's gospel was shaped by the question of whether and on what terms Gentiles could be regarded as acceptable to God. This is to say, as Krister Stendahl among others had insisted, that Paul's doctrine of justification by faith emerged out of, and as the solution to, that question.[75] This also implies that Paul in his gospel was continuing to react against that

---

72. See the survey in T. L. Donaldson, "Proselytes or 'Righteous Gentiles'? The Status of Gentiles in Eschatological Pilgrimage Patterns of Thought," *JSP* 7 (1990): 3–27.

73. See T. L. Donaldson, *Paul and the Gentiles: Remapping the Apostle's Convictional World* (Minneapolis: Fortress, 1997).

74. Kim, *The Origin of Paul's Gospel;* contrast H. Räisänen, "Paul's Call Experience and His Later View of the Law," in *Jesus, Paul, and Torah: Collected Essays,* JSNTSup 43 (Sheffield: JSOT Press, 1992), 15–47.

75. See Stendahl, *Paul among Jews and Gentiles.*

zeal-inspired tradition of his ancestral faith, which had insisted that separation from the nations was essential to the identity of the covenant people.

The dispute can be focused on what became a key phrase in Paul's theology: "works of the law" (Rom. 3:20, 28). Paul uses that phrase, and does so no less than three times, in Gal. 2:16—the first occurrence of the phrase in his theology. And in the sequence of Gal. 2:1–21, the conclusion that justification is not by "works of the law" (2:15–16) seems to be Paul's summing up of his argument that circumcision was not necessary for Gentile converts (2:1–10), and that Gentile converts should not be required to observe Jewish regulations governing table fellowship (2:11–14). In other words, "works of the law" is the phrase that Paul uses to characterize the counterinsistence that Gentile converts must be circumcised and observe purity and dietary rules. "Works of the law" seems to be code for Jewish insistence on maintaining the distinguishing marks of Israel, the boundary markers that preserved Israel's identity, not least the purity code, which still required Jews (including Peter and Barnabas) to "separate" from non-Jews (2:12). The theological logic recently has been illuminated by a sectarian scroll from the Dead Sea, 4QMMT, which uses the same phrase in the same way: "works of the law" as distinguishing the Dead Sea sect and requiring it to "separate" "from the multitude of the people" (4QMMT C7).[76]

This exegesis generally has not been well received in evangelical circles,[77] for it seems to reduce the fundamental Pauline/Protestant doctrine of justification by faith to a dispute about a few boundary issues between Jews and Gentiles. But such a response would be wrongheaded. On the one hand, Paul is actually bringing to bear on issues of the moment the more fundamental theological axiom that faith alone is the basis for relationship with God (Gal. 2:16). Whether that was an axiom that he shared with Israel's own fundamental understanding of election (Rom. 4:4–5)—just as the similar argument a few verses earlier (3:27–31) appeals to the shared confession that "God is one" (3:30)—or an axiom that Paul was (re)introducing is less relevant. And on the other hand, he is putting at the heart of that fundamental doctrine the equally fundamental assertion that fulfillment of God's covenant promise rules out continuing discrimination by any people claiming covenant relation with God against others who wish to claim that covenant promise (by faith alone) for themselves.[78]

76. See J. D. G. Dunn, "4QMMT and Galatians," *NTS* 43 (1997): 147–53; "Noch Einmal 'Works of the Law': The Dialogue Continues," in *Fair Play: Diversity and Conflicts in Early Christianity,* ed. I. Dunderberg, C. Tuckett, and K. Syreeni, NovTSup 103 (Leiden: Brill, 2002), 273–90.

77. See M. A. Seifrid, *Justification by Faith: The Origin and Development of a Central Pauline Theme,* NovTSup 68 (Leiden: Brill, 1992); D. A. Hagner, "Paul and Judaism: Testing the New Perspective," in Stuhlmacher, *Revisiting Paul's Doctrine of Justification,* 75–105; see also above, the last paragraph of "The Story of Israel."

78. For the fullest recent statement see Dunn, *Theology of Paul the Apostle,* 334–89; Stendahl's earlier contribution, *Paul among Jews and Gentiles,* has been insufficiently appreciated.

Paul's story does not end with the Antioch incident, of course; rather, it merges with the story of his churches. But it remains important to note how much of Paul's theology was shaped by his conversion and by the initial disputes with those who had come to faith in Jesus Messiah before him, and the extent to which these initial experiences imprinted a lasting mark on key features of his gospel.

The Story of Paul's Churches

This last of the five stories that form the warp and woof of Paul's theology/theologizing merges into a study of each of Paul's letters. For, of course, our main knowledge of these churches, apart from some fairly cursory information provided by Acts, is given by Paul's letters to these churches. From these letters we learn how these churches had been established and were, or were not, prospering: the gospel that they believed (e.g., 1 Cor. 15:3–5; Gal. 3:1; 1 Thess. 1:9–10); the power that wrought conviction in their hearts (1 Cor. 2:1–5; Gal. 3:2–5; 1 Thess. 1:5–6; 2:13); the importance and problems surrounding their experience of baptism and the Lord's Supper (1 Cor. 1:12–17; 10:16–17; 11:17–34); the character of the worship they enjoyed and abused (1 Cor. 12–14); and so on. All these have idiosyncratic features that remind us that Paul was writing to particular churches in particular circumstances. But enough of relevance beyond the particular is evident to enable us to speak in at least some measure of Paul's theology in all these cases.

At this point the temptation is to follow through the second approach to the analysis of Paul's theology suggested at the beginning of this essay. Having recognized the coherent character of Paul's theology in terms of the first four stories, it would be natural to explore how that theology came to contingent expression in specific cases (Beker). To do that approach justice at this stage is, of course, impossible. Yet, it is salutary to be reminded of how many themes of Paul's theology are dependent on the particular circumstances (problems and abuses) that required him to speak on that theme in a particular letter—notably his eschatological expectations (1 Thessalonians) and his understanding of the Lord's Supper (1 Cor. 10–11). In the present case, however, it will have to suffice to note how the story, or rather stories, of Paul's churches relate to the other four stories.

As we have already observed, the stories of Paul's churches are the obverse of Paul's own continued story as successful missionary and concerned pastor. The importance of this observation is to note that Paul's theology was not an ivory-tower production, dictated to secretaries in some garret hidden away from the world. On the contrary, his pastoral and practical theology, like his fundamental theology described in the previous sections, was hammered out in the fires of controversy, in response to often malicious attacks, disappointments, and betrayals, in situations of personal stress and hardship that would have tested the patience of a less passionate character than Paul. Equally important, however, is the reverse observation: Paul's pastoral and practical theology was always informed through and through by his basic conviction regarding his calling and the character of the gospel entrusted to him. Christianity should be grateful for the fact that there came a time when Paul concluded that he had done all he could in the Aegean area and determined to think through his gospel and to set it out as fully as necessary as he planned the next phase of his mission (Rom. 15:14–21). For it is the fruit of that decision—Paul's letter to the Romans—that demonstrates that Paul did indeed have a coherent and thoroughly thought-through theology in which the missionary and pastoral heart continued to beat strongly.

More to the point, Paul's gospel sought to reshape the stories of his churches, as it had done and was doing Paul's own life story, by tying them into the other, earlier stories. For Paul, it evidently was crucial for his converts' self-understanding that they should see themselves as those who were part of each of these stories, that these stories were incomplete without them. They were "in Adam" (1 Cor. 15:22): the story of creation was still being unfolded in them; the purpose of God in creating humankind would reach its climax in them; their own liberation would be incomplete without the liberation of creation from atrophy, the bondage to decay (Rom. 8:19–21). They were Abraham's seed (Gal. 3; Rom. 4): the story of Israel was still being unfolded in them; it was the promise to Abraham that was being fulfilled in them (Gentiles as well as Jews); it was the promise to Abraham—that the nations would be blessed through him—that would be fulfilled in and through them. Above all, they were "in Christ" (a much loved phrase in Paul): the story of Christ was still being unfolded in them; Christ's life was working out through them; they were already sharing his death, but with a view to sharing his life (Rom. 8:10–11, 17; 2 Cor. 4:10–12; Phil. 3:10–11).

The most far-reaching effects of so reading their own story within, and in relation to, the other stories came to expression in the paraenesis with which Paul always correlated his more cerebral theology. It was important to Paul that his converts understand the reality of their createdness: of bodily living, and the communication with fellow believers and others thus made possible (Rom. 6:12–13; 12:1–2); of the reality and danger of their being still in the flesh, and consequently still vulnerable to being tempted to be ruled by merely human appetites (Rom. 8:1–14; Gal. 5:13–26). Alternatively expressed, they had to live within the reality of a process of salvation already begun but not yet completed, to live the life of the Spirit through a body destined for death (Phil. 3:10–11). The life/death rhythm of creation had still to be played through to the end. And final judgment still lay ahead (Rom. 2:6–11; 14:10–12; 2 Cor. 5:10), whose outcome would depend on some kind of synergy between divine grace and human response (Gal. 3:3; Phil. 2:12–13; 3:12–14).

It was equally important that they appreciated and benefited from the immense heritage that was theirs by their integration into the inheritance of

Abraham. For although "the works of the law" no longer were relevant for Christian living, since their boundary-protecting role was at an end, the law had a continuing function as a definition of sin, quickener of conscience, and yardstick of final judgment (Rom. 2:12–16; 3:20; 7:13). Israel's law, particularly its warnings against idolatry and sexual license, was not to be disdained. The Scriptures, Israel's Scriptures, were their Scriptures, written for their instruction (Rom. 15:4; 1 Cor. 10:11).[79]

Most important of all was that they should read their story with and within that of Jesus, for the key to a realistic theological ethic was a life molded on the template of Christ. That included the echoes of Jesus' ethical teaching that appear regularly (e.g., Rom 12:14; 14:14; 1 Cor. 13:2; 1 Thess. 5:2, 4), the appeal to Jesus' example (Rom. 13:14; 15:1–3), to the law as modeled by Christ (Gal. 6:2), and the pattern of Jesus' prayer (Rom. 8:15–16; Gal. 4:6). But it included still more the recognition that what Christ had done for them constituted the starting point for their living, the indicative out of which emerged the imperative of ethical living.[80] Still more, it was the story of Christ that gave them a central model for living: the cruciform life, the cross as determining the character of self-sacrificing love, the story of discipleship as the story of Christ's self-giving being still lived out till that day when those who had shared in his dying would also share fully in his rising again (Rom. 6:5; Gal. 2:19–20; 6:14).[81] It is this understanding of Christian living as Christ-living that both explains and is enabled by the Pauline understanding of the motivating, empowering Spirit as the Spirit of Christ (Rom. 8:9; Gal. 4:6; Phil. 1:19), and the social support group of the church as the body of Christ (Rom. 12:6–8; 1 Cor. 12). For only that divine power which shaped Christ's own bodily existence is sufficient to re-form the image of God (Christ) in believers (2 Cor. 3:18; Gal. 4:19; Col. 3:9–10).

Not least of importance in this final reflection is that it shows how the five stories worked for Paul. It was by so relating their life stories individually and corporately to these earlier stories, by reading their life stories within these other stories, that Paul and his converts found meaning for their lives. By identifying themselves individually and corporately with Israel and Israel's Messiah, they found that purpose had been given to their existence. The stories would remain incomplete till they completed them in their own living.

---

79. See B. S. Rosner, *Paul, Scripture and Ethics: A Study of 1 Corinthians 5–7*, AGJU 22 (Leiden: Brill, 1994); R. B. Hays, "The Role of Scripture in Paul's Ethics," in *Theology and Ethics in Paul and His Interpreters*, ed. E. H. Lovering and J. L. Sumney (Nashville: Abingdon, 1966), 30–47.

80. See particularly R. Bultmann, "The Problem of Ethics in Paul" (1924), reprinted in *Understanding Paul's Ethics: Twentieth Century Approaches*, ed. B. Rosner (Grand Rapids: Eerdmans, 1995), 195–216; V. P. Furnish, *Theology and Ethics in Paul* (Nashville: Abingdon, 1968).

81. See R. B. Hays, *The Moral Vision of the New Testament: Community, Cross, New Creation* (San Francisco: HarperSanFrancisco, 1996); B. W. Longenecker, *The Triumph of Abraham's God: The Transformation of Identity in Galatians* (Edinburgh: Clark, 1998).

17

Luke

Darrell L. Bock

Luke's theological and pastoral concerns are evident in his emphases. Ever since W. C. van Unnik observed in 1966 that Luke-Acts was a "storm center" in NT studies, the climatic activity focusing on Luke's message and his pastoral concerns has not abated.[1] Methodological questions have run the gamut from discussions of the Greek text of Acts, to the import of Greco-Roman backgrounds, to the study of Jewish roots, to the pursuit of narratological readings, as well as the use of standard NT historical-critical methods, particularly appeals to redaction criticism rooted especially in the work of Hans Conzelmann in 1954.[2] Lukan studies, after having stood in Conzelmann's shadow for almost

1. W. C. van Unnik, "Luke-Acts, A Storm Center in Contemporary Scholarship," in *Studies in Luke-Acts,* ed. Leander Keck and J. Louis Martyn (1966; reprint, Philadelphia: Fortress, 1980), 15–32. Much of contemporary discussion also has roots in the work of Henry Cadbury, whose writings in the 1920s to 1950s have left a lasting impact on Lukan discussion, especially his *The Making of Luke-Acts,* published in 1927. It is Cadbury who made NT studies take notice that Luke should be studied as a literary unit, as Luke-Acts. This significantly impacted the way Luke and Acts were read and studied, as before, Luke was grouped with the Synoptics, while Acts was left to itself as a history of the early church. The unity of Luke-Acts has been challenged by M. C. Parsons and R. I. Pervo, *Rethinking the Unity of Luke and Acts* (Minneapolis: Augsburg, 1993). However, this position has not proved persuasive to most NT scholars. See J. Verheyden, "The Unity of Luke-Acts: What Are We Up To?" in *The Unity of Luke-Acts,* ed. J. Verheyden, BETL 142 (Leuven: Peeters, 1999), 5–7. In narrative readings, unity is usually assumed rather than argued.

2. For a full catalog of the range of discussion, see Verheyden, "The Unity of Luke-Acts," 3–56. Earlier survey works are François Bovon, *Luke the Theologian: Thirty-Three Years of Re-*

two decades, emerged in the 1970s with a vibrancy and activity that still has it going in several directions at once. The best way to assess what is taking place is not to concentrate so much on method, as these approaches are discussed and assessed well elsewhere,[3] but to stay focused on the issues that Luke's material itself raises, his themes, and how they are being discussed currently. My goal, then, is to proceed by tracing the debate as it falls out in the tackling of specific Lukan issues. In this way, the essay will serve its role as an introduction to Lukan studies and themes.

Issues Centering on Luke's Purpose

There are several proposals concerning Luke's purpose; not all of them are mutually exclusive in terms of thrust or methodological concerns. If there is some movement toward a general consensus on Luke, it is that his two volumes are an explanation of the origins of the new community now known as the church—an exercise in what today would be called sociological legitimization.[4] Luke is explaining how a seemingly new movement has roots in old divine

---

search (1950–1983), trans. Ken McKinney, Princeton Theological Monograph (Allison Park, Pa.: Pickwick, 1987); Mark Allan Powell, *What Are They Saying about Luke?* (New York: Paulist Press, 1989). Bovon's work is an update of his 1978 French edition. Conzelmann's work is found in English in its 1960 translation, *The Theology of Saint Luke,* trans. Geoffrey Buswell (New York: Harper, 1960). The English title is unfortunate, as the German title, *Die Mitte der Zeit* ("The Midst of Time"), highlights the central role that Conzelmann argues Luke gave to Jesus as part of a period distinct from both the era of Israel and that of the church. This threefold scheme was Luke's explanation for the delay of the parousia, which Conzelmann saw as the controlling pastoral concern and apologetic of Luke's development of salvation history. This explanation captivated Lukan studies until the 1970s, when other Lukan themes began to emerge as more significant than the issue of the delay. An important study examining key themes in Acts is I. Howard Marshall and David Peterson, eds., *Witness to the Gospel: The Theology of Acts* (Grand Rapids: Eerdmans, 1998). The present essay focuses on developments since the work of Conzelmann, developments that go in directions other than a concern for a "corrective" eschatology.

3. David Alan Black and David S. Dockery, eds., *Interpreting the New Testament: Essays on Method and Issues* (Nashville: Broadman & Holman, 2001). This work does a better job of surveying various methods of studying the NT than it does of treating the study of a particular Gospel writer, since it discusses the Synoptics as a unit—a move often made in NT surveys.

4. See Gregory E. Sterling, *Historiography and Self-Definition: Josephos, Luke-Acts, and Apologetic Historiography,* NovTSup 64 (Leiden: Brill, 1992). Sterling's work marked what was already an existing shift in Lukan studies toward examining Luke's purposes in terms closely tied to Greco-Roman historical method. Other studies have developed this approach, including Philip Esler, *Community and Gospel in Luke-Acts: The Social and Political Motivations of Lucan Theology,* SNTSMS 57 (Cambridge: Cambridge University Press, 1987); Loveday Alexander, "Luke's Preface in the Context of Greek Preface Writing," *NovT* 28 (1986): 48–74. The multivolume series edited by Bruce Winter, The Book of Acts in Its First Century Setting, jointly published by Eerdmans and Paternoster, also works in this approach, as does the recent work by the SBL Luke-Acts study group edited by David Moessner, *Jesus and the Heritage of Israel: Luke's Narrative Claim upon Israel's Legacy* (Harrisburg, Pa.: Trinity, 1999).

promises. In an ancient world, this is important because newer movements were viewed with suspicion. Luke's appeal to divine design, Scripture, and promise to describe the salvation that comes through Jesus argues that the movement that emerged from Jesus' ministry was a natural extension of Judaism. One can see how this description of Luke's purpose has moved significantly from the claim of Conzelmann that Luke's goal was to explain why Jesus had not yet returned. Whether this goal is seen as a form of theodicy,[5] a defense of Paul or the mission he represents,[6] an effort at conciliation with Judaism,[7] or a confirmation of the word of salvation,[8] the goal is to assure Theophilus about the divine roots and ancient pedigree of the new movement (Luke 1:4). Particularly significant is the explanation of how Gentiles could be included in what originally was a Jewish movement. Acts spends much time on this Gentile question. Yet, Acts keeps the door open to the inclusion of Jews, while at the same time explaining why the movement was rejected by most Jews.[9] This desire to explain the new movement and its roots helps us to appreciate why the design of God, the appeal to Scripture, and the detailed presentation of how Jesus preached, ministered, and was rejected are so important to Luke. The issue of Jewish rejection explains the pastoral concern to reassure Theophilus about the integrity of the movement and to call for perseverance.[10]

The God of Design: The Plan of God as an Extension of Promise

Luke's reassuring of Theophilus involves detailed discussion of God's plan.[11] Luke treats this theme more than do the other Synoptic evangelists. His concept

5. David Tiede, *Prophecy and History in Luke-Acts* (Philadelphia: Fortress, 1980).

6. A. J. Mattill Jr., "The Jesus-Paul Parallels and the Purpose of Luke-Acts," *NovT* 17 (1975): 15–46; Jacob Jervell, *Luke and the People of God: A New Look at Luke-Acts* (Minneapolis: Augsburg, 1972). Jervell's study highlighted the Jewish concerns evident in Luke-Acts in a significant way.

7. R. L. Brawley, *Luke-Acts and the Jews: Conflict, Apology, and Conciliation*, SBLMS 33 (Atlanta: Scholars Press, 1987).

8. I. H. Marshall, *Luke: Historian and Theologian* (Grand Rapids: Zondervan, 1970); Robert F. O'Toole, *The Unity of Luke's Theology: An Analysis of Luke Acts*, GNS 9 (Wilmington, Del.: Glazier, 1984).

9. Eric Franklin, *Christ the Lord: A Study in the Purpose and Theology of Luke-Acts* (London: SPCK, 1975); Darrell L. Bock, *Proclamation from Prophecy and Pattern: Lucan Old Testament Christology*, JSNTSup 12 (Sheffield: JSOT Press, 1987); R. C. Tannehill, "Israel in Luke-Acts: A Tragic Story," *JBL* 104 (1985): 69–85. The debate over how the Jews are portrayed in Luke-Acts is well surveyed in J. B. Tyson, ed., *Luke-Acts and the Jewish People: Eight Critical Perspectives* (Minneapolis: Augsburg, 1988).

10. See Schuyler Brown, *Apostasy and Perseverance in the Theology of Luke*, AnBib 36 (Rome: Pontifical Biblical Institute, 1969); Robert Maddox, *The Purpose of Luke-Acts*, SNTW (Edinburgh: Clark, 1982).

11. For this theme in Acts, see John Squires, "The Plan of God in the Acts of the Apostles," in Marshall and Peterson, *Witness to the Gospel*, 19–39. For the theme in Lukan theology as

of a plan involves a connection to scriptural hope, divine design, and elements of structure and progress within the Gospel's story. Again, legitimizing the new community and personal reassurance are the goals.

A number of uniquely Lukan passages include this theme (1:14–17, 31–35, 46–55, 68–79; 2:9–14, 30–32, 34–35; 4:16–30; 13:31–35; 24:44–49), while one text overlaps with the other Gospels (the inquiry from John the Baptist [7:18–35]). Luke utilizes the suffering Son of Man texts, a few of which are unique to him (9:22, 44; 17:25 [L]; 18:31–33 [L]; 22:22 [L]; 24:7 [L]). Acts also highlights the plan (2:23; 4:27–28; 13:32–39; 24:14–15; 26:22–23). Squires argues that the pivot of the plan in Acts comes in the turn to the Gentiles in Acts 8:4–12:25.[12] The church's missionary activity is being defended here, not so much Paul, but what he represents. Taking Luke-Acts as a whole, the major elements of the plan focus on the career of Jesus, including his role as Messiah-Lord and his suffering example, the hope of the spiritually humble and needy, the offer of God's blessings to Jew and Gentile, the new era's coming, and the division of Israel.

Supporting the theme of God's plan is that of promise and fulfillment, especially as it relates to the Scriptures.[13] Three areas are key: Christology, Israelite rejection/Gentile inclusion, and eschatological justice.[14] The latter two themes are more prominent in Acts. Nonetheless, the theme of Gentiles responding to the gospel while Israel stumbles is present in numerous Lukan

---

a whole, see I. Howard Marshall, *Luke,* 103–15. For a narratological look at this theme, see Robert L. Brawley, *Centering on God: Method and Message in Luke-Acts,* Literary Currents in Biblical Interpretation (Louisville: Westminster John Knox, 1990). On how the activity of God ties into the parables of Luke, see Greg W. Forbes, *The God of Old: The Role of the Lukan Parables in the Purpose of Luke's Gospel,* JSNTSup 198 (Sheffield; Sheffield Academic Press, 2000).

12. Squires, "The Plan of God," 28–31.

13. Paul Schubert, "The Structure and Significance of Luke 24," in *Neutestamentliche Studien für Rudolf Bultmann,* ed. W. Eltester, 2nd ed., BZNW 21 (Berlin: Töpelmann, 1957), is the foundational essay for these discussions, in which he discusses the issue of "proof from prophecy." Martin Rese (*Alttestamentliche Motive in der Christologie des Lukas,* SNT 1 [Gütersloh: Mohn, 1969]) challenged the view of Schubert. Darrell Bock (*Proclamation from Prophecy and Pattern*) responded to Rese and argued that the theme Luke develops using Scripture is more "proclamation from prophecy and pattern" versus mere prophetic proof. Charles A. Kimball (*Jesus' Exposition of the Old Testament in Luke's Gospel,* JSNTSup 94 [Sheffield: Sheffield Academic Press, 1994]) examines the issues tied to the Jewish form of these arguments. R. I. Denova (*The Things Accomplished among Us: Prophetic Tradition in the Scriptural Pattern of Luke-Acts,* JSNTSup 141 [Sheffield: Sheffield Academic Press, 1997]) looks at major themes of typology, including those from the second part of Isaiah. For a sample of a variety of studies on Luke's use of Scripture, see B. J. Koet, *Five Studies on Interpretation of Scripture in Luke-Acts,* SNTA 14 (Leuven: Peeters, 1989); Craig A. Evans and James A. Sanders, *Luke and Scripture: The Function of Sacred Tradition in Luke-Acts* (Minneapolis: Fortress, 1993).

14. Darrell L. Bock, "Proclamation from Prophecy and Pattern: Luke's Use of the Old Testament for Christology and Mission," in *The Gospels and the Scriptures of Israel,* ed. Craig A. Evans and W. Richard Stegner, JSNTSup 104, SSEJC 3 (Sheffield: Sheffield Academic Press, 1994); Craig A. Evans, "Prophecy and Polemic: Jews in Luke's Scriptural Apologetic," in Evans and Sanders, *Luke and Scripture,* 171–211.

Gospel texts (2:34; 3:7–9; 4:25–27; 7:1–10; 10:25–37; 11:49–51; 13:6–9, 23–30, 31–35; 14:16–24; 17:12–19; 19:41–44).

Various themes delineate the plan. The "today" passages show the immediate availability of the promise (2:11; 4:21; 5:26; 13:32–33; 19:5, 9; 19:42; 23:42–43). John the Baptist is the bridge between promise and inauguration (1–2; esp. 1:76–79; 3:4–6; 7:24–35; 16:16), the forerunner predicted by Malachi and the greatest prophet of the old era (7:27). However, the new era is so great that the kingdom's lowest member is higher than the greatest prophet of the old (7:28). In Luke 7:27 and 16:16, one finds the basic Lukan structure: the era of promise/expectation followed by the era of inauguration. The message of the gospel and Jesus' teaching about the end clarify the timing and structure of the new era. The plan still has future elements (2:38; 17:20–37; 21:5–36), but the basic turning point has come. So the plan's second portion is subdivided, even though all of that era represents fulfillment. The subdivisions are inauguration (Acts 2:14–40) and consummation (Acts 3:1–26), the already and the not yet.

Jesus' mission statements outline his task. Jesus preached good news to those in need (4:18–19), healed the sick (5:30–32), and was to be heard, whether his message was communicated through him or through his representative (10:16). He came to seek and save the lost (19:10). The geographical details trace the growth of the Jesus movement (e.g., the progress of the gospel from Galilee to Jerusalem and the necessity of Paul's going to Rome in Acts [Acts 1:8; 19:21; 23:11]). This journey toward the "ends of the earth" from Jerusalem's perspective is revealed in the drawn-out description of divine protection in the long sea voyage to Rome in Acts 27.[15]

Many passages declare that "it is necessary" (*dei*) that something occur. In fact, forty of the 101 NT uses of *dei* occur in Luke-Acts. Jesus *must* be in his Father's house (2:49), preach the kingdom (4:43), and heal the woman tormented by Satan (13:16). Certain events *must* precede the end (17:25; 21:9). Jesus *must* be numbered among the transgressors (23:37). The Christ *must* suffer and be raised, and repentance for the forgiveness of sins *must* be preached. The Son of Man's suffering is a divinely set forth necessity (24:7); the Christ *must* suffer and come into glory (24:26). At the climactic conclusion of the Gospel (24:44), it is noted that all of this took place because Scripture *must* be fulfilled. The fact that so many of these references appear in the last chapter of Luke underlines the importance of this theme right at the point where Luke creates a narrative bridge from Jesus to the story of the earliest church. Even as Acts closes, Scripture is cited to underscore that Jewish rejection of Jesus is also a part of the plan (Acts 28:25–28). In Luke-Acts, the plan indicates that God directs and is not surprised by what has taken place around Jesus. Then

---

15. On the backdrop to the sea voyage motif, see Charles H. Talbert and J. H. Hayes, "A Theology of Sea Storms in Luke-Acts," in Moessner, *Jesus and the Heritage of Israel*, 267–83. The essay explicitly ties the theme to that of the divine plan.

who is this major figure through whom God works? Does Luke have a unified portrait of Jesus and the salvation that God brings through the Promised One? Or does Luke simply randomly string together various disparate traditions?

Christology and Salvation

Jesus and deliverance stand at the heart of the plan. Central here are the themes of Jesus as Messiah-Lord, his teaching and work, and the blessings of the plan that come through him. In addition, Luke issues a call to respond to the opportunity that Jesus' invitation creates. There is a narrative unity and progression in the presentation of this understanding, although some have challenged the unity of Luke's christological portrait. Perhaps in no other place in Lukan theology and study does the issue of method become so prominent in how the text is being read.

Christology: Messiah-Servant-Prophet as Lord

Some say that Luke's Christology is more a patchwork than a unified whole; it is a collection of various traditions, "the most variegated christology in the NT."[16] The case relies on a view that a major key to understanding Luke is appreciating his sources and their differing perspectives. Luke is seen as "conservative" in taking these sources and simply placing them next to one another without trying to unify their differing perspectives. This approach makes several other points. First, there is a constant alteration of titles as Luke moves from one passage to another, so that a "development" of Christology is lacking. There also is the claim that if Luke is undertaking a "self-corrective" approach to Christology by highlighting the title "Lord," then this is a very subtle approach and ends up having earlier passages express an ultimately inadequate Christology, as the later, more developed perspectives reveal. However, the critique fails in part because it represents a caricature of the development view.[17] The point is that

16. This is stated most directly in these terms by C. F. Evans, *Saint Luke*, TPINTC (Philadelphia: Trinity, 1990), 56. The concept is thoroughly and vigorously defended by C. M. Tuckett, "The Christology of Luke-Acts," in Verheyden, *The Unity of Luke-Acts*, 131–64.

17. Tuckett's argument appears in four steps ("Christology of Luke-Acts," 150–52). His key claims are as follows: (1) an emphasis on "Lord" as the key title represents an abandonment of the title "Christ," which Luke worked so hard to affirm in his Gospel; (2) nowhere does Acts hint that "Christ" is an inadequate christological term; (3) Christology is dropped in the latter portions of Acts, and when it is raised, "Christ" is the key term used; and (4) it is doubtful that the Gentile mission is grounded in a Lord Christology. The fourth point fails to appreciate Acts 2 and 10 as linked and crucial pivots in the narrative. The importance of Acts 2 and 10 is not their location in the account, but their programmatic role in advancing the discussion of Jesus' work through the Spirit with an accompanying theological explanation that applies to all that follows in the narrative as it develops the rationale for the expanding and predominantly

Luke's Gospel is a narrative theology in which he reveals the person of Jesus in increments, with later portraits not so much "correcting" (i.e., rejecting) earlier expressions of Christology in his book as building upon their foundations. So it is not that Luke proclaims Jesus as Lord at the expense of a claim of Jesus as Messiah, but proclaims him as Lord-Messiah. Once having defined what kind of lordship the Messiah possesses, we see that the title "Christ" suffices because it has the proper, full content and understanding in it. We see such development in the understanding of the Christ in terms of his suffering—why should we not expect the same kind of clarification and development in terms of his rule and exaltation? Such a reading ends up not being as subtle as Tuckett implies. It also means that the "correction" is not as either/or as Tuckett's argument suggests. Rather, the argument is "See who this Messiah is: he is also Lord of all." So the gospel can go to all—precisely the emphasis of the key pivot speech of Acts 10. One can debate whether "Christ" or "Lord" is *the* key christological category for Luke, because in one sense they both are key and end up working in concert.[18] Here is where it is important to see Luke as an author presenting a theologically developing story in his Gospel and its sequel, and not merely an editor assembling disparate pieces of material.

So, is there a christological unity to the whole of Luke-Acts? Jesus is introduced as a regal figure (Luke 1–2). Here is Luke's foundation; but there are also hints of Jesus' uniqueness, as this birth comes through a virgin and the

---

Gentile mission. The third point is also not significant, for once having laid the christological foundation and having defined his terms, Luke moves on to other issues to which Christology connects. It is precisely this failure to appreciate Luke-Acts sufficiently as a synthetic narrative that allows Tuckett to cut up the material and construct his critique.

18. Two other key studies here try to develop the unity of Luke's Christology by appeal to Jesus' role as Messiah and the relationship to the work of the Spirit. Working with the messianic theme is Mark L. Strauss, *The Davidic Messiah in Luke-Acts: The Promise and Fulfillment in Lukan Christology*, JSNTSup 110 (Sheffield: Sheffield Academic Press, 1995); H. D. Buckwalter, *The Character and Purpose of Luke's Christology*, SNTSMS 89 (Cambridge: Cambridge University Press, 1996). Buckwalter develops the connection to Luke's pneumatology. Tuckett's critique ("Christology of Luke-Acts," 154) that Buckwalter's case depends on only a few texts, mostly in Acts, shows how nonnarratological his critique is, for it is the function of narrative to advance the story. His claim that Acts 2:36 is adoptionistic is questionable in light of the infancy material in Luke. However, even if it were correct, that still does not negate Buckwalter's claim that the exaltation of Jesus leaves the evangelist Luke affirming a "high" Christology. In Acts 2, Jesus is equal enough with God to be seated with him at his right hand—an extraordinary claim; see Darrell L. Bock, *Blasphemy and Exaltation in Judaism and the Final Examination of Jesus: A Philological-Historical Study of the Key Jewish Themes Impacting Mark 14:61–64*, WUNT 2.106 (Tübingen: Mohr Siebeck, 1998), 111–83. Tuckett's appeal to the range of use for the title "Lord" for all kinds of elevated human figures does not get at the point. This title is being applied to a Jesus who is uniquely seated next to God in heaven. Thus, it is not the mere use of the title that gives the Christology its exalted status, but the heavily laden theological context and imagery in which the title appears. The debate again underscores with regard to methodology how one can read Luke in terms of his sources or his story. The story as narrative needs to be recognized in order to appreciate the unity of Luke's effort. Here, critical readings that remain focused on sources distort the reading of the document as a unit.

work of the Spirit. The announcement to Mary and Zechariah's hymn make a Davidic connection for Jesus explicit (1:31–33, 69). The anointing of Jesus at his baptism recalls two OT passages, Ps. 2 and Isa. 42, fusing regal and prophetic images (3:21–22 ["Beloved Son" and "one in whom I am pleased"—an allusion to the divine Servant]). The images of servant and prophet are combined in Simeon's words (2:30–35), but the idea of a leader-prophet is a dominant christological theme in Luke. Jesus' sermon at Nazareth (4:16–30) also conjoins the regal and prophetic motifs. Though Elijah and Elisha are prophetic patterns for Jesus' work (4:25–27), the anointing described in the language of Isa. 61:1 refers to Jesus' baptism with its regal/prophetic motifs drawn from the baptismal declaration. The people recognize that Jesus is a prophet (7:16; 9:7–9, 19), but Peter confesses him as the Christ (9:20). Jesus further explains that he is the suffering Son of Man. In a tradition unique to his Gospel, Luke relates Jesus' title as "Son" to Jesus' messianic role (4:41). The regal/prophetic mix reappears with the heavenly voice at the transfiguration (9:35; cf. Ps. 2:7; Isa. 42:1; Deut. 18:15). Jesus is presented as a leader-prophet, one like Moses.[19] The themes of rule and direction are fundamental.

Jesus' messianic role is foundational for Luke. He spells out the nature of Jesus' messiahship, placing it alongside other christological categories. The prophetic motif also is important in the woes against the scribes (11:46–52), the mourning for Jerusalem (13:31–35), and the conversation on the Emmaus road (24:19, 21). Yet even in Luke 13:31–35, the appeal to Ps. 118 carries a regal overtone (cf. 19:38), since "the one who comes" is for Luke fundamentally an eschatological and messianic deliverer (3:15–18; 7:22–23; 19:38). On the Emmaus road the disciples associate their perception of Jesus as a prophet with the hope of national redemption (24:21). For Luke, the deliverer and regal imageries merge with the prophetic.

Luke emphasizes Jesus' elevated status. The authority of the Son of Man is introduced as early as 5:24 as possessing an authority to forgive sins, and this authority and his status as Lord become the focus of dispute in 20:41–44; 21:27; and 22:69 (worked out even more in Acts 2:30–36; 10:36). The significance of Ps. 110 and its reference to Jesus is of crucial importance. In three steps, the issue is raised (Luke 20:41–44), Jesus responds (22:69), and the message of Jesus' authority as Lord is proclaimed (Acts 2:30–36). The Synoptics share the first two texts, but Luke's sequence, ending with the detailed exposition of Acts 2, shows the importance of the dispute. Luke 22:69 makes it clear that "from now on" Jesus, the Messiah-Servant-Prophet, will exercise his lordship at and from the right hand of God. The ability to sit at God's right hand and do divine work shows how exalted Luke's Christology is as it rotates around the

---

19. The significance and uniqueness of this "prophet like Moses" theme and its overlapping with an eschatological prophetic category in Judaism is stressed in the work of David Moessner, *Lord of the Banquet: The Literary and Theological Significance of the Lukan Travel Narrative* (Minneapolis: Fortress, 1989).

idea of Christ who is Lord (Luke 2:11; 4:41; Acts 2:36). This is not to deny that Luke uses other titles. Jesus is Savior, or one who delivers (Luke 1:70–75; 2:11, 30–32), as well as Son of David (1:27, 32, 69; 2:4, 11; 18:38–39) or king (19:38). He is the Son, who relates to God as Father, just as the divine testimony declares (1:35; 2:49; 3:21–22, 38; 4:3, 9, 41; 9:35; 10:21–22). Yet he is also son of Adam, who grows in grace and overcomes the temptation of the devil (2:40, 52; 3:38; 4:1–13). He is compared to Jonah and Solomon (11:29–32). As Son of Man, he not only suffers and is exalted, but also ministers (5:24; 6:5, 22; 7:34; 9:58; 11:29–32; 12:8; 19:10). Another frequently used title is "Teacher" (7:40; 8:49; 9:38; 10:25; 11:45; 12:13; 18:18; 19:39; 20:21, 28, 39; 21:7; 22:11). Luke's portrait of Jesus is variegated but organized. The eschatological figures that Judaism discussed are collated in the unifying portrait of Jesus.[20] Jesus bears authority as well as promise. He is the divinely prophetic figure, a leader-prophet, who also is Messiah and Lord, now exalted and seated at God's right hand, doing his work of rule through the mediation of the Spirit. All of these claims were intelligible in the Jewish context of Jesus' ministry—a point on which Luke seems to be sensitive. This central eschatological claim leads us into what Jesus brings as a part of the promise: the kingdom of God.

The Kingdom in Jesus' Teaching and Work and the Spirit

The Messiah brings the kingdom of God (4:18, 43; 7:22; 8:1; 9:6; 10:11).[21] The kingdom is present now, but it comes fully in the future. It includes earthly hope, and yet has spiritual dimensions. The kingdom as present reality is associated with Jesus' authority, shown in his command over evil forces. Jesus can speak of the kingdom as "near" (10:9). He sees Satan fall as the seventy(-two) disciples exercise authority over demons (10:18–19). He says that if he casts out demons by the finger of God, then the kingdom has come (11:20–23). He can say that the kingdom is "among you" (17:21). A king, in one parable, departs "to receive a kingdom" (19:12). In his hearing before the council of Jewish elders, Jesus says that from now on he will be at God's side (22:69). Finally, the appeal to Ps. 110 depicts a regal authority, ruling from the side of God. This theme is picked up again in Acts 2:30–36, where Jesus exercises executive messianic authority in distributing the Spirit, just as John the Baptist said the Messiah would (Luke 3:15–17).

But the kingdom is also future. Luke 17:22–37 describes the judgment preceding its consummation. Luke 21:5–38 depicts the "time of redemption." Here

---

20. On the variety of views regarding Jewish messianic and eschatological figures, see John J. Collins, *The Scepter and the Star: The Messiahs of the Dead Sea Scrolls and Other Literature* (New York: Doubleday, 1995); J. Neusner, W. Green, and E. Frerichs, eds., *Judaisms and Their Messiahs* (Cambridge: Cambridge University Press, 1987).

21. On this theme, see Marshall, *Luke: Historian and Theologian*, 88–94.

the imagery of the Day of the Lord abounds; evil is to be decisively judged. In Luke 21:25–27, allusions appear, suggesting the cosmic disturbance associated with the Day of the Lord (cf. Isa. 13:10; Ezek. 32:7; Joel 2:30–31; Ps. 46:2–3; 65:7; Isa. 24:19 LXX; Hag. 2:6, 21; Dan. 7:13). Jesus will return to fulfill the rest of the promise, showing himself visibly on earth to all humanity while giving eternal benefits to believers.

The kingdom is earthly. Jesus will rule as a Son of David on the earth and yet will bring about total deliverance in the ministry that will follow that of John the Baptist (Luke 1:32–33, 46–55, 69–75). All this activity, both present and future, is Jesus' promised messianic work. The nation of Israel is the initial focus of such ministry (Luke 2:25, 38). The eschatological discourses and the statements of Acts 1:11 and 3:18–21 show that the future hope has not been absorbed in the theme of present inauguration but remains alive, connected to its OT roots. God brings all his promises to fruition, even those made to Israel.[22] Spiritual deliverance also comes from him through Christ. Zechariah's song (Luke 1:68–79) speaks of Jesus as the rising sun who leads those in darkness into peace. The promise of the Holy Spirit (3:15–17; 24:49; Acts 1:8) and the hope of forgiveness of sins (Luke 24:47) are elements of this deliverance, with mission to the world being the result. Jesus' authority over demons shows that he is able to fulfill these promises and that the longed-for promise of God's rule has come.

The subjects of the kingdom, who benefit from its presence, are the disciples of Jesus (18:26–30). Anyone who wishes to enter is a potential beneficiary (13:23–30; 14:16–24). But there are also unwilling subjects, those who are accountable to Jesus now and who one day will face his rule as the one appointed to be the judge of the living and the dead (19:27; 21:24–27; Acts 3:20–26; 10:42; 17:30–31).

---

22. There is a lively debate over whether Israel has been reconstituted by what Jesus does, or whether Israel, still seen in racial-national terms, has been dropped from view for rejecting Jesus. It seems more likely that Israel has a future in God's plan than that Israel has been dropped from view. Whether the church is to be seen as a "new Israel" or is a fresh work is a more complicated question. Luke's answer appears to be complex. The church is not what Israel once was, and it has been forced to become a distinct institution because of rejection from those who are racially Israel. This "new" entity is no surprise in God's plan and is somewhat distinct from Israel (because of its new racial makeup), and yet it has claims to God's promises of old. On the reconstitution of Israel, see Max Turner, *Power from on High: The Spirit in Israel's Restoration and Witness in Luke-Acts,* JPTSup 9 (Sheffield: Sheffield Academic Press, 1996). For the story of Israel as one of tragedy but with the potential for a future that remains open, see Robert Tannehill, "Israel in Luke-Acts: A Tragic Story," *JBL* 104 (1985): 69–85. For the argument that one must distinguish between the Jewish leadership and Israel in Luke, so that one must avoid condemning the nation as a whole, see Jon A. Weatherly, *Jewish Responsibility for the Death of Jesus in Luke-Acts,* JSNTSup 106 (Sheffield: Sheffield Academic Press, 1994). Arguing against a de-eschatologizing of history by Luke (as Conzelmann claimed) and for a salvation history that has both eschatological aims and a future for Israel is J. Bradley Chance, *Jerusalem, the Temple, and the New Age in Luke-Acts* (Macon, Ga.: Mercer University Press, 1988).

The coming of the Spirit is promised (Luke 3:15–17). He empowers and testifies to Jesus (3:21–22; 4:16–20). Many speak of the Spirit in Luke as the "spirit of prophecy," but this is too narrow a reading, as the Spirit also impels the new community to mission and empowers it to speak about the Messiah, as well as guides its way in that mission.[23]

Unlike the twofold division of promise and fulfillment that marks off the kingdom, Luke's presentation of the Spirit is marked out by a more complex scheme.[24] Initially, the Spirit leads to words of announced prophecy in figures such as Elizabeth, Zechariah, and Simeon (Luke 1–2). Yet much of what the Spirit is to be is yet anticipated, as John the Baptist's remarks in Luke 3:15–17 make clear. In the time of Jesus' ministry, the Spirit is God's enablement that anoints Jesus and points to his messianic function (Luke 3:21–22; 4:16–18). Beyond this connection to Jesus, the work of the Spirit is mostly left to the future, and the exact relationship between the Spirit and Jesus is not so clearly spelled out. The key work of the Spirit lies with the formation of the new community after Jesus' resurrection and exaltation. Here, the Spirit falls on all believers as the last days come (Luke 24:49 [promised]; Acts 2:1–41 [realized]). The Spirit is power (or enablement) from on high (Luke 24:49; Acts 2:30–36; 10:44–47; 11:15–16; 15:8). The Spirit's presence is evidence that Jesus is raised and that Jesus directs his new community from the right hand of God, primarily for proclamation and as a means of guidance. Though the Messiah has died and seems to be absent, the power of God is now present in the gift of the Spirit. The Spirit becomes the enabler of the kingdom, sent by the Messiah-Lord as the evidence that he has come and is active (Luke 3:15–17; Acts 2:14–39).

At the center of God's provision of salvation is the resurrection and ascension of Jesus. Among the Gospel writers, only Luke describes the ascension; it links Luke 24 and Acts 1.[25] The risen Savior is one who can both rule and consummate his promise. He is one who can forgive and signify forgiveness by bestowing blessings (Luke 24:47; Acts 2:21; 4:12; 10:43). He is one who can receive and give the Spirit, who empowers God's people to testify to him (Acts 2). In short, the ascension shows that Jesus is both Lord and Christ in conjunction with God's hope and promises (Acts 2:16–36).[26]

23. Correctly, Turner, *Power from on High.*

24. This division works better in thinking about the Spirit than in thinking of the Lukan scheme of salvation history and the kingdom as a whole. It is yet another indication of the careful nuances in Luke's theological expression. See J. A. Fitzmyer, "The Role of the Spirit in Luke-Acts," in Verheyden, *The Unity of Luke-Acts,* 165–83.

25. On the key role of this event in Luke-Acts, see Mikeal Parsons, *The Departure of Jesus in Luke-Acts: The Ascension Narratives in Context,* JSNTSup 21 (Sheffield: Sheffield Academic Press, 1987).

26. On the importance of covenant promise for these themes, see R. L. Brawley, "Abrahamic Covenant Traditions and the Characterization of God in Luke-Acts," in Verheyden, *The Unity of Luke-Acts,* 109–32.

Salvation in Jesus' Teaching and Work

Jesus brings both promise and salvation. Salvation involves sharing in hope, experiencing the kingdom, tasting forgiveness, and participating in the Spirit's enabling power, especially for mission. As we have seen, Jesus' teaching focuses on the offer of the kingdom. This offer is pictured as the release and healing of the Jubilee (Luke 4:16–21; cf. Lev. 25:10; Isa. 61:1–2), but it also includes a call to ethical honor reflecting the experience of blessing (Luke 6:20–49).[27] The parables show the same dual concern. A few parables deal with God's plan (13:6–9, 23–30; 14:16–24; 20:9–18), and in some of these a meal or feast scene is included. The feast displays the joy of salvation and the table fellowship of the future.[28]

Thus, the offer of salvation includes a call to an ethical way of life.[29] The life of relationship with God, engagement in mission, and ethical honor involves love, humility, service, and righteousness—the subject of most of the other parables (10:25–37; 11:5–8; 12:35–49; 14:1–12; 15:1–32; 16:1–8, 19–31; 18:1–8; 19:11–27). Jesus did not come simply to rescue people for heaven, but also to have them know God's transforming presence. This note is struck early on with the remarks about how John the Baptist will prepare people for God's coming in his Promised One (1:16–17). Here, themes pointing to human reconciliation, both to God and between people, are stressed. This different way of relating to God, the call to service versus power, and the road of suffering it entails will not be popular, and so commitment to Jesus' teaching and path is required (9:21–26, 57–62; 14:25–34; 18:18–30).[30]

In his survey of Jesus' work and teaching, as well as in his treatment of salvation, Luke says little about the cross.[31] Why is this, especially when Paul

27. On the Jubilee theme in Luke 4, see Robert B. Sloan Jr., *The Favorable Year of the Lord: A Study of Jubilary Theology in the Gospel of Luke* (Austin: Schola, 1977).

28. Moessner, *Lord of the Banquet,* gives much attention to the parables of the central section of Luke 9–19. See also Forbes, *The God of Old;* Denova, *The Things Accomplished among Us.*

29. See Christoph Stenschke, "The Need for Salvation," in Marshall and Peterson, *Witness to the Gospel,* 125–44. This essay focuses on the importance of forgiveness of sins, but it does not develop as much as it could the ethical dimensions of repentance and the forgiveness of sins as seen in the key early material in Luke tied to John the Baptist. Matthias Wenk, *Community-Forming Power: The Socio-Ethical Role of the Spirit in Luke-Acts,* JPTSup 19 (Sheffield: Sheffield Academic Press, 2000), emphasizes how mission and ethnic-racial reconciliation are a product of the Spirit's work for Luke.

30. See Charles H. Talbert, "Discipleship in Luke-Acts," in *Discipleship in the New Testament,* ed. Fernando F. Segovia (Philadelphia: Fortress, 1985); Richard N. Longenecker, "Taking Up the Cross Daily: Discipleship in Luke-Acts," in *Patterns of Discipleship in the New Testament,* ed. Richard N. Longenecker, McMaster New Testament Studies (Grand Rapids: Eerdmans, 1996).

31. This point is made not to say that Luke is silent about the cross, but that Luke gives it less emphasis than it receives elsewhere in the NT. An aspect of this difference is likely to be that Luke is aware that the emphasis on the cross is already well known, being grounded in the traditional kerygma, as 1 Cor. 15:1–3 indicates. So Luke takes the opportunity to develop

makes so much of it? It is because Luke gives Jesus' ascension and exaltation more prominence. Luke emphasizes the "who" of salvation. Deliverance comes from the exalted Lord, who functions as the promised Messiah (Acts 2:16–36). Paul explains how Jesus accomplished salvation from sin. Though the cross is less prominent for Luke than for Paul, it has more than an ethical or historical function; it still occupies a significant theological position in Luke's teaching. Jesus is the righteous sufferer (Luke 22–23). His death inaugurates the new covenant (Luke 22:20), and the church is "purchased" with his blood (Acts 20:28).[32] Covenant inauguration and a saving transaction take place in Jesus' death. Two other images reinforce this view. The substitution of Jesus for Barabbas illustrates the fact that Jesus took the place of the sinner (Luke 23:18–25). Jesus' offer of paradise to the thief as they die together (23:43) shows that Jesus, despite his death, can offer life. This last text is important, even for those who do not see atonement as prominent for Luke, because Jesus still offers and can deliver life despite his death.

Not only the resurrection, but also the miracles, in their demonstration of the arrival of the new era, authenticate Jesus' authoritative role in the divine plan that brings salvation (Luke 7:22; Acts 2:22–24). In fact, the scope of Jesus' healings shows the breadth of his authority. He heals the sick, exorcising evil spirits and curing a variety of specific conditions: a flow of blood, a withered hand, blindness, deafness, paralysis, epilepsy, leprosy, dropsy, and fever. He resuscitates the dead and exercises power over nature. The fact that Acts records the disciples' continuing to perform some of these works (Acts 3:6, 16) shows that Jesus' authority, and its authentication, continue after his ascension.

Luke's portrayal of Jesus is focused on his authority and the promise that he brings. Jesus' saving work inaugurates the kingdom, delivers the sinner, secures

---

and emphasize other soteriological themes. Still, an important case can be made for a coherent Lukan theology of the cross, as does Peter Doble, *The Paradox of Salvation: Luke's Theology of the Cross*, SNTSMS 87 (Cambridge: Cambridge University Press, 1996). He argues that although Luke does not develop Jesus' death as an atonement, Luke does see the event with the resurrection as a "turning of the ages" (235). It is a suffering of the "righteous" on the model of Jewish wisdom texts. Doble perhaps understates the significance of the new-covenant language of the Last Supper and of the picture of Barabbas, leaving too much distance between Luke and a belief in atonement. Acts 20:28 also speaks to this theme, which is not emphasized by Luke, but not absent either.

32. Although some scholars challenge the text-critical authenticity of both of these texts, each has a solid claim to being present. See Bruce M. Metzger, *A Textual Commentary on the Greek New Testament*, 2nd ed. (Stuttgart: Deutsche Bibelgesellschaft, 1994), 425–27, and the discussion in Ben Witherington III, *The Acts of the Apostles: A Social-Rhetorical Commentary* (Grand Rapids: Eerdmans, 1998), 623–24. That the cross involves more than the purchase of forgiveness for Luke is seen in the idea that forgiveness is associated with Jesus' death and his releasing of sin and the model of suffering that Jesus' death is. See David Moessner, "The Script of the Scriptures in Acts: Suffering as God's Plan (βουλή) for the World for the Release of Sins," in *History, Literature, and Society in the Book of Acts*, ed. Ben Witherington III (Cambridge: Cambridge University Press, 1996), 218–50.

forgiveness of sin, provides the Spirit, and calls for a committed and faithful life lived in the context of hope in the future consummation. Theophilus should be reassured that Jesus can and does fulfill these promises. But who makes up the new community? How does Christology relate to the task of this new community?

The New Community

The new community formed around Jesus is not really an organized entity in its earliest stages. There are the Twelve and the Seventy(-two), but beyond these basic groups there is no formal community structure in Luke. The term "church" does appear, but mostly in summaries or later in Acts (5:11; 8:1, 3; 9:31; 11:22, 26; 12:1, 5; 13:1; 14:23, 27; 15:3–4, 22, 41; 16:5; 18:22; 20:17, 28). Rather, those who will become the new community of Acts are called "disciples" in Luke's Gospel. This group is mostly Jewish, but a few hints reveal that Jesus' program can extend to Samaritans and non-Jews (Luke 3:4–6; 4:22–30; 7:1–10; 13:23–30; 14:16–24; 17:12–19; 20:15–16; 24:47).[33] This multiracial theme becomes prominent in Acts, but in Luke's Gospel the key fact is that Jesus' message touches the fringes of society.[34]

Luke focuses on outcasts as members of this blessed community: the poor, sinners, and tax collectors.[35] The poor are materially *and* spiritually impoverished (1:50–53 and 6:20–23, where the condition of the poor and humble is related to that of God's prophets). The poor or rejected are mentioned in several texts (1:46–55; 4:18; 6:20–23; 7:22; 10:21–22; 14:13, 21–24; 16:19–31; 21:1–4). The OT roots for this concept are in the Hebrew concept of the *ʿănāwim* (Isa. 61:1–2). Sinners are the special targets of the gospel (Luke 5:27–32; 7:28, 30, 34, 36–50; 15:1–2; 19:7). Tax collectors, regarded by most Jews as traitors, are potential beneficiaries as well (5:27–32; 7:34; 18:9–14; 19:1–10).

Finally, Luke features women (7:36–50; 8:1–3, 43–48; 10:38–42; 13:10–17; 24:1–12).[36] Often, widows are mentioned, since they are the most vulnerable

---

33. See Stephen G. Wilson, *The Gentiles and the Gentile Mission in Luke-Acts,* SNTSMS 23 (Cambridge: Cambridge University Press, 1973); Esler, *Community and Gospel in Luke-Acts,* 24–70, although Esler overplays Luke's differences with Matthew on the issue of table fellowship.

34. See David Seccombe, "The New People of God," in Marshall and Peterson, *Witness to the Gospel,* 349–72; Walter E. Pilgrim, *Good News to the Poor: Wealth and Poverty in Luke-Acts* (Minneapolis: Augsburg, 1981), esp. 17–84.

35. See Robert F. O'Toole, "Luke's Position on Politics and Society in Luke-Acts," in *Political Issues in Luke-Acts,* ed. Richard J. Cassidy and Philip J. Scharper (Maryknoll, N.Y.: Orbis, 1983), 1–17; Robert F. O'Toole, "Christ, the Savior of the Disadvantaged," in Verheyden, *The Unity of Luke-Acts,* 109–48.

36. One of the few monographs on this theme is written from a feminist perspective: Turid Karlsen Seim, *The Double Message: Patterns of Gender in Luke and Acts* (Nashville: Abingdon, 1994). The "double message" of Luke is that he is unusual in highlighting the role of women throughout his work while also giving men priority in the organization of the church in Acts (259).

of women (2:36–37; 4:25–26; 7:12; 18:3, 5; 20:47; 21:2–3). Most of these women in the Gospel are sensitive to Jesus' message. Though on the fringes of first-century society, women are a highly visible element in Luke's story. They are examples of faith, stewardship, and discipleship (cf., however, Acts 5:1–10). Often they are paired with men (Luke 2:25–28; 4:25–27; 8:40–56; 11:31–32; 13:18–21; 15:4–10; 17:34–35; cf. Acts 21:9–10).

In short, the makeup of the new community knows no boundaries. The good news is available to all, but society's weak and vulnerable often are most able to respond. Jesus shows them a special concern, just as the world seems to ignore or rebuke them. Luke uses three terms to describe the response to the message that brings one into the community: "repent," "turn," and "faith."[37] The term translated "repent" is rooted in the OT word for "turn around" (Luke 24:44–47). Repentance involves a reorientation of perspective, a fresh point of view. The call to repent is another way to call the people of God back to faithfulness, when this call is issued within Israel. For Luke, the fruit of repentance expresses itself concretely. In material unique to Luke, John the Baptist replies to those who desire his baptism and who inquire, "What should we do then?" by teaching that repentance expresses itself in everyday life, especially in how men and women treat each other (3:7–14).

Four pictures of repentance are significant. Luke 5:31–32 portrays Jesus as a physician healing the sick. Luke 15:17–21 describes the repentance of the prodigal and indicates that a repentant heart makes no claims, recognizing that only God and his mercy can provide relief. At the end of his Gospel, Luke summarizes the essence of the good news: "Repentance and forgiveness of sins will be preached in his name" (24:47). The parable of the tax collector who in the temple cries out "God, have mercy on me, a sinner" (18:9–14) demonstrates the penitent's response to God, although the term "repentance" is not used there (also 19:1–10). The word "turn," though rarely used in the Gospel (1:17; 17:4; 22:32), becomes prominent in Acts, where it denotes the fundamental change of direction that accompanies repentance (Acts 3:19; 9:35; 11:21; 14:15; 15:19; 26:18–20; 28:27). Faith for Luke expresses itself concretely, whether the faith of the paralytic's friends (Luke 5:20), the faith of the centurion (7:9), or the faith of the sinful woman who anoints Jesus (7:47–50). The Samaritan leper and the blind man also have faith that Jesus can restore them to wholeness (17:19; 18:42).[38] Faith believes and so acts. In short, faith is the recognition and conviction that God had something to offer through Jesus: forgiveness and the promised blessings of spiritual restoration

---

37. See Darrell L. Bock, "A Theology of Luke-Acts," in *A Biblical Theology of the New Testament,* ed. Roy B. Zuck and Darrell L. Bock (Chicago: Moody, 1994), 129–34; Stenschke, "The Need for Salvation."

38. On the relationship of salvation to wholeness, see Ben Witherington III, "Salvation and Health in Christian Antiquity: The Soteriology of Luke-Acts in Its First Century Setting," in Marshall and Peterson, *Witness to the Gospel,* 145–66.

before God. Such people "call on the name of the Lord" when they respond in faith (Acts 2:21; cf. Rom. 10:13).

Various terms denote the blessings given to community members: forgiveness or release (Luke 1:77; 3:3; 4:18; 24:47), life (10:25; 12:15, 22–25; 18:29–30), peace (1:79; 2:14; 10:5–6; Acts 10:36), the kingdom (1:33; 6:20; 7:28; 11:20; 17:21; 22:29–30), and the Spirit (3:16; 11:13; 12:12; 24:49).[39]

In addition, the community grows through the sharing of teaching, fellowship, the breaking of bread, and praying together (Acts 2:42). They also helped to meet their needs by praying for one another, especially in the difficult moments of mission, and by sharing material needs with each other (Acts 4:23–37; 11:29).

The Opponents of Salvation and the New Community

Luke identifies spiritual and human opponents of the new community. At the transcendent level, the spiritual forces of evil are resistant, though powerless to frustrate the plan (Luke 4:1–13, 33–37; 8:26–39; 9:1; 10:1–12, 18; 11:14–26; 22:3).[40] God's struggle involves not only reclaiming humanity's devotion, but also reversing the effects of the presence of evil forces. On a human level, the opponents are primarily the Jewish leadership of scribes and Pharisees, although in the Book of Acts they are seen with more sympathy and potential than the Sadducees, who lack the right kind of beliefs about spiritual forces and the resurrection to be responsive to Jesus and his message. After Jesus claims authority to forgive sin and challenges the Sabbath tradition (5:24; 6:1–11), opposition from the Jewish leadership becomes a regular feature of the narrative. Its roots go back to the rejection of John the Baptist (7:29–30; 20:1–8).

---

39. For a treatment of the theme of peace that overplays the political dimensions at the expense of the spiritual elements, but does examine the concept in Luke, see Willard M. Swartley, "Politics and Peace (*Eirēnē*) in Luke's Gospel," in Cassidy and Scharper, *Political Issues in Luke-Acts,* 18–37. A better balance appears in a more general discussion of community in Wenk, *Community-Forming Power,* 259–73.

40. See Susan R. Garrett: *The Demise of the Devil: Magic and the Demonic in Luke's Writings* (Minneapolis: Fortress, 1989); Weatherly, *Death of Jesus in Luke-Acts.* Too soft on Jewish responsibility in opposition to Jesus is Brawley, *Luke-Acts and the Jews.* Emphasizing the Jewish opposition to Jesus is Joseph Tyson, *The Death of Jesus in Luke-Acts* (Columbia: University of South Carolina Press, 1986). This is the other end of the responsibility spectrum in Lukan studies from Brawley. Jack Sanders, *The Jews in Luke-Acts* (London: SCM, 1987), goes even further, arguing that Luke is anti-Semitic. Yet another angle is found in Jacob Jervell, *Luke and the People of God* (Minneapolis: Augsburg, 1972). He contends that Jewish Christians are still a powerful minority at the time of Luke's writing. Israel en masse did not reject Jesus. So also David Tiede, *Prophecy and History in Luke-Acts* (Philadelphia: Fortress, 1980). These more nuanced positions about Jewish involvement are more likely on target in terms of Lukan themes. Weatherly's work is an important summary of this discussion, while the key seminal study of how Jews are portrayed in Luke is Jervell, *Luke and the People of God.* He makes it clear that the portrait of Jews is quite nuanced, not one of total rejection.

Three times Jesus warns the Pharisees (7:36–50; 11:37–52; 14:1–24). Often, the leaders are the object of Jesus' condemnation, expressed in the strongest of terms (11:37–52; 12:1; 14:14; 15:1–10; 16:14–15; 19:45–47; 20:45–47). Although the few exceptions, such as Jairus (8:41) and Joseph of Arimathea (23:50–53), catch the attention, the Jewish leadership as a whole opposes Jesus and plots his demise (6:11; 11:53–54; 20:19; 22:1–6, 21; 23:3–5).

The crowd's reaction to Jesus is mixed. They are interested, but their response is superficial and fickle.[41] A transition occurs in Luke 9–13. Jesus issues many warnings in Luke 12:49–14:24. He rebukes "this generation" in 11:29–32, condemns various cities of Israel in 10:13–15, and tells parables about the failings of the nation (13:6–9; 20:9–19). The crowd's eventual response in Luke 23 typifies the response of most people in Israel. Their rejection of Jesus brings early warnings of judgment, yet he yearns and weeps for those whom he warns (13:34–35; 19:41–44). In the end, the crowd shares the responsibility for Jesus' death by asking for Barabbas (23:18–25). So Jesus delivers a prophetic message of judgment to the daughters of Jerusalem and their children (23:27–31).

The response of most of Israel is tragic.[42] The nation was offered blessing, but has missed its day of visitation and now awaits exilic-like judgment in being defeated in a siege of Jerusalem, an allusion to 70 C.E. (19:44). Now it is the "time of the Gentiles" (21:24). Israel has not lost its place in God's plan, for the faithfulness of God's promise cannot be denied, but Israel is "desolate" until it acknowledges the Messiah (13:34–35; Acts 3:13–21). Luke has been wrongly accused of anti-Semitism; rather, he claims that the new community was persecuted by those rejecting the message of hope, even as that message continued to go out to Jews as Paul preached in the synagogues as well as to Gentiles. Jesus and the disciples offered the gospel to the nation and suffered for it. The disciples did not create the division or bring violence to Israel. The new community was not anti-Jewish; it was pro-promise. Its enemies were to be loved and prayed for, as Jesus made clear, and as Stephen exemplified during his martyrdom (Luke 6:27–36; 23:34; Acts 7:60).

One source of tension between the Jews and the new community was the law. Luke's precise understanding of this matter has been a subject of ongoing debate in Lukan scholarship.[43] It has been properly argued that Luke understands the law to be part of the old era and portrays the church in Acts as slowly coming to recognize that truth. The law was not regarded as binding,

41. See Robert C. Tannehill, *The Narrative Unity of Luke-Acts: A Literary Interpretation*, 2 vols., FF (Philadelphia: Fortress, 1986–90), vol. 1, *The Gospel according to Luke*, esp. 158–66.

42. Tannehill, *Narrative Unity of Luke-Acts*, 1:259–61.

43. See Craig Blomberg, "The Law in Luke-Acts," *JSNT* 22 (1984): 53–80; Stephen G. Wilson, *Luke and the Law*, SNTMS 50 (Cambridge: Cambridge University Press, 1983). Wilson argues the Luke is not consistent in his presentation of the issue of the law. Wilson is responding in part to work by Jacob Jervell (*Luke and the People of God*, esp. 136–44), who calls Luke's view of the law "conservative" and influenced by a Jewish-Christian perspective. The position of Blomberg and Jervell is the more sustainable one.

though the missionary praxis of the early church allowed its observance where issues central to the new faith were not at stake. So Gentiles did not need to be circumcised (Acts 15), but Jews could continue that practice. The law and its associated traditions, especially the Sabbath regulations and some traditional issues tied to purity (Luke 6:1–11; 11:37–53), are a major source of conflict in Luke's Gospel. Jesus' challenge to the Sabbath regulations comes after his proclamation that new wine must come in new wineskins, and that those who like the old will not try the new (5:33–39). This remark is part of a dispute centered on Jesus' neglect of Jewish traditions related to cleansing. Jesus challenged the law, or at least its first-century Jewish interpretation. Luke regards this challenge as an important element in Jewish opposition. Such charges also show up in Acts (6:13–14).

In the face of opposition, disciples were called to a strong commitment to Jesus. Opposition would come. Indications of division come early in Luke's Gospel (2:34–35) and continue throughout (8:14–15; 9:21–23, 61–62; 12:8–9; 22:35–38). Persecution can cause a lack of fruit for the seed of the word of the kingdom, as the parable of the sower makes clear. The disciples are pictured as shrinking back from a bold response, as in the account of Peter's denial. The exhortation to steadfast discipleship reveals one facet of the Gospel's origin. For Theophilus and others, the pressure of conflict was the occasion for reassurance.

Response: Luke's Call to Repentance, Faith, Ethics, and Perseverance

Luke is clear about how his readers should respond to Jesus and the difficulties arising from opposition to him. The community is called to a fundamental reorientation toward God, expressed in faith, repentance, and commitment. This attitude of trust both initiates and sustains their walk with God (Luke 5:31–32; 15:17–21; cf. 12:22–32). The path is difficult and requires self-examination, total commitment, daily dedication, and cross-bearing (9:23, 57–62; 14:25–35). The community is called to mission. Although Acts details the early missionary activity of the community, the call to preach repentance and forgiveness to all nations, beginning at Jerusalem, is spelled out in the Gospel (24:47). The parables of Luke 15 reflect Luke's focus on the lost, as do the clear statements of 5:31–32 and 19:10.[44] Jesus' disciples are to follow him in reaching out to others.

Love for God and for one's neighbor, including one's enemy, is part of the call. Luke 11:1–13 describes devotion to God expressed in dependent prayer. Devotion to Jesus is shown in Mary's choice to sit at his feet, absorbing his

---

44. See Craig Blomberg, *Interpreting the Parables* (Downers Grove, Ill.: InterVarsity, 1990).

teaching and enjoying his presence (10:38–42). In this she is an example of love for God and his way. In addition, the care of one's neighbor is enjoined in 10:25–37.[45] Jesus in his ministry demonstrates what he calls his disciples to be: neighbors to all, without distinction of race or class. The cross, as the expression of his willingness to die for others, shows him acting in love toward those who are his enemies.

Jesus encourages prayer (11:1–13; 18:1–14; 22:40).[46] Prayer does not demand; it requests, humbly relying on God's mercy and will. It trusts in God's care and provision of basic needs, and it looks with expectation to the eschatological consummation of God's kingdom. This mixing of trust and eschatology, as it emerges in 18:1–8, makes it clear that part of the issue tied to trust in God is being patient with the timing of God's plan.[47]

Under the pressure of opposition, the community is to remain steadfast and faithful (Luke 8:13–15; 9:23; 18:8; 21:19).[48] Disciples are to fear God, not mortals (12:1–12), recognizing that the Lord will return and that they are responsible to him (12:35–48; 18:8; 19:11–27). Like the seed on good soil, they hear the word, cling to it, persevere, and bear fruit (8:15). Exemplars such as Peter, Stephen, and Paul portray what the faithfulness and steadfastness of proclaiming the word is like and what it might require—imprisonment or death.[49] Their lives recall that of the suffering and rejection of the Lord. Jesus' promises are for both the present and the future. Those promises that remain unrealized will eventually be fulfilled (17:22–37; 21:5–38). The coming judgment on Jerusalem is the guarantee and picture of the final judgment as the eschatological discourse of 21:5–37 looks to the near and the far future in a complex typology that compares 70 C.E. to the events of the end. The return of Jesus will be horrific for unbelievers, who will be severely judged. Luke emphasizes that the coming of the Son of Man places a responsibility on his disciples to be faithful and on all humanity to respond to the gospel. Though the time of Jesus' return is unknown, it will come suddenly, and the disciples must be prepared (12:35–40).

The Lukan view of wealth warns against attachment to possessions (8:14; 12:13–21; 16:1–15, 19–31; 18:18–25), but some examples are given of the positive uses of money (8:1–3; 19:1–10; 21:1–4).[50] Scholars have debated

---

45. See J. D. M. Derrett, *The Law in the New Testament* (London: Darton, Longman & Todd, 1970), 223–24.

46. On Jesus and his unique role as messianic intercessor, see David Crump, *Jesus the Intercessor: Prayer and Christology in Luke-Acts*, WUNT 2.49 (Tübingen: Mohr, 1992).

47. See David Tiede, *Luke*, ACNT (Minneapolis: Augsburg, 1988), 304.

48. See John J. Kilgallen, "Persecution in the Acts of the Apostles," in *Luke and Acts*, ed. Gerald O'Collins and Gilberto Marconi, trans. Matthew O'Connell (New York: Paulist Press, 1991), 143–60.

49. See Martin H. Scharlemann, *Stephen: A Singular Saint*, AnBib 34 (Rome: Pontifical Biblical Institute, 1968).

50. See Luke T. Johnson, *The Literary Function of Possessions in Luke-Acts*, SBLDS 39 (Missoula, Mont.: Scholars Press, 1977); David Seccombe, *Possessions and the Poor in Luke-Acts*, SNTSU B.6 (Linz: Plöchl, 1982); Pilgrim, *Good News to the Poor*.

whether Luke decries wealth per se. Zacchaeus, who generously gives half of his possessions to the poor and repays those he has wronged, does not divest himself of every asset. His example suggests that the issue is what people do with their possessions and how they view possessions: do they hoard them or use them generously? The disciples are said to have "left all" for Jesus (18:28–30), family as well as resources. Yet, later in the Gospel, under the pressure of Jesus' arrest, they are afraid and deny him. The issue with resources, as with the other demands of discipleship, is not the perfection of the response, but rather its fundamental orientation. Several texts point to a reversal of roles in the judgment, warning that possessions and status are not automatic indicators of blessing (1:51–53; 8:14; 12:13–21; 16:19–30; 18:18–30). Disciples are called to recognize that all life belongs to God and comes from his hand. The rich man rejects Jesus' request to sell all, while the disciples and Zacchaeus begin to relinquish their possessions. Luke warns that hindrances to discipleship include not only misplaced confidence in resources, but also the fear of others' opinions (12:1–12) and the cares of life (8:14).

Issues of Setting and Genre

It is in this final area that the debates surrounding Luke swirl the most. The debates here reflect the kind of critical reconstructive work that appeals to the Jewish and/or Greco-Roman backgrounds. Where does Luke fit in relation to various cultural-historical and theological trajectories? Is he interacting with a Jewish setting, especially in the Gospel and early in Acts? Is it a mix of contexts? Or is he primarily set in a Hellenistic context? Such work also debates whether Luke is conservative with his tradition or is a writer working creatively, reading his setting in the early church back into the earlier period of Jesus. Debates center on the genre of Luke, the nature of the prologue, the dating of his work, and his audience. These issues are among the most difficult in Luke-Acts to tie down. In many ways, they impact many of the themes already covered, for the question becomes whether Luke, in making his theological points, does so with a careful eye on history or as a creative theologian interested less in historical issues and more in his current pastoral concerns. The spectrum of the debate runs the gamut of options. However, even posing the question in such either/or ways risks oversimplifying what has taken place, given the constant appeal to Jewish promise and history throughout Luke's two volumes.

The views on genre extend from Luke-Acts being a combination of solid biography and history to some form of sociological legitimization, to a romantic work largely of symbolic significance.[51] Those who see a solid historical base to Luke's work appear to have the better of the argument here. There was too

_____

51. The multivolume series edited by Bruce Winter, The Book of Acts in Its First Century Setting, has used both Greco-Roman and Jewish backgrounds to make a case for the solid his-

much at stake in the claims that Luke makes for him to be exclusively symbolic in his portrayal of this period. There also is evidence that the outlines of the material in Acts, especially the material in the early chapters, have solid historical roots.[52]

The role of Luke's prologue(s) in signaling the nature of his work has also been the subject of much discussion.[53] It seems clear that Luke's introduction recalls elements in both Greco-Roman and Jewish works, especially works such as Josephus and 2 Maccabees, and claims to have been careful while recognizing that exact citation is not always possible (as appears in Thucydides, *The Peloponnesian War* 1.22.1–2). There also is debate whether Luke's claim to have followed everything carefully is a claim about his experience of keeping an interested eye on such matters or is an allusion to actual research in earlier sources.[54] More recently, scholars have tended to favor an appeal to Luke's

torical grounding of Acts. On the role of speeches in Acts and this question, see Conrad Gempf, "Public Speaking and Published Accounts," *The Book of Acts in Its Ancient Literary Setting*, ed. Bruce Winter and Andrew Clarke, BAFCS 1 (Grand Rapids: Eerdmans, 1993), 259–303, which argues for a solid historical core in this material; so also Colin J. Hemer, *The Book of Acts in the Setting of Hellenistic History*, WUNT 49 (Tübingen: Mohr, 1989). For a survey of this debate with regard to Luke's method, see David Balch, "ἀκριβῶς . . . γράψαι (Luke 1:3): To Write the *Full History of God's Receiving All Nations*," in Moessner, *Jesus and the Heritage of Israel*, 229–50. Much of the Moessner volume deals with these issues and this approach. Gregory Sterling's *Historiography and Self-Definition* has made the most detailed case for legitimization. R. Pervo (*Profit with Delight: The Literary Genre of the Acts of the Apostles* [Philadelphia: Fortress, 1987]) places Acts in the ancient genre of literary romance, like the NT apocryphal books of Acts. For the Gospel, the whole issue of whether a Gospel fits the genre of a biography or a special category of material has been part of an ongoing discussion about the Synoptics in New Testament. Here Richard Burridge, *What Are the Gospels? A Comparison with Greco-Roman Biography*, SNTSMS 70 (Cambridge: Cambridge University Press, 1992), is an important study arguing that the ancient biography is the closest genre to what the Gospels are, despite years of denials of such connections in NT studies.

52. Hemer's *Book of Acts in the Setting of Hellenistic History* has not received due appreciation, perhaps because of his untimely death. For an opposite approach to this question, see Daryl D. Schmidt, "Rhetorical Influences and Genre: Luke's Preface and the Rhetoric of Hellenistic Historiography," in Moessner, *Jesus and the Heritage of Israel*, 27–60. Schmidt engages with Hemer, questions whether Greek historians such as Thucydides and his claims for "accuracy" were normative for Hellenistic historians, and challenges Hemer's idea that rhetoric and accuracy can be placed together. The debates here have to do with the relationship between the rhetorical and stylistic elements that are alleged to embellish such accounts and those claims tied to historicity. Are these opposing forces or complementary ones? Dealing with the Jewish roots of Christian tradition, Samuel Byrskog (*Story as History—History as Story*, WUNT 123 [Tübingen: Mohr Siebeck, 2000]) makes a more nuanced study of this question, showing that concerns for the core story are not ignored in this historiographic tradition.

53. The entire first part of Moessner, *Jesus and the Heritage of Israel*, covers the prologue issue with essays by Loveday C. A. Alexander, Daryl D. Schmidt, Vernon K. Robbins, and David P. Moessner. These essays focus mostly on Greco-Roman prototypes, but the importance of Jewish parallels should not be understated.

54. The key essay making a case for Luke's experience as one who comprehends the events as a credentialed figure is that of D. P. Moessner, "'Eyewitnesses,' 'Informed Contemporaries,'

credentials versus an emphasis on research, but this may be a question of emphasis rather than a real choice between the two. If Luke has qualifications to follow the story and to present it, where did those qualifications come from other than his very proximity to the tradition and those who formed it? Still, this is an area of ongoing discussion.

The issue of dating, and thus of setting, is tied to how one dates not only Luke, but also the entire Synoptic sequence—a discussion that moves well beyond the limits of this essay. For those who place Mark in the middle to late 60s, Luke and Acts must come later, anywhere from the late 60s to especially the 80s, although why the date should be this late is not so clear.[55] Others also argue that within Luke 21 and the addition of Luke 19:41–44 (not present in the Markan and Matthean parallels) there is evidence that Luke knows of the fall of Jerusalem in 70 C.E. These arguments lead many to prefer a date for Luke in the 70s or 80s and as a result to heighten the focus on a Gentile audience. On the other end of this spectrum are those who suggest that the end of Acts gives us our best clue for the date of Luke-Acts, for the story stops at the point that it has reached, with Paul in a Roman prison in the early 60s.[56] With Acts placed in the early 60s, Luke then is placed earlier. In this scenario, the Gospel is said to come from the late 50s to early 60s. For many, however, this is too early in light of Mark's likely date, which also is variously placed in late 60s or early 70s. It is possible that for Luke, Paul's arrival in Rome with the gospel and not his ultimate fate is the significant point of the end of Acts, meaning that the lack of resolution of his imprisonment is not a key factor in arguing about a date. It does seem that Luke makes little of 70 C.E. in terms of narrative elaboration—a point that is surprising if all that Jesus had predicted about it within Luke's Gospel had already taken place. This suggests completion

---

and 'Unknowing Inquirers': Josephus' Criteria for Authentic Historiography and the Meaning of ΠΑΡΑΚΟΛΟΥΘΕΩ," *NovT* 38 (1996): 105–22. This study was followed up by Moessner in "The Appeal and Power of Poetics (Luke 1:1–4): Luke's Superior Credentials (παρηκολουθηκότι), Narrative Sequence (καθεξῆς), and Firmness of Understanding (ἡ ἀσφάλεια) for the Reader," in Moessner, *Jesus and the Heritage of Israel*, 84–123. On the other side of this debate is Loveday C. A. Alexander, who also argues that the prologue is a credentialed claim, but to "fidelity and comprehension in transmission" rather than to personal research; still, the account promises "an account of tradition, carefully (or accurately) 'followed.'" See Loveday C. A. Alexander, "The Preface to Acts and the Historians," in Witherington, *History, Literature, and Society*, 73–103; idem, "Formal Elements and Genre: Which Greco-Roman Prologues Most Closely Parallel the Lukan Prologues?" in Moessner, *Jesus and the Heritage of Israel*, 9–26, where she compares the result to the "sense of security" that a BBC newsreader provides for an audience (25).

55. Esler (*Community and Gospel in Luke-Acts*, 27–30) offers a concise discussion, opting for 70–95 C.E., perceiving that a nonapocalyptic attitude has formed (à la Conzelmann) and also noting Luke's lack of appeal to the letters of Paul. The Pauline-letter argument is one from silence, on which too much should not be placed. These two factors together cause Esler to opt for a date in the 80s or early 90s. His argument is typical of those who place Luke-Acts in the latter portion of the first century.

56. Hemer, *Book of Acts*, 365–410. Hemer argues that Luke may have known of the development of Mark's work as it was being prepared.

of the volumes in the 60s, possibly in the mid-to-late 60s, when the clouds of war with Rome might have been on Israel's horizon.[57]

As we noted, the dating of these works impacts the view of what audience is in view. Generally speaking, the later that one fixes the date, the less likely one is to see Jewish concerns playing a significant role in the two volumes. Yet, the heavy use of the OT, the time spent on Jewish-Gentile relations, and the issues of Jewish dispute in Luke's Gospel, including the detail given to Jewish rejection, all suggest that the issue of Jewish influence is significant in the account.[58] The emphasis on themes such as perseverance seems to suggest an audience that needs to endure with the community in light of Jewish rejection rather than an audience to whom is directed a strictly evangelistic appeal to enter into salvation. Theophilus probably is a Gentile and may well be a God-fearer, one who came to Jesus after first having embraced the God of Israel. Luke's trip back to the roots of the movement is a way of assuring him and explaining to all how Gentiles should be included. These concerns appear to treat issues of an earlier period in the community's existence and point to an audience in the community. This observation means that Luke-Acts is not an invitation to enter the community.[59] The time spent on such concerns suggests that the audience has embraced the Christian view but is struggling with the adoption of that perspective. No doubt the social and spiritual pressures of Jewish-Gentile tensions played a major role here. Luke's journey through the community's roots says that both Jews and Gentiles belong, and that an effective reconciliation is necessary for effective mission and testimony. Luke's call is not so much, then, an invitation to participate in the beginnings of divine salvation in light of the divine plan worked out through Jesus, the messianic Lord; rather, it is an invitation to embrace and persevere in the faith, to experience that salvation to the full, recognizing that God has designed both Jew and Gentile to be a part of the new community.

Conclusion

Luke's work is pastoral, theological, and historical. The study of Luke and Acts works in many distinct thematic directions. God's plan affects how individuals see themselves and the community to which they belong. The message of Jesus is one of hope and transformation as well as the beginnings of the

---

57. Moessner, *Lord of the Banquet*, 308–15.

58. See Darrell L. Bock, *Luke 1:1–9:50*, BECNT (Grand Rapids: Baker, 1994), 14–15.

59. John Nolland has made the case that the primary reader of Luke's Gospel may well be a God-fearer (J. L. Nolland, "Luke's Readers: A Study of Luke 4:22–28; Acts 13:46; 18:6; 28:28 and Luke 21:5–36" [Ph.D. diss., Cambridge University, 1977]; *Luke 1–9:20*, WBC 35A [Dallas: Word, 1989], xxii–xxiii). Nolland opts for a date ranging from the late 60s to later 70s for Luke.

completion of promises made long ago. Anyone, Jew or Gentile, can belong to the new community, which was designed to be racially inclusive. Though Gentiles are included, Jews still can hope for the completion of promises made to them in the OT. At the center of this work stands the exalted Jesus, the promised Messiah-Lord, who sits at God's right hand, exercising authority from above. He will return one day, and all are accountable to him, as he will be the judge of the living and the dead. His life, ministry, resurrection, and ascension prove that he is worthy of trust and that he is still at work through the Spirit, who equips God's people for mission. Just as Jesus has inaugurated the fulfillment of God's promises, so he will bring them to completion. In the meantime, being a disciple is not easy, as the world has a distinct set of values that rejects the way of the Promised One. However, the new life of the Spirit-enabled community does bring many rich blessings that transcend anything else this life can offer.

18

The Petrine Epistles

Recent Developments and Trends

Robert L. Webb

The two letters ascribed to Peter often have been relegated to the backwater of NT scholarship due in part to their brevity, their perceived theological strangeness (often simply because they are distinct from Pauline thought), and possibly their inclusion with a group of "general" epistles.[1] But recent developments suggest a reversal in the fortunes of these two letters. The trend is toward a recognition of their individuality and distinctiveness, and an appreciation of how they represent other voices in the diversity of early Christianity.[2]

First Peter

In 1976, John H. Elliott lamented the neglect that 1 Peter had experienced in NT scholarship, but he noted that this sad situation was being addressed,

1. The term "general" (or "catholic") for these epistles is somewhat of a misnomer. Some of these letters, such as 1 Peter, appear to have been written to a wider audience than only one church (contrary to Paul's Letters), but this does not mean that they are universal in scope or general in content. The General Epistles are, like Paul's Epistles, "occasional" documents—written to a specific situation and occasion. See Robert L. Webb, "Epistles, Catholic," *ABD* 2:569–70.

2. This applies equally to a recognition that 2 Peter and Jude also are distinct from each other with respect to the social context of their readers and the rhetorical arguments of their authors. Unfortunately, a consideration of Jude is beyond the limitations of this essay, but some

and this "exegetical step-child" was experiencing "rehabilitation."[3] Recently, almost twenty-five years later, Elliott would be able to observe that 1 Peter has subsequently been the focus of numerous studies, which "have led to clearer insight into the letter's situation and strategy and, as a result, to a greater appreciation of 1 Peter."[4] I will trace here some of the paths taken since 1976 that have led to this exciting turn of fortune for 1 Peter.[5]

First Peter in Literary Context

Though 1 Peter manifests the features typical of a genuine Greco-Roman letter, it often has been suggested that this epistle is a composite work, with the epistolary format being imposed upon an earlier, different form. For example, R. Perdelwitz (1911) argued that 1:3–4:11 was a baptismal homily to which an author attached a letter of encouragement (4:12–5:14 and 1:1–2) when the

---

bibliographic notes are provided below in the discussion of 2 Peter. An interesting study that recognizes the individual distinctives of these letters but also suggests that they may have originated in a Petrine school is that of Marion L. Soards, "1 Peter, 2 Peter, and Jude as Evidence for a Petrine School," in *ANRW* 2.25.5:3827–49.

3. John H. Elliott, "The Rehabilitation of an Exegetical Step-Child: 1 Peter in Recent Research," *JBL* 95 (1976): 243.

4. John H. Elliott, *1 Peter: A New Translation with Introduction and Commentary*, AB 37B (New York: Doubleday, 2000), 6.

5. The focus of attention in this essay is those areas where significant development has taken place. Other subjects also could have been examined but were not included due to limitations of space or because no major advances have been made in their discussion (e.g., the authorship of 1 Peter). Other accounts of recent research in 1 Peter include Dennis Sylva, "1 Peter Studies: The State of the Discipline," *BTB* 10 (1980): 155–63; Troy W. Martin, *Metaphor and Composition in 1 Peter*, SBLDS 131 (Atlanta: Scholars Press, 1992), 3–39; Elliott, *1 Peter*, 1–152; Birger A. Pearson, "James, 1–2 Peter, Jude," in *The New Testament and Its Modern Interpreters*, ed. E. Epp and G. MacRae (Philadelphia: Fortress, 1989), 376–82; Edouard Cothenet, "La Première de Pierre: Bilan de 35 ans de recherches," in *ANRW* 2.25.5:3685–712.

Recent bibliographies include Dennis Sylva, "The Critical Exploration of 1 Peter," in *Perspectives on First Peter*, ed. Charles H. Talbert, NABPR Special Studies Series 9 (Macon, Ga.: Mercer University Press, 1986), 17–36; Anthony Casurella, *Bibliography of Literature on First Peter*, NTTS 23 (Leiden: Brill, 1996); Elliott, *1 Peter*, 155–304; Watson E. Mills, *1 Peter*, BBRNT 17 (Lewiston, N.Y.: Mellen, 2000).

The best recent technical commentaries include J. N. D. Kelly, *A Commentary on the Epistles of Peter and of Jude*, BNTC (London: Black, 1969); Norbert Brox, *Der erste Petrusbrief*, EKKNT 21 (Zürich: Benziger, 1979); Karl Hermann Schelkle, *Die Petrusbriefe, Der Judasbrief*, 5th ed., HTKNT 13.2 (Freiburg: Herder, 1980); J. Ramsey Michaels, *1 Peter*, WBC 49 (Waco, Tex.: Word, 1988); Leonhard Goppelt, *A Commentary on 1 Peter*, ed. and trans. J. E. Alsup (Grand Rapids: Eerdmans, 1993); Paul J. Achtemeier, *1 Peter*, Hermeneia (Minneapolis: Fortress, 1996); Elliott, *1 Peter*.

The best recent nontechnical commentaries include Wayne A. Grudem, *The First Epistle of Peter*, TNTC 17 (Grand Rapids: Eerdmans, 1988); Peter H. Davids, *The First Epistle of Peter*, NICNT (Grand Rapids: Eerdmans, 1990); I. Howard Marshall, *1 Peter*, IVPNTC (Downers Grove, Ill.: InterVarsity, 1991); Scot McKnight, *1 Peter*, NIVAC (Grand Rapids: Zondervan, 1996); M. Eugene Boring, *1 Peter*, ANTC (Nashville: Abingdon, 1999).

persecution, alluded to in the homily, actually began.[6] Several twists on this theme have been proposed: H. Preisker (1951) argued that 1 Peter contained an actual baptismal liturgy;[7] F. L. Cross's (1954) view was that this was a part played by a celebrant at a baptismal paschal Eucharist;[8] M.-É. Boismard (1961) proposed multiple hymnal fragments in 1 Peter taken from a baptismal liturgy.[9] C. F. D. Moule (1956) suggested that 1 Peter is a compilation of what was originally two letters: 2:11–4:11 was written to those for whom suffering was yet future, and 4:12–5:11 was written to those now experiencing persecution.[10]

Such theories were popular in the past, but recent studies have argued to the contrary that such composite theories not only were quite speculative, but also they forced the text in ways unnatural to the text itself. For example, J. N. D. Kelly observes that these "theses are impressive in their breath-taking ingenuity," and with respect to Preisker's view in particular, he comments that it "can only be described as a *tour de force* of subjective improvisation."[11] The text of 1 Peter refers only once to the term "baptism" (3:21), and while it does elsewhere make use of what appears to be traditional material, this hardly constitutes sufficient grounds to impose a baptismal grid (whether liturgical or homiletical) onto the text.[12] Furthermore, the language and themes of the epistolary framework of 1:1–2 and 5:12–14 are related to the body of the letter (1:3–5:11), and the doxology in 4:11 is not a break indicating two letters but a transition to a new unit of thought (along with the repeated direct address, "Beloved," from 2:11) that gives "a positive valuation of innocent suffering."[13]

6. R. Perdelwitz, *Die Mysterienreligion und das Problem des 1. Petrusbriefes: Ein literarischer und religionsgeschichtlicher Versuch*, RVV 11.3 (Giessen: Töpelmann, 1911). Various forms of this view became quite popular—for example, F. W. Beare, *The First Epistle of Peter*, 3rd ed. (Oxford: Blackwell, 1970), 25–28; Bo Reicke, *The Epistles of James, Peter, and Jude*, AB 37 (Garden City: Doubleday, 1964), 74–75.

7. H. Windisch and H. Preisker, *Die katholischen Briefe*, 3rd ed., HNT 15 (Tübingen: Mohr, 1951), 156–60.

8. F. L. Cross, *I Peter: A Paschal Liturgy* (London: Mowbray, 1954), esp. 31; cf. A. R. C. Leaney, "I Peter and the Passover: An Interpretation," *NTS* 10 (1964): 238–51.

9. M.-É. Boismard, *Quatre hymnes baptismales dans la première épître de Pierre*, LD 30 (Paris: Cerf, 1961).

10. C. F. D. Moule, "The Nature and Purpose of I Peter," *NTS* 3 (1956): 1–11.

11. Kelly, *Epistles of Peter and of Jude*, 18. Cf. the comments by David Hill, "On Suffering and Baptism in I Peter," *NovT* 18 (1976): 189. Cf. the criticisms by T. C. G. Thornton, "1 Peter, a Paschal Liturgy?" *JTS* 12 (1961): 14–26.

12. Kelly (*Epistles of Peter and of Jude*, 19) also rejects Cross's paranomasia of *pasch* (i.e., "paschal") and *paschein* ("to suffer"): "Not only is it hard to see how anyone could be expected to recognize it since the key-term *pasch* is nowhere used, but the references to suffering are naturally and adequately accounted for by the situation of the addressees." We may also observe that little is actually known about liturgy in the first century, let alone baptismal liturgy. To impose such a liturgical structure on the text may be somewhat anachronistic. See William J. Dalton, *Christ's Proclamation to the Spirits: A Study of 1 Peter 3:18–4:6*, 2nd ed., AnBib 23 (Rome: Pontifical Biblical Institute, 1989), 74.

13. Elliott, *1 Peter*, 9–10.

Thus, more recent studies have argued that 1 Peter is indeed a letter, and this should guide how it is to be understood.[14] In particular, 1 Peter is a paraenetic letter—that is, its mood is primarily one of exhortation.[15] As such, two matters become particular foci of attention: (1) the rhetorical arguments and literary devices used to support the paraenesis, and (2) the social context of the readers that provides the backdrop against which the paraenesis is understood. The first of these we turn to now, and the second we will examine in a separate section below.

Rhetorical criticism has become a popular means of analyzing biblical texts, and the fruitfulness of this approach has been evident. In general, the method examines the rhetorical situation assumed by the argument of the text and the "invention, arrangement, and style"[16] of a text in order to understand how it persuades its readers. Most applications of rhetorical criticism use the lens of how rhetoric was used and taught in the Greco-Roman world. Invaluable in this regard are the rhetorical manuals extant from this period.[17] Several rhe-

---

14. Most studies now take an epistolary view of 1 Peter. Recent examples of those who provide argumentation to support such a view include William L. Schutter, *Hermeneutic and Composition in I Peter*, WUNT 2.30 (Tübingen: Mohr [Siebeck], 1989), 19–32; Lauri Thurén, *The Rhetorical Strategy of 1 Peter: With Special Regard to Ambiguous Expressions* (Åbo: Åbo Akademis Förlag, 1990), 79–88; Martin, *Metaphor and Composition*, 41–79; Philip L. Tite, *Compositional Transitions in 1 Peter: An Analysis of the Letter-Opening* (San Francisco: International Scholars Publications, 1997).

One scholar who appears to have shifted his views on this subject is Ralph P. Martin. In an earlier publication ("The Composition of 1 Peter in Recent Study," in *Vox Evangelica: Biblical and Historical Essays,* ed. Ralph P. Martin [London: Epworth, 1962], 29–42), Martin argued for 1 Peter being a letter that includes two baptismal homilies, one for before baptism and one for afterward. More recently, however, Martin concludes that such views have been disproved—whatever traditional materials might have been used in 1 Peter, these "do not define the composition of the letter" ("The Theology of Jude, 1 Peter, and 2 Peter," in *The Theology of the Letters of James, Peter, and Jude,* ed. Andrew Chester and Ralph P. Martin, NTT [Cambridge: Cambridge University Press, 1994], 99).

15. See the sustained development by Martin, *Metaphor and Composition*, 81–134; on paraenetic letters, see Stanley K. Stowers, *Letter Writing in Greco-Roman Antiquity*, LEC (Philadelphia: Westminster, 1986), 94–106, esp. 96–97; and also on NT letters, including 1 Peter, see 96–97.

J. Ramsey Michaels (*1 Peter*, xlvi–xlix) has proposed that 1 Peter is "an apocalyptic diaspora letter to 'Israel.'" Similarly, Elliott (*1 Peter*, 12) views it as a Diaspora letter. However, Davids (*First Epistle of Peter*, 13–14) questions whether a Diaspora letter is a distinct genre. The apocalyptic character, however, certainly is not to be denied; on which, see Robert L. Webb, "The Apocalyptic Perspective of First Peter" (master's thesis, Regent College, Vancouver, 1986).

16. These three terms are derived from classical rhetorical manuals. "Invention" is concerned with developing proofs to support the argument. "Arrangement" is concerned with the order in which the proofs and other parts of the argument are arranged for best effect. "Style" is concerned with choice of proper language and figures of speech to best express the argument. A helpful discussion of these terms in the classical rhetorical manuals may be found in Duane F. Watson, *Invention, Arrangement, and Style: Rhetorical Criticism of Jude and 2 Peter*, SBLDS 104 (Atlanta: Scholars Press, 1988), 13–26.

17. Helpful introductions to rhetorical criticism include George A. Kennedy, *New Testament Interpretation through Rhetorical Criticism* (Chapel Hill: University of North Carolina Press,

torical studies have contributed significantly to our understanding of 1 Peter. John H. Elliott (1981) understands the letter to have been written to Gentile Christians whose social position as "resident aliens" and "visiting strangers" rendered them the object of social ostracism and verbal persecution.[18] The rhetorical strategy of 1 Peter in addressing this situation was "to reinforce the group consciousness, cohesion and commitment" of the Christians to their distinctive, sectarian Christian identity.[19] David L. Balch (1981), on the other hand, argues that the strategy (of at least the household code [2:13–3:12]) was "to reduce the social-political tension between society and the churches."[20] In other words, in order to stop the slander and abuse, the household code encouraged conformity to the expectations of society. Of these two views, Elliott's is preferable, for it takes into account the evidence of the entire letter, which stresses separation and sectarian identity.[21]

Lauri Thurén's doctoral dissertation (1990) also examines the rhetorical strategy of 1 Peter,[22] but takes as the starting point ambiguous expressions in 1 Peter that can have more than one meaning. He views 1 Peter as exhibiting epideictic rhetoric, encouraging the believers to continue exhibiting the values that they already know. But the letter addresses a composite audience and thus exhibits multiple exigencies (i.e., rhetorical situations being addressed). The ambiguous expressions aid the author in addressing the different rhetorical exigencies. Thurén followed up this work (1995) with an examination of how the

---

1984); Watson, *Invention, Arrangement, and Style*, 1–28; Burton L. Mack, *Rhetoric and the New Testament*, GBS (Minneapolis: Fortress, 1990); cf. the more advanced discussion in Stanley E. Porter and Dennis L. Stamps, eds., *Rhetorical Criticism and the Bible*, JSNTSup 195 (Sheffield: Sheffield Academic Press, 2002).

18. See below, under the section "First Peter in Sociohistorical Context."

19. John H. Elliott, *A Home for the Homeless: A Sociological Exegesis of 1 Peter, Its Situation and Strategy* (Philadelphia: Fortress, 1981), 107, cf. 101–64. He further explains, "The strategy . . . was to counteract the demoralizing and disintegrating impact which such social tension and suffering had upon the Christian sect by reassuring its members of their distinctive communal identity, reminding them of the importance of maintaining discipline and cohesion *within* the brotherhood as well as separation from Gentile influence *without*, and by providing them with a sustaining and motivating rationale for continued faith and commitment" (148).

20. David L. Balch, *Let Wives Be Submissive: The Domestic Code in 1 Peter*, SBLDS 26 (Chico, Calif.: Scholars Press, 1981), 81.

21. See the subsequent debate between Elliott and Balch in Talbert, *Perspectives on First Peter*: John H. Elliott, "1 Peter, Its Situation and Strategy: A Discussion with David Balch," 61–78; David L. Balch, "Hellenization/Acculturation in 1 Peter," 79–101. In the same volume, Charles H. Talbert ("Once Again: The Plan of 1 Peter," 146–48) attempts a mediating position. Steven R. Bechtler (*Following in His Steps: Suffering, Community, and Christology in 1 Peter*, SBLDS 162 [Atlanta: Scholars Press, 1998]) also attempts a mediating position through the anthropological concept of "liminal" existence. Cf. the comment by Leonhard Goppelt on 1 Pet. 3:13: "It is conduct that does justice to the institutions within which one lives and generally to the *justitia civilis* (cf. 4:15). It does not conform to the commonly accepted middle-class morality but, according to v. 16, is practiced with a 'good conscience' before God or 'in Christ,' i.e., in fellowship with Christ" (*1 Peter*, 240).

22. Thurén, *Rhetorical Strategy of 1 Peter*.

paraenesis functions in 1 Peter.[23] He develops a form of argumentation analysis designed to uncover the ideological structure of the motivation underlying the text. He finds three: (1) the believers have a new status, and appreciating it leads to obeying God; (2) God's intention and will, and Christ's example in suffering; and (3) supporting factors, such as allusion to Scripture.

Barth L. Campbell (1998) analyzes the rhetoric of 1 Peter, using classical rhetorical criticism as well as the lens of the cultural values of honor/shame.[24] He suggests that the situation may be clarified by the challenge/riposte exchange: society has issued a "challenge" to the Christians through slander, insult, and ostracization, but the author encourages them that the best "riposte" is virtuous living. Campbell's analysis of the rhetorical structure divides the letter into an *exordium* (1:3–12 [i.e., a prologue]) followed by three *argumentatio* sections (1:13–2:10; 2:11–3:12; 3:13–4:11), each of which has the same substructure: *propositio, ratio, confirmatio, exornatio,* and *complexio* (i.e., a proposition, reason, proofs or corroboration, embellishment, and summary). The final section in 1 Peter is a *peroratio* (4:12–5:14 [i.e., a conclusion]).

As a paraenetic letter, 1 Peter is unusually rich in the variety of literary motifs, themes, and techniques that it uses to put forward its arguments and exhortations. John H. Elliott's groundbreaking work (1981) argued that the terms *paroikos* ("resident alien") and *parepidēmos* ("visiting stranger") describe the social realities of the readers, and that "the household of God" provides the overarching metaphor for understanding the response of 1 Peter to the readers' social condition.[25] Responding in part to Elliott is the particularly valuable study by Troy W. Martin (1992) of the metaphors in 1 Peter.[26] He argues that there is one overarching metaphor controlling the entire book, and this metaphor is the Diaspora, as indicated by the language of the letter opening ("exiles of the Dispersion" [1:1]) and letter closing ("Babylon" [5:13]). In turn, the body of the letter develops this overarching metaphor with three metaphor clusters that dominate the three main sections of the letter. In 1:14–2:10, the dominant metaphor cluster is the elect household of God, which subsumes the metaphors of obedient children (1:14), children under a new *pater potestas* (i.e., an all-powerful father [1:17–21]), children in a new brotherhood (1:22–25), newborn babes (2:1–3), and living stones (2:4–10). The first three of these metaphors focus on the family relations that result from new birth, while the latter two focus on the concept of growth. The second metaphor cluster is aliens in this world (2:11–3:12). Included in this cluster are the metaphors of resident and

23. Lauri Thurén, *Argument and Theology in 1 Peter: The Origins of Christian Paraenesis,* JSNTSup 114 (Sheffield: Sheffield Academic Press, 1995).

24. Barth L. Campbell, *Honor, Shame, and the Rhetoric of 1 Peter,* SBLDS 160 (Atlanta: Scholars Press, 1998).

25. Elliott, *Home for the Homeless,* 101–266. On Elliott's argument, see below, under the section "First Peter in Sociohistorical Context."

26. Martin, *Metaphor and Composition,* 135–267. He also provides a helpful analysis of the letter structure of 1 Peter (41–79).

visiting aliens (2:11–15) and free people (2:16–17 with 2:18–3:12). Related to the first is the need for abstinence and submission, and to the second is the need to honor everyone. In 3:13–5:11, the dominant metaphor cluster is the sufferers of the Diaspora, which includes these metaphors: righteous sufferers (3:13–4:11), and partners with Christ in sufferings and glory (4:12–5:11). Martin concludes, "All of these metaphor clusters contribute to the author's primary objectives of exposing conduct appropriate for his readers on their eschatological journey and of dissuading them from defection while persuading them to steadfast allegiance to the faith."[27] Perhaps one weakness in Martin's invaluable contribution is the attempt to subsume all metaphors under the rubric of the one metaphor, Diaspora. For example, to view the metaphor of free people along with the household code (2:16–17 with 2:18–3:12) as somehow related to the metaphor of Diaspora is unconvincing.[28]

One literary technique employed to present arguments and exhortations that is particularly prominent in 1 Peter is the use of traditional material in general, and the use of the OT in particular.[29] William L. Schutter (1989) examines the letter's hermeneutical use of the Hebrew Bible and contends that what best accounts for this hermeneutical style is a form of homiletical midrash. He argues that the eschatological hermeneutic expressed in 1:10–12 and the "sufferings/glories" theme are used throughout the letter. His study highlights the importance of the "Temple-community motif" derived in particular from Ezek. 8–11.[30] He concludes that "the very close connexion between Christology and ecclesiology in the letter is seated in the hermeneutic of its author, and is an integral part of the way he read the scriptures."[31] Schutter's otherwise admirable work is marred by the imposition of the concept of "homiletical" midrash—a throwback to the older "liturgical" mode of thinking with respect to 1 Peter. It would have been better for him to simply discuss 1 Peter's hermeneutic as "midrash."[32] A comparable study by Sharon C. Pearson (2001)

---

27. Ibid., 266.

28. See J. Ramsey Michaels, review of *Metaphor and Composition in 1 Peter*, by Troy W. Martin, *JBL* 112 (1993): 358–60.

29. An important earlier study of the use of the OT in 1 Peter is John H. Elliott, *The Elect and the Holy: An Exegetical Examination of 1 Peter 2:4–10 and the Phrase βασίλειον ἱεράτευμα*, NovTSup 12 (Leiden: Brill, 1966). See also W. Edward Glenny, "The Hermeneutics of the Use of the Old Testament in 1 Peter" (Ph.D. diss., Dallas Theological Seminary, 1987). Equally important is Dalton's study of the traditions, biblical and extrabiblical, used in 3:18–22 and 4:6 (Dalton, *Christ's Proclamation to the Spirits*). His work is an invaluable contribution to understanding the perplexing and complex issues surrounding 3:18–22.

30. Schutter, *Hermeneutic and Composition*, 161–63, 176–77.

31. Ibid., 171. On the apocalyptic eschatological orientation of 1 Peter, see Webb, "Apocalyptic Perspective."

32. Schutter (e.g., *Hermeneutic and Composition*, 109–23) does use the term "pesher-like exegesis." Following up on Schutter's work, Elliott (*1 Peter*, 12–17) provides a helpful summary and categorization of the uses of the OT in 1 Peter. For other secondary literature on this subject, see Elliott, *1 Peter*, 17 n. 2.

highlights the significance of Isa. 53 for the christological passages in 1 Peter. This otherwise helpful analysis is marred, similarly, by viewing these passages as having a "hymnic" pattern.[33]

Another component of 1 Peter's use of tradition is the relationship between the letter and other early Christian literature. The history of 1 Peter scholarship is rife with proposals of the letter's dependence on one or more NT books, based on the "parallels" between them.[34] But it has become evident in biblical studies that "parallelomania" leads scholars to claim more than the evidence actually supports. John H. Elliott provides a helpful survey of these parallels that have led many to make claims of literary dependency.[35] But most recent studies, such as that by Jens Herzer (1998), argue against dependence,[36] though Rainer Metzner (1995) has proposed 1 Peter's dependence upon Matthew (initial reviews have not found Metzner's work convincing).[37] A much more helpful approach is to understand these parallels to be the joint use of early Christian tradition by both parties.[38]

Strides have been made also in understanding the conceptual world underlying 1 Peter. It has always been evident that eschatological thought marks the letter, but more recently the apocalyptic character has been recog-

---

33. Sharon C. Pearson, *The Christological and Rhetorical Properties of 1 Peter,* SBEC 45 (Lewiston, N.Y.: Mellen, 2001). Unfortunately, the title of this work is somewhat misleading, for it is not a rhetorical analysis. The title used in the text of the work itself is "The Christological Hymnic Patterns of 1 Peter" (4).

34. For example, Francis W. Beare (*First Epistle of Peter,* 219) understands the author of 1 Peter to have known and used much of the NT.

35. Elliott, *1 Peter,* 20–30.

36. Jens Herzer, *Petrus oder Paulus? Studien über das Verhältnis des Ersten Petrusbriefes zur paulinischen Tradition,* WUNT 2.103 (Tübingen: Mohr [Siebeck], 1998). Cf. the helpful studies by Kazuhito Shimada, "Is I Peter Dependent on Ephesians? A Critique of C. L. Mitton," *AJBI* 17 (1991): 77–106; idem, "Is I Peter Dependent on Romans?" *AJBI* 19 (1993): 87–137; and the older study by Edward G. Selwyn, *The First Epistle of St. Peter: The Greek Text with Introduction, Notes, and Essays,* 2nd ed. (1947; reprint, Grand Rapids: Baker, 1981), 365–466. Cf. the idiosyncratic thesis by Winsome Munro (*Authority in Paul and Peter: The Identification of a Pastoral Stratum in the Pauline Corpus and 1 Peter,* SNTSMS 45 [Cambridge: Cambridge University Press, 1983]) that the household codes in both the Pauline Epistles and 1 Peter (i.e., 2:13–3:12) were a later redactional addition to the letters made by the same source as that responsible for the Pastoral Epistles.

37. Rainer Metzner, *Die Rezeption des Matthäusevangeliums im 1. Petrusbrief: Studien zum traditionsgeschichtlichen und theologischen Einfluß des 1. Evangeliums auf den 1. Petrusbrief,* WUNT 2.74 (Tübingen: Mohr [Siebeck], 1995). See the review of Metzner by John H. Elliott, *RBL,* July 31, 2000 (online: http://www.bookreviews.org/pdf/2578_1811.pdf).

38. For example, Goppelt (*1 Peter,* 36) states in his conclusion concerning these parallels: "I Peter is furnished in many ways with early Christian streams of tradition and the religious backgrounds mediated to it by them. . . . I Peter draws on a tradition going back directly to Palestinian origins that have been in conversation with the Hellenistic Christianity represented by Paul. I Peter then shaped this tradition independently into a fundamental, Church-wide form of address that nevertheless addressed a particular historical situation." See also Elliott, *1 Peter,* 30–37.

nized. J. Ramsey Michaels (1988) views the letter as an "apocalyptic diaspora letter."[39] The apocalyptic character of 1 Peter is explored by Peter H. Davids (1990), whose viewpoint is that "apocalyptic eschatology colors the whole of the epistle."[40] Davids's work builds on my own work (1986), which applies the definition of apocalypticism developed by the SBL Apocalypse Group[41] to 1 Peter. It becomes evident that numerous motifs of the apocalyptic paradigm may be observed in 1 Peter. With respect to the temporal axis, 1 Peter alludes to protology (the opposite of eschatology), in which primordial events are understood to have paradigmatic significance (3:18–22). At the other end of the temporal axis, the suffering alluded to in the letter is understood as an eschatological crisis, and it leads to both eschatological judgment (e.g., 2:12; 3:16–17; 4:5, 17–18; cf. 1:17; 2:15) and eschatological salvation (e.g., 1:5, 9–12; 3:20–21; 4:18). These are understood to function within a spatial axis involving otherworldly beings and regions (e.g., 1:12; 3:19–20, 22; 5:8–9).[42] This has been expanded more recently by Mark Dubis (2002), who focuses on the use of the "messianic woes" motif as expressed particularly in 4:12–19.[43] He understands the phrase "you share Christ's sufferings" (4:13) as a reference not only to the passion of Jesus Christ but also to the "messianic woes," or the eschatological time of suffering that God's people were expected to undergo prior to the coming of the messiah (in Judaism this was understood to be simply the coming of the messiah, whereas in 1 Peter this alludes to the second advent). This motif not only informs our understanding of 4:12–19, but also it may be seen reflected in 1:10–12 and 5:1.[44] Dubis places the use of this motif within the larger context of 1 Peter's use of the "overarching motif of exile and restoration," which also may be seen in the citations and allusions to Isa. 40–55. "First Peter claims that Isa. 40–55's hopes of restoration are being realized in Christ."[45] This motif provides the readers not only with a theological understanding of their suffering, but also with hope that their suffering is both temporary and anticipates glory. Furthermore, it motivates them to stand firm in their faith and not be ashamed.

An examination of 1 Peter's paraenetic emphasis, its rhetorical structure and argument, its use of metaphor, and its use of traditions demonstrates the rich character of this letter's literary context. But as a letter, it also has a social context, and to this we now turn.

39. Michaels, *1 Peter*, xlvi–xlix; cf. lxix–lxxi.
40. Davids, *First Epistle of Peter*, 17. Cf. Achtemeier, *1 Peter*, 105–7.
41. See John J. Collins, "Introduction: Towards the Morphology of a Genre," *Semeia* 14 (1979): 1–20.
42. See the extensive development by Webb, "Apocalyptic Perspective."
43. Mark Dubis, *Messianic Woes in First Peter: Suffering and Eschatology in 1 Peter 4:12–19*, Studies in Biblical Literature 33 (New York: Lang, 2002).
44. I suggest that it also forms the background of 1:3–9, especially vv. 5–6.
45. Dubis, *Messianic Woes*, 187.

First Peter in Sociohistorical Context

Prior to the mid-1970s, the common view of the sociohistorical situation of 1 Peter's readers was that they were suffering under official Roman persecution, and the debate was over whether this persecution occurred during the reign of Nero (54–68 C.E.), Domitian (81–96 C.E.), or Trajan (98–117 C.E.).[46] The evidence for this in 1 Peter is essentially fourfold. First, in 3:15 the readers are exhorted to "be ready to give a defense," which is interpreted as a courtroom defense. Second, the description of their suffering as a "fiery trial taking place among you" in 4:12 is understood as literal fire (a possible allusion to the burning of Christians). Third, the reference to the possibility that one might suffer "as a Christian" in 4:16 is understood to parallel the charge in 4:15 to "not suffer as a murderer, or a thief, or a criminal," thus suggesting that being "a Christian" was also a criminal offense. Fourth, 5:9 indicates that this suffering is worldwide in scope. However, this view has come to be increasingly rejected for three reasons. First, the evidence for a widespread, official Roman persecution of Christians is lacking for the time period during which 1 Peter was written. Rather, persecution of Christians was localized, informal, and frequently generated by mob rule rather than Roman rule.[47] Second, the texts above can better be interpreted as signifying informal suffering rather than formal persecution.[48] Third, nowhere in 1 Peter is the source of the suffering identified as the Roman government. In fact, the letter speaks quite positively of the emperor and government officials in 2:13–14, and in 2:17 it exhorts the readers to "honor the emperor."

The letter uses the verb *paschein* ("to suffer") twelve times and the noun *pathēma* ("suffering") four times. Of these, seven uses refer to the suffering of Christ (1:11; 2:21, 23; 3:18; 4:1a, 13; 5:1), and the remaining nine are used with reference to Christians suffering (2:19, 20; 3:14, 17; 4:1b, 15, 19; 5:9, 10).[49] These references identify the effect upon these Christians as "suffering," but they do not identify the specific nature of what is causing the suffering. These references, therefore, while highlighting the experience of suffering, do not aid in clarifying the cause of that suffering. Elsewhere in the letter, however, are seven references that do make specific allusions to the type of suffering, using six different words: "to speak against, slander" (2:12; 3:16), "insult" (3:9), "to denounce, mistreat" (3:16),[50] "to

---

46. See, for example, Beare, *First Epistle of Peter,* 30–34.

47. Elliott (*1 Peter,* 98) points out that "the first worldwide persecution of Christians officially undertaken by Rome did not occur until the persecution initiated by Decius (249–251 C.E.) in 250 C.E."; he cites Eusebius, *Hist. eccl.* 6.39.1–42.6; 7.1; *Sib. Or.* 13:81–88. See also Kelly, *Epistles of Peter and of Jude,* 5–11; Ernest Best, *1 Peter,* NCB (London: Oliphants, 1971), 36–42; Achtemeier, *1 Peter,* 28–36.

48. See the commentary on these texts in Michaels, *1 Peter;* Davids, *First Epistle of Peter;* Goppelt, *1 Peter;* Achtemeier, *1 Peter;* Elliott, *1 Peter.*

49. One could also add to these the two uses of "test" (*peirasmos* [1:6; 4:12]).

50. This could refer to either verbal abuse or physical abuse, but in this context it is verbal abuse because it is explaining the slander earlier in the verse: "in order that when you are *slandered,* the ones who *denounce* your good conduct in Christ might be put to shame."

malign, injure the reputation" (4:4), "to reproach, insult" (4:14), and "to beat" (2:20). Of these seven references, six are specifically to verbal abuse. Only the last reference ("to beat" in 2:20) is to physical abuse, and this is abuse arising in the context of a specific social relationship within the household: masters abusing slaves.[51] The evidence indicates that the social situation that these Christians are facing is not official Roman persecution, but rather slander and verbal abuse intended to demean and discredit them (with the possibility of physical abuse in household social relationships).[52]

Apparently, two factors led to this abuse. First, it appears that the ethical behavior of these Christians had changed. They were suffering "for the sake of righteousness" (3:14) and "for doing what is right" (3:17). Their persecutors were slandering their "good conduct in Christ" (3:16; cf. 2:12, 19–20; 3:6; 4:4, 15–16). In 4:3–4 there is information that helps to clarify this change: prior to their conversion, these Christians had engaged in behavior that was accepted and practiced by many people around them; but after their conversion, they no longer practiced these things, and so their persecutors "are surprised that you no longer join them in the same outpouring of dissipation, and so they malign you" (4:4). The second factor is implied by this same text: their social relationships had changed. The behavior described in the preceding verse was previously common ground shared between them. This behavior was not only social common ground, but also religious common ground, for some of these practices would have been expressed in local religious activities. The change in the ethical behavior and the consequent change in social relations would have been viewed as rebellion against social harmony.[53]

With the recognition that the recipients of 1 Peter were not the focus of official Roman persecution but rather of localized verbal abuse, the way was cleared for some significant advances in further understanding this social context. Here, the groundbreaking work by John H. Elliott (1981) made a significant impact.[54]

---

51. First Peter 3:6b suggests that wives are afraid. This may imply physical abuse as well. If it does, the same conclusion applies: the references to physical suffering in 1 Peter arise in the context of specific relationships within the household.

52. See Webb, "Apocalyptic Perspective," 86–107; Elliott, *1 Peter*, 100–101. Cf. the helpful discussion of suffering in 1 Peter and the NT in Davids, *First Epistle of Peter*, 30–44.

53. The comments by Leonhard Goppelt (*The Variety and Unity of the Apostolic Witness to Christ*, vol. 2 of *Theology of the New Testament*, ed. Jürgen Roloff, trans. John E. Alsup [Grand Rapids: Eerdmans, 1982], 163) are worth noting: "Hence contradiction and suspicion had to surface in everyday life since here [in 1 Peter] not the members of a foreign people, the Jews, distanced themselves personally as Christians from the ways of living in their environment, but one's very fellow citizens, neighbors, and relatives. And it was these very people who let it be known that they, like already the Jews, laid claim to this offensive notion of religious absolutism. Christianity had to have appeared more or less as that which Celsus repeatedly labled as *stasis*, rebellion against the divine harmony (*C. Cels.* 5.33ff., 41; 8.14) in which all people were to live together tolerantly in a fundamental syncretism. Hence Christianity looked like a 'new and mischievous superstition' (Suetonius *Nero* 16 = LCL, II,111)."

54. Elliott, *Home for the Homeless*.

He applied "sociological exegesis" to 1 Peter in a study of how the Christian community becomes a "home for the homeless." Elliott examines the two terms used in 1 Peter to describe the readers: "resident aliens" and "visiting strangers"[55] (2:11; cf. 1:1, 17). He concludes that "the addresses of 1 Peter were *paroikoi* by virtue of their social condition, not by virtue of their 'heavenly home.'" In other words, this was their social situation prior to conversion to Christianity. This affects how the strategy of 1 Peter is understood. Elliott continues: "The alternative to this marginal social condition of which 1 Peter speaks is not an ephemeral 'heaven is our home' form of consolation but the new home and social family to which the Christians belong here and now; namely, the *oikos tou theou* [the household of God]."[56] Elliott's sociological analysis also shows that "the communities addressed in 1 Peter most closely resemble sects which promote a conversionist type of sectarian response to the world."[57]

The significant contributions of Elliott's work to the development of 1 Peter studies cannot be overestimated, for it probably has done more than any other single work to contribute to the "rehabilitation of [this] exegetical step-child."[58] Not everyone agrees with Elliott, but his work did lead to new ways of looking at the text. Two elements of Elliott's work came in for criticism. First, his argument that the overarching metaphor in 1 Peter is "the household of God" has been questioned, but this was discussed above.[59] Second, it is more probable that the language describing the readers as "resident aliens" and "visiting strangers" should not be taken literally as referring to their social situation prior to conversion. Elliott is correct to highlight the social realities that these terms indicate, rejecting the tendency to spiritualize them as alluding to Christians as strangers in the world away from their heavenly home.[60] However, as we saw, it is their conversion to Christianity that has led to their experience of social alienation (cf. 4:3–4).[61] This has been argued most extensively by Reinhard Feldmeier (1992) in his study on the metaphor of foreigner.[62] He examines the terms "resident alien" and "visiting stranger" both in a literal sense as having reference to one's sociocultural setting, and in a variety of metaphorical uses, in particular in Greek

55. Ibid., 23; cf. 21–100.
56. Ibid., 130; cf. 42–47.
57. Ibid., 77.
58. This alludes to Elliott's now famous dictum mentioned at the beginning of this essay (Elliott, "Rehabilitation," 243–54).
59. See the discussion of metaphor, above, in the section "First Peter in Literary Context."
60. As in, for example, Beare, *First Epistle of Peter*, 135.
61. Cf. the arguments by Webb, "Apocalyptic Perspective," 91–93; Paul J. Achtemeier, "Newborn Babes and Living Stones: Literal and Figurative in 1 Peter," in *To Touch the Text*, ed. Maurya P. Horgan and Paul J. Kobelski (New York: Crossroad, 1989), 215–18; Achtemeier, *1 Peter*, 55–57; Martin, *Metaphor and Composition*, 142–44. Cf. Elliott's recent defense of this position in *1 Peter*, 101–3. For a nontechnical explanation and defense of Elliott's view, see McKnight, *1 Peter*, 23–26.
62. Reinhard Feldmeier, *Die Christen als Fremde: Die Metapher der Fremde in der antiken Welt, im Urchristentum und im 1. Petrusbrief,* WUNT 64 (Tübingen: Mohr [Siebeck], 1992).

philosophical texts and Second Temple Jewish texts. With respect to 1 Peter, he argues that the use of these terms is metaphorical rather than literal, and they do not present the idea that the Christian's identity is a "citizenship in heaven." Rather, the metaphor highlights the fact they are noncitizens, and this brings them inevitably into conflict with the society around them. The metaphor, then, is not intended to provide heavenly comfort; rather, it is to help them realize that their identity is no longer derived from their former social status, but from their new status as the people of God. Furthermore, this new status shapes not only their new identity, but also their response.

With this new understanding of the sociohistorical context of 1 Peter, the literary context (whether the use of metaphor, traditions, or apocalyptic perspective) can be appreciated in a fresh light as providing a nuanced and sophisticated response to the readers' social situation. This response provides the readers not only with a new interpretive grid that gives meaning to their social situation but also with the motivation for them to continue in their radical Christian ethic and to maintain their sectarian Christian identity.[63]

Second Peter

The letter of 2 Peter has suffered from being one of the most neglected books in the NT—a fate it shares with Jude.[64] Although some interesting research has contributed to our understanding of 2 Peter, the letter has not experienced the renaissance that 1 Peter has. This is a most unfortunate situation, for 2 Peter bears some quite interesting and distinctive characteristics that warrant closer attention.[65]

63. Webb, "Apocalyptic Perspective," 129–33, 164–71, 241–60. The most helpful works that explore how the literary context responds to the social situation are Elliott, *Home for the Homeless*; Martin, *Metaphor and Composition*; Feldmeier, *Die Christen als Fremde*; Campbell, *Honor, Shame*; Bechtler, *Following in His Steps*.

64. The focus of the present essay is on 2 Peter. For recent discussion of research in Jude, consult Richard J. Bauckham, "The Letter of Jude: An Account of Research," in *ANRW* 2.25.5:3791–826; Roman Heiligenthal, "Der Judasbrief: Aspekte der Forschung in den letzten Jahrzenten," *TRu* 51 (1986): 117–29; Pearson, "James, 1–2 Peter, Jude," 385–87. See also the bibliography by Watson E. Mills, *2 Peter and Jude*, BBRNT 19 (Lewiston, N.Y.: Mellen, 2000).

Recent important works on Jude include Watson, *Invention, Arrangement, and Style;* Richard J. Bauckham, *Jude and the Relatives of Jesus in the Early Church* (Edinburgh: Clark, 1990); J. Daryl Charles, *Literary Strategy in the Epistle of Jude* (London and Toronto: Associated University Presses, 1993); Kenneth R. Lyle, *Ethical Admonition in the Epistle of Jude*, Studies in Biblical Literature 4 (New York: Lang, 1998); Ruth Anne Reese, *Writing Jude: The Reader, the Text, and the Author in Constructs of Power and Desire*, BIS 51 (Leiden: Brill, 2000).

The best commentaries on Jude include Richard J. Bauckham, *Jude, 2 Peter*, WBC 50 (Waco, Tex.: Word, 1983); Jerome H. Neyrey, *2 Peter, Jude*, AB 37C (New York: Doubleday, 1993). Also, forthcoming is Robert L. Webb, *Jude, 2 Peter*, NICNT (Grand Rapids: Eerdmans).

65. Space constraints require that I exclude some topics here. Other accounts of recent research in 2 Peter include Richard J. Bauckham, "2 Peter: An Account of Research," in *ANRW* 2.25.5:3713–52; Pearson, "James, 1–2 Peter, Jude," 382–85. Recent bibliographies include

The letter has been neglected perhaps because of its size, its polemical character, and its seeming repetition of much of the contents of Jude. But one particularly significant reason is the evaluation of its theological character as "early catholic," on the basis of which it has been deemed second rate. Characteristic and influential in this regard is Ernst Käsemann's 1952 lecture in which he described 2 Peter as "an apologia for primitive Christian eschatology" and "a document expressing an early Catholic viewpoint," and thus found it to be "perhaps the most dubious writing in the canon."[66] He identifies the opponents as gnostics who "proclaim the message of redemption under the slogan 'Freedom from the transitory.'"[67] Käsemann proceeds to evaluate the eschatology of 2 Peter: "The real theological problem of the epistle . . . lies in the fact that its eschatology lacks any vestige of Christological orientation."[68] Given such an evaluation, it is no wonder that 2 Peter has suffered neglect.

Recent developments in the study of 2 Peter have begun to shake off this quite unfortunate characterization of 2 Peter. This may be traced in particular to two works, both written in 1977. First, Tord Fornberg (1977) places 2 Peter in a specific sociocultural context: the church is now predominantly Gentile, with the Jewish influence having been in decline for some time.[69] Under Hellenistic influence, the church is under pressure to conform to non-Christian values and ideas. The author writes in opposition to this Hellenizing, and yet at the same time "translates" the gospel into Hellenistic terms: "2 Peter is one of the most important documents for our knowledge of a fairly early stage in this translation process. It represents a distinctly Christian line, without thereby rejecting those features of the Hellenistic culture which were acceptable."[70] Fornberg has been criticized, however, for neglecting to give due credit

---

Michael J. Gilmour, "2 Peter in Recent Research: A Bibliography," *JETS* 42 (1999): 673–78; Neyrey, *2 Peter, Jude*, 252–60; Mills, *2 Peter and Jude*.

The best recent technical commentaries include Kelly, *Epistles of Peter and of Jude*; Schelkle, *Die Petrusbriefe, Der Judasbrief*; Bauckham, *Jude, 2 Peter*; Eric Fuchs and Pierre Reymond, *La deuxième épître de saint Pierre: L'épître de saint Jude*, 2nd ed., CNT 2.13b (Geneva: Labor et Fides, 1988); Henning Paulsen, *Der zweite Petrusbrief und der Judasbrief*, KEK 12.2 (Göttingen: Vandenhoeck & Ruprecht, 1992); Neyrey, *2 Peter, Jude*.

The best recent nontechnical commentaries include Michael Green, *The Second Epistle General of Peter and the General Epistle of Jude*, 2nd ed., TNTC 18 (Grand Rapids: Eerdmans, 1987); D. Edmond Hiebert, *Second Peter and Jude: An Expositional Commentary* (Greenville, S.C.: Unusual Publications, 1989); Douglas J. Moo, *2 Peter and Jude*, NIVAC (Grand Rapids: Zondervan, 1996); Steven J. Kraftchick, *Jude, 2 Peter*, ANTC (Nashville: Abingdon, 2002). Note also Webb, *Jude, 2 Peter*.

66. Ernst Käsemann, "An Apologia for Primitive Christian Eschatology," in *Essays on New Testament Themes*, trans. W. J. Montague, SBT 41 (London: SCM, 1964), 169.

67. Ibid., 171.

68. Ibid., 178.

69. Tord Fornberg, *An Early Church in a Pluralistic Society: A Study of 2 Peter*, trans. J. Gray, ConBNT 9 (Lund: Gleerup, 1977).

70. Ibid., 148. Cf. his discussion of the inappropriateness of the term "early Catholic" as a designation for 2 Peter (3–6).

to the Jewish apocalyptic material present in 2 Peter, especially 2:4–22 and 3:3–13, and for failing to recognize that this "translation" process had also been undertaken within Hellenistic Judaism, on which the author may have been dependent.[71] Nevertheless, Fornberg's work represents an advance beyond the past consensus.

Further development was made by Jerome H. Neyrey (1977, 1980), who provides a careful study of the polemic in 2 Peter.[72] He sees the background of the opponents in 2 Peter in certain Hellenistic and Jewish polemics against divine judgment, the afterlife, and postmortem retribution. In response, the author provides an apology for divine judgment in 2:3b–9; 3:7, 9–13, for the afterlife and/or another world in 3:7, 10–13, and for postmortem retribution in 2:4, 9, 17; 3:7, 10.[73] This analysis leads Neyrey to conclude that "the presumed lack of christological focus does not stem from the ineptitude of an 'early catholic' writer; the criticism is misplaced since the polemic confronting 2 Peter was a specific attack on theodicy, not christology: the issue was divine judgment in general, not Christ's in particular."[74] Furthermore, it becomes clear that the opponents should not be characterized as gnostic at all.

Neyrey also provides a careful analysis of the form of the debate in 2 Peter, noting in particular the distinction between explicit statements by the opponents (1:16, 20–21; 2:3b; 3:3–4, 9a), indirect references by the opponents (2:1, 19; 3:16), apologetic responses by the author (1:16–19, 20–21; 2:4–10; 3:5–7, 8–9, 10–13), and polemical attacks by the author (2:15–16, 19–22).[75] This analysis helps to clarify the cut and thrust of the debate between the author and his opponents.

A third component of Neyrey's study is a redaction-critical analysis of 2 Peter's use of Jude. As a result, he concludes that "the historical situation of Jude and 2 Peter are quite different, and the respective opponents of the two letters must also be considered as different."[76]

These two works shake things up considerably with respect to 2 Peter. First, rather than being characterized as "early catholic" and theologically suspect, 2 Peter may now be considered theologically astute and quite sophisticated. Second, the opponents are not gnostic, but rather are to be found represented in various forms of Hellenistic thought. Third, Jude and 2 Peter are recognized as different, not only in identity of opponents and sociocultural context, but

71. See Bauckham, "2 Peter: An Account of Research," 3732.

72. Jerome H. Neyrey, "The Form and Background of the Polemic in 2 Peter" (Ph.D. diss., Yale University, 1977); "The Form and Background of the Polemic in 2 Peter," *JBL* 99 (1980): 407–31. Cf. his recent commentary, *2 Peter, Jude,* which applies this earlier work to a sustained exposition of the text.

73. Neyrey, "Polemic in 2 Peter" (1980), 423, cf. 423–31.

74. Ibid., 430.

75. Unfortunately, this analysis is available only in the unpublished form of Neyrey's dissertation, "Polemic in 2 Peter" (1977), 12–118.

76. Ibid., 167, cf. 119–67.

also in terms of theology and argumentation. Now the way is paved for further developments.

Significant in this regard is the commentary by Richard Bauckham (1983). He argues that from a genre perspective, 2 Peter is both a letter and a testament (or farewell speech). The testament was a well-known genre in the intertestamental period, in which the last words of renowned OT saints were recorded for later readers. In 2 Peter, this combination "created a genre with a unique communicative capacity: a testamentary letter could communicate at a distance *in space* (like all letters) and also at a distance *in time*, for in a written testament it is possible explicitly to address not only those who read it immediately but also those who will read it after the testator's death (as 1:12–15 makes very clear)."[77] Bauckham also concludes (as do most recent scholars) that 2 Peter is dependent upon Jude for some material (particularly in ch. 2), but "the literary relationship between 2 Peter and Jude does not justify the common habit of classing the two works together as similar works. . . . The reuse of some of the material in one work by the writer of another no more proves that in this case than it does in the case of, e.g., Kings and Chronicles, or Mark and Luke. . . . Jude and 2 Peter are very different works, from very different historical contexts."[78] Contrary to Fornberg (see above), Bauckham views 2 Peter as combining both Hellenistic and apocalyptic traditions. The author interprets the gospel from a Hellenistic perspective for his Gentile audience, but "he must defend the eschatological content and the eschatologically motivated ethical content of the apostolic teaching."[79] Playing the Hellenistic perspective against the apocalyptic character is what makes 2 Peter special. Bauckham also rejects the gnostic identity for the opponents in 2 Peter. Rather, they may "be seen as aiming to disencumber Christianity of its eschatology and its ethical rigorism, which seemed to them an embarrassment in their cultural environment, especially after the evident failure of the Parousia expectation."[80]

Building upon Neyrey's analysis of the form of the polemic in 2 Peter, Bauckham sees the structure of the letter body to revolve largely around the apologetic defense and the polemic attack by the author:

Reply to Objection 1:
   (a) Apostolic Eyewitnesses (1:16–18)

---

77. Bauckham, *Jude, 2 Peter*, 133. He also concludes that 2 Peter is probably pseudepigraphical and would have been recognized as such by its readers (134–35, 158–62). The debate over the issue of authorship has not seen any significant developments in the past twenty-five years. Bauckham presents the best arguments for pseudepigraphy, while Michael Green (*Second Epistle General*, 13–39) presents the best case for Petrine authorship.

78. Bauckham, *Jude, 2 Peter*, 143.

79. Ibid., 154. On the eschatology of 2 Peter, see John I. Snyder, *The Promise of His Coming: The Eschatology of 2 Peter* (San Mateo, Calif.: Western Book, 1986).

80. Bauckham, *Jude, 2 Peter*, 156.

(b) The Value of OT Prophecy (1:19)

Reply to Objection 2: The Inspiration of OT Prophecy (1:20–21)

Peter's Prediction of False Teachers (2:1–3a)

Reply to Objection 3: The Certainty of Judgment (2:3b–10a)

Denunciation of the False Teachers (2:10b–22)

Peter's Prediction of Scoffers (including Objection 4 [v. 4]; 3:1–4)

Reply to Objection 4:

    (a) The Sovereignty of God's Word (3:5–7)

    (b) The Forbearance of the Lord (3:8–10)

Exhortation (3:11–16)[81]

More recently, Duane F. Watson (1988) has analyzed the rhetoric of 2 Peter.[82] He concludes that 2 Peter is deliberative rhetoric: "It is clearly intended to advise and dissuade the audience with regard to a particular way of thinking and course of action."[83] The rhetorical situation faced in 2 Peter is the presence of false teachers who have led others astray with their false teaching and immoral practice. The basis for their false teaching is a denial of Christ's parousia and the judgment to accompany it, and this in turn justifies their ethical libertinism.[84] Watson's analysis leads him to propose the following rhetorical outline:[85]

    I. *Exordium* (1:3–15; with the letter opening, 1:1–2, as a quasi-*exordium*)

    II. *Probatio* (1:16–3:13)

        A. First accusation and refutation (1:16–19)

        B. Second accusation and refutation (1:20–21)

        C. Counteraccusation (2:1–3a)

        D. Third accusation and refutation (2:3b–10a)

        E. *Digressio* (2:10b–22)

        F. *Transitio,* or secondary exordium (3:1–2)

        G. Fourth accusation and refutation (3:3–13)

    III. *Peroratio* (3:14–18)

This outline is similar to that proposed earlier by Bauckham except that it makes explicit the rhetorical function of the various sections, and it proposes a different substructure for the elements in ch. 3.

---

81. Ibid., 135.

82. For an explanation of rhetorical criticism and relevant bibliography, see above, under the section "First Peter."

83. Watson, *Invention, Arrangement, and Style,* 85. He does observe sections of 2 Peter that are judicial rhetoric (1:16–2:10a; 3:1–13) and epideictic rhetoric (2:10b–22).

84. Ibid., 81–82.

85. Ibid., 141–42.

Watson also examines the relationship of 2 Peter and Jude, combining rhetorical criticism and redaction criticism. He makes no assumption concerning priority, but rather examines each correspondence to determine which author is more likely redacting the other text to conform with his rhetorical purposes. Watson concludes that with some correspondences the evidence is inconclusive: occasionally Jude appears dependent upon 2 Peter, but in most instances of correspondence 2 Peter is more likely redacting Jude.[86]

In *Virtue amidst Vice* (1997), J. Daryl Charles has contributed a series of essays on 2 Peter that, although subtitled *The Catalog of Virtues in 2 Peter 1*, actually discusses a variety of topics with respect to 2 Peter.[87] Most significant among his contributions is the emphasis upon the ethical issues underlying 2 Peter. He argues that "ethics, not doctrine, is the cause of fomentation within the community."[88] He provides considerable background to the ethical world of the Greco-Roman thought and Stoicism in particular as a context in which to understand the virtue list in 1:5–7. Although 2 Peter's perspective and emphasis differ from this background, the letter does share a common moral language with the broader Greco-Roman ethical discourse.[89] Charles's emphasis on the ethical component of 2 Peter is helpful, but his dichotomy of ethics versus teaching and his corresponding rejection of the doctrinal elements prove less so. For in 2 Peter, belief and behavior are intertwined, each influencing the other.[90]

Conclusion

The history of the study of 1 and 2 Peter in the past twenty-five years reveals how the understanding of each letter in its own way has broken free of an entrapping consensus and has moved on to fresh perspectives. These new developments show how 1 and 2 Peter each sound a distinct voice in the development of early Christianity—voices that deserve to be heard.

---

86. Ibid., 168–87. Watson also applies the results of his rhetorical analysis to the question of the literary integrity of 2 Peter and Jude (147–59).

87. J. Daryl Charles, *Virtue amidst Vice: The Catalog of Virtues in 2 Peter 1*, JSNTSup 150 (Sheffield: Sheffield Academic Press, 1997). He argues for a rejection of the "early catholic" understanding of 2 Peter (11–43). He also argues against understanding 2 Peter's genre as a testament (49–75).

88. Ibid., 49; cf. 84–98.

89. Ibid., 99–152; cf. J. Daryl Charles, "The Language and Logic of Virtue in 2 Peter 1:5–7," *BBR* 8 (1998): 55–73.

90. Other recent contributions to the study of 2 Peter include James M. Starr, *Sharers in Divine Nature: 2 Peter 1:4 in Its Hellenistic Context*, ConBNT 33 (Stockholm: Almqvist & Wiksell, 2000); Thomas J. Kraus, *Sprache, Stil und historischer Ort des zweiten Petrusbriefes*, WUNT 2.136 (Tübingen: Mohr [Siebeck], 2001); Anders Gerdmar, *Rethinking the Judaism-Hellenism Dichotomy: A Historiographical Study of Second Peter and Jude*, ConBNT 36 (Stockholm: Almqvist & Wiksell, 2001); Michael J. Gilmour, *The Significance of Parallels between 2 Peter and Other Early Christian Literature*, Academia Biblica 10 (Atlanta: Society of Biblical Literature, 2002).

19

Mark's Gospel

Peter G. Bolt

A great deal has been written on the Gospel of Mark in recent years. After a brief look at the earlier periods, for which numerous surveys already exist,[1] this essay will especially focus on the last twenty years or so in order to assess the current state of Markan studies.

The Early Period

Surveys of the history of interpretation of the Gospel of Mark chart a fairly well-defined course. This history has been characterized as "one of long-standing neglect and recent rediscovery."[2] In the early church, the paucity of evidence suggests that Mark was rather neglected. In the fourth century, Eusebius mentions the five-volume work on the Gospels written by Papias (ca. 130 C.E.), *Exposition of the Oracles of the Lord,* which, although nothing more is known of it, may have been the first commentary written on the Gospels.[3] Augustine's statement that

---

1. For the history of interpretation of Mark, see the following: W. R. Telford, *Mark*, NTG (Sheffield: Sheffield Academic Press, 1995); idem, introduction to *The Interpretation of Mark,* ed. W. R. Telford, IRT 7 (London: SPCK, 1985; rev. ed., 1995), 1–61; F. J. Matera, *What Are They Saying about Mark?* (New York: Paulist Press, 1987); S. P. Kealy, *Mark's Gospel: A History of Its Interpretation from the Beginning until 1979* (New York: Paulist Press, 1982); R. P. Martin, *Mark, Evangelist and Theologian* (Exeter: Paternoster, 1972).
2. Telford, *Mark,* 26.
3. Kealy, *Mark's Gospel,* 11.

"Mark follows [Matthew] closely and looks as if he were his servant and epitomist" (*De consensu evangelistarum* 1.2 [4]) perhaps illustrates one reason for the neglect: Mark was regarded simply as an abbreviator of Matthew.[4] Furthermore, given Augustine's influence, his statement appears to have contributed to many more years of neglect among those who followed him. This neglect received explicit comment in the late fifth century when Victor of Antioch complained of the total lack of commentary on Mark before attempting to rectify the situation by compiling incidental comments that the church fathers made on Mark in the process of commenting on the other Gospels.[5] Two disciples of Gregory the Great (bishop of Rome, 590–604) followed the same procedure, compiling Gregory's comments on Mark from his homilies on Job and Ezekiel.[6] Since such compilations can hardly be called a commentary proper,[7] it appears that the first actual commentary on the Gospel that has survived is the document formerly known as *Pseudo-Jerome,* which was written in the early seventh century.[8] The fact that the author viewed his work as the first commentary on Mark indicates that he was unaware of the existence of any other commentary at that time.[9] In the medieval and Reformation periods, Mark received some attention, but usually as part of commentary on a harmony of the Gospels, which meant that comment was made only on those portions not found in Matthew. From the sixteenth century, Mark was singled out for individual attention,[10] but Markan study did not really come into its own until the nineteenth century. At that stage, as scholars attempted to solve the question of how Matthew, Mark, and Luke were interrelated (the "Synoptic problem"), they found new impetus for the study of this previously much neglected Gospel.

The Modern Period

Nineteenth-century scholarship established that Mark was the first Gospel to be written, and that it was then used by Matthew and Luke. Markan prior-

4. This certainly is the reason for the neglect of Mark postulated by the author of *Pseudo-Jerome,* for example.

5. Kealy, *Mark's Gospel,* 28. Victor's sources are documented in H. Smith, "The Sources of Victor of Antioch's Commentary on Mark," *JTS* 19 (1918): 350–70.

6. Kealy, *Mark's Gospel,* 29.

7. Although Victor's work often has been given the status of "commentary" (e.g., Kealy, *Mark's Gospel,* 28; Telford, *Mark,* 10), this is a rather loose use of the term; see M. Cahill, "The Identification of the First Markan Commentary," *RB* 101 (1994): 264–67.

8. See M. Cahill, trans. and ed., *The First Commentary on Mark: An Annotated Translation* (New York: Oxford University Press, 1998). The suggestion that the author was an Irish monk, Cummeanus, is disputed, even though this suggestion has been "prematurely 'canonized'" by inclusion in the later volumes of *Votus Latina.* See Cahill, *First Commentary on Mark,* 5 n. 6; "First Markan Commentary," 262. This may account for Kealy (*Mark's Gospel,* 36) mistakenly citing Cummeanus and *Pseudo-Jerome* as separate entries.

9. Cahill, "First Markan Commentary," 263–64.

10. See Kealy, *Mark's Gospel,* 48–49.

ity, combined with the postulate of Q (the source behind Matthew and Luke's common material) gave rise to the "two-document hypothesis." Later, in the twentieth century, Synoptic studies also spoke of sources of special material from Luke and Matthew, referred to as L and M. Although Markan priority generally has been assumed, a substantial case for Matthean priority has also been persistently argued, and this position gained considerable support in the last decades of the twentieth century.[11]

In the nineteenth century, once Mark was regarded as the earliest and the most primitive of the Synoptics, this provided great impetus for its close study in pursuit of "the quest for the historical Jesus." Prodigious efforts were mounted to discover the author's sources—perhaps there was an original Mark (*Ur-Markus*)?—and to construct an outline of historical fact about Jesus. Once this outline was delivered, a succession of "lives of Jesus" were constructed upon this base. It was with this "life of Jesus movement" that Mark's Gospel came into its own after centuries of neglect.[12]

So far, modern scholarship had assumed that Mark provided almost direct access to historical information about Jesus. In 1901, William Wrede[13] challenged this assumption by arguing that Mark's "messianic secret" theme was imposed upon the traditions by Mark himself to suit his own theological purposes. Although the details of Wrede's theory have not survived, after him it became a commonplace that the author of Mark was not simply a collector of historical traditions, but a creative writer whose theological purposes contributed to the final shape of the Gospel.

Between the two world wars was the era of form criticism. K. L. Schmidt[14] drew attention to the "pearls and string" character of the Gospel, in which units of tradition were strung together by a loose geographical and temporal framework. M. Dibelius and R. Bultmann[15] isolated and classified the forms, established the *Sitz im Leben* (the setting in life in which the forms were used and shaped) of the tradition, and reconstructed the tradition history. One major result of the form critics' work was that Mark was no longer regarded as eyewitness testimony, but as a community product, written at some distance from the events that it purports to narrate. These conclusions helped to shake

11. W. L. Lane ("The Present State of Markan Studies," in *The Gospels Today: A Guide to Some Recent Developments*, ed. J. H. Skilton [Philadelphia: Skilton House, 1990], 69–72) refers to a series of conferences and publications discussing Synoptic relations in the 1970s and 1980s. This discussion continues; see, for example, G. Strecker, ed., *Minor Agreements: Symposium Göttingen 1991* (Göttingen: Vandenhoeck & Ruprecht, 1993).

12. Martin, *Mark, Evangelist and Theologian*, 37.

13. W. Wrede, *The Messianic Secret*, trans. J. Greig (1901; reprint, Cambridge: Clark, 1971).

14. K. L. Schmidt, *Der Rahmen der Geschichte Jesu* (1919; reprint, Darmstadt: Wissenschaftliche Buchgesellschaft, 1964).

15. M. Dibelius, *From Tradition to Gospel*, trans. B. Lee (1919; Cambridge: Clark, 1971); R. Bultmann, *The History of the Synoptic Tradition*, trans. J. Marsh, 2nd ed. (Oxford: Blackwell, 1968).

confidence in the historical value of the Gospel, even if some using form criticism were not as skeptical about the historicity of the Gospel account (e.g.,
V. Taylor).

Redaction criticism arose after World War II. Its concerns were anticipated
in the pioneering work of E. Lohmeyer,[16] R. H. Lightfoot,[17] H. Riesenfeld,[18]
and J. M. Robinson,[19] although it is Willi Marxsen[20] who usually is credited
for setting new directions for Markan studies.[21] Redaction critics regard Mark
as a product of a creative author who pursued a definite theological purpose
in writing the Gospel. The Gospel contains three levels of life situation: that
of Jesus, that of the church in which the tradition circulated, and that of the
evangelist and the community to which the Gospel was addressed. The Gospel no longer witnesses primarily to Jesus, but to the situation of the original
community addressed by the evangelist.

The combination of source, form, and redaction criticism has proved to be
a formidable force in Gospels studies. Numerous full-scale studies and articles
continue to be written from this perspective. However, even though these
methods continue to be used with great confidence, the long period in which
they have been practiced has allowed their many weaknesses to emerge.

To take one example, the tendency toward the fragmentation of the
Gospels, which was recognized as problematic for a long time, gradually
caused interest to turn to the Gospel as a whole. The prodigious efforts of
the redaction critics gave rise to what John Barton deemed—albeit referring
to a similar problem in OT study—the case of "the disappearing redactor."[22]
Originally, source criticism was prompted by various textual phenomena
that were viewed as discrepancies and clumsy stitching together of original
sources. Eventually, redaction criticism reached the stage of recognizing how
artfully the original sources were woven together. Ironically, the better the
redactor had done his work, the less need there was to postulate his existence
in the first place!

16. E. Lohmeyer, *Galiläa und Jerusalem*, FRLANT 52 (Göttingen: Vandenhoeck & Ruprecht, 1936).

17. R. H. Lightfoot, *History and Interpretation in the Gospels* (London: Hodder & Stoughton,
1934); *Locality and Doctrine in the Gospels* (London: Hodder & Stoughton, 1938); *The Gospel
Message of St. Mark* (Oxford: Clarendon, 1950).

18. H. Riesenfeld, "On the Composition of the Gospel of Mark," in *The Gospel Tradition*, trans.
E. Rowley and R. Kraft (1954; Oxford: Blackwell, 1970). Riesenfeld draws upon Lightfoot.

19. Robinson's thesis was written in 1954, accepted in 1955, and partially translated and
published as *Das Geschichtsverständnis des Markus-Evangeliums* in 1956. A compressed version
was published as *The Problem of History in Mark* in 1957. See *The Problem of History in Mark
and Other Marcan Studies* (Philadelphia: Fortress, 1982), 9 n. 3.

20. Willi Marxsen, *Mark the Evangelist: Studies on the Redaction History of the Gospel*, trans.
J. Boyce et al. ([1956]; Philadelphia: Fortress, 1969).

21. Kealy, *Mark's Gospel*, 159–61.

22. J. Barton, *Reading the Old Testament: Method in Biblical Study* (London: Darton, Longman & Todd, 1984), 56–58.

In 1995, Richard Bauckham seriously questioned one of the major assumptions of redaction criticism in particular.[23] For decades, scholars had assumed that the Gospels were written not for a general and indefinite audience, but for a particular and specific audience—usually a small group of churches struggling with some particular set of issues. "Almost all contemporary writing about the Gospels shares the unargued assumption that each evangelist, himself no doubt a teacher in a particular church, wrote his Gospel for that particular church, with its particular situation, character, and needs at the forefront of his mind."[24] So, for example, this assumption is evident in the various debates about whether Mark was written for Rome, Galilee, or Syria.[25]

Although older scholarship also had asserted that a Gospel was written in and for a particular location, redaction studies made this assumption an axiom upon which interpretation was built. In the late 1960s and early 1970s,[26] this assumption "became the basis for interpretative strategies that found the specific circumstances and needs of a particular community addressed in a Gospel."[27] It was as if the defunct task of using the Gospels to reconstruct the historical Jesus had been replaced with the quest for the historical communities supposedly addressed by them.[28] This led to a type of allegorical reading in which characters and events were regarded as "code" for what was occurring in the Markan community.[29] A narrative that seems to be about Jesus ends up being about the church.

When Bauckham argued that this assumption was by no means self-evident, and that it makes better sense to see that the Gospels were written, from the beginning, for a general and indefinite audience, the response among British scholars was reminiscent of that when the little boy cried out, "The emperor's got no clothes on!" It seems that, by 1995, this aspect of standard Gospels criticism, as with many other aspects, had already become suspect in the minds of many. Voices arguing for a general audience had been raised many years before. So, for example, in 1981, Robert Fowler had stated,

23. See R. Bauckham, "For Whom Were Gospels Written?" in *The Gospels for All Christians: Rethinking the Gospel Audiences*, ed. R. Bauckham (Grand Rapids: Eerdmans, 1998), 9–48. A version of this essay was originally presented at the British New Testament Conference in 1995.

24. Ibid., 11.

25. For a summary of the debate over the location of Mark's supposed community, see J. R. Donahue, "The Quest for the Community of Mark's Gospel," in *The Four Gospels 1992*, ed. F. Van Segbroeck et al., 3 vols., BETL 100 (Leuven: Leuven University Press, 1992), 2:817–38.

26. Markan scholarship led the way in this move—for example, T. J. Weeden, *Mark—Traditions in Conflict* (Philadelphia: Fortress, 1971); K.-G. Reploh, *Markus, Lehrer der Gemeinde: Eine redaktionsgeschichtliche Studie zu den Jungerperikopen des Markus-Evangeliums* (Stuttgart: Katholisches Bibelwerk, 1969); H. C. Kee, *Community of the New Age* (Philadelphia: Westminster, 1977).

27. Bauckham, "For Whom Were Gospels Written?" 19.

28. Ibid., 20.

29. Ibid., 19–20.

Exactly where the Gospel was written is impossible to tell. The language of the Gospel, although expressive and vigorous, is unpolished and shows no great learning. Consequently, the Gospel could have been written almost anywhere in the Roman Empire where a writer could have received a grade school education in Greek (almost anywhere).[30]

Anticipating Bauckham by some five years, Mary Ann Tolbert exposed the unexamined assumption of Gospels research that the Gospel of Mark was written to "some identifiable, individualized local group—that is, a *specific* community."[31] This is a genre mistake, treating a Gospel as if it were a Pauline letter, when in fact Mark "was *not* written in response to the problems of a specific local community but was intended, as were the ancient erotic novels, for a wider readership."[32]

This move toward a more generalized understanding of these questions had also begun to appear in the commentaries. So, for example, in 1991, Morna Hooker had noted that "the [G]ospel was composed somewhere in the Roman Empire."[33] The paradigm in which Gospels study was operating had been shifting for some time.[34]

The Period of Shifting Paradigms

Signs of a "paradigm shift" include not only the emergence of problems with the former paradigm, but also the rise of new theories. Daniel Harrington notes that from 1975 to 1984, several monographs were published using new methods: Kee[35] adopted a "socio-cultural-historical" method, Kelber[36] drew on oral-tradition research by social scientists, and Robbins[37] used "socio-rhetorical

30. R. M. Fowler, *Loaves and Fishes: The Function of the Feeding Stories in the Gospel of Mark*, SBLDS 54 (Chico, Calif.: Scholars Press, 1981), 183. This is the published version of Fowler's 1978 doctoral dissertation.

31. M. A. Tolbert, *Sowing the Gospel: Mark's World in Literary-Historical Perspective* (Minneapolis: Fortress, 1989), 303. Bauckham ("For Whom Were Gospels Written?" 17 n. 16) notes appreciatively Tolbert's contribution.

32. Tolbert, *Sowing the Gospel*, 304.

33. Morna Hooker, *A Commentary on the Gospel according to St. Mark*, BNTC (London: Black, 1991), 8. "A conclusion that scarcely narrows the field at all!" Hooker adds.

34. The older view of a distinct community dies hard. It is still perpetuated by, for example, W. R. Telford, *The Theology of Mark* (Cambridge: Cambridge University Press, 1999), 15–17; and the commentaries by J. R. Edwards, *The Gospel according to Mark*, PNTC (Leicester: Inter-Varsity, 2002); and J. R. Donahue and D. J. Harrington, *The Gospel of Mark*, SP (Collegeville, Minn.: Liturgical Press, 2002).

35. Kee, *Community of the New Age*.

36. W. H. Kelber, *The Oral and Written Gospel: The Hermeneutics of Speakers and Writing in the Synoptic Tradition, Paul, and Q* (Philadelphia: Fortress, 1983).

37. V. K. Robbins, *Jesus the Teacher: A Socio-Rhetorical Interpretation of Mark* (Philadelphia: Fortress, 1984).

analysis."[38] William Lane comments that in the years under his scrutiny (1978 to 1987), "new and creative approaches" were developed, citing "narrative criticism and structural exegesis" as "viable alternatives to the historical-critical paradigm."[39]

What was occurring was a shift from studying the Gospels (or, indeed, the whole Bible) under the paradigm of "history" to studying them under the paradigm of "literature." This paradigm shift had already been noticed in 1976,[40] and it has continued ever since. Norman Perrin was one of the most influential scholars in this shift, and the period 1975–84, at least in America, has been called the "post-Perrin" era of Markan research,[41] when Perrin's emergent interest in the literary study of Mark was developed by several of his students. Rather than seeing Mark's Gospel as a set of edited traditions, this new literary criticism considered the book to be a genuine narration. Mark the evangelist was increasingly regarded as Mark the author of a compelling story. The analogy of the text as window or as mirror is often invoked to describe the difference between the historical-critical and the literary-critical enterprises. Whereas historical criticism looked *through* the text, as if it were a window to the history (or theology) behind the text, narrative criticism sought to look *at* the text "as a mirror on whose surface we find a self-contained world."[42]

This post-Perrin era clearly was an overlapping period. Although historical-critical works continued to be published, other works showed an interest in, and a move toward, literary concerns. This period saw the call for Markan studies to set aside a perceived overinterest in history in order to deal first with the text itself.[43] At first, the new literary methods were recruited to solve problems raised during the reign of the historical-critical method. This can be seen in a collection of essays edited by W. H. Kelber, *The Passion in Mark*,[44] as well as in J. Dewey, *Markan Public Debate*,[45] and R. M. Fowler, *Loaves and Fishes*.[46] Gradually, literary studies became legitimate in their own right, and a "torrent" of studies appeared.[47]

38. D. Harrington, "A Map of Books on Mark (1975–1984)," *BTB* 15 (1985): 13.

39. Lane, "Present State of Markan Studies," 60.

40. See D. Robertson, "Literature, the Bible as," in *The Interpreter's Dictionary of the Bible, Supplementary Volume,* ed. K. Crim et al. (Nashville: Abingdon, 1976), 547–51.

41. Harrington, "Map of Books on Mark," 12. Cf. Donahue and Harrington, *Gospel of Mark,* 12.

42. Lane, "Present State of Markan Studies," 60.

43. See N. R. Petersen, *Literary Criticism for New Testament Critics* (Philadelphia: Fortress, 1978).

44. W. H. Kelber, ed., *The Passion in Mark: Studies on Mark 14–16* (Philadelphia: Fortress, 1980).

45. J. Dewey, *Markan Public Debate: Literary Technique, Concentric Structure, and Theology in Mark 2:1–3:6,* SBLDS 48 (Chico, Calif.: Scholars Press, 1981).

46. See n. 30, above.

47. C. L. Blomberg, "Synoptic Studies: Some Recent Developments and Debates," *Them* 12 (1987): 43. The torrent has not subsided.

By 1985, Harrington noted the "growing scholarly tendency in the late 1960s and early 1970s to attribute more and more literary creativity to the Evangelist and to do away with the idea of pre-Markan traditions wherever possible."[48] Across the ten years of his survey he noted "an increasing recognition of Mark as a literary artist and the need for interpreting his work with the aid of literary criticism."[49] During this time, more literary approaches emerged, reflected in the works of scholars such as Bilezekian,[50] Standaert,[51] Kermode,[52] Rhoads and Michie,[53] and Stock.[54] The transition into the postmodern world was well under way.

The Postmodern Period

The world of this new paradigm has also been called the era of "poststructuralism." Certain features of structuralism were adopted in biblical studies under methods known as "structural exegesis," a term that is peculiar to the world of biblical studies and looks rather odd in the light of the agenda of the secular structuralism that it appropriated. Structuralism seeks to uncover the "deep structures" that universally describe human thought patterns and are expressed in all aspects of human culture, including literature. A piece of literature can be carefully analyzed to yield the "surface structures," but, for the structuralist, this is merely a preliminary step toward uncovering the "deep structures" expressed in the text. This enterprise should not be confused with historical criticism's search for the history behind the text. The deep structures of interest to the structuralist are the deep "mythic" structures of the human mind that enable thought. Structuralism is not interested in discerning the history behind the text—in fact, its critics are quick to point out the ahistorical nature of the movement.

By coining the term "structural exegesis," biblical critics reveal that their interest has tended to remain at the surface level, where some of the insights of structuralist analysis have been appropriated. Structuralist exegesis has been used especially to elucidate the meaning of parables. Daniel and Aline Patte

48. Harrington, "Map of Books on Mark," 12.

49. Ibid., 13.

50. G. G. Bilezekian, *The Liberated Gospel: A Comparison of the Gospel of Mark and Greek Tragedy* (Grand Rapids: Baker, 1977).

51. B. Standaert, *L'Évangile selon Marc: Composition et genre littéraire* (Nijmegen: Stichting Studentenpers Nijmegen, 1978). A version of this original thesis was later published as *L'Évangile selon Marc: Commentaire* (Paris: Cerf, 1983).

52. F. Kermode, *The Genesis of Secrecy: An Interpretation of Narrative* (Cambridge, Mass.: Harvard University Press, 1979).

53. D. Rhoads and D. Michie, *Mark as Story: An Introduction to the Narrative of a Gospel* (Philadelphia: Fortress, 1982).

54. A. Stock, *A Call to Discipleship: A Literary Study of Mark's Gospel* (Wilmington, Del.: Glazier, 1982); *The Method and Message of Mark* (Wilmington, Del.: Glazier, 1989).

used structuralist insights drawn from A. J. Greimas to analyze Mark 15 and 16.[55] Fernando Belo yoked insights drawn from another French structuralist, R. Barthes, with dialectical materialism.[56] Elizabeth Malbon provided what was the first—and probably the last—full-scale structural analysis of Mark,[57] in which she focused upon the "narrative space" (geopolitical, topographical, architectural) that shapes the Gospel of Mark and gives access to its "mythic meaning."

Although few studies adopted a fully structural approach, structuralism gave way to the many literary studies of this poststructuralist era. In 1987, Craig Blomberg spoke of two forms of poststructuralism in Gospels studies: reader-response criticism and deconstruction,[58] both exemplifying another feature of this period: the shift toward the reader.

Deconstruction is "a highly flexible strategy of reading,"[59] influenced by the thinking of Jacques Derrida and Paul de Man. In approaching a text, deconstruction follows Derrida in not "concentrating"—that is, focusing upon what is important, crucial, or central to the work itself; but rather in "de-concentrating"—that is, focusing upon "the secondary, eccentric, lateral, marginal, parasitic, borderline cases," upon "the excluded, the marginal, the blind spot, the blank."[60] The aim of such readings may simply be the production of pleasure for the deconstructer. At other times, such readings have a more serious intent, such as that of Tat-Siong Benny Liew, *Politics of Parousia* (1999),[61] which combines deconstruction with sociopolitical concerns with regard to colonialism.

Studies adopting a deconstructive stance have been rare in Markan studies.[62] Nevertheless, its influence is felt in numerous postmodern studies that assume that the meaning of a text resides in the reader, and also in those that adopt a reading of Mark "from the margins." Since Mark can be read from a

55. D. and A. Patte, *Structural Exegesis: From Theory to Practice: Exegesis of Mark 15 and 16, Hermeneutical Implications* (Philadelphia: Fortress, 1978).

56. F. Belo, *A Materialist Reading of the Gospel of Mark,* trans. M. O'Connell (Maryknoll, N.Y.: Orbis, 1981).

57. E. S. Malbon, *Narrative Space and Mythic Meaning in Mark* (San Francisco: Harper & Row, 1986; reprint, Sheffield: JSOT Press, 1991).

58. Blomberg, "Synoptic Studies," 38–45. At this stage, the recent developments were known as the "newer literary criticism"—"newer" to distinguish this discipline from the older literary (i.e., source) criticism.

59. S. D. Moore, "Deconstructive Criticism: The Gospel of the Mark," in *Mark and Method: New Approaches in Biblical Studies,* ed. J. C. Anderson and S. D. Moore (Minneapolis: Fortress, 1992), 85.

60. Moore, "Deconstructive Criticism," 85–86. The first series of terms is cited from Derrida, the second is Moore's.

61. Tat-Siong Benny Liew, *Politics of Parousia: Reading Mark Inter(con)textually,* BIS 42 (Leiden: Brill, 1999).

62. See Moore, "Deconstructive Criticism," 84–102; *Mark and Luke in Poststructuralist Perspectives: Jesus Begins to Write* (New Haven: Yale University Press, 1992).

variety of reading stances, these studies often are somewhat defensive about their particular stance, insisting that no one should take them as saying that their reading is for anyone else.[63] With such studies, the analogy of the text as mirror becomes all the more appropriate, in a sense, for it is as if the reader looks at the "mirror" and sees only an image of his or her own circumstances reflected back.

This postmodern view of texts has generated readings of Mark from a variety of particular stances: ideological readings,[64] feminist readings,[65] Buddhist readings,[66] black readings,[67] and even a reading of Mark from the stance of a recovering alcoholic.[68] Here it is often not a case of listening to what Mark has to say, but of utilizing Mark for a particular end. So Liew, writing from a deconstructive position, states, "I want to use Markan studies to facilitate liberation rather than legitimate oppression. For me, simply ignoring or 'trashing' such an instrumental book is counter-productive." He therefore seeks to "re-vision . . . to read an old, perhaps even familiar, text like Mark with new critical eyes so that I may engage it in the flesh and blood struggles of human beings for liberation."[69]

Many such studies are, of course, deliberately committed to a subjective reading—that is, where the contemporary reader determines the meaning of the text. A focus on the reader does not, however, always tend toward subjective readings and to solipsism. In recent years there have been many studies assuming that Mark is a work of literature written in such a way that the text itself exerts control of the reading experience so as to make an impact upon its readers. On such a view, narratives "work" on their readers, and the study of narrative seeks to uncover how they work. These reader-centered approaches

63. For example, under pressure from the variety of feminisms, Janice Anderson insists that her reading is not the only feminist reading possible; see J. C. Anderson, "Feminist Criticism: The Dancing Daughter," in Anderson and Moore, *Mark and Method*, 103–34.

64. For example, Belo, *Materialist Reading of the Gospel of Mark*.

65. For feminist readings of Mark, see, for example, Anderson, "Feminist Criticism," and the essays in A.-J. Levine, ed., *A Feminist Companion to Mark* (Sheffield: Sheffield Academic Press, 2001). Feminist studies have appeared on particular passages in Mark (e.g., M. A. Beavis, "From the Margin to the Way: A Feminist Reading of the Story of Bartimaeus," *JFSR* 14 [1998]: 19–39), on the whole of Mark (J. L. Mitchell, *Beyond Fear and Silence: A Feminist-Literary Reading of Mark* [New York: Continuum, 2001]), and from even more refined feminist perspectives (e.g., H. Kinukawa, *Women and Jesus in Mark: A Japanese Feminist Perspective* [Maryknoll, N.Y.: Orbis, 1994]; L. M. Harder, *Obedience, Suspicion, and the Gospel of Mark: A Mennonite-Feminist Exploration of Biblical Authority,* SWR 5 [Waterloo, Ont.: Canadian Corporation for Studies in Religion, 1998]).

66. J. P. Keenan, *The Gospel of Mark: A Mahayana Reading* (Maryknoll, N.Y.: Orbis, 1995).

67. B. K. Blount, *Go Preach! Mark's Kingdom Message and the Black Church Today* (Maryknoll, N.Y.: Orbis, 1998).

68. J. C. Mellon, *Mark as Recovery Story: Alcoholism and the Rhetoric of Gospel Mystery* (Chicago: University of Illinois Press, 1995).

69. Liew, *Politics of Parousia*, 21.

to narrative can be classified into two broad streams: narrative criticism and reader-response criticism.

Treating the text as a whole, narrative criticism looks at "the surface structures," such as the characters and the interaction between them, the plot, the narrated events, the temporal, geographical, and topographical settings, and movement, in order to establish what happens within the story-world. Dealing with the text as literature in this way, narrative criticism seeks to unlock the meaning that resides in the story.[70] The slim volume by David Rhoads and Donald Michie, *Mark as Story*,[71] has proved to be enormously influential in the narrative analysis of Mark. It recently has been revised, in conjunction with J. Dewey, in the light of further developments in literary studies. In the second edition, even though postmodern issues are not stressed, the influence of postmodern readings is explicitly mentioned: "We have learned that every reading is a reading through a particular lens. There is no 'objective' reading and therefore no single 'legitimate' reading. Rather, everyone reads from a particular social location—in regard to gender, age, race, ethnic group and nationality, social class, and economic level, education, religious affiliation, and so on—and the social location affects how each person interprets a narrative."[72] From this stance, the authors remind readers that "our reading is one among many" and that it "inevitably reflects . . . our particular social location."[73] Nevertheless, they are keen for readers to read Mark on its own terms.[74]

In 1996, Stephen Smith published a narrative-critical treatment of Mark, with chapters on characters, plot, time, and space, as well as on "author, reader, and text," "point of view," and "irony."[75] With these latter concerns we have moved from narrative criticism proper to reader-response criticism. Reader-response criticism includes the work of the narrative critic, but goes beyond it to ask how the narrative impacts the reader.

The variety of reader-response criticisms, each ascribing a different relation of text to reader,[76] can be conceived along a spectrum from a "subjective" end, where meaning resides in the reader, to an "objective" end, where the text controls the reader through textually embedded devices oriented toward the

---

70. For introductions to narrative criticism, see E. S. Malbon, "Narrative Criticism: How Does the Story Mean?" in Anderson and Moore, *Mark and Method*, 23–49 (reprinted in E. S. Malbon, *In the Company of Jesus: Characters in Mark's Gospel* [Louisville: Westminster John Knox, 2000], 1–40); M. Powell, *What Is Narrative Criticism?* (Minneapolis: Fortress, 1990).

71. Philadelphia: Fortress, 1982.

72. D. Rhoads, J. Dewey, and D. Michie, *Mark as Story: An Introduction to the Narrative of a Gospel*, 2nd ed. (Minneapolis: Fortress, 1999).

73. Ibid., xii; cf. 147.

74. Ibid., 147.

75. S. H. Smith, *A Lion with Wings: A Narrative-Critical Approach to Mark's Gospel* (Sheffield: Sheffield Academic Press, 1996).

76. See J. L. Resseguie, "Reader-response Criticism and the Synoptic Gospels," *JAAR* 52 (1984): 307.

reader.[77] A narrative can be conceptualized as having two levels: the "story," which is the *what* of the narrative, and the "discourse," which is the *how* of the narrative.[78] Reader-response criticism is especially concerned with the discourse, for it is here that the narrative makes contact with the reader and draws the reader into the narrative in order to achieve its impact.

Insights from reader-response criticism began to be applied to the study of Mark in 1981, with Robert Fowler's *Loaves and Fishes*.[79] By that time, however, reader-oriented approaches were so much taken for granted in nonbiblical literary circles that one author could discuss its "now hackneyed theses . . . of a commonplace nature."[80] Initially, there was a tendency to use reader-response insights for historical critical ends, but gradually these insights were utilized simply to elucidate the Markan reading experience. Bas van Iersel was the first to provide a reader-response commentary, in his 1986 popular-level commentary,[81] which was preliminary to his full-scale commentary published in 1998.[82] In 1992, J. P. Heil published *The Gospel of Mark as a Model for Action*,[83] which, although subtitled *A Reader-Response Commentary*, is not methodologically rigorous; its "reader-response" element consists merely in each character in a story being used for some exemplary model vis-à-vis the modern reader. In the same year, Robert Fowler published *Let the Reader Understand*, which sought to uncover the many textual devices by which Mark engages readers, such as explicit and implicit commentary, the "rhetoric of indirection," ambiguity, and opacity. So far, this book remains the only sustained treatment of Mark's discourse.[84]

77. See R. M. Fowler, "Who Is 'the Reader' of Mark's Gospel?" *SBLSP* 22 (1983): 31–53. Fowler mentions W. C. Booth, *The Rhetoric of Fiction* (Chicago: University of Chicago Press, 1983), and S. E. Fish, *Self-consuming Artifacts: The Experience of Seventeenth-Century Literature* (Berkeley: University of California Press, 1972), as two text-controlled critics who believe in the "rhetorical power of the text" (43). See Fowler's table classifying critics (35).

78. S. Chatman, *Story and Discourse: Narrative Structure in Fiction and Film* (Ithaca, N.Y.: Cornell University Press, 1978).

79. See his introduction to the method: Fowler, "Reader-Response Criticism: Figuring Mark's Reader," in Anderson and Moore, *Mark and Method,* 50–83. For an analysis and critique of the influence of poststructural criticism on Gospel studies, see S. D. Moore, *Literary Criticism and the Gospels: The Theoretical Challenge* (New Haven: Yale University Press, 1989).

80. J. Slawinski, "Reading and Reader in the Literary Historical Process," *New Literary History* 19 (1988): 521.

81. B. M. F. van Iersel, *Reading Mark,* trans. W. H. Bisscheroux ([1986]; Edinburgh: Clark, 1989).

82. B. M. F. van Iersel, *Mark: A Reader-Response Commentary,* trans. W. H. Bisscheroux, JSNTSup 164 (Sheffield: Sheffield Academic Press, 1998).

83. J. P. Heil, *The Gospel of Mark as a Model for Action* (New York: Paulist, 1992).

84. R. M. Fowler, *Let the Reader Understand: Reader-Response Criticism and the Gospel of Mark* (Minneapolis: Fortress, 1992; reprint, Harrisburg, Pa.: Trinity, 2001]). My own work also examines the discourse of Mark, paying special attention to the notions of focalization and distance: P. G. Bolt, *Jesus' Defeat of Death: An Analysis of the Role of the Suppliants in the Persuasion of Mark's Early Graeco-Roman Readers*, SNTSMS 125 (Cambridge: Cambridge University

Reader-response theory's significant contribution to the world of criticism is its attention to "the richness and the dynamism of the temporal experience of reading."[85] This dynamism in the reading experience can be analyzed using a model of the parties involved in a narrative transaction that is now fairly commonplace among reader-response critics (see fig. 19.1).[86] The inner box represents the text itself, with the real author and reader existing in the real world outside of the text and thus not being easily accessible through simply reading the text. On the other hand, the implied author and reader are textual constructs—that is, their portraits are painted by the text itself. The implied reader, therefore, "amounts to the textual elements that invite the actual reader to respond to the text in certain ways."[87]

Narrative Text

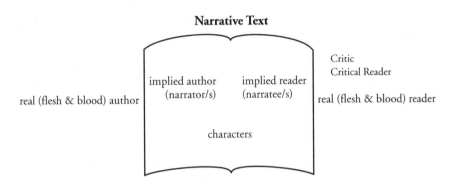

real (flesh & blood) author

implied author (narrator/s)

implied reader (narratee/s)

characters

Critic
Critical Reader

real (flesh & blood) reader

Fig. 19.1 Chatman's Narrative Dynamics

"Flesh-and-blood" readers certainly can read "against the grain," becoming "resistant" rather than "ideal" readers, but in order to experience the narrative in its fullest measure, they must be prepared to become the "implied reader,"[88] in a

---

Press, 2003). For a discussion of reader-response theory and its application to Mark, see W. R. Tate, *Reading Mark from the Outside: Eco and Iser Leave Their Marks* (Bethesda, Md.: Christian Universities Press, 1995).

85. Fowler, "Who Is 'the Reader' of Mark's Gospel?" 49.

86. This is a modification of Chatman's diagram (*Story and Discourse*). I have added "characters," for they can operate on either "side" of the equation, speaking for the author or being aligned with the reader. Fowler discusses the place of the "critic" and the "critical reader" ("Who Is 'the Reader' in Reader Response Criticism?" *Semeia* 31 [1985]: 5–10; *Let the Reader Understand*, 4–5, 263–64). Chatman's diagram is also used with slight modification by, among others, Paul Danove and van Iersel (see van Iersel, *Mark*, 16–21). The "narrator/narratee" axis is not useful for Mark, for the transaction simply involves the implied author/reader (Fowler, "Who Is 'the Reader' of Mark's Gospel?" 40).

87. Van Iersel, *Mark*, 17–18.

88. Fowler, "Who Is 'the Reader' in Reader Response Criticism?" 12. As a preliminary move, the "critic" must first become a reader, albeit a "critical reader"; cf. Fowler, "Who Is 'the Reader' of Mark's Gospel?" 32–38; Moore, *Literary Criticism and the Gospels*, 98–107.

move often called the "suspension of disbelief." This assumes that the narrative has something to say, and that the flesh-and-blood reader needs to be prepared to enter the narrative world in order to receive the full impact of the narrative.

Narrative-reader studies have continued to be published, dealing with individual passages as well as some of Mark's narrative methods, such as characterization,[89] irony,[90] and the "sandwich" device, in which one story is intercalated with another, forcing the reader to read both stories together.[91] Narrative-critical perspectives also have aided the understanding of various Markan themes, such as faith and unbelief,[92] time,[93] envy,[94] conflict,[95] and wonder.[96]

Given the importance of characters to a narrative, it is not surprising that the various characters and character groups in Mark also have received a good deal of attention. The major characters, such as Jesus, the disciples,[97] and his opponents,[98] provide continuity to the narrative by being present from start to finish. The disciples were of interest also to redaction critics, for whom they tended to stand allegorically for figures in the church of Mark's day.[99] Narrative critics, however, focus upon their role within the story, but they have also favored them for their role with regard to the readers. Apart from the three major characters, all other characters have tended to be lumped together as the "minor characters,"[100] although special attention has been given to some, such

89. See the essays in D. Rhoads and K. Syreeni, eds., *Characterisation in the Gospels: Reconceiving Narrative Criticism*, JSNTSup 184 (Sheffield: Sheffield Academic Press, 1999).

90. J. Camery-Hoggart, *Irony in Mark's Gospel: Text and Subtext*, SNTSMS 72 (Cambridge: Cambridge University Press, 1992).

91. J. R. Edwards, "Markan Sandwiches: The Significance of Interpolations in Markan Narratives," *NovT* 21 (1989): 193–216; T. Shepherd, *Markan Sandwich Stories: Narration, Definition, and Function* (Berrien Springs, Mich.: Andrews University Press, 1993).

92. C. Burdon, *Stumbling on God: Faith and Vision in Mark's Gospel* (London: SPCK, 1990); C. D. Marshall, *Faith as a Theme in Mark's Narrative*, SNTSMS 64 (Cambridge: Cambridge University Press, 1989; reprint, 1994); M. R. Thompson, *The Role of Disbelief in Mark: A New Approach to the Second Gospel* (New York: Paulist Press, 1989).

93. B. D. Schildgen, *Crisis and Continuity: Time in the Gospel of Mark*, JSNTSup 159 (Sheffield: Sheffield Academic Press, 1998).

94. A. C. Hagedorn and J. H. Neyrey, "'It Was out of Envy That They Handed Jesus Over' (Mark 15:10): The Anatomy of Envy and the Gospel of Mark," *JSNT* 69 (1998): 15–56.

95. J. D. Kingsbury, *Conflict in Mark: Jesus, Authorities, Disciples* (Minneapolis: Fortress, 1989); J. S. Hanson, *The Endangered Promises: Conflict in Mark*, SBLDS 171 (Atlanta: Society of Biblical Literature, 2000).

96. T. Dwyer, *The Motif of Wonder in the Gospel of Mark*, JSNTSup 128 (Sheffield: Sheffield Academic Press, 1996).

97. See, for example, E. S. Malbon, "Disciples/Crowds/Whoever: Markan Characters and Readers," in *In the Company of Jesus*, 70–99. See also Kingsbury, *Conflict in Mark*.

98. E. S. Malbon, "The Jewish Leaders in the Gospel of Mark: A Literary Study in Markan Characterization," in *In the Company of Jesus*, 131–65. See also Kingsbury, *Conflict in Mark*.

99. See, for example, Weeden, *Mark: Traditions in Conflict*.

100. E. S. Malbon, "The Major Importance of Minor Characters in Mark," in *In the Company of Jesus*, 189–225; J. F. Williams, *Other Followers of Jesus: Minor Characters as Major Figures in Mark's Gospel*, JSNTSup 102 (Sheffield: JSOT Press, 1994).

as the women[101] and the crowd.[102] However, the "suppliants"—those thirteen characters who come to Jesus in some need and find help—ought to be distinguished as a special group. They have an important role in Mark's communicative dynamics.[103] It is these characters with whom the implied reader is aligned, thus providing some kind of "entry point" into the movement of the narrative.

Whereas in the postmodern period interest often has been directed toward the contemporary reader, it is also entirely possible, having analyzed the narrative of Mark at both story and discourse levels, for the exegete to continue to move from the text toward Mark's early readers. Studies in Mark's narrative rhetoric begin with an understanding of Mark and his narrative world, and then seek to understand how the Gospel would have made its appeal to the ancient reader. This requires recourse to Greco-Roman materials as part of a process of reconstructing the "repertoire" that the ancient reader might have been expected to bring to a reading of Mark. This too has been an emergent trend.

Mark and the Greco-Roman World

The trend toward understanding Mark in its Greco-Roman context rightly includes the discussion of its genre. Richard Burridge has mounted a sustained argument that Mark (and the other Gospels) ought to be understood as a form of Greco-Roman *bios,* or "life" (loosely, "biography").[104] Although this is not a new suggestion, Burridge's careful treatment of the question has managed to persuade many. Others have argued for a biography of a particular kind, such as an "aretalogical biography" associated with a type of hero cult.[105] Others have gained insight into Mark from Greek theater, arguing that Mark is like a Greek tragedy,[106] or from the erotic novels.[107] More recently, Dennis MacDonald[108] has argued that Mark is directly influenced by both the LXX and

101. For a sample from a vast number of studies, see E. S. Malbon, "Fallible Followers: Women and Men in the Gospel of Mark," in *In the Company of Jesus,* 41–69.

102. See, for example, Malbon, "Disciples/Crowds/Whoever."

103. See Bolt, *Jesus' Defeat of Death.*

104. R. Burridge, *What Are the Gospels? A Comparison with Graeco-Roman Biography,* SNTSMS 71 (Cambridge: Cambridge University Press, 1992; reprint, 1995). See also D. Dormeyer, *Das Markusevangelium als Idealbiographie von Jesus Christus, dem Nazarener* (Stuttgart: Katholisches Bibelwerk, 1999).

105. L. M. Wills, *The Quest of the Historical Gospel: Mark, John, and the Origins of the Gospel Genre* (London: Routledge, 1997).

106. For example, Bilezekian, *Liberated Gospel;* Stock, *Call to Discipleship;* S. H. Smith, "A Divine Tragedy: Some Observations on the Dramatic Structure of Mark's Gospel," *NovT* 37 (1995): 209–31; M. A. Inch, *Exhortations of Jesus according to Matthew; and, Up from the Depths: Mark as Tragedy* (Lanham, Md.: University Press of America, 1997).

107. Tolbert, *Sowing the Gospel.*

108. D. R. MacDonald, *The Homeric Epics and the Gospel of Mark* (New Haven: Yale University Press, 2000).

the Homeric epics. Although Adela Yarbro Collins prefers to think of Mark's genre as "history in apocalyptic mode,"[109] with a background in apocalyptic texts such as *Enoch* and especially Daniel, she is nevertheless sensitive to the Greco-Roman context of Mark's readership.[110]

Mark's relation to the literature and culture of the Greco-Roman world has been explored in a number of ways.[111] Herman Waetjen, for example, combines the reader-response approach of Wolfgang Iser with a sociological model indebted to the Lenskis' study of peasant society in order to paint a picture of Mark's readers' social world.[112] Whitney Shiner attempts to examine the readers' role in the rhetoric, utilizing comparative material drawn from the Greco-Roman world.[113] Timothy Dwyer[114] has dealt with "wonder," and Kathleen Corley with "women,"[115] in the ancient world and in the Gospel of Mark. In my own work, I have assessed the healing and exorcism stories in the light of ancient understandings of disease, magic,[116] and the Roman imperial system.

The reading experience can be seen to have two movements.[117] If the text is constructed in such a way as to make an impact upon its readers, then the axis "text to (implied) reader" can be analyzed. This axis includes both story and discourse, but special attention is paid to how the text makes its impact upon the implied reader. The second axis is "(flesh-and-blood) reader to text." Since flesh-and-blood readers bring certain understandings to the reading experience, this "repertoire" will be part of the transaction as they "become" the implied

109. A. Y. Collins, "Is Mark's Gospel a Life of Jesus?" in *The Beginning of the Gospel: Probings of Mark in Context* (Minneapolis: Fortress, 1992), 1–38.

110. In other writings, Collins sets Mark in the Greco-Roman context. See, for example, "Apotheosis and Resurrection," in *The New Testament and Hellenistic Judaism,* ed. P. Borgen and S. Giversen (Aarhus: Aarhus University Press, 1995), 88–100; "The Signification of Mark 10:45 among Gentile Christians," *HTR* 90 (1997): 371–82.

111. Apart from those mentioned here, others have utilized Greco-Roman materials in their studies of Mark—for example, Robbins, *Jesus the Teacher;* M. A. Beavis, *Mark's Audience: The Literary and Social Setting of Mark 4:11–12,* JSNTSup 33 (Sheffield: JSOT Press, 1989); Tolbert, *Sowing the Gospel.*

112. H. C. Waetjen, *A Reordering of Power: A Sociopolitical Reading of Mark's Gospel* (Minneapolis: Fortress, 1989).

113. W. T. Shiner, *Follow Me: Disciples in Markan Rhetoric,* SBLDS 145 (Atlanta: Scholars Press, 1995).

114. Dwyer, *Motif of Wonder in the Gospel of Mark.*

115. K. E. Corley, *Private Women, Public Meals: Social Conflict in the Synoptic Tradition* (Peabody, Mass.: Hendrickson, 1993).

116. To date, there has been no sustained treatment of Mark and magic, although it is touched upon by studies dealing with magic and the Synoptics or the historical Jesus: M. Smith, *Jesus the Magician: Charlatan or Son of God?* (Berkeley, Calif.: Seastone, 1978; reprint, 1998); J. M. Hull, *Hellenistic Magic and the Synoptic Tradition,* SBT 2.28 (London: SCM, 1974); M. E. Mills, *Human Agents of Cosmic Power in Hellenistic Judaism and the Synoptic Tradition,* JSNTSup 41 (Sheffield: JSOT Press, 1990); B. Kollmann, *Jesus und die Christen als Wundertäter: Studien zu Magi, Medizin und Schamanismus in Antike und Christentum,* FRLANT 170 (Göttingen: Vandenhoeck & Ruprecht, 1996).

117. For this paragraph, see Bolt, *Jesus' Defeat of Death.*

reader at least for the time it takes to read Mark's story. Although the repertoire of the early readers of Mark probably never will be fully recovered, recovery certainly is possible in principle. And in practice, an attempt can be made to reconstruct this repertoire, at least partially, from our expanding knowledge of the ancient world. This is an exercise in social history.[118]

In keeping with the idea that Mark's audience was general and nonspecific from the beginning, this social history needs to aim at uncovering broad social phenomena that can be assumed to be in the repertoire of the average hearer of Mark in the first century.[119] Particular interest should be given to the social phenomena that automatically would be invoked by the kind of language and conceptual material found in Mark. Presumably, this is where Mark's narrative would have made a direct and immediate impact on the flesh-and-blood reader.

This journey in recent Markan scholarship from narrative to implied reader to flesh-and-blood reader has brought us full circle, back to Mark as a historical document.

The Return to History

We have already noted the silence about Mark in the early years. Nevertheless, a revival of interest in the reception history of Mark[120] has been assisted by Michael Cahill's publication of the first commentary on Mark, and by Thomas Oden and Christopher Hall providing citations from Mark in the church fathers.[121] Brenda Schildgen has examined the reception of Mark into later times,[122] but presumably Mark was being read from its production date, despite the difficulty we have in accessing these earliest reading experiences. An interest in the earliest flesh-and-blood readers is the first stage of a "reception history" of Mark.

This return to history answers a common objection to literary studies. After the paradigm shift from history to literature, some literary critics dismissed

118. For an introduction, see D. Rhoads, "Social Criticism: Crossing Boundaries," in Anderson and Moore, *Mark and Method,* 135–61 (although Rhoads deals with more than social history in this essay).

119. See Bauckham, "For Whom Were Gospels Written?" 46.

120. Cahill, "First Markan Commentary," 258 n. 1: "This post-modern age of biblical scholarship is marked by some indications that the history of exegesis is set to make a comeback as a matter of hermeneutical principle." He cites the use of older commentaries and Ulrich Luz's "history of influence" (*Wirkungsgeschichte*) as an attempt to overcome the deficiency of historical-critical interpretation.

121. T. C. Oden and C. A. Hall, eds., *Mark,* ACCS 2 (Downers Grove, Ill.: InterVarsity, 1998).

122. B. D. Schildgen, *Power and Prejudice: The Reception of the Gospel of Mark* (Detroit: Wayne State University Press, 1999).

historical inquiry altogether, and others so focused on literary inquiries that the historical questions were eclipsed. Many scholars familiar with the former paradigm therefore objected to the question of history being neglected.[123] In 1990, William Lane observed that this could not last:

> It may even become respectable once more to ask historical questions about the earthly Jesus with the recognition that Mark is narrating history. The current neglect of historical questions must ultimately be redressed.[124]

But the suggestion that Markan scholarship ought to recover a historical consciousness should not be taken as a call to return to the historical criticism from which it has come.[125] Even though studies from this perspective continue to be published, the problems with the historical-critical method that contributed to the rise of other paradigms still remain. In addition, the focus on narrative has contributed to indisputable advances in our understanding of Mark as a coherent whole. This cannot be ignored by simply returning to a method that, by its very nature, never adequately dealt with Mark holistically.

The return to history after holistically studying the narrative of Mark will be a return to a different kind of historical enterprise. This return should be a "postnarrative" move. That is, after the study of Mark as narrative, questions then can be asked about the reception of this whole narrative in the ancient world.

In this new environment, the question of Mark's purpose looks very different than it did under the previous paradigm. Approaching Mark from the perspective of first-century hearers requires paying attention to the overlaps in vocabulary and concepts between Mark and the hearers' probable repertoire. For example, the language that Mark uses to describe the illnesses of the suppliants was common to the first-century world—they knew what it meant to suffer fever, paralysis, or blindness. Craig Evans's Mark commentary, which completes the Word Biblical Commentary begun by Robert Guelich, is very helpful in drawing conceptual links between Mark and the ancient world. The early readers would not have missed the fact that much of the language used of Jesus intersects with the propaganda of the Roman imperial system.[126] They would have perceived that Mark was presenting Jesus as an alternative

123. Frank Matera frequently refers to the concern about loosing Gospel research from its historical moorings (*What Are They Saying about Mark?* 74, 91, 92).

124. Lane, "Present State of Markan Studies," 72.

125. Since Gospels study has resorted to the methods of source, form, and redaction criticism for so long, it is difficult for some to conceive of approaching the question of Mark's history without resorting to these methods once again. See Matera, *What Are They Saying about Mark?* 74.

126. See C. A. Evans, *Mark 8:27–16:20*, WBC 34B (Nashville: Nelson, 2001), lxxx–xciii; Bolt, *Jesus' Defeat of Death*; A. Dawson, *Freedom as Liberating Power: A Socio-Political Reading of the Ἐξουσία Texts in the Gospel of Mark*, NTOA 44 (Freiburg: Universitätsverlag: Göttingen: Vandenhoeck & Ruprecht, 2000).

to the Caesars. According to Anne Dawson, Mark proclaimed a freedom that was radically different from that espoused by the dominant ideology of the Roman culture, as expressed in the *Res gestae* of Augustus. Against the imperial propaganda that Augustus had inaugurated a golden age of liberty, Mark proclaimed that it was Jesus of Nazareth who had brought a new age of freedom within the kingdom of God.[127] In my own view,[128] Mark perceives that the experience of the kingdom is still future, but it is inaugurated and guaranteed by the resurrection of a crucified man. Whereas the imperial rhetoric proclaimed the "gospel" of Caesar,[129] the "Savior" who brought life to a world on the brink of death, Mark's "Son of God," through acts such as healing and exorcism, brought people out from under the shadow of death. This was a foretaste both of Jesus' own resurrection and of the future resurrection of others into the coming kingdom of God.

Mark's narrative, in its original context, made some radical claims that struck at the core of the politico-religious system endemic to the world inhabited by its Greco-Roman audience. This does not mean that the Gospel of Mark was simply a kind of political manifesto. Despite their very real political and social implications, these claims were in fact, at their core, theological claims.

Return to Theology

Since Wrede, if not before, there has been a tendency to draw a dichotomy between history and theology. Some later narrative studies made it a trichotomy by adding the category of narrative. But rather than pitting these three against one another, we should see it as eminently more sensible to recognize them as three aspects of the Gospel of Mark. Mark is a narrative about theologically significant historical events.

The recent emergence of a new series from Cambridge University Press testifies to a revival of interest in the theology of the NT. The volume contributed by W. R. Telford[130] approaches the issue from the stance of historical-critical method, though acknowledgment of the newer literary approaches is made at various points. First, Telford discusses the historical setting; the theology of Mark, in which he deals with the person, message, and mission of Jesus; the characters, reporting largely on redaction-critical discussions; and the purpose of Mark. Next, Telford discusses Mark's contribution to the theology of the NT, and in the final chapter provides a brief overview of the reception of Mark

127. Dawson, *Freedom as Liberating Power.*
128. Bolt, *Jesus' Defeat of Death.*
129. See the list of parallels in language and concepts between Mark's portrayal of Jesus and the imperial rhetoric in Evans, *Mark,* lxxx–xciii. Still more parallels could be added.
130. Telford, *Theology of Mark.*

throughout the centuries, and the contribution that Mark has to make in the contemporary world.

Telford's approach is that of a former era in which the theology of Mark was gained by an analysis of Mark's redactional activity in relation to the reconstructed audience to whom he was supposedly writing. But, as we noted with respect to the return to history, any return to theology should now be done as postnarrative study. Careful attention to Mark's narrative and to its rhetoric, as well as to its intertextual links to the OT,[131] should open up the theological significance of the historical events portrayed. Numerous "theological" themes continue to be discussed, but there is plenty more that can be done in this regard.

In particular, attention should continue to be paid to Mark's Christology. As we saw, one of the unfortunate results of redaction criticism was that the Gospel, while purporting to be about Jesus, was treated as if it was about the church. The shift toward narrative, with its recognition that Jesus is Mark's central character, as well as the renewed respectability of the view that Mark's genre is akin to biography, have reasserted the importance of Jesus to the theology of Mark.

It is no surprise, therefore, that studies in Mark's Christology continue to be published. The shift to narrative has also seen a corresponding shift in approach. Whereas Christology under the historical-critical paradigm mainly focused upon Jesus' titles and their history, in 1975 Robert Tannehill began a new trend when he briefly explored Mark as "narrative Christology."[132] Once Mark's narrative Christology has been explored, the titles then can be revisited in a postnarrative perspective that seeks to expose their contribution to Mark's overall portrayal of Jesus.[133]

As other themes are studied, it will be important for interpreters to analyze these themes by reference to Mark's overall message about Jesus.

Resources for the Study of Mark

At the beginning of the twenty-first century, students of Mark are well served with resources. Monographs devoted to particular passages of Mark

131. According to Mark, the theological significance of the events associated with Jesus' life, death, and resurrection is gained largely by reference to the OT. Mark's text forms clear intertextual links with a number of OT books, perhaps especially Isaiah (see R. E. Watts, *Isaiah's New Exodus and Mark*, WUNT 2.88 [Tübingen: Mohr, 1997; reprint, Grand Rapids: Baker, 2000]; S. E. Dowd, *Reading Mark: A Literary and Theological Commentary on the Second Gospel* [Macon, Ga.: Smyth & Helwys, 2000]; R. Schneck, *Isaiah in the Gospel of Mark I–VIII*, BIBALDS 1 [Vallejo, Calif.: BIBAL Press, 1994]), Psalms, and Daniel.

132. R. C. Tannehill, "The Gospel of Mark as Narrative Christology," *Semeia* 16 (1975): 57–95.

133. See E. Broadhead, *Naming Jesus: Titular Christology in the Gospel of Mark*, JSNTSup 175 (Sheffield: Sheffield Academic Press, 1999).

continue to be published from a variety of methodological perspectives, as well as linguistic[134] and textual studies.[135] If lack of commentary was the problem in the early years, the current problem probably is oversupply! In 1985, Daniel Harrington noted the appearance of four scholarly commentaries in German since 1974 and several excellent popular commentaries in English, even if no major English scholarly commentary had appeared.[136] Since 1985, a veritable flood of commentaries has continued to flow, both at the scholarly and the popular levels. Scholarly commentaries in English include those by Mann,[137] Guelich and Evans,[138] Hooker,[139] Gundry,[140] Witherington,[141] van Iersel,[142] Marcus,[143] Donahue and Harrington,[144] Edwards,[145] and France.[146] Commentaries by Adela Yarbro Collins (Hermeneia) and R. Barbour (ICC) also are in preparation.[147] In 1991, Morna Hooker gently brought in some of the results of the literary perspective on Mark, recognizing that the nature of the questions asked by scholarship were changing,[148] but by 2002, such results have well and truly become a standard feature of the commentary.[149] Other specialty commentaries have emerged, such as that by Ben Wither-

134. See Lane, "Present State of Markan Studies." In reviewing the period 1978 to 1987, Lane summarizes the work of E. J. Pryke (1978), P. Dschulnigg (1984) on Mark's style, and E. C. Maloney (1979) and M. Reiser (1984) on Semitic influence on Mark.

135. See K. and B. Aland, *Text und Textwert der griechischen Handschriften des Neuen Testaments, IV. Die synoptischen Evangelien*, vol. 1.1–2, *Das Markusevangelium* (Berlin: de Gruyter, 1998).

136. Harrington, "Map of Books on Mark," 12, referring to commentaries by Pesch (1976–77), Gnilka (1978–79), Schmithals (1979), and Ernst (1981).

137. C. S. Mann, *Mark: A New Translation with Introduction and Commentary*, AB 27 (Garden City, N.Y.: Doubleday, 1986). This has now been replaced by the commentary written by Joel Marcus.

138. R. A. Guelich, *Mark 1–8:26*, WBC 34A (Dallas: Word, 1989); Evans, *Mark 8:27–16:20* (WBC 34B).

139. Hooker, *Gospel according to St. Mark*.

140. R. H. Gundry, *Mark: A Commentary on His Apology for the Cross* (Grand Rapids: Eerdmans, 1993).

141. B. Witherington III, *The Gospel of Mark: A Socio-Rhetorical Commentary* (Grand Rapids: Eerdmans, 2001).

142. Van Iersel, *Mark*.

143. J. Marcus, *Mark 1–8: A New Translation with Introduction and Commentary*, AB 27A (Garden City, N.Y.: Doubleday, 1999). This replaces the commentary by Mann, which adopted the "two-Gospel hypothesis" that Mark used Matthew and Luke. Marcus adopts the more usual position of Markan priority.

144. Donahue and Harrington, *Gospel of Mark*.

145. Edwards, *Gospel according to Mark*.

146. R. T. France, *The Gospel according to Mark*, NIGTC (Grand Rapids: Eerdmans; Carlisle: Paternoster, 2002).

147. See Telford, *Mark*, 11.

148. Hooker, *Gospel according to St. Mark*, 2–5.

149. According to Edwards (*Gospel according to Mark*, 3), Mark is "a skilled literary artist and theologian." Donahue and Harrington (*Gospel of Mark*, 1) describe their approach in terms of "intratextuality and intertextuality."

ington III, which purports to be the first commentary from a sociorhetorical perspective,[150] and that by Bas van Iersel, which is the first written from
a reader-response perspective.[151] The flood of popular commentaries has
been even greater: my very rough count indicates that at least fifteen were
published in the 1970s, about twenty in the 1980s, and more than thirty-
six since 1990.

The Encounter with Mark

In 1990, William Lane ended his survey by saying that "the greatest
challenge to Markan studies will be the avoidance of an approach to the
text which precludes a living encounter with its claim and witness."[152] If
anything, the recent approaches to Mark have brought Markan studies to
a position of renewed openness to this encounter. This is the explicit argument of at least one study on Mark's Christology.[153] Other studies have
discussed the literary impact of Mark on its readers.[154] The rediscovery
of the rhetorical power of Mark has led to an interest in the retelling of
Mark's stories and in the "performance" of Mark's story, in part or whole.[155]
There is also a continued interest in preaching from Mark.[156] In addition,
Telford concludes his volume on the theology of Mark by drawing out the
implications of Mark's theology for the contemporary world, commenting

150. Witherington, *Gospel of Mark.*
151. Van Iersel, *Mark.*
152. Lane, "Present State of Markan Studies," 72.
153. L. T. Johnson, *Living Jesus: Learning the Heart of the Gospel* (San Francisco: HarperSan-
Francisco, 1999). Although only part of Johnson's book is on Mark, he discusses the mystery of
Jesus being a living person in the present.
154. M. I. Wegener, *Cruciformed: The Literary Impact of Mark's Story of Jesus and His Disciples*
(Lanham, Md.: University Press of America, 1995); M. L. Minor, *The Power of Mark's Story* (St.
Louis: Chalice, 2001), which argues that the storytelling of Mark has enduring power, enabling
us to gain new insights into what it is to be human as God created us to be; J. G. Cook, *The
Structure and Persuasive Power of Mark: A Linguistic Approach,* SBL Semeia Studies (Atlanta:
Scholars Press, 1995), which proposes that the governing speech-act in Mark encourages the
reader to accept the text as good news.
155. See T. E. Boomershine, *Story Journey: An Invitation to the Gospel as Storytelling* (Nashville:
Abingdon, 1988); D. Rhoads, "Performing the Gospel of Mark," in *Body and Bible: Interpreting
and Experiencing Biblical Narratives,* ed. B. Krondorfer (Philadelphia: Trinity, 1992), 102–19.
Boomershine also explored the rhetoric of Mark in his doctoral thesis, "Mark, the Storyteller:
A Rhetorical-Critical Investigation of Mark's Passion and Resurrection Narrative" (Ph.D. diss.,
Union Theological Seminary, New York, 1974), and has been working with the American Bible
Society on a multimedia "translation" of Mark.
156. B. Thurston, *Preaching Mark* (Minneapolis: Fortress, 2002); R. S. Reid, *Preaching
Mark* (St. Louis: Chalice, 1999); D. J. Ourisman, *From Gospel to Sermon: Preaching Synoptic
Texts* (St. Louis: Chalice, 2000); R. A. Jensen, *Preaching Mark's Gospel: A Narrative Approach*
(Lima, Ohio: CSS, 1996).

upon various issues for discipleship, ethics, politics, gender, and the church's relationship to Judaism.[157]

Markan studies have come a long way. At the beginning of this new century, Mark should be respected as a narrative that purports to tell an account of the historical events surrounding the life of Jesus, and a narrative with a theological purpose for those living in the first-century Greco-Roman world. Mark proclaimed Jesus to be the Christ, the Son of God—crucified and then raised. According to Mark, these events have enormous theological significance, for they are God's events that hold promise for the coming kingdom. Future Markan studies will, no doubt, have much more to say about "the beginning of the good news" that was launched upon the ancient world and even today still manages to turn heads and touch lives.

157. Telford, *Theology of Mark*, ch. 4.

20

Hebrews in Its First-Century Contexts

Recent Research

George H. Guthrie

The Book of Hebrews has been called "the Cinderella" of NT studies,[1] and, as research on the book progresses, the word picture increasingly fits on several levels. In the middle part of the twentieth century this Cinderella was seen as somewhat out of place in her home of the NT canon. She was, like the Melchizedek of whom she speaks, a mystery, a puzzle, without clear origin or agreed-upon purpose, living in the shadow of aggressive research especially on Paul and the Gospels (not that Paul and the Gospels are analogous to the wicked stepsisters!). No readily identifiable author, few firm clues as to date and recipients, patterns of thought that seemed to place her outside the mainstream of NT theology, and a style clearly superior to the bulk of the first Christians' literature all marked Hebrews as an anomaly. She had her admirers, but, based on volume of research, they were comparatively few.

Yet, at the dawn of the twenty-first century, we may be turning a page to another development in the story—this Cinderella seems to have come out of obscurity and to be on her way to the ball. The past fifteen years have witnessed a steady stream of commentaries, monographs, and articles on Hebrews, and dis-

1. J. C. McCullough, "Hebrews in Recent Scholarship," *IBS* 16 (April 1994): 66.

sertation research focused on the book seems to be on the rise. As demonstrated in this essay, she has been the object of literary analyses, studies in comparative backgrounds, rhetorical analyses, sociorhetorical analyses, discourse analyses, and a host of conceptual studies. Not that Hebrews, for all her eloquence and depth, will garner the center place of attention in the dance of biblical studies, but she is coming out of the shadows, and those committed to the advance of biblical studies should note and celebrate the heightened attention. What is emerging is an understanding that Hebrews' background of thought is complex and read inadequately against a simple or single cultural or theological context. Hebrews forms a point of convergence for several first-century "worlds." Further, recent research demonstrates that for all its mysteries and unique features, Hebrews has a more systemic connection with the rest of NT literature, and therefore with emergent first-century Christianity, than previously suspected and therefore has much to offer to broader conversations on NT thought.

The purpose of this essay is to portray the state of research on the Book of Hebrews, as that research sheds light on the book's relationship to Greco-Roman, Jewish, and early-Christian contexts. We begin with a brief survey of articles and works that provide an overview of study accomplished on Hebrews' background and framework of thought. Then, working our way from the broadest sociophilosophical context—the Greco-Roman world itself—to Hebrews' most immediate context as part of the first-century Christian movement, we consider the various cultural and theological contexts to which Hebrews might be said to relate, attempting to highlight the recent trends and the trajectories to which contemporary scholarship seems to be leading.

Overviews of Hebrews Research

To put the larger context of Hebrews research in perspective, we begin with several previous overviews that present recent scholarly discussions on the book.[2] In the past quarter century, and in addition to treatments in major commentaries, there have been at least five such attempts in the form of articles and monographs. In 1980–81, J. C. McCullough wrote a two-part article in *Irish Biblical Studies*[3] covering the topics of authorship, religious background

---

2. The current discussion focuses especially on work accomplished since the mid-1980s. For important earlier overviews on Hebrews research, see Erich Grässer, "Der Hebräerbrief 1938–1963," *TRu* 30 (1964): 138–236, now republished in Erich Grässer, *Aufbruch und Verheißung: Gesammelte Aufsätze zum Hebräerbrief,* ed. Martin Evang and Otto Merk, BZNW 65 (Berlin and New York: de Gruyter, 1992), 1–99; Ceslas Spicq, "Hébreux (Épître aux)," *DBSup* 7:226–79; G. W. Buchanan, "The Present State of Scholarship on Hebrews," in *Judaism, Christianity, and Other Greco-Roman Cults,* ed. Jacob Neusner, 4 vols., SJLA 12 (Leiden: Brill, 1975), 1:299–330.

3. J. C. McCullough, "Some Recent Developments in Research on the Epistle to the Hebrews," *IBS* 2 (1980): 141–65; 3 (1981): 28–43. The layout of the article may seem a bit quirky

(with discussions of Hebrews and Philo, Hebrews and Qumran, gnosticism, and Merkabah mysticism), the date and the area to which Hebrews was sent, literary genre, literary structure, use of the OT (the focus of McCullough's doctoral dissertation[4] and including the issues of text and exegetical methods), and a review of work on "Individual Themes and Passages" (specifically, treatment of the theme "covenant" and the passage 6:4–6). As the title suggests, McCullough was not attempting to be comprehensive. Rather, he focused on contributions made in the areas considered over roughly the prior two decades. His sections on religious background and use of the OT are the most helpful.

A much more extensive review of Hebrews research came in 1985 with Helmut Feld's *Der Hebräerbrief.*[5] Feld specifically reviewed work accomplished since the publication of Erich Grässer's great *Forschungsbericht,* "Der Hebräerbrief 1938–1963,"[6] while drawing in older works that demanded attention as formative to contemporary discussion on a given topic. Under questions concerning the historical backdrop of Hebrews, Feld addressed authorship, the recipients and destination, date, the occasion and intention, genre, literary structure, the religious and literary-historical background (including use of the OT, contours of ancient Judaism, gnosticism, and relation to broader NT thought), and history of interpretation. The balance of the book, some eighty pages, covers a helpful section on theological issues and an extensive bibliography. The theological issues addressed are Hebrews' primary, or fundamental, motif; the significance of the OT; the book's Christology (including the Son of God, the earthly Jesus, and the high priest motif); the heavenly cult and the new covenant; creation and eschatology; the Christian life (including faith, apostasy, and life in the community of faith); and evaluations of Hebrews' thought and logic. Feld's review of literature, though wide-ranging and aware of the most important research done on Hebrews in recent decades, has a firm orientation toward German scholarship on the book, that stream of research anchored especially by the influence of Ernst Käsemann and Erich Grässer.

---

at first glance because the author addresses "Authorship," followed by an extended section on "Religious Background," then "Date and Audience," but McCullough's prime conclusion on date and audience stems from the discussion of religious background. That conclusion—that little can be said on the book's date and audience—is accented by little else than the oft-quoted terminus ad quem of 96 C.E., the supposed date of *1 Clement.* Also, the section on "Individual Themes and Passages" in reality focuses on one theme (the concept "covenant") and one passage (6:4–6), but the discussions there, although somewhat out of step with an article meant to be a general review, are nonetheless helpful.

4. J. C. McCullough, "Hebrews and the Old Testament" (Ph.D. diss., Queen's University, Belfast, 1971).

5. Helmut Feld, *Der Hebräerbrief,* EdF 228 (Darmstadt: Wissenschaftliche Buchgesellschaft, 1985).

6. Erich Grässer, "Der Hebräerbrief 1938–1963," *TRu* 30 (1964): 138–236.

A book of a different nature, yet vitally important for our current project, is Lincoln Hurst's rigorous work.[7] Shortened from Hurst's doctoral thesis accomplished under the direction of G. B. Caird at the University of Oxford, the monograph is, nonetheless, a detailed and insightful delving into the various suggestions made concerning the framework of Hebrews' thought. Hurst approaches his treatment in two major movements. The first, "Non-Christian Backgrounds," considers in order "Philo, Alexandria and Platonism," "Qumran," and "Other non-Christian backgrounds," including "Gnosticism," "The Samaritans," and "*Merkabah* mysticism." The section on "Christian Backgrounds" constitutes the book's second main movement. Here, Hurst reflects on "The Stephen Tradition," Hebrews' connections with "Pauline theology," and "First Peter." Hurst concludes that Hebrews has been influenced especially by christological reading of sections of the LXX, the Christian traditions preserved in Acts 7, interaction with "Paul-like" theology, and Jewish apocalyptic.[8] Perhaps one of Hurst's most significant contributions is his building on earlier work, especially that of Ronald Williamson,[9] whom some consider to have devastated the seemingly unassailable position, held at the middle part of the last century, that Hebrews is essentially Platonic/Philonic in nature. In an extensive treatment of those passages said to mark Hebrews as in line with Philo's thought-world, and extending Williamson's work by a thorough consideration of the terms ὑπόδειγμα, σκία, ἀντίτυπος, ἀληθινός, and εἰκών, Hurst has shown these terms, as used in Hebrews, to fit quite adequately within a Jewish apocalyptic framework.

In April and June of 1994, J. C. McCullough revisited and updated aspects of his examination of Hebrews scholarship, again with a two-part article in *Irish Biblical Studies.*[10] Here, McCullough documented the "mini revival in interest in Hebrews" in the thirteen years since his previous articles were published. Whereas the period from 1960 to 1979 saw fewer than twenty commentaries and fewer than ten monographs published, the years 1980 to 1993 witnessed the release of approximately forty commentaries—some of them quite substantive—and nearly forty monographs. McCullough's two-part article focused on the commentaries, monographs, and articles of this latter period. With the exception of "Use of the Old Testament in Hebrews" and his treatment of "individual themes and passages," McCullough retraced the primary issues of background covered in the earlier two-part article: authorship, recipients

---

7. L. D. Hurst, *The Epistle to the Hebrews: Its Background of Thought*, SNTSMS 65 (Cambridge: Cambridge University Press, 1990). On the background of Hebrews' thought, see also Jeremy Punt, "Hebrews, Thought-Patterns and Context: Aspects of the Background of Hebrews," *Neot* 31 (1997): 119–58.

8. Ibid., 133.

9. Ronald Williamson, *Philo and the Epistle to the Hebrews*, ALGHJ 4 (Leiden: Brill, 1970).

10. J. C. McCullough, "Hebrews in Recent Scholarship," *IBS* 16 (April 1994): 66–86; (June 1994): 108–20.

(including issues of ethnicity, destination of the book, and occasion), genre and structure, and date. The important topic of the book's background of thought was covered under discussion of the author's profile (rather than his identity), which, as McCullough pointed out, has become the central discussion on the authorship of Hebrews. The omission of a discussion on use of the OT in Hebrews perhaps reflects a lack of wide-ranging advances being made in that area of research during this thirteen-year period.[11]

Also published in 1994 was Craig Koester's survey,[12] which nicely complements McCullough's articles. In addition to a section on the "Historical, Social and Religious Context" of Hebrews, he evaluates a few of the recent commentaries on the book, addresses literary and rhetorical studies of Hebrews, considers certain theological themes and important passages, and offers a brief section on the "History of Interpretation and Influence." The section on theological themes and important passages provides a brief review of numerous monographs and essays in recent study. Koester extends this overview greatly in his recently published commentary in the Anchor Bible series.[13] There, he covers a helpful "History of Interpretation and Influence," discussing four major eras of church history, the "Social Setting" of Hebrews, "Formal and Rhetorical Aspects" of the book, "Selected Issues in the Theology of Hebrews," and the "Text of Hebrews."

In addition to Koester's, three major commentaries demand mention at this point. The magisterial two-volume commentary by William L. Lane offers a prodigious introduction to Hebrews, which is detailed, lucid, and thorough.[14]

11. Yet, work was being done on several levels. See R. E. Clements, "The Use of the Old Testament in Hebrews," *SwJT* 28 (1985): 36–45; M. L. Loane, "The Unity of the Old and New Testaments as Illustrated in the Epistle to the Hebrews," in *God Who Is Rich in Mercy*, ed. P. T. O'Brien and D. G. Peterson (Homebush West, N.S.W.: Lancer, 1986), 255–64; P. G. Müller, "Die Funktion der Psalmzitate im Hebräerbrief," in *Freude an der Weisung des Herrn*, ed. E. Haag and F. L. Hossfeld, SBB 13 (Stuttgart: Katholisches Bibelwerk, 1986), 223–42; M. R. Cosby, *The Rhetorical Composition and Function of Hebrews 11 in Light of Example Lists in Ancient Antiquity* (Macon, Ga.: Mercer University Press, 1988 [publication of his 1985 dissertation done at Emory University]). Other dissertations from the period include Herbert W. Bateman, "Jewish and Apostolic Hermeneutics: How the Old Testament Is Used in Hebrews 1:5–13 (Dead Sea Scrolls)" (Ph.D. diss., Dallas Theological Seminary, 1993; published by Lang, 1997); Dale Leschert, "Hermeneutical Foundations of the Epistle to the Hebrews: A Study in the Validity of Its Interpretation of Some Core Citations from the Psalms" (Ph.D. diss., Fuller Theological Seminary, 1991; published by Mellen, 1994); Charles P. Baylis, "The Author of Hebrews' Use of Melchizedek from the Context of Genesis" (Ph.D. diss., Dallas Theological Seminary, 1989); Fred A. Malone, "A Critical Evaluation of the Use of Jeremiah 31:31–34 in the Letter to the Hebrews" (Ph.D. diss., Southwestern Baptist Theological Seminary, 1989).

12. Craig R. Koester, "The Epistle to the Hebrews in Recent Study," *CurBS* 2 (1994): 123–45.

13. Craig R. Koester, *Hebrews: A New Translation with Introduction and Commentary*, AB 36 (New York: Doubleday, 2001), 19–168.

14. William L. Lane, *Hebrews 1–8*, WBC 47A (Dallas: Word, 1991); *Hebrews 9–13*, WBC 47B (Dallas: Word, 1991).

Lane's great strength is the combination of his grasp of the significance of background issues with exegetical insights and theological reflection. His arguments concerning aspects of the backdrop of Hebrews' thought-world and circumstances are thought through well and are, to my mind, often convincing.

Although his introduction to the book is thin compared to the treatments of Lane and Koester, there is nothing thin about the exegetical interaction with ancient contexts and literatures in Harold Attridge's commentary.[15] It is replete with cross-references to the OT and Apocrypha, the Pseudepigrapha, Qumran literature, Talmud, Mishnah, Josephus, Philo, and a host of Greek and Latin authors. Also see Hans-Friedrich Weiss's commentary, which, in almost one hundred pages, covers Hebrews' literary character and structure, the book's foundational concern and purpose, its place in early Christianity, its place in the broader religious world of the time, its history of reception in the church, and its text.[16]

None of the works mentioned here is comprehensive, but taken together, they provide a strong introduction to work done on Hebrews in the past, and thus they are recommended reading for those beginning to consider research on the book.

Hebrews in Its First-Century Contexts

Hebrews and Greco-Roman Conventions

Students of the book have long recognized Hebrews as exceptional for its excellent Greek, use of numerous stylistic devices, methods of argument, and expansive vocabulary, all of which mark the book as the product of someone widely read and highly educated in Greco-Roman forms. What studies of recent years have made abundantly clear is that these features constitute the prime connecting point between Hebrews and its broad social context. That is, Hebrews' skill in the employment of broadly used linguistic and rhetorical conventions stands as the most obvious influence of the Greco-Roman world on our author.

Examples of Rhetorical Conventions and the Author's Rich Vocabulary

As one example of a rhetorical convention, a number of scholars have noted the use of *synkrisis*, or comparison, in Hebrews.[17] Timothy W. Seid has given

---

15. Harold Attridge, *The Epistle to the Hebrews: A Commentary on the Epistle to the Hebrews,* Hermeneia (Philadelphia: Fortress, 1989).

16. Hans-Friedrich Weiss, *Der Brief an die Hebräer: Übersetzt und erklärt,* KEK 13 (Göttingen: Vandenhoeck & Ruprecht, 1991), 35–132.

17. For example, Attridge, *Epistle to the Hebrews,* 104; David E. Aune, *The New Testament in Its Literary Environment* (Philadelphia: Westminster, 1987), 213; Thomas H. Olbricht, "Hebrews

this rhetorical device extensive treatment in his dissertation.[18] Seid argues that Heb. 7—in its detailed treatment of parentage, genealogy, birth, death, office, actions, status, ancestry, and achievements—conforms to the genre of *synkrisis* in line with Greco-Roman epideictic oratory.

Another example of a rhetorical convention is the use of *exempla,* and at least three works have focused specifically on the rhetorical force of the *exempla* in Heb. 11. In 1985, Michael R. Cosby produced an Emory University dissertation, later published as a monograph and summarized in a *Journal of Biblical Literature* article.[19] Cosby demonstrated that the pronounced use of anaphora, asyndeton, and other techniques was present widely in example lists of the ancient world. Rather than intending simply to inform, the author constructed the example list of Heb. 11 for rhetorical force through a dynamic building up of evidence presented with repetition of certain clausal patterns. The effect was to overwhelm the hearers with the rightness of responding to God in faith, so that they might emulate those who serve as examples from the past.

A decade later, Alan D. Bulley attempted to extend Cosby's work by examining features of epideictic rhetoric related to orations given in celebration of the dead, and demonstrating the interrelationship of the concepts of faith, suffering, and death.[20] Bulley concluded that in form the *exempla* of Heb. 11 is epideictic, but in function it is deliberative rhetoric, and suggested that the themes of suffering and death form a key connecting point between the expositional and hortatory movements of the book.

Finally, Pamela Eisenbaum wrote a dissertation that sought to demonstrate the use of the heroes of Heb. 11 to denationalize biblical history.[21] Eisenbaum perceptively raised the question concerning the criteria by which these heroes and their specific highlighted characteristics were chosen. She concludes that the key criterion in a profile of these people is their marginalization in relation to the nation of Israel. Thus, they are "transvalued"—that is, the value

---

as Amplification," in *Rhetoric and the New Testament: Essays from the 1992 Heidelberg Conference,* ed. S. E. Porter and T. H. Olbricht, JSNTSup 90 (Sheffield: JSOT Press, 1993), 375–87.

18. Timothy W. Seid, "The Rhetorical Form of the Melchizedek/Christ Comparison in Hebrews 7" (Ph.D. diss., Brown University, 1996). See also idem, "Synkrisis in Hebrews 7: The Rhetorical Structure and Strategy," in *The Rhetorical Interpretation of Scripture: Essays from the 1996 Malibu Conference,* ed. S. E. Porter and D. L. Stamps, JSNTSup 180 (Sheffield: Sheffield Academic Press, 1999), 322–47.

19. Michael R. Cosby, *The Rhetorical Composition and Function of Hebrews 11, in Light of Example Lists in Antiquity* (Macon, Ga.: Mercer University Press, 1988); idem, "The Rhetorical Composition of Hebrews 11," *JBL* 107 (1988): 257–73.

20. Alan D. Bulley, "Death and Rhetoric in the Hebrews 'Hymn to Faith,'" *SR* 25 (1996): 409–23.

21. Pamela M. Eisenbaum, "The Jewish Heroes of Christian History: Hebrews 11 in Literary Context" (Ph.D. diss., Columbia University, 1996); published in summary form as "Heroes and History in Hebrews 11," in *Early Christian Interpretation of the Scriptures of Israel: Investigations and Proposals,* ed. Craig A. Evans and James A. Sanders, JSNTSup 148 (Sheffield: Sheffield Academic Press, 1997), 380–96.

normally placed on these people as national heroes has been transformed into another value: they were faithful as the marginalized. Thus, the author of Hebrews uses them as good examples to Christians who are struggling with being marginalized, giving them a biblical ancestry without national identity. So on Eisenbaum's reading, Heb. 11, by its use of *exempla,* is an innovative Christian interpretation of biblical history.

N. Clayton Croy provides yet other examples of Hebrews' use of rhetorical conventions.[22] First, he considers the image of Jesus as the model athlete in Heb. 12:1–3, which the author has shaped according to rhetorical theory of *exempla,* to challenge the hearers to endurance as those running a race. The Hellenistic moralists often used athletic imagery to encourage endurance. Second, Croy demonstrates that the use of *paideia* in Heb. 12:4–13, rather than being intended as punitive, is a nonpunitive, educational notion that has precedent in both Jewish and Greco-Roman writings, but especially can be found in the later Stoics. Further, Croy shows that athletic imagery and nonpunitive forms of moral discipline often were used together as mutually reinforcing concepts.[23]

Highlighting prominent social dynamics as used in Hebrews has been the focus of David deSilva in a number of works. His dissertation under Luke Timothy Johnson has been published, and he has authored a sociorhetorical commentary that incorporates his insights on this dynamic.[24] DeSilva has worked out a model for analyzing how honor/shame language works in ancient Greco-Roman societies. From deSilva's perspective, the original hearers of Hebrews were challenged to value honor in relation to God in light of the patron-client relationship established by Christ, and therefore to choose to be shamed by the world. Although such a model, when overdone, lends itself to reductionism in the particulars of Hebrews interpretation, deSilva has fashioned a lens through which a very fresh reading of parts of Hebrews may be accomplished.

All of the studies mentioned in this section demonstrate that Hebrews utilizes certain rhetorical devices commonly found in the literature and oratory of the Greco-Roman world. In addition, I mention the following stylistic

22. N. Clayton Croy, *Endurance in Suffering: Hebrews 12:1–13 in Its Rhetorical, Religious, and Philosophical Context,* SNTSMS 98 (Cambridge: Cambridge University Press, 1998); based on Croy's "Endurance in Suffering: A Study of Hebrews 12:1–13 in Its Rhetorical, Religious, and Philosophical Context" (Ph.D. diss., Emory University, 1995).

23. Ibid., 217.

24. David deSilva, *Despising Shame: Honor Discourse and Community Maintenance in the Epistle to the Hebrews,* SBLDS 152 (Atlanta: Scholars Press, 1995); based on deSilva's "Despising Shame: The Social Function of the Rhetoric of Honor and Dishonor in the Epistle to the Hebrews" (Ph.D. diss., Emory University, 1995); *Perseverance in Gratitude: A Socio-Rhetorical Commentary on the Epistle "to the Hebrews"* (Grand Rapids: Eerdmans, 2000); see also idem, "The Epistle to the Hebrews in Social-Scientific Perspective," *ResQ* 36 (1994): 1–21; "Exchanging Favor for Wrath: Apostasy in Hebrews and Patron-Client Relationships," *JBL* 115 (1996): 91–116.

devices, all found in the rhetorical handbooks of the era, which have been identified as present in Hebrews.[25] The author crafts his text with various uses of rhythm, periodic style (linking of numerous clauses, covering various topics in a well-rounded unity, knit together in a complex construction [e.g., 1:1–4]), rhetorical questions, alliteration, anaphora (repetition of a certain word), antithesis (juxtaposition of contrasting concepts), assonance (repetition of sounds in words or syllables), asyndeton (clauses, or words in a list, juxtaposed without intervening conjunctions), polysyndeton (repetition of conjunctions in clause after clause), brachylogy (simplifying an expression to a type of shorthand), chiasm, ellipsis, hendiadys (communicating a single idea with two terms), hyperbaton (separating words that naturally belong together), isocolon (parallel clauses that are equally balanced), litotes (use of a double negative), *inclusio* (presenting a statement at the beginning of a section, an approximation of which is repeated at the end of the section), "hook-words" (a transition using a term, or terms, at the end of one section and the beginning of the next), and paronomasia (etymological play on words). To these basic features of style can be added figures of speech such as metaphor, metonymy (replacing a word with another that has some relation to it), synecdoche (a part of something represents the whole), hyperbole, and antonomasia (replacing a name with a paraphrase).

Further, researchers have long recognized Hebrews' rich and varied use of vocabulary, with some 169 terms that occur nowhere else in the NT. Studies continue on the meanings of certain obscure terms, some giving insight to issues of interpretation and translation. For example, in a 1997 essay, John Lee considers the author's use of the word ἕξις at Heb. 5:14, demonstrating that the common translation of the term along the lines of "practice" has no basis in the word's use in the ancient world.[26] Yet, this mistranslation and its related misinterpretation are ubiquitous, and the history of misunderstanding dates back to the Vulgate. Rather, the term connotes a state or condition. Thus understood, the author of Hebrews asserts that the spiritually mature, by virtue of their *state of maturity*, possess senses trained to discern the difference between good and evil.

Hebrews' Structure and Greco-Roman Conventions

Works on the structure of the book have done much to demonstrate the author's expertise, his command of complex and interwoven techniques, in crafting a discourse. Approaches to Hebrews' structure can be divided into those that essentially are thematically oriented, literary approaches, rhetorical

25. Among recent commentaries, see especially Attridge, *Epistle to the Hebrews*, 20–21; Koester, *Hebrews*, 92–96.

26. John A. Lee, "Hebrews 5:14 and ῞ΕΞΙΣ: A History of Misunderstanding," *NovT* 39 (1997): 151–76.

approaches, those in which key OT passages are seen as providing a framework for the book, and linguistic approaches.[27] Of these approaches, the rhetorical, literary, and linguistic all depend to some extent on rhetorical features borrowed from the Greco-Roman world.

First, attempts at pegging Hebrews with the species of rhetoric or a pattern of the oratorical speeches of the day have been less than successful. Such attempts are nothing new. The older works of Niels Hemmingsen, Hermann F. von Soden, Theodore Haering, and Hans Windisch presented the structure of Hebrews according to patterns in ancient Greek oratory.[28] More recently, Barnabas Lindars sought to review the Book of Hebrews by examining the rhetorical impact of each section of the book on the first hearers. Although not addressing a coherent structure for the whole book, he concludes that Hebrews falls in line with deliberative rhetoric, a species of rhetoric that sought to challenge the hearers to follow a course of action.[29] Others have understood Hebrews to be more in line with epideictic rhetoric, a species that sought to shore up the values of the hearers by exalting those characteristics that were worthy of praise and condemning actions that were shameful.[30] Harold Attridge contends, "It is clearly an epideictic oration, celebrating the significance of Christ and inculcating values that his followers ought to share."[31]

Like the older works of von Soden and Haering, other recent studies have sought to identify Hebrews' structure according to oratorical patterns from types of speeches. Walter G. Übelacker offers an extensive treatment that addresses Hebrews' structure.[32] Übelacker also reads Hebrews

27. See George H. Guthrie, *The Structure of Hebrews: A Text-Linguistic Analysis*, NovTSup 73 (Leiden: Brill, 1994), 23–41; Albert Vanhoye, *La structure littéraire de l'Épître aux Hébreux*, 2nd ed. (Lyon: Desclée de Brouwer, 1976), 13–15; Walter G. Übelacker, *Der Hebräerbrief als Appell: Untersuchungen zu exordium, narration und postscriptum (Hebr 1–2 und 13,22–25)*, ConBNT 21 (Stockholm: Almqvist & Wiksell, 1989), 40–48. For those who have sought to assess Hebrews' structure on the framework established by key OT texts in the book, see G. B. Caird, "The Exegetical Method of the Epistle to the Hebrews," *CJT* 5 (1959): 44–51; R. N. Longenecker, *Biblical Exegesis in the Apostolic Period* (Grand Rapids: Eerdmans, 1975), 175–85; R. T. France, "The Writer of Hebrews as a Biblical Expositor," *TynBul* 47 (1996): 245–76; John Walters, "The Rhetorical Arrangement of Hebrews," *AsTJ* 51 (1996): 59–70.

28. Niels Hemmingsen, *Commentaria in omnes Epistolas Apostolorum, Pauli, Petri, Iudae, Ioannis, Iacobi, et in eam quae ad Hebraeos inscribitur* (Frankfurt: Georg Corvinus, 1579), 831 (quoted in Kenneth Hagen, *Hebrews Commenting from Erasmus to Bèze, 1516–1598*, BGBE 23 [Tübingen: Mohr Siebeck, 1981], 80–81); Hermann F. von Soden, *Urchristliche Literaturgeschichte: Die Schriften des Neuen Testaments* (Berlin: Alexander Duncker, 1905), 8–11, 127–28; Theodore Haering, "Gedankengang und Grundgedanken des Hebräerbriefs," *ZNW* 18 (1917–18): 153; Hans Windisch, *Der Hebräerbrief*, HNT 14 (Tübingen: Mohr Siebeck, 1931), 8.

29. Barnabas Lindars, "The Rhetorical Structure of Hebrews," *NTS* 35 (1989): 382–406.

30. On the various suggestions concerning Hebrews' species of rhetoric, see Koester, *Hebrews*, 82; Lane, *Hebrews 1–8*, lxxviii–lxxix.

31. Attridge, *Epistle to the Hebrews*, 14.

32. Übelacker, *Der Hebräerbrief als Appell*, 66–138.

as a deliberative discourse, identifying a *prooemium* (1:1–4), *narratio* with *propositio* (1:5–2:18), *argumentatio* with *probatio* and *refutatio* (3:1–12:29), *peroratio* (13:1–21), and *postscriptum* (13:22–25). His treatment of 1:1–4 and to a lesser degree 1:5–2:18 constitute the focus of his monograph, and the analysis of the rest of the book flows from his detailed examination of these two sections.

Seeking to understand the function of the high priest motif in the book, Keijo Nissilä also has produced a rhetorical analysis of Hebrews.[33] He examines nine passages in Hebrews, taking each through a *Textanalyse* and *Motivanalyse,* the latter always ending with a consideration of *die rhetorische Anwendung* (the rhetorical use of the high priest motif in that passage). Nissilä's outline of Hebrews divides the book into an *exordium* (1:1–4), *narratio* (1:5–2:18), *argumentatio* (3:1–12:29), and *epilogus* (13:1–25).

One trend in Hebrews research, even among those sympathetic to insights from rhetorical criticism, is to recognize that attempts either at identifying Hebrews with one species of rhetoric or at superimposing a set rhetorical pattern on the book are, in the end, not helpful.[34] William Lane states flatly, "Hebrews cannot be forced into the mold of a classical speech."[35] Nevertheless, the extensive use of rhetorical *style* is beyond question.

Literary analyses of Hebrews, anchored especially in the influential work of Albert Vanhoye, identify key literary dynamics in the text that mark the text's divisions. Vanhoye offered five literary devices as keys to understanding Hebrews' structure: the announcement of the subject, hook-words, change in genre, characteristic terms, and uses of *inclusio.*[36] More recently, I offered an eclectic approach combining identification of techniques highlighted by earlier literary approaches, identification of types of transition techniques, and various other linguistic methods in a discourse analysis of the text.[37] I challenged Vanhoye's work at a numerous points, preeminently his lack of attention to a prominent *inclusio* at 4:14–16 and 10:19–25. However, both Vanhoye's work and mine make clear that the use of techniques such as *inclusio* and hook-words, which were employed widely in ancient Greek literature,[38] plays a significant role in marking the structure of Hebrews.

33. Keijo Nissilä, *Das Hohepriestermotiv im Hebräerbrief: Eine exegetische Untersuchung,* Schriften der Finnischen exegetischen Gesellschaft 33 (Helsinki: Oy Liiton Kirjapaino, 1979), 1–5.

34. See, for example, David A. deSilva, *Perseverance in Gratitude,* 57; Koester, *Hebrews,* 82. Koester notes that the classical handbooks recognized that deliberative and epideictic rhetoric were found often in the same speech (see Aristotle, *Rhetoric* 1.9.36; Quintilian, *Inst.* 3.7.28).

35. Lane, *Hebrews 1–8,* lxxix.

36. Vanhoye, *La structure littéraire de l'Épître aux Hébreux,* 37.

37. Guthrie, *The Structure of Hebrews.*

38. See Richard Volkmann, *Die Rhetorik der Griechen und Römer in systematischer Übersicht* (Leipzig: Teubner, 1885), 438, 471; Heinrich Lausberg, *Handbuch der literarischen Rhetorik: Eine Grundlegung der Literaturwissenschaft* (Munich: Hueber, 1960), 1.

Conclusion

Various works in recent years on Hebrews' stylistic and structural techniques, vocabulary, and rhetorical conventions clearly demonstrate that the book's author was highly educated and highly skilled in written and spoken discourse of the Greco-Roman world. Thus, that world provided the author with the means for dynamic and complex communication of his message. As we move to the next first-century context—the influence of broader Judaism—we continue to deal with methodologies of communication but also begin to confront questions of Hebrews' background of thought.

Hebrews and Broader Judaism

On even the most casual reading of Hebrews, one cannot miss the book's orientation toward Jewish concerns, both in its extensive use of the Jewish Scriptures and in its theological interests. Thus, attempts at narrowing the scope of influences on Hebrews have focused on various expressions of Judaism in the first century, some with more success than others.

Merkabah Mysticism, Gnosticism, and Qumran

For instance, the endeavor to put forward Merkabah mysticism as a primary backdrop for the book's thought must be said to have failed, as Craig Koester recognizes: "Mystic traditions . . . are now widely acknowledged to be of little help in interpreting Hebrews."[39] This was done first by H.-M. Schenke, and later by Ronald Williamson and O. Hofius.[40] Lincoln Hurst has demonstrated that the parallels suggested by Williamson and others can be explained by sources or influences common to both Merkabah mysticism and Hebrews, such as the psalms and writings from apocalyptic Judaism; Williamson himself concedes the point.[41] Further, most of the literature to which these writers appeal for insights into Merkabah mysticism is post-NT, which raises the question whether there was an entity in existence in the first century that can be labeled "Merkabah mysticism."[42]

This state of affairs is very similar to that surrounding suggestions of a gnostic backdrop for Hebrews. The gnostic proposition has been especially popular in

---

39. Koester, "Hebrews in Recent Study," 132.

40. H.-M. Schenke, "Erwägung zum Rätsel des Hebräerbriefes," in *Neues Testament und christliche Existenz,* ed. H. D. Betz and L. Schottroff (Tübingen: Mohr Siebeck, 1973), 433–34; Ronald Williamson, "The Background of the Epistle to the Hebrews," *ExpTim* 87 (1975–76): 232–37; O. Hofius, *Der Vorhang vor dem Thron Gottes: Eine exegetisch-religionsgeschichtliche Untersuchung zu Hebräer 6:19f. und 10:19f.,* WUNT 14 (Tübingen: Mohr Siebeck, 1972).

41. Hurst, *Epistle to the Hebrews,* 82–85; Williamson, "Background of the Epistle," 236.

42. Hurst, *Epistle to the Hebrews,* 84–85.

German scholarship, running from Ernst Käsemann's 1939 monograph *Das wandernde Gottesvolk* (translated as *The Wandering People of God* in 1984) to the major works in the 1960s by Erich Grässer and Gerd Theissen.[43] On the surface, the gnostic interpretation model as applied to Hebrews seems suggestive at points. The "wandering people" motif, with its subtopic of "rest,"[44] parallels the gnostic idea of the journey of the soul from the dark material world to the heavenly realm, and Jesus' journey and work can be read against the backdrop of the "redeemer myth." Yet, the difficulty of establishing the origin, nature, and exact era of gnosticism, and a "redeemer myth," is notorious. Moreover, the purported parallels have reasonable explanations in mainline Jewish currents of the first century. One scholar has stated: "One may wonder how fragmented, how significant, and how widespread a 'movement' it was," and "theories of first-century Christian debt to 'a Gnostic myth' assume a very significant degree of influence from a group which was evidently writing nothing of consequence and against whom we do not possess unambiguous examples of polemic."[45] As Hurst notes, "With a few exceptions, the gnostic approach to Hebrews has made little impact upon responsible interpretation."[46]

Potentially more compelling have been attempts to find Hebrews' background of thought at Qumran.[47] Here is a body of literature with a number of parallels with Hebrews, such as a significant role for angels, various messianic conceptions, aspects of eschatological outlook, the significance of Moses and the prophet(s), and uses of the OT.[48] Especially attractive in light of the exposition of Melchizedek texts in Heb. 7 is 11QMelchizedek.[49] Yet, these at-

43. Erich Grässer, *Der Glaube im Hebräerbrief,* Marburger theologische Studien 2 (Marburg: Elwert, 1965); Gerd Theissen, *Untersuchungen zum Hebräerbrief,* SNT 2 (Gütersloh: Mohn, 1969). See the discussion in Weiss, *Der Brief an die Hebräer,* 103–6.

44. See Judith Hoch Wray, *Rest as a Theological Metaphor in the Epistle to the Hebrews and the Gospel of Truth,* SBLDS 166 (Atlanta: Scholars Press, 1998).

45. Jon Laansma, *"I Will Give You Rest": The Rest Motif in the New Testament with Special Reference to Mt. 11 and Heb. 3–4,* WUNT 98 (Tübingen: Mohr Siebeck, 1997), 151.

46. Hurst, *Epistle to the Hebrews,* 74.

47. See Y. Yadin, "The Dead Sea Scrolls and the Epistle to the Hebrews," *Scripta Hierosolymitana* 4 (1958): 36–53; F. C. Fensham, "Hebrews and Qumran," *Neot* 5 (1971): 9–21; P. E. Hughes, *A Commentary on the Epistle to the Hebrews* (Grand Rapids: Eerdmans, 1977), 10–15; S. Kistemaker, *The Psalm Citations in the Epistle to the Hebrews* (Amsterdam: van Soest, 1961), 74. H. Kosmala, in *Hebräer, Essener, Christen: Studien zur Vorgeschichte der frühchristlichen Verkündigung,* SPB 1 (Leiden: Brill, 1959), suggested that the recipients were from the Essenes and had not yet converted to Christianity but were undergoing basic instruction in the faith.

48. For discussion and bibliography see Koester, *Hebrews,* 62–63; Lane, *Hebrews 1–8,* cvii–cviii, 161; Hurst, *Epistle to the Hebrews,* 43–66; Punt, "Hebrews, Thought-Patterns and Context," 137–40.

49. M. de Jonge and A. S. van der Woude, "11QMelchizedek and the New Testament," *NTS* 12 (1965–66): 301–26; Y. Yadin, "A Note on Melchizedek and Qumran," *IEJ* 15 (1965): 152–54; R. Longenecker, "The Melchizedek Argument of Hebrews: A Study in the Development and Circumstantial Expression of New Testament Thought," in *Unity and Diversity in New Testament Theology,* ed. R. A. Guelich (Grand Rapids: Eerdmans, 1978), 173–79.

tempts also have failed to convince, because genuine parallels once again can be explained from the broader milieu of Judaism in the Mediterranean world at the time,[50] and conceptual differences between Hebrews and Qumran must be taken seriously.

Hellenistic Judaism

More convincing is the insight that a number of prominent characteristics in Hebrews mark the work as having been written under the general influence of currents in broader Hellenistic Judaism.[51] The author's Bible is an Old Greek version, the version used in the Hellenistic synagogue, and that version has influenced his language at numerous points. Further, William Lane and others have noted at least three other characteristics that mark Hebrews as a product in line with the thought of Hellenistic Judaism. First, in introducing the "Son" in 1:1–4, the author's expressions seem to be influenced by the divine wisdom tradition of Hellenistic Judaism.[52] Second, 2:2 speaks of God's angels as mediators of the law, and this conviction seems to have been prominent especially among Hellenistic Jews of the period.[53] Third, Moses, who serves as such a prominent exemplar in Hebrews (3:1–6; 8:3–5; 11:23–29), held a place of great veneration in Hellenistic Judaism as one of great authority and access to God. In some branches of Jewish tradition he is considered to be the greatest person of history, and a wealth of literature focuses on him as the primary figure.[54] Lane marks these features as placing Hebrews squarely in that broad stream of first-century Hellenistic Judaism.[55]

Philo of Alexandria or Jewish Apocalyptic?

Among the prominent intellectual voices of Hellenistic Judaism of the first century, preeminent was that of Philo of Alexandria. In the sixty years leading up to the middle of the last century, the view that Philo's thought, method of

---

50. See Herbert Braun, *Qumran und das Neue Testament*, 2 vols. (Tübingen: Mohr Siebeck, 1966), 241–78; Grässer, "Der Hebräerbrief 1938–1963," 171–217.

51. See especially Lane, *Hebrews 1–8*, cxlvii–cl; also John and Kathleen Court, *The New Testament World* (Cambridge: Cambridge University Press, 1990), 322; Marie Isaacs, *Sacred Space: An Approach to the Theology of the Epistle to the Hebrews*, JSNTSup (Sheffield: JSOT Press, 1992), 48–49; Barnabas Lindars, *The Theology of the Letter to the Hebrews*, New Testament Theology (Cambridge: Cambridge University Press, 1991), 22–23. On caution in how one should use the designator "Hellenistic Judaism," see Punt, "Hebrews, Thought-Patterns and Context," 122–24.

52. W. L. Lane, "Detecting Divine Wisdom in Hebrews 1:1–4," *NTS* 5 (1982): 150–58.

53. Lane, *Hebrews 1–8*, liv, noting Acts 7:38, 53; Gal. 3:19; Josephus, *Ant.* 15.136.

54. M. R. D'Angelo, *Moses in the Letter to the Hebrews*, SBLDS 42 (Missoula, Mont.: Scholars Press, 1979), 95–131.

55. Lane, *Hebrews 1–8*, liv.

interpretation, and vocabulary held extensive influence on the author of Hebrews had all but reached the level of scholarly consensus, and no pen heralded that influence more forcefully than that of Ceslas Spicq. In his two-volume commentary on Hebrews, published in 1952, Spicq marched through extensive parallels between Hebrews and Philo in the areas of interpretive method, vocabulary, and worldview.[56] On the strength of this data, Spicq concluded that Philo had strongly influenced the author, and yet the author was a convert to Christianity who under the influence of the Christian movement had adopted a typological method.

As Lane and Hurst both note, two forces started to chip away at this seemingly unassailable position. First, the finding and study of the Qumran writings brought to light another Jewish backdrop against which Hebrews could be considered. Spicq himself responded to insights from the Qumran findings by adjusting his position, saying that Hebrews was addressed to a group of priests who had been in contact with Qumran.[57] Second, a series of studies called into question the validity of Spicq's research. C. K. Barrett, although still holding that Hebrews contains elements of Philonic idealism, demonstrated that many of the concepts in Hebrews that formerly had been read as Platonic/Philonic should actually be read in light of Jewish apocalyptic thought. He concluded, "Certain features of Hebrews which have often been held to have been derived from Alexandrian Platonism were in fact derived from apocalyptic symbolism."[58]

Further damage to the case for Philonic influence was done in 1959 by R. P. C. Hanson and then by F. Schröger almost ten years later;[59] both writers found great dissimilarities between Hebrews and Philo. Yet, the work most damaging to Spicq's position came in 1970 with the publication of Ronald Williamson's detailed analysis.[60] Williamson dismantled Spicq's research, analyzing Hebrews and Philo for their respective worldviews, uses of terminology, and exegetical methods. Williamson showed Spicq's research and logic to be flawed.

In the past quarter century, great strides have been made in the study of Jewish apocalyptic,[61] strides that have shown Jewish apocalyptic to be, among

---

56. Ceslas Spicq, *L'Épître aux Hébreux,* 2 vols., Études bibliques (Paris: Gabalda, 1952), 1:39–91.

57. Ceslas Spicq, "Le' Épitre aux Hébreux, Apollos, Jean-Baptiste, les Hellénistes et Qumran," *RevQ* 1 (1959): 365–90.

58. C. K. Barrett, "The Eschatology of the Epistle to the Hebrews," in *The Background of the New Testament and Its Eschatology,* ed. D. Daube and W. D. Davies (Cambridge: Cambridge University Press, 1956), 393.

59. R. P. C. Hansen, *Allegory and Event: A Study of the Sources and Significance of Origen's Interpretation of Scripture* (Richmond, Va.: John Knox, 1959); Friedrich Schröger, *Der Verfasser des Hebräerbriefes als Schriftausleger* (Regensburg: Pustet, 1968).

60. Ronald Williamson, *Philo and the Epistle to the Hebrews,* ALGHJ 4 (Leiden: Brill, 1970).

61. When addressing apocalyptic thought, we immediately are confronted with the problem of terminology, a problem that has been discussed at least since the early 1970s with Klaus Koch's *The Rediscovery of Apocalyptic.* Koch made a distinction between the literary

other characteristics, highly spatial, focusing on the distinctions between the heavenly and the earthly realms. In line with this trend, Lincoln Hurst has extended Barrett's and Williamson's work by further demonstrating the cogency of Hebrews' use of terminology with the spatial and temporal dualism of Jewish apocalyptic. In his conclusion on the matter he states:

> In all of this there is nothing *distinctly* "Platonic," "philosophical" or "noumenal"; much of it is drawn from the OT. Enough indications exist to point to a reasonable conclusion that *Auctor* developed certain OT ideas within the Jewish apocalyptic framework, while Philo developed the same themes within a Platonic framework.[62]

This trend toward reading Hebrews against the backdrop of Jewish apocalyptic thought has had great influence in Hebrews research of the past few decades.[63] Hurst has provided a thorough treatment of the case that must be answered by those who wish to hold to Philonic influence on Hebrews' background of thought. His suggestion that a common dynamic shared by Hebrews and Philo was their respective endeavors at handling the Jewish Scriptures brings us to another aspect of Jewish life and culture of the first century, the Jewish synagogue context.

---

genre of apocalypse and the historical movement that he called apocalyptic. P. D. Hanson later would argue for a threefold delineation between the literary form of apocalypse, the theological perspective of apocalyptic eschatology, and the socioreligious movement of apocalypticism. With Hanson's delineations, however, one still sees no distinction between those apocalyptic elements of a writing that are specifically eschatological and those that are not. Consequently, the helpful distinction has been made more recently between *apocalypse* as a particular genre of writing, *apocalypticism* as a social movement, *apocalyptic* as an adjective used either of the genre or of the theological perspective behind it, and *apocalyptic eschatology* as a way of referring to a particular kind of eschatology concerned with how God will put things right at the end of the age. See K. Koch, *The Rediscovery of Apocalyptic*, SBT 2.22 (London: SCM, 1972); P. D. Hanson, *The Dawn of Apocalyptic: The Historical and Sociological Roots of Jewish Apocalyptic Eschatology*, rev. ed. (Philadelphia: Fortress, 1979), 429–44; L. J. Kreitzer, "Apocalyptic, Apocalypticism," in *Dictionary of the Later New Testament and Its Developments*, ed. Ralph P. Martin and Peter H. Davids (Downers Grove, Ill.: InterVarsity, 1997), 55–68.

62. Hurst, *Epistle to the Hebrews*, 42.

63. In spite of this great turn in opinion, all heads have not been turned entirely in that direction, and many scholars still hold to some connection between the cultural context of Philo and the Book of Hebrews. James Thompson (*The Beginnings of Christian Philosophy: The Epistle to the Hebrews*, CBQMS 13 [Washington, D.C.: Catholic Biblical Association, 1982]) continues to argue for Philonic components in Hebrews' thought. George MacRae ("Heavenly Temple and Eschatology in the Letter to the Hebrews," *Semeia* 12 [1978]: 179–99) has suggested that the author, whose thought was Platonic, was addressing a group that was apocalyptic in orientation. Thus, the current state of the question may be considered somewhat mixed. Yet, I suggest that the weight must go to the perspective that reads Hebrews, in regard to its framework of thought, in line with apocalyptic Judaism. That there are parallels in vocabulary between Hebrews and Philo is undeniable, but this must be treated separately from the conceptual framework.

The Synagogue Context

It is a widely published observation that Hebrews begins like a sermon rather than a letter, and that the author of the book calls Hebrews a "word of exhortation," a designation that Acts 13:15 shows could be used of a synagogue homily. Therefore, many modern interpreters have followed the lead of Hartwig Thyen, who in 1955 demonstrated that Hebrews contains numerous characteristics that mark it as a homily. He even went so far as to say that Hebrews is the only fully preserved homily we have from the period.[64] A host of modern commentators have identified Hebrews with the homily form.[65] L. Wills has shown that homilies of the era moved from *exempla*, to a conclusion, to a final exhortation. Wills noted that the author of Hebrews uses this pattern generally but modifies it to his own purposes.[66] C. C. Black follows Wills's conclusion but notes the influence of, and congruence with, aspects of classical rhetoric in the patterns identified by Wills. Thus, Black suggests that Hebrews is an example of early Christian preaching but with incorporation of sophisticated aspects of rhetorical argumentation.[67] The material discussed above on Hebrews' use of rhetorical and stylistic conventions from the Greco-Roman world offers resounding support for the latter.

Use of the Old Testament

There is perhaps no topic more important to Hebrews' interpretation than the book's uses of the OT.[68] The author makes extensive use of quotations, allusions, general references, and echoes as a basis of authority, a tool for rhetoric and exhortation, a source of materials for building a structural framework, and a wellspring for theology. Thus, research into Hebrews' appropriation of the OT text is vital for ongoing interpretation of the book, and certain strides have been made in recent years. In light of the topic's importance, it is surprising, however, to find that recent overviews of the topic are scarce. In 1985, R. E. Clements offered a brief article on the topic.[69] Paul Ellingworth provided an overview of the phenomena surrounding Hebrews' appropriation of the Jewish Scriptures without delving into the author's use of various methodologies.[70]

---

64. Hartwig Thyen, *Der Stil des jüdisch-hellenistischen Homilie,* FRLANT 65 (Göttingen: Vandenhoeck & Ruprecht, 1955), 106.

65. See the discussion in Lane, *Hebrews 1–8,* lxix–lxxv; Koester, *Hebrews,* 80–82.

66. L. Wills, "The Form of the Sermon in Hellenistic Judaism and Early Christianity," *HTR* 77 (1984): 277–99.

67. C. C. Black II, "The Rhetorical Form of the Hellenistic Jewish and Early Christian Sermon: A Response to Lawrence Wills," *HTR* 81 (1988): 1–18.

68. For work done on the use of the OT in Hebrews in recent years, see n. 11, above.

69. R. E. Clements, "The Use of the Old Testament in Hebrews," *SwJT* 28 (1985): 36–45.

70. Paul Ellingworth, *The Epistle to the Hebrews: A Commentary on the Greek Text,* NIGNT (Grand Rapids: Eerdmans, 1993), 37–42.

William L. Lane, in the first volume of his magisterial commentary, provided extensive treatment on the author's handling of scriptural texts by considering "The Function of the OT Texts in the Structure of Hebrews," "The Extent of the Writer's Indebtedness to the OT," "Primary Sources for the Writer's Theology," "The Writer's Preferred Text," and "The Writer's Appropriation of the OT Text."[71] As Lane pointed out, the last of these subsections is heavily indebted to material, unpublished at the time, from my dissertation, "The Structure of Hebrews: A Text-linguistic Analysis." The dissertation, for which Lane served as an outside reader, was near the time of submission when Lane used it in his introduction, but due to length restrictions, my chapter on Hebrews' use of the OT was not included in the final form of the dissertation. That chapter later formed the basis for my 1997 article on the "Old Testament in Hebrews" in the *Dictionary of the Later New Testament and Its Developments.* In that article I overviewed current thinking on the phenomena surrounding Hebrews' use of the Jewish Scriptures, the author's text type, general forms used in the author's appropriation of the text (specifically, midrash, chain quotations, and *exempla*), principles used in interpretation of the text (e.g., verbal analogy, argument from lesser to greater, and dispelling confusion), and the theological implications that can be derived from the author's handling of his text.[72] Most technical commentaries, as they deal with individual passages, treat the author's uses of certain techniques and forms found in Jewish exegesis of the day—especially verbal analogy, argument from lesser to greater, and chain quotations. Drawing on the work of Dan Cohn-Sherbok, I added reflection on principles such as dispelling confusion, reinforcement, and drawing out implications, found at various points in the book.[73] As we saw above under consideration of Greco-Roman conventions (a number of which have been shown to have had influence on the Jewish practices of the Second Temple era), both Michael Cosby and Pamela Eisenbaum have done significant work on the *exempla* of Heb. 11.[74]

One of the best recent works on methodological parallels between Hebrews and other branches of Judaism is that of Herbert Bateman in his examination of Heb. 1:5–14. Bateman has demonstrated extensive parallels between midrashic characteristics found in 4QFlorilegium and Heb. 1:5–14.[75] Both texts use the catena form, also referred to as a "chain quotation" or *ḥaraz* ("to string"); both use introductory formulae to introduce scriptural passages; and

---

71. Lane, *Hebrews 1–8,* cxii–cxxiv.

72. G. H. Guthrie, "Old Testament in Hebrews," in Martin and Davids, *Dictionary of the Later New Testament,* 841–50.

73. See Dan Cohn-Sherbok, "Paul and Rabbinic Exegesis," *SJT* 35 (1982): 117–32.

74. Cosby, *Composition and Function of Hebrews 11;* Eisenbaum, "Jewish Heroes of Christian History."

75. Bateman, *Early Jewish Hermeneutics and Hebrews 1:5–13: The Impact of Early Jewish Exegesis on the Interpretation of a Significant New Testament Passage,* AUS 193 (New York: Lang, 1997): 56–77, 149–206.

both draw passages together based on conceptual parallels. Bateman's work, as well as the other studies listed above, underscores Hebrews' place as part of a broader methodological fabric of Judaism of the era.

As to text type, it is almost universally assumed that the author's text form was Greek. Discussions of the past century and a half have focused on which Greek text is most closely aligned with the text used by the author of Hebrews, most discussions centering on LXXA or LXXB. In 1980, J. C. McCullough concluded that for several books of the OT, such as Jeremiah and Psalms, the recension from which the quoted text is taken is fairly clear, but definite conclusions concerning other OT books were elusive. Therefore, he emphasized the need to study the Greek text forms on a book-by-book basis, rather than drawing wide-ranging conclusions concerning specific recensions of the Old Greek text.[76]

More recently, scholars have looked for other explanations of the differences between the author's quotations and known forms of the ancient Greek text of the OT, fixing especially on the author's freedom to make adjustments to his quotations for stylistic reasons and his freedom to paraphrase in order to highlight certain aspects of theology. In his monograph on the hermeneutical foundations of Hebrews, Dale Leschert suggests that the author handled the OT as authoritative and, generally, followed it consistently. However, the author may have altered the text slightly to improve on its literary style or to emphasize points of theology. Yet, it is difficult, Leschert notes, to determine which departures from the Septuagintal texts we have were actually in his form of the Greek text and which were his own adjustments.[77] Bateman concludes the same: in keeping with his historical milieu, the author freely edits his OT both for stylistic balance and for theological emphasis.[78] Graham Hughes suggests that by doing new-covenant reflection on the old-covenant text, the author of Hebrews creates a new logia, and this process may, in line with the techniques utilized by exegetes of the day, involve altering the text to suit the author's interpretation.[79] Very similar is Peter Enns's conclusion regarding the author's use of Ps. 95 in Heb. 3. Enns states, "Apparently, the author seems to have no difficulty in taking certain liberties with the text in order to make his theological point. His exegetical technique is similar to what we find, for example, in the commentaries of the Qumran community."[80] Karen

76. J. C. McCullough, "The Old Testament Quotations in Hebrews," *NTS* 26 (1979–80): 363–79.

77. D. F. Leschert, *The Hermeneutical Foundations of Hebrews: A Study in the Validity of the Epistle's Interpretation of Some Core Citations from the Psalms*, NABPR Dissertation Series 10 (Lewiston, N.Y.: Mellen, 1994), 245–47.

78. Bateman, *Early Jewish Hermeneutics and Hebrews 1:5–13*, 240.

79. Graham Hughes, *Hebrews and Hermeneutics: The Epistle to the Hebrews as a New Testament Example of Biblical Interpretation*, SNTSMS 36 (Cambridge: Cambridge University Press, 1979), 59.

80. Peter Enns, "The Interpretation of Psalm 95 in Hebrews 3:1–4:13," in Evans and Sanders, *Early Christian Interpretation of the Scriptures*, 362.

Jobes proposes that the changes we find in the author's quotation of Ps. 40 create a phonetic assonance, a pleasing style, and she notes similar dynamics in five other quotations in Hebrews. Further, Jobes suggests that such changes accomplish a theological purpose: they highlight the discontinuity between the old and the new eras.[81]

These authors feel varying degrees of comfort in suggesting that the author of Hebrews is making substantive changes in the message of the OT text. Most argue that he makes interpretive renderings that in essence are in line with the basic meaning of the OT text but bring out the greater significance of that meaning as fulfilled in Christ. At the same time, they acknowledge that the variants in the textual histories of both the Hebrew and the Old Greek texts may account for some of these changes.

The question of Hebrews' christological hermeneutic brings us to a third and more narrow cultural context for Hebrews: its place in emergent first-century Christianity.

Hebrews in Emergent First-Century Christianity

As we have noted, Hebrews exhibits the artistry of an author highly educated in the rhetorical conventions of Greco-Roman culture and one greatly influenced, especially in his use of the Greek OT, by the Hellenistic Jewish synagogue context. Further, the author's framework of thought was strongly influenced by apocalyptic Judaism, with its spatial and temporal dualisms. Yet, for the author of Hebrews, all these dynamics cohere in a vibrant Christian view of reality and find their impetus in a pastoral situation. It can be argued that Hebrews' most immediate theological context was the crucible of emergent first-century Christianity,[82] in spite of objections that the term "Christian" as an all-inclusive moniker for the first followers of Jesus suggests, undemonstrably, that the movement was a monolithic entity.[83] The author is a preacher/leader of the church, vying for his hearers' perseverance in Christian belief and practice.

A Christological Hermeneutic

What most sets Hebrews apart from its broader Jewish currents of thought, of course, is its christocentric orientation. The author reads the OT text with the eyes of a believer in Jesus as the Christ, the Son of God. With the shift from the older wisdom on Hebrews' exegesis—a wisdom assessing the author's

81. K. Jobes, "The Function of Paronomasia in Hebrews 10:5–7," *TJ* 13 (1992): 181–91.
82. Lindars, *Theology of the Letter to the Hebrews,* 25; Ellingworth, *Epistle to the Hebrews,* 47.
83. So Punt, "Hebrews, Thought-Patterns and Context," 149.

methods as essentially Philonic in nature—researchers have grappled with how to understand this early Christian author's hermeneutical system. In the past half century there have been numerous ways of assessing his system of hermeneutics,[84] but here we focus on four of the most significant in recent years.

First, the "proof-texting" approach suggests that the author of Hebrews forces texts of the OT to meet his current need in Christian preaching. For instance, in Weiss's assessment of Hebrews' hermeneutic, the author cares little or nothing for original context and the constraints of the OT language.[85] Rather, Hebrews forces Scripture's contents to match his own presuppositions.[86]

Second, Paul Ellingworth suggests the preexistence of Christ as a key to unlocking the hermeneutics of Hebrews:

> The author's approach to the OT may be summarized as follows: Christ, by whom God has now spoken his final word (1.1f.), was alive and active in creation (1.2) and throughout Israel's history. Any part of the OT may thus in principle be understood as speaking about Christ, or as spoken to or by him. Clues within the text may show to what parts of the OT it is most appropriate to apply this principle in practice. Indeed, since Christ was already at work in OT times, even an OT text without a future reference . . . may be applied to Christ.[87]

Motyer correctly points out two problems with this approach: (1) Hebrews' application of texts such as Ps. 22 to the person of Christ does not claim, nor does it depend upon, the doctrine of Christ's preexistence (any more, I would add, than the application of Ps. 95 or Prov. 3 to us requires our preexistence); (2) there is, in the revelation of God, both continuity and strong elements of discontinuity, and a sharp sense of demarcation between the age prior to

84. In addition to those sketched here we could add the *sensus plenior* approach of many Catholic scholars, and the "dialogical hermeneutics" proposed in Markus Barth, "The Old Testament in Hebrews: An Essay in Biblical Hermeneutics," in *Current Issues in New Testament Interpretation,* ed. W. Klassen and G. F. Snyder (New York: Harper & Row, 1962), 65–78.

85. Weiss, *Der Brief an die Hebräer,* 181.

86. Stephen Motyer raises two objections to this critique. First, it greatly underestimates Hebrews' clear sense of *Heilsgeschichte,* which retains a clear sense of historical distance and historical progression. Second, rather than simply plundering the OT and reassigning passages according to new intentions, the author of Hebrews does detailed work on the OT text in mounting his arguments. In other words, he does an exegesis that his audience could understand and follow. His rhetorical program could have been severely hampered by arbitrary use of his materials. Hebrews appeals to principles embraced in historical grammatical exegesis, such as sensitivity to context, specific word meanings, and inherent logic in a passage. Thus, to ascribe to the author a simple proof-texting approach is itself too simplistic. Consequently, this critique of the author has receded somewhat in the face of extensive work on the details of Hebrews' use of the OT and nuanced investigations into his hermeneutic system. See Stephen Motyer, "The Psalm Quotations of Hebrews 1: A Hermeneutic-Free Zone?" *TynBul* 50 (1999): 3–22, esp. 7–8.

87. Ellingworth, *Epistle to the Hebrews,* 41–42.

Messiah's coming and the current age.[88] Such historical distinctions are treated more clearly in the work of Graham Hughes.

Third, Graham Hughes identifies the crux of the hermeneutical question in Hebrews as follows:

> What is the relationship between the conceptual "frames"—which certainly are there independently of the interpreter and between which, when it is drawn to our attention, there can be seen an intriguing connectedness—and the faith-convictions of the interpreter apart from which this connectedness is at best but latent, suggestive?[89]

For Hughes, the historical frames of the OT text are distinct from, but correspond to, the historical framework inherent in the interpretive program of the early church. The connection between the two are not discernible by mere historical scrutiny. Yet, the OT forms "permit" to the new-covenant interpreter the meanings that may be found in light of Christ. Thus, Hughes calls this approach a "hermeneutic of permission." What draws the word of

---

88. Motyer, "Psalm Quotations of Hebrews 1," 9–10.

89. Hughes, *Hebrews and Hermeneutics,* 105. See also Thomas Ladd Blackstone's interaction with Hughes in his 1995 doctoral dissertation, done at Emory University, "The Hermeneutics of Recontextualization in the Epistle to the Hebrews." Drawing from contemporary theories of intertextuality, Blackstone examines Hebrews' approach to recontextualization—the movement of words or ideas from one literary expression to another—categorizing the quotations as static, surface, or fluid. Static recontextualization constitutes those cases in which the author sticks closely to the original contextual meaning of the OT text. Surface recontextualization, on the other hand, involves the author working with the original form of the text, the thrust of the original text being left intact, while the reference points historically are modified. This especially relates to those passages that the author sees as being fulfilled in the new-covenant community. Finally, fluid recontextualization constitutes those instances where the OT context is not brought explicitly to the surface of the author's discussion. Blackstone embraces many of Hughes's suggestions but qualifies his "hermeneutic of permission," suggesting that "permission," as used by Hughes, is a static quality from the realm of human contracts. A "living voice," on the other hand, is organically related to the organism from which it originates. God is speaking; he speaks old words with new meanings at points; but, for Blackstone, it is important to grasp that the author presents the living voice of God as speaking in, and at the same time encompassing the breadth of, biblical history. I believe that this thought actually is present in Hughes's work, and I wonder if, in this sense, Blackstone really has made any advance on Hughes. Blackstone's conclusion, in which he seeks to give an overarching construct to the hermeneutic of Hebrews, is not as strongly developed as one would have wished. However, two aspects of Blackstone's research are quite suggestive. First, his analysis of recontextualization in Hebrews shows that most of the quotations from the Pentateuch are static, the author focusing on the historical facts, while all of the quotations from Psalms and the Prophets are either surface or fluid. This, of course, may be due to the genre of narrative in the Pentateuch, but making these distinctions gives another angle on the data. Second, Blackstone has demonstrated that noncited portions of the OT material exert influence on the development of the writer's thought. The broader contexts of his OT quotations come into play, producing echoes in his discussions and exhortations. This second contribution is also present in an article by Motyer, who is one representative of our last category of hermeneutic approaches to Hebrews.

the OT and the word in and through Christ together is that God is speaking consistently through both and gives continuity to them. Thus, for Hughes, real historical continuity exists between the OT text and the NT interpretation. This continuity is seen in part by the inherent expectations found in the OT text of something future that would constitute their fulfillment, and by the specific ways in which Jesus Christ actually fulfills those expectations. At the end of the day, for Hughes, a Christian hermeneutic "cannot be other than a hermeneutic of faith."[90] He argues against Bultmann, saying that theology must not be reduced to anthropology. Thus, his hermeneutic of permission is in essence a christological hermeneutic.

Finally, we come to what normally is called typological hermeneutics. One of the more helpful works in this approach is Motyer's 1999 article on the Psalms quotations of Heb. 1.[91] Following G. B. Caird, Motyer notes the OT has built into itself a note of inadequacy, which, if fulfilled, must be fulfilled by some means other than the institution, person, or event immediately in view. He proposes that there are three categories of passages in Heb. 1. First, there are those texts generally held as messianic either in Judaism of the day or at least in early Christianity. Psalm 2:7 and 2 Sam. 7:14, twin quotations in Heb. 1:5, fall into this category. These texts both appear in 4QFlorilegium. The hermeneutic at play here goes something like this: Ps. 2 builds on the 2 Sam. 7 promise to David regarding dynastic dominance of the world. Yet, this was not realized by any of the Davidic kings. Thus, the text must have anticipated a greater fulfillment, and therefore it sets up a typological construct adopted by the author of Hebrews. Also, in this category would be Ps. 110:1, quoted in Heb. 1:13. Although evidence for the messianic reading of this text in early Judaism is minimal, its prominence in the NT may be due to Jesus' appropriation of the text for his own significance. Motyer notes the interpretation of this psalm in Acts 2:32–34, where Peter states that David did not fulfill the psalm, since he never ascended to heaven. Thus, these messianic texts also display Caird's concept of the OT texts' self-confessed inadequacy.

Motyer's second category identifies texts that, on the same principle, may be readily understood as messianic. We have no evidence that Ps. 44:7–8 LXX, quoted in Heb. 1:8–9, was interpreted as messianic in Judaism or elsewhere in the NT. Yet, like the texts in the previous category, it promises universal victory and rule to the Davidic king.

The third category involves those texts that, in Motyer's words, "stretch and tease but extend the same line of thought." Here we have the two remaining passages of the catena, Deut. 32:43, quoted in Heb. 1:6, and Ps. 101:26–28 LXX, presented in Heb. 1:10–12. Motyer disputes that the quote at Heb. 1:6 is from Deuteronomy, although he suggests that the language of the quote has been influenced by Deut. 32:43, opting instead for Ps. 96:7 LXX as the parent

---

90. Ibid., 104–7, 118.
91. Motyer, "Psalm Quotations of Hebrews 1."

text. In the LXX this psalm has a heading indicating that this passage was for David upon his appointment over the land. The heading of this text, therefore, moves it into the same realm of Davidic dynastic rule that we have seen in the other passages quoted in Heb. 1. Motyer suggests that the author's use of Ps. 101:26–28 LXX at Heb. 1:10–12 may be understood similarly. Motyer notes that the broader context of that psalm includes the Lord's deliverance of Zion, which will involve bringing the kings and nations of the earth to fear his name (Ps. 101:16 LXX). I would add that verse 18 of that psalm specifically states that this work will be accomplished for another generation and a people being created to praise the Lord. The emphases in this psalm, according to Motyer, parallel the other texts of the catena nicely.

Thus, Motyer argues that the author of Hebrews mixes accepted messianic passages with others that he adds on the basis of his own reflection, "but which are interpreted by employing the same hermeneutic as the widely-used texts."[92]

On this reading, the use of the OT by the author of Hebrews is christological and typological in that it interprets with new-covenant eyes, seeing in Christ the fulfillment of what obviously is left undone in the former era. Yet, the author's hermeneutic, at the same time, consistently emphasizes context, word meanings, and analogy between various parts of Scripture. Another designation, perhaps "new-covenant hermeneutic," might be better, since there are uses of the OT in Hebrews that, while fitting into the broad typological framework, are not based on typology.

Other Connections with Emergent Christianity

The Stephen Tradition

At mid-twentieth century, William Manson delivered a seminal address suggesting extensive theological contacts between Hebrews and the early Hellenists, represented by Stephen and his associates. The driving force for the development of this theological orientation, in Manson's view, was reflection on the advance of a worldwide mission.[93] The office and significance of Messiah should be understood as "more-than-Jewish," and thus not limited to traditional Jewish orientations such as the law, the temple, and the land. As seen in Stephen's speech of Acts 7:2–53, this theological orientation reads Israel's history against a framework that evaluates religion in terms of an obedience/disobedience grid. The people of God are called to be a people on pilgrimage, a pilgrimage in which they are characterized by obedience to the word of God as a word

92. Ibid., 21.
93. W. Manson, *The Epistle to the Hebrews: An Historical and Theological Reconsideration* (London: Hodder & Stoughton, 1951), 25–46.

of promise for the obedient (Acts 7:5–7, 17, 37–38, 52), which is a major motif found in Hebrews (3:7–4:13). Thus, God's revelation is not limited to a given place, whether the temple or the land. The law of God is not merely to be received, but must be kept. Moses, rather than being primarily the giver of the law, is paradigmatic of an obedient servant of God who points to the one to come (Acts 7:37; Heb. 3:1–6). Obedience ultimately comes in submitting to God's Christ as Lord.[94]

The contacts between Hebrews and the so-called Stephen tradition seem unmistakable, and many modern scholars have been convinced of their adherence to a common tradition. The extent to which Luke may have shaped the speech of Acts 7 is a difficult and abiding question, but the connections are there nonetheless. Others remain unconvinced of the significance of the connections; however, to suggest literary dependence is not necessary, nor—against Martin Scharlemann—is the suggestion that Hebrews must correspond at every point with the Stephen episode of Acts 7.[95] Differences between Hebrews and the speech given by Stephen include different conceptions of the fulfillment of God's promise, different views about the binding nature of the first covenant, and different assessments of the tabernacle.[96] Yet, it should not be surprising that this tradition was adapted and developed by the author of Hebrews in distinct ways.[97] The evidence suggests that Hebrews fits within a stream of early Christianity strongly influenced by a Hellenistic form of Judaism grown disillusioned with static, traditional institutions. Whether or not this was a movement outside of early Christianity is unclear, but Hebrews suggests its significance within the Christian movement.

Pauline Christianity

Parallels between Hebrews and Paul are extensive, and Windisch, Hurst, Koester, and others have produced impressive lists. These include elements such as the various aspects of "The Way of the Son": his preexistence and role in creation, his incarnation, his obedience to the point of death, his sacrificial death, his exaltation and heavenly intercession for his people, his defeat of the evil powers, and the anticipation of his second coming. All things will be subjected to him. Further, both Paul and Hebrews celebrate the superiority of the new covenant, gifts distributed by the Holy Spirit, Abraham as an exemplar of faith, the wilderness wanderers as exemplars of disobedience, and the Christian life as a race. Hebrews' ending has both structural elements and vocabulary that mirror Paul, and the reference to Timothy (Heb. 13:23) is

94. Lane, *Hebrews 1–8*, cxlvi–cl.
95. So Hurst, *Epistle to the Hebrews,* 106.
96. Koester, *Hebrews,* 57.
97. So Lane, *Hebrews 1–8,* cxlvi–cl.

striking. Adding to Windisch's list, Hurst produces no fewer than twenty-six parallels, and Koester offers twenty-nine.[98]

At the same time, the significant differences between the two have led to a virtual consensus among modern scholars that Paul did not write Hebrews.[99] Many of the images, theological themes, and words are not found in the Pauline literature. For example, the high priest motif, as used of Christ, is unique to Hebrews. Some 169 words used in Hebrews find no expression elsewhere in the NT, and the Greek of Hebrews is superior to that of the Pauline literature. Further, both the author's Greek text and his manner of quoting the Jewish Scriptures vary from Paul. Paul customarily uses the phrase "It is written," while Hebrews, following the style of sermons in the Greek-speaking Jewish synagogues of the Mediterranean world, introduces scriptural quotations with some manner of God speaking (e.g., "He says"). Finally, and for many most significantly, the author of Hebrews presents himself as having received the gospel from the original witnesses (Heb. 2:3). In light of his strong assertions to have received the gospel directly from Christ, it is difficult to imagine Paul making such a statement (see, e.g., Rom. 1:1; 1 Cor. 15:8; Gal. 1:11–16).

Upon further examination of three sample themes developed by both Paul and Hebrews (the destiny of humankind; Christ's humiliation, with his obedience and exaltation; and the role of faith in the Christian life), Hurst concludes that the themes are developed similarly. At points the same ideas are expressed by various uses of the same terminology, or by different terminology and imagery. Hurst rules out direct literary dependence[100] but suggests that it is not beyond reason that the author of Hebrews could have been a disciple of Paul at one time. Thus, Hurst leaves open the possibility of Paul's influence on Hebrews apart from literary dependence.[101] Another viable option is that each, independent of the other, utilized significant parts of common Christian tradition.[102]

First Peter

The other NT writing shown to have extensive verbal and conceptual parallels with Hebrews is 1 Peter.[103] Past studies have suggested numerous correspon-

---

98. Hurst, *Epistle to the Hebrews*, 107–8; Koester, *Hebrews*, 54–55.

99. However, see D. A. Black, "Who Wrote Hebrews? The Internal and External Evidence Reexamined," *Faith and Mission* 18 (2001): 3–26.

100. Although, see the case for Hebrews' literary dependence on Galatians made by Ben Witherington, "The Influence of Galatians on Hebrews," *NTS* 37 (1991): 146–52.

101. Hurst, *Epistle to the Hebrews*, 124.

102. See Koester, *Hebrews*, 56 n. 20; F. Schröger, *Der Verfasser des Hebräerbriefes als Schriftausleger*, Biblische Untersuchungen 4 (Regensburg: Pustet, 1968), "Hebräerbrief," 216–17; Weiss, *Der Brief an die Hebräer*, 88.

103. A case also has been made for connections with John. See E. Cothenet et al., *Les écrits de Saint Jean et l'Épître aux Hébreux* (Paris: Desclée, 1984); C. J. A. Hickling, "John and Hebrews: The Background of Hebrews 2:10–18," *NTS* 29 (1983): 112–16.

dences, and the proposal has been given fresh currency by commentators such as Koester and Attridge,[104] and, once again, by Hurst's exploration of Hebrews' background of thought.[105] Conflating the lists of previous studies, Hurst lists thirty-eight parallels, Attridge lists some thirty-two, and Koester focuses on approximately twenty-three. As presented by Attridge, the correspondences can be divided roughly into (1) ways of presenting Christ and his work (e.g., he was "manifested" [Heb. 9:26; 1 Pet. 1:20; 5:4]; his death was "once for all," providing salvation [Heb. 7:27; 9:26; 10:12; 1 Pet. 3:18] and involving the "sprinkling of blood" [Heb. 10:22; 12:24; 1 Pet. 1:2]); (2) the significance of his work for a persecuted community in need of encouragement (e.g., they are "aliens and strangers" [Heb. 11:8–16; 12:22; 13:14; 1 Pet. 2:11], part of God's household [Heb. 3:2–6; 1 Pet. 2:5], who are called to endure [Heb. 10:32, 39; 12:2–3, 7; 1 Pet. 2:20] as they look to Christ [Heb. 12:3; 1 Pet. 2:21], their great "shepherd" [Heb. 13:20; 1 Pet. 5:4]); and (3) the desired outcome for the follower of Christ (e.g., they can anticipate an "inheritance" [Heb. 1:4; 6:12; 9:15; 1 Pet. 1:4–5; 3:9] at the end of the age [Heb. 10:25; 1 Pet. 4:7]).

Many of the parallels may be due to a common stock of Greek idiom, independent uses of the OT, common Christian tradition, and Pauline influence.[106] Yet, both the number of verbal parallels and their depth of theological correspondence at points seem impressive and suggest some form of literary connection, though the nature of the connection probably is beyond the reach of modern research.

Hebrews' Specific Circumstances

As for the specifics of Hebrews' original circumstances, much remains unanswered by modern scholarship due to lack of clear evidence, and little progress has been made in recent years. On the question of authorship, research has moved away from attempts to identify a specific person as author to a focus on the author's profile. Suggestions for the date of Hebrews generally may be divided according to pre- and post-70 C.E., although most now agree that the references in Hebrews to the defunct status of the tabernacle cannot be related to the destruction of the temple in Jerusalem. The recipients have been understood as Jewish, Gentile, or a mixed group, and the majority of commentators now place them in the city of Rome, though other opinions still are put forward.[107]

Suggestions concerning the occasion for Hebrews are more interesting and mostly center in some way on the issue of apostasy. The apostasy is understood

---

104. Attridge, *Epistle to the Hebrews*, 30–31; Koester, *Hebrews*, 57–58.
105. Hurst, *Epistle to the Hebrews*, 125–30.
106. Ibid., 130; Koester, *Hebrews*, 58.
107. On these topics, see the introductions by Lane, Koester, Attridge, Weiss, and Ellingworth.

as stemming perhaps either from persecution from without the church or from a breakdown in the community itself.[108] Lane proposes that the resolve to follow Christ was waning in the face of increased persecution under Nero's reign.[109] Rejecting the idea that the first recipients of Hebrews were in danger of lowering their valuation of Christ, Marie Isaacs, in her excellent monograph on "sacred space" in Hebrews, suggests instead that these Jewish Christians were mourning the loss of Jerusalem and the temple. The purpose for the book, therefore, was to raise their eyes to "the only sacred space worth having"—heaven.[110] Barnabas Lindars proposes that an overwhelming sense of sin and guilt had caused those in the community to resort to Jewish customs that would give them a tangible sense of relief, and Hebrews answers by presenting Jesus' death as a once-for-all atoning sacrifice.[111] By way of his reading of Hebrews along sociorhetorical lines, David deSilva suggests that the first hearers were struggling with a loss of status in the society. Rather than struggling against violent persecution or the draw of Judaism, they were giving way to the normal "pedestrian" desires for esteem and goods lost by their association with the church.[112]

Studies in Hebrews' Theology

One of the gains of the past two decades of Hebrews research is a renewed interest in the book's theology.[113] Lindars's *Theology of the Letter to the Hebrews*, Feld's review of past research on theological questions,[114] and theological introductions in several major commentaries have been helpful in this regard.[115] In addition, a number of monographs have taken up specific issues in Hebrews' theology. Here I can mention but a few. As we noted, Marie Isaacs has shown the importance of "sacred space" in Hebrews, proposing that God's promises of land and the tabernacle, as well as access to God himself, were to be reinterpreted in light of Jesus' exaltation to the heavenly place.[116] Jon Laansma has accomplished an extensive treatment of the "rest" motif in Heb. 3–4.[117] Following his introduction, Laansma covers the motif in the Hebrew OT, in the LXX,

---

108. Attridge, *Epistle to the Hebrews*, 12–13.

109. Lane, *Hebrews 1–8*, lx–lxvi.

110. Isaacs, *Sacred Space*, 67.

111. Lindars, *Theology of the Letter to the Hebrews*, 10.

112. DeSilva, *Perseverance in Gratitude*, 19.

113. In addition to the monographs listed below, see the review by Koester, "Hebrews in Recent Study," 133–36.

114. H. Feld, "Der Hebräerbrief: Literarische Form, religionsgeschichtlicher Hintergrund, theologische Fragen," in *ANRW* 2.25.4:3564–88 (cf. 3522–3601).

115. For example, Lane, *Hebrews 1–8*, cxxv–cxlvii; Ellingworth, *Epistle to the Hebrews*, 63–77; Koester, *Hebrews*, 96–128.

116. Isaacs, *Sacred Space*, 131–33.

117. Laansma, *"I Will Give You Rest."* Laansma's study is superior to that of Wray, *Rest as a Theological Metaphor*.

and in other Jewish and Christian literature. Chapter 7 specifically focuses on the motif in the context of Heb. 3–4 and the various proposals that scholars have offered concerning the κατάπαυσις. Christian Rose, focusing especially on Heb. 10:32–12:3, has addressed "the cloud of witnesses" in Hebrews;[118] and David Wider, in a monograph based on his University of Bern dissertation, examines the nature, means, and effects of God's speech.[119] Victor Rhee has revisited the nature of faith in Hebrews, seeking to push an understanding of faith in Hebrews beyond an ethical view, and even beyond an eschatological view, to a conception of faith that is christocentric at its core—that is, a faith that finds in Jesus not only its model but also its object.[120] John Dunnill reads Hebrews as a "covenant renewal rite," the Christian kerygma proclaimed in the language of the OT cultus.[121] Finally, Hermut Löhr has addressed the twin topics of repentance and sin.[122]

Conclusion

At the beginning of this essay, Hebrews was likened to a "Cinderella" of biblical studies, and it is clear from the amount of attention she has enjoyed in recent years that this is the case and should be celebrated. From this review of recent research on Hebrews, we see that the book clearly has systemic connections with each of its first-century contexts. Our understanding of its place in those contexts moves forward under the steam of good work done in recent years. Let us hope for, and work toward, greater understanding of this complex and compelling book in the years to come. Yet, for those who still consider this word of exhortation as authoritative, the goal is not to force Hebrews "under us," to wrestle it to the ground and wring from it its secrets, its history, and its proclamations, as if we could pin it down with our array of research tools. Rather, sitting under its word, we should seek to hear it more clearly as those who have grasped the new-covenant message and to follow its exhortation more faithfully as those on pilgrimage to the heavenly city. As Markus Barth stated at the end of an essay on the use of the OT in Hebrews,

118. C. Rose, *Die Wolke der Zeugen: Eine exegetisch-traditionsgeschichtliche Untersuchung zu Hebräer 10,32–12,3*, WUNT 60 (Tübingen: Mohr Siebeck, 1994).

119. D. Wider, *Theozentrik und Bekenntnis: Untersuchungen zur Theologie des Redens Gottes in Hebräerbrief*, BZNW 87 (Berlin and New York: de Gruyter, 1997).

120. V. Rhee, *Faith in Hebrews: Analysis within the Context of Christology, Eschatology, and Ethics*, Studies in Biblical Literature 19 (New York: Lang, 2001).

121. J. Dunnill, *Covenant and Sacrifice in the Letter to the Hebrews*, SNTSMS 75 (Cambridge: Cambridge University Press, 1992), 261.

122. Hermut Löhr, *Umkehr und Sünde im Hebräerbrief*, BZNW 73 (Berlin and New York: de Gruyter, 1994).

Ever changing "modern" critics of Hebrews come and go. The Epistle has survived them all. And it is still a living, unique, and indispensable power that draws attention to Israel and the OT, that creates knowledge and understanding of what the king of the Jews and the priest of all the weak is, and that proclaims Christ by saying words of comfort, guidance, encouragement. The witness born to Christ by Hebrews is still clearer, stronger, better than that of all commentaries written about or against it taken together.[123]

123. M. Barth, "The Old Testament in Hebrews: An Essay in Biblical Hermeneutics," in Klassen and Snyder, *Current Issues in New Testament Interpretation,* 78.

21

The Johannine Gospel in Recent Research

Klaus Scholtissek

The Johannine Gospel is a favorite subject of exegetical research.[1] This is evidenced not only by the essays that will be introduced here, but also by new literature reports,[2] bibliographies,[3] and publications that summarize the current state of research,[4] as well as the current debate about introductory questions

1. This essay is a continuation of the following research reports: Klaus Scholtissek, "Neue Wege der Johannesauslegung I–II," *TGl* 89 (1999): 263–95; 91 (2001): 109–33 (cf. the English translation in *CurBS* 6 [1998]: 227–59; 9 [2001]: 277–395; "Johannes auslegen I–II," *SNTSU* 24 (1999): 35–84; 25 (2000): 98–140; "Eine Renaissance des Evangeliums nach Johannes," *TRev* 97 (2001): 267–88.

2. See in the journals, Xavier Léon-Dufour, *RSR* 55 (1967)–82 (1994); Michèle Morgen, *RSR* 84 (1996)–89 (2001); cf. Léon Dufour, "Où en est la recherche johannique?" in *Origine et postérité de l'Évangile de Jean*, ed. A. Marchadour, LD 143 (Paris: Cerf, 1990), 17–41; Franz G. Untergaßmair, "Das Johannesevangelium: Ein Bericht über neuere Literatur aus der Johannesforschung," *TRev* 90 (1994): 91–108; Udo Schnelle, "Perspektiven der Johannesexegese," *SNTSU* 15 (1990): 59–72; idem, "Ein neuer Blick: Tendenzen der gegenwärtigen Johannesforschung," *BTZ* 16 (1999): 29–40; Francis J. Moloney, "Where Does One Look? Reflections on Some Recent Johannine Scholarship," *Antonianum* 62 (2000): 223–51.

3. Gilbert van Belle, *Johannine Bibliography 1966–1985*, BETL 82 (Leuven: Brill, 1988); W. E. Mills, *The Gospel of John*, BBRNT 4 (Lewiston, N.Y.: Mellen Biblical Press, 1995). See online: http://www.johannine.net.

4. See Robert Kysar, "John, the Gospel of," *ABD* 3:912–31; Jörg Frey, "Johannes I. der Evangelist," *DNP* 5:1056–58; Harold W. Attridge, "Johannesevangelium," *RGG* 4:552–62;

concerning the Johannine corpus[5] and the debate about exegetical methods.[6] During the last several years, exegetical efforts have been focused more on the Gospel of John than on the Synoptic Gospels. The reason for this might partly be an existing backlog demand, but is mainly caused by new starts in the research about the Johannine Gospel itself. New ways of asking questions lead to new and highly interesting discoveries in the text and its interpretations. Exegetical perspectives that have lasted for decades are closely questioned by these new approaches: for example, increasingly it is assumed that the evangelist John did have some knowledge of the Synoptic Gospels.[7] The classic literary criticism applied to the Gospel of John has severe difficulties in defending itself.[8] Attempts to assign the Johannine Gospel to specific religious contexts (typically, gnosticism) have turned out to be unreliable.[9] Clarifying the characteristics of the Johannine language, narration, and theology is understood more and more as a special task and a challenge for the interpretation of this Gospel.[10] The exegetical focus on a hypothetically reconstructed basic document, the

---

Martin Hengel, *Judaica, Hellenistica et Christiana 2*, WUNT 109 (Tübingen: Mohr Siebeck, 1999), 293–334. See also David E. Orton, ed., *The Composition of John's Gospel: Selected Studies from Novum Testamentum* (Leiden: Brill, 1999).

5. See Raymond E. Brown, *An Introduction to the New Testament*, ABRL (New York: Doubleday, 1997), 333–405; Ingo Broer, *Einleitung in das Neue Testament*, NEBNTSup 2.1 (Würzburg: Echter, 1998), 179–248. See also the extensive overview of different options to identify John the evangelist by R. Alan Culpepper, *John, the Son of Zebedee: The Life of a Legend*, 2nd ed., Studies on Personalities of the New Testament (Edinburgh: Clark, 2000).

6. See Fernando F. Segovia, ed., *"What Is John?"* 2 vols., SBLSymS 3 and 7 (Atlanta: Scholars Press, 1996–98); Johannes Nissen and Sigfred Pedersen, eds., *New Readings in John*, JSNTSup 182 (Sheffield: Sheffield Academic Press, 1999).

7. This view has been defended for many years by Frans Neirynck. See F. Neirynck, "John and the Synoptics in Recent Commentaries," *ETL* 74 (1998): 386–97; Manfred Lang, *Johannes und die Synoptiker: Analyse von Joh 18–20 vor markinischem und lukanischem Hintergrund*, FRLANT 182 (Göttingen: Vandenhoeck & Ruprecht, 1998).

8. See Jörg Frey, *Die johanneische Eschatologie*, 3 vols., WUNT 96, 110, and 117 (Tübingen: Mohr Siebeck, 1997–2000); Scholtissek, "Johannes auslegen I," 51–59.

9. Nor is the Johannine Gospel directly influenced by the writings from Qumran, but rather it arises from the same early Jewish context, which has left its traces in the entire Johannine Gospel. See Richard Bauckham, "The Qumran Community and the Gospel of John," in *The Dead Sea Scrolls: Fifty Years after Their Discovery 1947–1997*, ed. Lawrence H. Schiffman et al. (Jerusalem: Israel Exploration Society, 2000), 105–15.

10. Three new commentaries in the German language represent these developments: Ludger Schenke, *Johannes* (Düsseldorf: Patmos, 1998); U. Schnelle, *Das Evangelium nach Johannes*, THKNT 4 (Leipzig: Evangelische Verlagsanstalt, 2000); Ulrich Wilckens, *Das Evangelium nach Johannes*, NTD 4 (Göttingen: Vandenhoeck & Ruprecht, 2000). See also John Ashton, *Understanding the Fourth Gospel* (Oxford: Oxford University Press, 1993); D. Moody Smith, *John among the Gospels* (Columbia: University of South Carolina Press, 2001); idem, *John*, ANTC (Nashville: Abingdon, 1999); A. J. Köstenberger, *Encountering John: The Gospel in Historical, Literary, and Theological Perspective* (Grand Rapids: Baker, 1999); R. Alan Culpepper, Ruth B. Edwards, and John M. Court, eds., *The Johannine Literature* (Sheffield: Sheffield Academic Press, 2000); Marianne Meye Thompson, *The God of the Gospel of John* (Grand Rapids: Eerdmans, 2001).

so-called Semeia-Quelle (Signs Source), or changes in the orders of the chapters of the Johannine Gospel are no longer viable. The canonical text of the Gospel of John reaches authority again and is discovered anew and taken seriously as the primary subject of exegetical interpretation. The following essay attempts to take this current state of research in the Gospel of John into account. It introduces chosen central subjects of North American research in the Gospel of John. This is followed by a short presentation of the criticisms leveled at the classic research paradigms and of the new views that have gained their places. The essay then deals with prominent topics of research in the Johannine Gospel and concludes with some summarizing remarks.

Central Topics of North American Research in the Gospel of John

Since the publication of the important commentary on the Gospel of John by Raymond E. Brown, a considerable and internationally highly respected community of research in the Johannine Gospel has been established in the United States. It has contributed valuable essays and basic research to the exegesis of the Fourth Gospel and the Johanninne corpus.[11] Only a few can be chosen from the enormous number of titles, theses, and opinions.

History of Theology and of the Congregation—Raymond E. Brown

The most influential and balanced commentary that comes from North America has been written by Raymond Brown,[12] a leading figure among researchers who try to bring together the history of the tradition of the Johannine Gospel and the reconstructed history of the congregation.[13] Brown assumes a

11. See, for example, D. Moody Smith, *The Theology of the Gospel of John,* NTT (Cambridge: University Press, 1996); R. Alan Culpepper and C. C. Black, eds., *Exploring the Gospel of John* (Louisville: Westminster John Knox, 1996); T. L. Brodie, *The Gospel according to John: A Literary and Theological Commentary* (Oxford: Oxford University Press, 1993); Leon Morris, *Reflections on the Gospel of John,* 4 vols. (Grand Rapids: Baker, 1986–88); idem, *The Gospel of John,* rev. ed., NICNT (Grand Rapids: Eerdmans, 1995).

12. See R. E. Brown, *The Gospel according to John,* 2 vols., AB 29–29A (Garden City, N.Y.: Doubleday, 1966–70); *Introduction to the New Testament,* 333–405; *The Death of the Messiah: From Gethsemane to the Grave,* ABRL (New York: Doubleday, 1994); *Reading the Gospels within the Church: From Christmas through Easter* (Cincinnati: St. Anthony Messenger Press, 1996), 33–43; *A Risen Christ in Eastertime: Essays on the Gospel Narratives of the Resurrection* (Collegeville, Minn.: Liturgical Press, 1990), 65–80; *The Gospel and Epistles of John: A Concise Commentary* (Collegeville, Minn.: Liturgical Press, 1988); *An Introduction to New Testament Christology* (London: Chapman, 1994), 196–213.

13. See R. E. Brown, *The Community of the Beloved Disciple: The Life, Loves, and Hates of an Individual Church in New Testament Times* (New York: Paulist Press, 1979); *Introduction to the New Testament,* 373–76. Correlations between the history of the congregation and the theology of the Gospel of John are treated also in J. Louis Martyn, *History and Theology in the Fourth*

development in several stages. At first, the words and deeds of Jesus were passed on in the form of oral tradition—with some independence from the Synoptic tradition. Later, the specific experiences of life and of the congregation led to a revision of these traditions. Finally, the evangelist, a highly gifted preacher, shaped the written form of the Gospel. According to Brown, this history of tradition correlates with the following history of the congregation: At the first stage, Palestinian Judeo-Christians confess Jesus as the Davidic Messiah and even accept expulsion from the synagogue as a consequence (until about 70–80 C.E.). At the second stage, after a possible move to Asia Minor, with the written form of the Gospel being created by the evangelist, the universal dimension of the Gospel (cf. John 12:20–23) is reflected more clearly. The first two Johannine Epistles result from a schism within the congregation.[14] Finally, the third Johannine Epistle and the completion of the Gospel by its present final chapter (21) mark an "early catholic" turn of the Johannine tradition.[15] Brown states that the exegetical theses concerning the reconstructed history of the Johannine congregation, the sources, and the composition of the Gospel of John do not by themselves open up the intended message of the Gospel (cf. 20:31).[16]

Leading Figures in the Evangelical Interpretation of the Fourth Gospel

Stephen S. Smalley

Stephen Smalley recognizes in the Gospel of John "an independent and basically historical tradition which the evangelist has interpreted in his own way."[17] According to Smalley, the interest of the author of the Fourth Gospel

---

Gospel (Nashville: Abingdon, 1979); Rudolf Schnackenburg, The Gospel according to St. John, 3 vols. (London: Burns & Oats, 1968–82); R. Alan Culpepper, The Gospel and Letters of John, Interpreting Biblical Texts (Nashville: Abingdon, 1998), 54–61.

14. The current state of research concerning 1 John is treated reliably by Johannes Beutler, Die Johannesbriefe, RNT (Regensburg: Pustet, 2000), 11–33.

15. See Brown, Introduction to the New Testament, 363, 373–76.

16. Ibid., 378.

17. Stephen S. Smalley, John: Evangelist and Interpreter (Exeter: Paternoster, 1978), 7. See also further contributions by Smalley: "New Light on the Fourth Gospel," TynBul 17 (1966): 35–62; "The Johannine Son of Man Sayings," NTS 16 (1968–69): 278–301; "Diversity and Development in John," NTS 17 (1970–71): 276–92; "The Testament of Jesus: Another Look [on John 13–17: Response to E. Käsemann]," Studia Evangelica 6 (1973): 495–501; "The Sign of John XXI," NTS 20 (1974): 275–88; "Recent Johannine Studies," ExpTim 87 (1975–76): 247–48; "Johannine Spirituality," in The Westminster Dictionary of Christian Spirituality, ed. G. S. Wakefield (Philadelphia: Westminster, 1983), 230–32; "The Christ-Christian Relationship in Paul and John," in Pauline Studies, ed. D. A. Hagner and M. J. Harris (Exeter: Paternoster, 1980), 95–105; "The Johannine Community and the Letters of John," in A Vision for the Church, ed. M. Bockmuehl and M. B. Thompson (Edinburgh: Clark, 1997), 95–104; 1–3 John, WBC 51 (Waco, Tex.: Word, 1984).

as evangelist is focused mainly on securing and preserving "the historical and traditional basis on which all Christian faith rests," while as interpreter, "John presents and explains that gospel more fully for his congregation, relating it directly to their particular situation."[18] Yet, John is no historian in a modern sense, but a gifted theologian who is able to bring both together: "the historical basis of faith" and "its theological meaning and existential appeal for all time."[19] Smalley differentiates between John the son of Zebedee (the Beloved Disciple) and John the evangelist: whereas the apostle John had been responsible for preserving the Johannine tradition about Jesus, the Gospel itself has been written by one or more authors.[20] Smalley assumes that John passed on his writings to his disciples, who then became responsible for the edition and the revision.[21] On this view, the apostolic character of the Gospel of John can be preserved, which for Smalley is very much equated with the historical credibility of the narrations. He emphasizes the reliability of topographical details and the historical character of the "signs" of Jesus, as well as Jesus' sermons (note especially the misunderstandings, the "I am" and the "Amen, Amen" sayings, the prayer of Jesus in John 17).

George R. Beasley-Murray

George R. Beasley-Murray has presented a well-balanced commentary on the Fourth Gospel that takes into consideration German, English, and American research in the Gospel of John.[22] His opinion for a gradual, growing knowledge of the Synoptic Gospels by the Johannine congregation is well-founded. He represents a balanced trend of research as he nevertheless rejects the idea of direct use of sources by the Fourth Gospel.[23] Consequently, he also rejects the isolation of the Johannine Gospel as representative of a "sect" within early Christianity. He correctly points out the difficulty with all analyses in literary criticism and history of tradition concerning the Gospel of John that assume processes of growth during the emergence of the Gospel or later interferences by the evangelist himself or by a disciple acting according to the will of the evangelist. How can such processes reliably be recognized? Because of this difficulty, Beasley-Murray refrains from proposing far-reaching hypotheses about

18. Smalley, *John: Evangelist and Interpreter,* 150.
19. Ibid., 252.
20. Ibid., 81; cf. Smalley, *1–3 John,* xxii. In "John's Revelation and John's Community," *BJRL* 69 (1987): 551–71, Smalley believes that Revelation was the first writing of the Johannine corpus, written by the apostle John himself.
21. Smalley, *John: Evangelist and Interpreter,* 119–21.
22. George R. Beasley-Murray, *John,* WBC 36 (Waco, Tex.: Word, 1987). See also other works of his dedicated to the Gospel of John: "John 12:31–32: The Eschatological Significance of the Lifting Up of the Son of Man," in *Studien zum Text und zur Ethik des Neuen Testaments,* ed. W. Schrage, BZNW 47 (Berlin: de Gruyter: 1986), 70–81; *Gospel of Life: Theology in the Fourth Gospel* (Peabody, Mass.: Hendrickson, 1991).
23. See Beasley-Murray, *John,* xxxv–xxxvii.

the literary process that led to the Gospel of John. He pleads for a synchronic exegesis of the canonical text in its final form. This kind of exegesis takes seriously the preaching of the Gospel and the call for faith (20:30–31).[24] He rejects the view that the Gospel of John can simply be ascribed to one ancient religious context; rather, "it is rooted in the ancient religions of the nearer Orient in which ancient Israel was set, and from which the Greeks themselves learned."[25] The evangelist is not to be identified with the Beloved Disciple, who as a disciple of Jesus had been the deciding authority in the early Johannine congregation. The evangelist is to be understood as a "master interpreter of the school of the Beloved Disciple, among whom the Spirit showed his activity in large measure."[26] In general agreement with T. W. Manson, R. H. Lightfoot, and R. Schnackenburg, Beasley-Murray assumes a history of the Johannine congregation that started in Jerusalem and from there, via Antioch, reached Ephesus.[27]

D. A. Carson

In the beginning of his scholarly research, D. A. Carson tackled a classic topic of Reformed theology: How are God's providence and sovereignty related to human freedom (i.e., responsibility) in the Bible?[28] Carson gives an overview of OT, early Jewish, and rabbinical testimonies that offer emphases without resolving the tension between the two poles. The same is true for the Gospel of John: God asserts himself with his plan, and at the same time, humankind is responsible and can become guilty vis-à-vis God's call, which waits for a response. In his essays dealing with John, Carson develops a well-founded skepticism about the possibility of reconstructing sources of the Johannine Gospel (not about the existence of sources per se)[29] and affirms a comprehensive and reliable tradition of the Johannine version of Jesus' historical work. He formulates this last point by referencing the work of C. H. Dodd.[30]

---

24. Ibid., xxxviii–liii.

25. Ibid., lxv.

26. Ibid., lxxv.

27. Ibid., lxxx–lxxxi.

28. Donald A. Carson, *Divine Sovereignty and Human Responsibility: Biblical Perspectives in Tension* (Atlanta: Knox, 1981).

29. D. A. Carson, "Current Source Criticism of the Fourth Gospel: Some Methodological Questions," *JBL* 97 (1978): 411–29. See also idem, "Recent Literature on the Fourth Gospel: Some Reflections," *Them* 99 (1983): 8–18; "The Function of the Paraclete in John 16:7–11," *JBL* 98 (1979): 547–66.

30. See C. H. Dodd, *The Interpretation of the Fourth Gospel* (Cambridge: Cambridge University Press, 1953); *Historical Tradition in the Fourth Gospel* (Cambridge: Cambridge University Press, 1963); cf. D. A. Carson, "Historical Tradition in the Fourth Gospel: After Dodd, What?" in *Studies of History and Tradition in the Four Gospels,* ed. R. T. France and D. Wenham, Gospel Perspectives 2 (Sheffield: JSOT Press, 1981), 83–145; J. S. King, "Has D. A. Carson Been Fair to C. H. Dodd?" *JSNT* 17 (1983): 97–102; D. A. Carson, "Historical Tradition in the Fourth Gospel: A Response to J. S. King," *JSNT* 23 (1985): 73–81.

The characteristic Johannine misunderstandings are a stylistic device, yet in a modified manner Carson traces them back to the historical Jesus: "However worked over in Johannine idiom, they are grounded in the life-setting of the historical Jesus."[31] Also, for the farewell discourse (John 14–17) Carson allows more sayings to go back to the historical Jesus than is generally permitted by the exegetical mainstream.[32] Carson characterizes the purpose of the Gospel of John as the evangelization of Jews in the Diaspora as well as of proselytes and Gentiles converted to Judaism, and he gives as support for this view the Johannine exegesis of the Scriptures[33] and a problematic translation of John 20:31 that he nevertheless assumes to be correct: "in order that you may believe that the Christ, the Son of God, is Jesus" (versus "that Jesus is the Christ").[34] Unlike Smalley and Beasley-Murray, he identifies the apostle John with the Beloved Disciple *and* with the evangelist.[35]

Narrative Exegesis of John

The creativity of the new research in the Fourth Gospel shows itself in the energetic debates about methods in literary studies. The most fruitful of these methods seems to be the narrative interpretation of John.[36] Here, the presentation and the profile of the actors come to the foreground as the main questions, interlinked with the concept of *characterization*.[37] In this context, the importance of women in the Gospel of John is treated quite often.[38]

31. D. A. Carson, "Understanding the Misunderstandings in the Fourth Gospel," *TynBul* 33 (1982): 90.

32. D. A. Carson, *The Farewell Discourse and the Final Prayer of Jesus: An Exposition of John 14–17* (Grand Rapids: Baker, 1980). For Carson's hermeneutical approach, see *The Sermon on the Mount: An Evangelical Exposition of Matthew 5–7* (Grand Rapids: Baker, 1978), 139–49; "Recent Developments in the Doctrine of Scripture," in *Hermeneutics, Authority and Canon,* ed. D. A. Carson and John D. Woodbridge (Leicester: Inter-Varsity, 1986), 5–48 (notes on pp. 363–74).

33. D. A. Carson, "John and the Johannine Epistles," in *It Is Written: Scripture Citing Scripture,* ed. D. A. Carson and H. G. M. Williamson (Cambridge: Cambridge University Press, 1988), 245–64.

34. D. A. Carson, "The Purpose of the Fourth Gospel: John 20:31 Reconsidered," *JBL* 106 (1987): 639–51.

35. D. A. Carson, *The Gospel according to John* (Grand Rapids: Eerdmans, 1991), 69–81.

36. See Mark W. G. Stibbe, *John,* Readings: A New Biblical Commentary (Sheffield: Sheffield Academic Press, 1993); Francis J. Moloney, *Belief in the Word: Reading the Fourth Gospel, John 1–4* (Minneapolis: Fortress, 1993); idem, *Signs and Shadows: Reading John 5–12* (Minneapolis: Fortress, 1996); idem, *Glory Not Dishonor: Reading John 13–21* (Minneapolis: Augsburg Fortress, 1998); idem, *The Gospel of John,* SP 4 (Collegeville, Minn.: Liturgical Press, 1998); Dirk F. Gniesmer, *In den Prozeß verwickelt: Erzähltextanalytische und textpragmatische Erwägungen zur Erzählung vom Prozeß Jesu vor Pilatus (Joh 18,28–19,16a.b),* Europäische Hochschulschriften 23.688 (Frankfurt: Lang, 2000).

37. See David R. Beck, *The Discipleship Paradigm: Readers and Anonymous Characters in the Fourth Gospel,* BIS 27 (Leiden: Brill 1997); David Rhoads and Kari Syreeni, eds., *Characterization in the Gospels: Rediscovering Narrative Criticism,* JSNTSup 184 (Sheffield: Sheffield Academic Press, 1999).

38. See Colleen M. Conway, *Men and Women in the Fourth Gospel: Gender and Johannine Characterization,* SBLDS 167 (Atlanta: Society of Biblical Literature, 1999); Ingrid Kitzberger,

R. Alan Culpepper

The pioneer of the narrative interpretation of John is R. Alan Culpepper, whose 1987 volume *The Anatomy of the Fourth Gospel* still represents well the current state of research.[39] Many of his discoveries can be judged as today's standard knowledge for the exegesis of John. Culpepper provides useful insights about the narrator and the perspective of the narrative; the narrated time and the time of the narration; the plot, the characters, and the implicit comments (including misunderstandings, irony,[40] and symbolism); the comments of the narrator; and the implicit reader. These narrative signs, authorities, and effects allow the narrative anatomy of the Gospel of John to be seen in its entirety. The narrative coherence of the Fourth Gospel results not only from axes that run throughout the whole Gospel (plot, progression of action from scene to scene, thematic development), but also from subtle structures. These can be discovered by a narrative analysis of the characters and of the author's steering of the reader by the use of misunderstandings, symbols, and irony. Culpepper's narrative analysis and his interpretation of the Gospel of John can be used profitably in conjunction with insights from historical criticism about the emergence and the theology of the Johannine Gospel. His analysis clarifies and widens the historical-critical view in many respects.[41]

Francis J. Moloney

Francis J. Moloney has authored commentaries on the Gospel of John that apply methods of narrative interpretation.[42] His exegesis shows convincingly that this method is fruitful and suitable to the text, as it emphasizes the coherence of the Johannine theology without denying a process of growth of the Gospel of John. Moloney aims at showing the logical steering of the reader that culminates in John 20:30–31. Primarily, he does not want to describe the world "behind the text," but the world "in front of the text"; this means the reception[43] of the Gospel then and today. Moloney succeeds impressively in showing "that readers at the turn of the second and third millennia still find that their response to this gospel, in dialogue with the experience of almost two

---

"Synoptic Women in John: Interfigural Readings," in *Transformative Encounters: Jesus and Women Re-viewed*, ed. I. R. Kitzberger, BIS 43 (Leiden: Brill, 2000), 77–111.

39. R. Alan Culpepper, *The Anatomy of the Fourth Gospel: A Study in Literary Design* (Philadelphia: Fortress, 1987).

40. See K. Scholtissek, "Ironie und Rollenwechsel im Johannesevangelium," *ZNW* 89 (1998): 235–55.

41. See R. Alan Culpepper, *The Johannine School: An Evaluation of the Johannine-School Hypothesis Based on an Investigation of the Nature of Ancient Schools*, SBLDS 26 (Missoula, Mont.: Scholars Press, 1975); idem, *John, the Son of Zebedee; The Gospel and Letters of John*.

42. Moloney, *Belief in the Word; Signs and Shadows; Glory Not Dishonor*.

43. Moloney refers to Sandra M. Schneiders, *The Revelatory Text: Interpreting the New Testament as Sacred Scripture* (Collegeville, Minn.: Liturgical Press, 1999).

thousand years of Christian life, resonates with the experience of the implied reader and the original readers in the Johannine community."[44]

Old and New Paradigms of Research in the Gospel of John

Criticism of the Classic Points of View

The end of the twentieth century marks a shift in the research in John that erodes the dominating paradigms of literary criticism and of the history-of-religions approach. This new beginning is marked by a departure from the divisions that have been standard since Rudolf Bultmann in the study of the Gospel of John: the opposition of present and future eschatology, of faith and sacrament, of soteriology and ethics, and of Christology and ecclesiology. This shift is impressively displayed in the recent commentary of Ulrich Wilckens,[45] which stands in clear contrast to the commentary of, for example, Siegfried Schulz,[46] who followed his teacher Bultmann and whose volume appeared in the same series as that of Wilckens.

The Classic Literary Criticism

The classic position concerning Johannine literary criticism and history of tradition, which was formulated with enormous impact in the commentary on John by Rudolf Bultmann[47] and influenced important commentaries in the period following (Rudolf Schnackenburg,[48] Jürgen Becker),[49] is no longer accepted in new monographs as a self-evident precondition of interpretation.[50] The voices that question the existence of the Signs Source are growing in number and are making convincing arguments.[51] The classic paradigm of literary criticism is most extensively critiqued by Jörg Frey.[52] His magnum

44. Moloney, *The Gospel of John*, 19; cf. idem, *Belief in the Word*, 1–22.

45. Wilckens, *Das Evangelium nach Johannes*.

46. Siegfried Schulz, *Das Evangelium nach Johannes*, NTD 4 (Göttingen: Vandenhoeck & Ruprecht, 1987).

47. R. Bultmann, *Das Evangelium des Johannes*, KEK (Göttingen: Vandenhoeck & Ruprecht, 1950).

48. Schnackenburg, *The Gospel according to St. John*, vols. 1–2.

49. Jürgen Becker, *Das Evangelium nach Johannes*, 2 vols., ÖTK 4 (Gütersloh: Gütersloher Verlagshaus Mohn, 1979–81).

50. This is confirmed by Johannes Beutler, *Studien zu den johanneischen Schriften*, SBAB 25 (Stuttgart: Katholisches Bibelwerk, 1998).

51. See G. van Belle, *The Signs Source in the Fourth Gospel: Historical Survey and Critical Evaluation of the Semeia Hypothesis*, BETL 116 (Leuven: Peeters, 1994).

52. Frey, *Die johanneische Eschatologie*, vol. 1.

opus tackles the whole of modern research in John in extraordinary breadth and makes visible its roots in the history of modern thought.

In the first volume, which treats the history of research, Frey presents the exegesis of Johannine eschatology since the Enlightenment. Whereas H. S. Reimarus and J. S. Semler represent the questioning of NT eschatology in general, the philosophy of the Enlightenment (G. E. Lessing, I. Kant, G. W. F. Hegel, F. Schleiermacher) tends toward an interpretation that puts the focus of eschatology totally on the present.[53] This interpretation is characterized by a certain violence toward the text that adjusts the NT sayings to the prevailing worldview and its preconditions. In the time of the Enlightenment, this led to a lack of awareness of the temporal structure of the NT testimonies (according to Frey, they became "untemporalized"); their temporal structure, especially concerning the future, was neglected. Even the rediscovering of eschatology in the preaching of Jesus by Johannes Weiss could not destroy his and Albert Schweitzer's preference for an "un-eschatological" Gospel of John. Frey succeeds in showing how strongly the arising literary criticism applied to the Fourth Gospel (H. H. Wendt, J. Wellhausen, E. Schwartz) was marked by systematic interests. The early research in the history of religions (W. Bousset, A. Schlatter, W. Bauer, R. Bultmann, H. Odeberg), in all its diversity, is interested in an eschatology that is related to the present as well.

Frey gives a detailed description of the exegesis of Bultmann. According to Bultmann, the evangelist boldly transformed eschatology into history, put it in the present, and thus eliminated the traditional eschatology with its focus on the future.[54] Easter, Pentecost, and the parousia therefore form one and the same point in the work of the evangelist. This exegesis and its implications (concerning the history of literature, of religions, of tradition, and of theology) are criticized intensely by Frey. His remarks could not be sharper and more apt. According to Frey, literary criticism became the instrument of a projection that ascribes the Lutheran doctrine of justification to the theology of the evangelist himself and the traces of early catholicism to a postulated "revision of the Church." In contrast to this trend, Frey mentions the positions of G. Stählin, W. G. Kümmel, J. Blank, and R. Schnackenburg, who, with different emphases, assume certain temporal dialectics in Johannine eschatology, and O. Cullmann, whose interpretation is oriented toward the history of salvation. A new beginning can also be found among those authors who for different reasons and out of special interests lean toward a synchronous reading of John. But they are in danger of neglecting the historical context and the historical interpretation of the Fourth Gospel.

53. Ibid., 1:13.
54. Ibid., 1:108.

John in the Ban of Gnosis?

Since the commentary of Bultmann, the Gospel of John often is understood against the backdrop of the ban of, or dispute with, gnosis.[55] The historical and religious context from which gnosis originated is understood by a large number of researchers in the following way: "Gnosis is a syncretistic phenomenon, a mixture of religions: dualism from Iran, vulgar platonic philosophy, various myths of the ancient world, from the OT, especially from fringe groups out of Judaism: apocalyptic and wisdom traditions, finally also out of the emerging Christianity."[56] The characterization of the Gospel of John as gnostic or antignostic depends on the question of whether or not pre-Christian origins of gnosis, particularly forms of gnosis parallel to Christianity but outside of it, can be assumed. According to Christoph Markschies, "Pre-Christian gnosis is very unlikely, as we have no sources for this."[57] There are strong objections against seeing a dispute with gnosis as the background for the Gospel of John. Today, the gnostic texts are mostly dated from the second and third centuries C.E. The dualism of John (light/darkness, children of God/children of the devil, etc.) can be explained from Jewish sources (apocalyptic circles, Qumran). The dualism of spirit and matter, which is fundamental to the whole gnostic system and can be derived from Platonic philosophy, cannot be found in the Gospel of John. John's anthropology is biblical. The Johannine image of God is rooted in its Jewish tradition. Again and again researchers claim to find a doctrine of providence in the Gospel of John, but this would be a direct contradiction of the main headlines of Johannine theology. An exegesis of John having been formed to combat gnosis therefore has to be rejected.

However, a plausible case can be made for a gnostic reception of the Gospel of John. Titus Nagel has written a detailed volume about the reception of John in the second century.[58] He maintains that only after the middle of the second century does an exact way of preserving the text start to develop that is inter-

55. See Scholtissek, "Johannes auslegen I," 36–51; cf. the early history of the reception of the Fourth Gospel: Titus Nagel, *Die Rezeption des Johannesevangeliums im 2. Jahrhundert,* ABG 2 (Leipzig: Evangelische Verlagsanstalt, 2000); Ansgar Wucherpfennig, *Heracleon Philologus: Gnostische Johannesexegese im zweiten Jahrhundert,* WUNT 146 (Tübingen: Mohr Siebeck, 2002).

56. Hans-Josef Klauck, "Gnosis als Weltanschauung in der Antike" (1993), in *Alte Welt und neuer Glaube: Beiträge zur Religiongeschichte, Forschungsgeschichte und Theologie des Neuen Testaments,* NTOA 29 (Freiburg: Universitätsverlag; Göttingen: Vandenhoeck & Ruprecht, 1994), 177–78; cf. idem, *Die religiöse Umwelt des Urchristentums,* 2 vols. in 1, StTh 9.1–2 (Stuttgart: Kohlhammer 1995–96), 2:145–98; in English, *The Religious Context of Early Christianity: A Guide to Graeco-Roman Religions* (Edinburgh: Clark, 2000); see also Pheme Perkins, *Gnosticism and the New Testament* (Minneapolis: Fortress, 1993).

57. Christoph Markschies, "Gnosis/Gnostizismus," *NBL* (Zürich: Benziger, 1991): 1:868–71, esp. 869; cf. idem, *Die Gnosis* (Munich: Beck, 2001). See also the early criticism of the gnostic hypothesis by E. M. Yamauchi, *Pre-Christian Gnosticism: A Survey of the Proposed Evidences* (Grand Rapids: Eerdmans, 1973).

58. Nagel, *Die Rezeption des Johannesevangeliums.*

ested in retaining every word. Prior to that time, oral and written traditions existed side by side. Concerning the question of gnostic traces in the Gospel of John itself, Nagel convincingly argues for a later gnostic coloring and use of Johannine terms and texts but against their having a gnostic character per se. Nagel's analyses show the very early and broad knowledge and reception of the Gospel of John in the church (in Asia Minor, Syria, Rome, Egypt). That the Fourth Gospel dates from about 100–110 C.E. and was written in Asia Minor is made even more plausible by these results. The broad reception of the Gospel of John in Christian-gnostic literature, according to Nagel, does not originate in an affinity of John's Gospel to the gnostic system, but in the fact that many Christian-gnostic texts have an exegetical tendency and character. Obviously, in these circles there was keen interest to incorporate the Gospel of John as an authority (or to reject it polemically).

John and the Synoptic Gospels

The vast majority of researchers in John in the twentieth century were convinced that the Gospel of John was written without any knowledge of the Synoptic Gospels. For a long time, only Frans Neirynck had rejected this consensus.[59] Today many German-speaking researchers assume in their new commentaries that the evangelist knew at least one, or maybe even more, of the Synoptics (e.g., L. Schenke, U. Schnelle, U. Wilckens). A middle position assumes common traditions, predating the written versions of the Gospels, which are used by Mark and John and include "traditions incorporated later into Luke."[60] A prominent feature of Wilckens's exegesis is the belief that the Gospel of John resulted in a deeper theological interpretation of the Synoptics.

New Positions

The "Johannine Question"

The introductory questions concerning the Gospel of John continue to be addressed.[61] After the volume by Martin Hengel in which he argues for an edition of the Gospel of John at the end of the first century in Ephesus,[62] there

---

59. See, among the numerous publications of Neirynck, "John and the Synoptics 1975–1990," in *John and the Synoptics,* ed. A. Denaux, BETL 101 (Leuven: Leuven University Press, 1992), 3–62; idem, "John and the Synoptics in Recent Commentaries." See also the other essays in Denaux, *John and the Synoptics.*

60. See Brown, *Introduction to the New Testament,* 365.

61. See J. Beutler, "Johannesevangelium (u. -Briefe)," *RAC* 141 (1997): 646–63, 668–70.

62. M. Hengel, *The Johannine Question* (Philadelphia: Trinity, 1989); in German, *Die johanneische Frage: Ein Lösungsversuch,* WUNT 67 (Tübingen: Mohr Siebeck, 1993); cf. the critique by Culpepper, *John, the Son of Zebedee,* 304–7.

are still proposals that find reasons for Syria[63] or Egypt[64] as the place of origin of the Fourth Gospel. Hengel considers the evangelist to be a disciple of the historical Jesus during his last time in Jerusalem, someone who saw and heard Jesus and has written his Gospel after a long period of mature reflection. His disciples then edited his writings. This evangelist, who is also responsible for the emergence of 1–3 John, is identified by Hengel as the "presbyter" John who is mentioned by Papias (cf. 2 John 1; 3 John 1). With this view, Hengel rejects a collective and more or less anonymous "Johannine school."[65] More cautious is the judgment of R. E. Brown, who says that the Beloved Disciple was a disciple of the historical Jesus and later became the chief authority in the Johannine congregations. According to Brown, the evangelist was a disciple of the Beloved Disciple, and Brown assumes the existence of a "Johannine school."[66] Udo Schnelle calls Ephesus the place of origin of the Fourth Gospel, where, according to him, it was written ca. 100–110 C.E. The evangelist is no eyewitness of the life of Jesus but belongs "to a circle of teachers who are gifted by the Spirit and who—relying on the Paraclete themselves—commit the congregation to the exclusive authority of Jesus."[67] Against the broad agreement of the scholarly community that judges the Gospel of John to be the youngest, only a few, and hardly convincing, voices are heard that plead for an earlier date for the origin of the Johannine Gospel, some going back as far as the time before the Jewish-Roman war.[68]

Johannine Form and Tradition History

Despite the new trend to interpret the Gospel of John synchronically, some researchers still opt for a tradition history of the Fourth Gospel, which they believe can be reconstructed. Michael Labahn dedicates himself to the analy-

63. See J. Becker, "Geisterfahrung und Christologie—ein Vergleich zwischen Paulus und Johannes," in *Antikes Judentum und Frühes Christentum*, ed. B. Kollmann, W. Reinbold, and A. Steudel, BZNW 97 (Berlin: de Gruyter 1999), 439–42.

64. See Klaus Berger, *Im Anfang war Johannes: Datierung und Theologie des vierten Evangeliums* (Stuttgart: Quell, 1997); Marco Frenschkowski, "(Joh 12,13) und andere Indizien für einen ägyptischen Ursprung des Johannesevangeliums," *ZNW* 91 (2000): 212–29.

65. Cf. Culpepper, *The Johannine School*. For a recent overview of the current research, see Christian Cebulj, "Johannesevangelium und Johannesbriefe," in *Schulen im Neuen Testament? Zur Stellung des Urchristentums in der Bildungswelt seiner Zeit*, ed. T. Schmeller, HBS 30 (Freiburg: Herder, 2001), 254–342.

66. Brown, *Introduction to the New Testament*, 368–71. See also the debate presented by Theo Heckel, *Vom Evangelium des Markus zum viergestaltigen Evangelium*, WUNT 120 (Tübingen: Mohr Siebeck, 1999), 106–44, 246–65. Moloney (*The Gospel of John*, 6–9) sees the Beloved Disciple as the evangelist.

67. See Schnelle, *Das Evangelium nach Johannes*, 1–27, esp. 5; cf. idem, *Einleitung in das Neue Testament*, UTB 1830 (Göttingen: Vandenhoeck & Ruprecht, 1999), 495–584.

68. See John A. T. Robinson, *The Priority of John*, ed. J. F. Coakley (Oak Park, Ill.: Meyer-Stone, 1987); Berger, *Im Anfang war Johannes* (cf. the critique by Scholtissek, "Neue Wege der Johannesauslegung I," 281f.).

sis of the form history and to the interpretation of the Johannine miracles.[69] Labahn considers the form history to be indispensable for shedding light on the history of the Johannine congregation and on the Johannine Gospel itself. The analyses and interpretations of all seven miracles (John 2:1–12; 4:46–54; 5:1–9, 10–16 [and 7:21–24]; 6:1–15, 16–21;[70] 9:1–41; 11:1–54) form a closed presentation that describes comparable formal developments of the seven "signs" until they reach their canonical and final version. The classic problem of Johannine literary criticism appears again. In regard to John 9, Labahn, on the one hand, assumes a quite homogenous entity, and on the other hand, he postulates four stages that for the form history have to be differentiated. But he cannot present these stages exactly, because the evangelist, according to Labahn, has revised them with his own language and style. For Michael Theobald, literary criticism produces some fanciful theories (e.g., the proposal that all texts that mention the Beloved Disciple were inserted after the completion of the Gospel),[71] and he assumes that the history of the tradition of the Johannine sermons of Jesus can be reconstructed, beginning with some crucial sayings in these sermons.[72]

The Coherence of the Canonical Text

Following the international trend, German-speaking researchers picked up methods for the synchronic interpretation of the Gospel of John. Jörg Frey advocates a thesis that is supported more and more in current research and that was emphasized by his teacher Martin Hengel: the Gospel of John is coherent in rhetorical and pragmatic respects; a uniform concept stands behind the whole work. Only John 21 probably was added by editors of the Johannine school, according to Frey. His studies are a forceful plea to take the canonical text seriously as a whole—with its tensions and its theological claims—and to interpret it in the framework of its own thought forms and temporal structure.

Thomas Popp[73] succeeds impressively in showing the coherence of the canonical text of the Fourth Gospel. He convincingly demonstrates, for example,

---

69. Michael Labahn, *Jesus als der Lebensspender: Untersuchungen zu einer Geschichte der johanneischen Tradition anhand ihrer Wundergeschichten*, BZNW 98 (Berlin: de Gruyter, 1999); see also idem, "Between Tradition and Literary Art," *Bib* 80 (1999): 178–203; *Offenbarung in Zeichen und Wort: Untersuchungen zur Vorgeschichte von Joh 6,1–25a und seiner Rezeption in der Brotrede*, WUNT 2.117 (Tübingen: Mohr Siebeck, 2000).

70. On John 6, see Scholtissek, "Die Brotrede Jesu in Joh 6," *ZTK* 123 (2001): 35–55.

71. M. Theobald, "Der Jünger, den Jesus liebte," in *Geschichte—Tradition—Reflexion*, ed. H. Cancik, H. Lichtenberger, and P. Schäfer (Tübingen: Mohr Siebeck, 1996), 3:219–55.

72. M. Theobald, "'Spruchgut' im Johannesevangelium," in *Das Urchristentum in seiner literarischen Geschichte*, ed. U. Mell and U. Müller, BZNW 100 (Berlin: de Gruyter, 1999), 335–67; *Herrenworte im Johannesevangelium*, HBS 34 (Freiburg: Herder, 2002).

73. Thomas Popp, *Grammatik des Geistes: Literarische Kunst und theologische Konzeption in Johannes 3 und 6*, ABG 3 (Leipzig: Evangelische Verlagsanstalt, 2001).

that John 2:23–3:36 and 6:1–71—often underestimated with regard to their artistic form and theological concept (which are inseparably linked)—can be read and understood as documents of the spiritual and anamnestic interpretation of the gospel of Jesus Christ itself. The Spirit of God—that is, of Jesus Christ—who is the source of the Johannine Gospel and whose guidance the Fourth Gospel announces emphatically in the time after Easter, is the dynamic driving force that formed the Johannine theological and literary presentation of the gospel. The Gospel of John, as the written form of the faith in Christ that was brought by the Spirit, bears witness to the "grammar of the Spirit" after Easter (Popp references Martin Luther: *Spiritus sanctus habet suam grammaticam*). To decode this grammar, one is required "to listen," "to recognize," and "to believe" in guidance by the Spirit. Pneumatology assumes a vital role for the evangelist himself, both in the actual form of the text of the Johannine Gospel and in its reception. Form and content are taken seriously in their inseparable mutual relationship. The so-called grammar of the Spirit can be identified more specifically in methodological and hermeneutical aspects and in content. The Johannine stylistic devices (repetition, amplification, variation, parallelism, the spiral movement of thought, misunderstanding, irony, the semantic ambiguity of some terms, *inclusio,* chiasm, composition using a headword or a net of headwords, metaphor) are included in this "spiritual grammar." Popp emphasizes that the Gospel of John invites the reader to read it numerous times, each time obtaining a deeper understanding. This way of reading leads to the encounter with Jesus Christ, who is revealing himself. Therefore, the Gospel of John has to be taken seriously as a work of literary art (H. Strathmann). *Poiesis* on the side of the author and of the text and *aesthesis* and *katharsis* on the side of the recipients belong together. In methodological and hermeneutical respects, the uniform literary and theological concept of John and its coherence are demonstrated by the examples from John 2–3 and 6, and Popp presents a convincing case. A result of this investigation is the emphasis on the "aspectual" and "synthetic way of thinking" in the Gospel of John. The Johannine Gospel can be characterized as "a new interpretation of Christ in continuation with the apostolic Christology, but as a new exegesis written in review and given by the Spirit to open up anew the sense and meaning of Christ."[74]

Relecture and Réécriture

One of the most promising new contributions in research in John is the paradigm called *relecture:* the history of the growth of the Johannine tradition of Jesus is understood not as a dispute between opposite positions, but as a creative process of continuation. There is no rejection, but rather a reception, of earlier stages: they are picked up, they become incorporated and included and deepened

---

74. Ibid., 40.

by new challenges. In this sense, the process of growth of the Johannine Gospel can be considered as a process toward maturity. This concept is developed especially by Jean Zumstein.[75] Zumstein's student Andreas Dettwiler has used *relecture* for the interpretation of Jesus' farewell discourse.[76] Dettwiler is able to present a new perspective on reading the complex text in John 13:31–16:33. The movement of the theological thought and the history of the growth of the farewell discourse is no longer seen as the history of competing positions, but as an organic process of continuation that picks up the earlier version and unfolds it. The exegetical thesis of Dettwiler is highly plausible: 15:1–7 is a *relecture* of 13:1–17, 34, and 16:4b–33 is a *relecture* of 13:31–14:31. *Relecture* in Johannine understanding means the process of self-interpretation of the risen Christ—a process that is guided by the Spirit. Zumstein shows the possibility of combining narrative interpretation of John with the paradigm of *relecture*. Its basic principle is: "Relecture does not simply repeat a text, but puts it back into a context"[77]—in the context of a new situation or of a new question. The coherence of the content of the Johannine theology, according to Zumstein, can be seen "in an independent exegesis of the Christian faith that is based on itself."[78] In the perspective of faith that developed after Easter, John presents the way of faith in "a hermeneutic of stages"; the Johannine "strategy of faith" aims at two things: to deepen the gospel personally and to make it more accessible. These aims are illustrated by the different persons who meet Jesus in the Gospel of John. The Johannine Gospel therefore has to be understood "as a mediating authority that tries to awaken *the faith of the faithful*."[79]

Besides the *relecture* that reflects the diachronic relationship of two texts, there can be found, in my view, an analogous process in the synchronic relationship of texts in the Gospel of John: *réécriture*. Here, one basic principle is taken up, varied, and expressed differently by one and the same author.[80] The character of *réécriture* in Johannine thought can be demonstrated by the use of language: repetitions of quotations, of sentences or parts of sentences, or of

75. Jean Zumstein, *Kreative Erinnerung: Relecture und Auslegung im Johannesevangelium* (Zürich: Pano, 1999).

76. Andreas Dettwiler, *Die Gegenwart des Erhöhten: Eine exegetische Studie zu den johanneischen Abschiedsreden (Joh 13,31–16,33) unter besonderer Berücksichtigung ihres Relecture—Charakters,* FRLANT 169 (Göttingen: Vandenhoeck & Ruprecht, 1995). For a further description of *relecture,* see K. Scholtissek, "Relecture—zu einem neu entdeckten Programmwort der Schriftauslegung," *BL* 70 (1997): 309–15; idem, "Relecture und Réécriture: Neue Paradigmen zu Methode und Inhalt der Johannesauslegung aufgewiesen am Prolog 1,1–18 und der ersten Abschiedsrede 13,31–14,31," *TP* 75 (2000): 1–29. Cf. Konrad Haldimann, *Rekonstruktion und Entfaltung: Exegetische Untersuchungen zu Joh 15 und 16,* BZNW 104 (Berlin: de Gruyter, 2000); Susanne Ruschmann, *Maria von Magdala im Johannesevangelium: Jüngerin, Zeugin, Glaubensbotin,* NTAbh 40 (Münster: Aschendorff, 2002).

77. Zumstein, *Kreative Erinnerung,* 20.

78. Ibid., 13.

79. Ibid., 36.

80. See Scholtissek, "Relecture and réécriture."

specially marked words. In the sermon of Jesus in John 6, the "I am" saying of 6:35 is taken up again in 6:41, 48, 51. The basic principle that is varied again and again by the evangelist is expressed in the saying of John the Baptist in 1:26: "Among you stands the one you do not know." This messianic rule of the Baptist is a basic principle that is unfolded by narration in nearly all Johannine scenes, including the Easter tradition.[81]

The "Johannine Way of Watching"

Franz Mussner has introduced the helpful term "Johannine way of watching."[82] It refers to the hermeneutic vantage point of the evangelist: he "watches" the life and work of Jesus before Easter and the reality of the risen and glorified Christ "syn-optically" together. This view is deepened and exemplified in some studies that we review here.

METAPHORS AND AESTHETICS

Otto Schwankl[83] has presented an important contribution to the debate about the use of metaphor in the Gospel of John by his research in the metaphors of light and darkness in the Johannine corpus. The possibilities for variation of metaphor, its vitality and creativity, open up new territory. Metaphor "is one of the most important means to create a naming for an imagination that has no adequate name yet."[84] Schwankl defines the metaphor of the light as a "language of disclosure." He reflects upon the Johannine relationship of seeing and believing. The "Johannine way of watching" can be understood as a "metaphorical watching and seeing." Therefore, not only the specifically metaphorical sayings, but also the whole Johannine language, have this disclosure character. "The metaphor of the light in John contains the whole dramatic process of the world history, of the history of salvation and of the individual history of everyone's life. This process is represented, concentrated, deepened and decided by the use of the dramaturgy of this metaphor."[85] The "metaphorical potency" of the Johannine language is, at the same time, a hermeneutical program. The Gospel of John is an "ecumenical forum" that shows an "evangelizing" interest: "The Gospel's process of becoming part of a cultural area results from the incarnation."[86]

---

81. See K. Scholtissek, "'Mitten unter euch steht der, den ihr nicht kennt' (Joh 1,26): Die Messias-Regel des Täufers als johanneische Sinnlinie," *MTZ* 48 (1997): 103–21.

82. Cf. Franz Mussner, *Die johanneische Sehweise und die Frage nach dem historischen Jesus,* QD 28 (Freiburg: Herder, 1965); cf. Clemens Hergenröder, *Wir schauten seine Herrlichkeit: Das johanneische Sprechen vom Sehen im Horizont von Selbsterschließung Jesu und Antwort des Menschen,* FzB 80 (Würzburg: Echter, 1996).

83. Otto Schwankl, *Licht und Finsternis: Ein metaphorisches Paradigma in den johanneischen Schriften,* HBS 5 (Freiburg: Herder, 1995).

84. Ibid., 31.

85. Ibid., 354.

86. Ibid., 400.

Jan van der Watt has presented the first detailed investigation into the Johannine family metaphors.[87] He is able to show that the family metaphors in the Gospel of John are the continuous leading metaphors and comprise a constantly recurring motif. The other metaphors can be grouped, netlike, around this motif. The motifs of father, mother, son, children, wedding, bridegroom, love, birth-life-death, friends, servants, orphans, house, bread (food), water (drink), property, the householder's right, education, tradition of knowledge, mutual honor and respect, protection, and the Paraclete belong to the inner circle of the family metaphors. Correctly, van der Watt emphasizes that the evangelist uses these metaphors for his exegesis of the gospel. He uses them as far as they are useful *for* him: "The form of the imagery is dominated by the message. John adapts and develops his imagery in such a way that it communicates what he wants to say in the most effective way."[88]

PNEUMATIC ANAMNESIS AND HODEGY

Christina Hoegen-Rohls demonstrates that the point of view of the evangelist after Easter is his own chosen view that forms the framework in which he wants to understand and to present his material.[89] In the Gospel there are many hints that underline this role of the evangelist: the narrator's comments, which explicitly differentiate between the situation before and after Easter; the promises of Jesus that are not part of the farewell discourse and that are already looking toward the time after Easter; the five promises of Jesus in the farewell discourse to send the Paraclete; statements in the review and in the prayer of Jesus in John 17; and the confessions in the "we"—or "I"—sayings and the other Johannine sayings about the work of the Spirit. Analyzing and interpreting the Johannine pneumatology, Hoegen-Rohls works with suitable criteria to show the caesura, the continuity, and the interconnection of times in the Gospel of John, and explicates her thesis that the farewell discourse is the hermeneutical key to the Johannine way of presenting the Gospel. John 13–17 is the touchstone for all methodological and hermeneutical attempts at interpretation, as well as for attempts at exegesis of the content. Johannine theology understands itself as "seeing" and "recognizing," resulting from the prophetic work of the Spirit, and keeps both together: the work of the earthly Jesus as the authoritative (but not the only) place of God's final revelation and the situation after Easter as the time to meet Jesus and the Father anew.

---

87. Jan G. van der Watt, *Family of the King: Dynamics of Metaphor in the Gospel according to John*, BIS (Leiden: Brill, 2000). On the Johannine family metaphors, see also K. Scholtissek, "Kinder Gottes und Freunde Jesu," in *Ekklesiologie des Neuen Testaments*, ed. R. Kampling and T. Söding (Freiburg: Herder, 1996), 184–211; idem, *In ihm sein und bleiben: Die Sprache der Immanenz in den johanneischen Schriften*, HBS 21 (Freiburg: Herder, 2000), 162–65, 179–84, 222–53.

88. Van der Watt, *Family of the King*, 413.

89. Christina Hoegen-Rohls, *Der nachösterliche Johannes: Die Abschiedsreden als hermeneutischer Schlüssel zum vierten Evangelium*, WUNT 2.84 (Tübingen: Mohr Siebeck, 1996).

The more recent publications concerning the Johannine farewell discourse investigate its form[90] and narration,[91] understand it as *relecture*,[92] or present a continuous commentary[93] on the text.[94]

Prominent Topics in Contemporary Johannine Research

John and His Jewish Roots

The issue of John's relation to Judaism corresponds to the growing importance of the Jewish-Christian dialogue and to the interest in questions of biblical theology such as the relation between OT and NT, the description of the "Jewish roots" of the Christian gospel, and the NT authors' exegesis of OT Scripture. The research in John participates in this process.[95] One of the crucial topics is the question of a hostile attitude toward Jews in the Gospel of John, arising especially from the use of the term "the Jews." New studies in different fields of the Fourth Gospel present convincingly the Jewish roots of the evangelist and of his tradition of Jesus. Often, the Johannine exegesis of Scripture is investigated in these studies.[96]

---

90. See Martin Winter, *Das Vermächtnis Jesu und die Abschiedsworte der Väter: Gattungsgeschichtliche Untersuchung der Vermächtnisrede im Blick auf Joh. 13–17*, FRLANT 161 (Göttingen: Vandenhoeck & Ruprecht, 1994).

91. See D. Francois Tolmie, *Jesus' Farewell to the Disciples: John 13:1–17:26 in Narratological Perspective*, BIS 2 (Leiden: Brill, 1995).

92. See Dettwiler, *Die Gegenwart des Erhöhten*.

93. See Christian Dietzfelbinger, *Der Abschied des Kommenden: Eine Auslegung der johanneischen Abschiedsreden*, WUNT 95 (Tübingen: Mohr Siebeck, 1997); see also idem, *Das Evangelium nach Johannes*, 2 vols., ZBKNT 4 (Zürich: Theologische Verlagsanstalt, 2001).

94. See H.-J. Klauck, "Der Weggang Jesu," *BZ* 40 (1996): 236–50; Haldimann, *Rekonstruktion und Entfaltung*.

95. See U. Schnelle, "Die Juden im Johannesevangelium," in *Gedenkt an das Wort*, ed. C. Kähler, M. Böhm, and C. Böttrich (Leipzig: Evangelische Verlagsanstalt, 1999), 217–30; K. Scholtissek, "Antijudaismus im Johannesevangelium?" in "*Nun steht aber diese Sache im Evangelium . . .*": *Zur Frage nach den Anfängen des christlichen Antijudaismus*, ed. R. Kampling (Paderborn: Schöningh, 1999), 151–81; Thomas Söding, "'Was kann aus Nazareth schon Gutes kommen?': Die Bedeutung des Judeseins Jesu im Johannesevangelium," *NTS* 46 (2000): 21–41; Andreas Lindemann, "Mose und Jesus Christus: Zum Verständnis des Gesetzes im Johannesevangelium," in Mell and Müller, *Das Urchristentum in seiner literarischen Geschichte*, 309–34; Urban C. von Wahlde, "Die Darstellung von Juden und Judentum im Johannesevangelium" (1993), in *Studien zu einer neutestamentlichen Hermeneutik nach Auschwitz*, ed. P. Fiedler and G. Dautzenberg, SBAB 27 (Stuttgart: Katholisches Bibelwerk, 1999), 89–114.

96. See Bruce G. Schuchard, *Scripture within Scripture: The Interrelationship of Form and Function in the Explicit Old Testament Citations in the Gospel of John*, SBLDS 133 (Atlanta: Scholars, 1992); Andreas Obermann, *Die christologische Erfüllung der Schrift im Johannesevangelium: Eine Untersuchung zur johanneischen Hermeneutik anhand der Schriftzitate*, WUNT 2.83 (Tübingen: Mohr Siebeck, 1996); Maarten J. J. Menken, *Old Testament Quotations in the Fourth Gospel: Studies in Textual Form*, CBET 15 (Kampen: Kok Pharos, 1996); idem, "Observations on the Significance of the Old Testament in the Fourth Gospel," *Neot* 33 (1999): 125–43; Margaret

Johannine Monotheism

Ulrich Wilckens considers the language and the topics of the Gospel of John to be thoroughly biblical. The evangelist knows liturgical traditions of Judaism and is a recipient of these traditions himself, as he reflects the liturgical customs of his congregation. According to Wilckens, the major theological challenge to which the evangelist had to respond was the accusation of blasphemy expressed by the Jewish side.[97] The evangelist brings forward this accusation expressed during the trial of Jesus in order to illuminate the whole work of Jesus. His main interest is to declare the only God and the unity of Father and Son (cf. John 10:30) as noncontradictory. The sayings about the mutual immanence of the Father and the Son, and in particular of the Son and the faithful, are the way to cope with this theological task. Jesus was sent to let the faithful take part in the unity and community of the Son with the Father. Wilckens mentions the Jewish-Christian dialogue that already can be found in the Johannine Gospel: "Both, Jews and Christians, are absolutely bound to this one and only God and are therefore bound together in their disputes in a depth that no other disputing parties in the world can share."[98]

Anti-Judaism in the Gospel of John?

The twenty-five essays in the volume edited by Reimund Bieringer and others and dedicated to the question of anti-Judaism in the Gospel of John[99] are introduced by a thoughtful foreword. The editors present the different positions of the contributors and formulate a critical judgment on each essay. The various positions that occur in the research in John are categorized according to how they respond to five main questions:

1. *Is the Gospel of John hostile toward Jews?* This question has to be differentiated in terms of the interpretation of John, the text itself, and the author of the text. The history of the interpretation of John shows that not only some individual exegetes, but also whole communities of exegetes de facto, have interpreted the Fourth Gospel with the attitude

---

Daly-Denton, *David in the Fourth Gospel: The Johannine Reception of the Psalms,* AGJU 47 (Leiden: Brill, 2000).

97. See U. Wilckens, *Das Evangelium nach Johannes;* idem, "Monotheismus und Christologie," *JBTh* 12 (1997): 87–97; cf. Tobias Kriener, *"Glauben an Jesus"—ein Verstoß gegen das zweite Gebot? Die johanneische Christologie und der jüdische Vorwurf des Götzendientes,* NTDH 29 (Neukirchen-Vluyn: Neukirchener Verlag, 2000).

98. Wilckens, *Das Evangelium nach Johannes,* 126.

99. Cf. R. Bieringer, D. Pollefeyt, and F. Vandecasteele-Vanneuville, eds., *Anti-Judaism and the Fourth Gospel,* Jewish and Christian Heritage Series 1 (Assen: Van Gorcum, 2001); cf. the short version: *Anti-Judaism and the Fourth Gospel* (Philadelphia: Westminster John Knox, 2001). See also R. Kysar, "Anti-Semitism and the Gospel of John," in *Anti-Semitism and Early Christianity: Issues of Polemic and Faith,* ed. C. A. Evans and D. A. Hagner (Minneapolis: Fortress, 1993), 113–27.

of anti-Judaism. According to the editors, however, this cannot result only from the history of interpretation after John. The position that the text of John contains judgments that are hostile toward Jews, but the evangelist as the author of the text is free from anti-Judaism, is rejected by the editors as an apologetic strategy. Nor is it sufficient to explain the thinking of the author as a result of a controversy within Judaism (J. D. G. Dunn; U. C. von Wahlde) or as the result of a special situation within the author's context (M. de Boer), especially concerning the polemical sayings in John 8:31–59. Finally, it is by no means evident that the parting of the ways of Judaism and Christianity was already completed when the Gospel of John was written (A. Reinhartz). The editors do not acquit the Gospel of John and its author of the charge of anti-Judaism.

2. *Who are "the Jews" in the Gospel of John?* They are variously defined as opponents within Christianity (H. J. de Jonge), as the Jewish authorities in Jerusalem (U. C. von Wahlde), as the Jewish neighborhood of the Johannine congregations (S. Motyer), or as the inhabitants of Judea. Against these options, the editors point to the fact that the "Jews" of Jesus' time and the "Jews" of the time of the evangelist cannot be differentiated. According to the editors, the popular solution of seeing the Jews as "those representing disbelief" does not reduce the potential of anti-Judaism in the term "the Jews."

3. *How should the conflict between the Johannine congregation and "the Jews" that is reflected in the Fourth Gospel be understood?* If one does not want to deny the historical conflict and opts for describing it as literal and within Christianity (H. J. de Jonge), there are the possibilities of interpreting it either as a conflict within Christianity (J. D. G. Dunn) or as a Jewish-Christian conflict (J. Zumstein) about Christology.

4. *Do the Johannine Christology and the Christian faith take the place of the Jewish faith in the sense of a replacement (model of substitution)?* While some scholars take the view that the Johannine Christology claims the heritage of the promises of Israel in such a way that the Jews who do not believe in Christ are excluded from salvation (R. A. Culpepper), other scholars support the view that the Johannine Christology aims at the "restitution of Israel" (G. van Belle) or the "accomplishment" (not the "fulfillment") and the "summit" of Israel's history of salvation (J. Zumstein). Against this last option, the editors point to the fact that "fulfillment" and "replacement," at least in the perspective of history, have shown themselves to be siblings.

5. *Which hermeneutical insights are fruitful when reading the Gospel of John today?* Together with R. Burggraeve, the editors affirm that the central message of John asserts itself despite self-contradictions within the Gospel. With regard to hermeneutical procedure, they plead for a theological understanding of revelation that does not grant equal au-

thority of revelation to every verse of the Scripture. According to them, it is possible and necessary to interpret John against John. The main message contains a normative "alternative world of all-inclusive love and life which transcends anti-Judaism."[100]

John and the Rabbinical Exegesis of Scripture

Klaus Wengst explains the Gospel of John completely on the background of rabbinical testimonies.[101] He presupposes as the basic model of the Jewish-Christian relationship that the "people of the nations" are led to confidence in God by Jesus—a confidence that already exists in Israel and that will exist in Israel without the necessity of the Son.[102] Wengst refers to the famous saying of Franz Rosenzweig that believing Jews are already with the Father, so they do not need the mediation of Jesus Christ.[103] Above all, he understands Jesus in the Gospel of John to be the "messiah coming out of Israel" for the nations as "savior of the world" (cf. John 4:42), but not to be the messiah for Israel.[104] The numerous references to rabbinical texts do not show dependence, but Wengst wants to point out the "possibilities of Jewish expressions and Jewish thinking."[105] Of course, it is problematic to neglect (nearly all) other texts in the religious context of early Christianity. In line with his monograph on the Jewish and Judeo-Christian *Sitz im Leben* of the Fourth Gospel,[106] Wengst locates the emergence of the Gospel of John in the dispute between Pharisaic Judaism after the Jewish-Roman war (70 C.E.) and the predominantly Judeo-Christian congregation that, as a minority excluded from the synagogue, considered itself hard pressed. Concerning content, the question of the Messiah is the focus of the Johannine Gospel, which is written especially for those Judeo-Christians who are in danger of joining the Jewish-Pharisaic majority again. Wengst considers the Johannine Christology to be a strictly God-centered messianology—more exactly, a Christology that emphasizes the Son as the one who was sent. The reason for it is the endeavor to counter Jewish objections concerning the messianic dignity of the one "who so shamefully has been executed on the cross."[107] All other titles of Christ are subsumed under this pattern. This is a consequent interpretation of the Gospel of John and not a suitable one.

---

100. Bieringer, Pollefeyt, and Vandecasteele-Vanneuville, *Anti-Judaism and the Fourth Gospel*, 44.

101. V. Klaus Wengst, *Das Johannesevangelium*, 2 vols., THKNT 4 (Stuttgart: Kohlhammer, 2000–2001).

102. Ibid., 1:149.

103. Ibid., 2:119–21.

104. Ibid., 2:254.

105. Ibid., 1:28.

106. V. Klaus Wengst, *Bedrängte Gemeinde und verherrlichter Christus: Ein Versuch über das Johannesevangelium*, 3rd ed. (München: Kaiser, 1990).

107. Wengst, *Das Johannesevangelium*, 1:34.

Johannine Eschatology

The eschatology of the fourth evangelist is one of the most frequently discussed topics in Johannine studies. In his exegesis of John 5:28–29, Udo Schnelle argues for a genuine Johannine "synoptic" view of eschatology that refers both to the present and to the future: "The perspective of the narrator who deliberately has taken the view after Easter and the Paraclete who announces the things to come . . . emphasize the careful reflection of the evangelist about the temporal situation of his congregation. He does not intend to place the faith out of history, but aims at understanding the different factual, local, and temporal levels of the work of Christ."[108]

1. Jörg Frey chooses the Johannine expression "the time is coming and has now come" (John 4:23; 5:25) as the basic principle for his exegetical reconstruction of Johannine eschatology.[109] He starts convincingly with the question of the Johannine understanding of time—this is the guideline for his interpretation of Johannine eschatology. Frey investigates the use of the temporal in the Fourth Gospel and shows that the Johannine usage has a differentiating ability. Concerning the bitemporal sayings in 4:23 and 5:25, Frey perceives a tension in the theological meaning that was intended by the evangelist and therefore must not be resolved in one direction or the other. Temporal paradoxes are not signs of clumsiness on the part of the evangelist (or a reviser), but a "deliberately chosen means of expression."[110] Together with Josef Blank, Frey contends for the "Christological"—that is, "personal"—implication of Johannine eschatology: in the person of Jesus Christ, "times meet, therefore the presence of the eschatological salvation results from the presence of the risen Christ."[111] Sayings that refer to the present and those that refer to the future do not exclude each other, but rather confirm and stimulate each other.

Frey's third volume is dedicated to the eschatological sayings in 1–3 John and in the Gospel of John. He tries to ascertain the view of the recipients, in this case for eschatological traditions in the Johannine congregations. Frey, who considers the Johannine Epistles to be older than John's Gospel, analyzes the schism caused by docetic opponents and its apocalyptic dimensions according to the author of the letter (cf. 1 John 2:18–19; John 11:24), the expectation of the parousia (1 John 2:28) and of the judgment (1 John 4:17), and the eschatological tradi-

---

108. See Schnelle, *Das Evangelium nach Johannes,* 108–10, esp. 110.
109. Cf. Frey, *Die johanneische Eschatologie,* vols. 2, 3.
110. Frey, *Die johanneische Eschatologie,* 2:151.
111. Ibid., 2:243. Cf. Schnelle, "Perspektiven der Johannesexegese"; idem, "Johannes als Geisttheologe," *NovT* 40 (1998): 17–31.

tion of the congregation in 1 John 3:1–2. Frey correctly observes that the certainty of salvation and the expectation of the future in 1 John 3:1–2 do not compete with each other. The farewell discourse[112] in John 13–17 is the hermeneutical key for the Gospel of John, as it shows the typical Johannine interconnection of times very clearly.[113] Frey calls it a "temporale . . . Stereoskopie" and a "programmatic *interconnection of the temporal and factual horizons of Jesus' time and the congregation's time.*"[114]

Interpreting John 13:31–14:31, Frey convincingly rejects the thesis of Jürgen Becker[115] that the evangelist dismissed the eschatological saying referring to the future in 14:2–3 in favor of the saying that refers to the present in 14:23.[116] He points to the "temporal double perspective" in 13:31–32 that marks the entire farewell discourse. The often postulated identification of Easter, Pentecost, and parousia in the Gospel of John is dismissed in his exegesis and replaced by a "synoptic view that at the same time differentiates" the times.[117] The detailed interpretations of the eschatological texts in John 3, 5, and 11 confirm this pattern. John 5:19–30 makes apparent the primacy of Christology before eschatology: the Son of God, who predominates over time and who bears the authority of God, stands in a unique relation to God that is not merely functional[118] but has to be understood ontologically. Starting from this point, Frey interprets the eschatological sayings in 5:24–25 (referring to the present) and 5:28–29 (referring to the future) as explications of Jesus' christological authority: the present communication of life, its eschatological final effect, and the promise of the resurrection of the dead at the end of time complete and confirm each other.

2. Disagreeing with Frey, Hans-Christian Kammler[119] describes the Johannine eschatology as referring completely to the present. Sayings that refer to the future are not omitted by methods of literary criticism, but their content is interpreted as referring to the present (but Kammler's exegesis is unconvincing). According to Kammler, this is

---

112. The sense of the Gospel of John allows us to assume with confidence one farewell discourse in John 13–17; for the reasons, see K. Scholtissek, "Abschied und neue Gegenwart: Exegetische und theologische Reflexionen zur johanneischen Abschiedsrede Joh 13,31–17,26," *ETL* 75 (1999): 332–58, esp. 348–50.

113. Cf. Hoegen-Rohls, *Der nachösterliche Johannes;* Scholtissek, "Abschied und neue Gegenwart."

114. Frey, *Die johanneische Eschatologie,* 3:234.

115. Becker has reaffirmed his thesis in "Die Hoffnung auf ewiges Leben im Johannesevangelium," *ZNW* 91 (2000): 192–211.

116. Likewise, Scholtissek, *In ihm sein und bleiben,* 210–74.

117. Frey, *Die johanneische Eschatologie,* 3:167.

118. Contra Wengst, *Das Johannesevangelium,* 1:226–27.

119. Hans-Christian Kammler, *Christologie und Eschatologie: Joh 5,17–30 als Schlüsseltext johanneischer Theologie,* WUNT 126 (Tübingen: Mohr Siebeck, 2000).

true not only for John 5:17–30, but also for 6:39c, 40c, 44c, 54b; 11:25–26; 12:48c; 14:2–3; 17:24. For Kammler, the central message of 5:17–30 is the unity of Father and Son, and therefore the deity of Jesus. An eschatology with a focus only on the present is an explication of this high Johannine Christology. With this questionable view, Kammler connects the problematic thesis of a strict predestination in the Gospel of John that totally omits human free will. The universal will of God to bring the whole creation into salvation is replaced by a particular one. Kammler wants to confirm this with an exegesis of John 3:16 and of the whole Johannine Gospel, but his views are to be emphatically rejected.

The Outstanding Role of Women

Compared to the Synoptics, the role of women in the Gospel of John (the Samaritan woman; Mary and Martha from Bethany; Mary of Magdala)[120] is striking. Both traditional and feminist exegetes examine these important testimonies about women in the Gospel of John.[121] Sandra Schneiders[122] criticizes the traditional exegeses that neglect the Johannine emphasis on women as actors and preachers. She exposes the patriarchal exegesis of the Fourth Gospel (and the whole NT) as a consequence of culturally influenced views. Schneiders states that the author of the Fourth Gospel was sensitive to female religious experiences. Consequently, women occur as partners in theological discussions, as gifted preachers of the gospel, as public confessors of faith, and as servants at the table of the Lord. They have direct relations with Jesus and act independently of male disciples. In Martha's "serving" she recognizes eucharistic implications. Mary of Magdala is identified as the primary Easter witness and as the one who guarantees the apostolic tradition. Schneiders characterizes the figure of the Beloved Disciple as a "textual paradigm" with striking parallels to Mary of Magdala. This textual paradigm identifies the authority of the Johannine school and also includes the ideal of discipleship for both males and females. Schneiders casts the Samaritan woman as "the evangelist's *alter ego.*"

---

120. On Mary of Magdala in the Gospel of John, see Ruschmann, *Maria von Magdala im Johannesevangelium.*

121. See R. E. Brown, "Roles of Women in the Fourth Gospel," *TS* 36 (1975): 688–99; Adele Reinhartz, "The Gospel of John," in *Searching the Scriptures,* ed. E. Schüssler Fiorenza, 2 vols. (New York: Crossroad, 1994), 2:561–600; Rut Habermann, "Das Evangelium nach Johannes," in *Kompendium Feministische Bibelauslegung,* ed. L. Schottroff and M.-T. Wacker (Gütersloh: Kaiser, 1999), 527–41.

122. See S. M. Schneiders, *Written That You May Believe: Encountering Jesus in the Fourth Gospel* (New York: Crossroad, 1999), 93–114, 126–48, 189–201, 211–32.

Johannine Spirituality

"To Awaken the Faith of the Faithful"

Readers have a certain confidence in the theological and spiritual competence of the Johannine Gospel. Jean Zumstein has admirably summarized the intention of the Fourth Gospel: "To awaken the faith of the faithful."[123] The Gospel of John has to be read and interpreted as the "Gospel of meetings," as a Gospel that invites its readers to meet with the risen Jesus and involves its readers in such a meeting.[124] Sandra Schneiders[125] starts her interpretation with the correct assumption that the Gospel of John is the consequence of, and points to, a special spiritual experience of faith.[126] To take this spiritual dimension into account is compatible with the historical-critical method, and is in fact demanded by the text itself. In doing this, the faith of the community that has caused the emergence of the Johannine Gospel is taken seriously for the hermeneutical task of interpretation. Christians then and now read the Gospel of John in this community of faith. The classic interpretation of Scripture until the Enlightenment[127] aimed at "personal and communal transformation,"[128] whereas the modern historical-critical research sought historical information instead. This led to an "increasing religious and theological sterility of academic work on the Bible."[129] Schneiders wants to oppose this loss of personal and communal "spiritual meeting" and of the "existential carrying out" of the biblical message. Therefore, she emphasizes the canonical character—that is, the normative character—of the Fourth Gospel as sacred Scripture in the exegesis of John 20:30–31, which is "the hermeneutical key to the Gospel."[130] In this final and solemn declaration, the text of the Fourth Gospel itself is established as the place for meeting Christ and revealing Christ.[131] People will be changed and converted by meeting Jesus. Also, the literary character of the Johannine Gospel points to "its immense power to engage the deepest spiritual dynamics of the reader."[132] The various stylistic means of the evangelist seek to lead the readers each time to a new meeting

---

123. Zumstein, *Kreative Erinnerung*, 36.

124. For more on this topic, see Peter Dschulnigg, *Jesus begegnen: Personen und ihre Bedeutung im Johannesevangelium,* Theologie 30 (Münster: LIT, 2000).

125. Schneiders, *Written That You May Believe.*

126. See S. M. Schneiders, "The Johannine Resurrection Narrative: An Exegetical and Theological Study of John 20 as a Synthesis of Johannine Spirituality," 2 vols. (S.T.D. diss., Pontificia Universitas Gregoriania, 1975).

127. See S. M. Schneiders, "Scripture and Spirituality," in *Christian Spirituality: Origins to the Twelfth Century,* ed. B. McGinn and J. Meyendorff, World Spirituality 16 (New York: Crossroad, 1985), 1–20.

128. Ibid., 16.

129. Ibid., 20.

130. Ibid., 5.

131. On this, see further Schneiders, *The Revelatory Text.*

132. Schneiders, "Scripture and Spirituality," 4.

with Jesus, in which their previous convictions are disturbed and questioned. The theology and spirituality of the Fourth Gospel,[133] according to Schneiders, develop around the two aspects of the relationship between Jesus and his disciples that is based, on the one hand, on the revelation of Jesus Christ and, on the other hand, on the continuation of this relationship in the time after the death and the resurrection of Jesus. Basically, God's revelation in Jesus Christ is defined as "self-revelation," "self-communication, self-opening, self-gift." The studies by Schneiders impress us by their determination to address exegetically and hermeneutically anew the "transforming" dynamic of the Gospel of John that is directed toward the faith and the life of the readers. The form of the Johannine stories of meetings with Jesus, which refers to the faith experiences of the individual and of the church and accompanies them, must not be omitted or relegated as a spiritual amendment, but honored as the deep basic principle of the Johannine theology.

The Sayings about Immanence

Distinctive among the features of the Johannine corpus are the expressions of the mutual inhabitation, the sayings about mutual immanence. My study *In ihm sein und bleiben*[134] treats in detail texts for comparison from the OT, early Judaism, and the Hellenistic world; it investigates equivalents and metaphors of these sayings and interprets and analyzes all testimonies about immanence in the Johannine corpus. The sayings about mutual immanence, which are transferred from the relationship between the Father and the Son to the relationship between the Son and the Christians in the time after Easter, lead to the central focus of the Johannine theology. These sayings describe the experience of the Christian faith as being safe in God and as God being present deep down inside humans.

Mysticism?

One of the most challenging and interesting topics of research in John is the question of whether there is mysticism in the Gospel of John (and if so, in what sense).[135] Whereas NT exegetes traditionally have been skeptical in this

---

133. See K. Scholtissek, "Mystagogische Christologie im Johannesevangelium?" *GuL* 68 (1995): 412–26; cf. idem, "'Mitten unter euch steht der, den ihr nicht kennt' (Joh 1, 26)," 103–21; idem, "'Er kam in sein Eigentum und die Eigenen nahmen ihn nicht auf' (Joh 1,11)," *GuL* 72 (1999): 436–51.

134. See Scholtissek, *In ihm sein und bleiben;* idem, "'Rabbi, wo wohnst du?' Zur Theologie der Immanenz-Aussagen im Johannesevangelium," *BL* 74 (2001): 240–53.

135. See K. Scholtissek, "Mystik im Johannesevangelium?" in *Pneuma und Gemeinde: Christsein in der Tradition des Paulus und Johannes,* ed. J. Eckert, M. Schmidl, and H. Steichele (Düsseldorf: Patmos, 2001), 295–324.

area, Jey Kanagaraj[136] and April DeConick,[137] who investigate early Jewish and rabbinical ascent and vision mysticism, conclude that there is indeed mysticism in John. Bernhard Neuenschwander[138] attempts a comparison between Buddhist Zen-mysticism and the Gospel of John. The works of these authors are, in many or most parts, highly questionable.

Concluding Observations

The positions of the new research in John reveal a clear trend favoring a synchronic interpretation. Today there is more trust in the canonical text of the Gospel of John (and with some caution, in John 21) and in the evangelist as the author of this text than there was in earlier stages of the history of research. Tensions concerning form, language, and content are mostly explained synchronically. The eschatological sayings, for example, which up to now have mostly been omitted by literary criticism, can be understood as being charged with inner tensions but nevertheless having a consistent message. The Gospel of John as a whole, with all its distinctive features and tensions, is the object of exegetical interpretation. This new approach to the Gospel of John discovers phenomena in the text that up to now had been hiding in the background: narrative structures and compositions, metaphorical nets and processes, irony and change of roles, theologically important continuations accomplished through *relecture* and *réécriture*. Nevertheless, in today's research in John opinions vary about the possibilities of literary criticism and of tradition history. The research paradigm that works with antagonistic and competing theologies to explain a passage in John is confronted with an opposite approach that itself works in two different ways: some researchers opting for *relecture* assume a creative process of continuation, which at the same time is bound to tradition; others opting for the unity of the text are skeptical about attempts to reconstruct pre-Johannine texts and processes of literary growth within the Gospel. The details of the emergence of the Johannine text will remain controversial also because the evangelist himself has marked these traditions on their way in the Gospel.

The different methodological approaches need an integration that evaluates the capacities of each approach critically and realistically. A narrative

136. Jey J. Kanagaraj, *"Mysticism" in the Gospel of John: An Inquiry into Its Background*, JSNTSup 158 (Sheffield: Sheffield Academic Press, 1998).

137. April D. DeConick, *Seek to See Him: Ascent and Vision Mysticism in the Gospel of Thomas*, VCSup 33 (Leiden: Brill, 1996); *Voices of the Mystics: Early Christian Discourse in the Gospels of John and Thomas and Other Ancient Christian Literature*, JSNTSup 157 (Sheffield: Sheffield Academic Press, 2001).

138. Bernhard Neuenschwander, *Mystik im Johannesevangelium: Eine hermeneutische Untersuchung aufgrund der Auseinandersetzung mit Zen-Meister Hisamatsu Shin'ichi*, BIS 31 (Leiden: Brill 1998).

interpretation, for example, must also address the classic questions of the *Sitz im Leben* and the theological concept of the Gospel of John. The history of the historical-critical method is characterized by the ability to recognize appropriate new approaches and to integrate them into the structure of different methodological steps.

One of the changes in the research in John is much more openness to the question of whether the fourth evangelist had some knowledge of one or more of the Synoptic Gospels and if he used materials of them. Today it is increasingly assumed that he knew one or more of the Synoptics and that he was able to handle, shape, and use them according to his own theological intentions.

The many studies on special topics of the Johannine corpus point, in their strengths and in their weaknesses, to the necessity of keeping an eye on the overall theological concept of the Fourth Gospel. Detailed exegesis and an integrating view correspond to each other. One of the basic principles of Johannine theological thinking is the biblical monotheistic image of God. The Christology is integrated in this image as the eschatological doctrine of salvation, and biblical anthropology and the history of God's promises to his chosen people Israel also have their places in this image.

It is part of the interpretation of John to perceive the hermeneutical position of the evangelist, his way of seeing and watching. The Johannine writing develops from the anamnesis of the work of Christ after Easter, which is guided by the Spirit. Local and temporal dimensions become interconnected in this kind of theological language. This synthetic way of thinking derives from a long process within early Christianity and is the reason for the central place occupied by the Fourth Gospel in the canon of the NT. The steering of the readers by the evangelist aims at convincing them of his own point of view and convictions (cf. John 20:31). The addressees will share the Johannine way of watching and seeing in order that they, like the evangelist himself, as watchers, listeners, and believers, may find what they are looking for: "life to the full" (John 10:10).

22

Recent Trends in the Study of the Apocalypse

Grant R. Osborne

We are part of the greatest explosion of biblical knowledge in history. Never before has so much been discovered and published in the same generation. For virtually every book of the Bible major projects are coming to light, and commentaries benefiting from them are being written. This is nowhere more evident than with the Book of Revelation. After the magisterial works of H. B. Swete in 1906 and R. H. Charles in 1920, it was seventy years before a major commentary from the original language was published. Then, in just a short period, 1992–99, four major works on the book were published by R. L. Thomas, H. Giesen, D. E. Aune, and G. K. Beale,[1] and another appeared in 2002.[2] Moreover, many of the older theories on the book have been challenged and overturned, and certain consensus positions (if such a thing is possible in the world of scholarship) are beginning to emerge.

It is the task of this essay to summarize the highly creative last couple of decades and to ascertain the state of research on the Book of Revelation. In doing so, I will choose only those issues that have surfaced as major foci for

---

1. R. L. Thomas, *Revelation 1–7: An Exegetical Commentary*, 2 vols. (Chicago: Moody, 1992–95); H. Giesen, *Die Offenbarung des Johannes*, RNT (Regensburg: Pustet, 1997); D. E. Aune, *Revelation*, 3 vols., WBC 52A–C (Dallas: Word, 1997–98); G. K. Beale, *The Book of Revelation*, NIGTC (Grand Rapids: Eerdmans, 1999).

2. G. R. Osborne, *Revelation*, BECNT (Grand Rapids: Baker Academic, 2002).

attention and debate. The goal is to help the reader to see the multifaceted nature of this book and how to make sense of it.

Genre and Mind-Set

It has always been known that Revelation's genre is apocalyptic; however, it also has both epistolary and prophetic features. In fact, Ladd suggested in 1957 that the book be labeled "prophetic-apocalyptic."[3] However, the understanding of what genre implies has developed tremendously in recent years.[4] This is partly due to the challenge of critics from the deconstructionist school who argue that since genres intermix, they are no longer pure and cannot be classified. Rather than providing interpretive keys, genre is characterized by interpenetration and confusion.[5] Therefore, no unifying criteria exist. They argue that no *telos* or "achieved configuration" of any text can be said to achieve a synthesizing/systematizing function, and this can provide a "provisional generality for the text"; thus, there is no normative theory that can cover the internal operation of a text.[6] In other words, genre cannot function as a classification device to help a person interpret a text. This challenge had a positive effect on scholarship; as a result, conceptions of genre have moved more into the epistemological and ontological function of genre upon the reader. Now, we see genre as (1) classificatory, describing the basic historical categories for defining the mimetic (i.e., the historical type of literature imitated) background to a text; (2) epistemological, describing how the ancient minds stated and interpreted the message within a framework of thought; and (3) ontological, describing the categories in the mind that allowed ancient writers to communicate meaning and significance.[7] With respect to apocalyptic,[8] a great deal of

3. G. E. Ladd, "Why Not Prophetic-Apocalyptic?" *JBL* 76 (1957): 92–200.

4. See D. Hellholm, "Methodological Reflections on the Problem of Definition of Generic Texts," in *Mysteries and Revelations: Apocalyptic Studies since the Uppsala Convention,* ed. J. J. Collins and J. H. Charlesworth, JSPSup 9 (Sheffield: Sheffield Academic Press, 1991), 135–63. Hellholm argues for the interdependence of diachronic and synchronic considerations.

5. J. Derrida, "The Law of Genre," *Glyph* 7 (1980): 207–9; Geoffrey Hartman, preface to *Deconstruction and Criticism,* ed. H. Bloom et al. (New York: Seabury, 1979), vii–ix.

6. D. Kambouchner, "The Theory of Accidents," *Glyph* 7 (1980): 150–55.

7. G. R. Osborne, "Genre Criticism—Sensus Literalis," *TJ* 4 (1983): 23.

8. Revelation as apocalyptic has been challenged from three directions: (1) B. W. Jones ("More about the Apocalypse as Apocalyptic," *JBL* 87 [1968]: 325–27) denies its apocalyptic nature because it is not pseudonymous. But that elevates one characteristic over the others; there is no apocalyptic work that fits every characteristic. Moreover, as Aune demonstrates (*Revelation,* lxxxviii), it is a Christian not a Jewish apocalypse and parallels the *Shepherd of Hermas,* which also is not pseudonymous. (2) F. D. Mazzaferri (*The Genre of the Book of Revelation from a Source-Critical Perspective,* BZNW 54 [Berlin: de Gruyter, 1989]) argues that Revelation is more in line with OT prophecy than apocalyptic. This, however, is a disjunctive fallacy, for the book follows both prophecy and apocalyptic. (3) B. J. Malina (*On the Genre and Message of Revelation: Star Visions and Sky Journeys* [Peabody, Mass.: Hendrickson, 1995], 10–18) believes

work went into the understanding of the genre in the years 1979–89, beginning with the SBL genre project, resulting in *Semeia* 14 (1979) on *Apocalypse: The Morphology of a Genre,* which sought to define more accurately Jewish apocalyptic in distinction from Jewish prophetic literature. Two years later came the International Colloquium on Apocalypticism in Uppsala, Sweden, in August 1979, resulting in *Apocalypticism in the Mediterranean World and the Near East* (1983), which sought to understand the origins of apocalyptic more carefully on the basis of ancient parallels from Egypt, Akkadia, and Persia. A further SBL consultation and then seminar on early Christian apocalypticism from 1981 to 1987 resulted in *Semeia* 36 (1986), on *Early Christian Apocalypticism: Genre and Social Setting,* to define the social environment behind the early Christian form. Finally, an SBL symposium was held in 1989 to define more carefully the contours of Jewish apocalypticism itself, resulting in *Mysteries and Revelations: Apocalyptic Studies since the Uppsala Colloquium* (1991).

Two important results of that creative decade may be noted. First, the misuse of the term "apocalyptic" as a theological concept (by, e.g., Schweitzer, Bultmann, and Käsemann) having any number of definitions and no controls (i.e., it meant different things to every scholar) has been corrected by restricting the term to a body of literature, a genre.[9] However, it must be said that this misuse continues to this very day in many scholarly publications. Second, the interrelationship between the categories of form, content, and function within the concept of genre has been developed. In his (already) classic article, Collins proposes the primary aspects of form (visions and epiphanies, otherworldly journey, heavenly book, otherworldly mediator, human recipient, pseudonymity) and content (temporal axis—protology and cosmogony, primordial events, review of history, present salvation through knowledge, eschatological crisis, eschatological judgment, the wicked and the world, eschatological salvation; spatial axis—otherworldly elements, otherworldly regions, otherworldly beings).[10] These are more or less still accepted, although Aune would add: in terms of form—the presentation of the narrative in first-person autobiographical form and a deliberate structure of the revelatory vision in such a way "that the central revelatory message constitutes a literary climax"; in terms of content—the communication of a transcendent (eschatological) perspective on

---

that its designation as apocalyptic has resulted from "spurious information" derived from the nineteenth century, and that the ancients would have seen it as "astral prophecy" centering on celestial visions and cosmic symbolism. However, the parallels with Jewish apocalyptic certainly outweigh the supposed parallels with astral cults of the first century, and too many sections do not even occur in a heavenly sphere (see the critique in Beale, *Revelation,* 42–43).

9. See R. E. Sturm, "Defining the Word 'Apocalyptic': A Problem in Biblical Criticism," in *Apocalyptic and the New Testament,* ed. J. Marcus and M. L. Soards, JSNTSup 24 (Sheffield: JSOT Press, 1989), 37; J. J. Collins, "Genre, Ideology, and Social Movements in Jewish Apocalypticism," in Collins and Charlesworth, *Mysteries and Revelations,* 13.

10. J. J. Collins, "Introduction: Toward the Morphology of a Genre," *Semeia* 14 (1979): 6–8.

human existence.[11] Both Hellholm and Aune demand that genre also contain the aspect of function. Hellholm argues that purpose or function is an essential element of every genre and suggests that apocalyptic intends to exhort and console a group in crisis by means of divine authority.[12] Aune would add a threefold function: to legitimate the transcendent message, to mediate a new actualization of the original revelatory experience by concealing what the text reveals, and to encourage the recipients to modify their thinking and behavior on the basis of the transcendent perspective.[13] On this basis, I recommend the following summary definition of the apocalyptic genre:

> Apocalyptic entails the revelatory communication of heavenly secrets by an otherworldly being to a seer who presents the visions in a narrative framework; the visions guide readers into a transcendent reality that takes precedence over the current situation and encourages readers to persevere in the midst of their trials. The visions reverse normal experience by making the heavenly mysteries the real world and depicting the present crisis as a temporary, illusory situation. This is achieved via God's transforming the world for the faithful.[14]

In this sense, apocalyptic entails both a formal type of literature and a mind-set held by the group that adheres to the belief system. This is not a radical departure from the views of apocalyptic as a genre in older studies such as those by Charles, Lohmeyer, and even Beasley-Murray or Mounce, but it has a precision that is missing in these earlier studies. More and more, the Book of Revelation is interpreted on the basis of the body of Jewish apocalyptic literature that flourished from about 200 B.C.E. to 100 C.E., along with biblical prototypes such as Isa. 24–27, Ezek. 37–39, Zechariah, and Daniel.[15] In virtually every verse of the critical commentaries mentioned above, generic and conceptual parallels are adduced, often with several books together. In fact, Bauckham[16] argues that the parallels are so numerous that it is likely that John often draws much of his imagery from common apocalyptic tradition rather than from specific works.

11. D. E. Aune, "The Apocalypse of John and the Problem of Genre," *Semeia* 36 (1986): 86–87.

12. D. Hellholm, "The Problem of Apocalyptic Genre and the Apocalypse of John," *Semeia* 36 (1986): 27.

13. Aune, "Problem of Genre," 89–91.

14. Osborne, *Revelation*, 14. Here I combine the definitions of Collins, Aune, and also C. Rowland, *The Open Heaven: A Study of Apocalypticism in Judaism and Early Christianity* (London: SPCK, 1982).

15. On the protoapocalyptic biblical texts of the exilic and postexilic period, see S. L. Cook, *Prophecy and Apocalypticism: The Postexilic Social Setting* (Minneapolis: Fortress, 1995). Cook argues that the millennial groups originated primarily in an Israelite priestly (Zadokite) setting rather than through Persian influence.

16. R. Bauckham, "The Use of Apocalyptic Traditions," in *The Climax of Prophecy: Studies on the Book of Revelation* (Edinburgh: Clark, 1993), 39.

Revelation is not simply apocalyptic but could viably be labeled "apocalyptic prophecy"[17] or, perhaps better, "prophetic apocalypse"[18] due to the centrality of prophetic material. One could say that prophecy is more oracular and optimistic (if the people repent, then judgment will not take place), while apocalyptic is more visionary and negative (little hope in the present, yet future vindication and judgment guaranteed). Yet both center on future salvation for the faithful and certain judgment for the unfaithful. A good argument can be made that apocalyptic developed originally as a subset of the prophetic movement and "originated parallel to Iranian and Near Eastern ideas primarily in a prophetic milieu from the eighth to the sixth centuries B.C."[19] In most apocalyptic writings there is also a prophetic air, and it is useful for us to look briefly here at the prophetic nature of Revelation.

In the prologue and the conclusion John calls his book "prophecy" (1:3; 22:7, 10, 18, 19), and he likely was a leader of a circle of prophets who ministered to the churches in the Roman province of Asia (22:6, 9).[20] In 22:6, "the Lord God of the spirits of the prophets" means that God superintends the revelation of his end-time secrets through "the spirits of the prophets," most likely referring to "'the prophetic Spirit' by which each of them speaks through his or her own spirit."[21] In 22:9, the angel is "a fellow servant" with John and "your brothers the prophets," who could be faithful saints (so Beale), but are more likely the circle of prophets administered by John, who provided leadership for the churches and opposed the false teachers (so Bauckham, Giesen, Aune). The members of the church often are divided into "the saints and prophets" (11:18; 16:6; 18:24) or "saints and apostles and prophets" (18:20). Bauckham believes that the prophets not only read the book to the churches, but also expounded and explained it, thus forming a circle of teachers.[22] John

17. R. Bauckham, *The Theology of the Book of Revelation* (Cambridge: Cambridge University Press, 1993), 2. J. R. Michaels (*Revelation*, IVPNTC [Downers Grove, Ill.: InterVarsity, 1997], 14–16) goes so far as to call it a "prophetic letter" due to the "I" style narration of the book. He believes that it is not truly apocalyptic but is the one book of "written prophecy" in the NT.

18. Aune, *Revelation*, lxxxix. See also Ladd, "Why Not Prophetic-Apocalyptic?" 92; G. A. Krodel, *Revelation*, ACNT (Minneapolis: Augsburg, 1989), 51.

19. G. R. Osborne, "The Origins of Apocalyptic," in *The Hermeneutical Spiral: A Comprehensive Introduction to Biblical Interpretation* (Downers Grove, Ill.: InterVarsity, 1991), 233. See also D. Hellholm, ed., *Apocalypticism in the Mediterranean World and the Near East* (Tübingen: Mohr, 1983), especially the articles by J. Bergman on Egyptian parallels, by H. Ringgren on Akkadia, and by A. Hultgård on Persia; and Collins, "Genre, Ideology, and Social Movements," 25–32, where he builds on the work of Helge Kvanvig to argue for a wide range of Near Eastern and Hellenistic influences on Jewish apocalyptic. Beale (*Revelation*, 37) calls apocalyptic "an intensification of prophecy" and refuses to separate them.

20. On the prophetic circle in the province of Asia, see D. E. Aune, "The Prophetic Circle of John of Patmos and the Exegesis of Revelation 22:16," *JSNT* 37 (1989): 103–16.

21. This definition is found in G. D. Fee, *The First Epistle to the Corinthians*, NICNT (Grand Rapids: Eerdmans, 1987), 696.

22. Bauckham, *Climax of Prophecy*, 86–87.

was commissioned to his prophetic ministry (10:8–11) in a way deliberately reminiscent of Ezekiel (Ezek. 2:8–3:3) and was told to "prophesy against many peoples, nations, languages, and kings" (10:11).

The letters of the seven churches are best known for their prophetic material, written in third-person form (Jesus as the "one who") with a prophetic call to hear as well as a call to repentance and ethical responsibility.[23] In addition, direct first-person prophetic oracles are given by Jesus to the church through John (1:8, 17; 16:15; 22:7, 18–19) similar to the "Thus says the Lord" prophecies of the OT. This helps the reader to understand that John is not simply producing his own epistle with advice for the church (à la Peter or Paul), but rather has become the prophetic channel of messages (and visions) directly from God and Christ. As Schüssler Fiorenza says, the book is both a literary product of early Christian prophecy and a product of early Christian apocalyptic traditions as taught by the prophetic circle led by John.[24]

It is helpful also to observe that the book is epistolary in form. The normal greeting formula is found in 1:4–5 ("John to the seven churches. . . : Grace and peace"), but it is uncharacteristically placed after the prologue. Also, there is a brief benediction at the close (22:21), so John has encased his work in epistolary form. Moreover, the seven letters of chs. 2–3 are indeed epistles from Christ to each church in turn. This is important because the language of these letters is reflected often in the rest of the book, showing that the visions are addressed to local problems that the churches are currently experiencing. So it is right to call this a "prophetic letter" (so Aune) intended not so much as a casebook for identifying future events but as a theological workbook addressing the church in the present via the prophecies of the future. The function is paraenesis: challenging the Christians of John's day (and our day) to live differently in light of the apocalyptic times in which they live. The ethical mandate to persevere and overcome is essential, for apocalyptic literature has a distinct ethical component demanding faithfulness on the part of the people of God.

> The fundamental perspective of the book is the exhortation to endure persecution on the basis of the transcendent reality of God's kingdom in the present as grounded in God's control of the future. Therefore the temporal world of temptation and pressure to conform to secular demands can be endured when one realizes that God is "the one who is and who was and who is to come" (1:4b), that is, the same God who controlled the past and will control the future is still in control in the present, even though it does not seem like it.[25]

23. See especially U. B. Müller, *Prophetie und Predigt im Neuen Testament: Formgeschichtliche Untersuchungen zur urchristlichen Prophetie*, SNT 10 (Gütersloh: Mohn, 1975), 47–107. Müller does a form-critical study of the seven letters and argues that they preserve early Jewish prophetic forms, in particular a sermon of repentance and a sermon of salvation.

24. E. Schüssler Fiorenza, "Apokalypsis and Propheteia: Revelation in the Context of Early Christian Prophecy," in *L'Apocalypse johannique et l'apocalyptique dans le Nouveau Testament,* ed. J. Lambrecht et al., BETL 53 (Leuven: Leuven University Press, 1980), 121–28.

25. Osborne, *Revelation,* 14–15.

Finally, we should note the intriguing thesis of D. L. Barr that the Apocalypse is also narrative.[26] The key is that it is a series of actions related sequentially, with the content being primarily a story about Jesus: his cosmic struggle against the evil powers of this world. It contains a plot and developing narration: a three-act play moving from scenes of direct revelation (1–3) to scenes of heavenly worship (4–11) to culminating scenes of holy war (12–22).[27] Although the details leave lots of room for disagreement, a narrative approach certainly will produce valuable insights.

Date and Social Situation

Four different dates for Revelation were proposed by early Christian writers (tagged by the Roman emperor in whose reign it would have been written): Claudius (41–54 C.E., by Epiphanius), Nero (54–68, by the Syriac versions), Domitian (81–96, by Irenaeus, Victorinus, Eusebius, Clement of Alexandria, Origen), and Trajan (98–117, by Donotheus, Theophylact).[28] However, the scholarly debate has always centered on whether the book is set during the Neronian persecution (66–68 C.E.) or the Domitianic (92–95 C.E.). The Neronian view dominated scholarship of the nineteenth century, and the Domitianic that of the twentieth. Those who take the book as a prophecy regarding the destruction of Jerusalem and as a diatribe against Jewish apostasy tend to place the book in the latter part of Nero's reign.[29] Also, those who believe that Nero led the only true persecution place the book around 67–68 C.E.[30] However, the historical data and the preponderance of the evidence for the situation behind the book (see below) have led the vast majority of scholars to the later date.

26. See D. L. Barr, *Tales of the End: A Narrative Commentary on the Book of Revelation* (Santa Rosa, Calif.: Polebridge, 1998); "The Apocalypse of John in the Light of Modern Narrative Theory," in *1900th Anniversary of St. John's Apocalypse: Proceedings of the International and Interdisciplinary Symposium* (Athens: Holy Monastery of St. John, 1999), 259–71. See also J. R. Michaels, *Interpreting the Book of Revelation* (Grand Rapids: Baker, 1992), 95–106, which discusses "Narrative Criticism: The Voices of the Revelation"; and C. W. Hedrick, "Narrative Asides in the Gospel of John," in *1900th Anniversary of St. John's Apocalypse,* 650–53.

27. Barr, *Tales of the End,* 1–2, 10–15; "Modern Narrative Theory," 262–65.

28. D. A. Carson, D. J. Moo, and L. Morris, *An Introduction to the New Testament* (Grand Rapids: Zondervan, 1992), 473–74.

29. See J. Massyngberde Ford, *Revelation: Introduction, Translation and Commentary,* AB 38 (Garden City, N.Y.: Doubleday, 1975); J. A. T. Robinson, *Redating the New Testament* (Philadelphia: Westminster, 1976), 221–53; Rowland, *The Open Heaven,* 403–13; D. C. Chilton, *The Days of Vengeance: An Exposition of the Book of Revelation* (Fort Worth, Tex.: Dominion, 1987); K. L. Gentry, *Before Jerusalem Fell: Dating the Book of Revelation* (Tyler, Tex.: Institute for Christian Economics, 1989).

30. E. Lipinsky, "L'apocalypse et la martyre de Jean à Jérusalem," *NovT* 11 (1969): 225–32; A. A. Bell, "The Date of John's Apocalypse: The Evidence of Some Roman Historians Reconsidered," *NTS* 25 (1979): 93–102; R. B. Moberley, "When Was Revelation Conceived?" *Biblica* 73 (1992): 376–93; J. C. Wilson, "The Problem of the Domitianic Date of Revelation," *NTS* 39 (1993): 587–605.

The social situation itself has been the primary focus of scholarly dialogue in the last two decades. In the past it usually was assumed that the book was occasioned by a major outbreak of official Roman persecution under the anti-Christian emperor Domitian (so Swete, Beckwith, Charles). This came under considerable fire in the 1980s, when a group of studies demonstrated that there was virtually no official persecution of Christians under Domitian. The leading figure in this reconfiguring of the historical background was L. L. Thompson, who examined the data in a new way, noting that the standard sources for the negative portrayal of Domitian as a cruel despot came from a circle of writers gathered around Pliny the Younger during the reign of Trajan: Tacitus, Suetonius, Dio Chrysostom, and, a century later, Dio Cassius. Thompson[31] argued that their portraiture of Domitian—a lover of flattery, suspicious of (and insanely savage to) his perceived enemies, jealous of his brother Titus, power hungry, and a plunderer of the provinces—was entirely political rather than substantive. These writers sought to make Domitian a foil to Trajan and paint him as evil in order to make Trajan look good. However, on the basis of coinage, epigraphic evidence, and other writers of his own time (e.g., Quintilian, Frontinus, Statius, Martial, Silius Italicus), a quite different picture emerges: a Domitian who was modest, respectful of his father (Vespasian) and brother Titus, militarily successful, and a benign politician who ruled well. His decisive actions against the senate were occasioned by concern for the welfare of the lower-class provincials, demonstrating a concern for justice.[32] Moreover, Thompson goes on to say, Christians participated fully in urban Roman life, and all opposition was local rather than imperial in origin. Though there was Jewish opposition, Christians generally lived peacefully in the Roman social order.[33] In short, there was no official persecution at that time (for reaction to this view, see below).

A similar debate surrounds the issue of the imperial cult—that is, the worship of the emperor as a god. It is clear from the Apocalypse that this was a major problem in the province of Asia (13:4, 14–17; 14:9; 15:2; 16:2; 19:20; 20:4). Historically, Rome did not participate in the ancient Near Eastern view of kings as gods (e.g., Egypt, Persia), but with the end of the republic and the onset of the empire (after the death of Julius Caesar and the emergence of his nephew Octavius, who became the emperor Augustus in 27 B.C.E.), this view began to make inroads. It began when the common people included Julius Caesar and Augustus (and later Claudius and Vespasian) among their household gods, and it quickly spread to the main families as well. However, the practice was to deify

---

31. L. L. Thompson, *The Book of Revelation: Apocalypse and Empire* (New York: Oxford University Press, 1990), 96–101. See also A. Y. Collins, *Crisis and Catharsis: The Power of the Apocalypse* (Philadelphia: Westminster, 1984), 69–73; D. Warden, "Imperial Persecution and the Dating of 1 Peter and Revelation," *JETS* 34 (1991): 207–11; Barr, *Tales of the End*, 165–69.

32. Thompson, *Book of Revelation*, 102–9; Aune, *Revelation*, lxviii.

33. Thompson, *Book of Revelation*, 116–32.

an emperor after his death (Tiberias and Claudius had refused the honor while they were alive). Nero was not deified. To be sure, the emperor was seen not so much as a god but as the earthly representative of the gods,[34] but this role was popularly seen as divinity, evidenced in the temples and idolatrous images/statues. Soon, cities vied with each other to be labeled *neokoros,* or temple warden—that is, to be allowed to build a temple to one of the emperors. There is some evidence that Domitian wished to be recognized as *deus praesens* (present deity) and to be called "our Lord and god," and coins have him enthroned as "father of the gods."[35] However, Thompson argues that Domitian did not wish to be deified.[36] As we saw, it is the group of writers connected to Pliny that disparages Domitian as arrogantly requiring titles for himself. Such titles are missing from the writings of Domitian's supporters, such as Statius and Quintilian, where one would expect to find them if Domitian had demanded such. Thus, there is no incontestable evidence that Domitian ever sought deification or demanded titles such as *dominus* ("Lord") or *deus* ("god") for himself.

However, this new view of the persecution setting and of the imperial cult has been challenged of late from several perspectives. Beale[37] believes that Thompson overstated his case and that the truth lies in between the two extremes. Both Domitian's supporters and his later antagonists gave biased accounts, and though Domitian never demanded to be worshiped as a god, he did accept the title, and the negative evaluations of his reign have some basis in fact. There is evidence that he persecuted aristocrats who were Christians and that he was anti-Jewish. Beale finds "some evidence for a hardening of Roman policy, which became increasingly intolerant toward explicit Christian nonparticipation in the political-religious life of Greco-Roman society."[38]

Janzen[39] maintains that the coins point to a certain amount of megalomania on the part of Domitian; they show that even his wife is referred to as the mother of the divine Caesar. Botha[40] points out that there was no single "imperial cult." Instead, each city developed its own rituals, and though this was voluntary, it was also part of the benefactor system and thus was expected. So the pressure to participate was local and differed from city to city. Slater[41]

34. Giesen, *Die Offenbarung des Johannes,* 28–30.
35. D. L. Jones, "Roman Imperial Cult," *ABD* 5:807.
36. Thompson, *Book of Revelation,* 104–7.
37. Beale, *Revelation,* 6–12. He relies partly on S. R. F. Price, *Rituals and Power: The Roman Imperial Cult in Asia Minor* (Cambridge: Cambridge University Press, 1984), as well as S. J. Friesen, *Twice Neokoros: Ephesus, Asia, and the Cult of the Flavian Imperial Family,* Religions in the Graeco-Roman World 116 (Leiden: Brill, 1993).
38. Beale, *Revelation,* 9.
39. E. P. Janzen, "The Jesus of the Apocalypse Wears the Emperor's Clothes," *SBLSP* 33 (1994): 643–49.
40. P. J. J. Botha, "God, Emperor Worship, and Society: Contemporary Experiences and the Book of Revelation," *Neot* 22 (1988): 87–91.
41. T. B. Slater, "On the Social Setting of the Revelation to John," *NTS* 44 (1998): 234–38.

sums up the evidence well: Domitian was loved by the people in the provinces because he curbed the economic exploitation caused by the Roman governors, and thus the elite in Rome disliked him intensely. Although the Pliny circle did write under Trajan, when it was politically advantageous to disparage the Flavians, especially Domitian, at the same time the imperial cult did grow under Domitian. Biguzzi[42] provides a great deal of evidence: Asia was the epicenter of the imperial cult, and the major cities competed for the privilege of erecting a temple, beginning with Pergamum in 29 B.C.E., then Smyrna in 21 C.E. Ephesus was the third and was the core of anchoring for the Flavian dynasty in the province. The city erected a seven-meter-high statue of Titus (some think Domitian) in the temple, and emperor worship was seen there as a means of uniting the people under the Pax Romana.

In addition, the data, when examined more closely, does not prove that there was no persecution, but only that persecution was not officially instigated by Rome. The evidence of the book supports the presence of persecution, with passages referring to persecution in the recent past (1:9; 2:3, 9, 13; 3:8; 6:9; possibly ch. 13), and other passages warning of imminent systematic persecution to come (6:11; ch. 13; 17:6; 18:24; 19:2; 20:4).[43] Under the growing power of the imperial cult, especially in the province of Asia, such problems were growing under Domitian and came to a head under Trajan, as demonstrated by the renowned letter from Pliny to Trajan in 113 C.E., in which Pliny sought legal precedent for arresting Christians and bringing them to trial.[44] The principle given by Trajan was that he should not seek out Christians but should execute any who were brought to him and convicted. The pressure is also seen in the late first century in *1 Clem.* 1:1 ("sudden and repeated calamities" falling on the church) and 7:1 ("We are in the same arena, and the same struggle [as during the martyrdoms of Peter and Paul] is before us").[45] DeSilva[46] points out that there is no evidence of widespread persecution, but the relation between the state and Roman religious life placed tremendous pressure on all citizens to participate in the official religion, both in terms of temple worship and the idolatrous guild banquets that were at the center of daily life. Asia Minor was

42. G. Biguzzi, "Ephesus, Its Artemision, Its Temple to the Flavian Emperors, and Idolatry in Revelation," *NovT* 40 (1998): 280–89. See also A. Brent, "John as Theologos: The Imperial Mysteries and the Apocalypse," *JSNT* 75 (1999): 101–2. Brent believes that John was seen as the Christian counterpart to the *theologos*, the pagan official who oversaw the ritual, with Revelation meant to counter the mysteries of the imperial cult.

43. Beale, *Revelation,* 12 n. 65. Aune (*Revelation,* lxv) centers on 1:9; 6:9–11; 7:9, 14; 11:7–8; 12:11; 13:7; 14:13; 16:6; 17:6; 18:24; 20:4.

44. Pliny, *Letters,* 10.96 (reproduced in Barr, *Tales of the End,* 166–67). See also Krodel, *Revelation,* 39–42.

45. Beale, *Revelation,* 13, building on L. W. Barnard, "Clement of Rome and the Persecution of Domitian," *NTS* 10 (1964): 251–60.

46. D. A. deSilva, "The Social Setting of the Revelation to John: Conflicts Within, Fears Without," *WTJ* 54 (1992): 274–77. See also Michaels, *Revelation,* 22.

known for its pro-Roman zeal, and this was especially true of the imperial cult. So the nonparticipation of Christians in the imperial cult was a decisive test, and local persecution was likely. Reddish, in fact, goes so far as to describe the church there as "threatened by official persecution and martyrdom."[47] However, Massyngberde Ford is closer to the probable situation, saying that there was no systematic persecution under Domitian, but rather daily pressure and social ostracism that resulted from Christians refusing to participate in the Roman cults.[48]

The decision regarding the extent of the influence of the imperial cult and of the persecution that resulted from it makes all the difference in one's assessment of the social situation behind the book. For instance, A. Y. Collins[49] believes that there was very little persecution, so the feelings of alienation came from within the Christian community rather than from outside instigation. The believers did not perceive any crisis, so the author sought to awaken such an understanding. The problem was the "economic exploitation and cultural imperialism of Rome," and so the visions construct a symbolic universe under the control of God, with the faithful as God's priests who refuse to bow to Roman pressure.[50] In a similar way, Barr[51] believes that the book provided a "mythic therapy" intended to transform the perspectives of the readers and enable them to assimilate Christ's defeat of the dragon and thereby find victory in the struggle between "Roman culture and Christian conviction." For Schüssler Fiorenza,[52] the key is the "rhetorical strategy" of the book as it creates a new "symbolic universe" that enables the readers to enter the new world and alienate themselves from Roman power, thereby to accept the "deprivation and destitution" that goes with it. This is accomplished by constructing a new social reality, a world of future possibility in the midst of present oppression, a world in which

47. M. G. Reddish, "Martyr Theology in the Apocalypse," *JSNT* 33 (1988): 85.

48. J. Massyngberde Ford, "Persecution and Martyrdom in the Book of Revelation," *Bible Today* 29 (1990): 144–46; see also idem, "The Priestly People of God in the Apocalypse," *Listening* 28 (1993): 246–47.

49. Collins, *Crisis and Catharsis,* 141–60; see also Thompson, *Book of Revelation,* 27–28.

50. Collins, "Apocalypse and Politics," *Forum* 8 (1992): 302–5. Thompson (*Book of Revelation,* 169–70) claims that there was no crisis at all. Their identification with the crucified king separated them from society, so the author created a "feed-back loop" by developing an alternative symbolic world in which they would be the victors. E. Schüssler Fiorenza ("Epilogue: The Rhetoricality of Apocalypse and the Politics of Interpretation," in *The Book of Revelation: Justice and Judgment,* 2nd ed. [Philadelphia: Fortress, 1998], 231 n. 18) calls this "a depoliticizing trend in Revelation research."

51. Barr, *Tales of the End,* 178–80. See also idem, "The Apocalypse as a Symbolic Transformation of the World: A Literary Analysis," *Int* 38 (1984): 49–50, where Barr says that the book provides a "catharsis" that gives the Christians a new worldview in which the victims become the victors.

52. Schüssler Fiorenza, *Justice and Judgment,* 187–99.

God is supremely sovereign. Similarly, Giesen[53] argues that John does not
encourage the readers so much as warn them against the insidious nature
of the imperial cult, telling Christians to have nothing to do with it. The
danger is not martyrdom but attraction to the pagan world. Kraybill[54] believes that the problem is not persecution but compromise; the church had
become "cozy with the pagan world," and so the book demands that believers
choose between Christ and the emperor. There is a movement away from
the view that the problem is external pressure to accommodate with Rome
and toward the view of an internal battle between John's prophetic circle and
the Christian sect seeking accommodation with Rome. Le Grys[55] believes
that the issue is not external but internal, a crisis of prophetic authority: the
danger of the Nicolaitans (2:6) and their influence on Christian compromise. Harland[56] argues that John and his followers were a strong minority,
as most Christians then freely participated in the *polis* and were integrated
into the community, including membership in the guilds and honoring
the emperor. Koester[57] sums up this approach, noting three threats: seduc-
tion by false teaching that calls for cultural assimilation, conflict with local
synagogues and the danger of being denounced to the local authorities, and
complacency due to prosperity.

These theories regarding the social world behind the book certainly contain a great deal of truth. Yet there is much more to it than this. The seven
churches (indeed all the churches of the province of Asia) existed within a
hostile environment stemming from both the Jewish and Roman worlds. The
key is recognizing that persecution was not merely perceived but real. First,
the "synagogue of Satan" (2:9; 3:9) turned against them (as seen throughout
the Book of Acts), and the hostility increased in the last couple decades of

53. Giesen, *Die Offenbarung des Johannes*, 34–36; see also idem, "Ermutigung zur Glauben-
streue in schwerer Zeit: Zum Zweck der Johannesoffenbarung," *TTZ* 105 (1996): 61–63;
"Das Buch mit den sieben Siegeln—Heil für Aussenseiter," in *1900th Anniversary of St. John's
Apocalypse*, 592–601, where Giesen develops the reality of the imperial cult as "Gefährdung für
den christlichen Glauben."
54. J. N. Kraybill, "Apocalypse Now," *Christianity Today* 43 (1999): 37–38.
55. A. Le Grys, "Conflict and Vengeance in the Book of Revelation," *ExpTim* 104 (1992):
77–79. See also S. S. Smalley, *Thunder and Love: John's Revelation and John's Community* (Vancouver: Word, 1994), 121–28; H. O. Maier, "Staging the Gaze: Early Christian Apocalypses
and Narrative Self-Representation," *HTR* 90 (1997): 149–50.
56. P. A. Harland, "Honouring the Emperor or Assailing the Beast: Participation in Civic
Life among Associations (Jewish Christian and Other) in Asia Minor and the Apocalypse of
God," *JSNT* 77 (2000): 99–121. Harland draws much of his evidence from P. Trebilco (*Jewish
Communities in Asia Minor*, SNTSMS 69 [Cambridge: Cambridge University Press, 1991]),
who shows a similar assimilation of Jewish communities. This is a provocative possibility but
somewhat doubtful in light of the fact that the Nicolaitan cult, the major syncretistic Christian
cult, apparently is influential in only two of the churches, Pergamum and Thyatira, and has
already been defeated in the church at Ephesus.
57. C. R. Koester, "The Distant Triumph Song: Music and the Book of Revelation," *Word
and World* 12 (1992): 248–49.

the first century.[58] The special privilege accorded the Jews, allowing them to worship their God rather than the Roman gods, had been extended to Christians because the Romans generally considered them a Jewish sect. But the Jews had been denouncing Christians as non-Jews, and there is some evidence that this was starting to change Roman attitudes. Bredin[59] notes the Judean tax that the Romans imposed on the Jews for the rebuilding of the Capitoline temple. This tax allowed the Jews freedom from participation in the imperial cult. Christians refused to pay this tax, and the Jews denounced Christians as both non-Jewish and troublemakers against Rome. This caused many to turn against the Christians. So although there was no official persecution, there was intense economic and social pressure to participate in Roman life. Beale[60] describes the great pressure to compromise with the guilds, especially in the annual feast honoring each guild's patron deities (the Nicolaitan cult surrendered to this pressure). When believers refused, they experienced great antipathy and persecution, as is reflected in the seven letters. Hartman[61] finds three major factors in the religious situation: heresies (the Nicolaitan cult), oppression (not official but local, yet still real and soon to escalate), and lack of zeal (tendencies to compromise and assimilate to the majority ethos).

So the theses of Collins, Thompson, Barr, and others underestimate the situation. There is much more than a perceived crisis; the difficulties have actually begun and would intensify in succeeding years. Still, however, they are correct in saying that Revelation develops a "symbolic universe," a transcendent realm in which God's people are both a counterculture and a witness to the reality of the world of God and his people. As deSilva states, the church is told in the book to maintain its *communitas* in the midst of alienation and societal pressure, and to resist temptation to compromise and accommodate itself to societal mores.[62] This worldview is a new set of ethical standards that both resists accommodation and actually embraces societal rejection in allegiance to Christ. He calls the book an "honor discourse"[63] written to persuade the believers to oppose pressure to conform to pagan ways, to encourage perseverance, and to warn the weak against compromise.

58. For the view that Jews rather than Romans were the primary source of persecution in the book, see A. J. Beagley, *The "Sitz im Leben" of the Apocalypse with Particular Reference to the Role of the Church's Enemies*, BZNW 50 (New York: de Gruyter, 1987).

59. M. R. J. Bredin, "The Synagogue of Satan Accusation in Revelation 2:9," *BTB* 28 (1998): 161–64.

60. Beale, *Revelation*, 30.

61. L. Hartman, "The Book of Revelation: A Document for Its Time as John Sees It," in *1900th Anniversary of St. John's Apocalypse*, 207–10.

62. DeSilva, "Social Setting," 301–2; see also idem, "The Construction and Social Function of a Counter-Cosmos in the Revelation of John," *Forum* 9 (1993): 47–62.

63. D. A. deSilva, "Honor Discourse and the Rhetorical Strategy of the Apocalypse of John," *JSNT* 71 (1998): 80–87.

In conclusion, A. Y. Collins and Thompson are correct in stating that the book presents an alternative universe and a crisis not truly perceived by the churches. There is indeed a call to recognize the reality of the transcendent realm and its inevitable triumph as well as a challenge to refuse compromise with pagan society. Yet, the situation is not imagined but real. The Christians were undergoing immense pressure and sporadic local oppression for refusing to accommodate, and some of them (the Nicolaitans) had given in to that pressure. The pressure was not only social but also economic, for the trade guilds were part of the pagan order, and these included worship of both the patron deities and the emperor as a god. So Revelation is written to encourage the faithful that their perseverance would be rewarded, to comfort them that God was still sovereign and their vindication was assured, and to warn the vacillating and "cowardly" among them that apostates would suffer unbelievable torment for abandoning the faith (21:8).

Feminist Interpretation

Revelation has received a significant feminist response, but it has gone virtually unnoticed in the major works. For instance, T. Pippin's influential work[64] is not even mentioned in the recent commentaries by Aune, Beale, and Thompson, nor do they discuss feminist critique of the "whore of Babylon" metaphor in Rev. 17. A. Y. Collins did a study of women's history and the Book of Revelation,[65] based on the principle that the Bible is "a record of our oppression." She sees androcentric bias especially in John's attack on Jezebel in 2:20–23, which is much more severe than Paul's less critical stance regarding meat offered to idols in 1 Cor. 8–10. Even more so, Revelation's emphasis on sexual continence in 14:1–5 is mandated for the sake of purity and is an attack on women as the source of evil. So for this book, the ideal Christian is male because males are more pure, and women are dangerous.

Pippin provides an even stronger feminist reading of the Apocalypse that unlocks the gender codes and unmasks both the oppressive view of women in the book and the Western biases that provide a male-centered political interpretation of the book. She believes that the book centers on disaster and death rather than on salvation, and that it contains a misogynist substratum that "reads the lives" of the females in the book in terms of death and destruction. This is nowhere better seen than in the destruction of "the whore of Babylon" in ch. 17 and in the battle against the prophetess Jezebel, who is to be thrown upon a bed of suffering (2:22–23). Even the "woman" in 12:12 is banished to

---

64. T. Pippin, *Death and Desire: The Rhetoric of Gender in the Apocalypse of John* (Louisville: Westminster John Knox, 1992).

65. A. Y. Collins, "Women's History and the Book of Revelation," *SBLSP* 26 (1987): 80–91, esp. 81–84.

the wilderness for protection.[66] She sees an "apocalypse of women" even in the vision of the New Jerusalem, for the bride imagery is quickly replaced by the anthropocentric priestly imagery.[67] Elsewhere, Pippin[68] states that women are rendered absent from the purity of 14:4; and not only is the model Christian male, but also women are excluded from the New Jerusalem. Images are turned inside out, and women are displaced. Even the "heroine," the woman clothed with the sun in ch. 12, has no name and does nothing more than represent institutions. She has productive value only when reproductive (bearing the male son). J. Dewey[69] disagrees that women are excluded from the New Jerusalem but agrees that women are marginalized, seeing 14:4–5 as "the author's androcentric mindset in operation." In fact, since the Apocalypse exalts passive suffering and violence, it cannot liberate men or women. Similarly, J. K. Kim[70] argues that the "whore of Babylon" pictures colonized women who first were invaded by foreign men and then abandoned by their own men. As such, they were marginalized and then victimized.

Schüssler Fiorenza argues that this deconstructive approach of Pippin and others is a naturalized or literal reading that sees the female images of the book as "real women"—that is, feminine archetypes rather than symbols. She considers the sexual metaphor of whoring in chs. 17–18 as a "conventional metaphor." Thus, it is better to read it as gender-inclusive rather than gender-specific.[71] Though a literalizing hermeneutic is viable here, Fiorenza says, it is better to take a "critical rhetorical multisystemic interpretation" of the gender language "in terms of sociopolitical and cultural-linguistic systems of domination," namely, that of Roman imperialism. This then adds the issues of race, class, and economic oppression to the issue of gender.[72] In a critique

---

66. See Pippin, *Death and Desire;* see also idem, "The Heroine and the Whore: Fantasy and the Female in the Apocalypse of John," *Semeia* 60 (1992): 69.

67. Pippin, *Death and Desire,* 47–48.

68. Pippin, "The Heroine and the Whore," 69–71; see also idem, "Eros and the End: Reading for Gender in the Apocalypse of John," *Semeia* 59 (1992): 193–209. J. Schaberg ("Response to Tina Pippin's 'Eros and the End,'" *Semeia* 59 [1992]: 220–21) adds that women not only have to flee rather than triumph (12:6), but they also are not included in the 144,000 and actually flee right out of the text and are never seen again.

69. J. Dewey, "Response: Fantasy and the New Testament," *Semeia* 60 (1992): 87–88.

70. J. K. Kim, "'Uncovering Her Wickedness': An Inter(con)textual Reading of Revelation 17 from a Postcolonial Feminist Perspective," *JSNT* 73 (1999): 61–81.

71. E. Schüssler Fiorenza, "Only Justice Can Stop a Curse: Response to Tina Pippin's *Death and Desire*" (paper presented at the annual meeting of the Society of Biblical Literature, Washington, D.C., November 1993); *Justice and Judgment,* 208, 216.

72. Schüssler Fiorenza, *Justice and Judgment,* 218–19. She finds four areas of ideological struggle in Rev. 17–18: (1) Babylon is a city symbolized as a woman, and the thrust is justice for imperial oppression; (2) the idea of whoredom is taken from the OT and is a conventional symbol for idolatry as religious whoredom; (3) Jezebel was an actual woman prophet and shows that women had leadership in the early church; the problem is not gender but doctrinal and political-cultural; (4) there are three major figures: the Queen of Heaven (Rev. 12), the Queen of Earth (Rev. 17), and the Queen of the New Heaven and New Earth (Rev. 21); the contrast

of Pippin, Barr states that the evil woman is always paired with an evil man: Jezebel/Balaam, whore/beast, and "masculine evil characters predominate." There are also more positive women in the book: the woman of ch. 12 and the bride of ch. 19. A. Y. Collins[73] points out that the female personifications in the Apocalypse are borrowed from Greek tradition. For instance, the harlot in ch. 17 as an image of Rome and the goddess Roma has prophetic precedents and is linked to Greek ethical tradition, in which Virtue and Vice are seen as women. Thus, this provides a moral indictment of Roman culture. In short, the Apocalypse is not repressive of women. The whore of Babylon is a symbol drawn from OT and Greco-Roman metanarrative rather than being a misogynistic rejection of women.[74]

Interpretation

There are two separate issues here: deciding on the proper method(s) for approaching Revelation, and deciding how to interpret its symbols. I will try to present the state of scholarship on each of these in turn. Historically, choosing one of the four methods—historicist (Joachim of Fiore, the Franciscans, the Reformers, Scofield-type dispensationalists on the seven letters), preterist (Charles, Sweet, Roloff, Schüssler Fiorenza, Collins, Thompson, Barr, Christian reconstructionists such as Gentry and Chilton), idealist (Milligan, Hendriksen, Hoekema, Hughes), or futurist (Justin, Irenaeus, Ladd, Walvoord, Thomas)—has been crucial, with the choice of method determining one's understanding of the book in virtually every detail.

However, in the last thirty years it has become increasingly common for scholars to label themselves "eclectic," utilizing several of the methods (Morris, Johnson, Roloff, Giesen, Mounce, Beale, Osborne). Virtually all would eschew the historicist approach as having limited value if any at all, but they would combine the other three as best reproducing the perspective of the Apocalypse. The belief is that each of the methods becomes dangerous when taken to the extreme. For instance, Harrington says that the futurist method leads to "gross misinterpretation. . . . The idea of an elect minority being shunted to the safe regions of the upper air while a vengeful Lamb destroys the inhabitants of

---

is not between women but between the old world of injustice and the new world of justice, between power used for destruction and power used for well-being (ibid., 219–26).

73. A. Y. Collins, "The Apocalyptic Ekphrasis," in *1900th Anniversary of St. John's Apocalypse,* 462.

74. D. L. Barr, "Playing with Polyvalence or Master(bat)ing the Text? The Seductive Reading of the Apocalypse in Tina Pippin's *Death and Desire*" (paper presented at the annual meeting of the Society of Biblical Literature, Washington, D.C., November 1993). See also A. D. Callahan, "The Language of the Apocalypse," *HTR* 88 (1999): 57. Callahan responds that there are no prurient images here. "Forensic, not salacious, elements dominate the text." It is "the military language of urban siege."

the earth is scarcely Christian."[75] This, of course, is a caricature of the futurist position, but it could fit the extreme edges. So most today allow the preterist, idealist, and futurist positions to interact so as to maximize the strengths and minimize the weaknesses of each one. Still, in virtually every case one of the methods will dominate the others. For instance, Beale calls his approach a "redemptive-historical form of modified idealism."[76] However, in reality it is a blend of the idealist and futurist positions in an inaugurated sense, describing the church age from the present to the future. For instance, the "beast" of 13:1–10 refers both to the "many antichrists" throughout church history and to the final antichrist, who will appear at the end of history.[77] Mounce interprets the beast not as an individual who will appear at the end of history, but first as the Roman Empire and then as "the deification of secular authority" down through the ages, thus combining the preterist and idealist positions.[78] Still, he also embraces the futurist position in the sense that he believes that the book points to a cataclysmic end of the world order in the eschatological future.

My own position gives the futurist perspective primacy in the sense that John's visions are mainly intended to describe how God will end world history.[79] The beast is the final antichrist, and the seals, trumpets, and bowls symbolize a final series of judgments that will occur just before (and at the same time are part of) the eschaton (see more on this below). Yet the preterist aspect is also central, for the visions use these pictures of the future to describe the church of John's day as well. Obviously, the three aspects cannot be completely assimilated to one another, for the preterist says that the book relates past and present events, and the futurist that it relates future events. One perspective must predominate (for Beale, it is the idealist; for me, it is the futurist), but the book as a whole can relate to all three aspects. Most of the imagery in the book is drawn from first-century parallels, especially the Greco-Roman period and Roman rule. The beast is a final Nero-like figure, and Babylon is the final unholy Roman Empire. In this sense, the church in John's present situation is addressed and likened to the people of God at the final period of world history. In other words, John the author deliberately uses double entendre, wanting his readers to see both dimensions. Finally, the idealist position is also important because these visions of the future are also timeless symbols intended to address the church in every age. Though the beast is primarily the final antichrist, Beale is correct in saying that the figure applies to the "many antichrists" who appear throughout the church age.

75. W. J. Harrington, *Revelation*, SP (Collegeville, Minn.: Liturgical Press, 1993), 16.
76. Beale, *Revelation*, 48.
77. Ibid., 680–81.
78. R. H. Mounce, *The Book of Revelation*, 2nd ed., NICNT (Grand Rapids: Eerdmans, 1998), 246.
79. Osborne, *Revelation*, 22.

This brings us to the second issue: the interpretation of the symbols themselves. If there is any book that must be read carefully in terms of its background, it is Revelation. This is the primary error of the so-called prophecy movement today: the false assumption that the symbols are unlocked by current events, resulting in the failure of those who so read the symbols to go back to the original background. As Friesen[80] says, to understand the book, one must wed social history to the text itself—that is, bring background information to bear on the symbols of the book. The symbols had a particular communicative function in addressing the social situation of the original readers, thereby opening up a new symbolic world for them.[81] The key is actually quite simple: what function did each symbol have in the thought-world of the first century, and what background information can be utilized to unlock its meaning?

In taking this approach, we utilize "the language of equivalents" and wed our knowledge—of the apocalyptic world of the first century, of the use of the OT in the Jewish world of that time, and of Greco-Roman backgrounds—to the way the symbol is used in the context. Beale[82] argues that in 1:1, John uses *esēmanen* in light of its meaning in Dan. 2:28–30, 45, where God "signifies" truths through symbolic visions. Thus, it means "communicate through symbols" and demands that the reader interpret the reality behind the symbols. Beale distinguishes four levels of communication: the linguistic level (the exegetical study of the text), the visionary level (John's experience of the visions), the referential level (each symbol seen in terms of historical background), and the symbolic level (asking what is connoted by the symbol). The symbols of the book are metaphorical, and as such, they must be understood pictorially and then referentially.[83] In this sense, the old dichotomy between the "literal" and the "symbolic" breaks down. Recent commentaries, such as those by Giesen, Beale, and Aune, recognize that we are dealing with tensive symbols that take the readers into a new thought-world and yet still address the real world of which they are a part. The image of the two "beasts" (ch. 13) reaches back to Job 40–41 as well as to Dan. 7 and yet at the same time draws meaning from the first-century world, perhaps that of the "Nero redivivus" legend (the beast from the sea) and the priests of the imperial cult, especially the "high priest," the provincial governors, or the "*commune* of Asia," whose president was called the "Asiarch" (the beast from the land).[84] It is a complex task, but not an impossible one.

80. S. J. Friesen, "Revelation, Realia, and Religion: Archaeology in the Interpretation of the Apocalypse," *HTR* 88 (1995): 306–14.

81. See E. Schüssler Fiorenza, "The Followers of the Lamb: Visionary Rhetoric and Socio-Political Situation," *Semeia* 36 (1986): 125–30.

82. Beale, *Revelation*, 50–52.

83. On the referential dimension of metaphors, see especially J. M. Soskice, *Metaphor and Religious Language* (Oxford: Clarendon, 1985), 51–53.

84. For the latter, see D. A. deSilva, "The 'Image of the Beast' and the Christians in Asia Minor: Escalation of Sectarian Tension in Revelation 13," *TJ* 12 (1990): 185–208; Aune, *Revelation*, 756–57.

The sources for interpreting the symbols stem from the OT, intertestamental literature (especially the apocalyptic writings), and the Greco-Roman world (i.e., the social world of Revelation's original readers). The explosion of knowledge in these areas is mind-boggling, and much of it has been captured in the brilliant commentary by Aune, which certainly is one of the great scholarly achievements of our time. Yet this is where the actual problem lies: so many possibilities have been uncovered that it seems impossible to sift through the viable choices to select the best. Some are fairly simple—for example, the "hot" and "cold" and "lukewarm" of 3:15–16. Since the older articles of Rudwick and Green as well as Wood,[85] it has been commonly accepted that the church of Laodicea was being likened to its water supply.

Other decisions are far more complex, such as the twelve foundation jewels of 21:19–20. They could be (1) the reversal of a list of the twelve jewels linked with the twelve signs of the zodiac in ancient Egyptian and Arabic writings (so Charles, Lohmeyer, Farrer, Kiddle, Caird, Beasley-Murray, the earlier Morris, Johnson, Roloff); (2) the list of the jewels on the breastplate of the high priest, with eight of the twelve paralleling the LXX of Exod. 28:17–20; 39:10–13 (so Rissi, Glasson, Massyngberde Ford, the later Morris, Sweet, Krodel, Mounce, Beale, Aune); (3) a general depiction of the glory of the people of God (so Ladd, Wall, Giesen, Harrington). Of these, the closest parallels are with the breastplate of the high priest, since the four stones that are different might well be semantic equivalents of the ones in Exod. 28:17–20 LXX.[86]

The Use of the Old Testament

It is surprising how many recent commentaries have no discussion whatsoever of the use of the OT in Revelation (e.g., Beasley-Murray, Krodel, Roloff, Buchanan, Michaels, Aune), in spite of the centrality of the OT in the book.[87] There is virtually no agreement as to the exact number of allusions to the OT in the Apocalypse,[88] but all agree that there are far more than in any other NT book.

85. M. J. S. Rudwick and E. M. B. Green, "The Laodicean Lukewarmness," *ExpTim* 69 (1957–58): 176–78; P. Wood, "Local Knowledge in the Letters of the Apocalypse," *ExpTim* 73 (1961–62): 263–64.

86. See Beale, *Revelation*, 1080–88; J. Joosten, "χαλκηδών (Ap 21,19)," *RHPR* 79 (1999): 135–43.

87. See G. K. Beale, *The Use of the Old Testament in Revelation*, JSNTSup 166 (Sheffield: Sheffield Academic Press, 1998), 15–59, for extensive evaluations of the seven important monographs written on this topic since the mid-1980s: his own on Daniel, Vogelgesang on Ezekiel, Paulien on allusions in 8:7–12, Ruiz on Ezekiel, Fekkes on Isaiah, Bauckham in *The Climax of Prophecy*, and Moyise on the book as a whole.

88. Beale (*Revelation*, 77 n. 16) points out that UBS has 394; NA, 635; Kilpatrick's *HKAINH ΔIAΘHKH*, 493; Swete, 278; and Charles, 226.

As Paulien[89] points out, the problem is the difficulty of determining partial quotations, allusions, and echoes of the OT in specific passages. Even more interesting is the total absence of introductory formulae such as "it is written" or "the Spirit says." The allusions are woven directly into the tapestry of the text—a style that is sometimes called the "compositional use" of the OT.[90] There is some question as to which OT book is the most influential. Beale[91] believes that Daniel is primary because it has the highest incidence of use in Revelation in comparison to its size. He says that Revelation as a whole is a midrash on Dan. 2 and 7. However, this does not fit the statistics themselves: there are 46 references to Isaiah, 31 to Daniel, 29 to Ezekiel, 27 to Psalms; and in descending order of frequency, allusions also to Genesis, Deuteronomy, Jeremiah, Joel, and Zechariah.[92] As Moyise says, "Revelation is a fresh composition which has used Daniel as *one* of its significant sources."[93] For John, the entire OT was a source, and he used it freely. There has been an explosion of research into this topic, with major works on the use of Daniel, of Isaiah, and of Ezekiel in the Apocalypse.[94]

The major issue is the extent of John's freedom in using the OT. Scholars debate whether he was faithful to the original context and meaning of the texts he used. Schüssler Fiorenza speaks of the anthological style of the book, moving from one allusion to another without mentioning the context, and concludes, "He does not interpret the OT but uses its words, images, phrases, and patterns as a language arsenal in order to make his own theological statement or express his own theological vision."[95] Roloff adds that "the symbols and images of the Old Testament models are freely adapted and modified in the service of the author's compositional method and poetic power of expres-

89. J. Paulien, "Elusive Allusions: The Problematic Use of the Old Testament in Revelation," *BR* 33 (1988): 37–38.

90. See J. Paulien, "Dreading the Whirlwind: Intertextuality and the Use of the Old Testament in Revelation," *AUSS* 39 (2001): 9–10, utilizing the phrase created by D. Dimant, "The Use and Interpretation of Mikra in the Apocrypha and Pseudepigrapha," in *Mikra: Text and Translation, Reading, and Interpretation of the Hebrew Bible in Ancient Judaism and Early Christianity,* ed. M. J. Mulder (Philadelphia: Fortress, 1988), 381–84.

91. G. K. Beale, "The Use of the Old Testament in Revelation," in *It Is Written: Scripture Citing Scripture,* ed. D. A. Carson and H. G. M. Williamson (Cambridge: Cambridge University Press, 1998), 318–36.

92. According to the statistics in H. B. Swete, *The Apocalypse of St. John* (London: Macmillan), cliii n. 1. See also S. Moyise (*The Old Testament in the Book of Revelation,* JSNTSup 115 [Sheffield: Sheffield Academic Press, 1994], 16), who tabulates 122 from Isaiah, 97 from the Psalms, 83 from Ezekiel, 82 from the Pentateuch, 74 from Daniel, 73 from the Minor Prophets, and 48 from Jeremiah.

93. Moyise, *Old Testament in the Book of Revelation,* 63. See also J.-P. Ruiz, *Ezekiel in the Apocalypse: The Transformation of Prophetic Language in Revelation 16,17–19,10,* EHS 23.376 (Frankfurt: Lang, 1989), 121.

94. G. K. Beale, *The Use of Daniel in Jewish Apocalyptic Literature and in the Revelation of St. John* (Lanham, Md.: University Press of America, 1984); Ruiz, *Ezekiel in the Apocalypse;* J. Fekkes, *Isaiah and Prophetic Traditions in the Book of Revelation: Visionary Antecedents and Their Development,* JSNTSup 93 (Sheffield: Sheffield Academic Press, 1994).

95. Schüssler Fiorenza, *Justice and Judgment,* 135.

sion."[96] Beale lists four things that lead many to believe that John ignores the original context: (1) the informal nature of the citations; (2) centering on his own authority, rather than that of the OT, due to his prophetic spirit; (3) his Hellenistic, illiterate readers, who would have been unable to unlock such original meanings; (4) the lack of evidence that John is consciously interpreting the texts he cites.[97] It is common to cite the title of A. M. Farrer's book *A Rebirth of Images* to describe the use of the OT in Revelation. The emphasis is upon the imagination of the reader, who is asked to enter the new world of ideas created by the transformation of images from the OT.

However, does the data itself support the view that the author disregards the OT context and meaning of his allusions? Certainly, one can demonstrate John's creative use of an OT passage, such as the use of Zech. 12:10 in Rev. 1:7. Originally, it spoke of the revival of the "house of David" and the "inhabitants of Jerusalem" who "mourn" for their sins, but in 1:7 John has switched the image over to "the peoples of the earth" who mourn in light of imminent judgment. However, it is also possible that John uses it with a "double meaning," to introduce the two tracks taken by the nations, who will either mourn for sin (the path of salvation [cf. 5:9–10; 11:13; 14:6–7; 15:4; 21:24, 26]) or mourn because they have opposed God and now face his wrath (the path of judgment [cf. 6:15–17; 11:18; 14:8–11; 16:6; 18:2–3, 6–8]).[98] John does indeed transform the OT context by applying the Israel passage to the nations of the earth, but at the same time he remains faithful to its context. In short, John is fully cognizant of original context as he transforms texts by applying them to the new apocalyptic situation in his visions.

J. Fekkes argues that it is an error to "find prophetic activity and authority incompatible with exegetical activity."[99] Anthological style does not of necessity obviate contextual fidelity. Adapting OT contexts to John's contemporary situation does, of course, constitute interpretation, but John's prophetic spirit does not create *ex nihilo* and in fact expects the readers to understand the exegetical foundations of the transformed visions. Fekkes believes that the interpretive style of Revelation is in keeping with Matthew, Paul, and the author of Hebrews, who also transformed OT texts as fulfilled in the NT setting. G. W. Buchanan calls this interpretive style "typology,"[100] by which he means a correspondence between events in salvation history. Moyise calls it "intertextuality," defined by him as "the dynamic interaction of shared language."[101] However, this does

96. J. Roloff, *Revelation*, trans. J. E. Alsup, CC (Minneapolis: Fortress, 1993), 12.

97. Beale, *Revelation*, 81–86.

98. Osborne, *Revelation*, 26, 68–72.

99. Fekkes, *Isaiah and Prophetic Traditions*, 286–90.

100. G. W. Buchanan, *The Book of Revelation: Its Introduction and Prophecy*, Mellen Biblical Commentary (Lewiston, N.Y.: Mellen Biblical Press, 1993), 14.

101. Moyise, *Old Testament in the Book of Revelation*, 138 (see 108–38). See also J. R. Michaels, "Old Testament in Revelation," in *Dictionary of the Later New Testament and Its Developments*, ed. R. P. Martin and P. H. Davids (Downers Grove, Ill.: InterVarsity, 1997), 852.

not mean a lack of consideration for context. "The most fundamental thing is that John has built a bridge between two contexts, thereby setting in motion an interaction that continues to reverberate throughout the whole book," namely, a "dialectical imitation, in which the symbolic world of the Old Testament is dynamically used and a broad interplay occurs between two worlds."[102] This is a process of transformation as John applies the original context via typology to the visions that God has sent him. Beale concludes, "John's interpretation of the Old Testament shows respect for the . . . contexts, and his interpretation shows formative influence from the Old Testament itself."[103]

Perhaps the issue can be demonstrated by the debate between Moyise and Beale regarding the extent of John's faithfulness to the OT context. Moyise[104] says that John involves the readers in the process, leading them to create new meanings or new understandings. Therefore, the meaning is open-ended for the reader. Beale, of course, believes strongly that John is at all times sensitive to the original context, but Moyise[105] responds that in reality the NT does give the OT new meanings and take them out of context; meaning is not just in the author, but also in the reader. In return, Beale[106] argues that it is a question of one's epistemological approach as well as the data itself; if one follows the approach of E. D. Hirsch, K. J. Vanhoozer, or N. T. Wright, then the author must be allowed to speak, and therefore the interpreter's task is to separate meaning from significance. J. Paulien tries to find a middle ground, arguing that NT writers do indeed respect the larger context of OT writings, but the reader is always involved in the meaning. He states, "Far too often authoritative appropriations of Scripture . . . are based not on careful exegesis but on presupposition-laden 'reader responses,' treated as accurate reflections of the text's intent. The ground for such readings has often been the drive for power and control more than faithfulness to the authoritative text."[107] In conclusion, we can say that John uses the OT with faithfulness to the original context but at the same time with freedom to transform it so as to apply its larger thrust to the new context of his churches.

Finally, we note the many ways the OT is used in the book:[108]

---

102. S. Moyise, "Intertextuality and the Book of Revelation," *ExpTim* 104 (1993): 295.

103. Beale, *Use of the Old Testament in Revelation*, 45. He finds four presuppositions behind John's use: (1) Christ corporately represents the New Israel; (2) history is unified under God's plan, so that earlier parts typologically correspond to the later events; (3) Christ's first advent has inaugurated the age of end-time fulfillment; (4) so the latter parts of canonical history interpret the earlier parts, and Christ becomes the key for interpreting the OT.

104. Moyise, *Old Testament in the Book of Revelation*, 110–11.

105. S. Moyise, "The Old Testament in the New: A Response to Greg Beale," *IBS* 21 (1999): 54–58.

106. G. K. Beale, "Questions of Authorial Intent, Epistemology, and Presuppositions and Their Bearing on the Study of the Old Testament in the New: A Rejoinder to Steve Moyise," *IBS* 21 (1999): 152–80.

107. Paulien, "Dreading the Whirlwind," 21 (see 18–22).

108. Here I combine material found in Beale, *Use of the Old Testament in Revelation*, 60–128; idem, *Revelation*, 86–96; and Fekkes, *Isaiah and Prophetic Traditions*, 70–101.

1. Literary prototypes: OT passages can be models for major sections, such as Daniel for Rev. 13, Ezek. 37–48 for Rev. 20–22, or Ezek. 2:8–3:3 for Rev. 10:8–11.
2. Thematic analogues: clusters of traditional material develop certain themes, such as the "holy war" theme[109] or divine titles applied to Christ.
3. Typology or analogical fulfillment: OT figures such as Leviathan (= the dragon) or the little horn of Daniel (= the beast from the sea), as well as places such as the tabernacle/temple (= the heavenly temple) or things such as the horsemen of Zech. 1 and 6 (= the horsemen of Rev. 6:1–8), are fulfilled in the images of the book.
4. Universalization: taking what applied to Israel and applying it to the world or the church, such as Zech. 12:10 (Israel mourning) in Rev. 1:7, or Exod. 19:6 ("kingdom of priests") in Rev. 1:6; 5:10.
5. Indirect fulfillment: informal use of OT passages to heighten the imagery, such as Moses and Elijah behind the imagery of the two witnesses in Rev. 11, or an inaugurated use of Dan. 7:13 behind "the one like a son of man" in Rev. 1:12–13 (meaning that Jesus has begun to fulfill the exaltation aspect in that passage).
6. Inverted uses: the OT passage is actually reversed in the book—for instance, Rev. 3:9, in which the Jewish persecutors will bow down before the believers (the opposite of Jewish hopes in Isa. 45:14; 49:23; 60:14), or Rev. 12:7–8, the overthrow of Satan by Michael (the opposite of Dan. 7:21, where the horn overpowers the saints).
7. One final aspect may be noted: the tendency of John to utilize either the Hebrew OT or the LXX, depending on which one fits better in a given context.[110]

Unity and Structure

At first glance, the unity of language and thought in Revelation causes one to assume the unity of the book itself. Sweet responds to the kaleidoscopic changes in the book by saying, "A glance at other apocalyptic books shows that the genre is in its nature incoherent, with bewildering changes of scene and speaker, interjections, repetitions, and inconsistencies. . . . On our view, allowing for the looseness of the genre, Revelation is an impressively coherent

109. See R. Bauckham, "The Apocalypse as a Christian War Scroll," in *Climax of Prophecy,* 210–37; C. H. Giblin, *The Book of Revelation,* GNS 34 (Collegeville, Minn.: Liturgical Press, 1992), 25–36.
110. See S. Moyise, "The Language of the Old Testament in the Apocalypse," *JSOT* 76 (1999): 112–13. This topic is also highly debated, as several scholars believe that John used both but centered on the Hebrew texts—for example, J. P. M. Sweet, *Revelation,* PNTC (London: SCM, 1979), 40; Fekkes, *Isaiah and Prophetic Traditions,* 17.

whole, and can be taken as substantially the work of one mind."[111] In fact, the majority of commentators recently (Beasley-Murray, Krodel, Roloff, Mounce, Beale, Keener) assume unity and fail even to discuss redactional theories. However, there have been a steady number of attempts to discern source-critical layers through the years, and it is important to understand them.

Generally speaking, there are three types of source-critical theories.[112]

1. Compilation theories: several separate Jewish and Christian apocalypses were combined, either two Jewish works (Weyland) or Jewish and Christian works (Spitta, Weiss). Others believe that Christian works are combined, perhaps two written during Nero and Vespasian's reigns (Boismard) or by a member of the Baptist circle plus later disciples (Massyngberde Ford).

2. Revision theories: a single work was developed in a series of stages, perhaps a Jewish apocalypse by a Christian writer (Vischer, Whealen); a later disciple interpolating material into it after the author died (Charles); a single author writing in stages (Kraft); or two editions, with the second adding the seven letters, the epilogue, and a few interpolations (Prigent).

3. Fragmentary theories: fragments from Jewish apocalypses were incorporated into the original text (Bousset).

Aune has recently combined the three into a comprehensive redaction-critical theory.[113] According to him, Revelation is a composite of several different apocalyptic tracts composed by a single author over a twenty- to thirty-year period. The book was compiled in three stages:

1. Twelve self-contained units were combined from the 50s and 60s (7:1–17; 10:1–11; 11:1–13; 12:1–17; 13:1–18; 14:1–20; 17:1–18; 18:1–24; 19:11–16; 20:1–10, 11–15; 21:9–22:5), the author perhaps writing some while still a non-Christian Jew (7:1–8; 11:1–13) and the rest after converting to Christianity.

2. The first edition was compiled during the period 69–74 C.E., with further material intended to introduce the document (1:7–12a) and to unify it into a whole (4:1–22:5) by providing an eschatological framework (e.g., 20:4–6), binding together the sections (e.g., 1:20; 4:1, 5; 5:6; 9:4; 10:7; 11:7, 14a), and Christianizing Jewish texts (e.g., 12:11; 14:13; 16:6; 17:6).

111. Sweet, *Revelation*, 35.

112. Here I am drawing upon the excellent surveys in Schüssler Fiorenza, *Justice and Judgment*, 160–64; D. Guthrie, *New Testament Introduction*, 4th ed. (Downers Grove, Ill.: InterVarsity, 1990), 967–69; Aune, *Revelation*, cx–cxvii.

113. Aune, *Revelation*, cxviii–cxxxiv.

3. The final edition appeared after the turn of the century, with further material meant to frame the work (1:1–3, 4–6; 1:12b–3:22; 22:6–21) and emphasize the unity of Christ with God.

Such a theory is breathtaking in its scope and complexity, but, like many others, is too speculative and complex for its own good.[114] The movement of thought and the unity of the language bind the whole together too well to need so detailed a theory. For instance, the way the language of the seven letters reverberates throughout the rest of the book shows that the letters were composed before the material that follows them. Moreover, it is better to see deliberate doublets and repetitions for thematic purposes than separate recensions. The themes of the book—the sovereignty of God, Christ as both one with God and the Lamb who purchased souls for God, the futility of Satan, the mission of God to the world, the judgment and yet salvation of the nations—are woven so brilliantly and so neatly through the whole book that it is difficult to comprehend how it could have been compiled from isolated pericopes. It sounds too much like the older scissors-and-paste compilation theories of the form/tradition critics, and it partakes of the same weaknesses that led to redaction and then narrative criticism of the Gospels.

The structure of the book is an even more difficult issue. There seem to be as many structural suggestions as there are scholars working on the problem! Of course, the same is true of many NT books (e.g., Matthew), but Revelation is particularly problematic because of the subgenres combined (epistle, prophecy, apocalyptic) and because of the incredibly complex movements taking place as the story unfolds. Historically, the key has been whether to organize the book chronologically (R. H. Charles, as well as most dispensational approaches) or topically (especially in terms of recapitulation). If the latter, does the recapitulation control the whole of Rev. 4–20 or just the seals, trumpets, or bowls? Today, however, literary questions have taken center stage. In one sense, the movement of thought is easy to see, yet at every level there are complexities. Does the prologue consist of 1:1–8 or 1:1–10? The next three sections are simple to identify (1:9–20; 2:1–3:22; 4:1–5:14), but do we see the throne room vision of Rev. 4–5 as the third part that introduces the central section of the seals, trumpets, and bowls (1:9–5:14; 6:1–16:21) or as the first section of the central part (1:9–3:22; 4:1–16:21)? The latter would be the consensus today. Are the scrolls of Rev. 5 and 10 the same (there is no consensus here)? Are there two interludes (7:1–17; 10:1–11:13) or three (with 12:1–14:20), and how do they fit into the three judgment septets? Are the first two interludes part of the sixth seal and sixth trumpet (also highly debated)?[115] Finally, how do we

114. See also J. M. Court, *Myth and History in the Book of Revelation* (Atlanta: John Knox, 1979), 16. Court, after a survey of source-critical attempts, concludes, "The mathematical techniques of modern computer analysis indicate the substantial unity of the book."

115. Beale (*Revelation*, 108) says that there is a broad consensus on Rev. 1–16, with the following outline: 1:1–8 (prologue), 1:9–3:22 (seven letters), 4:1–8:1 (seven seals, with 4:1–5:14

structure 17:1–22:5—does the first section end at 18:24; 19:5; or 19:10; and does the second end at 19:21; 20:15; or 21:8?

Many scholars see literary features as the key to the book[116]—for instance, "I was in the Spirit" (1:10; 4:2; 17:3; 21:10, indicating a visionary experience), which would lead to an outline of 1:1–8; 1:9–3:22; 4:1–16:21; 17:1–21:8; 21:9–22:5; 22:6–21.[117] Or one could utilize the phrase "what must take place soon/after these things" (1:1, 19; 4:1; 22:6), leading to the outline 1:19–3:22; 4:1–22:6.[118] Another possibility is "Come and see," producing the outline 1:1–3:22; 4:1–16:21; 17:1–22:5; 22:6–21; or "And I saw, and behold," leading to six vision blocks (1:8–3:22; 4:1–6:17; 7:1–8; 7:9–15:4; 15:5–17:18; 18:1–22:21).[119] Though these phrases are important, it is unlikely that any of them are sufficiently central to control the outline of the book. It is better to see them as a stylistic feature of the author.

There are six basic types of outlines:[120]

1. Many find a chiastic structure in the book. The one who began this current trend of finding chiasm throughout Scripture was N. W. Lund, who also saw chiasm in Revelation:

A Prologue (1)
  B Seven letters (2–3)
    C Seven seals (6:1–8:1)
      D Seven trumpets (8:2–9:17; 11:14–19)
        E Church's witness to Rome (10:1–11)
          F Church's witness to Judaism (11:1–13)
          F′ Church's persecution in Judaism (12:1–17)
        E′ Church persecuted by Rome (13:1–18)
      D′ Seven angels (14:1–15:4)

---

sometimes taken as a separate section), 8:2–11:19 (seven trumpets), 12:1–14:20 (seven signs), and 15:1–16:21 (seven bowls). However, I do not see any consensus on this, as the outlines given below will demonstrate. Many outlines do not place 1:6–20 with the seven letters, and it is quite common for scholars to see two sections in the central portion: 4:1–11:19 and 12:1–16:21 (Bauckham, Aune, Osborne).

116. For an excellent overview, see U. Vanni, *La struttura letteraria dell'Apocalisse*, 2nd ed., Aloisiana 8A (Brescia: Morcelliana, 1980), 105–67. Vanni also discusses phrases such as "lightnings, voices, and thunders" (4:5; 8:5; 11:19; 16:18) and the doxologies of 4:8–11; 5:8–14; 7:9–12; 11:15; 15:3–4; 19:1–8 and their possible influences on the structure of the book.

117. Used by C. R. Smith, "The Structure of the Book of Revelation in the Light of Apocalyptic Literary Conventions," *NovT* 36 (1994): 384–87; also accepted by M. C. Tenney, *Interpreting Revelation* (Grand Rapids: Eerdmans, 1958), 32–34; G. E. Ladd, *A Commentary on the Revelation of John* (Grand Rapids: Eerdmans, 1972), 14–17.

118. So Beale, *Revelation,* 111.

119. R. J. Korner, "'And I Saw . . .': An Apocalyptic Literary Convention for Structural Identification in the Apocalypse," *NovT* 42 (2000): 160–83.

120. The first four are delineated in S. L. Waechter, "An Analysis of the Literary Structure of the Book of Revelation according to Textlinguistic Methods" (Ph.D. diss., Mid-America Baptist Theological Seminary, 1994), 173–82.

    C′ Seven bowls (15:5–16:21)
   B′ Seven angels (17:1–22:5)
A′ Epilogue (22:6–21)[121]

The chiastic scheme that is best known is that of Schüssler Fiorenza,[122] who argues that the patterns of seven, the two scroll visions, and the method of intercalation and interlocking produce four major units in the book: the inaugural vision and letter septet (1:9–3:22), the seven-sealed scroll (4:1–9:21; 11:15–19; 15:1, 5–16:21; 17:1–19:10), the small prophetic scroll (10:1–15:4), and the visions of judgment and salvation (19:11–22:9). Then by doing an actantial analysis of the book, she believes that the central section is 10:1–15:4, and the rest of the book falls into a sevenfold chiastic structure:

    A 1:1–8
      B 1:9–3:22
        C 4:1–9:21; 11:15–19
          D 10:1–15:4
        C′ 15:1, 5–19:10
      B′ 19:11–22:9
    A′ 22:10–21

Others propose an even more complex chiasm. The key is always to delineate the central section, for it becomes the pivot on which the book turns. Strand[123] sees an elevenfold pattern: A (1:1–11), B (1:12–3:22), C (4:1–8:1), Da (8:2–11:18), Db (11:19–14:20), E (15:2–4), Db′(15:1, 5–16:21), Da′ (17:1–18:24), C′(19:1–21:4), B′(21:5–22:5), A′(22:6–21). Lee[124] produces an even more complex model with twenty sections and a twofold central section, 13:1–18 and 14:1–20. The problem is that each proposed chiasm is no better than the connections it draws, and in each case here the choice of the central section appears strained. Most agree that the center of the book is chs. 12–13 and the battle between good and evil. So perhaps the most likely suggestion is that of Beale:[125]

121. N. W. Lund, *Chiasmus in the New Testament: A Study in Formgeschichte* (Chapel Hill: University of North Carolina Press, 1942), 323–30; idem, *Studies in the Book of Revelation* (Chicago: Covenant, 1955), 34–35.

122. Schüssler Fiorenza, *Justice and Judgment*, 174–77.

123. K. A. Strand, "Chiastic Structure and Some Motifs in the Book of Revelation," *AUSS* 16 (1978): 401–8; see also idem, *Interpreting the Book of Revelation: Hermeneutical Guidelines with Brief Introduction to Literary Analysis* (Worthington, Mich.: Ann Arbor Publishers, 1976).

124. M. V. Lee, "A Call to Martyrdom: Function as Method and Message in Revelation," *NovT* 40 (1998): 174–75.

125. Beale, *Revelation*, 131. He presents this as an interesting possibility rather than his own choice.

A Prologue (1:1–8)
  B Vision and letters (1:9–3:22)
    C Seven seals (4:1–8:1)
      D Seven trumpets (8:2–11:18)
        E War of the ages (11:19–14:20)
      D′ Seven bowls (15:1–19:10)
    C′ The world's final judgment (19:11–21:8)
  B′ Vision of the perfect church in glory (21:9–22:5)
A′ Epilogue (22:6–21)

Beale has the proper central section, but one still wonders whether the sections truly match—for example, B and B′, as well as C and C′. In the final analysis, such schemes are interesting and thought-provoking but not entirely convincing.

2. Others view the book as a dramatic play patterned after Greek theater. The best known is J. W. Bowman,[126] who believes that the book is constructed precisely as a seven-act play, with each act having seven scenes in it (framed by the prologue and epilogue, 1:1–8; 22:6–21): Act I: The Church on Earth (1:9–3:22); Act II: God's Purpose in History (4:1–8:1); Act III: The Church in Tribulation (8:2–11:18); Act IV: The Salvation of the Church (11:19–15:4); Act V: The World in Agony (15:5–16:21); Act VI: The Judgment of the World (17:1–20:3); Act VII: The Church in the Millennium (20:4–22:5). L. C. Spinks[127] recognizes certain weaknesses in the choice of categories but basically agrees with Bowman's structure. On the other hand, D. L. Barr[128] thinks of the book as a three-act play: the risen Christ dictates seven letters (1–3), the Lamb opens the sealed book (3–11), and the dragon makes war with the elect and loses (12–22).

3. Many organize the book as a series of sevens. We have already seen this with Schüssler Fiorenza's sevenfold chiasm, and even more with Bowman's seven-act play, with each act having seven scenes. One of the first to do this was E. Lohmeyer,[129] who divided what he believed to be the apocalyptic material (4:1–21:4) into seven sections (with 4:1–5:14 introductory to it): 6:1–8:1; 8:2–11:14; 11:15–13:18; 14:1–20; 15:1–16:21; 17:1–19:10; 19:11–21:4. Within each he also delineated seven subsections.[130] A. M. Farrer also found

126. J. W. Bowman, "The Revelation to John: Its Dramatic Structure and Message," *Int* 9 (1955): 440–43.

127. L. C. Spinks, "A Critical Examination of J. W. Bowman's Proposed Structure of the Revelation," *EvQ* 50 (1979): 211–22. See also J. L. Blevins, *Revelation as Drama* (Nashville: Broadman, 1984).

128. D. L. Barr, "The Apocalypse as a Symbolic Transformation of the World: A Literary Analysis," *Int* 38 (1984): 44–45.

129. E. Lohmeyer, *Die Offenbarung des Johannes,* HNT 16 (Tübingen: Mohr, 1926), 1–2. Lohmeyer offers no introduction but discusses his reasoning throughout the commentary.

130. For a similar attempt to find seven major sections with seven subsections, see E. R. Wendland, "7 X 7 (X 7): A Structural and Thematic Outline of John's Apocalypse," *Occasional Papers in Translation and Textlinguistics* 4 (1990): 371–87.

a sevenfold structure.[131] He divided the book into six (1949, where he organized the book liturgically on the basis of Sabbath visions) or four (1964) major sections, with each having seven subsections: 1–3; 4–7; 8:1–11:14; 11:15–14:20; 15–18; 19–22. A. Y. Collins[132] reworked Farrer on the basis of the key techniques of interlocking and recapitulation, finding six sevens: seven messages (1:9–3:22), seven seals (4:1–8:5), seven trumpets (8:2–11:19), seven unnumbered visions (12:1–15:4), seven bowls (15:1–16:20) with a Babylon appendix (17:1–19:10), and seven unnumbered visions (19:11–21:8) with a Jerusalem appendix (21:9–22:5). Massyngberde Ford[133] believes that the original work had a series of six septets, but the later redactor turned it into seven septets, each with an introduction: the seven letters (2:1–3:22) following 1:9–20; the seven seals (6:1–17 [7:1–17 an intermission]) following 4:1–5:14; the seven trumpets (8:7–11:14) following 8:1–6; the seven signs (12:1–14:20) following 11:6–19; the seven bowls (16:2–16) following 15:1–16:1; the seven stages in the fall of Babylon (17:1–19:5) following 16:17–21; and seven final events (19:11–22:5) following 19:6–10. As with other proposals, each has its strengths and makes sense of the data, but we must wonder about the corners that often are cut to arrive at sevens. When one is past the obvious four septets—the letters, seals, trumpets, and bowls—it is not so easy to find sevens everywhere. For instance, Bauckham[134] points out the difficulty of finding seven sections in chs. 12–14 (or 12:1–15:4) or in 19:11–21:8.

4. Some have seen Revelation as a liturgical work built on early liturgical and festal patterns. We have already seen this in Farrer's first work, but others have embraced this approach as well. J. J. O'Rourke[135] maintains that the author used preexisting liturgical sources in composing his book, contra D. R. Carnegie,[136] who believes that the hymns are an essential part of the structure but were composed by the author. P. Pokorny[137] speaks of "St. John's Revelation as Christian liturgy," arguing that liturgy is central to both the ecclesiology and the Christology of the book. P. Prigent[138] goes further, believing that the book has been organized along lines of the synagogue liturgy and that the hymns are at the heart of the book, with a Passover eucharistic liturgy behind chs.

131. A. M. Farrer, *A Rebirth of Images: The Making of St. John's Apocalypse* (Westminster: Dacre, 1949), 36–58; *The Revelation of St. John the Divine: Commentary on the English Text* (Oxford: Clarendon, 1964).

132. A. Y. Collins, *The Combat Myth in the Book of Revelation*, HDR 9 (Missoula, Mont.: Scholars Press, 1976), 16–44.

133. Massyngberde Ford, *Revelation*, 46–50.

134. Bauckham, *Climax of Prophecy*, 5–6, 15–18.

135. J. J. O'Rourke, "The Hymns of the Apocalypse," *CBQ* 30 (1968): 399–409.

136. D. R. Carnegie, "Worthy Is the Lamb: The Hymns in Revelation," in *Christ the Lord*, ed. H. H. Rowdon (Downers Grove, Ill.: InterVarsity, 1982), 243–56, esp. 246–47.

137. P. Pokorny, "St. John's Revelation: Structure and Message," in *1900th Anniversary of St. John's Apocalypse*, 504–7.

138. P. Prigent, *Apokalypse et Liturgie* (Paris: Delachaux et Niestlé, 1964), 39–79; see also idem, *L'Apocalypse de Saint Jean* (Paris: Delachaux et Niestlé, 1981).

4–5, as well as key confessions such as the trisagion of 4:8 and "Come, Lord Jesus" of 22:20. M. H. Shepherd[139] goes so far as to claim that the scheme of the book follows the church's paschal liturgy, with the Scrutinies (1–3), the Vigil and Lessons (4–5, 6), the Initiation (7, 8), the Synaxis—including the Prayers (8), Law (8–9), Prophets (10–11), Gospel (12–15, 16–18), and Psalmody (19)—and the Eucharist (19, 20–22). However, though liturgy and worship are critical, one must ask whether the book as a whole is structured around them. Shepherd's scheme seems quite speculative, and the liturgy itself developed after the first century. Thompson argues that worship is a unifying presence in the book, and Barr goes so far as to propose that proper worship of God is the central theme of the book.[140] However, neither scholar structures the book around that theme.

5. Several believe that recapitulation is the key to Revelation's structure. One of the first was G. Bornkamm,[141] who argued that the book is primarily a revelation of the contents of the seven-sealed scroll of Rev. 5. Therefore, 15:1–19:21 recapitulates 8:2–14:20 in unveiling the scroll. This was followed by a large number of commentators who took a similar approach (e.g., Lenski, Milligan, Morris, Caird, Mulholland, Beasley-Murray). Collins[142] finds recapitulation in five of the cycles—the seals, trumpets, bowls, and the two sets of unnumbered visions in 12:1–15:4 and 19:11–21:8. Giblin[143] sees recapitulation controlling chs. 4–22 in three stages: the acclamation and the seals in 4:1–8:6, the seven trumpet blasts in 8:7–15:8, and judgment and salvation in 16:1–22:11. As seen in Hendriksen and Hoekema,[144] recapitulation became the primary method of interpretation for the Dutch Reformed position. They see Revelation consisting of seven cycles, each one describing the period between the first and second advents of Christ. The key to this method, of course, is how far the recapitulation extends. Most agree on the seals, trumpets, and bowls, but beyond that there is a great deal of disagreement.

6. Finally, Waechter[145] has developed a text-linguistic approach. Using lexical and syntactical principles regarding word order and linguistic emphases, along with a careful delineation of discourse boundaries indicated by markers such as "after these things," "in the Spirit," and "seven" as well as paragraph

139. M. H. Shepherd, *The Paschal Liturgy and the Apocalypse* (Richmond: John Knox, 1960), 77–84.

140. Thompson, *Book of Revelation,* 53; D. L. Barr, "The Apocalypse of John as Oral Enactment," *Int* 40 (1986): 255.

141. G. Bornkamm, "Die Komposition der apokaplyptischen Visionen in der Offenbarung Johannes," *ZNW* 36 (1937): 132–49.

142. Collins, *Combat Myth,* 32–44.

143. Giblin, *The Book of Revelation,* 12–18; idem, "Recapitulation and the Literary Coherence of John's Apocalypse," *CBQ* 56 (1994): 94–95.

144. W. Hendriksen, *More Than Conquerors: An Interpretation of the Book of Revelation* (1939; reprint, Grand Rapids: Baker, 1967), 22–31; A. A. Hoekema, *The Bible and the Future* (Grand Rapids: Eerdmans, 1979), 221–23.

145. Waechter, "Analysis of the Literary Structure," 73–150.

groupings and unit relationships, he developed the following structure: Rev. 1 creates expectation, and Rev. 2–3 present the exposition or problem confronting the churches. This is followed by three major segments (4:1–8:1; 8:2–11:19; 12:1–18:24) that develop conflict and increased tension. There are two peaks: the peak/climax (19:1–10) has great vividness and rhetorical power; then an intervening episode (19:11–20:15) prepares for the peak/denouement (21:1–22:7), which provides final resolution, followed by closure (22:8–21). Though many details of this plan can be challenged, the method is a significant step forward, for it is based on the development of the text itself. However, final decisions must be made not on the basis of rhetorical emphases and paragraph groupings alone, but must flow out of a detailed exegesis of the book.

With all the complexity and multiplicity of approaches, one would be excused for giving up all hope of outlining a structural plan that can find general approval. Therefore, keeping in mind the issues of (1) recapitulation, (2) the introductory sections 8:1–5 (the trumpets) and 15:2–4 (the bowls), and (3) the three so-called interludes (7:1–7; 10:1–11:13; 12:1–14:20), one can only seek to do justice to the data. The biggest problem is that such outlines spring from Western linear thought, and it is doubtful that John's mind worked with such categories. No single plan will suffice, for passages such as 4:1–5:14 are part of the introductory material preparing for the judgment septets and also an intimate part of those septets, and 12:1–14:20 is an interlude and at the same time a separate vision of the opponents in the great cosmic battle. Still, my proposal is as follows:[146]

Prologue (1:1–8)
    I. The churches addressed (1:9–3:22)
        A. Inaugural vision (1:9–20)
        B. The letters to the seven churches (2:1–3:22)
    II. God in majesty and judgment (4:1–16:21)
        A. The sovereignty of God in judgment (4:1–11:19)
            1. The throne room vision—God and the Lamb in heaven (4:1–5:14)
                a. God on his throne (4:1–11)
                b. Christ the Lamb, worthy to open the seals (5:1–14)
            2. The opening of the seals (6:1–8:1)
                a. The four horsemen of the Apocalypse (6:1–8)
                b. The fifth seal—the martyred saints (6:9–11)
                c. The sixth seal—the shaking of the heavens (6:12–17)
                d. Interlude: the saints on earth and in heaven (7:1–17)
                e. The seventh seal (8:1)
            3. The sounding of the seven trumpets (8:2–11:19)

---

146. Osborne, *Revelation*, 30–31.

Subject Index

Author Index

515

Scripture Index

533

New Testament

John